X

SS REF
BUSN, PTN
PRO

Professional Practices Handbook

Sixth Edition

The College of Law ☒
14 S... ...treet
Bloomsbury
London
WC1E 7DE

FOR REFERENCE

ONLY

D1419974

The College of Law, Guildford

S15056

Professional Practices Handbook

Sixth Edition

Smith & Williamson

in association with

MAURICE | TURNOR | GARDNER

Bloomsbury Professional

Bloomsbury Professional Ltd

Maxwelton House
41–43 Boltro Road
Haywards Heath
West Sussex
RH16 1BJ

© Bloomsbury Professional Ltd 2011

Previously published by Tottel Publishing Ltd

All rights reserved. No part of this publication may be reproduced in any material form (including photocopying or storing it in any medium by electronic means and whether or not transiently or incidentally to some other use of this publication) without the written permission of the copyright owner except in accordance with the provisions of the Copyright, Designs and Patents Act 1988 or under the terms of a licence issued by the Copyright Licensing Agency Ltd, Saffron House, 6–10 Kirby Street, London, EC1N 8TS, England. Applications for the copyright owner's written permission to reproduce any part of this publication should be addressed to the publisher.

Warning: The doing of an unauthorised act in relation to a copyright work may result in both a civil claim for damages and criminal prosecution.

Crown copyright material is reproduced with the permission of the Controller of HMSO and the Queen's Printer for Scotland. Parliamentary copyright material is reproduced with the permission of the Controller of Her Majesty's Stationery Office on behalf of Parliament. Any European material in this work which has been reproduced from EUR-lex, the official European Communities legislation website, is European Communities copyright.

British Library Cataloguing-in-Publication Data

A CIP Catalogue record for this book is available from the British Library.

ISBN 978 1 84766 511 9

Typeset by Kerrypress Ltd, Luton, Beds

Printed and bound in Great Britain by Hobbs The Printers Ltd, Totton, Hampshire

Preface to the sixth edition

This is the sixth edition of a book first published in 1996, then entitled 'Professional Partnership Handbook'. Many changes have occurred in the legal, regulatory, taxation, and business environment that affect professional firms over the past fifteen years.

Since the last edition the trend has continued for professional firms to limit their liability. This may be as limited liability partnerships (LLPs) or limited companies, rather than as general partnerships, and more complex structures have become increasingly common.

There has been a very significant adverse change in the economic environment leading to firms focusing on cost, service delivery and people issues in the management of their practices. There has also been significant change in the taxation environment including rapidly changing rules affecting provision for retirement.

In the legal services field, a significant change in the marketplace is being precipitated by the implementation of the *Legal Services Act 2007*.

This edition has been updated to reflect the above as well as other relevant changes.

Simon Mabey

Preface to the first edition

Partnership is a form of business organisation which has enabled a variety of professional practices to flourish. Professional partnerships may be large, medium-sized or small and exhibit many different styles of management. This perhaps explains why remarkably little literature is available on the practical aspects of running a professional partnership. This handbook is designed to be of use to a broad range of individuals involved in the management of partnerships including senior and managing partners, finance partners and other partners as well as those considering partnership.

In the past, partners tended to consider themselves primarily as members of a profession, rather than as participants in businesses. In today's competitive environment, the reverse is more commonly true. Nevertheless whilst those responsible for the management of partnerships are generally highly expert in their own field, they have not always had the opportunity to acquire the range of skills needed to run a successful business.

While a handbook is no substitute for experience, this book is designed to provide information and advice on the wide range of issues that running a professional partnership involves. Between them, the contributors have many years' experience of advising professional partnerships as well as involvement in management in their own practices.

A professional partnership is a living entity that develops and succeeds through the skills and abilities of its people. This handbook is for all those who wish to ensure the success of their partnership.

Acknowledgements

The Professional Practices Handbook has been written primarily by teams of experts at Smith & Williamson and Maurice Turnor Gardner who advise professional practices. We are extremely grateful to Richard Turnor, Corinne Staves and the professional practices team at Maurice Turnor Gardner for their substantial contribution on the legal aspects of the Handbook, especially the first six chapters.

In addition, I should like to thank Tony Williams of Jomati for reviewing the chapters on profit shares, management and strategic planning; Steve Smith of Thirdperson for his review of the marketing chapter; and Mike Scurr of Aon Limited for his contributions on insurance.

I also wish to thank my many colleagues at Smith & Williamson who contributed significantly in their professional areas of expertise. I would particularly like to mention audit and accounting experts Giles Murphy, Nick Learoyd and Pambos Patsalides; tax specialists Richard Mannion, Helen Demuth, Mark Eade, David Hewison, Chris Lallemand, Tim Lyford, Pamela Sayers and John Voyez; pensions director Mike Fosberry; information systems specialist Roland Brook; people management director Rachel Stone; human resources director Karen Crossley; operations director David Smart; and director of marketing Ann Monks.

Simon Mabey

Chairman, Professional Practices Group

Smith & Williamson

Contents

Contents

Contents

Contents

Table of cases

Table of Statutes

References at the right-hand side are to paragraph numbers.

Table of Statutory Instruments

References at the right-hand side are to paragraph numbers.

Chapter 1 Introduction – The Evolving Structure of Professional Practices

The origin of the business model

1.1 Until relatively recently, the vast majority of professional practices were constituted as partnerships, often simply because this was a requirement of the relevant professional bodies, and sometimes because of the favourable tax treatment as compared to that of a company. As a business form, the partnership is ideally suited to professional practices formed of key skilled individuals who bring their individual talents to the common business in return for a share in the profits. Many professional practices are still constituted in this way and the concept of partnership is explored in CHAPTER 2.

As professional practices became larger, more complex and international, there was increasing concern about partners being jointly responsible for the global debts and liabilities of the firm. In the 1990s, the Government came under significant pressure from the major accountancy firms, which were concerned about vast claims being made against them at that time, to introduce an alternative business vehicle which offered better protection while benefitting from the tax treatment of a partnership. Following the example of some US States, Jersey created a form of limited liability partnership (LLP) for use by UK firms, but HM Revenue & Customs made the use of Jersey LLPs impractical by indicating that, like companies, they would be treated as opaque for tax purposes. Further, a potential £5 million capitalisation requirement made the vehicle unattractive for many, particularly small, businesses. However, in 1997 the Government of the day announced a consultation on the introduction of an LLP in England and Wales and Scotland. The *Limited Liability Partnerships Act 2000* was passed and came into force on 6 April 2001 and most major British professional practices now operate in this form. LLPs are considered in CHAPTER 3.

However, some professional practices are also conducted in the form of a company, and companies frequently form part of a hybrid structure, often with a company participating in one or more professional practices established as partnerships or LLPs. For example, the so called 'consolidators' set up companies to acquire accounting practices, raising the necessary funds through the issue of shares in the market and seeking to create value for investors through economies of scale and shared management expertise. Sometimes, partners or members participate in their firm both directly

1

and through a company, with profits being streamed to the individuals and the company as necessary depending on the funding requirements of the business and tax considerations (see CHAPTERS 18 TO 20). Such complex arrangements are likely to become more common from October 2011, as law firms seek to take advantage of the ability to form 'alternative business structures' (ABSs) under the *Legal Services Act 2007*, but they remain outside the scope of this handbook which focuses particularly on professional practices operated through a partnership or an LLP.

Separation of the professions

1.2   Historically, the different professions have practised separately, so that partnerships have tended to consist of partners from the same profession. There have been some exceptions. For example, surveying firms have often included partners who are qualified as chartered surveyors, land agents and auctioneers.

This separation of the professions has in some cases been a requirement of professional rules. For example, for many years solicitors were only permitted, by Law Society and Solicitors Regulation Authority rules, to enter into partnership with registered foreign lawyers and registered European lawyers. However, the accountancy profession has encouraged alternative business structures, such as multi-disciplinary partnerships, by reducing to 50 the required number of partners in a firm of chartered accountants that must be qualified as such.

The continuing evolution of legal professional practices

1.3   Following reviews by the Office of Fair Trading and the Law Society, Sir David Clementi reviewed, consulted and reported on the provision of legal services in England and Wales and, in particular, considered the availability of multi-disciplinary partnerships to legal service providers.

In response to the Clementi Report (Report of the Review of the Regulatory Framework for Legal Services in England and Wales, December 2004), in October 2005 the Government published a White Paper 'The Future of Legal Services: Putting Consumers First' (Cm 6679) and proposed the introduction of alternative business structures for legal service providers. On 30 October 2007, the *Legal Services Act 2007* received Royal Assent. The *Legal Services Act 2007* created the Legal Services Board, to supervise the provision of legal services by all approved regulators, as well as an independent Ombudsman service to handle consumer complaints about legal services.

On 31 March 2009, legal disciplinary practices (LDPs) were introduced. In LDPs, up to 25% of the partners can be lawyers (other than solicitors) and non-lawyers who are involved in the management of the firm. This has immediate practical benefits, such as removing the need for barristers and legal executives to re-train as solicitors before becoming partners in a firm of solicitors. However, it also enables firms to include key non-lawyer managers in the partnership. Many large professional practices have key managers who oversee the worldwide finance, HR or IT functions, and who are appropriately qualified and highly skilled – and arguably more significant to the professional practice's management than many of the partners – yet, until LDPs were introduced, these individuals could not be partners.

Although LDPs may have some impact on the legal profession, it is thought that the introduction by the *Legal Services Act 2007* of ABSs will have a much greater impact. In short, ABSs will allow lawyers to form multi-disciplinary practices which offer legal services in conjunction with non-legal services and which are owned by non-lawyers. This will allow non-lawyers, including commercial organisations, to own firms that provide legal services. Therefore, ABS firms will, when introduced, enable barristers, solicitors, patent and trademark attorneys and non-lawyers to practise on an equal and integrated footing and also to tap into external investment, both of which are currently restricted. It is hoped that ABSs will be permitted from late 2011 onwards. Until then, the Solicitors Regulation Authority (in its guidance on 'preparing for alternative business structures' issued in July 2009) is encouraging interested legal practices to prepare for the arrival of ABSs in the following ways:

- having discussions with potential business partners;

- considering a non-binding arrangement with a potential business partner for the setting up of an ABS, ie an arrangement 'subject to contract';

- registering LLP or company names, acquiring domain names, etc;

- considering agreements to enter into exclusive negotiations with a potential business partner; or

- considering certain conditional contractual arrangements to be activated once the regulatory requirements have been relaxed and all necessary approvals granted – eg an agreement to accept new non-lawyers, or an outside investor, into partnership.

Chapter 2 Partnerships

Definition of partnership

2.1 In everyday speech, the word 'partnership' is used to describe almost any relationship involving collective activity by people of equal standing. As a matter of law, however, it has a very particular meaning which is to be found in the *Partnership Act 1890* (see **APPENDIX 1**).

Section 1(1) of the *Partnership Act 1890* defines partnership as the relation which subsists between persons carrying on a business in common with a view of profit.

A partnership therefore involves three essential elements.

There must be a business

2.2 *Section 45* of the *Partnership Act 1890* states that the expression 'business' includes every trade, occupation or profession. Almost every commercial activity, including a one-off commercial venture, can be a business for this purpose.

Section 2 of the *Partnership Act 1890* provides that co-ownership of property, and investing jointly in property, does not necessarily imply the existence of a partnership (see **2.8** below).

The business must be carried on by two or more persons in common

2.3 For a partnership to exist, two or more persons must carry on the business in common (*s 1(1)*). The term 'persons' includes corporations and unincorporated bodies (such as partnerships), as well as individuals.

The persons carrying on the business must act as principals and agents for one another and not simply as agents or trustees for someone else A partnership will not exist simply because two or more agents carry on a business on behalf of a third party. Likewise, two executors carrying on the business of a deceased sole trader are not strictly partners as they carry on the business on behalf of the deceased person's estate.

The words 'in common' indicate the necessity for a single business carried on jointly. A partnership does not exist where each partner in fact carries on a different and distinct business and there is no mutual agency between them. However, this is often a fine distinction to draw. For example, where several separate firms agree to co-operate over the referral of business, training and the maintenance of business standards but there is no further integration, a single partnership is unlikely to exist. However, where those firms also use the same name and share profits and losses, the separate firms may in fact be in the same position as branch offices of a single partnership. In such circumstances, the separate firms may be surprised to find themselves jointly liable for one another's debts.

(See also CHAPTER 28, DEATH OF A PARTNER.)

The business must be carried on with a view of profit

2.4   In conducting a business in common, the partners must intend that the receipts of the business will exceed the expenses incurred in generating those receipts, leaving a profit. The profit motive of the partners, rather than the actual generation of profits, is essential. The making of a profit need not be the only motive. Even if the partners have an additional motive (eg administrative convenience or tax avoidance), the condition of conducting the business with a view to profit must be satisfied.

Prior to 1890, it was thought that no partnership would exist, unless the partners not only intend to make a profit but also intend to divide the profits between themselves. The *Partnership Act 1890* does not contain this requirement, and it is now thought that a partnership may exist even where one or more of the partners are excluded from the profits, and perhaps also where the partners agree to pay the profits to a third party (provided that collectively they are conducting the business as principals). Even so, sharing the profits of a business is prima facie evidence of partnership, although whether or not the recipients of those profits are all partners will be a question of fact. *Section 2(3)* of the *Partnership Act 1890* describes specific circumstances where profit sharing will not create a partnership. For example the following do not in themselves make the recipient a partner:

(a)   repaying a debt or liquidated amount by instalments out of the profits of a business;

(b)   paying an employee or agent a share of the profits of the business under his or her contract for remuneration; and

(c)   paying the widow or children of a deceased partner an annuity from the profits of the partnership.

A partnership will only exist at a time when the business is carried on. Therefore, even if the parties have entered into a partnership agreement, a partnership will not exist between them until such time as they begin to carry on a business together. This does not mean that actual trading must have commenced. In *Khan v Miah* [2000] 1 WLR 2123, which involved the establishment of a restaurant business, it was held by the House of Lords that preparatory activities, including fitting out premises in view of carrying on a trading business, were indicative of the existence of a partnership relationship. In *Goudberg v Erniman Associates Pty. Ltd* [2007] VSCA 12 (22 January 2007), however, the individuals had 'embarked on a project', but the Court did not agree that at the relevant time they were carrying on a business.

Similarly, there is a rebuttable presumption that the sale of all of the assets of a partnership will cause the partnership to dissolve (*Nirmal Singh Chahal v Krishan Dev Mahal, Pooja Deol (nee Linda Mahal)* [2005] WL 1630807). However, on the facts of that case, the Court of Appeal held that, even though the assets of a partnership had been transferred to a limited company in which two of the three partners held equal shares, since the third party had no knowledge of the transaction, the partnership through which the three partners previously traded had not been dissolved.

What is not a partnership?

2.5 The definition of partnership in *s 1(1)* of the *Partnership Act 1890* is very wide, but the Act expressly limits its scope. The following situations do not give rise to a partnership.

A company

2.6 *Section 1(2)* of the *Partnership Act 1890* specifically provides that the relationship between the members of a company (whether registered under the *Companies Act 2006* or incorporated under Royal Charter) or between members of other special types of company is not a partnership. The fundamental difference between a company and a partnership is that a company is a separate entity capable of acquiring rights and incurring liabilities which are separate from those of its members. However, partners jointly own the assets of and rights relating to the partnership and are jointly liable for liabilities incurred by it.

Limited liability partnership

2.7 As noted in CHAPTER 1, a limited liability partnership is not a partnership. *Section 1(5)* of the *Limited Liability Partnerships Act 2000* specifically provides that, except as far as otherwise provided by that Act or any other legislation, the law relating to partnerships does not apply to LLPs.

Joint holding of property

2.8   *Section 2(1)* of the *Partnership Act 1890* provides that joint tenancy, tenancy in common, joint property, common property, or part ownership does not of itself create a partnership as to anything so held or owned, whether or not the holders share any profits made by the use of these assets. In order for a partnership to exist, the holders of the property must be carrying on a business in common (see **2.2** and **2.3** above).

The sharing of gross returns

2.9   The mere sharing of gross returns, as opposed to profits, does not give rise to a partnership.

Clubs and societies

2.10   Clubs and societies are not partnerships even if carrying on a business, provided that their objects do not include making profits.

Formalities of forming a partnership

2.11   A partnership exists when the three essential elements of a partnership are in existence, irrespective of whether or not the partners have entered into a formal written partnership agreement or deed. It is therefore quite possible for a person to incur liability as a partner unintentionally, without realising that the nature of his relationship with another person amounts to a partnership.

In practice, however, it is important that partners should enter into a clear written agreement because of the difficulty of discerning the intention of the parties where the agreement is oral or derived from a course of dealing (see *Partnership Act 1890, s 19*). Subject to any express agreement, the default rules in *ss 24* and *25* of the *Partnership Act 1890* govern the partnership. These default rules rarely reflect what the parties would have expected and provide as follows:

  (i) capital, profits and losses are to be shared or borne equally (*s 24(1)*);

 (ii) a partner making an advance to the firm in excess of his agreed capital contribution is entitled to interest at 5 per cent per annum (*s 24(3)*);

(iii) there is no other entitlement to interest on capital (*s 24(4)*);

 (iv) every partner can take part in management (*s 24(5)*);

  (v) no partner is entitled to any salary or fixed share of profits (*s 24(6)*);

 (vi) no new partner can be admitted without unanimous consent (*s 24(7)*);

(vii) disagreements about ordinary matters relating to the business are decided by a simple majority, but no change can be made to the nature of the business without unanimity (*s 24(8)*);

(viii) no majority of partners can expel a partner (*s 25*);

(ix) any partner can dissolve a partnership at will by giving oral or written notice (in the event that the partnership is constituted by deed) (*ss 26, 32*);

(x) the partnership will be dissolved automatically by the bankruptcy or death of a partner, and may be dissolved if a partner charges his share for his separate debts (*s 33*).

Joyce v Morrissey [1999] EMLR 233 concerned a band, The Smiths. There was no formal agreement governing the relationship between the band members and therefore the relationship was governed by the *Partnership Act 1890*. *Section 24* states that there is a presumption of equality as to the distribution of profits between partners. The defendant argued that the profits should be shared unequally as a result of discussions between the band members. The judge held that the presumption in *s 24* could only be displaced if the plaintiff had actively accepted new terms of unequal profit sharing.

Where parties have entered into a partnership agreement but the three conditions are not satisfied, a partnership will not exist simply because the parties have said that it exists.

Name of partnership and business documentation

2.12   The partnership should ensure that it complies with the provisions of *Part 41* of the *Companies Act 2006* where the name does not consist of the surnames of all the partners who are individuals and names of all the partners that are corporate entities.

Part 41 largely restates the provisions of the *Business Names Act 1985* (now repealed) and provides that the approval of the Secretary of State is required where certain words or expressions are used as or as part of a firm's business name. In addition, all business letters, written orders for goods or services, invoices and receipts and other similar documents issued in the course of business must state, in legible characters, the name of each partner and an address in the United Kingdom for the service of process. This last provision does not apply to a document issued by a partnership of more than 20 people which keeps at its principal place of business a list of the names of all the partners if:

(i)   none of the partners' names appear in the document except in the text or as a signatory; and

(ii) the document states the firm's principal place of business and says that a list of the partners can be inspected at that address.

Number of partners

2.13 Since the *Regulatory Reform (Removal of 20 Member Limit in Partnerships etc) Order 2002*, which came into effect on 21 December 2002, there has been no restriction on the number of partners.

Categories of partners

2.14 In the context of a professional partnership, a person normally starts his professional life as an employee. Having earned his spurs, he may then be invited to become a partner. Before becoming a full partner, otherwise known as an equity partner, he will often spend a number of years as a salaried partner so as to enhance his status but without having all the authority of a full partner and usually remunerated by way of salary. At the end of his career, a partner in a professional firm will normally simply retire, thus becoming a retired partner and withdrawing his investment in the firm.

Who may become a partner?

2.15 Anyone except an enemy alien can be a partner in a partnership. However, special rules apply in a number of situations and the key rules are set out below.

Companies

2.16 Both limited and unlimited companies can become partners. A partnership may consist of corporate bodies, individuals or a combination of corporate bodies and individuals. A company should be authorised to enter into a partnership in its articles of association, however, whether a corporate entity has a constitutional authority to join a partnership is less important than previously, following the amendment of the ultra vires rules (see *Companies Act 2006, s 39*).

Limited liability partnerships

2.17 Limited liability partnerships formed under the *Limited Liability Partnerships Act 2000* have unlimited capacity. They are, therefore, able to become partners in much the same way as companies.

Persons of unsound mind

2.18   Where it is claimed by a partner that he was suffering from some form of mental disorder at the time he entered into the partnership agreement, he will continue to be bound by that partnership agreement unless he can show that his fellow contracting partners were aware of his disability at the time or that Court of Protection proceedings had been commenced before he entered into the agreement. Partnership agreements frequently provide for the automatic retirement of partners who are of unsound mind.

Children

2.19   A partnership can be formed where one or more of the partners is under 18 and is therefore a minor. However, for a number of reasons it is not advisable for a professional partnership to admit a minor as a partner. The first and most obvious reason is that a minor is unlikely to have the skills and experience to discharge his duties properly within the professional partnership. In addition, however, it is generally believed that minors will not share responsibility for the debts and liabilities of the firm.

Furthermore, a minor may repudiate the agreement before the age of 18 or within a reasonable time after attaining that age. However a minor cannot repudiate the agreement in part, for example, to take a profit share but without being responsible for his share of the firm's losses, and a minor partner who fails to repudiate or affirm the agreement promptly after attaining the age of 18 risks assuming liabilities as a partner due to the doctrine of holding out (see further **2.25** below).

Bankrupts

2.20   Bankrupts can be partners, although a bankrupt is likely to be guilty of an offence under *s 360* of the *Insolvency Act 1986* if he obtains credit on behalf of the firm without disclosing his status. Most partnership agreements will provide for the automatic expulsion of bankrupts, and will usually override *s 33(1)* of the *Partnership Act 1890*, which provides for the automatic dissolution of the partnership upon the bankruptcy of any partner.

Unqualified persons

2.21   It is important to ensure that each partner in a professional partnership holds the required professional qualifications. At worst, the inclusion of an unqualified person could lead to an automatic dissolution of the firm as an illegal partnership.

2.22   New legal practices, including LDPs, formed as partnerships must apply to the Solicitors Regulation Authority to practise as a recognised body under the *SRA Recognised Bodies Regulations 2009*. The forms are available on the Solicitors Regulation Authority website and there is a specific form for a recognised body formed as a partnership.

As a result of the *SRA Recognised Bodies Regulations 2009* and the *SRA Practising Regulations 2009*, firms are also required to renew their recognition by 31 October each year.

Liabilities of partners and partnerships

General liabilities of partnerships

2.23   Traditionally, young professional people have sought the status and rewards that are associated with becoming a partner in their firm, but an increasingly litigious culture has made the risks associated with partnerships the cause of great concern. Some firms have faced claims that substantially exceed their insurance cover. There have also been some high-profile partnership failures, in some cases leading to personal bankruptcies. That is why start-up professional firms tend nowadays to incorporate as limited liability partnerships. However, traditional partnerships retain some advantages, especially the fact that public disclosure of financial information is still generally unnecessary (see further CHAPTER 4, CHOOSING AN APPROPRIATE BUSINESS STRUCTURE). This section outlines the way in which the law deals with the liabilities of partnerships and refers to some of the problems that might be encountered in practice.

Power of partners to bind the firm

2.24   The general principle of agency in the context of partnerships is set out in *s 5* of the *Partnership Act 1890*. It is worth repeating that section in full:

> 'Every partner is an agent of the firm and his other partners for the purpose of the business of the partnership; and the acts of every partner who does any act for carrying on in the usual way business of the kind carried on by the firm of which he is a member, bind the firm and his partners, unless the partner so acting has in fact no authority to act for the firm in the particular matter, and the person with whom he is dealing either knows that he has no authority, or does not know or believe him to be a partner.'

This provision contains the following elements:

(a) *Actual authority.* Something done by a partner on behalf of his firm which is within the scope of his actual authority always binds the firm. This is so even if the action concerned falls outside the usual course of business of the firm. For example, if a firm of chartered accountants decides to hold a dinner dance for its staff, it might decide to authorise one of the partners to organise the evening. Even though the organisation of dinner dances might not be in the usual course of the firm's business, the firm would be bound by the acts of the organising partner since they would fall within his actual authority. Furthermore, the organising partner will be entitled to require the other partners to contribute their fair share of the costs.

(b) *Implied authority.* An act done in order to carry on business of the kind carried on by the partnership in the usual way binds the partnership even if the partner concerned had no actual authority to bind the firm. Even if a partner's actual or implied authority has been revoked, the partner will have apparent authority to carry on the business of the partnership in the usual way unless the third party knows that the partner does not have the requisite degree of authority. However, in these circumstances, the partner may have to indemnify the firm against any loss incurred by his actions. Whilst a partner in a firm of chartered surveyors specialising in land agency might not have actual authority to turn his hand to valuation work, if he does advise on valuation work his firm will be bound, unless (for example) the client knows that he is in fact moonlighting in his own capacity.

It follows that if a partner does something without authority and outside the ordinary course of the firm's business, the firm will not be bound, except perhaps on the grounds of holding out (see **2.25** below).

Furthermore, *ss 7* and *8* of the *Partnership Act 1890* expressly protect the firm where a partner uses the credit of the firm for a purpose which is apparently unconnected with the partnership business, or where the third party knows that the act contravenes an agreed restriction on the partner's purported authority. For example, if an architect agrees to make a loan to a builder without the authority of his co-partners, the firm is unlikely to be bound. Similarly, in *Hirst v Etherington* [1999] 3 All ER 797, the Court of Appeal held that it was not possible to rely on an undertaking where, having regard to the nature of the underlying transaction, it is clear that a solicitor should not have given such an undertaking. The decision in *Hirst* on this point was cited with approval in *Antonelli v Allen* [2000] All ER (D) 2040.

Holding out

2.25   Even where a person is not a partner at all, he may incur liability if he is held out as such. The general principle of holding out in the context of partnerships is set out in *s 14* of the *Partnership Act 1890* which commences as follows:

> 'Every one who by words spoken or written or by conduct represents himself, or who knowingly suffers himself to be represented, as a partner in a particular firm, is liable as a partner to anyone who has on the faith of any such representation given credit to the firm ...'

Liability under this section will arise where the following elements are present:

(a)   There must be a holding out. The person concerned must either hold himself out as a partner or allow himself to be held out as such by a partner. Holding out does not have to take any particular form, and can be done in writing, orally or even by conduct.

(b)   The third party must actually know that the person is held out as a partner, and rely upon it to his detriment.

(c)   There must be credit given to the firm. This expression should be given a wide meaning, and extends to any transaction giving rise to an obligation on the firm's part.

Liability through holding out could occur even where no partnership exists at all, but a third party is led to believe that one exists, and even where the person who is held out as a partner exceeds the authority actually conferred upon him. This could include a situation where a non-partnership business uses the term 'partner' to describe its principals as is frequently the case where a partnership has 'converted' to an LLP (see further Chapter 4).

Likewise, salaried partners (employees who are held out as partners) may incur liabilities to the outside world, which is why the full partners normally agree to indemnify them against any such liability arising which is not their own fault. The decision in *Nationwide Building Society v Lewis* [1998] 2 WLR 915 confirmed that liability for professional negligence could be attributed to a salaried partner who is held out as a partner of the firm even if he is in fact an employee. In that case, the salaried partner was not liable in negligence because the plaintiff could not show any reliance on the salaried partner being held out as a full partner. The Court of Appeal found that a plaintiff would have to establish reliance on that holding out in order to be able to recover from the salaried partner.

A salaried partner is defined in this book as a salaried employee who is held out as a partner. Sometimes the term is used in practice in respect of an equity partner whose profits consist principally of a fixed or prior share.

Contracts

2.26   A partner can generally bind his firm in contract under the principles discussed above. Even where there is no actual authority, there will generally be implied or apparent authority to issue invoices, to open bank accounts in the firm's name, write cheques and to borrow money for the purposes of the business. There will also be an implied power to hire and fire employees and to effect insurance. However, implied and apparent authority are always subject to the requirement that the action taken should not be unusual in the context of the firm's business. Furthermore, there is no general implied power to commit the firm to guarantees, or to a mortgage of the firm's property. Perhaps the kind of contract where problems most frequently arise, are leases and bank accounts.

Section 9 of the *Partnership Act 1890* provides that all partners are jointly liable for the debts of the partnership (but jointly and severally in Scotland). Joint liability means that any one or more of the partners can be sued and found liable for the whole debt, but those against whom the debt is enforced then have a right to recover from the other partners the contribution which they are obliged to make to ensure that profits and losses are shared in accordance with the partnership agreement (see **2.33** below).

Leases

2.27   Most professional partnerships occupy leasehold premises. Where there are more than four partners, *s 34(2)* of the *Law of Property Act 1925* provides that the leasehold property cannot be vested in more than four partners. Where there are four or more partners, frequently the legal title to the lease will be held in the name of four partners who act as nominees for themselves and their co-partners. Under normal principles of privity of contract, the nominee partners are liable on the tenant's covenants in the lease throughout the term of the lease, notwithstanding their retirement, the dissolution of the partnership or the assignment of the lease to a third party.

The liability of the other partners to the lessor depends on the form of the lease. If it is a deed, and only the four nominee partners are parties, the lessor may have no contract with the unnamed partners. This is because there is generally no implied authority to bind a firm by deed. Furthermore, under common law as preserved by *s 6* of the *Partnership Act 1890*, even if the nominee partners had express authority from the firm and even if the deed makes it clear that the nominees are acting on behalf of the firm, the firm may not be bound unless the covenant is expressed to be made by the firm, and not merely on its behalf. If it is not a deed, the firm (ie the partners at the time when the lease is entered into) will be bound if the nominee partners had express or implied authority to enter into the lease, and the existence of implied authority to do so may depend upon the nature of the firm's business, the length of the lease and other factors.

Even if the firm is not bound as far as the lessor is concerned, the partnership agreement will generally give the nominee partners a right of indemnity from the firm. Nevertheless, problems can arise for nominee partners, who may have no right of recourse against anyone who was a partner at the date of the lease but has since retired, and who may have difficulties enforcing the indemnity if the partnership has been dissolved or is insolvent.

In order to avoid these problems, from the point of view both of the landlord and of the nominee partners, modern leases generally provide for all the partners to guarantee the obligations of the nominee partners, or to be parties to the lease and bound by its covenants. Provision is also often made for new partners to enter into guarantees and for retiring partners to be released from their obligations, usually subject to the number of partners remaining in the partnership being greater than a stated minimum. Alternatively, a nominee company, perhaps an unlimited company owned by all the partners, may be substituted for the nominee partners, with the individual partners being guarantors.

Bank loans

2.28 When money is borrowed by a partnership, everyone who is a partner at the date when the debt is incurred will normally be subject to the obligation to repay. Retiring partners will remain bound unless expressly released, although they will normally be entitled to an express or implied indemnity from the continuing partners. New partners will have no direct obligation to the lender, unless they expressly or impliedly agree with the lender to be bound, but they will generally agree with the other partners to share in the firm's assets and liabilities, including the loan. The repayment of a partnership debt by one partner extinguishes the liability of the firm as a whole if the object of the payment is to repay the debt, or if partnership funds are used.

It can be very difficult to decide who is responsible for the outstanding debit balance of an overdraft facility where partners come and go and the firm is then dissolved. It is then necessary to match drawings under the facility with amounts paid in to reduce the borrowing, in order to determine who is responsible for the outstanding amount. Amounts paid into the account will generally be treated as discharging the earliest amounts borrowed under the facility.

In order to reduce some of these difficulties, many loan documents provide for outgoing partners to be released from all their obligations, and for all new partners to sign documents agreeing to be bound, subject perhaps to the total number of partners remaining above a particular level.

Duration of a partner's liability

2.29   A new partner is not directly liable to third parties for the debts of the firm incurred before he became a partner merely by reason of the fact that he becomes a partner (*Partnership Act 1890, s 17(1)*) although the partnership agreement will generally provide for the new partner to contribute a share of those liabilities to the extent that they are to be taken into account in computing the profits and losses of future years. The agreement may also provide for incoming partners to undertake direct contractual obligations, for example to bankers and landlords.

When a person ceases to be a partner, the authority of the continuing partners to bind him and his authority to bind the firm will both come to an end. However, third parties dealing with the partnership may be entitled to assume that the outgoing partner remains a partner (ie there may be continuing ostensible authority) until actual notice is given of the change (*Partnership Act 1890, s 36(1)*).

Notice is not required to prevent liability for future obligations (*s 36(3)*) being incurred:

(a)   on the death of a partner;

(b)   on the insolvency of a partner; or

(c)   on the retirement of a truly dormant partner, who was not known to the outside world to be a partner.

Furthermore, *s 36(2)* of the *Partnership Act 1890* provides for an advertisement in the London Gazette (or Edinburgh Gazette in Scotland) to be sufficient notice of partnership changes to anyone who had no dealings with the firm before the date of the change concerned. Even so, it is important, for the protection of the continuing partners and of the outgoing partner alike, that an advertisement should be placed in the London Gazette, and that the main suppliers and creditors of the firm should be notified of the change (see, for example, *Hamerhaven Pty Ltd v Ogge* [1996] 2 VR 488).

It is also important that the outgoing partner should not be held out as a continuing partner, eg by omitting to change the notepaper or the list of partners at the principal office (see **2.25** above).

A partner who ceases to be a partner does not automatically cease to be liable to third parties for partnership debts incurred before he ceased to be a partner (*Partnership Act 1890, s 17(2)*) (although he would normally have an express or implied right of indemnity against his former partners).

That is why the personal representatives of deceased former partners are sometimes unable to distribute a deceased former partner's estate for many years. If the firm faces claims in respect of a period before the deceased former partner left the firm, which exceed the available insurance cover, and the continuing partners of the firm are unable to meet the claim in full, the estate of the deceased former partner could be exposed to liability. If the personal representatives have made distributions, they may face personal liability. Of course, the creditor, the continuing partners and the outgoing partner can agree that the outgoing partner will be released, and provisions to this effect are frequently included in leases and loan facility letters. Indeed, *s 17(3)* of the *Partnership Act 1890* expressly recognises that this may be achieved by express agreement, or inferred from the course of dealing between a creditor and the firm as newly constituted.

Unless expressly released, a former partner cannot regard himself as free from claims relating to his period as a partner until those claims have been satisfied, become statute barred, or have otherwise lapsed.

Wrongful acts and omissions

2.30   The principles that govern the treatment of wrongful acts and omissions, like torts and frauds, are set out in *s 10* of the *Partnership Act 1890* which reads as follows:

> 'Where, by any wrongful act or omission of any partner acting in the ordinary course of business of the firm, or with the authority of his co-partners, loss or injury is caused to any person not being a partner in the firm, or any penalty is incurred, the firm is liable, therefor, to the same extent as the partner so acting or omitting to act.'

As in the case of *s 5* of the *Partnership Act 1890* and contracts (see **2.26** above), a partner must be acting with the authority of the firm or in the usual course of business, the firm is to incur liability.

There are many examples of cases in which a firm has been held vicariously liable for torts committed by partners acting in the usual course of the business. Perhaps the most relevant one in the context of a professional partnership is that of a tortious claim in respect of negligent advice. For example, if a solicitor fails to act on instructions to draw up a will and the testator dies, the disappointed beneficiaries may be able to recover from the solicitor and his firm.

The scope of *s 10* was considered by the House of Lords in *Dubai Aluminium Co Ltd v Salaam and Livingston* [2003] 2 AC 366. It was held that the meaning of wrongful acts or omissions should be widely construed and its applicability should not be confined to torts properly so called and frauds. Consequently, the firm and its innocent partners are vicariously

17

liable for a partner's conduct under *s 10*, provided three conditions are satisfied: (i) the conduct is wrongful; (ii) it causes damage to the claimant; and (iii) it is carried out in the ordinary course of the firm's business. The House of Lords decision in the *Dubai Aluminium* case was applied in *Eamon McHugh* (High Court) 2003 WLR 2293614. In *Walker v Stones* [2001] QB 902 the Court of Appeal considered the question of whether a breach of trust by a partner in a firm of solicitors acting as trustee for a family trust fell within the ordinary course of business of the solicitors firm. It was held that it fell outside the ordinary course of the business of the firm, and therefore the firm could not be held vicariously liable for the wrongdoing of the partner by virtue of *s 10*.

Misapplication of money and property

2.31   *Section 11* of the *Partnership Act 1890* provides that where one partner acting in the scope of his apparent authority receives the money or property of a third person and misapplies it, or a firm in the course of its business receives money or property of a third person and misapplies it while in the firm's custody, then the firm is liable to account for the money it had received.

Once again, the underlying principles that lie behind *ss 5* and *10* of the *Partnership Act 1890* apply, in that the firm is only liable where the money is received within the scope of the partner's express or implied authority and it also has to be in the context of the carrying on of the partnership's usual business. Thus, if a client pays money to an architect to enable the firm to discharge a quantity surveyor's bill on his behalf, and the architect uses the money for his own purposes, the architect's firm will be liable to account for the money it had received. However, if the money was received to enable the architect to place a bet on a horse on the client's behalf, the firm would not be liable.

Breaches of trust

2.32   *Section 13* of the *Partnership Act 1890* provides that:

> 'If a partner, being a trustee, improperly employs trust property in the business or on the account of the partnership, no other partner is liable for the trust property to the persons beneficially entitled therein.'

However, there are a number of provisos. *Section 13* does not prevent the trust money being followed and recovered from the firm if it is still in its possession and under its control. In addition, it does not affect any liability incurred by any partner by reason of his having notice of the breach of trust. Liability in these circumstances will be governed by the general doctrines of 'knowing assistance' and 'knowing receipt'.

Most professions have their own rules which tend to be more stringent than the general provisions in *s 13*. Therefore, any potential transgression is likely to involve relevant rules of professional conduct as well as liabilities for breach of trust.

Sharing of liabilities

2.33   Under *s 9* of the *Partnership Act 1890*, partners are jointly liable with one another for the obligations of the partnership. As far as third parties are concerned, any partner is liable, without limit, for the firm's debts incurred when he was a partner and a creditor may recover a partnership debt by enforcement against an individual partner's assets without first enforcing against the partnership's assets. As a default rule, a partner who discharges a partnership liability is entitled to an indemnity from the firm (*Partnership Act 1890, s 24(2)*) and has a right to contribution from the other partners. However, it is open to the partners to agree between themselves how liabilities are to be borne. This is generally achieved through the sharing of profits and losses and set out in the constitutional document of the partnership. The partnership's liabilities will be reflected in its profit and loss account and will therefore lead to an increased loss or decreased profit to be shared between the partners as noted in CHAPTER 8, PROFIT SHARES. The sharing of profits and losses is deemed by *s 24(1)* of the *Partnership Act 1890* to be equal unless the partnership agreement provides differently. A consistent contrary course of conduct, such as sharing profits and losses exactly in proportion to unequal capital contributions, will operate to disapply *s 24(1)* (*Partnership Act 1890, s 19*).

However, where a partner incurs a liability for the firm which falls outside the scope of his actual authority, the other partners will generally be entitled to seek an indemnity from him in respect of that liability, assuming that he has sufficient assets to meet his obligations. Similarly, the partners will often agree to indemnify non-partners who might be held out as partners, eg salaried and retired partners. The partners will also generally agree to provide for certain liabilities (eg claims for professional negligence) through insurance. Further discussion of professional indemnity insurance is set out in CHAPTER 16, INSURANCE.

Limiting liability by contract

2.34   An obvious way for a firm to control exposure to claims by third parties is to include a term in its conditions of business or letter of engagement limiting liability to a particular sum.

The extent to which this can be a solution to the problem of unlimited liability depends to a large extent on whether clients are prepared to agree to such limitations. However, it is now becoming much more common for professional firms to limit their exposure to claims by contract. For example, the maximum liability is often limited to a multiple of the fee, to an insurable amount, or to loss of a particular description. Clauses of this nature may be subject to statutory control under the *Unfair Contract Terms Act 1977*. For example, any exclusion clause contained in a firm's written standard terms of business must be reasonable having regard to all the circumstances, such as the availability of insurance. (*Unfair Contract Terms Act 1977, ss 3, 11*). It is therefore essential to seek legal advice before relying on such clauses.

Section 60(5) of the *Solicitors Act 1974* provides that any provision limiting the liability of solicitors in contentious business is void. *Section 532* of the *Companies Act 2006* prevents auditors from being indemnified against or exempted from any liability resulting from their negligence or breach of duty.

Other methods of protection of partners

Insurance

2.35 Professional indemnity insurance remains a very important means of protection and for further discussion of this, see **CHAPTER 16**. Some professional firms may be unable to obtain adequate cover for certain high-risk areas of practice. Insurance cover is provided on a claims made basis, ie a given policy covers claims made in that policy year, not negligent advice given in that policy year. Even if negligent advice is given in a year when the partnership has adequate cover, that cover may no longer be available by the time the claim is made. As a result of the problems with professional indemnity insurance in the market some partnerships have set up their own captive insurance companies, or mutual insurance companies shared with others, to provide for future uninsured claims.

Professional indemnity policies only cover professional indemnity claims and cannot protect against the claims of banks, landlords and other general trade creditors. Care must also be taken when taking on lateral hire partners from firms against which claims are existing or likely. In some circumstances, for example, where the number of partners taken on exceeds a threshold or the merged firm will use the other firm's name or former premises, it may be that such potential liabilities will need to be insured by the acquiring firm by virtue of the applicable professional indemnity insurance regulations. See, for example, the minimum terms and conditions of professional indemnity insurance in *Solicitors Indemnity Insurance Rules 2009, Appendix 1.*

Debts

2.36 Although all partners are jointly liable for the partnerships debts, partners can agree to share responsibility for debts in any way they like (see **2.33** above). Careful drafting of the partnership agreement can provide protection for particular partners through indemnities and profit and loss sharing arrangements. Of course, an individual partner will still be fully responsible for the partnership debts as far as third parties are concerned, and the value of his rights against fellow partners will depend on whether they and the firm have sufficient personal assets to meet claims brought by him under the partnership agreement.

Asset protection

2.37 Asset protection involves the transfer of assets to a spouse, or into a trust for the benefit of the partner and his family. The intention is to protect those assets from creditors and ensure that they are available for the partner's family should the worst happen. These arrangements involve substantial civil and even potential criminal law risks.

Reasons for insolvency

2.38 A partnership may suffer financial difficulties, perhaps because it has undertaken fixed overheads in better times, which are now difficult or impossible to reduce, despite falling turnover and pressure on profit margins. For example, many firms have entered into leases in respect of their premises which can run for up to 25 years and contain upwards-only rent review clauses. The market demands that many professional support staff are entitled to relatively high salary levels with little or no discretionary or bonus element. Many firms have committed themselves to making inflation adjusted annual payments to their former partners and their spouses, although this is becoming increasingly rare in practice. Some firms have very substantial borrowings, in addition to individual partners' borrowings taken up in order to finance the acquisition of their homes and their shares of equity in the partnership. In these circumstances, a downturn in business can be catastrophic. Once a firm's profits are under pressure, those partners who are practising in an area which remains profitable are often not prepared to continue to work hard for less reward than is available in competing firms. Such partners may be tempted by an offer from a competitor firm which remains more profitable, with the consequence that a dwindling group of partners remains responsible for the same fixed overheads. Once the spiral of decline has started it can be very difficult indeed to pull out of it.

Action required

2.39 A well-managed firm ensures that it has accurate and detailed management information available at all times, which will enable it to detect a downturn in profits very early on. It can then respond, eg by investing in new business areas, by carefully controlling costs and partner drawings, by supporting and encouraging partners to enable them to achieve maximum profitability, and perhaps by encouraging underperforming partners to leave or, as has been seen in recent years, actively reducing partner numbers through programmes of compulsory retirement. In some cases, it may be appropriate at an early stage to try to prevent the spiral accelerating by all the partners mutually agreeing that there are to be no resignations, or reduced drawings, for a period which is thought to be sufficient to enable the business as a whole to weather the crisis. It is essential that the financial position of the firm should be monitored closely during a difficult period, and that appropriate insolvency advice should be obtained. Individual partners will be subject to the provisions of the *Insolvency Act 1986* relating to bankruptcy offences, including the offences relating to obtaining credit and failure to keep proper accounting records. It should also be borne in mind that, in the event of an insolvency, the court now has power to make a disqualification order against a partner whose conduct as an officer of the partnership makes him unfit to be concerned in the management of a company or LLP, although such a disqualification order will only have the effect of preventing the partner from acting as a director of a limited company or a member of an LLP and not from acting as a partner during the period of disqualification. It is also possible that the wrongful and fraudulent trading provisions of the *Insolvency Act 1986* could apply to a partner if the partnership goes into liquidation, although this is by no means clear.

Voluntary arrangements

2.40 It will rarely be in the interests of creditors to force a professional firm and its members into insolvency, which may prevent the partners from practising under their professional rules and therefore destroy the earning power on which creditors depend. Recognising that fact, *art 4* of the *Insolvent Partnerships Order 1994* provides that the provisions of the *Insolvency Act 1986* dealing with company voluntary arrangements apply to insolvent partnerships (subject to some modifications). Essentially, voluntary arrangements involve debtors agreeing new terms for the repayment of debts with their creditors under the supervision of a qualified insolvency practitioner, and the *1994 Order* facilitates voluntary arrangements with a firm as a whole, which may be easier to achieve than a series of interlocking voluntary arrangements with each member of the partnership. The procedure is that, if the proposed arrangement is approved by a majority of over 75 per cent by value of those creditors attending and voting at a special creditors' meeting (whether in person or by proxy), then all creditors of a partnership who were given notice of the meeting and were entitled to vote will be bound by the arrangements. In this way, the partnership may avoid being wound up, and be able to trade out of its difficulties.

The *Insolvency Act 2000* contains provisions which provide for a moratorium on creditor action for certain eligible companies whilst proposals are put together for a voluntary arrangement. By virtue of the *Insolvent Partnerships* (*Amendment*) (*No 2*) *Order 2002*, the moratorium is also available to eligible partnerships whilst they are putting together a proposal for a partnership voluntary arrangement. The *Insolvency Act 2000* also contains provisions which would make the voluntary arrangement binding on all creditors, not just those with notice of the meeting, if the requisite majority votes in favour of the proposals.

Administration procedure

2.41 The *Insolvent Partnerships Order 1994* also provides that the administration procedure available to companies under the *Insolvency Act 1986* will now also be available to partnerships. An administration order may be made by the court if it considers that it is likely to achieve one or more of the three statutory purposes set out in the *Insolvency Act 1986*, namely the survival of the whole or any part of the partnership business as a going concern, the approval of a voluntary arrangement or the disposal of the partnerships' property in a more advantageous way than would be the case on a winding up.

An administrator, who must be an independent insolvency practitioner, will have control of the partnership during the course of the administration and while the administration order is in force no order can be made for the winding up of the partnership. Furthermore, no steps may be taken to enforce any security over the partnership property, and no other proceedings can be commenced or continued against the partnership, without the leave of the administrator or the consent of the court. This provides a useful breathing space during which the administrator can attempt to achieve the purpose for which the administration order was made.

It should be noted that far-reaching reforms to the *Insolvency Act 1986* have been made in the *Enterprise Act 2002*. These reforms have streamlined the administration process by introducing a new out-of-court route into administration in addition to the existing court route into administration. The purposes for which an administration order can be obtained have also been replaced with a single, three-part purpose with the primary emphasis on rescue. Although the *Enterprise Act 2002* refers to corporate insolvency (rather than partnership insolvency), it takes effect by amending the provisions of the *Insolvency Act 1986* and so, by virtue of the *Insolvent Partnerships Order 1994*, the *Insolvent Partnerships (Amendment) Order 2005* and the *Insolvent Partnerships (Amendment) Order 2006* the new streamlined administration procedure under *Schedule B1* to the *1986 Act* will also be available (subject to certain modifications) to partnerships.

Winding up

2.42 If all else fails, the creditors or the partners themselves may be forced to petition for a winding up. There are various different ways in which a partnership can be wound up. Following the *Insolvency Act 1986* and the *Insolvent Partnerships Order 1994*, all partnerships of whatever size are now subject to the regime affecting unregistered companies. This regime is concurrent with the provisions relating to the insolvency of individual partners, and it is possible to present an application to wind up a partnership as an unregistered company concurrently with insolvency petitions being presented against two or more of the partners. It should be noted, however, that it is possible for a partnership to be unable to pay its debts for the purposes of the *Insolvency Act 1986* notwithstanding that the value of the assets of one partner are greater than the partnership's liabilities. It makes no difference that the creditors of the partnership have full recourse against that partner. A detailed review of the law of insolvency in relation to partnerships is outside the scope of this book. However, broadly speaking, the partnership's assets are used first to meet the debts of the partnership, and only then to meet the separate debts of individual partners. The separate estates of the individual partners are used first to meet individual debts and only then to meet the debts of the partnership.

On a winding up of a partnership, by virtue of *s 38* of the *Partnership Act 1890*, the authority of the partners to bind the partnership and the other partners continues notwithstanding the dissolution, but only so far as necessary to wind up the affairs of the partnership and to complete unfinished transactions.

Professional implications of insolvency

2.43 Insolvency may have serious implications under the professional rules applicable. For example, under *s 15(1)* of the *Solicitors Act 1974*, a solicitor's practising certificate is automatically suspended if he is adjudicated bankrupt, and remains suspended until the bankruptcy is annulled.

The Law Society has power to hear applications to have a practising certificate reinstated notwithstanding bankruptcy. If this is refused, a further appeal may be made to the High Court.

Similarly, under Bye-law 7(a) of the ICAEW Principal Bye-laws, a chartered accountant automatically ceases to be a member of the institute on his bankruptcy. The council has power to readmit former members on the terms they think fit.

In either case, the bankruptcy may trigger the automatic dissolution of the firm under *s 33* of the *Partnership Act 1890*, subject to contrary agreement.

If a partner enters into a voluntary arrangement he is likely to avoid these professional problems, although the professional body is still likely to take note of the partner's conduct. For example, a solicitor's practising certificate will not be suspended but the Solicitors Disciplinary Tribunal has power to impose conditions on the solicitor concerned. Furthermore, the Law Society has power to intervene in the solicitor's practice, and will do so if it considers that there is evidence that clients' money may be at risk.

Application of Financial Services and Markets Act 2000

2.44 A partnership may be a collective investment scheme for the purposes of the *Financial Services and Markets Act 2000* (*FSMA 2000*) as an arrangement with respect to property (its goodwill, debtors and cash, for example) the purpose or effect of which is to enable the participants (the members) to participate in its profits arising from the acquisition, holding, management or disposal of that property (*FSMA 2000, s 235(1)*). If it is, then the 'operator' of the scheme will require authorisation by the Financial Services Authority (FSA), something which will rarely be desirable for a professional firm. However, in the context of a professional firm, the exemption where all the partners have day-to-day control over the management of the property should be available provided that the partnership agreement provides for all partners to work in the business and to be able collectively, by a specified majority, to override management decisions by any executive appointed under the agreement. The provisions could equally catch LLPs where members do not participate in day–to-day management, and this is discussed in some detail in Whittaker and Machell *The Law of Limited Liability Partnerships* (3rd Edn) at 18.21–18.28.

Partnership Law Reform

2.45 Partnership law was extensively reviewed by the Law Commission jointly with the Scottish Law Commission and a joint report was published on 10 October 2003 (Law Com No 283 and Scot Law Com No 192). The Report reviewed the law as it then stood, reported on feedback from the consultation undertaken, made recommendations and proposals and set out a draft Partnership Bill. In April 2004, the Department of Trade and Industry (DTI) initiated a further consultation into the economic impact of the reform of partnership law (URN04/966). The responses indicated that the proposed reforms to partnership law were highly controversial (especially as it was proposed to afford separate legal personality to English partnerships for the first time) but generally supported the reforms to the limited partnerships regime. In light of this, the Government decided to drop the proposed reform of partnership law generally and to take forward the proposed reforms for limited partnership law only. The programme of reform of the law applicable to limited partnerships is discussed further in CHAPTER 4, CHOOSING AN APPROPRIATE BUSINESS STRUCTURE.

Chapter 3   Limited Liability Partnerships

Introduction

3.1   Limited liability partnerships (LLPs) were introduced into English law by the *Limited Liability Partnerships Act 2000* (*LLP Act*), which was brought into effect by ministerial order on 6 April 2001.

The *LLP Act* is accompanied by a series of statutory instruments, especially the *Limited Liability Partnerships Regulations 2001* (*LLP Regulations 2001*) and the *Limited Liability Partnerships (Application of Companies Act 2006) Regulations 2009* (*LLP Regulations 2009*). These provide for the regulation of LLPs by applying to them, with modifications, the appropriate provisions of the existing law which relates to companies and partnerships largely contained in the *Companies Act 2006*, the *Insolvency Act 1986*, the *Income and Corporation Taxes Act 1988* and the *Taxation of Chargeable Gains Act 1992*.

Until October 2009, the *LLP Act* applied to England, Wales and Scotland, and the *Limited Liability Partnership Act (Northern Ireland) 2002* and associated regulations applied in Northern Ireland. From 1 October 2009, all LLPs will be incorporated under the *LLP Act*, and LLPs incorporated under the Northern Ireland Act prior to 1 October 2009 are treated as registered and incorporated under the *LLP Act*.

The basic structure

3.2   The name 'limited liability partnership' reflects the fact that LLPs were introduced in response to demands from partners in professional firms for a suitable form of limited liability vehicle, but in fact an LLP is much more like a company than a partnership. It is a separate legal entity and a body corporate able to enter into contracts and hold property in its own right. It continues in existence despite any change in membership and third parties contract with the LLP rather than with the individual members. Members of an LLP, like shareholders of a company, generally have limited liability in the event of insolvency of the LLP (subject to the rules on insolvency and especially to a special 'clawback' regime which applies to LLPs only – see **3.16** below). LLPs can do anything which a partnership could have done. Partnership law generally has no application to LLPs, except as mentioned at **3.3** below (*LLP Act, s 1(5)*). However, large sections of the *Companies Act 2006* and the *Insolvency Act 1986*, as they apply to companies, are adapted for the purposes of LLPs. For example, an LLP is required to file audited accounts and an annual return (subject to special rules for small LLPs) at Companies House.

What is a limited liability partnership?

3.3 An LLP is a body corporate with legal personality separate from that of its members and which is formed by being incorporated under the *LLP Act* (*LLP Act, s 1(1), (2)*). It has unlimited capacity (*LLP Act, s 1(3)*) and is therefore able to undertake a full range of business activities. The members have 'such liability to contribute to its assets in the event of the LLP being wound up as is provided for by virtue of [the *LLP Act*]' (*LLP Act, s 1(4)*). There is no express statement that members will have limited liability, but since the *LLP Act* provides for members to be agents for the LLP and not one another (see *LLP Act, s 6* and **3.10** below), and the regulations introduced in relation to *s 14* of the *LLP Act* apply the insolvency regime applicable to companies with some important modifications, the effect is to give members limited liability in a similar way to shareholders in a company – hence the name 'limited liability partnership'.

Furthermore, in order to eliminate the risk that members might otherwise incur joint and several liability through the common law rules on mutual agency, it is expressly stated that partnership law does not apply to LLPs except as expressly provided by the *LLP Act* or any other enactment (*LLP Act, s 1(5)*). The only provisions based on partnership law are the 'default provisions' applicable to the extent that there is no members' agreement, as discussed at **3.9** below.

When is LLP status available?

3.4 For an LLP to be incorporated, 'two or more persons associated for carrying on a lawful business with a view to profit must have subscribed their names to an incorporation document' (*LLP Act, s 2(1)(a)*). It will be noted that the wording is similar to *s 1* of the *Partnership Act 1890* and that partnership case law would probably be used as a guide to interpretation accordingly. It was intended that LLPs should only be available in circumstances where there might have been a partnership, so **2.2–2.4** will be equally applicable to LLPs in relation to what is a business for this purpose. As a result of the 'business' requirement, therefore, LLPs will not be suitable for organisations where there is no profit motive, like mutual trading arrangements, members' clubs and charities or arrangements where there is no 'business', such as mere asset holding structures. However, the LLP structure is available to any business conducted by two or more persons all of whom have a view to profit and is not restricted to the regulated professions.

Incorporation of an LLP

3.5 An 'incorporation document' (Form LL IN 01) signed by the persons associated to carry on the lawful business with a view to profit, or an authenticated copy, must be delivered to the Registrar (*LLP Act, s 2(1)(a)*, (*b*)). In addition, a subscriber to the incorporation document, or a solicitor engaged to form the LLP, must certify that two or more persons named in the form are associated for carrying on lawful business with a view to profit (*LLP Act, s 2(1)(c)*). The incorporation document must state:

(a)   the name of the LLP;

(b)   whether the LLP will have a registered office situated in England and Wales, in Wales, in Scotland or in Northern Ireland;

(c)   the address of the registered office;

(d)   the required particulars of each of the members on incorporation; and

(e)   the names of the designated members or that all the members are to be 'designated members' (*LLP Act, s 2(2)(e)*, and see **3.12** below for a discussion of designated members).

Making a false statement will be an offence punishable by imprisonment or a fine or both (*LLP Act, s 2(3), (4)*). Thus, solicitors and others engaged in the formation of the LLP will need to take care to ensure that the incorporation document is correct and that the requirements of *s 2(1)(a)* really are satisfied.

Assuming that the Registrar is satisfied that the requirements of *s 2* of the *LLP Act*, are met, he then registers the incorporation document, and issues a certificate of registration which is conclusive evidence that the LLP has been incorporated by the name specified in the incorporation document (*LLP Act, s 3*).

Register of Members

3.6 The required particulars of members to be included on the incorporation document are the same as the details to be included in the LLP's register of members and the LLP's register of members' residential addresses (*LLP Act, s 2(2ZA)*).

The requirement to maintain these two registers was introduced on 1 October 2009, to bring LLPs into line with companies, and the registers are analogous to the register of directors and the register of directors' residential addresses maintained by companies (*Companies Act 2006, ss 162, 165*).

The register of members must be kept available for inspection at the LLP's registered office or at another place notified to Companies House as an inspection location. The register may be inspected by members of the LLP for no fee, and by any other person on the payment of a fee (*Companies Act 2006, s 162(4), (5)*).

Failure to comply with the requirements may result in a fine for the LLP and every designated member of the LLP who is at fault (*Companies Act 2006, ss 162(6), (7) and 165(4), (5)*).

For individuals, the details to be included in the LLP's register of members are:

(a) name and any former name used for business purpose in the past 20 years (although married women need not state their maiden name unless it was used for business purposes);

(b) service address;

(c) the country or state (or part of the UK) in which he is usually resident;

(d) date of birth and the required particulars of each of the members on incorporation; and

(e) whether he is a designated member.

For corporate members and firms, the details included in the LLP's register of members are:

(a) corporate or firm name;

(b) registered or principal address (this cannot be a PO box);

(c) in the case of an EEA company to which the First Company Law Directive (EC/151/EEC) applies,

   (i) where the company file is kept; and

   (ii) the registration number in that register,

(so, in the case of a company incorporated at Companies House in England & Wales, 'England' then its company number, eg '1234567').

(d) in other cases (which includes corporate members which are not companies, such as LLPs acting as a corporate member):

   (i) the legal form of the company and the law by which it is governed;

   (ii) the register in which it is entered and the registration number in that register; and

(e) whether it is a designated member.

The register of members' residential addresses applies only to members who are individuals and must state the usual residential address of each of the LLP's individual members (*Companies Act 2006, s 165(1), (2)*). The reason for maintaining the residential addresses register separately from the register of members is to protect the personal information of LLP members. The members' service addresses are publicly available, whereas the residential addresses are protected from disclosure in all but very limited circumstances (see below).

Accordingly, if a member chooses to disclose that information by using his usual residential address as his service address, the register of residential addresses need only contain an entry stating that his residential address is 'the same as the service address' (*Companies Act 2006, s 165(3)*).

If he would prefer greater confidentiality, he may choose to state in the register of members that his service address is 'the LLP's registered office' and only include his residential address in the register of members' residential addresses.

A member's residential address, or the fact that a member's service address is his residential address, is 'protected information' and it remains protected information even after the member has ceased to be a member of the LLP (*Companies Act 2006, s 240*). Unless the member (or former member) consents, LLPs must not disclose protected information other than to communicate with that member, to comply with the *LLP Act* or the *Companies Act 2006* or in order to comply with a court order (*Companies Act 2006, s 241*). The Registrar of Companies may only disclose protected information to public authorities, to credit reference agencies or to comply with a court order (*Companies Act 2006, ss 242, 243*). However, if it appears that members are not receiving communications at their service address, the Registrar may begin a procedure to replace the member's service address with his usual residential address (*Companies Act 2006, ss 245, 246*).

If the member of the LLP considers that there is a serious risk that the member, or a person living with him, will be subjected to violence or intimidation as a result of the activities of the LLP, an application may be made to prevent the Registrar of Companies from disclosing that member's residential address to credit reference agencies (see further *Companies Act 2006, s 243*, and the *Companies (Disclosure of Address) Regulations 2009*).

The new procedures relating the register of residential addresses replace the previous system whereby members applied to the Secretary of State for a confidentiality order (as set out in the *Limited Liability Partnerships (Particulars of Usual Residential Address) (Confidentiality Orders) Regulations 2002*). LLP members who had the benefit of a confidentiality order prior to 1 October 2009 are treated as if they had made a successful application under *s 243* as described in the paragraph above, and the requirement to include their residential address in the register of residential addresses does not extend to these members.

The registers may be kept in hard or electronic form, provided that the information is adequately recorded for future reference and, where the registers are kept in electronic form, these are capable of being reproduced in hard copy form (*Companies Act 2006, ss 1134, 1135*).

Name and registered office

3.7   *Section 1(6)* of the *LLP Act* introduces the Schedule to the Act, which contains provisions relating to the name and registered office of an LLP. The name of the LLP must include the expression 'Limited Liability Partnership', 'LLP' (in upper or lower case) or Welsh equivalents. The Registrar will not incorporate an LLP with a name which does not comply with the rules set out in the *Companies Act 2006* and the *Company and Business Names (Miscellaneous Provisions) Regulations 2009*. The key restrictions are on names which:

- would constitute a criminal offence or are offensive;

- suggest a connection with the Government;

- include 'sensitive' words or expressions (such as 'Bank', 'Charity', 'Fund', 'Holding' or 'International', although some sensitive words and expressions may be used if permission is sought from the body specified in the Appendices to the *Company, Limited Liability Partnership and Business Names (Sensitive Words and Expressions) Regulations 2009*);

- are the 'same as' another name appearing on the registrar's index of names (eg where there is an existing company or LLP on the register and the only difference between its name and the proposed LLP's name is a word such as: 'biz', 'co', 'co uk', 'co.uk', 'com', 'company', 'UK', 'United Kingdom', 'Wales', 'Cymru', 'net', 'GB', 'Great Britain', 'org.uk', 'services' or 'international'), unless the proposed LLP will form part of the same group as the LLP or other body that already 'owns' that name and that body has agreed to the proposed name; and

- include an expression or abbreviation that implies it has a different legal status (eg using public limited company, plc, limited partnership or LP in the name).

It is also advisable: (1) to check the Trade Marks register at the UK Intellectual Property Office prior to incorporating an LLP to see if the proposed name is identical or similar to a registered trade mark which could lead to trade mark infringement proceedings; and (2) to conduct an internet search of the proposed name to establish whether another business uses the name for a similar type of business or in a similar geographical area.

LLPs must have a registered office at all times in the United Kingdom, and the incorporation document has to state whether it is in England and Wales, in Wales, in Scotland, or in Northern Ireland. Notice has to be given of changes of registered office, although valid service may be made on the LLP at the previous address for 14 days after the change of address is registered. Note that it is not necessary for an LLP to have an actual place of business in the UK, and that the LLP as a business organisation may be a possibility for firms practising only outside the UK, depending on the regulations applicable to them in their home jurisdiction.

Membership of an LLP

3.8 Initially, the members are those who subscribe their names to the incorporation document, assuming they are still living or in existence (*LLP Act, s 4(1)*), but any other individual or corporate body can become a member of the LLP if so agreed with the existing members. The agreement to introduce the new member, rather than registration of a new member with the Registrar of Companies, creates the new membership but the appointment of a new member must be notified to the Registrar within 14 days (*LLP Act, s 9(1)(a)*). Any change in the particulars contained in the register of members or the register of members' residential addresses must also be notified within 14 days (*LLP Act, s 9(1)(b)*). The notice must contain a statement that the member consents to acting in that capacity and should state the particulars of the new member that are required in the register of members and the register of members' residential addresses (*LLP Act, s 9(3)(a)*). If a notice is delivered providing that a member's service address has changed, but no change to the member's residential address has been notified, a statement that no change has been made to the register of members' residential addresses must also be included (*LLP Act, s 9(3ZA)*). Failure to comply with these rules is an offence (*LLP Act, s 9(4)*). A member ceases to be a member on death or dissolution of that member or in accordance with agreement with the other members, and, in the absence of agreement to the contrary, a member can cease to be a member on giving 'reasonable notice' to the other members (*LLP Act, s 4(3)*).

A member of an LLP is not regarded for any purpose as employed by the LLP, unless he would have been regarded as employed by the LLP if he and the other members were in fact partners in a partnership (*LLP Act, s 4(4)*). This provision is confusing given that partner and employee status are, generally, mutually exclusive, but the effect appears to be that the member will not be an employee by reason only that he is a member of the LLP, but he may be an employee as well as a member if he has a contractual relationship with the LLP which would have amounted to a contract of employment if the relationship had been one with a partnership instead. Employed members will have statutory employment rights, and care must be taken in drafting the members' agreement to avoid an employment relationship unless employed status is intended. Whether or not an employment relationship is intended, in order to protect the limited liability of the members it should be made clear that no partnership is intended and that neither the LLP nor any of its other members has authority to act as agent for the salaried member. If an employment relationship is intended, factors indicative of employment (see *Chitty on Contracts* (29th Edn) 39–010 to 39–028) should be built into the relationship. If an employment relationship is not intended, on the other hand, this should be expressly stated and such factors should be avoided. In *Kovats v TFO Management LLP* [2009] ICR 1140, the Employment Appeal Tribunal set out a list of factors that could indicate that a partnership relationship was intended. These included: the fact that the parties intended a partnership-like relationship, signature of a partnership/LLP agreement, payment of drawings gross, the member accounting for income tax himself, and provision of capital of some sort. The tax status of members with an employment relationship with the LLP is considered in CHAPTER 19.

Relations between members, and between the LLP and the members

3.9　Except as otherwise expressly provided in the *Act*, relations between members and between the LLP and its members are to be governed by agreement between the members, or between the LLP and the members, or in the absence of agreement, by *regs 7* and *8* of the *LLP Regulations 2001,* which contain the default regime (similar to the default regime applicable to partnerships) and which provide that:

'7. The mutual rights and duties of the members and the mutual rights and duties of the LLP and the members shall be determined, subject to the provisions of the general law and to the terms of any LLP agreement, by the following rules:

(1) All the members of a limited liability partnership are entitled to share equally in the capital and profits of the limited liability partnership.

(2) The LLP must indemnify every member in respect of payments made and personal liabilities incurred by him:

(a) in the ordinary and proper conduct of the business of the LLP; or

(b) in or about anything necessarily done for the preservation of the business or property of the LLP.

(3)　Every member may take part in the management of the LLP.

(4)　No member shall be entitled to remuneration for acting in the business or management of the LLP.

(5)　No person may be introduced as a member or voluntarily assign an interest in an LLP without the consent of all existing members.

(6)　Any difference arising as to ordinary matters connected with the business of the LLP may be decided by a majority of the members, but no change may be made in the nature of the business of the LLP without the consent of all members.

(7)　The books and records of the LLP are to be made available for inspection at the registered office of the LLP or at such other place as the members think fit and every member of the LLP may when he thinks fit have access to and inspect and copy any of them.

(8)　Each member shall render true accounts and full information of all things affecting the LLP to any member or his legal representative.

(9)　If a member, without the consent of the LLP, carries on any business of the same nature as and competing with the LLP, he must account for and pay over to the LLP all profits made by him in that business.

(10)　Every member must account to the LLP for any benefit derived by him without the consent of the LLP from any transaction concerning the LLP, or from any use by him of the property of the LLP, name or business connection.

8. No majority of the members can expel any member unless a power to do so has been conferred by express agreement between the members.'

It will be noted that these provisions are broadly based on the provisions of *ss 24* and *25* of the *Partnership Act 1890*.

The *LLP Regulations 2009* also provide minority protection in the form of *s 994* of the *Companies Act 2006* as it applies to LLPs. This allows a member to apply for a court order where the LLP's affairs are conducted in a manner which is unfairly prejudicial to the interests of the members generally or some part of them. This provision may, however, be excluded by the unanimous decision of the members and a provision to that effect is often included in the members' agreement so that the agreement itself sets out an exclusive code for dispute resolution.

As can be seen, the *LLP Regulations 2001* only set out the most basic rules regulating relations between members, which will rarely be sufficient or, in most cases, appropriate and will at best constitute only a basic code for the simplest situation. Furthermore, the general guidance of the rules of equity and law governing partnerships is expressly excluded by *s 1(5)* of the *LLP Act,* and there will be no general duty of good faith between members and only the most basic minority protections. In these circumstances, a detailed and comprehensive agreement setting out the rights and obligations of each member and the LLP itself will, in practice, be essential in order to avoid uncertainty and the risk of litigation (see **3.18** below and APPENDIX 5).

Relationship with third parties – limited liability

3.10   As the name 'limited liability partnership' implies, the key objective of the legislation is to create limited liability for members of the LLP and, as noted at **3.3** above, this is achieved by a combination of factors. *Section 1* of the *LLP Act* provides for the LLP to be a separate legal person and for partnership law (and, therefore, rules about mutual agency between partners and joint and several liability) to be excluded. *Section 6* of the *LLP Act,* provides (at *sub-s (1)*) for members to be agents of the LLP. Nowhere is it provided that there is any implied agency between the members themselves. Therefore, when a member enters into a contract with a third party on behalf of the LLP, the member generally binds the LLP and not the members personally. Thus the LLP, and not the members, will be bound. Furthermore, as noted at **3.16** below, there are limited obligations on the members to contribute to the assets of an LLP on its insolvency. The effect is to create a limited liability regime which is very similar to that applicable to companies under the *Companies Act 2006* (but note the unique 'clawback' rule discussed at **3.16** below).

It should be noted that the LLP will not be bound where a member deals with a third party if the member in fact had no authority to act on behalf of the LLP in that way and the third party either knows that the member has no authority, or does not know or believe him to be a member of the LLP (*LLP Act, s 6(2)*). However, if a member commits a wrongful act or omission in the course of the LLP's business or with its authority, the LLP will be liable in any event (*LLP Act, s 6(4)*). Because of the implied agency of members, it will be very important to ensure that the actual scope of the authority of members is clearly set out in the members' agreement.

Third parties are entitled to assume that a member is still a member, even if they have in fact ceased to be a member, unless they have actual notice that the member has ceased to be a member or the Registrar of Companies has been notified that the former member has ceased to be a member (*LLP Act, s 6(3)*).

While third parties will generally only have contractual claims against the LLP, and not its members, a member who is personally negligent or who otherwise causes loss to clients of the LLP or third parties may still be personally liable in tort. In the House of Lords case of *Williams v Natural Life Health Foods Ltd* [1998] 1 WLR 830, it was held that, in deciding whether a person is personally liable to a client, the courts will have regard to various factors including whether that person has assumed a personal responsibility for the advice given so as to create a special relationship, whether the client has in fact relied on the advice and whether that reliance was reasonable. The factors outlined in *Williams v Natural Life Health Foods Ltd* were affirmed by the High Court and the Court of Appeal in the case of *Partco Group Ltd and another v Wragg and Scott* [2002] 1 Lloyd's Rep 320 and [2002] 2 Lloyd's Rep 343.

In *Merrett v Babb* [2001] 3 WLR 1, the Court of Appeal considered that the defendant's liability would not necessarily depend on his active assumption of responsibility for the advice, but that such assumption of personal responsibility may be recognised or imposed by law by reference to the nature of the relationship. The question was stated as being whether the professional is to be taken to have assumed responsibility to the client to guard against the loss for which damages are claimed. In *Merrett v Babb*, the claim arose from a negligent property valuation that was prepared for the lender, but also supplied directly to the buyers by the individual property surveyor in his own name. Even though there was no direct instruction from the borrower to the surveyor (having been instructed by the lender), as a matter of fact the borrower had relied upon the professional skill and care expected of a surveyor and of that individual as a member of that profession and that it was reasonable for them to have done so in the circumstances.

The law is developing and lawyers are still debating how these two cases should be reconciled, but *Merrett v Babb* at least demonstrates that it will be easier to establish personal responsibility in the case of professional staff, whether members or employees, of a professional LLP because of the fiduciary relationship between client and professional adviser. In the professional context, therefore, it is particularly important to consider making it clear in the engagement letter with the client that the client is contracting solely with the LLP and that no member or employee of the LLP assumes a personal duty of care. Engagement letters and other correspondence, such as email footers and websites should also clarify that references to a partner mean references to a member of the LLP. It is also important, if (as is often the case) the engagement letter expressly excludes third party rights, to make it clear that members and employees can take the benefit of this provision of the engagement letter. While such provisions may be regulated by the *Unfair Contract Terms Act 1977*, which seeks to prevent the unreasonable exclusion of liability for negligence, it is thought that in most cases it ought to be reasonable to include such a provision where it is properly drawn to the attention of the client, the LLP retains liability for the negligence and the LLP carries reasonable professional indemnity insurance to cover claims. For a fuller discussion of these issues, see Whittaker and Machell *The Law of Limited Liability Partnerships* (3rd Edn) at 16.5–16.31.

Ex-members

3.11   A shareholder of a company continues to be a shareholder and to have full economic and voting rights, until he ceases to be registered as a shareholder upon his successor or assignee successfully applying to be registered in his place. The right of a successor or assignee to be registered as a shareholder will depend upon the terms of the company's articles of association. These are implied by regulations contained in the relevant model articles under the *Companies Act 2006*, if not otherwise expressly provided in the company's articles of association.

The position for LLPs is very different. *Section 7* of the *LLP Act* applies where a member ceases to be a member in accordance with the agreement with the other members, or on death or dissolution ie under *s 4(3)* of the *LLP Act* or where his interest vests by operation of law in a third party on death, or insolvency, or where he has assigned the whole or any part of his share in the LLP to a third party (*LLP Act, s 7(1)*). Thus, ceasing to be a member depends on these events rather than any entry on the register. The former member or his successor is prevented from interfering in the management or administration of the business or affairs of the LLP (*LLP Act, s 7(2)*), but this does not affect any right to receive a payment from the LLP (*LLP Act, s 7(3)*). Thus former members and their successors in title may continue to have the economic rights associated with membership, but will not hold any other rights, and the successor will not automatically become a member itself. Of course, the other members may agree to admit the successor in title as a member of the LLP (*LLP Act, s 4(2)*) whereupon the successor in title will have all the rights of membership.

It is therefore important that the members' agreement should set out expressly when membership begins and ends. In most cases, for professional LLPs, it will be appropriate to state expressly that membership terminates on bankruptcy and death and that there can be no assignment of membership interests. The rights and obligations of the parties where a member ceases to be a member, dies, becomes bankrupt or assigns his membership rights also need to be spelt out.

Designated members

3.12   The *LLP Act* introduced the concept of 'designated members' whose role is to perform certain administrative and filing duties. In particular, the designated members have duties and functions which include the duty:

(1) to sign the annual accounts (*Companies Act 2006, s 414(1)*);

(2) to ensure that the LLP maintains a register of members and a register of members' residential addresses. Failure to do so results in the designated members being guilty of an offence and liable to a fine (*Companies Act 2006, ss 162* and *165*);

(3) to ensure annual accounts and auditor's report are delivered to the Registrar. Failure to do so results in the designated members being guilty of an offence and liable to a fine for the period of default (*Companies Act 2006, ss 441* and *451*);

(4) to ensure that the LLP delivers its annual returns to the Registrar. Failure to do so results in the designated members being guilty of an offence and liable to a fine for the period of the default (*Companies Act 2006, s 858*);

(5) to ensure that the LLP appoints auditors where necessary. Failure to do so amounts to the LLP and the designated members being guilty of an offence and liable to a fine for the period of the default (*Companies Act 2006, s 486*);

(6) to fix remuneration of the auditors (*Companies Act 1985, s 492(1)*);

(7) to give notice to the Registrar of Companies of an auditor's resignation or removal (*Companies Act 2006, ss 517(1)* and *512(2)*);

(8) to deliver a notice of an auditor's resignation to the Registrar. Failure to do so results in the designated members being guilty of an offence and liable to a fine for the period of default (*Companies Act 2006, s 518*);

(9) to submit a proposal for voluntary arrangement to nominee (*Insolvency Act 1986, s 2*);

(10) to sign statutory declaration of solvency. Failure to do so results in the designated members being guilty of an offence and liable to a fine for the period of the default (*Insolvency Act 1986, s 89*); and

(11) to lay statement of affairs before the creditors. Failure to do so results in the designated members being guilty of an offence and liable to a fine (*Insolvency Act 1986, s 99*).

A designated member may, in relation to some of these duties, have a defence against liability if it is shown that he is not 'in default'; that is, he has not authorised, permitted, participated in or failed to take reasonable steps to prevent the contravention of the relevant statutory provision.

In addition, the designated members' powers include:

(1) to deliver additional copies of the accounts to the Registrar of Companies in euros (*Companies Act 2006, s 469*); and

(2) to reasonably determine that audited accounts are unlikely to be required (*Companies Act 2006, s 485(1)*).

The accounting provisions relating to LLPs are discussed in greater detail in CHAPTER 14, ACCOUNTING.

Initially, the designated members are those identified as such in the incorporation document, but members become and cease to be designated members in accordance with the members' agreement (*LLP Act, s 8(1)*). Unless there are at least two designated members, or if the incorporation document states that every member of the LLP is to be a designated member, then all the members from time to time are designated members (*LLP Act, s 8(2), (3)*). It is therefore important that the members' agreement should deal with the identity of the designated members.

The LLP can notify the designated members from time to time to the Registrar (*LLP Act, s 8(4)*) and this takes effect as if included in the incorporation document. Anyone who ceases to be a member automatically ceases to be a designated member (*LLP Act, s 8(6)*) and this also takes effect as if included in the incorporation document. Where anyone becomes or ceases to be a designated member, the Registrar must be notified within 14 days (*LLP Act, s 9(1)(a)*) but, where all the members from time to time are designated members, there is no need to give separate notice of changes of designated members just because members change (*LLP Act, s 9(2)*). Again, failure to comply is an offence (*LLP Act, s 9(4), (6)*).

Membership changes

3.13 As noted at **3.8** above, changes of members and designated members, and in the members' particulars, must be notified to the Registrar within 14 days, and the register of members and the register of members' residential addresses must be updated.

Taxation of LLPs

3.14 See CHAPTERS 18 TO 20.

Application of Company Law

3.15 As mentioned above, a series of statutory instruments, and especially the *LLP Regulations 2001* and the *LLP Regulations 2009,* apply large parts of the *Companies Act 2006* and the *Insolvency Act 1986* to LLPs with appropriate modifications. The *Limited Liability Partnerships (Accounts and Audit) (Application of Companies Act 2006) Regulations 2008* cover the application to LLPs of the rules on accounts and auditing, together with the *Small Limited Liability Partnerships (Accounts) Regulations 2008* and the *Large and Medium-sized Limited Liability Partnerships (Accounts) Regulations 2008*. *Regulation 5* of the *LLP Regulations 2001* covers the application to LLPs of certain provisions of the *Insolvency Act 1986*; *regs 6* and *7* deal with 'default' rules to apply to relations between members except as otherwise expressly agreed, and are broadly based on certain provisions of the *Partnership Act 1890*.

Further amendments have been made by virtue of other regulations, including those made under the *Companies Act 2006* and the *Insolvency Act 1986*.

Accounts and audit

3.16 See CHAPTER 14.

Application of the Companies Act 2006 (other than accounts and audit requirements)

3.17 As mentioned above, the *LLP Regulations 2009* apply certain specified, generally non-accounting, provisions of the *Companies Act 2006* to LLPs by setting out the relevant provisions in full in the *LLP Regulations 2009*.

Any person involved with the establishment or operation of an LLP will need to familiarise themselves with all the relevant provisions of the *Companies Act 2006*. The following is a summary of some of the most significant provisions of this legislation which apply to LLPs.

The *LLP Regulations 2009* contain a number of regulations, each regulation setting out sections of the *Companies Act 2006* as they apply to LLPs; for example, *reg 4* sets out *ss 43–47* of the *Companies Act 2006* as they have been modified to apply to LLPs. To avoid confusion, only the *Companies Act 2006* provision number is set out in the list below.

Sections 43–52: The rules regarding formalities for execution of documents, presumptions of due execution and use of seals apply to LLPs. A document is executed by an LLP by affixing its common seal or by being signed by two members or a member of the LLP in the presence of a witness who attests the signature (*s 44*). Where a person signs a document on behalf of the LLP and in another capacity, for example, on behalf of a company, it must be signed separately in each capacity (*s 44(5)*). A document is validly executed by an LLP as a deed where it is duly executed as a deed and delivered as a deed (*s 46*). An LLP may appoint an attorney to execute documents or deeds on its behalf provided that the instrument empowering the attorney is executed by deed (*s 47*). A contract entered into on behalf of an LLP before its incorporation has the effect of giving personal liability to the person purporting to contract on behalf of the LLP (*s 51*).

Sections 53–57 and *65–74*: Provisions relating to LLP names (discussed at **3.7** above) and the adjudication procedure for objection to an LLP name.

Section 82: This applies the *Companies (Trading Disclosures) Regulations 2008* to LLPs, modified as set out in *s 82*. These regulations require an LLP to display its registered name at its registered office, at locations at which it carries on business and on business communications. An LLP is also required to show its registered name, number, registered address and the part of the UK in which it is registered on it business letters, order forms and websites. If the LLP's business letter contains one of the member's names, other than in text or as a signatory, then all of the members' names must be disclosed, unless the LLP has more than 20 members in which case a list of the members can be maintained for inspection at the LLP's principal place of business. Small professional partnerships often use one or more of the members' names in the name of the LLP so it should be ensured that business letters include a list of all members' names, for example at the foot of the page. Failure to comply with the regulations is an offence committed by of the LLP and its designated members.

Sections 86–88: These require LLPs to have a registered office in the UK.

Sections 162–165: LLPs must maintain a register of members and a register of members' residential addresses (see **3.7** above).

Sections 738–750 and *752–754*: Provisions regarding debentures, the requirement to register an allotment of debentures and the debenture register inspection requirements.

Sections 854–858: The LLP must prepare and deliver an annual return on the return date, being the anniversary of the LLP's incorporation or, if the LLP's last return was made up to a different date, the anniversary of that date. Failure to do so is an offence of the LLP and the designated members.

Sections 860–892: Any charge (for example, by way of security) made over assets of an LLP must be registered with the Registrar of Companies. This is often done by the beneficiary of the charge but the LLP itself has the legal obligation to ensure registration. A charge not registered within the relevant time limits may be void. The LLP must keep a register of charges, and copies of instruments creating charges, at the LLP's registered office or other place notified as an inspection location.

Section 895–900: Provisions on arrangements and reconstructions which apply where a compromise is proposed between the LLP and its creditors or members (or any class of either).

Section 993: This deals with punishment for fraudulent trading by LLPs.

Sections 994–997: These are minority shareholder protection provisions which enable a member to apply to the court for an order on the grounds of unfair prejudice to the interests of some or all of the members in the conduct of the LLP's affairs. The application of these provisions to the LLP can be excluded by unanimous agreement of the members.

Sections 1000–1011: The Registrar of Companies has the power to strike off the register any LLP which he has reasonable cause to believe is not carrying on a business or operating. There is also a procedure whereby the LLP may be struck off following an application by the members.

Sections 1024–1034: Procedure to restore to the register an LLP which has been struck off.

Sections 1121–1122 and *1126–1133*: Provision relating to offences and the liabilities of LLPs and members who are in default under the *Companies Act 2006*.

Sections 1134–1142: Provisions relating to LLP records, which may be kept in hard or electronic form, provided that the information is adequately recorded for future reference, and, where kept in electronic form, these are capable of being reproduced in hard copy form. Documents may be served on LLPs by leaving them at or sending them to the LLP's registered office.

Insolvency of LLPs

3.18   The *LLP Act* provides for the introduction of regulations relating to the insolvency and winding up of LLPs (*LLP Act, s 14*). It also provides for regulations to be introduced in relation to the insolvency and winding up of 'oversea limited liability partnerships' – ie limited liability partnerships incorporated or otherwise established outside the United Kingdom but having a connection with the United Kingdom. *Regulation 5* of the *LLP Regulations 2001* applies large sections of the *Insolvency Act 1986* to LLPs, subject to the various amendments set out in *reg 5(2)* of, and *Sch 3* to, the *LLP Regulations 2001*.

A detailed review of the insolvency regime which applies to limited partnerships is outside the scope of this chapter. The following is only a summary.

(1)   *Insolvency procedures*

LLPs are broadly subject to the same insolvency procedures as companies including:

(a) voluntary arrangements (including the moratorium procedure for small LLPs);

(b) the streamlined administration regime which came into force on 1 October 2005 under the *Limited Liability Partnerships (Amendment) Regulations 2005* (and the old regime where the petition for an administration order was presented before that date);

(c) receivership, including administrative receivership (but note that *s 72A* applies to LLPs and prohibits the appointment of an administrative receiver except where the exemptions (designed to protect the financial markets) apply, which will rarely if ever be the case for professional firms); and

(d) liquidation (although members are free to determine how and when an LLP is voluntarily wound up without any necessary formality).

Note that EC Council Regulation 1346/2000 on insolvency proceedings applies to LLPs, and gives the courts of member states within the territory of which is the centre of an LLP's main interests jurisdiction to open insolvency proceedings. Where a member state has such jurisdiction, proceedings in other member states (including the UK) are restricted to assets situated in those other member states. An LLP with its centre of main interests outside the UK and no establishment in the UK cannot be wound up in England and Wales except in a member's voluntary winding up.

(2) *Adjustment of prior transactions*

The insolvency regime for LLPs also contains provision for the adjustment of prior transactions taking place in the period leading up to insolvency. As in the case of companies, there are four principal categories into which transactions which may be set aside by a liquidator fall:

(i) transactions at an under value, ie gifts or transactions for insufficient consideration;

(ii) preferences, ie anything done or allowed to be done which has the intended effect of putting a particular creditor or guarantor in a better position than he would have been in on an insolvent liquidation;

(iii) floating charges created within 12 months of the onset of insolvency, except to the extent that the charge secures new indebtedness; and

(iv) transactions entered into for the purpose of putting assets beyond the reach of a person who also is making, or may make, a claim or of otherwise prejudicing the interests of such a person in relation to a claim.

There are detailed time limits within which claims to set aside such transactions must be brought, except in the case of category (iv) which is available without time limit.

(3) *The position of the members*

As is the case for directors of companies, members or shadow members of LLPs may be ordered to contribute to the assets of an insolvent LLP in the following cases:

(a) misfeasance;

(b) wrongful trading; or

(c) fraudulent trading.

However, the *LLP Regulations 2001* introduced *s 214A* to the *Insolvency Act 1986*, relating to the 'adjustment of withdrawals' or 'clawback'. This is unique to LLPs and applies to a member or shadow member where, in the course of winding up, it appears that, during the period of two years ending with the commencement of the winding up, he withdrew property of the LLP, whether in the form of a share of profits, salary, repayment of a loan (or interest thereon) or any other withdrawal.

If the liquidator proves to the satisfaction of the court that, at the time of the withdrawal, the member or shadow member knew or had reasonable grounds for believing that the LLP was at the time of its withdrawal unable to pay its debts, within the meaning of *s 123* of the *Insolvency Act 1986*, or became so unable to pay its debts after the assets of the LLP had been depleted by the withdrawal and any other withdrawals made by members contemporaneously with that withdrawal or in contemplation when that withdrawal was made, the court can order the member to make such contributions to the LLP's assets as it thinks proper. For these purposes, a withdrawal occurs if property of the LLP is withdrawn in the form of share of profits, the payment of interest on a loan to the LLP or any other withdrawal of property. Aggregate contributions cannot exceed withdrawals made during the two-year period prior to a winding up. In making such an order, the court must decide whether the particular member knew or ought to have concluded that there was no reasonable prospect of avoiding insolvency. A member will be expected to reach the conclusions that a reasonably diligent person would reach with the same

45

level of experience as that member and, if higher, the actual level of knowledge and skill of that member.

In addition, it should be noted that a member may be liable under the common law for negligence if he fails to show the degree of care and skill reasonably expected from a person of his knowledge and experience.

The *Company Directors Disqualification Act 1986* is also applied to LLPs and will enable the court to impose a disqualification order on any member (not just the designated members) of an LLP from being concerned in any way in, or taking part in the promotion, formation or management of any LLP or company if the member is found culpable of improper conduct leading up to the insolvency of the LLP.

All these rules will apply equally to members and shadow members. A shadow member is defined as 'a person in accordance with whose directions or instructions the members of the LLP are accustomed to act' (but so that a person is not a shadow member by reason only that the LLP members act on his professional advice).

(4)   *Conduct when an LLP is in difficulty*

The overall effect of the proposed insolvency regime for LLPs is that all members of an LLP in financial difficulty will be in a very similar position to directors, although they will also face the additional risk of clawback of their drawings for a potentially lengthy period. Considerable care must therefore be taken in such circumstances, and it will generally be essential for members to seek appropriate professional advice.

Legal practices – registration

3.19   New legal practices, including LDPs, formed as LLPs and partnerships wishing to convert to an LLP must apply to the Solicitors Regulation Authority to practise as a recognised body under the *SRA Recognised Bodies Regulations 2009*. Form RB1 is used for partnerships wishing to apply for approval as a new partnership, and form RB2 is used for a new LLP wishing to apply for approval, as well as existing partnerships wishing to 'convert' to an LLP. The forms are available on the Solicitors Regulation Authority website at www.sra.org.uk.

Need for an agreement

3.20   There is no statutory requirement of an agreement between members, although *s 5* of the *LLP Act* provides for the mutual rights and duties of an LLP and its members to be governed by agreement between the members or, in the absence of agreement, by the regulations discussed in **3.9** above. Paragraph 17 of the explanatory notes to the *LLP Act* notes the 'clear advantages in having a formal written agreement between members to regulate the affairs of the undertaking and to avoid disputes between them', and that 'the formal procedures needed to establish an LLP, including the need for an application to the Registrar of Companies, are likely to encourage the members to set up a formal arrangement before the LLP commences business'. Partnership and LLP agreements are discussed in more detail in CHAPTER **5**.

Chapter 4 Choosing an Appropriate Business Structure

Adopting a limited liability model

Use of LLPs

4.1 LLP status has a number of advantages over a partnership structure, including the following:

(a) *Limited liability* – by far the most important benefit is that only the LLP will be responsible for its own contractual obligations and only a member who is personally negligent will be potentially exposed to claims in tort, and even this may perhaps be eliminated or significantly reduced through carefully worded engagement letters. This is of course the key reason for adopting an LLP structure.

(b) Like a company, an LLP will be able to contract in its own name so that there will be no need to deal with novation of contracts every time partners retire or are appointed. Neither will there be a complex web of indemnities between generations of partners (see **CHAPTER 2**).

(c) The LLP will have unlimited capacity (see **3.3**), including the ability to grant floating charges.

(d) The tax position of members of an LLP is very similar to that of the partners in a partnership. In order to benefit from some of the advantages of practising through a body corporate, individuals who are accustomed to practising through a partnership may feel more comfortable transferring the partnership business to an LLP, rather than a company.

However, there may be a number of reasons why a firm will decide not to convert to an LLP (which is the short-hand phrase often used to describe the process whereby the partnership business is transferred to an LLP), and these are discussed in the following section.

What might prevent a partnership converting to an LLP?

4.2 Potential barriers to conversion include the following:

(a) *Current partners* – most partnership agreements will require a very substantial majority before the partnership can dispose the whole of its business to an LLP (see **4.3** below), as a separate corporate body, and be dissolved. Some even require unanimity, and unanimity will be required if there is no partnership agreement. Is there a danger that a disaffected minority may use the exercise of an effective veto as a weapon in a dispute on something completely unconnected? It is important to think through the decision that will be required and how to achieve it.

(b)   *Retired partners* – in some (increasingly rare) cases, retired partners are entitled to an annuity from the current partners. Sometimes they are even given the right to a lump sum if the firm is ever dissolved or its business transferred, and this may give retired partners an effective veto. In these circumstances their agreement should be obtained, and ideally they should be asked to release the partners from their personal obligations in return for a covenant from the LLP. However, the obligation to pay the annuities will then have to appear on the LLP's balance sheet (see (e) below) and in many cases it may be appropriate for the members to retain the liability to pay the annuities personally out of their profit shares, with the LLP having no liability at all. Arrangements will have to be made to release retiring members and to bind incoming members.

(c)   *Banks* – banks are likely to have two levels of exposure, loans to partners individually to finance their capital contributions and facilities provided to the partnership itself. In an ideal world, from a limited liability standpoint, the bank would be asked to provide facilities to the LLP or company, rather than to each individual member who would then have a personal liability, and to release the partners personally from any continuing liability. However, banks may insist on security and on continuing personal guarantees from the partners. Their attitude will depend very much on their perception of the firm and its management. Many larger and better managed firms are often able to take facilities for the LLP without any requirement for personal guarantees, provided that the balance sheet of the LLP is strong enough.

(d)   *Landlords* – landlords generally have direct personal covenants from at least some of the partners, who, in turn, have rights of contribution from the other partners. In many cases, landlords will be reluctant to give up these rights and may insist on being given equivalent protection in the form of personal guarantees. Some far-sighted firms may have negotiated leases in a form which allows them to substitute an LLP as tenant unilaterally. Either way, the position of landlords needs to be considered.

(e)   *Accounts* – the requirement of filing accounts may be a major issue for many firms. Furthermore, the requirement that the accounts comply with UK generally accepted accounting practice may be a barrier to conversion. For example, if provision has to be made on a capitalised basis for retired partners' annuities, or vacant property, will this make the LLP's balance sheet look so bleak as to preclude incorporation at all? Can the offending liabilities be kept off the balance sheet of the partnership and retained by the partners, or will this mean that the LLP does not provide sufficient protection to make conversion worthwhile? Can other steps be taken to address the problem? These issues need to be reviewed with the firm's accountants.

(f) *Clients* – experience suggests that limited liability in itself is unlikely to lead to the loss of clients, provided that it is handled carefully. Clients tend to choose their professional advisers on the basis of the strength of the relationship and their track record, rather than because each partner will be jointly and severally liable if something goes wrong. But, especially if the firm is heavily dependent on a small number of major clients, it will be as well to sound major clients out before incurring substantial expense. The need to enter into new engagements with all clients post-conversion may be a daunting prospect, but is unlikely to be significant enough to be a barrier to conversion. While the process may be laborious, it can present a business development opportunity as contact is re-established with all clients.

(g) *Tax and regulations* – more complex overseas structures may be required if LLP or company status is adopted. For example, a firm with overseas offices which incorporates as an LLP may find that it is treated as a company for tax purposes in some countries and the risk is obviously much higher where a partnership incorporates as a company. Companies and LLPs may also be prohibited from practising at all in others by local regulations. This may mean that the business in such jurisdictions will have to continue to be conducted in partnership. Running an LLP and one or more partnerships in parallel gives rise to a number of significant issues. How can it be ensured that clients know when they are being advised by the partnership or by the LLP? How can the 'holding out' risk associated with referring to all 'partners' by that term whether they are partners in the partnership or members of the LLP, or both, be minimised? How can profits generated by the partnership and the LLP be shared on a combined basis without tax and liability issues arising? How can those practising in the partnership be compensated for the loss of a right to a contribution to losses from those who are no longer partners in the partnership? How can the risk of double taxation be minimised? Major international professional practices have had to cope with these and many other issues when they have transferred the bulk of their practices to an LLP. Expert advice should be sought at an early stage.

Incorporating an existing partnership business as an LLP

4.3 This will involve four key steps:

(1) drawing up the members' agreement;

(2) registration of the LLP;

(3) transfer of the business of the partnership to the LLP; and

(4) winding up the old partnership.

The steps to be taken to register the LLP are discussed at **3.5**. Issues arising on drawing up a members' agreement are discussed in **CHAPTER 5**, together with a commentary on the model LLP agreement set out in **APPENDIX 5**.

Turning to the business transfer, the process of incorporation as an LLP is very similar to incorporating as a company.

Accordingly, the business of a partnership will actually have to be transferred to the LLP as a separate legal entity. This should make it much less likely that foreign courts will refuse to recognise the limited liability of an LLP, any more than they would in the case of a company, and contrasts with the situation in most states of the USA where application is simply made to register an existing partnership as an LLP.

The following issues arise as a result:

(a) The assets which are to be transferred to the LLP must be identified and, if third party consents are required, the consents obtained. Plenty of time must be allowed in the conversion timetable to allow the consents to be obtained. Some assets may deliberately be left behind in the partnership – for example, it may be appropriate to leave some debtors in the partnership so that the cash eventually realised could be used to pay creditors (to the extent that the LLP does not undertake to pay creditors pursuant to the transfer agreement).

(b) It will be necessary to identify liabilities and obligations of the partnership which are to be assumed by the LLP (and therefore reflected in its accounts), and any which are to be retained by the partnership. If a particular liability is to be transferred, in some cases it may be sufficient for the LLP simply to covenant to indemnify the partners in the partnership in respect of those liabilities. In other cases it may be desirable to ask the third party creditors concerned to release the partners in the partnership from liability, in return for a substitute covenant from the LLP. Unless creditors (like banks or landlords) release the partners from the partnership, they will remain at risk from personal claims even after incorporation as an LLP. This means that there may have to be detailed negotiations with major creditors who may, in some cases, insist on continuing liability from the partners. Time must be built into the timetable to allow for this.

(c) Clients will have to authorise the assumption of responsibility for client assignments by the LLP and to release the partnership. This provides an opportunity to regularise all client relationships, and to build in terms and conditions reflecting the fact that the LLP, and not its members and employees, are responsible for advice given to the client. It will be necessary to identify all clients with ongoing engagements or relationships. In order to avoid clients being troubled several times by different contacts, it will also be necessary to identify the relationship partner who will be responsible for managing the relationship with each client. The form and timing of communications with clients will need careful planning, taking into account the fact that the final decision to convert sometimes takes place only a few weeks or even days before actual conversion. In the case of law firms, the Solicitors Regulation Authority will expect former clients for whom documents or client monies are held to be informed of conversion. In the case of audit assignments, shareholder consent will be required. Where no authorisation is forthcoming, the partnership will have to complete that assignment (either directly or through the agency of the LLP). Again, the amount of time and resources required to handle client relationships should not be underestimated.

(d) Employees of the partnership who are to transfer to the LLP will need to be identified. It is likely that all or most of the business of the partnership will be transferred to the LLP. In this case, it should be expected that all the employees of the business will transfer automatically to the LLP by operation of law pursuant to the *Transfer of Undertakings (Protection of Employment) Regulations 2006*. Under these regulations, the LLP will have responsibility generally for employees from the date of the transfer. It may be appropriate for the LLP to assume in addition all past liabilities of the partnership to employees. Where staff are employed by a service company, title to the shares in the service company will need to be transferred to the LLP and the service agreement with the partnership will need to be novated by the LLP. The details should be set out in the transfer agreement.

(e) *Other contracts.* Contracts entered into on behalf of the partnership in relation to the operating requirements of the business may or may not require the consent of the third party to the assignment. Each contract will need to be identified and a decision taken about whether the contract is a material contract which should be novated by the LLP. Consideration should be given to the criteria for materiality and, in relation to each material contract, as to whether consent should be sought in advance of assignment to the LLP. For non-material contracts it may be appropriate for the LLP simply to indemnify the partnership in relation to ongoing obligations and (possibly) past obligations (although it should be noted that the former partners will then remain liable under the contracts). The partnership should hold the benefit of the relevant contracts on trust for the LLP. If contracts are still to be performed at the point where the original partnership is to be dissolved, then the assignment may need to be perfected at that time.

(f) *Consideration.* If all the partners in the partnership become members of the LLP with interests in the same proportions, the 'consideration' for the transfer to the partnership will, for each partner, be his membership of the LLP. The transfer agreement will generally provide for each partner's accounts with the LLP to be credited and debited with the sums previously credited and debited to the partnership. If the proportionate shares are altered at the time of conversion, or some partners are not to go forward as members of the LLP, this will need to be reflected in the transfer agreement.

(g) *Stamp duty and VAT.* See CHAPTERS **22** and **23**.

(h) Regulatory issues may also be important. For example, if the partnership is a firm of solicitors, the LLP will need to seek recognition as a recognised body (see **3.17**) and, if it is authorised under the *Financial Services and Markets Act 2000* (*FSMA 2000*), the *Consumer Credit Act 1974* or similar legislation, the same authorisation will have to be obtained for the LLP before it starts business. If the firm has overseas offices, it will need to think about local professional and tax rules.

(i) Especially where the firm has overseas branches, taxation will be an important issue. It will be necessary to obtain local advice about whether conversion will involve any taxation on disposal of assets by the partnership or will affect the tax treatment of partners' shares of profits and losses in the future. Tax clearances may be needed and, in some cases, may take months or even years to obtain.

While none of the above involves anything unduly complex, there will be a lot to do. Some tasks depend on co-operation from other parties (such as novations with landlords and suppliers). Other tasks depend on successful completion of earlier steps. A comprehensive project plan should therefore be prepared so that the critical path to completion can be mapped out and monitored and all deadlines met. Plenty of time needs to be allowed for third party consents, tax clearances and other matters outside the firm's control, and sufficient flexibility built into the timetable and project plan to allow adjustments as matters progress.

A team needs to be established with responsibility for driving the project through, and a project leader appointed with overall responsibility for the project and the authority necessary to ensure that all fee earners, support staff and external advisers play their part. If there is no-one suitable within the firm, an external project manager may be desirable, and ideally he should have prior experience of LLP conversion. The team needs to meet regularly throughout the project so that all members understand how their contribution fits in and is affected by what others are doing, and vice versa.

Most firms find that this process has collateral benefits. Once a full list of clients, relationship partners, suppliers and so on has been established, it is relatively easy to keep up to date. Once engagement letters are in place, it is relatively easy to require and police complete coverage by engagement letters. Procedures and practices will need to be established to ensure that the firm's processes are maintained and improved beyond conversion.

The final act is to wind up the old partnership. In some cases, even after the business has been transferred to the LLP, the partnership may be left with assignments to run off, debts to collect, creditors to pay and potential exposure to past claims where the transfer of these assets and liabilities to the LLP is impossible or undesirable. Some issues may take years to work themselves out. Sometimes the old partnership may deliberately be left in place for years, so that it can deal with liabilities which are to be kept off the LLP's balance sheet, such as retired partners' annuities.

It will be important to agree before incorporating an LLP how the business of the partnership is to be wound up, and the insurance arrangements to be put in place to cover any residual liability in respect of professional indemnity claims against the partners. In practice, running off of the old partnership business is likely to be undertaken by the LLP as agent for the partners at the date of incorporation and it is important to ensure that the LLP has the necessary authorisations and access to sufficient finance to enable it to conduct this process efficiently and smoothly.

Use of companies

4.4 The benefit of a company is similar to that of an LLP, because third parties can generally only recover from the assets of the limited company (being a separate legal entity) and not from the personal assets of the non-negligent members of the company.

Even after incorporation, directors of a company whose personal negligence leads to loss may be personally liable jointly with company and negligent directors or employees may be liable either to the company under their employment contracts or to the aggrieved third party in tort. However, at least incorporation protects those other director shareholders who were not themselves involved in giving negligent advice.

Directors, like members of an LLP, also owe fiduciary and statutory duties to the company and to third parties.

The tax treatment of a company is generally thought to be less favourable than is the case for a partnership or LLP and this is the main reason why companies have not been more widely used. These tax consequences are considered in CHAPTER 20, TAXATION OF CORPORATE ASPECTS. However, as noted in CHAPTER 1, companies are increasingly used in hybrid structures, and are sometimes incorporated by a partnership or LLP to conduct the part of its business which is most prone to professional indemnity claims (eg the audit practice of an accountancy firm). The shares are generally then held as a partnership or LLP asset. However, partial incorporation needs to be structured very carefully to ensure that a third party cannot argue, for example, that he thought he was dealing with the partnership or that the company itself has a claim against the partnership. Otherwise, the third party may be able to pierce the ring fence provided by the company. The company must ensure that it clearly operates discrete services on its own behalf and that it employs all persons providing advice on that area of the business itself, in order to minimise the risk of claimants piercing the ring fence that protects individual partners from claims after partial incorporation.

As noted in CHAPTER 1, typically professional partnerships have remained partnerships or have converted to LLPs, rather than companies. The key steps for conversion set out above are therefore described in the context of an LLP conversion, although many of the same issues would arise upon a transfer to a company.

Why are limited partnerships not used?

4.5   Limited partnerships are an important exception to the rule that all partners of a general partnership are jointly liable for obligations incurred by the firm, as is a limited partner in a limited partnership formed under the *Limited Partnerships Act 1907* (*1907 Act*). However, limited partnerships are very rarely used in a professional partnership context, for reasons that are explained below.

A limited partnership is no more than an ordinary partnership which satisfies certain characteristics required by the *1907 Act*.

A limited partnership must consist of one or more general partners and one or more limited partners. A general partner is liable for the obligations of the firm in the same way as a partner of any other partnership whereas a limited partner is generally only liable for the debts of the firm to the extent that he has agreed to contribute to its capital or has withdrawn capital from it. Under *s 4(2)* of the *1907 Act* a limited partner must contribute at least a nominal amount of capital to the partnership but there is no statutory obligation on the general partner to contribute to the partnership capital. A limited partnership must be registered with the Registrar of Companies.

As a result of amendments made by the *Legislative Reform (Limited Partnerships) Order 2009*, from 1 October 2009, the information to be registered consists of:

(a) the firm's name (which must end with 'limited partnership' or 'LP' or if registered in Wales, 'partneriaeth cyfyngedig' or 'PC' – each in upper or lower case with or without punctuation);

(b) the general nature of the business;

(c) the address of the principal place of business;

(d) the full name of each general partner and each limited partner;

(e) the term, if any, of the partnership, beginning with its date of registration; and

(f) details of the sum contributed by each limited partner and whether paid in cash or otherwise.

Until 1 October 2009, it was thought likely that limited liability of limited partners is lost if the information held by the Registrar becomes out of date and/or inaccurate, by virtue of *s 5* of the *1907 Act*. However, owing to an amendment made to *s 5* under the *Legislative Reform (Limited Partnerships) Order 2009*, this now seems unlikely.

Generally speaking, there is no obligation to file accounts (unless all of the partners are themselves limited companies or unlimited companies whose members are limited companies), in which case the general partner will be (subject to certain exemptions) required by the *Partnerships (Accounts) Regulations 2008, SI 2008/569*, to produce and file a full set of accounts for the partnership. General partners can become limited partners, and vice versa, provided that the required details are registered, although a general partner who becomes a limited partner should take the same precautions as a partner in an ordinary partnership who retires (see **2.6**). A company can be a general or a limited partner.

Section 6 of the *1907 Act* provides that a limited partner has no implied power to bind the firm, and cannot take part in the management of the partnership business. The partnership agreement can give express authority to the limited partner to act on behalf of the firm, in which case the firm will be bound by his actions in the same way as it would be bound by the acts of any employee or other agent. The danger from his point of view is that his actions will amount to management of the partnership business, thus forfeiting the benefit of his limited liability status. The *1907 Act* contains no definition of what is meant by taking part in the management of the partnership business, but it is generally thought that being involved in anything which amounts to an ordinary matter connected with the partnership business will be likely to amount to taking part in management. The draft legislation issued by the Department for Business, Enterprise and Regulatory Reform (BERR) in August 2008, as part of the consultation on the reforms to limited partnership law, set out a non-exhaustive list of activities which would could be undertaken by limited partners without being considered to be involved with management. If this list of 'permitted activities' is introduced as part of the proposed programme of reforms discussed below, this will add clarity on this point.

If it were not for *s 6* of the *1907 Act*, limited partnerships might be a very helpful way of limiting partners' liabilities; for example, it might be possible to form a limited partnership with a corporate general partner which also enjoyed limited liability. However, the fact that the limited partners are unable to participate in management has effectively prevented the use of limited partnerships for active professional partnerships and their partners.

A further concern is that a professional practice constituted as a limited partnership would almost certainly be a collective investment scheme for the purposes of *s 235* of *FSMA 2000*, and would have to comply with the consequent regulatory requirements. The characteristics of a collective investment scheme are: (i) that the contributions of the participants and the profits or income out of which payments are made to them are pooled; and (ii) that the property in question is to be managed as a whole by or on behalf of the operator of the scheme.

Since limited partners are excluded from participating in the management of the affairs of the partnership, and the general partners are regarded as the operator of the scheme, a limited partnership will be a collective investment scheme unless exempted for constituting a particular type of arrangement. Such arrangements are listed in the *Schedule* to the *Financial Services and Markets Act 2000 (Collective Investment Schemes) Order 2001* which rarely apply in the professional context.

If the partnership constitutes a collective investment scheme, the general partner must, unless it already has appropriate authorisation, seek authorisation under *FSMA 2000* to operate collective investment schemes. Alternatively, the practice of many general partners is to delegate the functions which constitute regulated activity to an appropriately authorised firm. Authorisation is generally sought from the Financial Services Authority, and this is a procedure which can take six months or more. Otherwise, the operation of the partnership will be illegal and the partnership agreement may be unenforceable.

In addition, the marketing of unregulated collective investment schemes (which would include limited partnerships) is very difficult within the UK regulatory framework unless marketing is limited to institutional investors only.

The Law Commissions' joint report on Partnership Law (Law Com No 283) proposed extensive reform of limited partnership law and, although the reforms proposed for general partnerships were not taken forward, the Government decided that the reforms for limited partnerships should be implemented. A BERR consultation document issued in August 2008 contained draft legislation intended to implement all of the proposed reforms, but, since then, BERR and its successor, the Department for Business, Innovation and Skills (BIS), have taken a less ambitious approach. On 1 October 2009, the first instalment of the proposed reforms was brought into effect by the *Legislative Reform (Limited Partnerships) Order 2009*, and it is intended that the other reforms to the limited partnerships regime will be introduced in two or three further instalments, although the precise scope and timing of the proposed reforms is still a subject for consultation.

Chapter 5 Issues Covered by a Standard Partnership or LLP Agreement

The importance of a written agreement

5.1 As noted in **2.11** and **3.9**, there is no legal requirement for a firm to have a formal written partnership or LLP agreement. The rights and obligations of the partners, members and LLP may be agreed orally and an agreement may be inferred from a course of dealing. In the absence of agreement on specific issues, *s 24* of the *Partnership Act 1890* governs the rights and obligations of the partners, and *s 5(1)* of the *LLP Act* and associated regulations govern the rights and obligations of the LLP and its members.

However, a modern professional firm should always have a well-drafted written agreement. The following are some of the main benefits:

(a) *Certainty.* In the event of a dispute, a written agreement is prima facie evidence of the terms upon which the partners or members have agreed to carry on business together. Note that the terms of the agreement may be varied by consent of the partners, which may be express or inferred from a course of dealing. *Section 19* of the *Partnership Act 1890* expressly sets out this principle in the case of partnerships, but an LLP agreement, like any contract, can also be varied expressly or by implication.

(b) *Concentrating the mind.* Discussing the terms of a draft agreement and updating an existing agreement forces the partners or members to concentrate on the issues that concern them and to think through how the business will be run, and what their respective rights and obligations should be.

(c) *Overriding the legislation.* There are many provisions in the *Partnership Act 1890*, the *LLP Act*, the *LLP Regulations 2001* and the *LLP (Application of Companies Act 2006) Regulations 2009* which will apply if not excluded by contrary agreement. The main provisions are set out in **2.11** and **3.9**. Many of these provisions are wholly inappropriate for a modern professional partnership, and should be excluded by a carefully drafted written agreement.

(d) *Avoiding disputes.* Few things can be more disruptive to a business than litigation between partners or members, and a clear agreement is the single most important way of avoiding this, because it helps partners or members to know exactly where they stand.

(e) *Evidence of the existence of the partnership.* Although not conclusive, a written agreement is evidence of the existence of the partnership and its date of commencement. An LLP's incorporation is evidence of the existence of an LLP.

An agreement is often made as a deed, although this is not strictly necessary. If a deed is used, a debt owed under the agreement will be a specialty debt and will become time barred after 12 years rather than the normal six-year limitation period. If an agreement includes a power of attorney, for example to execute documents or deeds on behalf of the LLP or partnership, or to sign documents on behalf of a retiring partner, then the power will only be valid if it is made by deed (*Powers of Attorney Act 1971, s 1(1)*). Otherwise, a written agreement is perfectly adequate.

It is common for supplemental agreements to be entered into, especially when a new partner or member joins the firm, or an existing partner or member retires from the firm, or the capital contributions or profit-sharing ratios of the partners or members are altered. Provision is often made for the partnership agreement to be capable of being amended by a resolution of a specified majority the partners or members (see **5.46** below). It is often helpful to produce regular consolidated versions of the agreement, as amended by supplemental agreements and resolutions. One partner or member may be made responsible for maintaining an up-to-date record of the agreement and its accompanying documents.

As explained above, a written agreement can be varied with the consent of all the partners, and such consent inferred from a course of dealing, even if the formal amendment procedures established in the agreement have not been followed. It is therefore important to review the agreement regularly to ensure that its terms reflect the firm's current practice. This is of particular significance when new partners or members are introduced to the firm, as they will be bound by the terms of the agreement as presented to them (usually the existing written agreement) until it is varied again with the agreement of all the partners (including the new partner), whether by way of resolution or by inference from conduct.

Typical clauses in a well-drafted partnership/LLP agreement

5.2 Model partnership and LLP agreements are set out in APPENDICES 4 AND 5, and a checklist for preparation of agreements is set out at **5.48** below. Every professional partnership is unique and will have its own individual requirements, and the model agreements have been included for illustration purposes only. It is important that partners seek professional advice when preparing the agreement. Modern professional firm's agreements normally include clauses dealing with the matters described in the following paragraphs of this chapter.

The parties to the agreement

5.3 The parties will be those who are engaged jointly in the business as principals, ie the equity partners or members. Those who are not engaged in the business as principals, such as salaried partners or members who are in fact merely employees and not in receipt of any profit share although they are held out as if they were partners, need not be parties, although their rights and obligations should be fully set out in separate agreements if they are not. Unlike a partnership, but like a company, the LLP itself is a legal person, and it should be a party to the LLP agreement which should set out its rights and obligations. For example, the LLP may provide an indemnity to the members and the members may be obliged to contribute to the LLP's capital. Note that the *LLP Act* expressly provides that an agreement made between members before incorporation of an LLP can bind the LLP itself after its incorporation (*LLP Act, s 5(2)*).

The business to be carried on (model clauses 1(1) and 2(1))

5.4 Third parties can often assume that the partner or member has the necessary authority to bind the firm. It is therefore important to set out very clearly in the agreement the scope of the business, and the extent to which the partners or members actually authorise one another to bind the partnership or LLP.

Section 5 of the *Partnership Act 1890* provides that:

'Every partner is an agent of the firm and his other partners for the purpose of the business of the partnership; and the acts of every partner who does any act for carrying on in the usual way business of the kind carried on by the firm of which he is a member, bind the firm and his partners, unless the partner so acting has in fact no authority to act for the firm in the particular matter, and the person with whom he is dealing either knows that he has no authority, or does not know or believe him to be a partner.'

Further, *s 6* of the *LLP Act* provides that:

'(1) Every member of a limited liability partnership is the agent of the limited liability partnership.

(2) But a limited liability partnership is not bound by anything done by a member in dealing with a person if–

(a)   the member in fact has no authority to act for the limited liability partnership by doing that thing, and

(b)   the person knows that he has no authority or does not know or believe him to be a member of the limited liability partnership.'

61

Therefore, a partnership or the LLP will be bound by the acts of the partners or members where those acts fall within the usual scope of the partnership or LLP's business, even if the acting partner or member is not actually authorised to carry out that particular act, unless the third party is aware of the acting partner's lack of authority (see CHAPTERS 2 AND 3).

Name of the firm (model clauses 1(1) and 2(1))

5.5   The professional practice's name should be stated in the agreement. There may be statutory restrictions on the name that may be used and these are discussed in CHAPTERS 2 AND 3.

The name may be the firm's most valuable asset. It is important to protect the name and any abbreviations or combinations of it by registration as a service mark, worldwide if appropriate. It is also important that the agreement states that the name is a partnership or LLP asset, and as such may only be assigned or licensed to third parties in agreed circumstances. The agreement should provide that the name cannot be used by a partner or member who has retired and, in the case of a partnership, provision should be made for devolution of the name to the continuing partners on the retirement of a partner. Agreements also often provide expressly for what is to happen to the rights to the name on dissolution of the firm. Where the partnership or LLP forms part of a national or international organisation which uses a common name, the agreement between member firms may dictate terms regulating and protecting the use of that name.

Duration of the partnership (partnership model clauses 2(4) and 2(5))

5.6   In the case of a partnership, the agreement should state the date of commencement of the partnership (although this will not be conclusive proof of the actual date of commencement if it is not borne out by the facts: *Khan v Miah* [1998] 1 WLR 477) and the circumstances in which the partnership will be dissolved. Such circumstances may be, for example, a fixed date, the passing of a partnership resolution or the occurrence of specified events.

If the duration of the partnership has not been agreed, the partnership will be a partnership at will and can be dissolved by any one partner giving notice to that effect (*Partnership Act 1890, ss 26(1)* and *32(c)*). In the absence of an express provision to the contrary, a partnership will be dissolved by the death or bankruptcy of a partner (*Partnership Act 1890, s 33*). A partnership (whether or not of a fixed or certain duration) is also technically dissolved under general law whenever there is a change in the composition of the firm, for example, as a result of retirement, expulsion or the introduction of a new partner.

It is therefore important to override the position in law, as in most cases it will be intended that the partnership business should continue when only some of the partners leave or new partners are appointed. They will certainly want to avoid giving a single partner the ability to dissolve the firm unilaterally, thereby forcing the disposal of the firm's name and goodwill. This point should be addressed in the partnership agreement by providing either that the partnership is to have a fixed duration, or more usually that the firm is to exist so long as there are any two or more living partners. Either way, it should be specifically agreed that the partnership will not terminate when new partners join or existing partners leave the partnership, or where one partner serves notice of dissolution.

5.7 An LLP is a separate legal entity. The LLP exists from its date of incorporation and continues until it is wound-up. The LLP agreement will usually provide for the decision making process required in order to wind-up the LLP voluntarily (see **5.42** below). An LLP is often incorporated a little while before it actually commences business but the LLP agreement is then often expressed to take effect on an 'effective date', being the time when it starts to acquire assets and become subject to liabilities in furtherance of its business.

Place of business (model clause 3)

5.8 It is usual to describe the place where the business is to be carried on, which in the case of the partnership is the place where the books must be kept, subject to contrary agreement (*Partnership Act 1890, s 24(9)*). For an LLP, the place where the business is carried on is often the LLP's registered address, although it need not be. LLP records, including the register of members, the register of charges and register of debenture holders, should be kept in hard or electronic form at the LLP's registered office unless they are kept at an alternative inspection location which has been notified to Companies House (*Companies Act 2006, Pt 37* and *Companies (Company Records) Regulations 2008, SI 2008/3006*).

Property and goodwill (partnership model clause 4)

5.9 In the case of a partnership, and especially where some of the property used by the partnership is owned by individual partners, the partnership agreement should make clear what is partnership property and what is property belonging to the individual partners. It is assumed, subject to evidence of contrary intention, that property acquired with the firm's money belongs to the partnership for use in the partnership business (*Partnership Act 1890, ss 20, 21*). The agreement should also state whether the goodwill of the partnership belongs to one or more of the partners separately or is a firm asset, and whether or not an outgoing partner is entitled to a sum representing the value of his share of the goodwill.

Legal title to land can be vested in a maximum of four individuals and it is often desirable for such property to be held in the name of one or more nominees (often four of the partners) on trust for the partnership. Since those four partners will remain liable under the lease even after they have ceased to be partners, and will have to rely on the indemnity from the continuing partnership, it may be preferable for the lease to be held in the name of a nominee company on trust for the partnership, and to be guaranteed by the partners for the time being. It should be made clear in the title documentation, and possibly in the partnership agreement itself, that partnership land is held for the benefit of the partnership as a whole. In the absence of an express statement, it is assumed that partnership property is owned by partners as beneficial tenants in common, and not as joint tenants, so that the rights of survivorship of the continuing beneficial partners would not apply on the death of one of the partners. However, this presumption is rebuttable in the event of clear evidence that the partners intend to hold partnership property as beneficial joint tenants (*Bathurst v Scarborow* [2005] 1 P & CR 4). Where land is held in the names of four nominee partners, they will in any event hold the legal title as trustees for the firm, and as trustees they are likely to hold as joint tenants. The general rules of law as to title to land will apply (*Partnership Act 1890, s 20(2)*).

5.10 An LLP is a separate body corporate. Therefore, LLP assets should be held in the name of the LLP, rather than the name of individual members. This means that counterparties, such as landlords and banks, enter into a contract directly with the LLP. In many cases, landlords or banks will seek personal guarantees from members of the LLP, as LLPs are subject to no capital maintenance requirements and the counterparties may have concerns about the LLP failing to meet its obligations. Where personal guarantees are given, the agreement may include a provision to ensure that the members who have given personal guarantees will be indemnified by the LLP, and sometimes even by the other members in respect of losses relating to those guarantees (although note that this would mean that members are personally liable to meet the guaranteed liabilities with consequent loss of limited liability protection, in respect of those liabilities, so legal advice is required before undertaking such a commitment). Care is also needed to ensure that new members accede to the indemnity arrangements and that, on retirement, the relevant members are released from the guarantee and remain beneficiaries of the indemnity to the extent necessary.

The LLP agreement should also state clearly whether the goodwill generated by the members belongs to the LLP or to the individual members.

Designated members (LLP model clause 4)

5.11 LLPs are required to have at least two designated members, who have the duties described in CHAPTER 3. Unless it is intended that every member should be a designated member, the LLP agreement should identify the designated members and include a procedure governing their appointment and retirement. Changes to the designated members must be notified to Companies House (*LLP Act, s 9(1)*), although a person will automatically cease to be a designated member when he or she ceases to be a member of the LLP (*LLP Act, s 8(6)*). The LLP should normally agree to indemnify the designated members for liabilities incurred by them in the proper execution of their duties as designated members.

Capital (model clause 5)

5.12 A key decision for every professional firm will be how to finance the practice. The partners or members will have to decide whether to contribute equity or loan capital, and in what proportions and whether to finance the firm through retained profits. They should also agree the extent to which the members' capital contributions are to be funded by means of loans from third parties, such as a bank.

(a) *Capital contributions.* The agreement should specify how much capital is to be contributed, by whom, whether by way of equity or loan, whether in cash or in kind, how it should be owned and when contributions and withdrawals should be made. The agreement should also set out how the partners or members are to be credited with paid-in capital, because if this is not dealt with, their entitlements will be treated as equal under *s 24* of the *Partnership Act 1890* and *reg 7(1)* of the *LLP Regulations 2001*. For partnerships, this is so even where partners have made unequal capital contributions (*Popat v Shonchhatra* [1997] 3 All ER 800, CA). The statutory provision that, in the absence of express agreement to the contrary, equality should prevail between the partners, reflects the fact that a partner's contribution to the partnership cannot be evaluated in purely monetary terms. The Court of Appeal noted in *Popat*, however, that this default rule can be displaced easily, particularly where there is a significant disparity in the shares in which partners have contributed capital. It is widely believed that the same reasoning would be applied to LLPs given the similarity between the position set out in *s 24* and *reg 7(1)*, and that therefore paid-in capital would be likely to be credited to members of an LLP equally regardless of the proportion of the contribution made by each member in the absence of any evidence of a contrary intention (such as accounts providing to the contrary and agreed by all the members).

(b)   *Interest on capital.* Sometimes firms agree to pay interest on the capital contributions made, particularly if capital is contributed in proportions that are different from the proportions in which profits and losses are to be shared. If the partnership agreement remains silent on this issue, no interest will be payable under the *Partnership Act 1890* unless the advance is greater than the partners' agreed capital contribution (*Partnership Act 1890, s 24(3), (4)*). Unless the LLP agreement makes provision for interest to be payable, no interest will be paid on capital contributions made to an LLP. It may be appropriate to provide for partners or members who make late capital contributions or early capital withdrawals to be charged interest.

(c)   *Outgoing partners.* The agreement should provide for what happens to the capital contributed by an outgoing partner or member. This is usually dealt with in the outgoing partner or member provisions (see **5.31** below).

(d)   *Changes in capital.* The agreement will usually provide future flexibility by way of periodic revisions of the amount of capital needed (perhaps at the end of every accounting year). Unless provision is made for additional capital contributions or withdrawals of capital, individual partners or members cannot be compelled to provide additional capital at a later date and no contributing partner is entitled to make a withdrawal. Agreements should normally specify what effect (if any) changes in the profit sharing ratios have on the capital contributions, and the time and manner in which additional capital is to be contributed or withdrawals made. In the model agreements, the capital contribution is linked to profit share, so that, if a partner's or member's profit share decreases, he receives back a corresponding proportion of his capital contribution but the capital base remains unchanged because one or more of the other partners or members will have correspondingly increased profit shares and will have to make corresponding capital contributions.

Sometimes, agreements provide for periodic revaluations of the partnership or LLP property, possibly including goodwill, with consequent debits and credits to the partners' or members' capital accounts, but this is unusual because a capital gains tax charge may then arise on a subsequent change in profit sharing ratios (see **CHAPTER 8**). When provision is made for revaluations, it should be made clear when the resulting capital profits can be withdrawn, whether as a return of capital or as an allocation of profit.

In an LLP context, the agreement should make it clear whether a member is entitled in any circumstances (including retirement) to require the LLP to pay him the whole or any part of his capital, in which case, in the light of FRS 25, such balances will appear in the balance sheet as debt to that extent. To the extent that it is wished to ensure that balances appear as equity, the LLP will need to be given the discretion to decide when and whether to redeem capital. For a fuller discussion see **CHAPTER 14, ACCOUNTING**.

Profits and losses (model clause 6)

5.13 The agreement should clarify how profits and losses are computed. Where a partner or member receives directors' fees from a client company, or holds shares in a company in connection with the partnership's business, the partner has a duty to account for such fees and any dividends or for any other income to the firm, so that they form part of the firms accrued income, unless the agreement expressly provides that he can treat them as his own.

Under the default regimes, profits and (in the case of a partnership) losses are to be shared equally, but this is rarely what the parties intend. It is therefore also important to agree how profits thus computed are to be shared. *Joyce v Morrissey* [1999] EMLR 233 illustrates that, where partners intend to displace the presumption of equality, it has to be made absolutely clear to, and agreed by, all the partners that profits and losses are to be shared on an unequal basis. Simply circulating accounts to the partners showing an unequal distribution is not enough.

The profits and losses of a professional firm may be made up of profits or losses of a capital or a revenue nature. Capital profits or losses are those profits or losses arising on the realisation of capital assets (eg the sale of goodwill). Revenue profits or losses are those profits or losses arising from the firm's trading or professional activities (eg professional fees and income on cash deposits).

The agreement should state clearly how both capital and revenue profits are to be shared and (in the case of a partnership) losses are to be borne. **CHAPTER 8** discusses profit and loss sharing in more detail.

Both individual members of an LLP and partners are subject to income tax on revenue profits computed on an earnings basis, and to capital gains tax on capital profits, and taxable profits (including work-in-progress) are computed for tax purposes on the basis of generally accepted accounting practices (see **CHAPTER 19, INCOME TAX**). An LLP's statutory accounts are also prepared on this basis (see **CHAPTER 14, ACCOUNTING**). Firms can agree to compute profits differently for the purposes of internal accounts used to determine partners' and members' entitlements if they wish, although this can lead to allocations of profit being greater or smaller than the profits shown in the accounts prepared for tax and statutory purposes (see **CHAPTER 8, PROFIT SHARES** and **CHAPTER 14, ACCOUNTING**). For an LLP, it will be very important to ensure that limited liability protection is preserved. Whereas partnership agreements generally provide for partners to contribute to losses, and to indemnify retiring partners against future losses, if the LLP has power to require members to contribute to losses, the limited liability of the members will be destroyed.

However, the LLP agreement should nevertheless tackle the treatment of losses. The simplest approach is to provide for members to have no liability for losses, which are simply to be financed by the LLP out of its capital. Because this could result in insolvency, or in the LLP having insufficient working capital, provision could be made for members to contribute additional capital if so decided by a particular majority (eg because it is thought that the LLP can trade out of its difficulty). However, because members have the fiduciary and statutory duties equivalent to those of a director, it may be arguable that they have a duty to require the contribution of capital in an insolvency, which also has the potential to destroy limited liability protection. It would therefore be safer to specify that such a power to require capital contributions is only exercisable where the LLP is not insolvent.

Some LLP agreements provide for losses to be met out of future profits (if any) so that there is an agreed procedure for trading out of difficulties. For example, provision can be made for losses to be allocated notionally between members, but without any obligation to contribute cash in respect of those losses. Provision can then be made for each member's share (if any) of profits of future accounting periods in excess of a specified sum to be used to meet the losses. It is necessary to consider what happens to any balance of unmet losses when a member retires. Should he lose his capital to that extent? Note that, whichever way losses are dealt with for liability purposes, the losses will need to be allocated for tax purposes in the firm's tax return.

Some agreements provide for partners or members to have guaranteed entitlement regardless of profits (akin to a salary), sharing any surplus profits in accordance with their agreed profit sharing ratios. If the profits fall short of the aggregate guaranteed salaries, it is important to agree how the shortfall will be financed.

Many professional firms operate a 'lockstep' basis of profit sharing. The *Equality Act 2010* (see **5.32** below) provides that it is unlawful to discriminate on the grounds of age; because sharing profits in a way which depends on length of service indirectly discriminates against younger partners, professional firms need to be satisfied that the lockstep arrangement is a proportionate means of achieving a legitimate aim and, assuming that the individual's length of service exceeds five years, the award fulfils a business need of the firm, for example by encouraging the loyalty or motivation or rewarding the experience of some or all workers. The damages that can be awarded in relation to age discrimination will be unlimited.

Agreements generally provide for a partner's or member's share of profits to be credited to a current account (although sometimes the capital account is used to record capital contributions and allocations of profit). Likewise, any shares of losses are debited to the partner's or member's current account but so that (in the case of an LLP and in order to protect limited liability) the current account balance cannot be reduced below zero. In an LLP context, current account balances are generally repayable at some point following retirement, and FRS 25 therefore has the effect that such balances will appear in the balance sheet as debt. To the extent that it is wished to ensure that such balances appear as equity, or reserves, the LLP will need to be given the discretion to decide when and whether to allocate the profits between the members and credit them to current accounts, thus creating a reserve of unallocated profits. For a fuller discussion, see CHAPTER 14, ACCOUNTING.

Drawings (model clause 7)

5.14 The profits of a professional partnership for a particular year of account may not be agreed for months after the year end, but the partners or members will need to draw money on account in their respective profit shares throughout the year even if they are not entitled to a guaranteed salary. Even when profits have been agreed, it may be desirable for the firm to retain a proportion of the profits of preceding years, whether to meet working capital requirements or to provide for tax liabilities of the members or partners, or both.

Therefore, the agreement should set out the partner's respective drawings entitlements very clearly, and deal with the consequences of over-drawings and under-drawings.

Books and accounts (model clause 8)

5.15 In the case of a partnership, the partnership agreement will usually specify the firm's accounting date and state that annual accounts are to be prepared. There may also be provision for the accounts to be audited. The agreement should state whether the accounts are to take into account the value of work-in-progress and goodwill. As from the tax year 1999/2000, partnerships have been required to take into account work-in-progress for income tax purposes.

As there is no statutory basis of accounting for partnerships, it is important that the partnership agreement reflects the firm's accounting practices and, where it is intended that the accounts are produced on a different basis, that this is set out clearly in the agreement. This was highlighted in *White v Minnis* [2000] 3 All ER 618, CA. In that case, the agreement required that each year's accounts should show its assets on the basis of a just valuation.

Over the years, the firm's accounts had always been drawn up on the basis of historic cost. The personal representatives of a deceased partner argued that, for the purposes of calculating the deceased partner's share in the capital of the partnership, the accounts should be shown at market value. The Court of Appeal held that, as the partners had dealt with the property in the accounts on an historic basis for many years, that was a just valuation within the meaning of the agreement.

Agreements often name the firm's accountants and set out the process for replacing them and most agreements also specify where the books are kept. Each partner normally has a right to inspect and take copies of the partnership books. If particular partners' or members' rights of inspection are to be restricted, this should be specified.

The accounting treatment of partnerships is discussed more fully in CHAPTER 14, ACCOUNTING.

In the case of an LLP, the auditing and accounting provisions will need to take into account the relevant requirements of the *Companies Act 2006* which apply to LLPs, and the desired accounting treatment of issues such as member's capital, reserves (including tax reserves and undivided profits). These are also discussed in more detail in CHAPTER 14. The *Companies Act 2006* requirements in relation to LLP records (discussed in CHAPTER 3) will also need to be included.

An LLP's year-end date is usually set out in the LLP agreement. The default accounting reference date is the end of the month in which the LLP is incorporated. The accounting reference date can, however, be changed, and this is discussed further in CHAPTER 14.

Provision for tax liabilities (model clause 9)

5.16   Under the self-assessment regime, income tax is the responsibility of the individual partners or members. However, many professional firms continue to provide for tax retentions to be held by the firm until needed by the individual partner or member to meet his tax liability, and many have chosen to continue the practice of the firm meeting the individual partner's or member's tax liabilities by direct payments to HMRC. A typical tax retention clause will provide for the partnership or LLP to retain amounts necessary to provide fully for all tax due and payable on all profits earned up to the end of each accounting period in that year's accounts. If the accounts date does not fall at the end of a tax year, consideration needs to be given to providing for a reserve for anticipated tax liabilities on the basis that a partner may retire in that accounting period. Thought needs to be given to the repayment of any excess retentions, interest on tax reserves, and whether the amount retained should be set aside in a separate ring fenced trust account or can be used as working capital of the firm or LLP.

The appointment of a partner with responsibility for ensuring compliance with any statutory and HM Revenue & Customs requirements is also necessary. The professional firm should provide the nominated partner or member with all necessary information and indemnify them in respect of liabilities incurred in the course of that role (other than those liabilities occasioned by his own wrongdoing). For a fuller discussion of the treatment of tax retentions, see **CHAPTER 14**.

Bank accounts (model clause 10)

5.17 The agreement normally names the firm's bankers, sets out a procedure for appointing new bankers and identifies the partners or members who are to be authorised to sign cheques. Provision may be made for different levels of approval and different partners' or members' signatures, depending upon the value of the cheque.

Insurance (model clause 11)

5.18 Most agreements contain provisions setting out the scope of the basic insurance cover to be maintained by the partnership, including employer's liability insurance, professional indemnity cover, third party liability insurance and cover for partnership assets.

Many agreements provide for former partners and members to be given the protection of any insurance cover to the extent that they are liable for any partnership-related claims.

Restrictions and duties (model clause 12)

Duty of good faith

5.19 Even though there is no express duty of good faith in the *Partnership Act 1890*, it is a fundamental principle that partners in a partnership must act with the utmost good faith towards each other (*Helmore v Smith* (1885) Ch D 436). The duty amounts to an obligation to be entirely honest, straightforward and open in all dealings between partners and to disclose all material facts.

Related fiduciary duties will bind the partners, such as *s 28* of the *Partnership Act 1890* which obliges partners to render true accounts and full information of all things affecting the partnership to any partner or his legal representatives. Although this is implied in any event, most agreements include an express provision to remind parties of this important duty. A partner is also under an obligation not to make private profits at the expense of the firm, not to compete with the firm's business and, to the extent that he does so, to share with the firm any private profits made in the

71

course of the firm's business or a competing business (see *Partnership Act 1890, ss 29, 30*). A partner who uses information gained during the course of the partnership business to acquire a personal benefit will normally have to account for the profit that he makes. Similarly, a partner who obtains a directorship of a client company will generally be accountable for the fees that he earns.

All of these duties to account may be overruled by contrary agreement. For example, the agreement should specify if a partner is to be allowed to keep any directors' fees or other profits for his own benefit. It is important to have regard to any professional rules which may restrict the freedom of the firm or an individual partner in the firm to act for a client where a directorship or appointment is held with that client.

Unlike company directors or trustees, partners in breach of these fiduciary duties have no defence against such claims, even if they have acted honestly and reasonably, as this defence is only available to directors and trustees under statute (*Companies Act 2006, s 1157*; *Trustee Act 1925, s 61*).

5.20   For members of an LLP, the position is different. *Section 6* of the *LLP Act* provides that every member of the LLP is an agent of the LLP. Therefore, members have an implied duty of good faith to the LLP under the common law. The legislation does not provide for a duty of good faith between members, although sometimes LLP agreements include an express duty of good faith in order to provide members, as well as the LLP, with a remedy in the event of a breach (see, for example, clause 12(1)(b) of the model LLP agreement). Many firms, however, prefer that such remedies should be under the control of the LLP's management and do not therefore provide members with a remedy as well. It is also thought that a kind of duty of good faith, namely an obligation to exercise voting rights in the best interests of the LLP, rather than in order to secure a personal benefit or pursue an ulterior motive, would be implied in respect of decisions which require a majority vote. This is discussed in detail in Whittaker and Machell *The Law of Limited Liability Partnerships* (3rd Edn) at 12.27.

Default rules 8 to 10 applicable to LLPs (see **3.9**) reflect *ss 28–30* of the *Partnership Act 1890*, although members must account to the LLP rather than to the other members. The LLP agreement often includes an express provision dealing with these duties (especially if the LLP agreement excludes the default rules generally), and makes provision for circumstances in which the members will not be obliged to comply with these duties, for example allowing them to retain directors' fees.

Members acting in breach of fiduciary duties may have a defence against claims where they can show that they have acted honestly and reasonably (*Companies Act 2006, s 1157*).

The *Companies Act 2006* codified many of the fiduciary duties owed by directors of a company. The codified duties do not extend to members of an LLP.

Full time and attention

5.21 In the absence of any statutory duty to devote full time and attention, it will normally be appropriate to specify in the partnership or LLP agreement that the partners' or members' whole time and attention should be devoted to the business. In the absence of such a provision, it may be impossible to show that a lack of commitment to the business amounts to a breach of duty.

The full time and attention clause will generally be coupled with an express prohibition against pursuing outside business interests, so that a partner or member who is in breach of this obligation can be forced to stop pursuing those interests by injunction, or required to compensate the firm for loss.

In some cases, partners or members need the freedom to pursue outside business interests, and the agreement therefore contains a mechanism to allow them to do so without being in breach.

To ensure that offices and appointments can be monitored, agreements sometimes require partners or members to obtain the consent of the managing partner or of a committee before accepting directorships and other positions and to specify whether the position is held for the account of the partnership/LLP or personally. If it is a professional practice appointment, the partner or member is generally fully indemnified by the firm in respect of all costs and liabilities incurred in that capacity. This consent requirement can help the firm to become aware of any appointments which give rise to conflicts of interest between the partner or member and the firm or its clients.

Especially in the case of partnerships, agreements often prohibit partners or members from joining any syndicate at Lloyd's, conducting any other business or holding any share in a company with unlimited liability, in order to reduce the risk of partners or members becoming personally insolvent and therefore being unable meet their commitments to the firm.

Restrictions

5.22 As noted at **2.24**, *s 5* of the *Partnership Act 1890* states that every partner is an agent of the firm and his other partners for the purpose of the business of the partnership, and *s 6* of the *LLP Act* provides that a member of the LLP is an agent of the LLP, and that the LLP will be bound by acts done by a member unless the member has no authority and the third party knows he has no authority or does not believe that the person is a member of the LLP.

Agreements, therefore, usually restrict a partner's or member's ability to bind the firm without the other partners' or the LLP's prior consent. Such restrictions may include preventing a partner or member from compromising, compounding, releasing or discharging any debt, entering into any bond, bail, security or surety, lending any money or property of the partnership or LLP, or giving credit or acting for or having any dealing with any person whom the partner or member has been requested not to deal with by the other partners or members.

Dealings with partnership/LLP interests

5.23 Partnership is essentially a personal relationship, and the *Partnership Act 1890* recognises this. *Section 31* provides that, subject to any contrary agreement, an assignee will have no right to participate in the management of the business, or even to inspect the books. He is simply entitled to his share of the partnership profits and, on dissolution, assets. Similarly, *s 7* of the *LLP Act* contemplates the assignment of a membership interest, although, if not excluded, default rule 5 requires the consent of all members for an assignment. Again, an assignee may not interfere in management or administration of the LLP (*LLP Act, s 7(2)*), although this does not affect the assignee's right to receive amounts from the LLP (*LLP Act, s 7(3)*).

In the context of a professional firm, it is normally appropriate to go further and to specify that partnership or LLP interests are non-assignable and that the partners or members may not charge their interests in the partnership or LLP. However, if capital contributions are to be funded through borrowings, the lender will often insist upon express agreement from the partners or members and the LLP that the firm will repay the capital directly to the lending bank when a partner or member retires. Especially where the firm also borrows, the bank may further require personal guarantees from the partners or members and perhaps a charge on personal assets, other than the partnership or LLP share itself. The agreement should not prevent the partners or members from agreeing suitable terms with lenders.

Professional and regulatory rules

5.24 Agreements usually provide that partners or members must comply with all regulatory and professional obligations. The inclusion of such a clause gives each partner or member a contractual duty to comply with these obligations, and in default other partners or members may be able to expel the defaulting partner or member, or to obtain damages or an order for specific performance.

Confidentiality

5.25 A partner or member, like anyone who occupies a fiduciary position implying trust and confidence, will be subject to a duty under general law not to disclose confidential information, and this is often supplemented by express wording in the agreement. This may make it easier for the firm to prevent a disaffected partner or member from disclosing confidential information to the press, or to obtain damages if the partner or member acts in breach of the restriction and the firm suffers loss.

Indemnity

5.26 Agreements usually provide for partners or members to be indemnified in respect of expenses incurred by them in the course of the ordinary and proper conduct of the firm's business. In the case of an LLP, it is important that the indemnity is provided by the LLP, not its members, because otherwise all members may become liable to third parties where one of their number gives negligent advice with consequent loss of limited liability. The question arises whether such a clause would, or should, provide protection from liability where the partner or member causes loss by his own negligence, and consideration might be given, for example, to providing for the indemnity to be dependent on a decision of the firm or of a committee where the loss arises from negligence of the member or partner himself. Sometimes, agreements also provide for each of the partners or members to indemnify the firm from any loss caused if he breaches any of the obligations contained in the agreement or the firm suffers loss owing to his own acts or omissions.

Management and decision making (model clauses 14 to 16)

5.27 *Section 24(5)* of the *Partnership Act 1890* and default rule 3 set out in the *LLP Regulations 2001* provide that, in default of any other agreement, every partner or member has a right to take part in the management of the business. *Section 24(8)* and default rule 6 provide that differences between the partners in relation to ordinary matters connected with the partnership business may be resolved by majority decision, except that a change in the nature of the partnership business can only be resolved by unanimous decision. Whether a decision relates to an ordinary matter connected with the partnership business is a question of fact and there is no statutory guidance. The basic position set out in the *Partnership Act 1890* and the default rules under the *LLP Regulations 2001* is rarely sufficient for a modern firm, and most day-to-day decision-making in firms of any size is delegated to a management team; in an era of fast-growing national and international practices, it is increasingly difficult and ill-advised for all the partners or members of the firm to be involved actively in the management of its day-to-day, firm-wide affairs.

Many agreements, therefore, specify that certain decisions will be taken by a senior or managing partner, or a committee or board, whilst other more important decisions require a specified majority vote of the partners or members. These important decisions might include, for example, dissolving the firm, admitting or expelling equity partners, appointing salaried partners, acquiring a company or business, merging with another firm, amending the terms of the agreement, and acquiring or disposing of freehold or leasehold property. Some agreements contain a requirement for certain very important decisions to require unanimity or the support of all but one or two partners, but such provisions may allow a capricious or dissident partner or member to block decisions which are in the general interests of the firm.

Striking a balance

5.28 The agreement must find a balance between:

(a) enabling the firm to make fast and effective management decisions in an increasingly competitive marketplace;

(b) enabling the firm to deal with sensitive issues, such as an underperforming individual, decisively but fairly; and

(c) preserving the fragile atmosphere of cooperation and mutual benefit, known as the partnership ethos, which is so important, whether the firm is structured as a partnership or an LLP.

The larger the firm, the harder it becomes to achieve the first two objectives without sacrificing the third. Those professional partnerships that choose to move towards a complex, corporate governance style of management must ensure that the management structure remains fully accountable to, and in touch with, the partners or members. Some of the larger professional firms achieve this by establishing a policy board in addition to a management committee. The board represents the professional practice as a whole, holding the management committee to account and providing strategic direction to the professional practice. Whatever governance structures are chosen, it is important that they are described fully and clearly in the agreement.

Deadlocks may arise where decisions have to be taken by majority decision. Possible ways of resolving deadlock include the following:

(i) not having any specific provision in the agreement dealing with deadlock but trying to resolve problems as they arise by negotiation (although, if the negotiations fail, then dissolution of the partnership or winding up the LLP may be the only practical answer);

(ii) providing a senior or managing partner with a casting vote in the event of a deadlock;

(iii) giving partners or members differing numbers of votes depending on their capital contributions, seniority within the firm or some other factor; or

(iv) giving a particular class of partners/members the right to veto certain decisions.

Partnership and committee meetings

5.29 The *Partnership Act 1890* and *LLP Act* say little about the conduct of meetings, although in the case of a partnership the implied duty of good faith confers a right on every partner to have his point of view heard and discussed. Especially in the context of larger professional firms, it is desirable to agree some procedures, and the agreement can usefully set out a code governing the conduct of meetings and committees. Such codes will deal with issues such as the notice required for meetings, quorum requirements and voting procedures including proxy voting, and voting rights where a partner or member declares an interest in the question to be decided. Minutes of these meetings should be taken and circulated to the partners or members.

Incoming partners (model clause 17)

5.30 The agreement should make provision for the admission of new partners or members. Otherwise, a dissident partner or member may be able to block the appointment of a new partner who may be important to the future of the firm.

The agreement should deal with the manner in which new partners or members will be admitted. A large majority in favour (such as 75%) is sometimes required, although larger firms often delegate the power of appointment to a committee or board. In the absence of agreement, unanimity will be required. It is important to note that, since 1 October 2006, it has been necessary to be able to justify any criteria for new partners based on age or length of service in the light of the *Employment Equality (Age) Regulations 2006* and, since 1 October 2010, the *Equality*

Act 2010. Any form of discrimination on the grounds of age would need to be demonstrated, on an objective basis, to be a proportionate means of achieving a legitimate aim.

In the case of a partnership, a new partner does not become directly liable to the creditors of the firm for any debts and obligations incurred before he became a partner (*Partnership Act 1890, s 17(1)*). However, liabilities incurred before a partner's or member's appointment, but first provided for in the profit and loss account after his appointment, will normally have the effect of making him indirectly liable by decreasing the profits or increasing the losses of the firm for the relevant period in which he shares. In the case of an LLP, it, and not the members, is liable for the LLP's debts and obligations in any event.

The agreement should establish how much capital (if any) the new partner or member must contribute on admission, and the new partner's or member's profit and (in the case of a partnership) loss sharing ratios. In order to ensure that the new partner or member is bound by the terms of the existing agreement, he is likely to be asked to sign a supplemental deed confirming that the terms of the main agreement apply to him, noting any new provisions which apply by way of custom and practice but which are not yet reflected in the main agreement, and setting out any particular issues that relate solely to him.

It can sometimes be helpful to attach, as a schedule to the agreement, a standard form of supplemental accession deed for use when new partners or members join the partnership or LLP. A form of supplemental deed, called a deed of accession, is attached to each of the models.

The admission of salaried partners or members as employees is normally effected by a separate contract with the salaried partner or member concerned. The agreement will often provide for a special majority decision of the partners or members to approve the appointment of a salaried partner or member.

Outgoing partners or members (model clauses 18 to 21)

5.31 The agreement should specify the circumstances in which partners or members cease to be partners or members and the rights and obligations of outgoing partners or members. Under the general law, a partnership for an indefinite term is dissolved when a partner retires or dies, and it is important to exclude the general law and to provide in the agreement that, in these circumstances, the partnership continues between the remaining partners. Unlike a partnership, an LLP is not dissolved upon a member ceasing to be a member of the LLP, so there is no need to specify that it will continue.

Expulsion and compulsory retirement

5.32 *Section 25* of the *Partnership Act 1890* and *reg 8* of the *LLP Regulations 2001* provide that no majority of the partners members can expel any partner/member unless a power to do so has been conferred by express agreement between the partners or members.

Therefore, unless the agreement makes express provision for expulsions, or the exit arrangements for a partner or member are agreed, the only way to expel a partner or member would be to dissolve the partnership or to petition the court for a just and equitable winding up of the LLP, as applicable. This could lead to the forced disposal of all the assets, including goodwill. However, the courts have a discretion to make an order in respect of a partnership that, on dissolution, one partner's share is valued and bought out by the continuing partners instead of a full winding up (*Syers v Syers* (1876) 1 App Case 174). A *Syers v Syers* order does not have the effect of preventing a technical dissolution of a partnership; the continuing partnership is a 'new' partnership. This may mean that assets and liabilities held for or owed by the 'old' partnership will need to be transferred to or novated by the new partnership. It is thought that a *Syers v Syers* order could be applied to a LLP, although obviously there would be no technical dissolution, as the LLP is a body corporate and continues until wound up.

In practice, most agreements include an expulsion provision providing that a partner or member may be expelled with immediate effect or on notice, where all or a substantial majority of the other partners agree. The agreement normally sets out a list of grounds for expulsion for cause, such as criminal activities, loss of any necessary professional qualification, infringement of the rules of any professional body regulating the firm, a serious or persistent breach of the agreement or insolvency and mental or physical incapacity. In the absence of such a clause, the mental incapacity of a partner can cause considerable inconvenience, making it necessary for the firm to deal with the relevant partner's attorney under an lasting power of attorney (where available), or with a Court of Protection Receiver. Note also that loss of a required professional qualification may mean that, unless the miscreant is automatically expelled, the partnership or LLP is conducting its business unlawfully and (in the case of a partnership) it is automatically dissolved.

One of the most difficult management issues is how to deal with underperforming partners or members who have not actually committed a breach of the agreement. Of course, prevention is better than cure, and a well-managed firm will monitor the performance of individual partners or members and give them the help and support they need to contribute everything that is expected of them. Unfortunately, however, it may be impossible for some partners or members to address the performance issues which are causing concern, and it is important to ensure that the firm can avoid a situation in which underperformers hold the firm back to such an extent that the firm cannot satisfy the aspirations of its high-fliers. It is normally possible to resolve the situation by mutual agreement, but ultimately the firm must have the means to secure the compulsory retirement of a partner or member where it is impossible to reach agreement. This will generally require a substantial majority of votes, but some larger firms now delegate this decision to a committee.

Whether a partner or member is being expelled or compulsorily retired, this must of course be handled with the utmost good faith. It must be fully debated, and, in the case of an expulsion for cause, the outgoing partner or member must be given the opportunity to put forward his case. If reasons are in practice put forward to justify compulsory retirement from an LLP, the member concerned should be given an opportunity to respond. Since 1 October 2006, when the *Employment Equality (Age) Regulations 2006* came into effect, it has become very important to ensure that no practice develops of encouraging or forcing partners to leave at a particular age, as it is unlikely that the practice could be justified as a proportionate and legitimate means of achieving the firm's business needs.

The *Equality Act 2010*, which replaced the *Employment Equality (Age) Regulations 2006*, applies to partnerships and LLPs and will prevent discrimination on the grounds of age, unless the particular provision or practice can be justified as a proportionate means of achieving a legitimate aim. Unlike the position for employers, no provision has been made to allow compulsory retirement of partners at 65; however, the Employment Appeal Tribunal observed in *Seldon v Clarkson Wright & Jakes* [2009] 3 All ER 435 that, although the choice of a compulsory retirement age of 65 could not be justified on an untested assumption that performance would drop at 65, the age of 65 has 'some, if limited, significance in circumstances where the partnership has been able to justify the adoption of a compulsory retirement age at some age'. In the relatively unusual cases where a compulsory retirement age is thought to be necessary, it is important to seek legal advice and to consider in the light of that advice whether the provision can be justified. Accordingly, the model agreements do not include a default provision for retirement upon reaching a specified age.

If, as will normally be the case, a compulsory retirement age cannot be justified, and so underperformance cannot be dealt with simply by leaving it to the passage of time, it will be all the more important to ensure that performance issues can be dealt with, for example by means of a compulsory retirement by notice procedure, a de-equitisation procedure and the introduction of flexible working practices, such as part-time or consultancy arrangements.

With a view to protecting the interests of the firm, partners and members should consider incorporating gardening leave provisions in their agreement. These may provide that, for the duration of any notice period, a partner or member who is subject to the notice may be denied access to the office, to clients and to staff, which helps isolate him. He could also be deprived of his right to participate in decision-making during this period. It may be thought to be unduly harsh to impose garden leave on an underperformer who is compulsorily retired.

Suspension

5.33 Some agreements provide for the suspension of partners or members for a period of time (for example, where a criminal investigation is pending or continuing but where no findings have been published or convictions obtained). Neither the *Partnership Act 1890* nor the *LLP Act* contemplates suspension, and suitable terms must be incorporated in the written agreement, where appropriate. The suspended partner or member may be excluded from the firm's offices, staff and clients during the period of suspension, may not be allowed to draw profits during the period of his suspension, and may be deprived of his right to participate in all decision-making, depending on the agreement reached. However, because of the obvious scope for abuse of such a clause, considerable care has to be taken to ensure that the power is exercised in the utmost good faith.

Voluntary retirement

5.34 The *Partnership Act 1890* makes no provision for the retirement of partners and, in the absence of such a clause, the only means available to a partner who wishes to leave the firm is to try to obtain an order to dissolve the firm. The partnership agreement should therefore set out the circumstances in which partners may retire from the firm. *Section 4(3) of the LLP Act* provides that a member of an LLP may cease to be a member of the LLP by giving reasonable notice to the other members. However, to avoid debate over what constitutes reasonable notice, the LLP agreement should set out the manner in which members may retire from the LLP.

Most agreements provide that partners or members can give notice to retire. Some still provide for compulsory retirement at a specified age, although this is increasingly less common, given the risk of being unable to justify an age-based provision as proportionate means of achieving a legitimate aim (see the discussion of the *Equality Act 2010* at **5.32** above).

Since the retirement of retiring partners or members can lead to serious cash flow problems, owing to falling revenues, fixed overheads and capital withdrawals, a limit may be imposed on the number of partners or members who may retire in a particular year. However, courts are generally reluctant to force partners to continue in partnership against their will, and the same reasoning is likely to be applied to LLPs. There is a danger that, in a situation where a partner or member is prevented from retiring from a firm in this manner, he could apply to the court to dissolve the partnership on the grounds that circumstances had arisen which made dissolution of a partnership just and equitable (*Partnership Act 1890, s 35*), or that a member might apply to wind up the LLP on just and equitable grounds. An alternative is to provide for the withdrawal of capital in fixed instalments, thereby controlling the cash flow situation, or even to require retiring partners to continue to contribute to specified expenses for a period while the firm adjusts (although this is rare). Sometimes, provision is made for retiring partners or members to be able to have a continuing involvement with the firm, perhaps as consultants.

Death

5.35 A partnership agreement should state that the partnership will continue after the death of a partner. Otherwise, under *s 33(1)* of the *Partnership Act 1890* the partnership will automatically dissolve, unless the deceased partner was a limited partner (*Limited Partnerships Act 1907, s 6(2)*). The agreement should also be clear that the deceased member's personal representatives do not become partners in his place.

Death will not dissolve an LLP, and the deceased member automatically ceases to be a member unless express provision is made for his personal representatives to become members (this is the effect of *s 4(3)* of the *LLP Act*). However, if the number of members falls below two, a sole member may become liable jointly and severally with the LLP for the LLP's debts (*LLP Act, s 4A*). As noted above, *s 7* of the *LLP Act* provides that the deceased member's personal representatives may not interfere with the management or administration of the LLP's business, but they may remain entitled to receive amounts from the LLP.

The agreement should also deal with the right of the estate of the deceased partner or member to payment of his current and capital account balances. It may also provide for any annuities that might become payable to the deceased partner's dependants, although annuity payments are becoming increasingly rare in the context of professional firms.

Bankruptcy

5.36 If it is intended that a partnership should continue, following the bankruptcy of one of the partners, this must be clearly stated in the partnership agreement. Otherwise, *s 33(1)* of the *Partnership Act 1890* provides for the partnership to dissolve.

An LLP will not be wound up on the bankruptcy of a member. *Section 7(2)* of the *LLP Act* provides that a trustee in bankruptcy may not interfere with the management or administration of the LLP's business, but *s 7(3)* of the *LLP Act* provides that this does not affect his rights to receive amounts from the LLP.

Entitlement of outgoing partners (model clause 22)

5.37 The agreement should deal with the financial entitlements of outgoing partners or members and, where a partner or member has died, the entitlement of his personal representatives. Such entitlement may include a return of capital, the withdrawal of any share of retained revenue or capital profits, and accrued interest on the partner's or member's capital account (if any). The agreement should also deal with how any advances made to, or over-drawings made by, the outgoing partner or member should be repaid (normally by way of deduction from the outgoing partner's or member's other entitlements).

Often, the agreement will provide for the withdrawal of capital in instalments (with or without interest) in order to assist with the cash flow issues. Sometimes, there is a very long delay before these balances are released, but the managing committee or board is permitted to authorise early release, in order to improve the negotiating position of the firm when a partner or member leaves and to provide a fund from which the firm can be compensated for any damage caused by the outgoing partner's or member's breaches.

It would even be possible to provide for a share of some expenses of the firm (eg rent under an onerous lease) to be debited to these retained balances, in order to ease cash flow problems and disincentivise early retirement. Onerous provisions of this kind could be expressed only to apply if the partner is retiring voluntarily, to discourage partners from leaving the firm to join a competitor.

Agreements generally provide for the outgoing partner's or member's share to accrue automatically to the other partners or members. Note, however, that providing for automatic accruer on death amounts to a 'buy and sell' agreement, which would mean that the deceased partner's partnership interest, or deceased member's LLP interest, would not enjoy relief as 'relevant business property' for inheritance tax purposes (see CHAPTER 23). Some agreements therefore provide for the continuing partners or members of the LLP to have the option to buy out the deceased partner's or member's interest, failing which the estate will retain an investment in the firm without remaining a partner or member.

Care needs to be taken to ensure that, where the continuing partners or members can effectively buy out a bankrupt partner's or member's share, the transaction is not vulnerable to attack by the trustee in bankruptcy as a transaction at an undervalue for the purposes of the *Insolvency Act 1986*. This is unlikely to be a problem if all outgoing members are entitled to equivalent rights and there are no special arrangements on a bankruptcy.

It is important that the agreement clarifies whether an outgoing partner's or member's rights are to be calculated by reference to the value of the assets that appear in the firm's annual accounts or whether full market value is to be substituted. Sometimes, it is intended that the assets should be revalued on a partner or member ceasing to be a partner or member, so that any increase or decrease in value can be debited or credited to the outgoing partner's or member's capital account on his departure. The capital gains tax consequences of such a provision are discussed in CHAPTER 21.

As noted above, to the extent that it is intended to ensure that capital and current account balances appear as equity in the accounts of an LLP, the LLP will need to be given the discretion to decide when and whether to allocate profits and redeem capital. For a fuller discussion, see CHAPTER 14.

If retired partners or members and their dependants are to be entitled to an annuity from the firm, this should be spelt out in the agreement, but this is increasingly rare, and partners or members are normally encouraged to make their own provision for retirement.

Debt exposure

5.38 The exposure of an outgoing partner to debts of the firm is fully discussed in CHAPTER 2.

Outgoing partners' liabilities

5.39 In the case of a partnership, an outgoing partner remains liable to third parties for the partnership debts and obligations, breaches of trust and contract, fraud (in the course of the partnership business) and negligence incurred while he was a partner, except to the extent that contrary agreement is reached with a particular creditor (*Partnership Act 1890, ss 9, 10* and *11*). Thus, outgoing partners may remain liable for continuing obligations, for example, under the covenants of a firm's lease or under hire-purchase agreements. Similarly, it is the partners who were partners at the time of a negligent action who are liable, not the partners in the firm at the time the claim is made (although the firm will normally be sued in its own name). The partners who are personally liable to the creditor, including the former partner, will normally be entitled to be indemnified by the continuing partners through the profit and loss sharing mechanism.

Under *s 9* of the *Partnership Act 1890*, an outgoing partner ceases to be liable for any partnership debts or obligations incurred after he ceases to be a partner, but he will continue to be exposed in contract (not tort) if he is held out as being a continuing partner or is an apparent partner, for example, because existing clients and contacts have not been informed that he has left the firm.

Given the above, most partnership agreements include an express indemnity for outgoing partners, although a right to indemnity from the continuing partners is generally implied in any event by the fact that the outgoing partner ceases to have a share in the firm's profits and losses. The rationale for such an indemnity is that it achieves a clean break.

Sometimes, however, agreements provide for outgoing partners to remain liable for the consequences of their own personal professional negligence or breach of duty. An account is drawn up as at the date when the partner leaves the firm, and provision is made for any known liabilities before he withdraws his capital and current account balances from the firm. Sometimes, sums are retained to provide for unknown liabilities as well (see **2.33**).

Although the members are not personally liable for the debts and obligations of the LLP, an outgoing member generally continues to have the benefit of an indemnity from the LLP (but see **5.26** above).

Restrictive covenants (model clause 23)

5.40   In an age of increasing mobility of partners and members, firms are anxious to minimise the loss of clients that can result from a partner or member leaving to join a rival firm, and a clear set of restrictive covenants can help to avoid damage to the business of the partnership or LLP.

Restrictive covenants

5.41   Most major UK professional firms have restrictive covenants, although most US law firms tend not to place restrictions on outgoing partners acting in competition with the firm, owing to the difficulty of enforcing such restrictions in the USA.

Some argue that it is wrong as a matter of principle to interfere with a partner's right to work after his departure, or with a client's right to choose its adviser, and that a firm should inspire, rather than force, partners or members to stay. On the other hand, partners or members are stakeholders in their firm and, unless reasonable restrictive covenants are included in the agreement, the danger is that a firm may become inherently unstable as partners or members seek to leave the business rather than help the firm work through a period of financial difficulty. Where outgoing partners or members have a complete indemnity, partner or member defections leave the remaining partners or members to meet the same overheads out of diminished turnover, and a trickle of defections could turn into a flood. Generally, in the UK it is thought perfectly legitimate for a firm to seek to protect its goodwill, or at least to maximise its negotiating position when a partner or member leaves, by discouraging defections and minimising the damage when they occur, especially as the courts have shown themselves willing to enforce reasonable restrictions and the trend in the marketplace is to include them.

The basic legal principle is that covenants are inherently anti-competitive, and they are therefore viewed as contrary to public policy and unenforceable if they go further than is strictly necessary to protect the legitimate interest of the ongoing business. In the context of professional firms, restrictive covenants should be no more onerous than is reasonable to protect the firm's goodwill.

Three kinds of restrictive covenants are often used.

The model agreements include a traditional clause seeking to prevent an outgoing partner or member from practising at all in a specified area for a limited period. Such clauses must be very limited in terms of the geographical area and the period of application if they are to be reasonable. A more general non-competition clause, which simply prevents acting in competition with the business anywhere for a specified period, is sometimes included as well, or instead, given that it is relatively easy for the firm to show that the effect of such restrictions is reasonable. Non-competition covenants prevent a partner or member from competing directly or indirectly with the firm for a fixed period of time after leaving the partnership or LLP. In a franchise case, *Kall-Kwik Printing (UK) Ltd v Rush* [1996] FSR 114, the courts interpreted 'competition' to mean carrying on a business capable of competing with the business being protected and not simply a business of the same type. The courts view non-competition covenants as inherently self-limiting, and geographical limitation on their operation is therefore less important.

Provisions preventing solicitation of, or dealing with, partnership or LLP clients and client prospects aim to prohibit a partner or member from soliciting clients or dealing with clients and client prospects for a fixed period of time, irrespective of whether or not the partner or member initiated the approach. Careful consideration needs to be given to the definition of a 'partnership or LLP client' and 'client prospect' in this context, to ensure that the restriction is no wider than is reasonable, and the restriction is generally applied only to clients and prospects with whom the outgoing partner or member had direct personal dealings in the period immediately preceding his departure. If the services to be supplied by an outgoing partner or member to a partnership or LLP client are not the same as those that the partnership or LLP supplies, any attempt to rely on such a restriction would be likely to be unreasonable.

Further, if there is a possibility of a transfer of the partnership or LLP business to a new entity, it is important that covenants are drafted by reference to the business, rather than partnership or LLP itself, so that the restriction can also protect the transferee. Note the strict interpretation of the restrictive covenants in *Prescott v Dunwoody Sports Marketing* [2007] EWCA Civ 461.

Clauses preventing solicitation of partners, other members and staff prevent a partner or member from encouraging another partner or member or a current employee to join him in a different business venture. Sometimes, this is coupled with a restriction against acting in partnership with, or in the same entity as, any person who was employed by, or was a partner or member, of the firm at the same time as the outgoing partner or member. This is designed to discourage team moves.

The period within which restrictive covenants apply has been a matter for debate in recent years. The current view is that, notwithstanding the five-year term upheld in the Privy Council decision in *Bridge v Deacon* [1984] 2 All ER 19, partnerships and LLPs should generally opt for a shorter term and thereby increase the likelihood of being able to enforce the covenants. The principle borne out by subsequent cases is that such covenants will be enforceable only if they are reasonable, in the interests of the parties and the public, and no wider than is required for the proper protection of the covenantee. The more onerous the covenant, the shorter the period should be.

The *Competition Act 1998* affects agreements containing non-competition clauses. *Chapter I* of the *1998 Act* prohibits agreements which have as their object or effect the prevention, restriction or distortion of competition within the UK or a part of it. However, *s 60* of the *Competition Act 1998* provides that, in applying the *Act*, a court must ensure that it is interpreted consistently with European law, the relevant provisions being Article 81(1) (formerly Article 85(1)) of the EC Treaty, and the rules interpreting the EC Merger Regulation.

Article 81(1) prohibits agreements which have as their object or effect the prevention, restriction or distortion of competition within the EU or part of it. However, in the context of sale and purchase agreements, agreements containing restrictive covenants have been held to fall outside Article 81(1) of the EC Treaty where such clauses are reasonable in time and scope. This may shed some light on the provisions relating to the transfer of a partner's interest in the business to the other partners on his retirement. Under the EC Merger Regulation, specific provision is made in relation to non-competition clauses where they can be seen as ancillary restrictions. The legal rationale is that they guarantee the purchaser the full value of the asset acquired. To be enforceable, however, the restriction must be limited to a reasonable duration, geographic scope and subject matter.

Even if reasonable restrictive covenants are included, in practice it can be very damaging to the partnership or LLP to insist that a particular client ceases to use the outgoing partner's or member's services, and the partnership or LLP may feel that it cannot seek an injunction preventing this. In those circumstances, it may be necessary instead to claim damages for breach from the outgoing partner or member. Sometimes, agreements specify how such damages are to be computed. The method of computation must be a genuine pre-estimate of the actual loss that the firm will suffer, as the court may otherwise strike it down as an unenforceable penalty, and exercise its own discretion to quantify the damage.

The individual restrictive covenants should be drafted as separate clauses, so that if the court thinks that any one of the covenants is unreasonable, then it can be struck out, leaving the remainder intact. This approach facilitates the inclusion of a matrix of covenants of varying terms and scope, some of which may arguably be unreasonable but which collectively have a deterrent effect.

An agreement may encourage the partners or members to adhere to the restrictive covenants by way of financial incentives, for example, denying outgoing partners or members in breach of such restrictions some part of their financial package (see **5.37** above), but care should be taken to ensure that the amount retained is a reasonable pre-estimate of loss. Otherwise, it may be unenforceable as a penalty.

Generally, a well-drafted agreement will also prohibit an outgoing partner or member from representing himself as a partner or member or using the partnership or LLP name in any way. An outgoing partner or member should also be prevented from disclosing information that is confidential to the partnership or LLP, and many agreements expressly require such partners or members to return to the continuing partners all documents, records and other papers in their possession which relate to the partnership business. Provision is sometimes included for there to be no announcement or disclosure of the retirement to clients, staff or the press, except as agreed in writing by the partnership or LLP.

Dissolution and winding up (model clause 24)

5.42 As noted above, in the context of a partnership, the expulsion, retirement, death and bankruptcy of a partner will lead to the automatic dissolution of the partnership, unless the agreement provides otherwise.

Dissolution may also be caused by expiration of the term of a fixed-term partnership or, in the case of an indefinite term partnership, by any partner giving notice to the other partners of his intention to dissolve the partnership. If an individual partner has power to dissolve the firm unilaterally, and thus perhaps to force a sale of the firm's assets, including goodwill, he will have a very powerful weapon in the event of a dispute. To avoid this, the partnership agreement should normally provide that the partnership may only be dissolved if dissolution is approved by all or a significant majority of the partners.

Whatever the partnership agreement says, *s 35* of the *Partnership Act 1890* provides that any partner may apply to the court for a decree of dissolution of a partnership in one of a number of situations, including where:

(a)   a partner becomes permanently incapable of performing his part of the partnership agreement;

(b)   the conduct of a partner is felt to be prejudicially affecting the conduct of the business, or a partner conducts himself in such a way that it is not reasonably practicable for the other partners to carry on business with him;

(c)   the partner is persistently in breach of his obligations under the partnership agreement or the business of the partnership can only be carried on at a loss; or

(d)   it is just and equitable that the partnership be dissolved.

The partner seeking dissolution cannot be the partner creating the reasons for dissolving the partnership. Dissolution may also be brought about by rescission for fraud or misrepresentation or by repudiation of the partnership agreement.

5.43   The concept of 'dissolution', as it applies to partnerships, does not apply to LLPs, so the LLP agreement should deal with the winding up of the LLP and will need to reflect the relevant *Insolvency Act 1986* requirements. The winding-up clause will be very different from that in a partnership agreement. In particular, provision should be made for the mechanics by which the LLP and its members will determine that a voluntary winding up should occur, and whether and to what extent members are to contribute to a winding up. Provision could be made for contribution of a nominal sum to ensure that members are contributories for the purposes of *s 79* of the *Insolvency Act 1986,* and individual members can therefore petition the court for a winding up, but some LLPs may prefer not to allow individual members to have that power and to leave such matters to a collective decision.

5.44   The agreement should set out the procedures to be followed on dissolution or a winding up, and should state how specific assets (eg goodwill, the name and the firm's intellectual property rights) are to be dealt with on winding up. It will often be appropriate for the agreement to provide for goodwill etc to be sold to the highest bidding group of former partners or members, in the event of a dissolution.

Mediation and arbitration (model clause 25)

5.45   To prevent a public airing of disputes in the court and to encourage the preservation of relations between partners or members wherever possible, it is usual to include a private dispute resolution process.

In the hope of restoring the trust and confidence that underlies a successful firm and to keep dispute resolution as inexpensive, quick and informal as possible, many agreements now provide for the parties to attempt to resolve disputes by mediation in the first instance. Mediation involves a neutral third party who clarifies the objectives of the parties, seeks to find common ground between them, does not impose a solution on them, and encourages them to resolve their points of difference by agreement in a way which avoids more formal means of dispute resolution, such as arbitration or court proceedings. Mediators can be appointed with the assistance of, among other bodies, the Centre for Dispute Resolution or by consulting directories of mediators and arbitrators such as the one maintained by the Association of Partnership Practitioners. In case mediation proves unsuccessful, the partnership agreement will also need to provide for a form of binding dispute resolution by arbitration or the courts.

An arbitration clause will provide for any dispute to be heard in private by an arbitrator or panel of arbitrators. In the case of a professional partnership, provision is often made for the arbitrator to be appointed by the President of the relevant professional body, or of the Chartered Institute of Arbitrators. The parties may provide that the arbitration rules of an arbitration institution will regulate the procedures to be adopted for the arbitration. The statutory rules relating to arbitration proceedings are contained in the *Arbitration Act 1996* and in a substantial body of court decisions.

Furthermore, the agreement can require that technical matters, valuation issues and other matters relating to the exercise of professional judgement or expertise should be referred for expert determination. This method of dispute resolution is particularly helpful for dealing with disputes about matters relating to accounting standards and practice. The agreement should specify how the expert is to be chosen and what issue is required to be determined and should confirm that the expert does not act as arbitrator. It should also specify that the expert's decision is final and binding.

Alterations to the partnership agreement (model clause 26)

5.46   In the absence of any contrary agreement, the agreement can only be changed by unanimous agreement. This may cause considerable practical problems if a dissident minority stands in the way of a change which is viewed as important by the vast majority of the partners or members. It is therefore common to provide for the agreement to be capable of being altered by a particular majority, say 75% of the partners or members.

It can be helpful to include a simplified procedure for correcting obvious errors and making 'non-substantive' changes, perhaps delegating the power to make such changes to a management committee or board.

Other clauses

5.47   The agreement may deal with many other issues in particular cases, including the following:

(a)   Holidays and other leave, such as sick leave, sabbaticals, maternity and paternity leave.

(b)   Flexible working arrangements.

(c)   Partners' or members' pensions, life assurance and health insurance. For a fuller discussion of these issues, see **CHAPTERS 16, INSURANCE** and **27, RETIREMENT PLANNING**.

(d)   Cars provided to partners or members.

(e)   The right of partners or members to the provision of free services for themselves and their families, perhaps subject to an overall limit, although this is increasingly rare.

(f)   Costs of drawing up the agreement.

(g)   Whole agreement clause providing that the terms of the agreement govern the professional partnership to the exclusion of all earlier agreements, except where otherwise stated.

(h)   Clause preventing any third parties having any rights under the agreement, although *s 6(2A)* of the *Contracts (Rights of Third Parties) Act 1999* provides that rights cannot be conferred on third parties by an LLP agreement.

(i)   In an LLP agreement only, members of an LLP will often wish to deal with minority protection expressly in the agreement, and to exclude *s 994* of the *Companies Act 2006* so that disputes have to be enforced through the mechanisms expressly contained in the agreement.

(j)   A counterparts clause providing for different parties to be able to sign different copies, all of which will be treated as part of the same document. This avoids having to circulate a single document to all the parties.

Written agreement checklist

5.48   It may be helpful to refer to the following checklist when reviewing a written agreement or preparing a new one:

1   *The partners or members*

Do all the partners or members have the necessary professional qualifications and, where appropriate, the qualifications required to carry on regulated activities under *FSMA 2000*?

2   *The business*

(1)   What will the business be?

(2)   What sort of majority will be required to change the nature of the business?

3   *The name*

(1)   Under what name will the business be carried on?

(2)   Does the name comply with the statutory restrictions / requirements?

(3)   Does the stationery comply with the statutory restrictions?

(4)   Has the name been protected by registration as a service mark wherever necessary?

(5)   Does the name comply with any contractual obligations owed to associated firms and others?

4   *Duration of the partnership*

(1)   Does the agreement make clear when it is to take effect?

(2)   Partnership only: Should the partnership be expressed to exist for a fixed term or while there are two or more current partners?

(3)   Partnership only: Has it been made clear, where appropriate, that death, retirement, expulsion and bankruptcy of a partner will not lead to dissolution of the firm?

(4)   Has it been made clear, where appropriate, that the firm cannot be dissolved or wound up except by specified majority decision?

5   *Place of business*

    (1)   Where will the firm carry on business?

    (2)   If new partnership premises are to be established, what kind of majority will be required for the decision to be effective?

6   *Property and goodwill*

    (1)   Is it clear what assets are partnership/LLP assets?

    (2)   Do the premises belong to the firm or to individual partners or members?

    (3)   If the premises belong to an individual partner or member, should the firm enter into a lease or licence enabling it to occupy the property? Will it pay rent? What other terms should apply to the right to occupy the premises?

    (4)   How is any interest in land held? If held in the name of a trustee or nominee for the partnership or LLP, what happens if the trustee or nominee dies or retires?

    (5)   Does the goodwill associated with the business belong to the firm as a whole?

    (6)   Should any other important assets (eg wholly owned companies) be mentioned?

7   *Capital*

    (1)   How much capital will the firm require?

    (2)   How is capital to be contributed?

    (3)   In what shares should capital be owned?

    (4)   Should partners or members receive any interest on capital, whether correctly provided or over-provided?

    (5)   Should partners or members be obliged to pay interest on capital under-provided?

    (6)   What happens to the capital of a partner or member on his death, retirement or expulsion?

    (7)   When will the firm's capital increase, and how will this be decided?

    (8)   Will changes in profit-sharing ratios affect capital-sharing ratios, and what contributions and withdrawals should be made when profit shares change?

(9) Should the firm's assets be revalued from time to time, and should the amount of any increase or decrease be credited or debited to capital accounts or even recognised as a profit or loss?

(10) LLP only: Should capital balances appear as equity? Should the LLP be given the discretion to decide when and whether to redeem capital?

8   *Profits and losses*

(1) How are profits and losses to be computed in the firms accounts (eg on an earnings, cash receipts or bills delivered basis)?

(2) How are profits to be shared?

(3) When should profits be allocated to the partners or members – immediately they are recognised, or on a subsequent decision to divide the profits?

(4) How are losses to be dealt with?

(5) Are any partners or members to be entitled to a first guaranteed slice of profits, and if so, what happens if there is a shortfall?

(6) Is there to be any additional reward for good performance, and if so, how is this to be achieved?

(7) Should partners or members account to the firm for, or retain personally, any remuneration earned through directorships and other external offices and employments?

(8) Can any direct or indirect discrimination in the way profits are shared, based on age or length of service, be justified in the light of the *Equality Act 2010*?

9   *Drawings*

(1) How much can partners or members draw on account of their profit shares each month?

(2) What happens if a partner or member has drawn too much?

(3) What happens if, when the accounts are prepared, it emerges that a partner or member has drawn too little?

(4) Should there be a compulsory retention for the tax liabilities of individual partners or members, and if so, how should it be calculated?

(5) Should any amount retained to meet tax liabilities be retained in a separate trust account, or can it be used by the firm as working capital?

10   *Books and accounts*

   (1)   Where should the books be kept?

   (2)   Who should have access to the books and when?

   (3)   What should be the accounting reference date?

   (4)   Who should be the firm's accountants and auditors?

   (5)   Should the accounts take into account goodwill?

   (6)   How should the accounts be agreed and who will oversee the approval and, if required, filing within the applicable deadlines?

   (7)   Will the accounts and partnership/LLP returns be available by the statutory self-assessment deadlines?

   (8)   Will the accounts and records meet the statutory requirements regarding production and inspection?

11   *Bankers*

   (1)   Who will be the firm's bankers?

   (2)   Who has authority to sign cheques, and for how much?

   (3)   How many partners or members have to sign each cheque, and should this vary according to the amounts involved?

   (4)   Will client accounts be needed?

12   *Insurance*

   (1)   Has provision been made for professional indemnity insurance?

   (2)   Has provision been made for public liability insurance?

   (3)   Has provision been made for employer's liability insurance?

   (4)   Has provision been made for insurance of valuable assets?

   (5)   Should any other form of insurance be provided for, eg key-man insurance, permanent health insurance?

13   *Duties*

   (1)   Is it clear that a partner or member must act with the utmost good faith?

   (2)   Is it clear that partners or members must devote their full time and attention to the business?

   (3)   What about exceptions to that rule? Has flexibility been included, where necessary, to enable partners or members to pursue agreed outside interests?

(4) Has provision been made, where appropriate, to prevent partners entering into other hazardous business ventures, such as underwriting at Lloyd's?

(5) Has provision been made to prevent partners or members assigning or charging their share of the firm's interest?

(6) Has provision been made for partners or members to comply with professional and regulatory rules?

(7) Has provision been made for partners or members to keep information confidential?

14 *Management and decision-making*

(1) What decisions require the approval of a simple majority of the partners or members?

(2) What decisions require the approval of a special majority of the partners or members?

(3) Should a partner or member be unable to vote on certain resolutions, eg a resolution to expel him?

(4) What are the rules for the conduct of meetings?

(5) Should any management decisions be delegated to the senior or managing partner or a committee or committees?

(6) Has an appropriate individual been appointed for tax return purposes?

15 *New partners/members and salaried partners/members*

(1) What sort of majority is required for the appointment of new partners or members?

(2) What capital will have to be contributed by a new partner or member?

(3) What will the new partner's or member's share of profits be?

(4) What documentation should be signed by a new partner or member?

(5) Can any criteria for appointment of partners based on age or length of service be justified in the light of the *Equality Act 2010*?

(6) How will salaried partners or members be appointed?

16 *Outgoing partners/members*

(1) When can partners or members be expelled, and what majority decision is required?

(2)   Should a majority of partners or members be entitled to require a partner or member to retire early, and if so, in what circumstances and what period of notice is required?

(3)   Should provision be made for partners or members to be suspended in appropriate circumstances, and what majority decision is needed?

(4)   How can a partner or member resign from the firm, and what period of notice should be required?

(5)   Will retired partners or members have a right to participate in any consultancy arrangements?

(6)   Should the firm have the ability to exclude a partner or member from the firm's offices, from its clients and from its employees, where that partner or member has given notice to leave to join a competitor?

17   *Entitlement of outgoing partners/members*

(1)   Will a retiring partner's or member's share accrue automatically to the shares of the continuing partners or members, or (in the case of death of a partner or member) will the continuing partners or members have an option to acquire it?

(2)   How will the firm finance the payment of an outgoing partner's/member's share of the firm?

(3)   Should the payment of an outgoing partner's or member's capital be made in instalments?

(4)   How and when will an outgoing partner or member be paid his outstanding entitlement to accrued profits?

(5)   Will any revaluations be required when computing the value of a retiring partner's or member's share in the firm?

(6)   Should an outgoing partner or member or his dependants be entitled to an annuity from the firm?

(7)   Should an outgoing partner or member have a consultancy arrangement with the firm after his retirement?

(8)   What will happen to any property belonging to the firm but held in the outgoing partner's name following his retirement?

(9)   What will happen to books and papers in the custody of the outgoing partner or member after his retirement?

(10) Should the outgoing partner be indemnified in respect of all debts of the firm, whether past or future, where he is also personally liable? What if a particular liability arises through his own fault?

18 *Restrictive covenants*

(1) Will an outgoing partner or member be prevented from competing with the firm?

(2) Will an outgoing partner or member be prevented from soliciting clients and employees of the firm?

(3) Will an outgoing partner or member be prevented from representing himself as a partner or member in the future?

(4) How long should the restrictive covenants bind the partner or member?

19 *Dissolution or winding up*

(1) Partnership only: Should the agreement prevent dissolution on the expulsion, retirement, death or bankruptcy of a partner?

(2) Partnership only: Will the firm dissolve on the termination of a fixed term?

(3) Partnership only: Should the agreement prevent an individual dissolving the firm?

(4) How should the firm's assets be treated on a dissolution or winding up?

(5) What sort of decision should be required for a voluntary dissolution or winding up?

(6) LLP only: Should members agree to contribute a sum on winding up?

20 *Arbitration*

(1) Has provision been made for disputes to be resolved by arbitration (and possibly mediation)?

(2) Who is to appoint the arbitrator or mediator?

(3) What rules will govern the arbitration or mediation proceedings?

(4) Can the arbitrator or mediator dissolve the firm?

21   *Alterations to the agreement*

What partner majority will be required to amend the agreement?

22   *Other clauses*

Has provision been made for the following matters:

    (i) Holiday entitlements?

    (ii) Sick leave and the consequences of long-term absence?

    (iii) Sabbatical leave?

    (iv) Maternity and paternity leave?

    (v) Flexible working arrangements?

    (vi) Life insurance and health insurance of partners?

    (vii) Savings by partners for their retirement?

    (viii) LLPs only: should *s 994* of the *Companies Act 2006* (minority protection) be excluded?

    (ix) Execution of counterpart copies, to avoid protracted circulation of a single execution copy.

Chapter 6 International Aspects

Introduction

6.1 Successful UK professional practices often seek to expand overseas, for two principal reasons:

(a) *Servicing UK clients' international needs*. UK clients of the partnership may have international needs which cannot be serviced effectively from the UK. The professional practice may therefore need to develop a capability in the relevant locations.

(b) *Exploiting international marketing opportunities*. An overseas presence may be essential in order to capitalise on opportunities to sell the firm's skills to new clients overseas.

Different approaches to developing an international capability

Worldwide professional practices

6.2 One way to develop an international capability is for the parent practice to set up local branch offices overseas, while remaining a single worldwide entity. Most of the large City of London law firms originally expanded internationally in this way. The overseas branch offices can be staffed either by posting partners or members from head office, by local recruitment, by merger, or by a combination of all three.

However, conducting business through a single multi-branched partnership or LLP can give rise to considerable tax and regulatory issues, and the use of LLPs may involve particular problems. In certain jurisdictions, it is impossible or highly impractical to carry on business as an LLP. For example, in some jurisdictions, legal practitioners are prohibited from practising through a limited liability entity, and tax authorities in some jurisdictions have not yet agreed to treat a UK LLP as if it was a partnership.

In these circumstances, it may be necessary to establish separate structures (often a partnership) to conduct business in the problem jurisdictions, these structures practising in parallel with the main LLP or partnership. This may mean that partners in those parallel partnerships remain exposed to unlimited liability. It may be possible to reduce any unfairness for such partners by ensuring that the worldwide assets of the organisation are available to help them meet claims, and perhaps by the protected LLP members covenanting to 'look after' the dependants of an exposed partner who has become bankrupt owing to a claim. Insurance cover for this kind of covenant is available. Care will have to be taken to integrate the separate structures into the profit sharing, governance and know-how sharing of the worldwide organisation.

Another solution is sometimes to set up a locally incorporated company to carry on business in that location. This company would normally be owned by the main partnership or LLP itself, or alternatively by another company owned by the main partnership or LLP.

Multinational organisations of independent firms

6.3 An alternative approach is to meet the need for overseas expansion by forming alliances with local firms overseas, and developing a multi-national organisation of independent firms. Often, such organisations agree to use a common brand name. There may or may not be some sort of worldwide umbrella entity. There will (or should) certainly be a series of inter-firm agreements governing the relationship (including the mainte-nance of international standards, the use of intellectual property, shared know-how, training and the secondment of partners and staff) between the members of the multinational organisation and the umbrella organisation. Most of the larger international firms of chartered accountants have developed in this way.

European Economic Interest Groupings (EEIGs)

6.4 The formation of an EEIG may be an attractive umbrella organisation to establish links between practices in European Union member states without losing individual identity and independence, although an EEIG cannot be established for the purpose of profit-making activities of its own (see further **6.17** below).

Developing a worldwide professional practice

6.5 Before establishing any permanent presence in an overseas juris-diction, the local conditions will have to be studied and local advice obtained. Some of the key factors to be considered are set out below.

(a) *Licences to practise.* Local law may impose restrictions on the practice of certain professions by foreign nationals, and licences may be needed. In some jurisdictions (eg in Japan), it may not be possible to open a branch office of a worldwide legal partnership or LLP, and the local law may force the use of a separate entity under local control.

(b) *Partnership and LLP law.* Local rules on the rights and obligations of partners or members, both between themselves and in relation to clients and other third parties, should be considered. It will be important to put in place appropriate professional indemnity arrangements, having regard to local conditions.

(c) *Immigration and employment law.* Local law may impose restrictions on partners and staff from the UK going to the new country to live and work. Whether or not staff are to be recruited locally, local advice on the applicable employment regulations will be needed.

(d) *Property law.* The branch office will need premises from which to operate. Local advice will be needed on the full range of property issues, eg applicable landlord and tenant rules, occupier's liability, and health and safety regulations.

(e) *Tax.* Local advice will be needed on the foreign tax treatment of the profits and losses of the branch office, and the foreign personal tax position of the partners or members and staff posted there. UK tax factors will also have to be considered.

Profit sharing and status

6.6 When expanding overseas, the question of the status of the personnel in the overseas office and the profit and loss sharing rules applicable to them will be of key importance. Assuming a single worldwide practice is intended in substance, if not in form, a number of options are available.

(a) *Worldwide equity partners or members.* Full equity partners or members of the worldwide practice could be posted to or recruited to the overseas offices, sharing worldwide profits and losses together with all other partners or members. Special additional remuneration arrangements may be needed (eg expatriate package for those posted overseas or modified profit shares, taking into account local profitability) depending on local conditions. The worldwide equity approach may be the least divisive initially, but can lead to problems if the contribution made by those in one overseas office is very different from the contribution made by those in other offices.

(b) *Local equity partners or members.* Partners or members in the overseas office could be restricted to sharing in the profits and losses of that office. Alternatively, part of the profits or losses of the overseas office could be allocated for sharing only between the partners or members in that office, the balance forming part of a worldwide pool. The approach adopted will be a matter for agreement.

(c) *Salaried partners/members and employees.* The partners or members staffing the overseas office could be salaried partners or members, who are held out to the outside world as partners, but paid a salary rather than having a profit share. This approach may not, however, satisfy the requirements of the partners or members concerned, and some equity participation or salary reflecting profitability may become essential to retain them. The overseas office will need staff. These may be employed directly by the firm or by a service company established in the jurisdiction and owned by the firm.

UK tax consequences of a single worldwide professional partnership

6.7   The main advantage of establishing a single worldwide partnership or LLP is that the results of the operations in overseas branches will normally be treated as an extension of the trade of the UK partnership or LLP and not a new trade. Accordingly, the loss (or profit) of the overseas branch (before deducting local partners' or members' share of profits and allowances treated as profit share) will be treated as part of the taxable profit in the UK. In the early years of an overseas branch, it is likely there will be a UK tax advantage as, initially, the branch is likely to operate at a loss. However, a non-resident individual partner or member in the worldwide firm would be liable to UK income tax on his or her profit share in the firm, in the same manner as a UK partner or member. This may be advantageous or disadvantageous, depending on where the overseas partners or members are based. For example, in the Netherlands the locally based equity partners may be exempt from Netherlands tax on their UK source income, with the result that they may suffer a lower effective rate of tax. In Hong Kong, exposure to UK taxation may lead to a higher effective rate of tax. For capital gains tax purposes, partners or members resident and ordinarily resident outside the UK are still liable to the tax on disposal of the firm's UK assets because of the situs of the assets in the UK. For other assets, there may be a charge on the partner's or member's return to the UK if that occurs within five complete tax years of the partner's or member's date of departure from the UK.

Partners or members assigned to an overseas branch are often made employees or members to avoid exposure to UK tax. So long as the individual becomes non-resident, by spending at least one complete tax year outside the UK and the duties are wholly rendered outside the UK, his or her salary (and bonus) would be liable to local taxation only. Although it is now possible to have a corporate partner or member of a UK law firm, this remains rare. However, for some professions a non-resident partner's interest in a UK partnership or LLP might be held through a non-resident corporation or even a non-resident trust. In such cases, the corporation and the trust are liable to income tax at the basic rate (and not at the higher rate) on their share of partnership or LLP profits arising. This is on the basis that the corporation and/or the trust is non-UK tax resident and, in the case of a foreign corporation, has no branch, agency or place of business in the UK. If the foreign corporation has such a branch, then its profit share becomes liable to corporation tax.

Local tax advice should be taken in the particular territory in which the branch is set up. In some circumstances, the office can be characterised as a representative office and hence, under the appropriate double tax agreement (if one exists), would be exempt from foreign tax. The double tax agreement would also give the UK partnership or LLP the opportunity to credit, against UK income tax, the foreign taxes chargeable on the same income. The credit is restricted to income tax on the foreign source of income and the top rate of income tax. If the foreign tax is at a higher rate than UK income tax, no credit is obtained for the excess.

In some territories, the local company might be used to conduct the practice. Dividends from such a company paid to a UK resident firm comprised of individual members do not carry with them the right to any underlying tax credit for the tax suffered in the foreign country; the tax credit is restricted to withholding tax on the dividend. Accordingly, such a company would often be held by a UK incorporated and resident company, so that that company would obtain underlying tax credit as well as a tax credit for withholding tax as dividends are paid. In addition, the firm would endeavour (within arm's-length pricing criteria) to charge costs incurred in the UK to the foreign firm.

Sharing liabilities

6.8 The way in which worldwide and local practitioners will be exposed to claims against the local branch or entity and against the worldwide practice will need careful analysis, and the agreements will need to ensure that ultimate liability is shared appropriately without breaching the protection afforded by limited liability entities (see **6.2** above).

The general principles of holding out have been considered at **2.25**. Where personnel in an overseas office are referred to as partners, even though they may not have full or any equity participation and there may be no partnership, they will be potentially liable as partners and will have implied authority to bind the other individuals who are held out as partners. This will make it crucial to make clear in client engagement letters that the term 'partner' is only an indication of status and (except in the case of an actual partnership) means an employee entity practising in that jurisdiction.

Indemnity insurance

6.9 It will probably be essential (and, in the case of many professional partnerships, required under the applicable professional rules) for the practitioners and entities in overseas offices, as well as the main firm, to be covered by appropriate professional indemnity insurance. Local law and market conditions will need to be checked in this respect.

Central controls

Decision making and local autonomy

6.10 The written agreement will have to spell out how the decision-making apparatus applies to the overseas office. While the worldwide firm as a whole will wish to retain control over many of the most important matters, eg the appointment of new partners or members in the overseas office, other decisions regarding local management may well be delegated to the local office. It would normally be appropriate to impose some reporting requirements on the local partners or members.

In overseas jurisdictions where regulatory constraints prevent local practitioners from being members of the worldwide firm at the same time, or where non-local practitioners cannot be partners or members, appropriate contractual arrangements will have to be made to ensure that governance of the local office is integrated with the worldwide structure.

Name and goodwill

6.11 The use of the worldwide firm name and ownership of goodwill will be of critical importance. Assuming that local law allows the local office to practise under the name of the worldwide firm, the worldwide firm will want to ensure that the name and goodwill belongs to itself and cannot be exploited by the partners or members in the local office if they break away. Therefore, the written agreement should make clear that the name and goodwill are owned by the worldwide firm.

It would be prudent to register the name locally as a trade or service mark, if the local conditions allow.

The local partners or members should be subject to central quality control, to avoid any damage to the firm's reputation as a result of disparities in standards of services available from different offices. Furthermore, the owners of the mark retain the right to monitor and control the quality of the goods or services for which the mark in question is being used. Failure to do so may undermine the enforceability of the registration and associated legal rights. It may be appropriate for service standards to be set out in a form of memorandum or charter for adoption by each office.

Discharging breakaways

6.12   The worldwide firm will also want to ensure that successful local offices do not break away, or at least that the potential damage if they do break away is minimised.

(a)   *Motivation and reward.* The most effective way to prevent individual partners or members in overseas offices, or even entire overseas offices, from breaking away from the parent will be to motivate and reward the local partners or members sufficiently. Shared goals and genuine mutuality of interest will be the best cement. For further information, see CHAPTER 13, HUMAN RESOURCES MANAGEMENT.

(b)   *Restrictive covenants.* Restrictive covenants can be an effective way of preventing former partners or members and employees from soliciting clients of the firm and exploiting the goodwill of the firm for their own benefit or the benefit of a competitor. It will be necessary to consider the local rules on restrictive trade practices.

Multinational organisations of independent firms

Ownership of name and international branding

6.13   It is often important that a multinational organisation of independent firms (whether formed by merger or by the establishment of a network of related but independent local offices) develops a strong international image, which will help member firms attract and retain clients. The ownership and protection of the name and goodwill will be key issues.

Different organisations adopt different approaches to the problem. One approach is for one or more of the member firms in the organisation to transfer or license its rights in a particular name or acronym to a central entity established in a country with favourable tax laws (which could be a company, foundation or trust). The tax consequences of such a transfer need careful consideration. That entity then licenses the use of the name to the various firms which participate in the multinational organisation for a fee, which is used to meet central costs. The name should be protected by registering all appropriate trade or service marks. The central entity must impose strict quality control procedures, to ensure that the reputation of the organisation is maintained and that its ownership of the name (and associated trade or service mark registrations) and goodwill is retained and remains enforceable. Agreement will be needed on the ownership of the entity, and for whose benefit the name and goodwill are held, if the multinational organisation structure breaks up.

An alternative approach is for one of the firms in the multinational organisation (the dominant or founder firm) to retain ownership of the name but to license it to the other participants, perhaps directly or perhaps through a central entity, which rests above it and the other member firms as an international coordinator. Again, the use of the name and the licensing arrangements will have to be carefully spelled out and policed, to ensure continued protection of goodwill and its ownership, and the appropriate trade and service marks should be registered. It will be essential in either case for appropriate recapture provisions to be included in the arrangements, so that the name and goodwill remain in the multinational organisation when member firms break away.

Profit and cost sharing

6.14   The agreements between the firms constituting the multinational organisation will need to spell out the profit and cost sharing arrangements. It may well be agreed that some costs, eg relating to training and know-how development, should be shared on a central basis, with all member firms contributing to a central fund. This could be consideration in return for the use of the name or could form an independent obligation.

In some cases, member firms may pay a commission on fees referred from other member firms to the organisation; they may even agree to share profits and losses on a worldwide basis to a greater or lesser extent. Care would be needed to ensure there was no worldwide partnership which could lead to one member firm incurring liability for the defaults of another (see CHAPTER 2). In addition, care should be taken that each member firm is taxed in its territory on its profit and obtains a deduction for contributions and losses. Furthermore, the firms should not expose themselves to overseas tax by the existence of the multinational organisations.

Sharing of liabilities: holding out and ring fencing

6.15   Assuming that the multinational contractual association between independent firms does not amount to a full partnership, it is possible that the use of a common name and the projection of a common identity will lead to a claim that the multinational organisation is held out as being an international partnership. The consequences of this are discussed in CHAPTER 2. The member firms should take steps to minimise the holding out risks, for example, by making clear in their contracts with clients, customers and suppliers that it is the relevant local firm which is contracting, not any multinational firm. The agreements between the member firms should also make clear that liabilities incurred are to be borne only by the firm which incurred them.

Escape routes

6.16 It may become necessary or desirable to expel a member firm, or a member firm may want to withdraw from the multinational organisation.

(a) *Expulsion.* The terms on which a member firm may be expelled should be spelled out in the agreements between the firms. Provisions will be needed regarding the recapture of the shared name and goodwill for the benefit of the continuing members of the organisation (or for distribution, if the entire organisation breaks up). Restrictive covenants should be imposed and consideration given to the enforceability of these provisions in all the relevant jurisdictions.

(b) *Voluntary withdrawal.* Provision may be included for voluntary withdrawal of member firms. Again, provisions for recapture of the name, goodwill and restrictive covenants will be needed. Similarly, if an individual partner or member in a member firm is also a partner or member in another connected firm, or has economic interests in another entity within the multinational organisation, it may be desirable to deem withdrawal from one firm to be withdrawal from the entire structure.

(c) *Cost of finding successor and financial penalties.* On expulsion or withdrawal of a member firm, it may be necessary to find a new firm to join the organisation in order to ensure continuity of cover for clients in the relevant jurisdiction. Therefore, it may be appropriate to impose the cost of finding a successor, and any other consequential loss, on the former member firm. Some organisations incorporate provisions for a departing firm to be liable to pay a sum calculated according to a formula, perhaps a multiple of fees for business referred to that member firm in the past year or two. A provision providing for payment of a liquidated sum on a breach of the international agreement may well be unenforceable under English law as a penalty, unless it represents a genuine attempt to pre-estimate loss suffered as a result of the breach. On the other hand, a provision for the payment of a particular sum, where a firm withdraws contractually from the organisation, is likely to be enforceable.

(d) *Restrictive covenants.* Restrictive covenants could be imposed on the activities of an expelled or withdrawn member firm to prevent continued use of the international name, and poaching of clients referred by other member firms. The enforceability of such covenants will depend on the law chosen by the member firms to govern the relationship between themselves and the enforceability of judgments under that law in the jurisdictions where the breaches occur.

European Economic Interest Groupings (EEIGs)

Formation

6.17 EEIGs are unincorporated associations formed by cooperation between two or more commercial organisations based in the EU, and are designed as convenient structures to carry on cooperative activities of existing enterprises. Professional firms in member states thinking of forming an EEIG should check their own professional rules to see if they allow formation.

An EEIG must comprise at least two members, each based in a different EU member state. Each member must be registered and formed according to the laws of one of the member states and must have its central administration, ie place of central management and control, within the EU. Any legal body (including a company or partnership) which carries on any industrial, commercial, craft or agricultural activity or provides professional or other services in the EU can therefore form an EEIG with at least one other similar body. The activities of an EEIG must relate to and be ancillary to the economic activities of its members, but it should not be established for profit-making activities. An EEIG cannot, therefore, be established to carry on a business wholly unrelated to that of its members.

EU member states can grant EEIGs the status of legal personality and, in the UK, a registered EEIG is accorded legal personality and the status of a body corporate. Companies House issued a useful guidance booklet about the main features of an EEIG and formalities for establishment in February 2005 which was republished in May 2009. There is nothing that prevents an EEIG from being subsequently incorporated and becoming an autonomous economic entity.

EEIGs cannot be formed with the object of making a profit (although they may do so in the normal course of operations), employ more than 500 persons, exercise any form of control over the management of their members, have any ownership interest in their members, be a member of another EEIG, and may not invite invitations from the public to invest in them. Neither may an EEIG be used to make loans to directors or transfer property from a company to a director that would otherwise be prohibited.

Formalities

6.18 The members of an EEIG are bound together by a contract of formation. The contract of formation must include the name of the EEIG, the official address of the grouping, the names and details of the group members, and the objects of the EEIG. Typically, the contract of formation will also include terms governing the sharing of profits and losses of the EEIG and the allocation of the EEIG's assets on termination, and rules on meetings and voting powers. It may provide that one or more particular members can exercise more than one vote, although no one member may exercise a majority of the votes, and there are some fundamental decisions which require unanimity.

The words 'European Economic Interest Grouping' or 'EEIG' must be included in the name. The name cannot include 'limited', 'unlimited', 'public limited company' or 'SE', or their abbreviations or Welsh equivalents.

The members of the EEIG must appoint managers to operate the EEIG on a day-to-day basis.

The contract of formation must be registered in the state in which the EEIG has its official address. This is either where the EEIG has its central administration or where one of its members has its central administration, as long as the EEIG carries on an activity there. Registration in England and Wales is at Companies House, Cardiff; registration in Scotland is at Companies House, Edinburgh; and registration in Northern Ireland is at Companies House, Belfast. A fee of £20 is payable on registration. If the EEIG opens an establishment in a member state other than the state in which it is registered, that establishment must be registered in that other state.

The creation and termination of an EEIG must be publicly announced in official publications. The relevant publication in England and Wales is the *London Gazette*. Various changes and other events must also be announced in these publications.

Further formalities in the running of an EEIG include registering details of the appointment or removal of managers; amendments to the formation contract; details of any judicial decision nullifying the EEIG; and notification of a member's assignment of all or part of its participation in the EEIG. The obligations are no more onerous than those imposed on a limited company registered in the UK.

Liabilities

6.19 An EEIG can sue and be sued and make contracts. The members of an EEIG have joint and several liability for its debts and other liabilities. Such liability will remain with any outgoing member who incurred liability before cessation of membership. Furthermore, unless exempted in the formation contract, an incoming member will be liable for debts previously incurred. Such liability can be avoided or at least apportioned by drafting the EEIG contract in such a way as to ensure that each member of the EEIG will share only a pro rata liability.

Accounts and taxation

6.20   An EEIG is not subject to any accounting or auditing requirements, such as the submission of an annual return. However, an EEIG registered in the UK is required to make a return to HM Revenue & Customs. Profits and losses resulting from the activities of an EEIG are taxable in the hands of its members as if the profits and gains had accrued to them directly.

Multinational professional practices

Regulatory environment

6.21   Professional restrictions often prohibit or impose conditions on the entry into partnership or co-membership of LLPs by UK professionals with foreign-qualified professionals in the same or other fields. Foreign-qualified professionals may be required to register with the relevant UK professional body.

The *Legal Services Act 2007* has changed the face of legal services in the UK, in particular as a result of the introduction of legal disciplinary practices and the forthcoming introduction of alternative business structures (see **CHAPTER 7**).

Chapter 7   Incorporation and External Investment

7.1   As discussed in CHAPTER 1, until relatively recently, the vast majority of professional practices were constituted as partnerships. Since 2001, it has been possible to form or convert to a limited liability partnership (LLP), and a great many professional practices have adopted this business structure in order to minimise the impact of professional indemnity and other liability problems (see CHAPTER 4).

In addition, some professional practices are also conducted in the form of a company, while still others employ a hybrid structure, often with a company participating in one or more professional practices established as partnerships or LLPs. Such complex arrangements are likely to become more common from October 2011, as law firms in particular seek to take advantage of the ability to form 'alternative business structures' (ABSs) under the *Legal Services Act 2007*.

This chapter deals with the influences on, and practical issues involved in, the incorporation of a professional practice. It also examines some of the particular changes affecting legal practices in this regard under the *Legal Services Act 2007*.

Incorporation

Strategic and commercial drivers

7.2   The first question that any firm must consider before restructuring is to decide whether such a course is in line with its strategic objectives. Incorporating the firm or seeking external investment is not a strategy in itself, but simply a means by which the strategy may be achieved. For further details on developing a strategic plan, see CHAPTER 10.

An overview of the commercial reasons for considering incorporation of a professional practice should include the following:

(a)   limitation of liabilities;

(b)   professional indemnity issues;

(c)   property factors;

(d)   ability to raise finance;

(e)   general management issues; and

(f)   stock exchange flotation.

Professional indemnity issues and limitation of liabilities

7.3   Professional indemnity issues have become more important as the commercial climate has become more litigious. The cost of professional indemnity insurance has become heavier. There have been claims many years after the event that incurred the loss, and this has increased the level of premiums. For example, architects may have problems with defective buildings, sometimes designed many years in the past.

The incorporation of a professional partnership as either a limited company or an LLP does not alleviate or alter the liability of pre-incorporation partners from their liability for such professional indemnity issues; but, from the moment of incorporation, there is a time cap on their liabilities. The limited liability of the incorporated professional firm provides the cap for post-incorporation events. Professional indemnity insurance is still needed for the business, so that the cost may not change. One possibility is that some firms may choose to reduce the top level of professional indemnity cover, relying on the limited liability cover of the incorporated business. However, those shareholders or members of an LLP who are former partners can sleep more easily since they know they will not be asked for the possible excess over the limit of professional indemnity cover arising after incorporation unless they owed the client a specific duty of care.

Property

7.4   If a professional partnership is, for example, taking on a long lease, then each and every partner is jointly and severally liable for the full rent, dilapidations payments and other onerous terms of the lease. For further discussion of the liabilities of partners and partnerships, see CHAPTER 2.

Raising finance

7.5   For firms with ambitions to expand and diversify their businesses, the opportunity to take external investment provides them with the resources to fund investment, while the creation of share capital provides a new currency to facilitate growth, and allow participation in that growth.

A limited company or LLP is a more straightforward, easier legal entity for banks and lending institutions to deal with than a partnership. In the case of a limited company, the ability, for example, to issue shares, loan notes and give charges over securities probably leads to the incorporated professional firm having the edge over a partnership. A commercial bank lending to a professional partnership will usually examine not only the partnership's balance sheet but also that of each individual partner. A company, on the other hand, would normally, depending on size and other factors, have its borrowings dealt with on a stand-alone basis. The individual shareholder's position would be considered separately (and not collectively) and then, normally, only in the context of his or her application for finance for acquiring shares or making loans to the company.

Management

7.6 Whilst it is perfectly possible for a partnership to be run on corporate lines with a board elected from the partnership, it is much easier for the limited company to be so run in accordance with the normal Articles of Association derived from the *Companies Acts* which give a legal framework for management. There are other aspects where a partnership or LLP have greater flexibility than a limited company.

Stock exchange flotation

7.7 Some professions have allowed, or will soon allow, the share capital of their incorporated members to be quoted on the stock exchange or held by third parties. Therefore, stock exchange flotation, and capital wealth creation for some of the members of the partnership who ultimately receive shares in the incorporated entity, must be considered as a major reason for incorporation.

Practical considerations on incorporating as a company

Valuation of a firm

7.8 For those firms seeking external investment, the value of the firm will be a critical issue in determining the amount of equity the partners are willing to give up in return for that investment. For most firms, the accounts are prepared on the historical cost convention, and therefore only record the recognised assets and liabilities of the firm at their historic cost. Typically, this means that property assets or investments in other businesses are not recorded at their current market value, and more significantly, in most cases, the goodwill of the firm is not recorded at all. The result is that the accounts do not reflect the real value of the firm.

Valuation of private businesses is inherently subjective, and the old adage, that something is only worth what somebody else is prepared to pay for it, remains true. From the perspective of the investor, there is no set methodology for valuing a professional firm; however, in the context of professional firms, it is likely that a valuer would evaluate earnings as the overarching determinant of value. Valuers therefore focus their expertise in determining the core factors affecting future earnings:

(a) Quality of earnings – In evaluating future earnings, a valuer will look to the historic earning trends and the pipeline of work to assess what might be called reliable maintainable earnings. The valuer will look at the quality of the firm's clients, the business relationships with those clients and the level of recurring fees.

(b) Adjustments to earnings – As most firms operate a full distribution policy, earnings will need to be calculated after deduction of notional salaries and bonuses to partners/directors. In addition, exceptional and unusual items would need to be adjusted for in order to assess the underlying earnings.

(c) Other factors affecting the valuation include reliance on key individuals as well as brand and reputation. If revenue generation is dependent on a number of key individuals, this will be a significant risk factor from the investor's perspective. Where firms have an established brand that transcends the individual partners, this can be seen as a substantial asset.

To arrive at a value for a business, the valuer would seek to identify the core underlying earnings of the business and capitalise these to obtain an enterprise value. The valuer would test the validity and integrity of this by comparison with listed businesses or recent market transactions for similar businesses.

Share ownership

7.9 Under partnership or LLP structures, the ownership of a firm is generally ill-defined. The reason for this lies in the dynamics of how professional practices have historically operated and organised their businesses, together with the culture of tenancy that prevails. It is clear what partners own as set out in the partnership accounts, with each partners 'share' of the recorded net assets being set out in their various capital, current and tax accounts, as well as receiving a share of future profits so long as they remain partners. On retirement or departure, typically they will lose the right to share in profit and have the balance of their various accounts paid out to them. What few firms record either in their partnership or LLP agreements is who owns the business over and above the recorded assets and liabilities, namely the goodwill built up in the business.

For firms considering taking external investment and using the corporate route, the issue of ownership will need to be addressed. Incorporation will crystallise the ownership of the business with the current population of partners, notwithstanding any arrangements to widen share ownership, leading potentially to divisive questions over who should receive what. Some agreements address the issue of ownership arising from the sale or partial sale of the business. However, whilst such agreements may represent the legal position, and therefore the starting point, in practical terms such a division of share capital on this basis may not prove acceptable to the wider partnership group. If, according to the partnership or LLP agreement, capital profits are divided in accordance with current profit sharing ratios, this is unlikely to be an acceptable method of allocating ownership to some partners, as this may not reflect partners' on-going interests in the firm. If the constitution of the firm requires a particular majority to approve any such fundamental change, a renegotiation of the ownership may be required.

At most professional practices, on retirement, notwithstanding any consulting or annuity arrangements, a partner leaves with only the capital they invested. Insofar as the business has grown into a stronger, better or more profitable business, the retiring partner receives no additional compensation for their contribution to this. Incorporation as a company creates a more formal structure for partners to benefit from growth in the business. On incorporation, the partners (and, potentially, other staff) receive shares in the company. Each share has a value based on the overall value of the business, including both the net tangible assets (such as fixed assets and debtors less any liabilities), but more importantly including the goodwill of the business. Insofar as the business subsequently develops and grows, so too does the goodwill and with it the value of the shares, and it is this that allows stakeholders to participate in the growth, through selling their shares to realise, hopefully, an enhanced value.

The value of any share in a corporate is also dependent upon the shareholder being able to realise their stake by transferring their holding to a willing buyer at the appropriate prevailing price. If the company floats on a stock market, then there is a market for shares to be traded. However, if the company remains private, then mechanisms will need to be put in place to ensure that partners can sell their shares on, say, retirement.

The crystallisation of ownership in the current group of partners and senior staff does raise a legitimate question of whether the interests of the business will diverge from that of its owners, as the current group of partners gradually retire from the business. It is important to note that there is something of a myth in the idea that crystallising ownership is only a means for the senior partners to cash in 'the family silver' by selling off the business and thereby deprive younger partners of their anticipated future returns. First, an investor is not looking to see their investment used to fund the retirement of partners, although there may be limited buy-out

116

to facilitate succession. Instead, the investor will expect to see the majority of their funding going into the business. Secondly, professional practices remain fundamentally people businesses, the long-term future of which is dependent on a succession of talent. It is therefore critical that mechanisms are put in place to incentivise talent and find the right balance between crystallising ownership at incorporation and providing the mechanisms for future generations to participate in continuing ownership.

Attracting external investment

7.10 In order to attract external investment, a firm will need to consider the perspective of the investor and what would make them an attractive investment. All firms should review their management structures and internal governance periodically; however, for those considering external investment, this is an absolute necessity. External investors will be looking for strong management and internal governance as a pre-requisite for any potential investment. Organisations that cannot demonstrate effective decision-making and efficient business practices may represent too great a risk for potential investors or suffer from a lower valuation than they might otherwise expect when seeking external investment.

Corporate governance

7.11 The Combined Code on Corporate Governance (and its successors) issued by the Financial Reporting Council is perhaps the most definitive guide to governance in the corporate sector. Whilst compliance with the Code is only obligatory for fully listed entities, and its provisions may be onerous for smaller private entities, it does provide a useful benchmark for how businesses can structure their governance arrangements. Some of the key principles of the Combined Code are particularly relevant to professional practices considering incorporation, as they may differ from the way in which many firms have traditionally been run. Examples of these include:

(a) a company should have an effective Board;

(b) the Board should include a balance of both executive and non-executive directors;

(c) there should be formal and transparent procedures for setting director remuneration; and

(d) there should be formal and transparent arrangements for oversight of financial reporting and controls.

Establishment of a Management Board

7.12   One of the most essential aspects of good management is the ability to deliver effective decision making over both the operation of the business and the strategic direction the business should take. For those concerned about investing too much power in a small group of individuals, a Management Board would usually have limits imposed on its authority, such that certain fundamental decisions could not be taken without recourse to the wider shareholder group. Typically, these might include the sale of the business, and material investment decisions such as mergers or dilution of interests.

For many firms, the roles of senior partner, equivalent to the Chairman, and managing partner, equivalent to the Chief Executive, are often rotated within the partner group. This short-term tenure can undermine the ability of a firm to develop a long-term strategy for the firm as a whole. Except in the largest firms, the roles of senior partner and managing partner are rarely separated completely from that of being fee-earners. The result is that managing the firm can be seen as a part-time role. From the perspective of an external investor, a constantly changing management team with potentially conflicting responsibilities represents a significant risk. Full-time management aligns the leadership of the firm with its long-term objectives.

Appointment of non-executives

7.13   The appointment of non-executives provides two very important benefits. First, part of the role of non-executives is to provide robust challenge to the executive Board. This ensures that the Board acts in the best interests of the firm as a whole and seeks to act as a control over potential Board excesses. Secondly, non-executives can be appointed from outside the profession to bring a wider commercial perspective to the strategic direction of the firm. Depending upon the nature and size of the stake of the external investor, they may also require Board representation. Significant care needs to be taken over the appointment of non-executive directors, as they have significant influence over the future direction of the firm.

Audit and remuneration committees

7.14   As authority is delegated to a smaller management group, investors as well as other stakeholders will need to have confidence that the Board is undertaking its responsibilities in an appropriate manner. While non-executives can perform this role in terms of day-to-day operations and strategy through their scrutiny and oversight, some functions require a more overt level of independence.

While the area of remuneration is discussed more fully in CHAPTER 9, the role of the Remuneration Committee to approve total remuneration is critical. To maintain confidence, the Committee should have clear terms of reference, including setting out the criteria to be used to evaluate performance. Similarly, it is recommended that the Audit Committee be populated by independent directors to ensure that it can fulfil its role of financial oversight free from any charge of vested interest.

Use of external managers

7.15 Within the largest professional practices, the employment of high-calibre support professionals in practice management is the norm; however, among many small and medium-sized firms, the practice of making partners responsible for certain practice management areas is still commonplace. While high-calibre managers may exist within the partner group, there is a risk that these functions will not operate as effectively as if they were run by experienced support professionals. The latter approach is likely to be preferred by external investors.

Reforming the reward structure

7.16 As discussed in CHAPTER 8, under the partnership or LLP model, partners receive their remuneration based on a share of the profits earned in the year. Most firms operate a full distribution policy, such that all profits are allocated to partners.

The partnership or LLP model does not distinguish between what partners receive in respect of their role as an 'employee' and their role as an 'owner' of the business. Under the corporate model, there will be a distinction between these roles, with partners becoming employees and receiving remuneration through a range of different means:

(a) Salaries – 'Partners' would become employees in a corporate structure and would receive a salary paid, usually, monthly after deduction of PAYE and National Insurance Contributions. This might be set so that the net salary broadly equates to what was previously received as monthly drawings.

(b) Bonuses – In addition to salaries, partners (and staff) would receive performance-related bonuses based on a set of criteria relevant to the specific role of that partner.

(c) Equity reward – In addition to salary and cash bonuses, the firm may reward partners and staff through equity participation schemes. Share options allow the holder to purchase shares at a fixed price, usually at some stage in the future. For tax reasons, the exercise price is usually set at the market value of the shares at the issue date. This encourages an interest in the long-term growth of the firm, where the future value of the share would be worth more than the cost to the employee. This provides a useful tool in terms of staff retention as employees accumulate options over several years.

As owners of the business, partners may also be entitled to receive dividends based on their respective shareholdings. On the assumption that the business generates significant profits after salaries and bonuses, the firm may elect to distribute profits to the shareholders via dividends; although, where firms have external investors, there is likely to be an expectation of dividend distributions set out in the dividend policy at the time external funds are raised. Different classes of share capital can be used to allow differing dividend distributions.

A key element of equity participation in a corporate as opposed to a partnership or LLP is the ability to benefit from increases in value of the underlying business and the shares themselves. However, the value of the shares can obviously go down as well as up.

Use of a corporate structure to enable growth

7.17 The use of a corporate vehicle and the creation of share capital provides firms with a new mechanism to build the business both organically from its existing pool of talent, and from the point of view of team hires and the acquisition of other businesses.

Staff retention

7.18 A critical part of the equation is the ability of professional practices to retain their existing high performers, who represent the future in terms of a firm's continuing success. The partnership model traditionally allows very limited participation for non-partners in the business with most firms being wholly owned by equity partners. By contrast, a corporate vehicle provides a model for allowing participation at almost any level through share ownership. One of the key advantages of widening the share ownership at incorporation is that this aligns the interests of the wider employee pool with the longer-term success and growth of the firm as a whole.

Going forward, equity participation, such as share options, provides a form of continuing remuneration that aligns the interests of the employee with a longer-term view, but also encourages loyalty to the firm. Share options usually have a time delay built in between the vesting period and the award (say, three years). Once a system of options awards is up and running, an individual will potentially have a pipeline of potential capital growth if the firm continues to succeed. This pipeline of options acts as a form of deferred loyalty remuneration, incentivising the holder to stay with the firm.

Aside from widening participation at the point of incorporation, a firm will need to put in place mechanisms to allow continuing flexibility to award new shares and to allow purchases and sales of shares. For private companies, this may mean creating an internal market for shares and the possible use of a (funded) Employee Benefit Trust to assist liquidity.

Individual and team hires

7.19 In terms of looking externally to hire new talent, the strength of resources afforded through external investment permits firms to make offers reflecting the long-term interests of the firm without regard to the immediate impact on profit dilution in the short term. In addition, the corporate vehicle has a whole new currency by comparison to the partnership model in terms of its ability to offer more than simply a profit share. A corporate firm will have the ability to offer an interest in the capital value of the firm with the benefit of growth thereon.

Acquisitions

7.20 The ability to offer shares is not only useful for incentivising current staff and potential hires, but also provides an alternative to cash for firms considering acquisitions. Historically, acquisitive consolidation within the industry has been hampered by the high cost and lack of availability of cash. Instead, consolidation has been dominated by mergers.

Managing conversion

7.21 Many of the changes required to convert a partnership or LLP into a company and take external investment appear radical. In an inherently conservative professional world, the process of change requires careful management at each stage of the process. Set out below is a list summarising the key aspects that professional practices will need to consider, although it is by no means exhaustive:

Planning

(a) Engage experienced advisers.

(b) Assess robustness of historic results and systems.

(c) Identify and assess the risk profile of the firm.

(d) Review the business plan for the next 3–5 years and identify key objectives and how incorporation will assist in delivery.

(e)   Obtain early mandate from all equity partners.

Initial Work

(f)   Clarify current ownership rights and approach to ownership transition.

(g)   Assess current valuation of business and the targets for value growth going forward.

(h)   Understand the financial implications of the proposed route.

(i)   Make sure all key parties have an understanding of the deal and the changes that lie ahead.

(j)   Provide regular communication to those affected.

(k)   Check your mandate from equity partners regularly.

(l)   Ensure regular communication of important points of detail.

(m)   Undertake due diligence on potential investors.

(n)   Review and agree on any changes to key management.

Implementation

(o)   Key management will be under extreme pressure towards closure and must be united throughout.

(p)   Make sure you can clearly articulate your business and its plans to potential investors.

(q)   Due diligence will be very time consuming and detailed.

(r)   Manage the communication to staff, clients, suppliers and the press.

(s)   Share, tax structuring and good/bad leaver provisions are complex and will need time to consult and draft.

(t)   Costs are high and abortive costs will have to be paid if the proposal is terminated.

Once incorporated as a company, continual planning and consideration of the structure will be required to ensure key objectives are achieved and relationships with external investors are strong.

Changes affecting legal practices under the Legal Services Act

7.22   Under the *Legal Services Act 2007* (*LSA*), the legal sector is in the process of undergoing substantial reform both in terms of its regulation and its operation. Historically, the legal profession has operated in an environment that imposes tight restrictions on the ownership of and participation in law firms, and therefore on who can provide legal services. Under the *LSA*, these restrictions have been substantially relaxed. At an operational level, the key provisions of the *LSA* applying to the structure and operations of solicitors' practices are as follows:

(a) non-lawyers may become partners in solicitors' practices (from 31 March 2009);

(b) legal disciplinary practices (LDPs) allow legal professionals to set up in business together, involving, say, barristers, solicitors and patent attorneys (from 31 March 2009); and

(c) alternative business structures (ABSs) allow non-lawyers including corporate entities to have an interest or stake in legal practices (from 6 October 2011).

Non-lawyers becoming partners

7.23 As firms move to a more business-focused approach to the delivery of services, the use of professional managers has become far more commonplace, with high-calibre professionals employed to manage finance, business development, HR and IT. Prior to the *LSA*, these professional managers could not participate in the ownership of the firm, and therefore could not be partners in the firm. The *LSA* allows such individuals to become partners or members and thereby align their interests with that of the firm and elevate their status.

Legal Disciplinary Practices

7.24 Since 31 March 2009, legal professionals from various disciplines have been permitted to enter into business together, overturning the prohibition that solicitors could only be in business with other solicitors, for example. This allows solicitors to enter into joint operations with barristers or patent attorneys. An application needs to be submitted and accepted by the Approved Regulator before a firm can set up an LDP. The *LSA* also permits up to 25% of an LDP's senior management to be non-lawyers.

Alternative Business Structures

7.25 Under *Part V* of the *LSA*, non-lawyers including corporates are (from 6 October 2011) able to take an ownership stake in legal practices. This creates the possibility of the so-called 'Tesco's Law', where businesses with strong brand image and marketing coverage could provide legal services. For the first time, firms are allowed to take external investment from third parties, and either partly or wholly disengage the ownership of a firm from those delivering legal services.

The SRA has indicated they would seek to minimise the number of restrictions on how an ABS may operate, so long as the organisation can satisfy the Approved Regulator that it is fit and proper for the purposes of providing legal services. In terms of ownership, there is no requirement for a lawyer to be an owner, and therefore the firm could be wholly owned by non-lawyers. In terms of operation, the requirement is that there must be at least one lawyer manager.

Due to the flexibility of both partnership and LLP agreements, the provisions of the *LSA* could easily operate within these structures. However, with regard to the prospect of external ownership, the preferred choice for investors is likely to be through a corporate structure where the concept of share ownership is widely understood and where rights and obligations are defined in company law.

Funding to law firms has historically been provided through either bank borrowings or partners' own funds. While bank borrowing has provided plentiful access to external finance, the general tightening of the debt markets at the time of writing has made this scarcer and more expensive. The cost of funding investment, combined with a generally low level of capitalisation in law firms in the harsher economic climate, led many firms to neglect investment in infrastructure. In addition, the short-term impact on profitability and the intergenerational partnership profile can lead to investment decisions being taken without regard to the long-term benefit to the business.

There are a number of reasons why external capital may therefore be an attractive alternative for some firms:

(a) Investment in growth – Historically, consolidation in the legal sector has been achieved through merger. The availability of external finance provides a new opportunity for a firm to reposition itself in a rapidly changing market through acquisition.

(b) Investment in resources – Firms may use external finance as a means of providing the capital to invest in new systems, new services and new products, and possibly to diversify away from the provision of legal services into complementary areas.

(c) Investment in systems and processes – This may require significant up-front expenditure, with payback over an extended period of time.

(d) Investment in people – Firms may use access to capital as a means to 'cherry pick' talent. An ambitious firm with significant capital backing could go out into the market place and 'buy up' some of this talent. The ability of firms to offer an equity interest, with potential for capital growth, may act as a significant factor in retaining newly acquired talent for the long term.

Chapter 8   Profit Shares

Agreeing sharing ratios

8.1   As indicated at **5.12** and **5.13**, *s 24* of the *Partnership Act 1890* states:

> '... subject to any agreement expressed or implied between the partners ... all the partners are entitled to share equally in the capital and profits of the business, and must contribute equally towards the losses whether of capital or otherwise sustained by the firm.'

In practice, there are very few professional practices where profits are shared equally, and this is because there has been an alternative agreement, either in permanent form or in the provision of a mechanism for regularly reviewing and agreeing profit shares. One such mechanism, a compensation committee that makes recommendations to the partnership or LLP, is suggested at **9.7**. Part of the difficulty in agreeing profit shares is that it is impossible, in most cases, for any partner or member to be objective as to what he considers his share should be, for example, whether he measures his entitlement by his assessment of his past and present contribution, his perceived value in the marketplace or what he requires to meet his living expenses. Indeed, in a typical partnership or LLP, the sum of the profit sharing percentages that would be proposed by each partner or member in respect of their own share would be considerably in excess of 100%, and may even approach 200%.

However, it is likely that the firms that will continue to prosper in the competitive environment which currently exists are those that are able to develop compensation systems for partners that are seen to be as fair as possible, and properly reward partners for activities that increase the firm's profits generally.

Criteria for fair profit shares

8.2   These will vary enormously from firm to firm. However, it is perhaps reasonable to break down criteria for rewarding partners into a number of different elements. Twelve such elements for a particular firm may be:

(a)   Past performance that has generated goodwill for the firm and thus, to some extent, the ability to earn current profits.

(b)   The provision of capital to the firm.

(c)   The skill of individual partners in attracting new business for themselves and other partners.

(d)   The amount of fee income brought into the firm, bearing in mind the profitability of that work.

(e)   The number of hours of work successfully billed to and collected from clients, and the recovery rate of such time.

(f)   The satisfaction of a partner's clients in relation to work done.

(g)   Contribution to the management of the firm or its individual departments.

(h)   Housekeeping skills in billing and collecting fees to minimise use of working capital.

(i)   Success in developing the skills of other partners and staff.

(j)   Contribution to the firm's external reputation through participation in high-profile activities.

(k)   Intellectual and technical contributions.

(l)   Other intangible qualities that increase the firm's strength.

Measurement of criteria

8.3   Some of these elements may be fairly judged using objective criteria, but many can only be viewed subjectively. Even with objective criteria, information is often unreliable or inadequate. Often, several different partners rightly claim some responsibility for the generation of new work. In other cases where responsibility is claimed, it may in fact be the firm's reputation that was the key determinant in new work coming in, and the recipient partner may simply be the lucky first port of call.

Judgment of criteria

8.4   It is important not to place too much reliance on any one factor, as this may lead to undesirable behaviour by partners which would be detrimental to the firm. For example, if a partner felt he was judged simply on fee income, then the temptation could be to hog work for himself. In addition, too much reliance on chargeable hours may encourage a partner to undertake less profitable work and may leave little time for other activities which, in the long run, would be more valuable to the firm. Alternatively, keeping an existing continuing client satisfied may be just as important as gaining a new client of equal value to the firm. Therefore, appropriate weight needs to be given to each factor considered relevant.

These factors may be a mix of objective and subjective but they should be consistently and fairly applied. Further factors should be considered when deciding fair methods of profit sharing. For example, it may benefit a firm of solicitors to provide some less profitable services as part of a comprehensive service offering, eg residential conveyancing, and it would be unfair to penalise an individual partner for his responsibility for providing those services.

Finally, some regard needs to be paid to profit shares in earlier years and likely shares in future ones, to avoid wild fluctuations. Whilst it may be motivating to appear more highly valued, it is likely to be demotivating to appear less highly regarded.

Partner mobility

8.5   A fair approach to profit sharing is particularly important in an age of increased partner mobility. The system should prevent partners leaving firms, simply because they feel they could get a 'fairer' reward elsewhere, and it should attract new partners who will need a certain remuneration level to be persuaded to join the firm. However, it is also important that the new partner's package should not upset the existing remuneration structure unduly, as this may cause unnecessary friction.

Commonwealth approach

8.6   Some firms find a semi-scientific assessment of fair profit shares all too difficult and have fixed percentages or formulae based on seniority. Such bases have the possible advantage of reducing time spent arguing, as debates may take place only every few years, and the partnership spirit and cooperation between partners and departments may be engendered. The so-called 'lockstep' sharing of profits based on years in the firm is reasonably simple to administer, although it only works effectively if all partners perform within a relatively narrow range of performance criteria. There may also be peer pressure to ensure underperforming partners contribute in proportion to their share. However, often an underperforming partner does not recognise failings that may be seen all too clearly by his peers. Therefore, fixed percentages and seniority schemes tend to work best in small or very profitable firms where all partners can be satisfied with their lot.

Equal shares

8.7   In the life of a professional practice, an equal sharing system is usually found at the beginning of a firm's life. Two or more individuals come together, recognise that their compatible qualities will lead to a successful business, and often, in the absence of knowledge or detailed consideration, or without the ability to devise an alternative basis, opt for equal sharing of profits. For example, two partners will take 50% of the profits each, or four partners 25% each, etc. Such founder partners of a successful firm are likely to be highly influential in the development of the firm for many years and, as a firm grows, successfully retain significant rights for themselves. This may be no more than their proper reward for the entrepreneurial flair that created the firm in the first place.

Unequal shares

8.8   As a firm develops, unequal shares may be the next step. This could be because of a mutual recognition, after a period, that the contribution of each partner to the generation of profits is not equal and equal sharing is unfair. This change may come about easily by agreement or when it becomes clear to the partners that the business will not thrive and prosper with unfair profit sharing and the only way to hold the business together is by adjusting profit shares. More often, particularly if the founder partners are few in number, the development to an unequal sharing system comes when the first new partner or member is admitted to the partnership or LLP, generally as a 'junior partner'.

A simple profit sharing example

8.9   To illustrate, we will consider a new partnership with a simple profit sharing basis over a number of years.

Stage 1

A partnership with two partners, A and B, introduces C as a new junior partner. A and B, who had 50% each of the equity, after four years' successful practice, each offer 10% of the profits to C, with the resulting profit shares:

Partner	Year 1	Year 4
A	50%	40%
B	50%	40%
C	—	20%
TOTAL	100%	100%

Part of the justification may be that C is unable to contribute capital, or not on the scale provided by A and B. In addition, A and B carried the risk of establishing the business and may have had lower profits in the years when the business was developing. They may feel that their larger share in the business represents a fair reward for the investment they made in the early years. However, as the matter is to be settled by agreement, A and B may make any offer they like to C. If C is an existing employee and the terms offered appear better than remuneration as a salaried employee, he is likely to accept.

Stage 2

As the partnership develops and prospers, new partners may be admitted, with profit shares coming mainly or exclusively from A and B. For example, a new partner D may be offered an 8% share and E a 6% share in Year 7, giving profit shares as follows:

Partner	Year 1	Year 4	Year 7
A	50%	40%	33%
B	50%	40%	33%
C	—	20%	20%
D	—	—	8%
E	—	—	6%
TOTAL	100%	100%	100%

Stage 3

Subsequently, F, G and H are admitted in Year 10, with 4% shares each coming from A, B and C unequally by agreement. This gives rise to respective shares of:

Partner	Year 1	Year 4	Year 7	Year 10
A	50%	40%	33%	28%
B	50%	40%	33%	28%
C	—	20%	20%	18%
D	—	—	8%	8%
E	—	—	6%	6%
F	—	—	—	4%
G	—	—	—	4%
H	—	—	—	4%
TOTAL	100%	100%	100%	100%

We have thus seen how a successful two-partner firm became an eight-partner firm over a ten-year period. How the firm develops from here may depend very much on the ages, personalities and ability of the partners, together with the success of the business. For example, H may feel well rewarded with a profit share of 40,000 per annum but resent the fact that the two most senior partners take profits of 280,000. Equally, A and B may be concerned about the future succession to the practice, and the ability of the remaining partners eventually to repay them their capital, let alone any value for the goodwill they have built up, either in capital profits or through annuities, if their partnership agreement so allows. The pressure is thus on for a new basis for sharing of profits and a negotiation amongst the partners.

Points scheme

8.10 It may be here that a points scheme comes into its own. Such schemes are particularly common amongst firms of solicitors and may be called lockstep arrangements. They often work as follows:

(1) Partners are awarded a particular number of points.

(2) Each partner's profit share is then calculated according to their number of points, expressed as a percentage of the total number of points held by all the partners.

Therefore, our points scheme example partnership may negotiate initial points and these percentages as follows.

Stage 1

Partner	Year 11
A	20%
B	20%
C	17%
D	12%
E	10%
F	7%
G	7%
H	7%
TOTAL	100%

Stage 2

The scheme involves each partner gaining two points a year, up to a maximum of 20. New partners will be introduced with seven points. A number of new partners join: I in Year 13, J and K in Year 14, L in Year 15, and M and N in Year 16. Two partners also retire: A in Year 15, and B in Year 16. This leads to a change in profit shares as follows:

Partner	Year 12		Year 13		Year 14		Year 15		Year 16	
	Points	%	Points	%	Points	%	Points	%	Points	%
A	20	20	20	16.8	20	13.7				
B	20	20	20	16.8	20	13.7	20	13.4		
C	17	17	19	16.0	20	13.7	20	13.4	20	12.4
D	12	12	14	11.9	16	11.0	18	12.1	20	12.4
E	10	10	12	10.1	14	9.6	16	10.7	18	11.2
F	7	7	9	7.5	11	7.5	13	8.7	15	9.3
G	7	7	9	7.5	11	7.5	13	8.7	15	9.3
H	7	7	9	7.5	11	7.5	13	8.7	15	9.3
I			7	5.9	9	6.2	11	7.4	13	8.1
J					7	4.8	9	6.1	11	6.8
K					7	4.8	9	6.1	11	6.8
L							7	4.7	9	5.6
M									7	4.4
N									7	4.4
TOTAL	100	100	119	100	146	100	149	100	161	100

Thus, by Year 16, succession is achieved, A and B have retired, C has become the most long-serving and probably senior partner, the partnership grows, and the differential in profit shares is reduced and is related to seniority within the partnership.

Interesting features

8.11   This scheme has a number of other interesting features:

(a)   As a partnership grows, even though an individual increases his number of points, his profit share may fall, eg D in Years 13 and 14.

(b)   The more junior members of the partnership's profit sharing percentage rises more rapidly than those nearing the plateau of 20 points.

(c)   Partners feel secure as their points rise each year, or at least the plateau does not fall.

(d)   The growth in the number of partners in the partnership will probably be possible as a result of rising profits. Otherwise, the firm may well feel there is not 'room' for new partners. Thus, even if a partners' profit sharing percentage is falling, commonly his share of profits may rise in monetary terms.

Escalators and ladders

8.12 Escalators and ladders are both points schemes. The scheme described at **8.9** above was an escalator scheme, as the increase in points was an automatic process (two points per year, leading in the seventh year to full equality with the most senior partners). This is a typical scheme, although the initial share in this case was only seven points, giving a differential of profit shares of almost three to one between the most junior and senior partners. The level of such differentials may depend on the profitability of the firm. More commonly, in a firm of solicitors, the starting point would be, say, 13 points (giving a differential of about 1.5 to one between lowest and highest sharing partners),although in more profitable firms a ratio of up to three to one is not uncommon. The partners in this escalator scheme would move one point a year, to reach full equality with the senior partners in seven years.

The essential difference between a ladder scheme and an escalator scheme is that the more junior partner must exert some effort to climb the ladder, as opposed to rising automatically to the desired destination. This means that additional points are only awarded on the basis of perceived merit or, for example, by meeting defined targets. This will be assessed by the managing partner, the compensation committee or the firm generally. Arguably, a ladder scheme carries with it the means to financial motivation and, therefore, may be better for the firm. However, if an individual partner fails to climb a ladder that his peers are climbing, he may be demoralised to the detriment of the firm.

Discretionary elements

8.13 As we have seen, a ladder scheme has a discretionary element to it, as there is a decision needed as to whether a particular partner is judged to merit the additional point and thus move up the ladder. However, the amount of profit share subject to discretion is limited.

A firm may feel a greater element of profit sharing needs to be discretionary. For example, if a firm takes the view that unequal shares is the appropriate profit sharing method and regular renegotiations are too divisive or damaging to the firm, it may consider that creating annual discretionary bonuses would be motivating and an appropriate means for rewarding partners' activities that significantly benefit the firm. Such a bonus scheme typically involves 5–10% of profits being set aside and distributed to a small number of partners judged to have materially increased profits for the firm, where partners feel that the basic profit sharing arrangements are not fair.

Fixed shares and prior shares

8.14   A fixed or prior share of profits is a first charge on the firm's profits. Often, a firm will consider equal prior shares as minimum 'salaries' to reflect time spent and work done, as opposed to the profitability of the firm. Such a scheme is a useful mechanism for ensuring junior partners still receive suitable remuneration in years when the firm's profits are low. An alternative is a safety net with a minimum level of profit for each partner (subject to the overall level of profits being adequate for each partner to receive a minimum share). Fixed shares can also be used to reflect particular onerous responsibilities, eg as senior partner or managing partner, where an additional 'salary' may be considered appropriate. Finally, fixed shares may be the principal element of the profit sharing of mezzanine partners (ie those whose status is generally seen as between that of salaried and equity partners). If a profit sharing agreement provides for fixed or prior shares, consideration needs to be given to how it should operate in the case of losses or inadequate total profits.

Interest on capital

8.15   If all capital is provided equally, in accordance with profit sharing ratios, there is no need to pay interest on capital. However, capital is often provided in a different ratio to profits. This may be because more junior partners do not have access to sufficient capital or borrowing powers. In the interest of equity, it is necessary to consider paying interest on capital. Such 'interest' is treated as a prior share of profits for both accounting and tax purposes.

Consideration needs to be given to the rate of interest payable on such capital. Arguably it should be at least equal to the individual partner's borrowing costs to provide such capital. Growing firms, and all firms in an era of inflation, tend to have a growing requirement for capital to finance the business's working capital requirements. In the absence of an interest provision, particularly if capital is not to be provided completely in accordance with profit shares, it may be hard to persuade partners to raise the additional capital the firm needs. Different partners may have different borrowing costs depending on their personal circumstances and, if interest is to be paid, it may need to be at a standard rate, eg bank base rate plus 2%. There is an argument that such capital should merit a much higher rate of return representing, as it does, risk equity.

There is also a good argument for paying interest on undrawn profits to encourage partners to keep funds in the business, as opposed to withdrawing them the moment they are released. If interest on such balances is paid at, say, bank base rate, both the firm and the individual may benefit. The firm benefits (and the partners generally benefit) because the firm may be financed with a permanent overdraft at an interest cost above base rate, and the partner benefits if he otherwise would have simply placed the funds on deposit in his own name at a rate of interest typically less than base rate. However, if partners choose to leave undrawn profits in the business, it may be a less secure loan than to a bank or building society.

Finally, the interest on capital concept can be used to deal with other issues involving equity between partners – eg cars, which are an emotive subject in many firms. Different amounts spent on individual cars can be treated as 'negative capital', giving an interest charge against individual profit shares.

Workers and owners

8.16 As indicated earlier, partners in a professional practice have the characteristics of both owners and workers. The analogy in a corporate environment is shareholders and employees. It is possible, and reasonable, to divide profit sharing into these two elements. In particular, it is generally hard to justify very large discrepancies in the profit share element between junior and senior partners which relate to how hard each works. The justification must relate more to both the value of that work with clients and contacts built up over many years, and the fact that more senior partners own a greater proportion of the business. If this is accepted, and it is not necessary for the junior partners, at least initially, to own the business and provide capital in the same proportions in which income is shared, schemes can then be devised that will enable junior partners to build up their capital over a period through retention of their profits or otherwise.

Salaried partners

8.17 The term 'salaried partners' is used in this book to describe senior employees held out by the practice as partners by 'being on the notepaper'. Such individuals do not strictly share in the profits at all. However, the term may also be used to define those partners whose profits consist principally of a fixed or prior share, with only a very small proportion of profits after fixed shares. Such partners have 'security' of profit share, as their 'take' in financial terms is not very dependent on the overall level of profits.

Losses

8.18 It is necessary to agree on the basis on which losses are to be shared. If this is not done, the provisions of *s 24* of the *Partnership Act 1890* come into play. These provide that losses are to be shared equally. Whilst professional practices may not normally contemplate making losses, they can arise – possibly as a result of a professional negligence claim greater than the level of insured cover. Normally, losses are shared on the same basis as profits (after any fixed or prior shares).

Capital profits and losses

8.19 The partnership or LLP agreement may provide that capital profits and losses are shared differently from revenue profits and losses. Capital profits and losses arise on disposals of capital assets, eg investments, properties or goodwill. Capital profits and losses would normally be shared on the basis on which capital is held which, as indicated at **8.16** above, may be different from revenue profit sharing. It may be important to distinguish between passive assets, possibly including premises and a sale of a part of the business, which will reduce future income flows.

Summary

8.20 As a collection of individuals, every professional practice is different and it is not possible to be prescriptive about how profits should be shared. There are many different bases in common use. Nevertheless, firms should be aware that the basis can have a significant effect on the firm's success because of the motivating or demotivating effect of the basis on individual partners or members.

Chapter 9 Management

Decision taking

9.1   As we have seen at **5.27**, *s 24*(*5*) of the *Partnership Act 1890* provides that, '... subject to any alternative agreement between the partners, every partner may take part in the management of the business'. This is normally impractical for medium-sized or large professional practices. In smaller firms of perhaps up to eight or ten partners, it sometimes remains possible for all the partners to be involved in the management of the business. In such firms it can be practical for decisions to be taken on management issues at daily, weekly or monthly meetings of all general or equity partners.

Senior partner

9.2   However, even in small firms, the position of a senior partner is generally recognised as one that carries particular responsibilities for the firm as a whole. Such responsibilities often extend to chairing partners' meetings, resolving conflicts and disputes between partners or members, where possible, and acting as the principal ambassador for the firm with the outside world, including the firm's professional body.

Committees

9.3   As a firm grows, it becomes normal for decision-making functions to be devolved to a number of committees. These would typically include a finance committee and a committee overseeing administration. There may also be committees responsible for the running of individual departments or functions, as well as a policy committee to which the more important decisions are devolved. An alternative structure involves an executive committee or board to whom important powers are delegated.

All powers of such committees would normally be devolved from the partners by one or more resolutions or in a general meeting. The firm may reserve certain powers or require certain decisions, for example, on capital expenditure or the admission or expulsion of partners, to be referred to themselves for final decisions.

Whilst such committees have the advantage of being able to involve partners in decisions, all too easily, such committees can behave in the ineffective way, so graphically described in *The Law* by Professor C Northcote Parkinson (Penguin Books). This can lead to a paralysis of decision-making.

Managing partner

9.4 As a firm grows further, the number of committees may increase until the firm reaches a critical size, typically perhaps 15 to 20 partners, when it becomes practical to appoint a managing partner (who may, or more usually may not, be the senior partner) for whom managing the firm can become a fairly full-time occupation. In addition to a managing partner, the governance or constitutional set-up can have a significant impact on the performance of firms. Even with a full-time managing partner, it is normal to involve a number of partners to some extent in the running of the practice. The length of appointment as managing partner, and the powers attached to the post, vary from firm to firm. Typically, the position may be held for between two and five years, with perhaps the need for re-election, although there seems to be a trend towards longer terms for managing partners or even a career role.

Professional practices need to consider carefully who to choose as managing partner. Personal qualities rather than technical abilities are the key determinant. A managing partner generally takes a considerable risk in giving up his client base, and he will deserve and welcome the commitment of the firm to making his role a success.

Outsiders

9.5 An alternative route for a firm is to have a professional manager. However, as the post-holder will usually not be qualified in the professional discipline of the firm, his status may be an issue in terms of gaining credibility within the firm. It is often very hard for such an individual coming in from outside to obtain the full confidence of the partners.

Another way in which an outsider may be involved in a senior capacity is as chairman of the firm, a role in lieu of the position of senior partner. Such an individual must be highly respected to enable the role to work. The responsibilities would typically be similar to those of a senior partner, although it is likely that a firm choosing this route would be looking for such an individual to have additional skills. Such an approach is relatively rare in professional practices although some do use a non-executive 'director' or adviser.

Governance

9.6 It is often helpful to divorce the positions of managing partner and senior partner. This enables the managing partner to have a separate sounding board. The senior partner will also generally be a conduit for channelling other partners' views. This more formal structure with a managing partner/senior partner relationship mirrors a corporate structure with a chief executive or managing director/chairman relationship. The managing partner/director's powers are generally attenuated and made accountable through the senior partner/chairman role.

As a professional practice grows larger, it tends to resemble a corporate entity, except that all partners or members are effectively both senior executives and shareholders. However, the unlimited liability consequences of the partnership vehicle will typically mean that, even in their shareholder role, partners are more active and interested than shareholders in companies.

Generally, best practice in governance in large partnerships and LLPs is evolving to come into line with corporate governance in large companies. To complement the roles of managing and senior partners in a larger firm, it is normal to have a board of partners or an executive committee that may be elected. Such a board may consider having non-executive members in order to make good use of outside experience. Even with this structure there are likely also to be other committees involving partners in decisions related to functions or departments. In any event, it is usual to have at least an annual meeting of all partners, akin to a company AGM. This meeting will be responsible for approving accounts and may be involved, for example, in electing board and committee members and approving remuneration arrangements.

The particular structure chosen by any firm will depend on history, the personalities of the partners and the stage of development of the firm. In the author's view, firms that thrive and prosper will be those with good management. This generally means the firms that are able to create structures that enable good and timely decisions to be taken.

Compensation committee

9.7 As discussions involving remuneration or profit sharing can be highly divisive matters, one way of reducing the risk of damaging disputes is to devolve responsibilities for relevant recommendations to a compensation committee. Typically, such a committee will include both partners chosen because they are highly respected, and partners representing different groups or interests in the firm.

Administration

9.8   Below partner or member level, there will be senior staff involved in administrative and support functions. Typically, they will not have the qualifications to be partners and careful consideration needs to be given to their status to ensure that they can work effectively. The most senior and effective members may best be motivated with some form of stake or profit share in the firm, such as a profit-related bonus. Such staff will report to the managing partner, other partners or committees, depending on the structure of the firm.

Partnership secretary

9.9   A well-recognised but less common role now is that of the partnership secretary. In some firms, this will be the most senior administrator, with responsibilities akin to those of a company secretary. This role generally involves attending meetings of partners, including in some cases committees of partners, recording decisions and ensuring that they are implemented. This role may be combined with others, for example responsibility for personnel, premises or insurances, depending on the size and structure of the firm. It is, however, increasingly common to divorce this role from that of heading up the finance function.

Head of finance

9.10   This role can have a variety of alternative titles, director of finance, partnership accountant or financial controller, depending on the size and structure of the firm and the degree of delegation from the partners. It is a critical role for any professional practice.

The head of finance will generally control day-to-day liaison with the firm's bankers and be responsible for the proper financial recordkeeping of the business and the annual accounts. He will also have the job of providing the firm's decision-makers with accurate and timely financial and other management information. External accountants may support and supplement this role. In a smaller firm, the individual may be responsible for IT and operations support as well.

If the firm chooses to delegate a considerable degree of responsibility for finance, then the individual's calibre must be very high. A good finance director will have to think strategically and the partners will increasingly rely on him or her for advice.

Other positions

9.11   These will vary from firm to firm and depend on the extent to which individual partners fill management functions. Other common senior roles in the larger firms will include head of personnel, head of marketing and head of IT, although exact titles may vary. In a larger firm, there is often considerable merit in employing professionals in these roles. It prevents partners being diverted from their client-facing roles and these professionals will bring best practice to their roles.

Departments

9.12   It is common for a professional practice of any size to divide itself internally into a number of departments. Typically, this will depend on the type of work. For example, a law firm may be divided into litigation, commercial, property and private client departments, with partners and staff allocated to departments according to their specialities. Similarly, a chartered surveyors' firm may be divided into residential property and commercial property, each subdivided according to property management, development or broking activities. Normally, one partner (typically called the head of the department) will take overall responsibility for the performance and management of each department. The firm's information systems will need to be designed to produce financial and other information on a departmental basis.

A departmental culture may be good for accountability and team building, as each department becomes a profit centre. Nevertheless, overemphasis on departmental culture may breed infighting, particularly if some departments, whilst essential for the firm, are known to be less profitable or loss leaders. Equally, overemphasis of the autonomy of departments and their role as separate profit centres will be damaging when clients need to be serviced by more than one department in the firm. Similarly, if departments are allowed complete autonomy in their marketing activity, confusing messages may be given to clients and the outside world. Appropriate profit sharing mechanisms can help to break down any potential silo approach.

To counter some of the effects of departmental marketing, a firm-wide plan and priorities should be established. Specialist cross-departmental groups of partners and staff, perhaps organised on an industry or other grouping from which clients come, may be needed to spread knowledge and ensure that a firm's resources are efficiently deployed. The administrative and support functions may also be subdivided into departments, for example finance, marketing, information technology and personnel.

Partners' meetings

9.13   The structure of the firm may mean that not all partners are fully involved in management. Nevertheless they invariably have certain powers of at least a reserve nature that will need exercising occasionally. Whilst sometimes this can be achieved through using written resolutions, normally there would be a partners' meeting which provides a forum for discussion as well as sometimes acting as a 'safety valve' mechanism. The partners' meeting is also important to help maintain a partner's sense of ownership of the business and to provide an opportunity to make the management directly accountable to the partnership or LLP.

The particular powers reserved to the partners as a whole will be determined in the constitution of the firm. This is likely to include admission and expulsion of partners, election of the board, choice of managing and senior partners, mergers, opening and closing branches or departments, approval of expenditure above a certain level and possibly choice of the firm's professional advisers. Particular majorities may be needed, especially on such sensitive items as elections or the expulsion of a partner. It may be wise to provide a mechanism for secret voting.

Conduct of partnership and committee meetings

9.14 As noted at **5.31**, there is little statutory guidance on how such meetings are to be conducted. Much will depend upon the detailed guidelines that may be set out in the partnership or LLP agreement or be a matter of custom and practice. Effective meetings will depend primarily on the skill of the meeting chairman to set the agenda and guide debate. Whilst it is important to allow all present to have a full say, most attendees will be very busy and the chairman must be able to keep a balance between a very full debate and ensuring that the meeting is not unnecessarily prolonged.

To ensure that action follows decisions taken by committees, accurate minuting of such meetings by the partnership or committee secretary and follow up by the meeting chairman and other partners or staff involved will be needed.

Functions of management

9.15 Management's functions may be defined as setting objectives, organising the business to meet such objectives, communicating those objectives to personnel and motivating them, measuring performance of parts of the business and taking necessary corrective action. To be able to do this, management must exercise control over the firm's affairs.

Within a professional practice, these functions are modified by the nature of the firm, its profession and the people in the firm. For example, the management of partners is always a delicate matter. The qualities that attract able individuals to practise in a profession may be such that subtle techniques need to be used by management to modify behaviour. Professional practices often attract successful partners who are 'prima donnas' and difficult to manage. Such partners may see management's role as simply ensuring necessary support. Nevertheless management has a valuable role to play in assisting every partner to develop personally for the benefit of the firm. Coordinating the activities of different departments to avoid duplication or conflicts will be a key management responsibility.

Planning and implementation

9.16   Strategic planning is important for the success of most organisations, including professional practices, resulting in the setting of key objectives. For example, these could include merger proposals, specific diversification of the firm's business through acquisitions of partners or practices, opening new branches in the UK or overseas, making strategic alliances or developing new specialities (see CHAPTER 10).

In the shorter term, all well-run organisations need more detailed business plans, annual budgets and targets, all stemming from the strategic plan, with regular monitoring of performance against such budgets and targets (see CHAPTER 15).

Financial control

9.17   A prime function of management of a firm, particularly as any partner may commit the partnership or LLP to liabilities, is to exercise proper control over the finances of the firm. Adequate procedures need to be in place to control expenditure and commitments, including offers of employment. Management will take responsibility for record-keeping and should have delegated responsibility for the partnership or LLP, with limits of responsibility and requirements to report to the partners generally. This is discussed in greater detail in CHAPTER 15.

Marketing

9.18   New profitable business is the life blood of a firm that relies on a number of discrete assignments. For those firms with continuing work for clients, new business is the prerequisite to a growing firm and is necessary to replace lost business. In practice, most firms generally have a mixture of discrete assignments and continuing work for clients, but all firms need to consider how to attract new work.

Marketing has become increasingly important for the success of professional practices as constraints placed by professional bodies have been steadily reducing. Whilst specific marketing may be the responsibility of individual fee-earning departments, central management's role, apart from providing support, is that of coordination and general promotion of the firm. This is discussed in greater detail in CHAPTER 11.

Information systems

9.19   For professional practices, information systems may represent a major investment of capital and commitment to revenue expenditure. Management must take overall responsibility for this and ensure that the investment provides an appropriate return (see CHAPTER 12).

Human resources

9.20   Professional practices are people businesses, and both partners and staff are demonstrably the major asset of a firm. To ensure the best return on the investment in this asset, careful attention needs to be paid by management to motivation, remuneration, training and development of partners and staff. See CHAPTER 13 for further detail.

Quality control and risk management

9.21   Management must take overall responsibility for the quality of advice or other services provided by a professional practice to its clients. Typically, detailed responsibility is delegated to fee-earning departments. This is partly to ensure the firm has happy clients, willing to pay professional fees. In the light of the growth of claims for professional negligence, it is also particularly important, as part of overall risk management, that the firm's management set the right tone and implement procedures to monitor and control the level of risk to which the firm is exposed. These procedures will span all aspects of the firm, such as, but not restricted to, recruitment, training, performance management and the use of standard methodology and documentation. Management will have responsibility for liaising with the firm's insurers. This is addressed in CHAPTER 16. Some firms may wish to introduce formal quality systems such as ISO 9000, both to reassure management as to the quality of work undertaken, and as part of a marketing drive to win new clients.

Premises

9.22   Management will need to ensure that there is an adequate amount of appropriate space for the firm in suitable offices in the right location.

Whilst some partners or members in professional practices still regard private offices as an important part of the status which comes with partnership, with property costs becoming a significant fixed cost of business, many firms have increasingly moved towards open plan office space. In addition, many firms are now pursuing more innovative approaches to offsite and home working or hot desking, to address office utilisation issues, with important systems and IT ramifications.

Premises are often a difficult issue for a partnership or LLP because they involve uncertain long-term commitments and liabilities that may outlive the working lives of individual partners. Indeed, managing premises requirements efficiently and negotiating effective lease terms can be a key factor in the success or failure of a business. Provision of suitable space for firms whose business is expanding (or contracting), and ensuring that it is well utilised, can also be difficult and expensive. Flexibility of lease terms, through the inclusion of break clauses for example, often comes at a price, and such terms will need to be carefully negotiated.

The opposite position is that premises may provide financial benefits for partners and firms at the times in the property cycle when significant inducements are offered to incoming tenants. The value of these inducements needs to be carefully balanced against long-term liabilities.

Property issues are also a key consideration in mergers and acquisitions of firms. Closing down offices can be a complex and expensive process.

Compliance with professional requirements and other legislation

9.23   Management will have overall responsibility for ensuring that the firm, its partners and staff comply with the responsibilities placed on them by the professional bodies of which they are members. This may extend to reports to such professional bodies, subscriptions, licences, registrations, and meeting obligations such as Continuing Professional Education, etc. A stream of new regulatory and criminal statutes place onerous obligations on professional practices, and management will need to ensure the firm complies with these as well as other legislation, such as employment law and health and safety legislation.

Business continuity and disaster recovery planning

9.24   Professional practices of all sizes need to have a business continuity plan in place in case of interruption to normal operations. Some regulatory bodies, such as the Solicitors Regulation Authority and Financial Services Authority, require firms to have a business continuity plan to ensure the resumption of business as quickly as possible.

Many firms do not treat business continuity plans seriously enough, yet they are essential for anything from relatively common problems such as viruses and software issues, security breaches, hardware failures, data corruption and supply chain issues, through to more catastrophic events such as natural disasters, fires, power interruptions, gas leaks, disease outbreaks and sabotage. However minor a threat may seem, if left unprepared in the event of a disaster, firms can lose credibility and goodwill among clients, face cash flow issues and payroll problems, incur financial loss and lose production and operational data. Ultimately, they could lose clients or even go out of business altogether.

Business, security and IT heads should together determine what kind of plan is necessary and which systems and departments are most crucial to the firm. Together, they should decide which people will be responsible for managing the aftermath of an event. A good disaster recovery plan will operate under a number of core principles. Staff safety should be of prime importance, critical business processes should be quickly recovered, and the impact of the emergency on the firm should be dealt with. Plans should also be in place to ensure that communication is well managed between clients, employees, counterparties, regulatory bodies and the press. The key to effective business continuity management is to have a small team to manage an event, with that team having the necessary responsibility and authority (or the knowledge and ability to access such authority quickly) to take the necessary actions to manage the disaster. Plans also need to be flexible to allow for any eventuality, rather than trying to second-guess specific circumstances.

Advice should be sought from insurance brokers to ensure that appropriate insurance cover is in place. Business continuity plans should also be tested regularly, and adapted as necessary. It is very easy to have plans in place which do not work when the pressure is on during an incident. IT systems should have a 24/7 back-up server. It may be necessary to take out a contract with a business recovery service that provides dedicated offices from which the firm can do business if its normal premises are rendered unusable.

Outsourcing

9.25 Firms are increasingly examining the benefits of outsourcing some administrative functions, such as IT, accounting, HR and marketing, to third parties. This can deliver substantial cost savings, as well as improvements in quality and timeliness of services through new computer hardware and software. Outsourcing to specialist external suppliers can also help to introduce industry 'best practices' to the firm. For law firms, for example, substantial savings can be made by outsourcing repetitive and process-driven work such as patent documentation, insurance claims, contract drafting and document reviews. Offshore outsourcers will be an option, but savings may also be made by using suppliers in low-cost areas outside London and other cities.

One of the most important aspects of successful outsourcing is having adequate controls in place over the work being undertaken, and clear roles and responsibilities for the management of relationships with any outsourcing company.

Corporate social responsibility

9.26 The development of a corporate social responsibility (CSR) agenda is an increasing priority for professional practices. CSR is essentially about how a firm maximises the benefits and minimises the downsides of its impact on society and the environment. Firms can take voluntary actions over and above meeting legal requirements to address their own business interests and how these affect society at large.

Clients and other stakeholders are taking an increasing interest in firms' CSR credentials and how their activities affect the environment, local communities and treatment of employees. Firms may wish to develop their charitable work and contributions. For example, through their HR policy, firms can offer employees the opportunity to take part in schemes where they spend time out of the office working on a voluntary basis, such as in schools or on environmental projects.

Facilities management

9.27 Primarily concerned with looking after a firm's premises, effective facilities management is vital to the success of any sizeable business. Facilities managers contribute to the delivery of strategic and operational objectives and are responsible for providing a safe and efficient working environment. Meeting the Carbon Reduction Commitment (CRC) obligations and other environmental concerns, such as recycling targets, will usually be the responsibility of facilities managers.

Chapter 10 Strategic Planning

Introduction

10.1 This chapter is intended as a general introduction to the concept and process of strategic planning in a professional practice. An in-depth analysis of the theory, methodologies and jargon of strategic planning is available in countless management books. This chapter has been written for the reader who probably has no previous direct experience of strategic planning but who wants a broad and practical understanding of it. Those intending to lead the development of a firm's strategic plan, or likely to be heavily involved in the planning team, should follow this chapter with further reading, training and advice from appropriately experienced consultants.

There is a fair amount of scepticism about the use of strategic planning. Professional practices have generally been less inclined to develop strategic plans than other types of business. This scepticism is often because of a number of factors, which might include the following:

(a) fears that the results of the work will be worthless;

(b) the fact that a previous strategic planning exercise has produced a voluminous tome which was never executed and now gathers dust on the shelf; or

(c) concern that discussion about the firm's direction and priorities will lead to unseemly squabbles.

In short, partners often feel strategic planning will be a worthless exercise involving uncomfortable navel gazing. These fears are fair ones. However, we believe that, if it is approached in the right way, strategic planning can have significant tangible benefits, both immediately and in the long term.

What is strategic planning?

10.2 At its simplest, strategic planning is thinking about how the firm is to move from where it is today to where it wants to be at some future point. However, strategic plans have characteristics which differentiate them from other tactical plans:

147

(a) *They tend to be about longer-term direction.* For most firms, the most appropriate planning horizon is no more than five years. The majority of strategic plans probably look forward three years.

(b) *Strategic plans always involve change.* Any firm which aspires to both survive and thrive will need to plan to change to meet the needs and pressures of a dynamic business environment. This is one of the many challenges of strategic planning. Handled inadequately, the planning process can cause a sense of unease and uncertainty in the firm. This potentially negative aspect of strategic planning can stop businesses initiating or fulfilling a vital process – planning their long-term future.

(c) A strategic plan should not be an introspective document. It should consider market trends, changes likely to affect clients, different buying habits, progress being made by competitors, potential new entrants to the market, and the impact of proposed changes in law.

(d) The final strategies and plans are heavily influenced by the values and aspirations of partners, staff and others involved in the process. Therefore, despite objective analysis of the firm's internal and external situation, there remains considerable subjectivity in the selection of the preferred strategy.

(e) The resultant actions are often complex because of the range of integrated issues which usually need to be addressed. These generally include marketing, human resources, business processes, finances, property and information systems.

(f) Strategic plans may create a high degree of uncertainty because they attempt to match the firm's activities and capabilities to a fast-changing environment. The shorter the plan's time span, the more certainty there can be about the outcome.

Why develop a strategic plan?

10.3 Strategic planning can be beneficial to professional practices of all sizes and in any sector, in good times and in bad. Some of the potential benefits include the following:

(a) *Ideas and initiatives are generated during the analysis, debate and discussion processes.* Action, with immediate benefits, is often stimulated even before the strategy is completed.

(b) *Partners and staff are given confidence in the future of the firm.* This can inspire greater levels of motivation, commitment and teamwork.

(c) *It helps to anticipate external changes which may be either opportunities or threats*. This might, for example, allow the firm to target new market opportunities before competitors or avoid exposing the firm to unnecessary risks.

(d) *Resources can be planned more effectively.* A clear view of the future for the firm might assist improved decision-making in terms of, for example, information systems, skills, numbers of staff, marketing, financing and property.

(e) It helps to resolve some of the debates and arguments which might have constrained the firm from making important decisions or even very basic ones.

(f) It helps to determine what the firm will not do, which is as important as, if not more important than, what it will do.

(g) The plan acts as a management tool – providing a mandate for management action, driving action and providing a basis for measuring the performance of the firm.

An effective strategic planning process can produce a coherent strategy for the firm, which gives it a competitive advantage in the marketplace. This is likely to provide immediate and practical benefits and increase the likelihood of achieving partners' common ambitions. There is no doubt that a firm can go a long way without going through a strategic planning process. But perhaps it would go further and faster in the right direction with one?

Who should be involved?

10.4 Everybody should be involved, although each person will be involved in different ways. Levels of involvement can be broadly segmented into three – planning, consulting and communication.

Planning

10.5 Here, we are referring to the team of people who will be directly involved in designing and leading the strategic planning process. It is vital that this team is carefully selected to ensure that it has an appropriate mix of personalities, business and creative/analytical skills, and 'political' representation from across the firm. Teams comprising solely of equity partners rarely have the mix needed. It is usually advantageous to have a team of between four and eight people. This might include some salaried partners and senior managers.

The planning team should ideally be led by the senior partner (chairman) or managing partner (chief executive). A valuable external and objective perspective can be added by co-opting people from outside the firm, eg either a consultant or the equivalent of a non-executive director, if the firm has one.

Consulting

10.6   The planning team will wish to consult colleagues across the firm. In an ideal world, it is best to give everybody an opportunity to contribute to the strategy development at some stage in its formulation. This encourages greater 'ownership' and commitment to the strategy. Such consultation might take place through a variety of processes such as group discussions, personal interviews/meetings and formal staff surveys. However, consultation with every member of staff is often not feasible. The planning team will need to ensure that the consultation net is thrown wide enough and that all key players are given an opportunity to contribute.

Communication

10.7   It is vital to communicate and 'sell' the strategy across the firm. The senior partners, management and planning team must demonstrate their commitment to the plan. Indeed, to ensure 'buy in', as many people within the firm as possible should be invited to provide input to the strategic review. Communication, through presentations and discussion, should ensure that there is understanding by all in the firm, and not just the partners, of the firm's direction and of each person's and department's role in it. It is surprising how many firms claim to have a strategy but their staff have no knowledge of its existence, let alone what it is. The need to communicate does not imply, of course, that certain plans and issues should not remain confidential to a smaller group of people.

The strategic planning process

10.8   The strategic planning process is never exactly the same from firm to firm. There is no single correct process. The process must be designed to take the following factors (among others) into account:

(a)   the size of the firm;

(b)   the complexity and sensitivity of the issues which need to be addressed;

(c)   the availability of internal and external data;

(d)   the firm's experience of planning;

(e)   existing planning and budgeting processes;

(f)   the firm's culture;

(g)   the action of the firm's competitors;

(h)   changes, and the speed of change, in the firm's operating environment;

(i)   changes in clients' buying habits;

(j)   changes to the client base, eg consolidation; and

(k)   likely regulatory changes that will impact the business.

It is vital to map the strategic development process at the outset. It is easy to lose your way unless there is a clear understanding of the steps and timetable. It is also important not to forget that, as you move through the strategic planning process, you will often want to reconsider assumptions, options and conclusions, or address new issues which arise.

Another danger with the process is that, understandably, the people involved are distracted by day-to-day issues which need to be addressed. This often causes significant delay. In addition, planners may not have time to think and develop the creative ideas which are so often essential to producing a strategy which is appropriate to a dynamic and highly competitive environment. One potential solution is to appoint an external person to facilitate the process and to keep the team on track.

Whatever the nature of the strategic planning process undertaken to suit the firm, the following are some of the factors that are usually considered:

(i)   *Aspirations/objectives.* In any professional practice (and most businesses), key drivers to a strategy are the aspirations and personal objectives of the key internal stakeholders (eg partners, managers, staff). Any strategy which does not take these into account is likely to be doomed. Therefore, it is vital that aspirations and objectives are understood. However, whilst being ambitious, such aspirations should be reasonably achievable, or the strategy may be dismissed as fantasy.

(ii)   *Mission and values of the firm.* There is normally considerable scepticism about the purpose and value of a 'mission statement' and it may be best to avoid that term. Nonetheless, some firms benefit from developing some form of written statement which summarises their firm's broad aims and philosophies in terms of, for example, markets, geography, services and values. Such a statement will provide the context for the development of the detailed strategy and plan.

(iii)   *Internal analysis.* This should identify the firm's internal resource strengths and weaknesses in relation to the competition and the likelihood of future change in the external environment. It will involve the gathering and interpretation of information relating to, for example, people (attitudes, numbers, skills, training, etc), property, management information and quality of services and client care, information systems and finances.

(iv) *External analysis.* A practical strategy must be based on an objective understanding of the business environment at three levels: the macro-environment, competitors and clients. Analysis of the macro-environment will involve examining the social, political, technological, economic and legal factors that may make an impact on the market-place. Also important is an analysis of both existing competitors and potential competitors to examine such issues as:

(a) their relative strengths and weaknesses;

(b) what they are doing new or differently; and

(c) their potential plans for the future.

Clients are, of course, fundamental to the future success of the firm, and client analysis would aim to answer questions such as:

(a) how they perceive the firm and its strengths and weaknesses;

(b) how their needs might change in the future;

(c) how they would like to see the firm develop in the future in terms of, for example, the range of services and method of service delivery; and

(d) how perceptions, needs and other factors vary across different types of client and market segments.

This external analysis will enable the firm to get the future changes to, and needs of, the business in perspective, and to take a view on the opportunities and threats that may arise in the future.

(v) *Strategy development.* This stage will involve consideration of all the data gathered to date. The aim of this stage is to reach broad agreement on issues such as:

(a) the firm's goals/objectives;

(b) the current situation, perhaps defined in terms of a SWOT analysis (strengths, weaknesses, opportunities and threats);

(c) critical success factors or issues which need to be addressed if the firm is to move successfully from its current position towards its objectives; and

(d) review of options for business development, possibly evaluated against various scenarios such as changes in the law, government, technology and the economy.

(vi) *Action planning.* Having agreed the broad strategy, it is important to develop a detailed action plan, incorporating clear responsibilities, timings and costs.

(vii) *Monitoring and review.* Strategic planning should not be a one-off exercise which is undertaken every few years. There should be regular monitoring of a firm's performance against the agreed performance targets and milestones. Progress against plan should be regularly reported to partners and staff. The strategy will probably require regular modification and refinement as performance targets are exceeded or missed and as the market and environment change.

The agreed strategy should not be set out in a lengthy and verbose document. A summary for internal consumption is often appropriate. This should include key elements of the strategy (goals, objectives, SWOT, strategic paths). It is very important that it also includes the action plan and performance targets which the firm is aiming to achieve as the firm moves towards its longer-term goals.

Typical components of a strategic plan

10.9 These components consist of:

(a) *Performance review.* A review of recent performance (overall, and in key areas of activity, eg products, customers, finances, people, etc). Such a review should also benchmark the firm against the performance of its key competitors.

(b) *Environment analysis.* Review of trends in the operating environment, eg social, legal, economic, political, technological. Review of competitors. Review of the markets, customer segments and relevant trends, etc. Identification of key opportunities and threats.

(c) *Internal analysis.* Review of the firm's resources (eg people, property, finances, products, services, information systems, etc) to identify principal strengths and weaknesses relative to the marketplace. This may result in a decision to exit weaker areas in order to put more resources into stronger and growing areas of the business.

(d) *SWOT analysis.* Summary of principal strengths, weaknesses, opportunities and threats.

(e) *Vision/Mission/Aims.* A statement of the firm's longer-term aspirations/aims, values, etc.

(f) *Strategy.* A series of strategic (or policy) statements regarding key issues such as markets/customers; products/services; quality; people; information systems; finances; method of development; property;

and geography (location, target areas). Options which might have been considered could be covered in this section.

(g) *Objectives/performance indicators.* A series of measurable objectives (or performance indicators) against which progress can be monitored.

(h) *Implementation plan.* Key actions with details of people responsible, timings and resource implications.

(i) *Appendices.* Appendices might be required, eg financial forecasts/scenario analyses; market data; sales data, etc.

Common pitfalls

10.10 Some common pitfalls that firms experience during the strategic planning process are given below:

(a) Inadequate internal consultation and consensus.

(b) Preparation is delegated with insufficient top management involvement and commitment.

(c) Too much time and effort spent on producing a voluminous report.

(d) The time frame of the plan is too short term (eg 1–2 years rather than 3–5).

(e) The plan is reliant on anecdotal and qualitative data which have not been substantiated with quantitative/objective data, including data from competitor benchmarking and client feedback.

(f) Lack of market and environment analysis.

(g) The planning process goes on for too long (eg 12 months rather than 3). People become bored with it, and the plan is out of date before it is finished.

(h) Failure to monitor progress against measurable milestones.

(i) Failure to review the strategy each year.

(j) Failure to communicate the strategy internally.

(k) Failure to incorporate a costed action plan with clear responsibilities.

(l) Failure to recognise the full range of key issues because the planning team was too narrow in its background and outlook.

(m) Failure to realistically consider the aspirations and objectives of all stakeholders.

(n) Potential future scenarios were not considered.

(o) Inadequate challenge of the strategy in terms of feasibility and practicality.

(p) Failure to develop and/or review the firm's strategy until the firm is in difficulty.

(q) Failure to make hard decisions, such as on exiting unprofitable or declining areas of the business and investing in more profitable and growing areas.

Chapter 11 Marketing and Business Development

Introduction

11.1 Marketing has become an increasingly important practice management issue. This is due to several factors, including:

(a) an increase in competition;

(b) a more sophisticated client base who select providers of professional services on criteria other than just habit or price; and

(c) a reduction in the regulations governing the ways in which professional practices promote their services.

This chapter provides an overview of the key marketing issues and suggests approaches to marketing planning and methodology.

What is marketing?

11.2 Perhaps the best and most succinct definition comes from the Chartered Institute of Marketing, which defines marketing as 'the management process responsible for identifying, anticipating and satisfying customer requirements profitably'. Marketing acts as the vehicle through which business development is delivered and provides the framework for execution and measurement.

Key goals

11.3 The key goals of a marketing-orientated practice can be broadly summarised as follows:

(a) to retain the firm's profitable clients;

(b) to generate more profitable business from existing clients; and

(c) to attract new clients to use the firm's services.

In order to achieve these goals, firms need to:

 (i) review the marketplace and identify those market segments which demonstrate similar characteristics (eg location, size, activities of clients);

 (ii) understand the needs of clients in each segment;

(iii) target those market segments whose characteristics best match the firm's skills, resources and services;

(iv) continue developing products and services to meet the needs of clients in the target segments;

(v) communicate with potential clients in the target segments, highlighting the benefits of using the firm;

(vi) understand and manage clients' expectations about the service they require and then ensure that the firm's service exceeds these expectations; and

(vii) monitor regularly service performance against client needs and expectations.

Marketing is central to all business activity and needs to be embraced by everyone in the organisation in order to realise its full potential.

Understanding the external environment

11.4　If a firm is to achieve long-term success, it is critical that it has a clear understanding of the external environment (see also **CHAPTER 10, STRATEGIC PLANNING**). Key questions for the firm might include, for example:

(a) *The market.* How big is it? What are the key segments? Which segments are growing or declining? How will the market and the business environment change?

(b) *Clients.* Who are they? How many are there? What are their needs and how well do we satisfy them?

(c) *Competitors.* Who are they? How big are they? What services do they provide and to whom? How do they charge for their services? What are their relative strengths and weaknesses?

(d) *Legislation.* What are the likely legal, economic and/or political changes that will affect the market? Will that effect be positive or negative?

Sources of information

11.5　There are a variety of sources of information a firm might use to gain a better understanding of the external environment. These include the following:

(a) *Media and social media.* Most business sectors have a range of media which provide informed comment on key developments within the market. These include trade press, business news websites and social media platforms.

(b) *Competitors.* Information on competitors can be derived from their websites, brochures, annual reports, advertisements, newsletters, etc, as well as through direct contact as a 'mystery shopper'.

(c) *Clients.* Information can be gained from clients on a structured basis, through targeted surveys, or through informal discussion as part of day-to-day business dealings.

(d) *Research.* A wide variety of intelligence is available online, as well as from research agencies and trade associations.

(e) *Internal sources.* All members of the firm, particularly those with direct contact with clients, are likely to gain useful external information on what is happening in their professional world. By creating effective internal communication networks, such data can be used to contribute to a firm's understanding of the market.

Having gathered the data, it is important to analyse the information carefully to see how the firm can enhance its services and market position, and counter potential threats from its competitors and others.

Marketing planning

11.6 Once the firm has an agreed strategic business plan and a clear understanding of the markets in which it operates, it can start compiling a marketing plan. This section specifies some of the key elements of the marketing plan but, first, it is worth considering the benefits of what some people may regard as a time-consuming and unnecessary distraction from fee-earning work. These are as follows:

(a) A marketing plan will help the firm to decide where it is going and to set specific and measurable objectives.

(b) Documenting the plan will help to build consensus among senior members of the firm.

(c) The plan will identify what individual members of the firm have to do, so the firm can achieve its goals.

Producing a plan

11.7 In the professional practices that prepare a marketing plan, it is often left to one individual to undertake the analysis and prepare the document. Although there are significant benefits in a single person coordinating the production of the overall plan, it is strongly recommended that all service providers are involved in the development of marketing plans for their respective areas. This will encourage greater realism and make people more committed to the final marketing strategy and its objectives.

Contents of a plan

11.8   Each firm will develop a plan format to suit its own requirements but, in the case of a professional service, this will usually include the following:

(a)   SWOT analysis (summary of the current position);

(b)   service/product range;

(c)   target clients;

(d)   the basis of charging for products/services;

(e)   promotion and communication;

(f)   key objectives;

(g)   action plan; and

(h)   analysis of expenditure (driven by the plan).

SWOT analysis

11.9   The firm will need to complete an audit of its marketing-related activities before it starts to compile a marketing plan. Many firms find the SWOT analysis a useful shorthand for summarising their current position and a constructive starting point for developing the future marketing direction of the practice. SWOT analysis identifies the relative internal strengths and weaknesses of the firm, as well as the key external (ie market/environment-related) opportunities for, and threats to, the business. The value of the SWOT analysis is that it provides an agreed position from which the marketing plan and its key objectives can be developed. The hypothetical example below demonstrates some of the points that may be included in a summary SWOT analysis.

An example SWOT analysis, ABC professional practice

Strengths	Weaknesses
• Wide service range	• Lack of service specialism
• Quality of service	• Over-reliance on a small number of clients
• Local market profile/reputation	• Low conversion rate of new sales leads
• Consistent income growth	• Poor cross-selling of services to existing clients

- Structured promotional programme
- Blue chip client base
- High level of retained clients

- Poor understanding of clients' future needs
- Uncompetitive pricing

Opportunities

- Market growth for XYZ services
- Expand into: – other UK regions
  – international

- Develop a service specialisation

Threats

- Increasing level of competition
- Loss of key staff to competitors
- Reduced demand for certain services as a result of new technologies

Service/product range

11.10   One of the most difficult aspects of marketing in a professional practice is that the service or product range is often relatively intangible. Not only are services harder to specify and define, but measuring their effectiveness is also more complex.

Therefore, from the outset, a professional practice needs to identify and clearly define the full range of services that it offers. Surprisingly, this often has the benefit of gaining internal consensus among the senior members of the firm on its activities, as well as assisting the communication of the service/product range to existing and potential clients. In defining the range, consideration should be given to:

(a)   the scope of activities;

(b)   the client benefits derived from using the service/product; and

(c)   how the service/product differs from, and (one hopes) is superior to, competing services/products.

Assuming the firm delivers more than one product or service, it may then be appropriate to prioritise the range. This will help management allocate resources appropriately (eg investment in staff, equipment, etc) and also assist in focusing the external communication of the firm by defining its 'brand' – what it stands for, how it wants to be perceived in the marketplace, and how it differentiates itself from its competitors.

How firms go about prioritising their services will vary, but it may involve judging how their practices, services or departments compare with each other in terms of:

(i)   the profitability of the service;

(ii) the level of technical skill within the firm;

(iii) the growth potential within the marketplace;

(iv) market share; and

(v) the level of competition.

Clients and prospective clients

11.11 Marketing plans should confirm precisely the firm's target audience for each product/service. Having reviewed the marketplace, the firm will have identified various market segments. Given that firms have limited resources, each of these sectors must then be prioritised so that the firm focuses on the most appropriate opportunities.

The criteria by which the firm undertakes such prioritisation will vary. The client sectors may be chosen according to, for example:

(a) the relative number of potential clients in each sector;

(b) the firm's existing experience in serving each particular sector;

(c) the perceived competition in each sector;

(d) the relative costs associated with targeting and serving the selected market segments; and

(e) the geographic concentration of clients.

An example of targeting

11.12 It is often useful to build a client profile so as to ensure the accuracy of targeting and to build internal consensus regarding the 'ideal' client. For example, an insurance broker wishing to sell life assurance cover might target:

(a) private individuals;

(b) men and women between 25 and 45 years old;

(c) individuals located within a 30-mile radius of the office; and

(d) those earning over £45,000 per annum.

Alternatively, a firm of engineers might target:

(i) manufacturing businesses;

(ii) organisations with a turnover of over £5 million;

(iii) businesses located in the West Midlands; and

(iv) firms with limited internal technical skills and resources.

The development of detailed target client profiles will enable all members of the firm to define their audience and will improve the accuracy of the organisation's targeting.

Pricing

11.13 Although many firms will consider that how they price their services and products is an integral part of the financial business plan, pricing also plays a key part in the organisation's marketing. From a marketing perspective, the firms need to look at pricing from the clients' point of view. How does the firm compare with the prices set by competitors? Given the quality of service, do clients think that they get value for money? Does the firm charge by the hour, or is there a fixed price for a standard service? Can discounts be offered for volume purchases or early settlement? Can different price scales be offered for 'premium', specialist and others types of work? Agreement on pricing policy will also help to determine the image of the firm in the marketplace. For example, a firm that charges high prices will be perceived differently from a firm with a low pricing policy.

Firms need to address these questions as part of the marketing plan in order to clarify how the income of the practice will be derived.

As an aside, it is worth noting that many firms do not review their prices often enough. An annual review of charge-out rates is a minimum requirement.

Promotional activity

11.14 All marketing plans include a promotional or communications programme designed to attract profitable new clients and retain existing ones. Before undertaking specific communication activity, firms must agree the key messages they need to communicate to clients and potential clients. To be effective, such messages need to concentrate on the major criteria by which clients choose professional practices. Areas where the firm believes it is better than its rivals and points of differentiation should be identified, where applicable.

For example, key messages might include:

(a) the widest range of services;

(b) the quickest service;

(c) the cheapest price; and/or

(d) the most local/convenient service.

Once the key messages have been agreed, they should be clearly and consistently communicated across all media. There is a wide and varied choice of media available to professional practices. Selecting the right medium for a particular firm will depend on the resources available, the clients being targeted and the promotional objectives and messages that the firm wants to get across. Some of the more common promotional tools are noted below, together with some of the typical advantages and disadvantages experienced by firms who have used them, although these will obviously vary from practice to practice and partner to partner.

Analysis of common promotional tools

Promotional tool	Advantages	Disadvantages
Advertising	• Communicates message to a wide audience	• Relatively high cost
	• Can build awareness and profile quickly	• Requires specialist implementation skills
	• Can be cost effective, particularly online compared to print	• Services may be too technically complex to communicate in an advert
Brochures	• Can give the firm 'stature' and credibility	• Relatively high cost
	• Opportunity to convey potentially complex messages	• Difficult to keep up to date (eg new services, personnel, clients, etc)
	• Flexibility of use (eg in meetings, at presentations, in mailings)	
Direct mail	• Relatively low cost	• Traditionally, response rates are low (c.2%)
	• Messages can be personalised	• May require follow up to be effective (eg by telephone)
	• Easy to monitor activity's effectiveness	

Entertainment	• Opportunity to build client/contact relations	• Can require a significant time investment
	• Variety of options (eg lunch, golf days) to suit all clients and budgets	• Some clients/contacts are becoming resistant to entertainment
Exhibitions	• Ability to target specific sectors	• Support material can be expensive
	• Brings the service provider into direct contact with potential purchasers	• Requires significant time investment
Newsletters	• Flexible format for regular contact	• Time investment required to write articles
	• Updates clients/contacts on issues and news	• Regular production required
	• Builds credibility	
	• Relatively low cost	
Personal selling	• Can be low cost	• Individuals may require training
	• Ability to tailor the message to suit each contact	• Potential personal resistance to a 'sales' role
Press relations	• Can demonstrate technical expertise	• Time investment required to target editors and write articles
	• Builds profile and credibility	• May need to support editorial copy with paid advertising
	• Relatively low cost	
Seminars	• Opportunity to demonstrate technical skills	• Requires significant management time
	• Builds personal profile and credibility	• Speakers may require training in presentation skills

	• Brings service provider into direct contact with potential purchasers	
Website/online media	• Makes information about the firm widely available	• Needs resources to keep it fresh and up to date
	• Can allow feedback from, and interaction with, visitors	
	• Can be tailored to suit the profile and needs of many different types of audience	

Websites, extranets and social media

11.15 Websites have become much more sophisticated among professional practices in recent years and can be very effective tools for providing information about the firm to clients, potential clients, suppliers, potential recruits, journalists and others. Typical information might include: details about services and specialist expertise, a profile of the firm and its people, articles, press releases and commentary on topical issues. Websites can also provide an effective means for delivering services and for engaging clients and others in an ongoing relationship with the firm. Website content should ideally incorporate 'calls to action', with links to offers, registration pages or dedicated subscriber-only pages.

Extranets are bespoke, private networks that use internet connectivity. They are often offered with 'client-only' areas to provide valuable information and encourage groups of users to share intelligence in an area secure from other web users.

Social media comprise interactive media which use web-based technologies enabling the creation and exchange of user-generated content. Increasingly, businesses are taking an interest in social networking platforms in order to maximise opportunities to reach large audiences, demonstrate thought leadership on topical issues, and encourage dialogue and interaction.

Although many professional services firms' websites are still effectively online brochures, firms are increasingly using their websites to deliver more engaging 'thought leadership' content to their various audiences.

Before producing a site, undertake research to get a feel for what good and bad sites are like, and seek professional advice to ensure that you make the most of the technology and web design expertise available. Some characteristics of the best websites are that they:

(a)   are easy to navigate and use;

(b)   have up-to-date information;

(c)   are quick to download;

(d)   have sufficient quantity of relevant information;

(e)   have some degree of interactivity;

(f)   encourage 'sales' opportunities;

(g)   track who is visiting and how they are using the site; and

(h)   are optimised for search engines.

Assessment of promotional tools

11.16   Whatever combination of promotional tools is used by the firm, it is important that the source of new business is tracked to establish the effectiveness of each communication channel, so that the overall promotional programme can be reviewed, developed and measured against investment.

It is strongly suggested, particularly for smaller, lower profile firms, that a structured programme of promotional activity is agreed for a year. This will encourage fee earners to undertake business development activity continuously and not solely when the level of chargeable time starts to dip.

Although this may mean spending time writing mailshot material or entertaining potential clients, for example, when the fee earner is already busy and probably wishes to concentrate on delivering the service, it should help to ensure that periods of 'feast and famine', so often experienced by smaller firms, are reduced.

Client care

11.17   Although proactive promotional activity is important, it must be recognised that the best source of business is from existing clients. Satisfied clients stay with your firm and can give it additional work. Delighted clients will also talk positively about your firm and recommend it to potential new clients. Thus, whatever your firm might invest in promotional activities, it must keep focused on delivering exceptional client care and service in order to delight its existing clients.

The firm should ensure that it knows what aspects of service are important to clients generally and also to specific clients. Perceptions of service quality should be monitored. Your quality of service goals will need to be supported by appropriate attitudes, behaviours and skills; investment will be needed to develop and maintain the appropriate culture, resources and skills to deliver exceptional service.

Brand

11.18 Brand is about the awareness and perceptions of the firm in the minds of clients, potential clients, intermediaries, staff and other stakeholders. Logos and visual image are only part of a brand. Values, ethics and business philosophy are vital elements of a firm's brand and greatly influence a firm's reputation. For clients, a strong brand can, for example, provide them with reassurance about quality, it can help influence their decisions when selecting a supplier and it can give psychological satisfaction by association. For the firm, a strong brand can, for example:

(a) attract profitable clients;

(b) enhance client loyalty;

(c) help to achieve higher fees or greater market share;

(d) increase the value of the firm; and

(e) assist with recruitment, motivation and retention of staff.

Some key issues to consider for effective brand development include:

(i) ensuring that top management are directly involved with, and are seen to lead, the brand development and management process;

(ii) understanding, measuring and monitoring the brand in terms of awareness of the firm and how the firm is perceived amongst key groups (this will normally involve qualitative and/or quantitative research);

(iii) developing a brand strategy in terms of how the firm wishes to be perceived, and how it wants to differentiate itself, in the minds of key audiences;

(iv) ensuring that the firm's values, culture and strategy are consistent with the brand strategy, and vice versa;

(v) ensuring that all communications and other direct contact (eg telephone handling style, offices, client care) with clients and others are consistent with the brand strategy and with each other; and

(vi) communicating with and training staff about the brand strategy and their role in implementing it.

Setting objectives

11.19   A marketing plan must include objectives and a time frame during which it is hoped they will be achieved. Objectives help endorse the plan which, in turn, drives the budget. Objectives, like the marketing plan itself, can cover a variety of time periods. Typically, however, objectives are normally set for the forthcoming 12 months and probably for the medium term, say three years. The objectives set will vary, depending on the firm, but they will probably include the following indicators or dimensions:

(a)   income and profitability;

(b)   clients (eg total number, number of new clients, new geographic regions);

(c)   products/services (eg income/profit from each service/product, launch of new products/services);

(d)   communications activity (eg campaign activities, goals, expenditure and messages); and

(e)   pricing/charging (eg achievement of rate increases, etc).

SMART objectives

11.20   Objectives can be set for almost any area of marketing activity but, in order for them to be effective, they should be SMART, ie:

(a)   Specific – the objectives should be clearly defined.

(b)   Measurable – each objective should be measurable (eg number of cases, value of income, etc).

(c)   Achievable – the objectives must be achievable, given the skills and resources of the firm.

(d)   Relevant – the marketing objectives should be relevant to the long-term strategy of the firm.

(e)   Timely – the time frame for achieving each objective should be clearly defined.

Action plan

11.21   The difference between a marketing plan which is an academic document and one which is a valuable management tool is often the inclusion of a practical action plan. The action plan should be driven by the marketing plan's objectives. In order to ensure the action plan is focused and easy to manage, it is suggested that it is constructed to include the following:

(a)   specific activity to be undertaken;

(b)   marketing objective to which the activity relates;

(c)   who is responsible for undertaking the activity;

(d)   the time by which the activity should be completed; and

(e)   an estimate of the resource implications/budget for undertaking the specific activity.

Organisation

11.22   For marketing to be effectively planned and implemented, it is very important to clarify the marketing organisation, particularly the responsibilities each person across the firm has for marketing. A common problem occurs when a firm appoints a Marketing Partner and/or a Marketing Director (or Manager/Executive) and then many partners and staff think that they no longer have to do it!

Firms have long recognised that an effective in-house marketing resource or use of experienced external consultants can be of great value. This is an important investment for any firm, and marketing needs to be embraced by everyone in the firm in order for this investment to support strategic objectives, to measure effectiveness and reap the rewards. Firms should ensure that, before recruiting marketing personnel, there are agreed job descriptions, performance objectives and candidate profiles, and that the senior members of the firm understand and are committed to marketing appointments. Embedding marketing professionals within practice areas and/or outsourcing specific marketing functions, such as PR, event management, client communications or design, are also worth considering.

Review and monitoring

11.23   The marketing plan of any professional practice can never be set in stone. The market will change, clients will require new products/ services, the firm's objectives will evolve. It is therefore important that the marketing plan is regularly reviewed. This will ensure that:

(a)   marketing activity continues to capitalise upon business opportunities;

(b)   the marketing plan supports the firm's business strategy; and

(c)   specific action which has been designed to achieve defined objectives is actually being undertaken within the timescales and resource constraints agreed.

The review period will largely depend on the dynamics of the marketplace and the firm's strategy. However, it is suggested that the plan is reviewed annually, with individual supporting activity reviewed on a monthly basis.

Internal marketing

11.24 Internal marketing is also an important concept for professional practices. The concept includes, for example:

(a) ensuring that everybody in the firm has a clear understanding about the firm's positioning in the market and its proposition (eg key values, competitive advantages/strengths and principal messages);

(b) ensuring that people internally have an appropriate understanding of the full range of services provided by the firm and of recent successes/achievements;

(c) providing means for all partners and staff to provide their ideas about how the firm can improve its service and about new market opportunities; and

(d) developing client care and other relevant marketing skills. Firms often set internal marketing objectives with an associated action plan covering, for example, internal communication and training.

Internal communications are at their most effective when the people within the firm responsible for HR, learning and development, corporate responsibility, and culture and values work closely together to deliver a consistent message.

Summary

11.25 Marketing is a broad and potentially complex subject and this chapter has only begun to scratch the surface. However, it has identified some of the priority issues which should be considered by firms which wish to achieve long-term success in the marketplace. There are a number of key points to remember:

(a) Understand your clients and potential clients, particularly with regard to:

　(i) their current and future needs;

　(ii) the key criteria by which they select a supplier of professional services; and

　(iii) what they think of your firm's services and quality of client care.

(b) Continually monitor trends in the marketplace to identify new opportunities and potential threats to the business.

(c)   Define and prioritise the firm's service range.

(d)   Agree the firm's key promotional messages and ensure they are consistently communicated in all media and by all members of the firm.

(e)   Develop an agreed marketing plan which includes objectives and a detailed action plan.

(f)   Ensure that everybody in the firm understands their role and responsibilities with regard to marketing.

(g)   Regularly monitor the effectiveness of the marketing plan in achieving the stated objectives and refine it, as appropriate.

(h)   Focus the firm's business development activity on the following groups, in order of priority:

   (i)   existing clients, to ensure that they are provided with excellent service in order to retain their custom and to ensure that their needs are understood, so that other services which the firm can provide are introduced to them, as appropriate;

   (ii)   intermediaries who may recommend your firm and influence purchasing decisions (eg accountants, lawyers, agents, etc); and

   (iii)   potential clients.

(i)   Involve everyone in the marketing of the business.

Chapter 12   Information Systems

Introduction

12.1   Good financial and management information, produced on a timely basis, is vital for modern professional practices. Proper information will help firms plan and monitor their business and assist the decision-making process. The right computer systems can assist with the preparation of this information.

In many professions, computers are not just a means for recording information about the activity undertaken, but are vital tools of the trade. Specialised document management systems are increasingly common, particularly in legal practices. Computer aided design (CAD) software is extensively used in architectural practices, and spreadsheet software is used throughout accountancy firms. Staff are increasingly able to access office-based systems direct from remote sites using a telephone landline, a smartphone or a personal digital assistant (PDA).

In addition to having a website, most firms have an internal intranet and some have an extranet for clients. Some forms are now offering the option of e-commerce transactions through the internet.

Scope of computer systems in professional practices

Time recording

12.2   In professional firms, time is the fee earners' most valuable resource. To maximise fees for any given activity, even if fees are not charged exclusively on a time basis, it is a prerequisite to keep a full record of the time each fee earner spends on both client and non-chargeable activities, and that this information is produced promptly. For firms of any size, it would be too time consuming to collate this information manually and errors may occur. Therefore, the use of a computer system becomes a necessity.

The speed and ease with which time information can be input are important considerations. Systems developed for some professions enable the fee earner to record time using hand-held systems or to use a scanning device that records bar codes attached to covers of files. The information can then be directly downloaded to the main computer system. It is increasingly common for staff to input the data from remote sites, including for instance their home. However, most professional firms still rely on traditional timesheets. There are a number of issues to consider when selecting a time recording system including the suitability of the base unit for charging time (eg minutes, six minutes, quarter hour) and the ability of the system to record different charge-out rates for different staff on similar activities. For instance, in a solicitors' practice, the legal aid charge-out rates will usually differ from those applied to non-legal aid work.

Work in progress

12.3   If the time records are computerised, then it is a logical extension for the amount of fees rendered to be offset against the time input, to provide an indication of time still to be billed. Disbursements chargeable to clients should also be recorded. Reports that combine information about unbilled time and disbursements can then be used in most professional practices as billing guides for raising fee notes. When selecting software to perform this function, it is important to ensure that reports produce sufficient detail about billed and unbilled staff time, and that the software processes under/over recoveries on interim and final fee notes in the way the firm requires.

Features checklist—Time recording and work in progress software

General	Essential	Desirable	Not required
Integration with payroll and ledgers			
Timesheet frequency			
Base unit of time			
Expenses/disbursements			
Non-chargeable time			
Data entry			
Timesheet media			
Speed of data entry			
Remote entry			
Narrative			
Charge-rates specified by:			
—staff member			
—staff grade			
—client			

	Essential	Desirable	Not required
—job type			
Charge-rate changes			
Processing			
Write-off procedures			
On account/final fee notes			
Valuation of fee earner time			
WIP valuation at cost			
Reporting			
Summaries			
Full detail			
Department totals			
Client totals			
Job analysis			
Billed and unbilled time			
Prior year or period information			
Billing guides			
Under/over-recoveries			
Recoverable disbursements			
Budgets, actual, variances			
Exception reports			

Financial accounting and reporting

12.4   If fee note details have been recorded for work-in-progress purposes, then duplication can be avoided if the fee ledger itself is computerised. For firms with a reasonable volume of transactions, it is sensible to computerise all the day books and ledgers. Other accounting areas may warrant computerisation, including the payroll and the fixed asset register.

It is sometimes suggested that accounts ledger software is all very similar and there are few real differences. However, features such as departmental reporting and multi-currency accounting are found in some ledger accounting packages but not in others. Firms holding client money will want a system that can handle the necessary requirements. Therefore, some care must be taken in assessing the suitability of software for performing even relatively straightforward tasks.

The speed with which data can be input on to a computer may not appear to be any faster than writing out the details of transactions in traditional ledgers and day books. However, the major benefit from using a computer arises when reports are required. Many packages have a limited range of standard reports already prepared. However, in many firms, the requests for information are likely to be diverse. They can range from detailed queries from fee earners about individual client accounts to aggregated summaries for the management about the performance of the firm as a whole.

Features checklist—Financial accounting software

General	Essential	Desirable	Not required
Accounting periods			
Password protection			
Integration with other modules			
Ledger codes:			
—Client and office accounts			
—Structures			
Multiple currency			
Multiple entity			
Internet enabled			
Data entry			
Batch posting			
Posting to future or past periods			
Sales or purchase invoices			
Single entry WIP update for expenses			
Cash book postings			
Cash allocation			
Journal postings:			
—multi-line			
—recurring			
—reversing			
Narrative			
Processing			
VAT cash accounting			
Brought forward or open item accounts			
Interest calculations			
Profit-share calculations			

	Essential	Desirable	Not required
Reporting			
Fee note production			
Cheque printing			
Aged debt listing			
Cash flow analysis			
Bank reconciliation			
Account history			
Audit trail			
Repeat period ends			
Consolidation			
By office, division			
Content and layout			
Budget, actual, variances			
Period, year to date, last year to date			
Report generator			
Data export to word processor or spreadsheet software			
Spooling to disk			

It is therefore likely that the content or layout of the standard reports are not what is needed, or that the reports do not incorporate the full range of analyses and ad hoc queries that may be requested from time to time. To mitigate these difficulties, packages often contain a report generator facility that enables users to design their own reports. The report generator may only permit reports to be designed using data from one part of the software, or alternatively it may allow data to be extracted from across the full range of the software modules.

Business intelligence

12.5 In the past, access to financial data tended to be restricted purely to the finance department or to partners. This was partly due to the traditional perceived need for privacy. But it was also due to the inability of software to present financial information in a manner comprehensible to non-financial persons.

Business executives then started using software that gave easy access to previously closed databases of financial information. This enabled both financial and non-financial data to be interrogated and presented in a visual way, comprehensible to people without a financial background. Other features that became more common included the ability to 'drill-down' to discover the detail behind any aggregated data. This type of software was initially termed 'executive information system' or 'EIS', but is now more commonly described as 'business intelligence' software. There are various business intelligence products available which create, manage and deliver information extracted from underlying information databases. However, the effective use of these products requires staff who have both a good understanding of the product as well as the field structures and relationships in the underlying database(s).

Contacts and client relationships

12.6 Existing clients and contacts are the principal sources of new work for a professional firm. It is therefore important that information on them is kept up to date and accurate, and is disseminated to all who would benefit from it. Many firms consider that the need to share information about clients and contacts justifies having a computerised database that centralises all knowledge about a particular client or contact and his business. It can also be used for marketing purposes to ensure that the contact is managed properly, with invitations to selected events, and is sent appropriate publications produced by the firm, or given a periodic telephone call. Such software is often described as CRM or customer relationship management software. In its broadest sense, this describes software that records data about any contact or transaction with a new or potential customer. As with any database, keeping it up to date takes administrative effort. It also requires the active cooperation of partners and other staff who should supply and update the required information.

A more recent phenomenon is social networking. Without proper controls, social networking tools can be seen as a threat to business efficiency, both in terms of wasted staff time and use of bandwidth. For this reason, many firms ban their use outright, or just during working hours. However, some firms see a benefit in developing an online community, for instance to stay in contact with alumni. Tools such as LinkedIn are more business-orientated, and are often seen as a valid basis for developing a business contact network, both for the purposes of new work but also, for example, listing and searching for jobs or potential candidates.

Word processing

12.7 Nowadays, nearly all word processing is performed using standard packages operating on personal computers. A standard package increases the chances that new staff or temporary assistants will already have the

177

necessary skills, and reduces the risk of compatibility and formatting problems when transmitting a document by e-mail. Microsoft Word^{TM} dominates across the professions.

The functionality of word processing packages has improved to such an extent that many are now quasi-desktop publishing packages, and improved tracking enables documents to be shared and updated across teams. However, this increased functionality has led to a need for hardware with a higher specification than previously required. Some professional firms wishing to upgrade their software may be inhibited by the additional cost of replacing their hardware on which it runs.

Spreadsheets

12.8 The basic design of spreadsheets has changed little since they were first launched in the late 1970s. However, spreadsheet packages now typically have additional features including graph facilities and a multi-sheet capability, as well as tools such as a spellchecker. Many spreadsheet packages also claim to have database features, although in reality these are quite primitive compared with software specifically designed as a database tool. Microsoft Excel^{TM} is the most widely used product in the professions.

Spreadsheet software is designed for the preparation of tabular analyses of financial data, and is ideal for budgets, forecasting, and sensitivity analyses. In partnerships and LLPs, profit share allocations are often calculated on a spreadsheet. Spreadsheets are also often used to remedy the shortfalls in the content or presentation of reports produced by accounting software and are extensively used by accountants.

Increasingly important is the ability to transfer data involving tables of information to and from other packages used for accounting, word processing and presentations. Dynamic links permit data to be transferred and then to change automatically if the data in the linked software also changes. Other links are less sophisticated, and might just comprise a file transfer routine or an import/export process without any subsequent update.

Presentations

12.9 The need for slides or slide handouts at initial proposal meetings, or when presenting results to clients, is now well recognised. Many firms now use presentation software as their main report production tool, particularly where there is the need to combine words, tables and charts.

Presentation software is available which makes the preparation of quite sophisticated outputs a relatively straightforward task. A number of different templates are usually provided, with varying backgrounds, bullet-point styles and slide transition characteristics.

Simple uncluttered slides can often be a more powerful tool than slides that appear very 'busy'. This is a situation where good design sense is required.

Desktop publishing

12.10   Many firms use desktop publishing (DTP) software to produce good quality proposals, newsletters, and printer-ready copy. However, for other firms, word processing or presentation software is sufficient.

DTP packages often have features designed for two subtly different purposes. The first purpose focuses on the creative design of single sheet documents using large numbers of graphic images and fonts. The second purpose focuses on the production of multi-sheet documents, for example, for producing booklets. DTP software is particularly memory and processor intensive, and a higher specification machine is sometimes necessary. Even with the right tools, it is very easy to produce desktop published documents that have an adverse visual effect. To use DTP software effectively, you need to have a member of staff with a good design sense.

Electronic mail and voice communications

12.11   E-mail systems either permit messages within the office environment across an existing network, or across the public telephone network using one of several e-mail carrying services.

E-mail is now the main form of data communication, and is clearly advantageous in situations where there is no need to send a hard copy of a message. Some firms have developed electronic communication further by incorporating 'instant messaging' into their communication systems.

The cost of any required hardware and other required infrastructure should not be overlooked when introducing a locally hosted e-mail system. It requires disciplined administration to ensure that emails have been properly authorised before transmission, and incoming messages are not left unread. There will be a need for services and/or tools to filter out viruses and general spam.

Voice and data communications were previously viewed as completely discrete services but are now starting to share common equipment and lines. Firms are starting to review their telecommunications and information strategies in tandem, and to address such issues as how partners and staff can most efficiently be contacted when away from the office or in meetings.

PDAs and smartphones enable staff to receive and respond to e-mails and update calendars. The increasing prevalence of such devices enables staff to keep working and stay in contact with clients even when out of the office, and can help improve client service. However, a decision to use such devices is not just about selection of hardware with the appropriate functionality, but also selection of an appropriate service provider, since the tariffs, coverage, transmission times and inter-operability can vary.

Sophisticated voicemail systems automatically notify the recipient by email when a message has been received, alerting staff with out-of-office access to emails that a telephone call has been received in the office.

Document management

12.12 As the volume of document files increases on networks and other multi-user systems, it becomes harder to manage, control and retrieve files. Well-developed file management and file-naming conventions are required, no matter what size the firm. However, document management software exists which allows the user to develop a profile for each document. It uses information such as subjects and keywords, and then allows the document to be retrieved using these search criteria. Such software can often also be used for version control to monitor the history of document amendments, as well as identifying documents due for archiving. It may also help users identify reports, letters and opinions that have previously been prepared on similar subject matter and therefore save repetition of research work already performed.

Workgroup tools enable users to share and comment on each other's documents without necessarily updating the document itself. At a later stage, the document author can review the comments and decide what further changes are required. More sophisticated software provides work-flow functionality which forces a particular type of transaction through a set routine of sign-offs and events.

External databases

12.13 Professional firms are increasingly being offered access to data-bases of information maintained by third parties such as newspaper and book publishers, or more specialised sources. The number of these third party database information providers is growing. The advantage of these databases is that they enable firms to access and extract more information than could be maintained internally, and will usually be more up to date. Well-established services for particular professions include LexisNexis, which offers a legal information service for lawyers covering UK and European Union case law and a range of other statutory and non-statutory document sources. Company financial information is provided by services such as Reuters or Bloomberg, often with the choice of direct internet access, delivery of a CD that is updated regularly, or e-mail newsfeeds. Compact discs are used in professional firms as a more portable substitute for traditional reference books and manuals, enabling fast searches for material which contains specified keywords even when staff are away from their desk.

Internet, intranet and extranet

12.14 Most Internet users are connected to the Internet by modem from their own computer to an Internet gateway computer run by an Internet Service Provider (ISP). Most users now access the Internet through broadband, which is faster compared with the slower dial-up lines, but may be more expensive for low volume usage. Larger businesses may have direct access to the Internet, but will need to provide sufficient capacity for a number of remote Internet users to access the system (for instance, to visit the business website).

An 'intranet' is in effect a business-wide implementation of the Internet from which the public is excluded. Uses include sharing manuals and documents that are updated centrally (for instance telephone lists, staff handbooks), helpdesk questions and answers, and as a method for distributing software updates. Newer intranet tools have the 'look and feel' of a website, and have better search capabilities. Aside from the selection of an appropriate intranet tool, there is also the need to consider who has responsibility for ensuring that the content is relevant and kept up-to-date.

The term 'extranet' merely recognises that many businesses are opening up their intranets to suppliers, customers and other contacts. Uses can include providing customer support, project-working, or giving clients direct access to documents. Confidentiality is an important issue to be considered when implementing an extranet.

E-business

12.15 E-business, or e-commerce, is a term used to describe the use of the Internet to sell products or services. In theory, e-commerce should provide a global presence at a reasonably low cost. However, the difficulty for professional firms is identifying services that can sensibly be sold over the Internet.

The e-commerce market is generally split into two categories: the retail end where goods and services are being sold to consumers (B2C), and transactions between businesses (B2B). The future expected growth of e-commerce is enormous, even allowing for slower than expected take-off in certain sectors. Perceived difficulties previously included poor security and lack of privacy, as well as slow response times. Major increases in available bandwidth continue, which help resolve speed problems, and will also act as the spur to provide other new services. Security scares may occasionally hold back growth, although the increasing sophistication of firewall software and encryption tools will help mitigate some of these concerns.

Whilst some firms are now starting to offer online services, for example for wills and contracts, it is still too early to ascertain the long-term viability of these services and whether they offer a fundamental shift from the core tenet of most professional firms to offer direct access to the services of skilled staff.

As mobile phone technology has advanced, we are seeing them increasingly being used to perform e-commerce transactions.

Types of software

Packaged software

12.16 Most purchased software is based on an existing package written by a software house that is sold to any number of potential customers. There are several advantages with packaged software. It is normally cheaper than bespoke software (because of economies of scale) and takes less time to get up to speed. Usually, many of the programme 'bugs' will already have been identified and corrected. There should also be the opportunity to contact and/or visit existing users of the software to discover how well it works in other businesses. However, the principal disadvantage of packaged software is that the customer is using a product that has not been specifically written for his particular business. So he will have to accept that it will probably not meet all his firm's individual requirements.

Bespoke software

12.17 Software written specifically for a particular customer is known as bespoke software. Its advantage is that, if it performs as expected, it will fit the requirements of a particular business much more closely than packaged software. However, the risks of developing bespoke software are much greater than when buying package software. There is a danger that the costs will overrun, that the software will not be delivered on time, or that it will fail to satisfy the specified requirements.

The development of bespoke programmes will probably involve a much higher degree of managerial involvement and require close supervision. Legally watertight contracts on a fixed-cost basis are advisable, with penalties for failure to deliver software that satisfies the specified requirements within an agreed timescale.

Any significant bespoke programme is usually developed in two stages. The first stage involves the preparation of a functional specification detailing the features of the proposed new software, including screen and report content and layouts. An alternative approach involves the supplier developing a prototype of the software. The second stage involves the programming itself.

Bespoke programmes are sometimes combined with a package solution if software is already available that satisfies part of the overall requirement. Alternatively, if a package already exists that satisfies most but not all of the requirements, the packaged software may be modified. When bespoke or modified software is acquired, it is particularly important to review the adequacy of future support arrangements. This is because a buyer of customised software will be heavily dependent on the software provider, and it may not be possible to install future off-the-shelf supplier upgrades. It is also often difficult, if not impossible, to transfer support to another supplier at a later stage.

General purpose software

12.18   Software that is designed for use in a wide range of different business environments is often described as general purpose software. However, this terminology can be misleading since no software package is suitable for all businesses.

Accounting software

12.19   Some professional firms use the same general purpose accounting software as commonly sold to the corporate sector. In relation to the ledgers, the only differences between the requirements of the firm and a company might be the need to replace the share capital account with a number of partner capital and drawings accounts, and to perform separate calculations of the journals necessary to record profit sharing arrangements.

However, many firms find general purpose accounting software does not have suitable time recording or billing features for a professional firm. Often, the time recording function only appears as a relatively insignificant part of a wider-ranging job cost module typically designed for manufacturing organisations, and the timesheet entry screens are not designed to allow large amounts of data to be input with the minimum keystrokes. In addition, time summary reports sometimes provide an overall total for net unbilled work in progress, but do not show sufficient information for billing purposes about which staff time has been billed and which has not.

Professional firms are often more discerning about the presentation of fee notes to clients than a company raising invoices in a typical manufacturing or distribution environment. Therefore, the content and layout of invoices produced from standard company orientated packages may not be considered appropriate. The recording and recharge of disbursements by professional firms is another area which may not be adequately satisfied by standard general purpose software.

Vertical market software

12.20 Software written for a specific profession or business sector is usually described as 'vertical market' software. The advantage of such software is that it should be more suitable for the businesses at which it is targeted. For instance, software written for the legal profession will probably include client account features not found in other software. On the other hand, software developed for surveyors and estate agents will typically include a property management capability. In addition, software for architects normally contains project information analysed into RIBA work-stages.

As vertical market software is targeted at a smaller overall market, it tends to be more expensive than the equivalent general purpose package. In addition, suppliers are also likely to be more specialised and could be financially less stable.

Integrated software

12.21 A problem faced by many professional firms is that a great deal of financial and other data is kept in different places, by different partners and members of staff. In the recent past, it was not unusual for the firm to have separate systems for ledger accounting, work in progress, publication mailing, marketing and archiving. Fee earners often also have separate listings for their own clients and contacts.

Maintaining the same data on separate systems is inefficient. Perhaps the most common example of duplicated data in a professional practice will be client details. It is likely that a client's name, address, telephone number and so on, is held in several separate databases. When these details change, it is not unusual to discover, for example, that some correspondence continues to be sent to an old address because not all the separate databases have been updated. This can give an adverse impression of the firm's efficiency. Separate work in progress and ledger software is also common, and leads to duplication.

Integrated software is designed to reduce these problems by ensuring that data is only entered onto a system once, with the entry of an amendment in one part of the software automatically updating the other functions. Recent software has often been developed so that all information is stored in one central database. Specific applications then extract and analyse data as required and present it either on the screen or in a report. Typically, staff from across a firm might access this data, but with carefully controlled permissions regarding what different grades of staff can access, edit or delete. After the core database has been acquired, it is not unusual for other additional applications to be purchased as individual modules which, when installed, integrate with the system as a whole.

Voice recognition software

12.22   Many people are still relatively slow when using computer key-boards. In the past, there has been little alternative except to dictate tapes or handwrite text for subsequent word processing input by a secretary. Devices have been available for some time which attempt to recognise the human voice, and to directly convert speech into computer text. However, these devices were not initially very successful, since they required the operator to talk very slowly in 'dalek-like' speech, and the word conversion success rate was low. The technology is now much improved, and the use of voice recognition software is becoming more commonplace in the professions. Relatively high specification machines are required, but the time taken for a computer to properly recognise a particular human voice is reducing, although still not insignificant. For many people, this is starting to become a viable method for communicating with their computer.

Networks, mid-range computers and Windows™

Networks

12.23   A network is usually made up of a fileserver connected to a number of desktop or portable computer workstations and other peripheral devices, such as printers. If the fileserver is 'dedicated', it acts as a repository for the data which is to be shared by the workstation users, and controls access and requests for files. A 'non-dedicated' fileserver will also act as a workstation. However, such fileservers are only advisable on small, low usage networks.

Networks are often introduced to enable users of several personal comput-ers to share resources such as access to a central library of client documents, or devices such as laser printers, or access to communications facilities. They typically exist in the office environment where the software being used comprises mainly desktop tools such as word processing and spreadsheets. In such cases, the processing of data will occur on the workstation, with the data file only being transferred across the network from/to the fileserver when it is being retrieved or saved.

Mid-range computers and open systems

12.24   Mid-range computers were preceded by the minicomputer, which filled the gap between micro-computer and mainframe technologies. They were previously considered the alternative multi-screen configuration to the network, typically comprising a relatively large central computer accessed by users through connected to dumb terminals, with all the processing and data handling functions being performed centrally.

In the past, there were was a cost advantages when large numbers of users were connected, as dumb terminals were cheaper than PC workstations; however, the difference is no longer so great. The use of dumb terminals could also lead to considerable strain on the central computer when processor-intensive applications such as spreadsheets and word processors were being used. Nevertheless, the mid-range computer configuration may still be appropriate, for instance, where access is required to a large central database with many accounting applications.

In practice, the differences between configurations of networked and mid-range/minicomputer systems are no longer so clear-cut, since the dumb terminals connected to the minicomputer have often been replaced by personal computers. The end result is that users can often now get the best of both worlds.

Reference is often made to the term 'open systems'. Previously, every hardware manufacturer appeared to develop their own proprietary operating system, and software was rarely transferable.

In its broadest sense, this refers to an environment where software is portable between a range of different hardware platforms and where there are standards for transferring information between databases.

Microsoft Windows™

12.25   Windows has become the dominant PC operating environment, and much application software has now been rewritten to take advantage of features such as the Windows' graphical interface, drop-down menus and improved data transfer. Various versions of Windows have been launched, the most recent consumer versions being Windows XP in 2001, Windows Vista in 2007 (albeit the latter's re-designed shell and user interface was not universally acclaimed), and then Windows 7. Different versions of Windows are used for fileservers, although most businesses still use Windows Server 2003 or later server releases.

The need to upgrade an operating system is now often dictated by software providers who eventually withdraw support for their packages running on older versions of an operating system. While later versions of operating systems provide additional functionality, and will usually increase platform stability, they may not be suitable for businesses with an installed base of older computers, due to the higher minimum recommended hardware specification.

The selection process

Strategy

12.26 Developing a strategy is an essential first step when deciding on the future direction for information systems in a firm. Whilst the business managers may be aware of the more obvious shortcomings of an existing system, they often fail to appreciate the wider perspective when considering what information is required to plan and control the business.

An IT strategy should not be developed in isolation from the aims and objectives of the firm's overall business plan. The IT strategy needs to react to and anticipate future changes in the direction of the business and its structure. Traditionally, once the business objectives had been agreed, then decisions were made about the information that is required to enable the managers to achieve these objectives. However, for some businesses IT is now itself the driver for business change, and not just a provider of information. In these circumstances, the IT strategy and the business plan may effectively be the same document.

The firm then has to assess the adequacy of its existing computer systems, and decide how it gets to where it wants to be in the future. This may involve deciding between having a new system or upgrading an old one.

In future, it is likely that some firms may subscribe to Software as a Service (SaaS) and use online versions of products hosted by their suppliers which would previously have operated on in-house servers. However, such arrangements need careful management, and many professional firms are still cautious about the perceived loss of control over client data which such arrangements might entail.

It may also be a good idea to consider the firm's telecommunication requirements at the same time, particularly if the firm has more than one office. In smaller firms, the use of manual systems for certain functions may remain an option, but only if the volume of transactions is relatively low.

An objective cost benefit analysis of the different alternatives may be difficult to achieve. Costs are relatively easy to quantify, but the benefits are often harder to measure. Outside professional advice may be needed.

Specification

12.27 Once a firm has decided to acquire a new system and knows what it wants that system to do, then the next step is usually to prepare a specification. This will define in detail what is required from the new system. The specification often comprises a formal document called a 'Statement of Requirements'. This describes what is wanted in commercial terms and may contain very little technical computer terminology. The contents normally comprise the following:

(a) *Introduction*. This section puts the proposed new system in context, and will comprise a summary of the business background, organisational structure, the scope of the system, areas of special importance and a brief outline of the existing systems.

(b) *Commercial constraints*. This section emphasises the business environment in which the new system will operate. Any relevant hardware requirements are analysed, including reference to the number of screens at each location and the need for peripheral resources such as printers. Details of existing hardware should be provided if it is anticipated this will be incorporated into the new system. Any specific security and performance parameters should be highlighted, and it is helpful if the skills of the project management team and the eventual end users are summarised.

(c) *System requirements*. This is the most important part of the Statement of Requirements. It should detail the data that the new system ought to contain, as well as all relevant processing routines, and prioritise between 'must haves' and 'nice to haves'. The scope and content of required reports should also be analysed.

The primary aim of a Statement of Requirements is to communicate the firm's IT needs to potential suppliers in a clear, precise way. This approach should minimise misunderstandings and will be the yardstick against which potential solutions will be evaluated at a later stage. Ultimately, the Statement of Requirements will form an important part of the contract with the selected supplier.

Preparing the Statement of Requirements will involve meetings and discussions with all key departmental managers. As a result, this process often provides a useful focus for the firm when discussing and agreeing the requirements for the new system.

Supplier selection

12.28 Shortlisting suitable suppliers for tender is a vital part of the overall process. Knowledge of the business and the computer market must be applied, and the shortlist should be software- not hardware-driven.

Initially, the computer marketplace should be reviewed to assess the availability of suitable software packages, or those which provide the closest fit and which, if necessary, can be modified. After identifying likely software solutions, potential software suppliers can be shortlisted. A supplier who will try to understand your requirements, and not simply sell you a system irrespective of its suitability, will be needed. Suppliers should also demonstrate in-depth experience of the proposed product. Such an initial shortlisting exercise should ensure that time is not subsequently wasted at a later stage.

The Statement of Requirements now becomes part of an Invitation to Tender, which will also detail the proposed selection and implementation timetable, as well as the key contract terms and the tender response. The Invitation to Tender will usually be sent to at least three shortlisted suppliers, and often more, depending on the overall value of the system. However, it is not helpful to adopt a scatter-gun approach, since suppliers may decide that the cost/success ratio is too high and therefore may not be prepared to devote the required resources to preparing a detailed response.

The tenders returned by the suppliers must be thoroughly reviewed. The evaluation should check the supplier's response to each stated requirement, taking care to look for any omissions.

Supplier tender checklist

- Understanding of the business requirements

- Overall solution fit

- Quality of solution

- Initial costs

- Recurring costs

- Financial stability of supplier

- Quality of supplier staff and technical competence

- Quality of implementation and training services

- Quality of ongoing support

- Quality of documentation

- Proposed timetable

- Expansion potential and costs

- Risk areas.

Ideally, the tender evaluation process will identify two or possibly three suppliers who merit further examination. Demonstrations of any packaged

189

software should now be organised, and contact made with existing users to ascertain their opinions about the supplier. As soon as a decision is made in principle, then all outstanding matters should be confirmed in writing and contracts reviewed in detail.

Contracts

12.29 Suppliers invariably offer their standard terms and conditions in the first instance. Not surprisingly, these are usually biased in their favour and often omit elementary protection for the purchaser. It is, therefore, wise to review contract terms from both a legal and a commercial viewpoint, particularly if a relatively high value is involved or if there is a significant degree of risk, such as with bespoke programmes.

Most supplier contracts are negotiable. For instance, the standard contract often specifies that final payment is due on delivery. This could cause problems as the purchaser will not, at that stage, have had the opportunity to test whether the system meets his stated requirements. It is quite normal for a retention to be negotiated, and for the final payment to be made when acceptance testing has confirmed that the system is working properly.

The contract should normally include a fixed cost for the supply of the deliverables, including services such as implementation, training and support. Suitable warranties, performance guarantees and a delivery timetable should be specified. The purchase contract should also specify the nature and cost of ongoing computer support, including any likely future price increases. It may also be appropriate to include an escrow agreement within the contract to ensure the source code of any software is available in the event that the supplier ceases trading, particularly if bespoke software is being bought.

If a completely new system (including both hardware and software) is being acquired, then there are often significant advantages in obtaining all parts of the system from one source under a 'turnkey' contract. This ensures that one supplier has sole responsibility for ensuring that all elements of the system work properly. It also means that a failure to supply one part of the overall system in accordance with the terms of the contract can result in the supplier having to pay the purchaser compensation based on the whole value of the system. This makes it much harder for a supplier to agree to pay compensation for one unsatisfactory element of the system (eg any software that fails to perform in accordance with the contract) while insisting that the customer hangs on to other parts of the system (eg the hardware) which do meet the contractual terms.

It may be appropriate for a lawyer to review the contract(s) if there is any chance that the matter may end up in the courts. To minimise legal costs, always ensure that the lawyer has previous experience with reviewing computer contracts.

Selecting smaller systems

12.30   Performing all the recommended selection procedures can be a time-consuming process. If the value of the system is relatively low, and only standard package software is being supplied, then it may not be appropriate to perform all these procedures in detail.

However, it will probably still be necessary to consider the principles underlying each procedure and how best to mitigate the risk of the wrong system being selected. For instance, whilst it may be inappropriate to prepare a complete Statement of Requirements detailing every part of the new system, the key areas and issues can be addressed in an extended letter to potential suppliers.

An alternative 'Request for Information' approach has been sponsored by the Business and Accounting Software Developers Association (BASDA). This essentially involves a streamlined selection process which is less time consuming but arguably also provides less assurance for the purchaser as compared with the traditional Invitation to Tender approach. More information can be obtained on the BASDA Help Line (tel 01494 868030; www.basda.org).

Sources of information

12.31   Whilst business managers may understand the principles of how to select a new system, they may nevertheless be unsure of the best way of obtaining information about the systems that are available.

(a)   *Directories.* There are several comprehensive computer and software listings available electronically on the Internet which detail the majority of the leading systems available in the United Kingdom. These are usually indexed by business sector, and are often a useful way of ascertaining quickly the names of relevant packages and suppliers for a particular profession. Due to space constraints, these directories inevitably only contain very cursory information but this should be sufficient to enable a firm to draw up a list of suppliers who merit a visit to their website or a telephone call to ascertain further details.

(b)   *Professional bodies.* Various professional bodies and trade associations have staff who deal with queries from their members about systems for their business sector, and these can be a useful point of initial contact. Many of the institutes, including the Institute of Chartered

Accountants in England and Wales (www.icaew.co.uk) and the Law Society (www.lawsociety.org.uk), give their members access to comprehensive software databases and reports about software written for a particular profession. Informal contact through regional or district societies can also be a useful way of ascertaining from like-minded professionals the names of suppliers worth considering and those best avoided.

(c) *Consultants*. Many business managers have neither the time, inclination nor confidence to select a suitable system. In these circumstances, they may look for third party assistance from a consultancy. However, although good consultancy advice can reduce the risk of a mistaken decision, it cannot guarantee that the right decision will be made. There are large numbers of consultants prepared to offer advice, but the quality varies and they are rarely cheap. Preliminary vetting will be required to ensure that the chosen consultants have experience in the relevant business sector and have a track record of satisfying their clients. Some assurance can be obtained if the consultants are themselves members of a professional body such as the Institute of Business Consulting (tel: 020 7497 0580; www.ibconsulting.org.uk). Always consider taking references from former clients and ensure that the scope and cost of the consultancy assistance are detailed in a letter of engagement.

Implementation

12.32 Selecting the right system is important. However, much can still go wrong if the implementation of the new system is not properly planned and controlled. There are a wide number of issues to consider, often within a very short timescale.

(a) *Personnel*. The selection and introduction of a new system will often impact on departments and their staff, right across the firm. An overall project manager should be appointed who is prepared to encourage constructive comments and to listen to a wide range of opinions, but who is also prepared to take responsibility and make decisions. Within a partnership, this position would normally be held by a partner or a senior manager. Each individual's responsibilities during the implementation phase should be clearly defined. Proper training is essential for the success of a new system, and a suitable training programme will be required for each affected member of staff. Any changes in job specification will require agreement with the staff concerned. Specific responsibilities will require allocation. For instance, a new network may require a network supervisor, whilst the task of controlling and monitoring a database may be devolved to a database administrator. A help desk may be required to deal with the inevitable volume of queries that will arise during the implementation of a new system.

(b) *Site*. Most computer systems now operate in a normal office environment, so there is less need these days for a separate computer room purely to ensure that proper temperature and air conditions are maintained. However, security issues may dictate that the computer is sited in a separate unit away from the main office. A clean power supply may be required. The introduction of a new system often involves comprehensive re-cabling of an office. It is usually preferable for cabling to be the responsibility of the new supplier, but sometimes a third party contractor is involved. This requires planning to ensure that there is the minimum disturbance, and that the cabling is installed and fully tested prior to the computer system being delivered.

(c) *Media*. The new system may require the redesign of pre-printed computer stationery such as fee notes, and liaison may be needed with a printer to ensure that the stationery is available when required. Other computer stationery such as tapes, disks, toner and ribbons may be required.

Security

12.33 Computer data is often one of the most valuable assets in a professional practice, and therefore proper procedures and controls are required to ensure its security. The importance of proper security over personal data is given statutory backing in the *Data Protection Act 1998*.

The need to raise internal awareness about good security has led many firms to distribute a document detailing procedures to be followed by partners and staff. This typically deals with the following issues:

(a) *Physical security*. The best form of security involves controlling access to buildings where computers are used. This may be through the use of staff monitoring every entry point to the building or by some form of electronic access control system. Access to a computer room containing important minicomputer or mainframe installations may also be controlled by physical security. The firm may insist that its staff lock away any portable computers that are not in use.

(b) *Passwords*. Good security measures often include the use of passwords to control access to programmes or individual data files. Passwords are particularly important where access can be obtained to a computer system from remote sites via a modem. Staff must be encouraged to keep passwords confidential, but at the same time the password must be obtainable if for some reason the individual cannot be contacted.

(c) *Viruses.* These are software programs designed to corrupt or destroy programs and data. Sometimes, the effects of a virus are immediately noticeable, or they may involve a more gradual and insidious process. They are usually transmitted on a USB data stick or via a modem. All computers are vulnerable to viruses, and special care must be taken when programs or data are received from outside computer systems. Games software is a notoriously high risk area for viruses. It is strongly recommended that every organisation with valuable data acquires software which can both detect and destroy at least the most common viruses. Connection to the Internet is another way that viruses can be transferred, for instance through the use of e-mail attachments, and can also enable unauthorised hackers to access a firm's computer systems. Firewall software is available which, when properly configured, helps minimise these risks, together with software designed to filter out unsolicited emails (spam).

(d) *Backup.* All media (whether documents, tapes or disks) which contain sensitive information must be controlled and physically protected. Computer magnetic media is particularly vulnerable to unintentional corruption. Users maintaining data on a hard disk or on just one USB disc must be encouraged to take a security copy on a regular basis, and to systematically rotate the backup disks or tapes.

(e) *Encryption.* The extensive use of laptop computers and other data devices such as USB sticks increases the risk that confidential data falls into the wrong hands if a loss or theft occurs. Many firms now make use of software tools to encrypt data held on such devices.

(f) *Disaster recovery.* Terrorism in the City of London and New York have emphasised the importance of fallback systems if access to an office is denied for whatever reason. Many firms now understand the importance of documenting procedures to minimise the effects of such a situation arising. Copies of vital data should be transmitted directly to a separate site, or alternatively disks and tapes should be taken off-site on a regular basis, and key personnel should know their tasks and responsibilities in the event that the fallback systems have to be used.

Various standards exist to assist the integration of technical, clerical, and managerial controls into one co-ordinated approach to information security, the most common of which is ISO/IEC 27001. Compliance with such standards may appear onerous, particularly for smaller firms, but can sometimes be a requirement when transacting or processing data for larger institutions or the public sector.

Data protection legislation

12.34 The *Data Protection Act 1984* introduced the requirement for most information about living individuals held on computer to be registered with the Information Commissioner (formerly the Data Protection Registrar), even if it only comprised a name and address. Registration also became necessary if data about individuals is processed by a third party, such as a computer bureau. Failure to register, or to re-register every three years, could lead to a prosecution by the Information Commissioner against a firm, followed by imposition of a severe fine.

There was previously no requirement to register manual records, eg a card index. However, the provisions of the EU Data Protection Directive have now been enacted in the United Kingdom, and the *Data Protection Act 1998* extended the scope of legislation to include certain manual records. Whilst there are some exemptions, many businesses consider it safer to prepare a catch-all registration rather than risk penalties for non-compliance.

The *Data Protection Act 1998* also specifies eight required principles of good practice. These refer to the need to collect and process data fairly and lawfully, and to ensure the data is accurate, relevant, protected by proper security and only disclosed to people described in the register entry.

The Act also gives rights to individuals about whom the information is recorded. They are entitled to see the information, challenge it, and have it corrected or erased if appropriate.

It is common for the person responsible for financial matters to also take overall responsibility for such tasks as ensuring that the *Data Protection Act 1998* registration is kept up to date. The Information Commissioner's Office can be contacted at Wycliffe House, Water Lane, Wilmslow, Cheshire, SK9 5AF (enquiry helpline 0303 123 1113; www.ico.gov.uk).

'Green' IT

12.35 IT is often seen as a significant element in a firm's carbon emissions. A common situation includes the use of servers for dedicated applications that are idle for much of the day. By using a technique known as 'virtualisation', multiple virtual servers can be combined into one physical server. Another way of reducing the need for servers is to outsource certain activities. 'Cloud computing' is an extension of the virtualisation concept, where the applications may run as an external service at a supplier.

Printers and related consumables are another common example of waste within the office environment. Some firms have introduced team or department printers to avoid waste.

Use of technology can, however, be a tool for reducing an organisation's overall carbon footprint. For instance, electronic transmission of documents such as fee notes and statements reduces printing and courier costs, and the use of tools which can transfer data between applications should reduce transcription errors and the associated costs.

Transport costs are a major contributor to the carbon footprint for many firms, but better use of video and tele-conferences can cut the need for superfluous travel to meetings. Similarly, webinars are becoming an increasingly popular method for delivering training.

Chapter 13 Human Resources Management

Introduction

13.1 Managing, improving and sustaining the performance of professional staff is a key issue for professional practices. Quality professional people are expensive and sometimes scarce. When highly motivated and effectively managed, they are the most important resource a firm has at its disposal and are the key to its success. This success is most likely to be achieved if a firm's human resource policies and procedures are based upon, and make a significant contribution to, the achievement of its corporate objectives and strategic plans.

Effective human resources management ensures that the way in which people are recruited, managed and motivated acts as a direct support to the business's strategic and operational objectives, both in the short and the long term.

To do this effectively, a firm needs to put in place sound policies, procedures and practices across some fundamental areas of people management. This chapter addresses each of these areas in turn, starting with recruitment, and moving on to look at retention, reward and development.

Recruitment

Determining staffing needs

13.2 Professional practices need to establish the levels of staffing they require to achieve the goals set out in their business plans. This process has two stages:

(a) determining how many people are needed, of what type, qualification, seniority and experience, to meet the business objectives; and

(b) analysing the skills and competencies which already exist within the firm and how they might be used most effectively.

The output from this process will be a clear picture of the overall staffing requirements, both for now and the future, and an identification of where gaps exist or may exist, ie where it may be necessary to recruit.

Recruitment steps

13.3 Recruitment is an expensive process, both in terms of money and time, so preparation is essential. A clear job description and person specification can make the whole process far more straightforward by clearly defining what is needed. Most firms establish a recruitment authorisation process to make sure that recruitment is controlled, and that employment costs are monitored and managed effectively.

Discrimination law applies equally to recruitment as it does to the treatment of existing employees, so do ensure that anyone involved in recruitment has appropriate training in interviewing, selection and avoiding discrimination in recruitment decisions. Discrimination on the grounds of race, sex, marital status, ethnic origin, age, disability, sexual orientation or religious belief is illegal.

Job description

13.4 A job description defines the job and its context. It should always include:

(a) the job title;

(b) basic organisation and reporting lines;

(c) statement of the overall purpose of the job;

(d) list of key responsibilities and tasks;

(e) decision-making authorities;

(f) information reflecting the size of the job (eg budgets, turnover, profits, number of staff, geography);

(g) key contacts; and

(h) any special requirements (eg significant travel or antisocial hours).

It helps to use a standard format for all job descriptions so that there is consistency across the firm.

Person specification

13.5 A person specification works alongside the job description. If the job description describes the job, then the person specification gives details of the attributes required in the job holder.

The information contained in a person specification would typically include:

(i) skills/expertise;

(ii) qualifications;

(iii)   previous training;

(iv)   experience (describe the type of experience rather than simply a number of years); and

(v)   personal attributes.

Together, the job description and person specification should provide a good picture of the job and the person required to do the job. You may also choose to include information on the firm and role priorities for the first year of the job, so that candidates understand how their performance will be judged and the context of the appointment. This information should be provided to candidates and to any agent who helps with the recruitment process.

Finding suitable candidates

13.6   When seeking to fill a particular vacancy, a number of potential sources exist. The most widely used methods include:

(a)   internal candidates;

(b)   advertising;

(c)   recruitment consultants;

(d)   executive search consultants; and

(e)   internet advertising.

Internal candidates

13.7   It is possible that the ideal candidate for a vacancy already works for the firm. However, it is prudent to check that this is indeed the case. Internal candidates' qualifications and experience should be compared with the job description and person specification. This will either confirm their suitability or demonstrate the value of attracting a wider range of candidates for comparison.

Advertising

13.8   There are specialist recruitment advertising agencies who can design, set and place recruitment advertisements on your behalf. Alternatively, a firm may decide to place advertisements directly with the relevant publication. Recruitment advertising should be seen as a way of enhancing the image of the firm, as well as attracting applicants for the particular vacancy. Bear in mind that a poorly drafted advertisement could lead to too many unsuitable applicants or too few of those you actually want to reach.

(a) The design of a job advertisement should create:

    (i) attention – the design should draw the eye and be easy to read;

    (ii) interest – by stating clearly the best points of the job;

    (iii) action – encouraging suitable applicants to apply or ask for further information.

(b) The advertisement will usually include:

    (i) a summary of your firm and the nature of the job;

    (ii) the qualifications/experience required;

    (iii) location and any special requirements;

    (iv) remuneration package;

    (v) closing date for response; and

    (vi) your firm's website address, so candidates can gather background information.

(c) The advertisement should also detail how potential candidates should respond, eg:

    (i) full CV;

    (ii) request for an application form and/or further information;

    (iii) letter of application;

    (iv) e-mail application attaching a CV;

    (v) online application.

Recruitment consultants

13.9 Using a recruitment consultant can reduce the time taken to find suitable applicants, particularly where there is intense competition for a limited pool of specialist or experienced staff. However, the quality of recruitment agencies varies tremendously, so it is vital that time is spent establishing which agency or agencies to use.

(a) As a starting point, consider consultants that you have used in the past, and who have given good service and know your sector.

(b) Obtain recommendations from other firms.

(c) Identify those selection consultancies which have particular experience in your sector.

(d) Ensure that you meet the consultant who is actually going to perform the assignment, and make sure that they understand your firm and the image you wish to present to candidates.

(e) Once a recruitment consultant has been selected, confirm the terms of the appointment in writing. This includes timescales, arrangements for advertising and the basis on which the candidate shortlist will be compiled.

(f) Establish the basis on which fees and expenses will be charged, and what will happen if the candidate leaves rapidly or proves unsuitable after appointment.

(g) Use the consultant's experience and expertise in drawing up the job description, person specification and level and content of the remuneration package.

(h) Obtain written confirmation of the terms of reference for the assignment.

(i) Be prepared to initiate a conversation to negotiate on fees.

Executive search consultants

13.10 Commonly known as headhunters, this type of consultant approaches candidates directly. They are of most value when there are only a limited number of potential candidates. However, headhunters should be used with care, as their fees are high and results cannot be guaranteed. The basis on which headhunters should be selected is the same as for recruitment consultants (see **13.9** above). Taking up references for executive search consultants is particularly important, as it is vital that they have a successful track record of finding good candidates in your sector.

Recruitment/selection procedures

13.11 All those involved in the recruitment process need training to make sure that they understand the process and that they are aware of the many legal obligations on them as they represent the firm, especially in terms of avoiding discrimination in the recruitment process. Every selection decision involves the firm in a significant financial commitment, so those involved must be competent and confident in their ability to make objective, fair and successful decisions. Information on selection decisions should be written down, as candidates have a legal right to see interview notes and details of how the selection decision was made. Using a common format for interview notes and for recording selection decisions will make it easier for the firm to show that it has followed a fair process.

Some firms use tests or exercises as part of the recruitment process. If this is the case for your firm, make sure that the tests confine themselves to skills, knowledge or experience that are directly relevant to the job in question, and always be prepared to give candidates feedback on their test results.

Interviews should be structured to make sure that each candidate is given the same opportunity to present themselves and their suitability for the job in question. The following points are key areas to consider when planning interview questions:

(a) *Attainments*. Educational, technical and professional.

(b) *Special aptitudes*. Particular skills/competencies required for the job.

(c) *Interests*. Particular interests outside the work field which may be of value. It is important to avoid questions of a personal nature that could suggest that the interviewer is discriminating on grounds that are not directly related to the requirements of the job.

(d) *Interpersonal skills*. The skills the job holder will need to work with colleagues, clients and contacts.

(e) *Circumstances*. What, in terms of personal circumstances, the job will demand.

It is often the case that better recruitment decisions are made when more than one person is involved in interviewing and selecting the right candidate. Joint interviews, or several one-to-one interviews that allow the candidate to meet several members of the firm, can be a helpful way to give the firm more than one point of view on each candidate, and to allow each candidate to get a better perspective on the firm as a whole.

Once a selection decision has been made, it is important the candidate receives full details of the offer in writing, together with details of any provisos that may affect their employment. For example, it is sensible to make an employment offer subject to the receipt of satisfactory references, evidence of the right to work in the UK, and evidence of qualifications.

Retention and reward

13.12   The recruitment process involves attracting the right people to your firm, and retention and reward processes address the important aspects of keeping and motivating those people.

This section looks at four areas:

(a)   performance management;

(b)   reward management;

(c)   policies and procedures; and

(d)   internal communication.

Performance management

13.13   The aim of a performance management system is not simply to maintain levels of performance, but to support their continuing improvement. Performance management is concerned with:

(a)   setting performance objectives;

(b)   measuring their achievement; and

(c)   rewarding the achievement of objectives.

Criteria for setting objectives

13.14   The criteria for setting objectives usually include some or all of the following:

(a)   billable hours worked;

(b)   hours billed;

(c)   effective hourly rate for business generation;

(d)   client responsibility;

(e)   non-billable hours, such as:

    (i)   firm management,

    (ii)   client development, and

    (iii)   professional activities;

(f)   delegation and effective utilisation of other staff;

(g)   billing efficiency and debtor collection;

(h)   length of time spent with the firm;

(i)   reputation; and

(j)   quality of work.

The criteria may also include a number of fairly broad categories, eg:

(a)   cooperation with other fee earners;

(b)   leadership ability;

(c)   dedication and efficiency;

(d)   training;

(e)   client management;

(f)   business development; and

(g)   historical contribution.

Reward management

13.15   Reward management focuses on the design, implementation and management of remuneration systems that support the achievement of the firm's business objectives. In order to do this, the systems must ensure that pay levels for fee earners and support staff are competitive and fair. They must also ensure that reward is linked to contribution and performance.

A reward system must have three qualities.

(a)   *It must be competitive.* High calibre people are scarce, even in difficult economic times. They are also fully aware of their value to the practice and expect to be rewarded accordingly. To attract and retain them, it is often necessary to match current market rates. Information on market rates can be gathered from a variety of sources including: job advertisements; remuneration consultants; published surveys; 'salary club' surveys; and bespoke surveys. It will usually be necessary to use a combination of these sources to discover the range of salaries/remuneration packages for a particular job. Having discovered the right salary range, a firm can then decide how much it wants to pay within those limits.

(b)   *It must be fair and be regarded by fee earners and support staff as fair.* If it is perceived to be unfair, it will demotivate staff and could lead to expensive discrimination claims. Often, staff dissatisfaction with salaries is not based on their actual salary level, but on their view of how they compare to others in the organisation.

(c)   *It must be able to provide rewards which are directly linked to levels of performance.* The design of performance-related pay systems takes much thought, as it is vital to measure aspects of performance that have most impact on overall results, rather than simply those that are easy to measure.

Reward structures

PROFIT SHARES

13.16   This is the subject of considerable debate and can sometimes cause animosity and upheaval in a professional practice. However, these feelings are seldom due solely to the fact that some fee earners believe they are being inadequately rewarded compared with others in the firm. Partners or directors who are unhappy about remuneration levels may also feel that there are problems in the systems used to determine their profit reward, or that the firm as a whole is not generating a satisfactory level of income. It is important that remuneration is considered as a whole, so that the right balance can be achieved between salary, profit, merit awards, bonuses and the like, in the light of each fee earner's contribution to the firm.

Systems used to reward partners or directors often seem to bear little relationship to the stage of the firm's development, except in a very broad sense. Younger and smaller firms tend towards the more straightforward systems, although there are also a number of larger firms which take this approach. The key lesson is that a firm must design and implement the reward system which is most beneficial to its own particular circumstances.

However, remuneration systems must be considered from a positive and constructive standpoint. The firm should look beyond the difficulties that may be encountered when changing existing arrangements, and persevere to achieve the longer-term improvements that can be anticipated for the future. The new system may bring benefits to the firm which may outweigh the practical difficulties of implementing change. It is worthwhile to give consideration to interim arrangements during such a change process, particularly where some individuals are more severely affected than others.

Detailed consideration is given to profit sharing in CHAPTER 8.

PROFESSIONAL FEE EARNING STAFF

13.17   An effective performance related reward scheme for professional staff should:

(a)   be part of total remuneration and be used to motivate and reward excellent performance;

(b)   be based on performance targets that reflect the firm's business objectives;

(c)   be based on both quantitative and qualitative performance measures that are non-discriminatory;

(d)   produce rewards at a sufficient level to motivate over the defined period;

(e)   be affordable and beneficial to the practice as a whole; and

(f)   be simple to communicate, administer and manage.

SCHEME DESIGN

13.18   The feasibility of including a performance related element in professional staff's remuneration package will depend on whether satisfactory responses can be obtained to the following questions:

(a)   Who is to be included in the scheme?

(b)   What are the most appropriate performance measures?

(c)   What standards of achievement are required for each measure?

(d)   To what extent will the measures be particular to each member of the scheme?

(e)   What is the scale of reward for achievement?

(f)   What types of reward will be used?

(g)   How will the scheme be communicated?

(h)   How will the scheme be managed, maintained and reviewed?

(i)   How can we assess the impact of the scheme on the firm's overall performance?

PROFIT RELATED PAY

13.19   At one stage, profit related pay (PRP) became a common feature of many remuneration packages, and professional practices of all sizes were quick to take advantage of the tax benefits available under these schemes. Whilst the tax-effective nature of these schemes has now been removed, some employers have continued with the schemes, as they enable reward to be linked to the firm's financial performance. This allows staff at all levels to share in the profitability of the firm they work for.

FLEXIBLE BENEFITS

13.20   With the phasing out of tax-free PRP, a number of firms have turned towards flexible benefit schemes as a way of attracting and retaining staff.

Flexible benefit schemes allow employees to choose the benefits they want from a range of choices so that the benefits they receive more closely match their individual needs. Schemes are tailored to each individual company and, as the purchasing power of organisations can often exceed that of the individual, firms can offer access to benefits such as healthcare, dental cover and critical illness cover at lower rates than the individual could achieve by going to the providers direct.

Other popular options are allowing staff to 'buy' extra holiday or 'sell' holiday in excess of the statutory minimum which they do not wish to utilise.

The use of software packages to administer flexible benefits allows for 'self service' facilities, so that staff can choose and review their own benefits, as well as reducing the administrative burden.

Policies and procedures

13.21   Over the last few years, there has been a steady increase in the volume of employment legislation in all areas of employment. Firms need to be aware of this legislation, to understand the impact of these developments and how they will be implemented in practice.

In addition, firms need to consider the impact of many significant decisions made by the courts and employment tribunals.

Whilst this chapter is not intended to provide a guide to employment legislation, it is important for firms to ensure that they comply with their responsibilities as employers, including:

(a)   issuing contracts and terms and conditions of employment information to all staff;

(b)   making sure that staff can exercise their statutory rights as employees – for example, rights to holiday, maternity leave and pay, right to request flexible working;

(c)   complying with the ACAS code of practice in terms of disputes, including disciplinary and grievance issues;

(d)   acting fairly and reasonably in connection with any form of dismissal or termination of employment; and

(e)   avoiding discrimination in the recruitment, employment, promotion and development of staff.

Finally, firms will need to ensure that they comply with legislation in respect of pensions, a subject dealt with in detail in CHAPTER 27, RETIRE-MENT PLANNING.

This area of law is evolving rapidly, and firms are strongly advised to seek specialist advice with regard to employment-related issues.

Internal communication and employee engagement

13.22   There are considerable day-to-day pressures at work in most professional practices, and it can be difficult for the partners or directors to find time to communicate effectively with their staff. However, the ability of a firm to keep its staff actively engaged and motivated in the work of the firm is an important part of achieving ongoing business success.

Whatever the size of the firm, communication with staff should be given regular thought, and the decisions of the partners or directors communicated in a positive and constructive way. This could include:

(a) team or department meetings on a regular basis;

(b) briefing meetings for all staff to update them on strategic goals, business objectives and yearly targets;

(c) firm newsletters or updates;

(d) sharing examples of client wins, successes and projects;

(e) recognition of outstanding performance by individuals or teams;

(f) information on what is happening in the professional services market;

(g) where possible, IT discussion boards or intranets, which can provide a useful forum for staff information; and

(h) staff surveys and the results of such surveys.

Most staff appreciate information on the goals, performance and activities of the firm that they work for, and respond well when given the chance to give their own feedback and comments to partners or directors.

Training and development

13.23 As with other human resource systems, the provision of cost-effective training and development activities is dependent upon a structured approach. To be effective, all development activity needs to be designed specifically to support the achievement of the firm's business goals.

A structured approach

13.24 Effective training is often described as a 'training cycle' of four stages. This involves:

(a) identifying training needs;

(b) planning the appropriate training activities;

(c) implementing the training; and

(d) evaluating the results.

Identifying training needs

13.25   A number of approaches exist for identifying training needs. The most effective approach looks at the overall picture in terms of the firm's business objectives, both short and long term, and what changes or additions to the skills, knowledge and qualifications of the workforce will be needed to achieve these objectives. This will normally produce some overall themes of training activity for the year. This should be accompanied by a review of each individual's job requirements and aspirations, often done as part of the appraisal process. Together, these two reviews will provide a good baseline for training planning and activity.

Analysis of job/role requirements

13.26   This involves identifying:

(a)   the job's component parts;

(b)   the tasks the job holder has to perform; and

(c)   the key responsibilities at each stage.

An analysis of job/role requirements ensures that training directly supports the achievement of the firm's business objectives. It also avoids providing training that might be generally useful but which has little or, at best, minimal impact on the job holder's performance. In most firms, there is scope for job roles to grow and develop over time, and effective training can support job holders as they expand their own skills and abilities.

Planning training activities and choosing training providers

13.27   It is vital that training activities achieve measurable results in a cost-effective manner. It is also essential that training disrupts the job as little as possible and that it equips those being trained with practical and versatile tools which will enhance job performance as much as possible. Planning training must take into account the work patterns and priorities of potential delegates and their departments, which often means flexibility in terms of training time, course structure, and how follow-up activities take place.

A good training provider will be able to appreciate these points and design training that fits around your firm's specific needs and operating requirements. Do choose training providers who have experience in your sector and can demonstrate that their training delivery style fits well with your staff. It is essential to see a trainer 'in action' before you choose to use them, either by asking them to deliver a short pilot workshop or by observing them training in another organisation. Always ask for recent references from organisations similar to your own, and ask about the outcomes of training as well as content and training style.

Before training starts, the training provider and the training sponsor should take time to agree the expected outputs and results that the training should achieve. Wherever possible, these should be tangible, so that agreement can be reached on whether or not these results have been achieved. If feedback will be subjective, a 'before' and after' assessment of views will give a baseline for assessing the impact of training.

Training and development activities

13.28   While most people still associate training with the provision of formal courses, a wide number of other options exist. Choosing the right approach obviously depends on the type of training to be provided, as well as the intended audience. Options include:

(a)   *Off-the-job programmes.* Group activities such as courses, workshops, group exercises and business simulations that take place away from the working environment.

(b)   *Presentations.* Information-delivering activities that can take place internally or externally. They include events such as seminars, lectures, conferences and meetings.

(c)   *Career planning.* Planned career development activities, including job rotation and secondment.

(d)   *Personal initiative.* Activities that individuals can initiate for themselves, such as distance learning, open learning and interactive video programmes.

(e)   *Coaching and mentoring.* Coaching and/or general guidance from a senior individual from within the organisation and who is not normally the person's direct line manager.

(f)   *Secondments.* Periods of time spent in other areas of the organisation or with other organisations (eg suppliers, partners, clients). This can include CSR activities that add value to the community within which your firm operates.

Evaluation

13.29   It is essential to evaluate the effectiveness of training and development activities. This will involve more than simply getting participants to complete the usual end-of-course assessment form. Although these forms will tell you about a participant's reactions to the actual training event, they cannot tell you whether the training will have a significant impact on job performance.

To know that, you have to look at how well an individual does their work after training has taken place. This is most easily done through the annual appraisal process, although it is advisable to review the performance of staff who have recently received training within two to six months of their having completed the course. This should ensure that training is producing demonstrable results and making a real impact on staff performance. Managers have an important part to play in encouraging staff to implement what they have learned when they return to the workplace.

Accreditation of your HR approach

13.30   There are a variety of accreditation schemes available that assess and accredit the quality of the HR approach in organisations. For example, Investors in People, ISO standards, Lexcel, Charter Marks and the Best Companies To Work For awards all provide a methodology to assess your firm against nationally recognised good practice. Before making a commitment to undertake any of these accreditation processes, decide whether you wish to gain recognition for existing good practice or use a set of standards to help your firm develop its people practices in a systematic way.

Speaking to other firms who have successfully completed an accreditation process will give you an accurate picture of the work involved, the level of commitment needed to work through the accreditation stages and the costs incurred.

The decision to undertake an external accreditation also provides an opportunity to build an internal project team to co-ordinate the process. Whilst senior level sponsorship and representation is vital, this type of corporate project work gives scope to provide development for 'rising stars' to help them appreciate the wider context in which the firm operates, and to build cross-departmental understanding.

Chapter 14 Accounting

Introduction

14.1 This chapter examines the requirements of a partnership and a limited liability partnership (LLP) in preparing annual accounts, and their relationships with accountants or auditors.

Partnerships

14.2 Under *s 28* of the *Partnership Act 1890*, 'Partners are bound to render true accounts and full information of all things affecting the partnership to any partner or his legal representatives'.

In addition to the legal requirements to maintain accounts, case law has developed further obligations on partners to maintain accounts. It is the duty of continuing or surviving partners to maintain accounts of the partnership so that it is possible to show the financial position at each date and the ownership of the partnership. Recognising in practice that some firms are less organised than is desirable, for example, where accounting records have not been maintained, or are so poorly maintained as to be unintelligible or have been destroyed or wrongfully withheld, subject to the direction of the court, those partners responsible for such a situation will be considered at fault. Where all the partners are at fault, this rule cannot be applied (*Walmsley v Walmsley* (1846) 3 Jo & Lat 556).

With regard to the right of inspection, *s 24(9)* of the *Partnership Act 1890* states that 'partnership books are to be kept at the place of business of the partnership (or the principal place if there is more than one), and every partner may, when he thinks fit, have access to and inspect and copy any of them'.

Whilst a partner cannot restrict access by his colleagues to the accounting records by keeping matters of a private nature within them, it is open to a partner himself to agree not to inspect the partnership's accounting records and to accept accounts prepared on his behalf (*Freeman v Fairlee* (1812) 3 Mer 29).

It is acceptable for a partner to engage an agent on his behalf to inspect the books and records of the firm, provided the agent is a person to whom no reasonable objection can be taken by the other partners (*Bevan v Webb* [1901] 2 Ch 59). As would be considered fair and just, access may be denied if the use of an agent is not reasonably required or the inspection is sought for an improper purpose. Naturally, the improper use of information so obtained is unlawful.

As mentioned in **CHAPTER 5**, the partnership agreement should include a clause on annual accounts. This clause should include reference to the date to which the annual accounts will be prepared, the scope of any third party examination and the scope of the information which should be included in the accounts. It should also make clear that, before the accounts are binding on the partners as between themselves, they have to be signed by all of the partners, unless there are provisions in the partnership agreement for approval by the majority and signing by a specific number of partner(s) on behalf of all.

The annual accounts will show how the partners stand as regards outsiders and as regards each other, and will also be required for tax purposes, whilst the underlying accounting records should be maintained to such a standard that they disclose with reasonable accuracy at any time the financial position of the partnership.

Partnership property

14.3 Unlike an LLP, a partnership is not a separate legal entity and therefore it is open to the partners to agree between themselves what assets are to be treated as partnership property. *Sections 20* and *21* of the *Partnership Act 1890* (see **APPENDIX 1**) provide a statutory framework which is helpful in considering what is and what is not partnership property when the appropriate treatment is ambiguous. However, where specific agreement exists, whether express or implied, that agreement will prevail over statute.

In the absence of an express agreement, the sections of the *Partnership Act 1890* referred to above highlight the important factors to consider. These are:

(a) the circumstances of the acquisition, in particular the source from which it was financed;

(b) the intention of the acquisition; and

(c) the manner in which the property has subsequently been dealt with.

By agreement between the partners, they may change the ownership of property, from partnership property to the separate property of a specified partner or partners, or vice versa.

Information in the partnership accounts

14.4   General partnerships are not subject to the same rigorous rules relating to the standardised presentation of balance sheets, or the same standard accounting policies, as are companies and LLPs. However, it is becoming more commonplace to provide greater disclosure within accounts to enable partners to have a good understanding of the financial performance of the firm and its standing at the year end date. There is also an increasing tendency to adopt the use of accounting policies which are generally accepted accounting practice (UK GAAP), not least because HM Revenue & Customs now require tax computations to be prepared under UK GAAP.

The annual accounts of a partnership will typically include the following:

(a)   statement of approval of the accounts by the partners;

(b)   report of the accountants or auditors;

(c)   balance sheet;

(d)   profit and loss account; and

(e)   notes to the accounts, including accounting policies.

Included as **APPENDIX 6** is an example set of partnership accounts.

Accounting policies

14.5   The accounting policies are the specific accounting bases judged to be appropriate to the circumstances of the partnership and which are adopted by the partnership for the purpose of preparing its accounts.

Accounting bases are diverse and numerous and, because they have evolved in response to many types of businesses and transactions, there may justifiably exist more than one recognised basis for dealing with particular items.

If the partnership wishes its accounts to show a true and fair view, it will need to prepare them in accordance with UK GAAP in a similar manner to that required for an LLP. This would, however, reduce the scope of the partnership to decide upon alternative accounting policies, which the partners may consider to be more equitable.

Role of accountants and auditors

14.6   The role of accountants when undertaking work for general partnerships is governed not by statute but by the instructions of each particular firm, defining the scope of the work to be done, and by the nature and extent of the records to be made available.

The Audit and Assurance Faculty of the Institute of Chartered Accountants in England and Wales (ICAEW) has issued a technical release on the compilation of historical financial information of unincorporated entities' (AAF 03/10) covering such situations. The technical release emphasises the need for a clear understanding of the scope of the work to be undertaken and that an engagement letter should be put in place to formalise the arrangements agreed with the client.

Any report issued by a firm of accountants will make clear the extent of the responsibilities which they accept for the accounts prepared by them and will provide an opinion only on accounts which they have audited or where additional relevant responsibilities have been agreed.

An audit is an independent examination and expression of opinion on the accounts of an enterprise. Companies and LLPs are required to have their accounts audited by a firm of registered auditors, except where the company or LLP is dormant or where it meets certain size criteria. However, some general partnerships may be required, either by the regulatory authority or by a term in their partnership agreement, to have an audit. In addition, provision of audited accounts by a specific date after the year end may be a condition of the granting of a loan by a bank or other lending institution.

Partners' accounts

14.7 Partners' accounts represent how the net assets of the business are financed by the partners. The partners' accounts (as shown in **APPENDIX 6**) are on the balance sheet as capital accounts, current accounts and, in some cases, taxation and other reserves. Former partners' accounts may be included or, alternatively, shown under current or long-term liabilities.

Capital and current accounts

14.8 In some firms, partners' capital is merged with the current accounts. Where it is separated, such capital accounts are intended to segregate an amount that is chosen to represent the 'permanent' capital of the business. In practice, even where such segregation has taken place, a significant proportion of current accounts often represent fairly permanent capital, in that they may not be drawable by the individual at the moment the amounts are credited to their current accounts.

An element of a partner's profit share is usually credited monthly, to enable drawings to be made on account during the year. The balance of the partner's share of profits would be credited annually after the final accounts are agreed; in practice, this means that profits not drawn during the year become a source of capital for the firm.

Capital accounts may consist of both paid-up capital, represented by cash paid in, and unpaid capital. This situation may exist where changes in the partnership profit sharing arrangements give rise to revaluations of goodwill. Where such changes are dealt with through a goodwill account, the transactions between partners will not be represented by cash, except in the case of incoming and outgoing partners.

In some firms, current accounts may be used to settle partners' benefits, such as health care, motor vehicle expenses and home telephone bills (to the extent that such items are not allowable against tax) and life assurance, together with interest on borrowings incurred to fund a partner's capital contributions. Current accounts for junior partners are sometimes allowed to run temporarily in debit whilst they contribute their capital at the same time as enabling them to maintain an acceptable level of drawings.

A sum representing interest may be paid on the balances on both capital and current accounts. Where the ratio of such balances is not consistent with profit sharing ratios, it enables equity to be maintained between partners. It also has the added benefit that it acts as an encouragement to leave funds in the business; the firm could justify paying a rate above that which could be earned by each partner on his own account but less than the partnership's cost of borrowing.

Taxation reserves

14.9 While it is partners, not the partnership, that are liable for taxation, historically, provisions for taxation have been made within the partnership accounts on behalf of the partners and, as such, can form significant sources of finance for a professional partnership. Inasmuch as tax provisions are debited to current accounts that partners may otherwise be allowed to draw upon, a prudent basis of providing for taxation liabilities is not only a sound policy to ensure partners have funds to settle their liabilities when they fall due, but can also provide useful cash flow funding for the firm.

There are various different ways in which a firm can provide for taxation, but it is best practice to provide on a prudent basis and to disclose in the balance sheet under current liabilities that element of the taxation provisions which is due and payable within the next 12 months. The excess element of reserves would normally be considered to be the 'prudent' element, and it is considered reasonable to disclose the amount under partners' reserves, although variations on where these amounts are disclosed on the balance sheet are common.

Amounts owing to former partners

14.10 Some firms allow for the prompt repayment of capital and undrawn profits held within a partnership to outgoing partners. More often, in order to protect the capital base of the firm, there will be a delay between the time a partner leaves and the time he receives the full amount owing to him. In some cases, this can be several years, with or without interest paid on outstanding amounts. Whilst for most firms this is not a significant source of finance, it can be important in smaller firms where a number of senior partners have retired or otherwise left the firm.

Limited liability partnerships

14.11 The annual accounting requirements for LLPs are set out in the *Limited Liability Partnership* (*Accounts and Audit*) (*Application of Companies Act 2006*) *Regulations 2008, Parts 1* to *9*. These regulations take *Part 15* (*Accounts and Reports*) of *CA 2006*, which deals with the requirements to prepare accounts, and make such modifications as are necessary to deal with the particular circumstances of LLPs. Detailed accounting provisions setting out the content of those accounts are no longer included in the schedules to *CA 2006*, as they were with *CA 1985*, but instead are included in secondary legislation such as the *Large and Medium-sized Limited Liability Partnerships* (*Accounts*) *Regulations 2008* and the *Small Limited Liability Partnerships Regulations 2008*. With the exception of the rules with respect to filing of accounts (which applied for periods beginning on or after 6 April 2008), all of the provisions are applicable to accounting periods that began on or after 1 October 2008.

For the first period after incorporation, the accounting reference date of an LLP (ie the date to which the accounts are prepared) is the last day of the month in which the anniversary of its incorporation falls. In the absence of any application to shorten or lengthen the accounting period (see below), the first accounting period will start on the date of incorporation and end on that accounting reference date. Subsequent accounting periods will then cover a year from the date of the end of the previous accounting period, unless an application is made to amend the accounting reference date.

The members are responsible for preparing at the end of each financial year a profit and loss account and balance sheet which give a true and fair view of the state of affairs of the LLP at the end of the financial period and of the profit or loss for the financial period. A report to the members (members' report) is also required. The form and content of the balance sheet, profit and loss account and notes to the accounts is set out in legislation. The fact that the accounts are required to give a true and fair view means that they also have to comply with all extant SSAPs, FRSs and

UITF Abstracts. Therefore, where required, they will also need to include a Cash Flow Statement and Statement of Total Recognised Gains and Losses.

The *Limited Liability Partnerships* (*Accounts and Audit*) (*Application of Companies Act 2006*) *Regulations 2008* permit the use by LLPs of International Financial Reporting Standards ('IFRS') on a voluntary basis. The SORP does not deal with the application of IFRS to LLPs and, to date, whilst some larger LLPs have chosen to prepare their accounts in accordance with IFRS, the majority remain with UK Generally Accepted Accounting Practice ('UK GAAP'). Once a decision has been taken to prepare the accounts in accordance with IFRS, an LLP must apply all the standards, and other than in exceptional circumstances it is not permitted to revert to UK GAAP.

The Accounting Standards Board ('ASB') have issued their proposals for the convergence of UK GAAP and IFRS, although this will not be implemented before 2012 at the earliest. Exactly how the change will be effected has still to be decided, but at some point in the relatively near future a large proportion of LLPs will be required to prepare their financial statements in accordance with the principles of IFRS.

Where, at the end of the financial period, an LLP is a parent undertaking, subject to certain size limits measured by reference to turnover, total assets and number of employees, both individual and group (consolidated) accounts are required.

The accounts of an LLP are required to be approved by the members and signed on their behalf by a designated member. The designated members are responsible for delivering the accounts to the Registrar of Companies. In practice, this will most probably be delegated to one person. Delivery to the Registrar must take place (unless newly incorporated) within nine months of the period end.

Where an LLP is within certain size criteria, it may be eligible to file abbreviated accounts with the Registrar of Companies, although it will have to produce full accounts for the members.

Statement of recommended practice (SORP) – accounting by limited liability partnerships

14.12   The SORP was first published on 29 May 2002 by the CCAB (the six major accounting institutes in the UK and Ireland), and is subject to periodic updates to reflect changes in accounting standards. The current version of the SORP was issued in March 2010 and applies for periods commencing on or after 1 January 2010.

The SORP does not provide details of all of the reporting requirements which are applicable to LLPs, but it does provide interpretation of those accounting standards where there are specific issues regarding their application to the circumstances of an LLP. One of the requirements of the SORP is that the note to the financial statements which deals with accounting policies should refer to the LLP's compliance with the SORP. Where there are any areas of non-compliance, this is required to be disclosed together with the reasons.

Some of the key areas dealt with within the SORP are as follows:

(a)   the contents of the annual report and financial statements; this section is fairly general and the SORP does not include an example set of accounts;

(b)   members' remuneration and interests;

(c)   retirement benefits;

(d)   taxation;

(e)   revenue recognition: stocks and long-term contracts;

(f)   business combinations and group accounts;

(g)   provisions and other implications of FRS 12; and

(h)   related parties.

The requirement to appoint auditors

14.13   Unless entitled to the exemptions included in the legislation, all LLPs are required to appoint auditors and have their accounts audited. Exemption from audit is available for LLPs with a turnover of £6.5 million or less and a balance sheet total (total assets before taking account of liabilities) that does not exceed £3.26 million. The exemption, however, is not available where the LLP is:

(a)   involved in banking or insurance;

(b)   enrolled under the list maintained by the Insurance Brokers Registration Council under *s 4* of the *Insurance Brokers (Registration) Act 1977*;

(c)   authorised under the *Financial Services and Markets Act 2000*;

(d)   a parent or a subsidiary unless:

(i)   throughout the financial period in which it was a subsidiary, it was dormant; or

(ii)   it is a parent or subsidiary in what is defined as a small group.

An LLP which is exempt from audit is still required to file accounts with the Registrar of Companies and must also circulate a full set of the accounts to each member.

Entitlement to exemption from audit is dependent on inclusion on the balance sheet of the statement set out below, which must be inserted immediately above the signature of the designated member(s):

'For the financial year ended [ ], the LLP was entitled to exemption from audit under Section 477 Companies Act 2006 (as applied to LLPs). The members acknowledge their responsibilities for ensuring that the LLP keeps accounting records which comply with Section 386 of the Act (as applied to LLPs) and for preparing accounts which give a true and fair view of the state of the affairs of the LLP as at the end of the financial year and of its profit or loss for the financial year in accordance with the requirements of Section 394 and 395 (as applied to LLPs) and which otherwise comply with the requirements of the Companies Act 2006 (as applied to LLPs) relating to accounts, so far as applicable to the LLP.'

The designated members of the LLP have ultimate responsibility for preparing accounts that give a true and fair view. This responsibility remains the same, even in circumstances where the audit firm may have been engaged to assist with the preparation of those accounts.

Communication between the auditor and LLP

14.14 Auditing standards require auditors to communicate with the members of the LLP on a range of matters throughout the audit process, including:

(a) the terms under which the auditor will act for the LLP, including the respective responsibilities of the auditors and the LLP and the limitations in the audit process;

(b) any relationships between the LLP and the audit firm that may affect, or be perceived to affect, the firm's independence;

(c) the nature and scope of the audit work to be performed;

(d) the findings from the audit, including:

    (i) the auditor's views about the quantitative aspects of the LLP's accounting practices;

    (ii) the written representations the auditor will be requesting from the management in respect of the audit (see below);

    (iii)   the uncorrected misstatements found during the course of the audit;

    (iv)   any expected modifications to the audit report; and

    (v)   material weaknesses in internal controls identified during the audit.

Changes to International Standards on Auditing (UK and Ireland), effective for periods ending on or after 15 October 2010, require additional matters to be referred to in the letter of representation. In addition, the revised standards require that auditors disclaim an opinion in circumstances where they either have doubt about management's representations in respect of responsibility for the financial statements and the provision of information to the auditors and the completeness of transactions and amounts in the financial statements, or where the members do not provide these representations.

The audit report

14.15   In addition to reporting on whether the accounts of the LLP give a true and fair view, there are certain other matters which legislation requires auditors to report on by exception. These are as follows:

(a)   whether adequate accounting records have been maintained;

(b)   whether the accounts are in agreement with the accounting records and returns; and

(c)   whether the auditors have obtained all of the information and explanations which they consider to be necessary to enable them to perform their audit.

Where the content of any other information accompanying the financial statements, including the members' report, is inconsistent with the accounts, the auditors may decide that this should be referred to in their audit report. This would also be the case where the financial statements do not comply with the SORP, unless the departure is considered necessary in order for the accounts to give a true and fair view and the accounts contain adequate disclosure of the reasons for the departure.

A variety of circumstances may lead to a modification of the audit report. Where the auditors have not been able to obtain all of the information they require ('limitation of scope'), or they disagree with the treatment or disclosure of an item in the accounts, a qualified audit report is issued. The qualification can take a number of forms:

(a)   *Except for.* Where the auditors have been unable to obtain sufficient evidence with respect to one or more items, but where they are satisfied with the evidence available in all other areas. This form of opinion is also used where the auditors disagree with the accounting treatment or disclosure in relation to an item in the accounts.

(b) *Disclaimer*. When the possible effect of a limitation in scope is so material or pervasive that the auditors have not been able to obtain sufficient evidence to enable them to form an opinion on the accounts.

(c) *Adverse opinion*. Where the auditors consider that the matter with which they disagree is so material or all-pervasive that the accounts are misleading. In these circumstances, the audit opinion will state that the accounts do not give a true and fair view.

In certain circumstances, there may be uncertainties surrounding an amount in the accounts, where the effect of the possible range of outcomes could be material. In these circumstances, where the auditors consider that this is a matter to which attention should be drawn, they will make reference to the existence of a *'significant uncertainty'* in their report by way of an 'emphasis of matter' paragraph, but this does not constitute a qualification of the audit opinion.

Current legislation means that audit reports have to identify the 'senior statutory auditor', who is the person within the audit firm who takes overall responsibility for the audit.

The audit and auditing standards

14.16 We have previously discussed the general requirement that the accounts of an LLP are subject to audit. At the most general level, an audit involves the collection and evaluation of sufficient evidence to enable auditors to express an opinion on whether the accounts are prepared, in all material respects, in accordance with the applicable accounting framework.

The auditors of an LLP are required to carry out their work in accordance with International Standards on Auditing (UK and Ireland) ('auditing standards') which are issued by the Auditing Practices Board. Whilst auditing standards do not dictate the exact nature of the work auditors should carry out, they do set out both principles and essential procedures which must be applied when carrying out audit work. Individual firms are then able to develop their own methodologies to comply with those auditing standards.

Whilst the methodologies of individual firms vary, all audits can be analysed broadly into the following stages:

(a) planning;

(b) obtaining audit evidence;

(c)   review; and

(d)   reporting.

Consolidated accounts

14.17   It is not unusual for an LLP to either set up other entities through which to carry out certain parts of its trade or acquire a controlling investment in another undertaking. Legislation and UK GAAP may, in such circumstances, require the LLP to prepare consolidated accounts, which aggregate the accounts of the LLP and the other undertakings, as well as its own entity accounts. The main accounting standard that governs the accounting for groups is FRS 2 'Accounting for subsidiary undertakings'.

Consolidation is the process of adjusting and combining financial information from the individual accounts of a parent LLP and its subsidiaries to prepare consolidated accounts that present financial information for the group as a single economic entity. In general, uniform group accounting policies should be used in preparing the consolidated accounts.

The date from which to commence accounting for an undertaking as a subsidiary is the date on which control of that undertaking passes to its new parent LLP.

The accounts of the subsidiaries to be used in preparing the consolidated accounts should have the same financial year end and be for the same accounting period as those of the parent LLP. Where the financial year end of a subsidiary is different, interim accounts for that subsidiary should be used. If this is impracticable, earlier accounts of the subsidiary may be used, provided that they are prepared for a financial year that ended not more than three months earlier.

Intra-group transactions may result in profits or losses being included in the book value of assets to be included in the consolidation. Such profits or losses should be eliminated in full, because, for the group as a whole, no profits or losses have arisen.

A parent LLP should prepare consolidated accounts unless it utilises one of the following exemptions permitted by the *Companies Act 2006*:

(a)   the group qualifies as small and does not constitute an ineligible group (see below);

(b)   the parent accounts are included in a larger group; or

(c)   all subsidiaries can be excluded from the consolidation under the following bases for exclusion:

    –   immateriality in the group context;

    –   severe long-term restrictions; or

    –   the LLP's interest is exclusively with a view to resale.

A group is ineligible if it contains:

(a)   a public company;

(b)   a body corporate (other than a company) whose shares are traded on a regulated market in an EEA State;

(c)   a person (other than a small company) who has permission under *Part 4* of the *Financial Services and Markets Act 2000* to carry on a regulated activity;

(d)   a small company that is an authorised insurance company, a banking company, an e-money issuer, a MiFID investment firm or a UCITS management company; or

(e)   a person who carries on insurance market activity.

Accounting policies

14.18   The accounting policies are the specific accounting bases judged to be appropriate to the circumstances of the LLP and which are adopted for the purpose of preparing its accounts.

Accounting bases are diverse and numerous and, because they have evolved in response to many types of businesses and transactions, there may justifiably exist more than one recognised basis for dealing with particular items.

In order for its accounts to show a true and fair view, the LLP will need to prepare them in accordance with UK GAAP and the provisions of the *Companies Act 2006*, together with the pronouncements issued by the Accounting Standards Board ('ASB'), including Statements of Standard Accounting Practice ('SSAPs'), Financial Reporting Standards ('FRSs') and other components of generally accepted accounting principles, including the SORP.

Accounting policies that are particularly relevant to the peculiarities of LLPs are discussed in detail under each separate balance sheet and profit and loss account heading in the paragraphs that follow.

Accounting concepts

14.19   Two accounting concepts play a pervasive role in the preparation of the accounts of any entity including LLPs. These are 'going concern' and 'accruals'.

The going concern concept assumes that the LLP will continue in operational existence for the foreseeable future.

The accruals concept recognises that the profit or loss for a period is the difference between income and expenditure – not the difference between cash receipts and payments. The accruals concept involves matching income with the costs incurred in producing that income.

In addition, in selecting accounting policies an LLP needs to judge their appropriateness against the following objectives:

(i)   relevance;

(ii)   reliability;

(iii) comparability; and

(iv)   understandability.

Financial information is relevant if it has the ability to influence the economic decisions of users and is provided in time to influence those decisions. Reliable financial information should be neutral, free from material error, complete and, where any uncertainty exists, it should be prepared on a prudent basis.

Comparability of financial information can usually be achieved through the consistent application of accounting policies year on year and disclosure. The information which is contained in the accounts of an LLP should be capable of being understood by those with a reasonable knowledge of business and accounting. The special interest of members in the financial performance of the LLP means that those responsible for the preparation of the accounts need to be prepared to explain the content in non-technical terms.

Accounting for members' interests

14.20   Within the balance sheet, amounts relating to the interaction of the LLP with the members are recorded in one of two places:

(a)   *Loans and other debts due to members.* Being amounts which are debts owed by the LLP to the member.

(b)   *Members' other interests.* Including, subject to the matters discussed below, capital introduced by members, unallocated profits, any revaluation reserves and other reserves which have been set aside from profits (for example, to cover the cost of retirement benefits).

The SORP requires the accounts of the LLP to include a comprehensive statement of the components of members' interests and movements during the year.

Accounting standards require that all financial instruments be classified either as a financial liability or equity. The definition of equity is very closely drawn and, as such, unless the LLP has an unconditional right to avoid paying cash (or, on occasion, another asset), the members' capital will probably be classed as debt and included within liabilities in the balance sheet.

Profit allocations

14.21   The basis on which profits will be allocated to individual members will be governed by the members' agreement. The amount of that profit for any particular year will, however, be known only when the accounts have been finalised. There is, therefore, an issue as to when the profits made by the LLP become a liability due to the members.

Legal advice taken during the development of the original SORP concluded that the profits of an LLP are only converted into a debt due to its members when the members have agreed to divide the profits among themselves. The implication of this opinion was that, unless the decision to divide profit had happened by the year end through some form of automatic agreement (eg an agreement simply to share all profits equally between all members as they arise) within the members' agreement, the profits due to members should not be regarded as a liability.

Where, however, profits are only divided following a decision of the LLP, these amounts would remain in equity (reserves) as unallocated profits, until the decision is made. The question then arises as to where unallocated profits should be included within the accounts. Considering the analogous position with a company, undistributed profits would be included within the profit and loss reserve. The regulations do not, however, permit an LLP to have in its balance sheet a separate heading 'Profit and loss account', so unallocated profits are included within other reserves.

Members' remuneration

14.22   The way in which members are remunerated will vary between LLPs but will reflect the fact that the members are in the position of both owning the LLP and, usually, working within it. The distinction between the rewards received as a result of ownership interests and those received from employment could well be blurred.

Whilst the intention will be for the members to share in the profits of the LLP, varying proportions of this may be guaranteed in the form of fixed payments. A further complication is that it is possible for a member to also be an employee of the LLP and, in these circumstances, there will be a contract of employment between the LLP and the member.

The principal ways in which members may obtain reward for their involvement with the LLP are as follows:

(a) *Fixed amount.* Members may be guaranteed a certain amount of remuneration each year, either within the membership agreement or through individual arrangements between the LLP and the member. This amount will be paid to them irrespective of the level of profits made by the LLP.

(b) *Allocation of profits.* Members are awarded a share of the profit made by the LLP, either on a pre-agreed basis or discretionary basis.

(c) *Combination of fixed amount and allocated profit.* In addition to receiving a fixed amount, members may also receive an allocation of the profit remaining after paying such amounts.

During the year, members may be entitled to receive cash from the LLP in lieu of remuneration they either expect to receive or which relates to an earlier year. Such amounts are referred to as drawings. Receipt of drawings will be particularly common where remuneration is either all, or predominantly all, in the form of profit share. Where drawings are made in advance of profit being allocated to the member, they form a loan repayable by the member, and therefore would appear as a debtor in the accounts of the LLP.

The way in which members' remuneration is accounted for largely depends on whether the related balance is accounted for as a liability or as equity. The regulations require that the profit and loss account disclose a total for 'Profit or loss for the financial year before members' remuneration and profit share'.

The notes to the accounts should analyse salaried remuneration of members between that which is paid under an employment contract and other. The average number of members during the year should also be disclosed in a note to the accounts. Whilst not required by either the regulations or the SORP, the members may wish to include details of average members' remuneration. Where this option is taken, the SORP states that it should be calculated by reference to the disclosed average number of members and the amount of profit before members' remuneration and profit shares shown in the profit and loss account.

Where the profit of the LLP before members' remuneration and profit share is greater than £200,000, the notes to the accounts are required to disclose the remuneration of the member with the highest entitlement to profit. As well as profit share and salaried remuneration from the LLP, this will also include any amounts paid to the member by a subsidiary undertaking or other third party. The member does not have to be named.

Borrowings of members within partnership

14.23 It is common practice for the partners to borrow in order to fund their interests in that partnership. These arrangements frequently involve the partnership entering into a guarantee, indemnity or similar arrangement with the provider of the funding. Similar arrangements arise in LLPs.

The fact that the members' interests have been funded by way of borrowings is not of itself something which requires disclosure in the accounts. Instead, it is necessary to look at the extent of the LLP's obligation to the provider of finance and how this should be treated. In the rare circumstances where the LLP has an obligation to repay the loan, then a provision should be recognised in the LLP's accounts. More commonly, the LLP will have guaranteed the borrowings but will only be liable if the member defaults on the loan. In these circumstances, the resultant contingent liability should be disclosed in the accounts.

Loans and other debts due to members

14.24　The SORP requires that the notes to the accounts disclose where amounts due to members would rank on a winding up in relation to other unsecured creditors. In the absence of any agreement to the contrary, amounts due to members will rank equally with other creditors.

Retirement benefits

14.25　The accounting treatment of retirement benefits within LLPs is probably one of the most complex and controversial areas. The accounting requirements with respect to retiring members, in particular, was the subject of much debate during the development of the original SORP, and the solution was not entirely in accordance with general accounting requirements applied to other types of entity.

Retirement benefits payable to former members will usually be of one of the following two types:

(a) *Pre-determined*. An amount which is fixed at the time of retirement. This may, for example, be by reference to the profits earned in the last year of membership. Alternatively, it could be a fixed sum, which may be index-linked or linked to some other measure which is independent of the profits of the LLP.

(b) *Profit-dependent*. An amount which effectively results in the member continuing to receive a share in the profits of the LLP post-retirement. This amount may be subject to some level of cap. There are a wide range of methods used to provide profit-dependent benefits, and these may include arrangements whereby the LLP has to achieve a certain level of profits before any payment is made.

Under the SORP, LLPs are required to accrue the estimated amount of retirement benefit payable to members from the point at which the obligation arises. In many cases, therefore, an LLP will be providing for annuities over the entire period during which it receives the services of the member. A further consequence of the requirement to make provision for retirement benefits is that LLPs with profit-dependent retirement benefit schemes need to make an assessment of their future profits in order to determine the level of provision. Whilst there is a certain amount of subjectivity attached to these estimates, it should be possible for the LLP to determine the range of potential outcomes from which a provision could be calculated.

The position within the accounts of the liability to pay retirement benefits will depend on whether it relates to former or current members. Former member provisions will be shown within either creditors or provisions for liabilities, with movements in the provision being shown as an operating expense, whilst obligations in respect of current members will be included within loans and other debts due to members, with movements in these amounts forming part of remuneration of members.

Revenue recognition and work in progress

14.26   Detailed guidance relating to this area can be found within FRS 5 'Reporting the substance of transactions' – Application Note G 'Revenue recognition' ('ANG') and UITF Abstract 40 'Revenue recognition and service contracts'.

Work in progress is time which has been spent by the LLP's employees on client affairs, but which has not yet been invoiced to the client. Work in progress, amounts recoverable on contracts, unbilled disbursements and unpaid invoices often represent the majority of the working capital of a professional firm. The existence of working capital is due to the time-lag between performing a piece of work and being paid for it. The largest item of expenditure in the profit and loss account of a professional firm will be staff salaries, with the majority of employees of a professional firm being paid monthly in arrears. Therefore, if the LLP is paid by its clients more than 30 days after the work is performed, it will need to find cash, usually from reserves or borrowings, to pay its staff until the clients' money is received.

Accrued income

14.27   Prior to the issue of ANG and UITF 40, accrued income arose under Statement of Standard Accounting Practice 9: Stocks and long-term contracts ('SSAP 9'), where a firm had long-term contracts. On such contracts, work is performed over a period of time, normally in excess of a year, and the pattern of invoicing may not reflect the performance of work on the contract. Under SSAP 9, where a business carries out long-term contracts and their outcome can be assessed with reasonable certainty before they are completed, profit should be recognised on a prudent basis as work on the contract progresses. This is done by recognising an appropriate proportion of total contract value as turnover in the profit and loss account as contract activity progresses; and, to the extent that turnover recognised exceeds amounts invoiced, this may give rise to accrued income (classified in the accounts as 'amounts recoverable on contracts').

Under ANG and UITF 40, the underlying principle is that income should be recognised when a business has earned the right to payment through performance of the underlying work, and long-term contracts are not the only situations where it may be appropriate to recognise income before it has been invoiced.

To the extent that a professional firm has performed work and the fee is not conditional on a future event outside the firm's control, this will normally represent earned income. As a result, the firm should accrue unbilled amounts at selling price, rather than simply deferring the cost of the work as work in progress to match against income in the future. UITF 40 makes it clear that the billing patterns agreed with the client are not relevant in determining whether income is earned.

Acceleration in the recognition of income and profits, as a result of applying UITF 40, had several practical implications for professional firms. The principal issue is that firms have had to decide how to allocate one-off, additional profit arising from first time application. Some firms have retained it as an asset of the firm in the form of an unallocated reserve within partners' interests, rather than allocating it to the members. Others have allocated it between members, but, as the additional profit has not been realised in cash, have not distributed it as part of the normal drawings cycle.

Work in progress

14.28 While most unbilled time is likely to be included within the accounts as accrued income, there may be circumstances where it is more appropriate to record this time as work in progress at the lower of cost and net realisable value.

In calculating the cost of work in progress, some firms take the value of unbilled fee earner time at charge rates as a starting point. They then reduce this value by the gross profit element included within the charge rates. Others build up an hourly cost for each fee earner from their salary and related costs plus an allocation of overheads. Where there is work in progress accounted for in accordance with SSAP 9 'Stocks and long-term contracts', members' time should be included to the extent it has been expensed in the profit and loss account as part of members' remuneration charged as an expense. Irrespective of whether time input by the member is included within work in progress, any overhead related to that time should be included.

Provisions

14.29 In accountancy, the term 'provision' can be used in two separate sets of circumstances. First, there are adjustments which are made to the amounts at which certain assets are included within the accounts. For example, provision for bad or doubtful debts or provision for obsolete stock. These are accounting adjustments and are not strictly provisions. Secondly, this term is reserved for those items which can be included on the balance sheet within the heading 'provisions for liabilities'. The accounting rules with respect to the recognition of such provisions are clearly defined in FRS 12 'Provisions, contingent assets and contingent liabilities'.

Before an LLP can recognise a provision within its accounts, it must be able to satisfy each of the three criteria set out in FRS 12:

(i)   there must be a legal or constructive obligation at the balance sheet date as a result of an event occurring before that date;

(ii) it must be probable that there will be a transfer of economic benefits (eg paying cash) to settle the obligation; and

(iii) a reliable estimate can be made of the amount involved.

A constructive obligation arises where, through custom and practice, the LLP has created a valid expectation on the part of the third party that their claim will be met.

Where the obligation to pay only becomes apparent after the balance sheet date, but it clearly arises as the result of an event before that date, a provision should be recognised. For example, an unexpected legal claim might be received after the balance sheet date in respect of damage alleged to have occurred before that date. In these circumstances, a provision would be recognised, but it would not be acceptable to create a general provision for possible legal claims arising from work performed.

It is appropriate to take into consideration contingencies existing at the balance sheet date when preparing financial statements. The term 'contingency' is normally applied to a condition which exists at the balance sheet date, where the outcome will be confirmed only on the occurrence or non-occurrence of one or more uncertain future events. Estimates of the outcome and of the financial effect of contingencies should be made by the LLP. These estimates will be based on consideration of information available up to the date on which the financial statements are approved, and will include a review of events occurring after the balance sheet date. Using the example of a substantial legal claim against a firm, the factors to be considered would include the progress of the claim at the date on which the financial statements are approved, the opinion of legal experts or other advisers and the experience of the firm in similar cases.

The appropriate treatment of a contingency existing at the balance sheet date would be considered in the light of its expected outcome. In addition to accruals, under the fundamental concept of prudence contingent losses would be accrued where it is probable that a future event will confirm a loss which can be estimated with reasonable accuracy at the date on which the financial statements are approved. A contingency may be reduced or avoided because it is matched by a related counter–claim, or claim by or against a third party. In such cases, any accrual would be reduced by taking into account the probable outcome of the claim.

Other accounting policies and disclosures

Going concern

14.30   Going concern is a fundamental principle underlying the preparation of the accounts of all entities. Accordingly, the majority of LLP accounts will be prepared on the basis that the LLP will continue in operational existence for the foreseeable future, known as the 'going concern basis'. Application of FRS 18 'Accounting policies' requires that an LLP should prepare its accounts on the going concern basis, unless the LLP is being liquidated or has ceased trading, or the members have no realistic alternative but to liquidate the LLP or cease trading. In these circumstances, it may be appropriate to prepare the accounts on an alternative basis.

When preparing accounts, the members are required to assess whether there are significant doubts about the LLP's ability to continue as a going concern. This assessment is required to be made for what is termed the 'foreseeable future'. This term is not defined in accounting standards; however, disclosure is required where the review period considered by members is less than one year from the date of approval of the accounts (not the accounting period end). Auditing standards require that, where the period considered is less than one year from the date the accounts are approved and this fact is not disclosed, it should be referred to in the audit report. As a consequence of these requirements, most LLPs will consider a period of at least 12 months from the date of approval of the accounts.

The extent of evidence required to support the members' assessment of going concern will depend on a number of factors. These include, but are not restricted to:

(a)   the extent to which the LLP's financial resources exceed its requirements;

(b)   the size and complexity of the LLP's operations; and

(c)   the extent to which the LLP is operating in a high-risk industry.

Where an LLP is trading profitably and it has adequate working capital, the
extent of documented evidence could be fairly minimal. In other cases,
where the position is less certain, it may be necessary to prepare cash flow
projections for subsequent periods comparing these with available, or likely
to be available, facilities. Such projections should take account of both
future trading and the impact of any major transactions, such as proposed
acquisitions or major capital investment programmes.

Once the members have carried out their assessment, there are three
possible conclusions:

(a)   there are no material uncertainties that lead to significant doubt about
the LLP's ability to continue as a going concern;

(b)   there are material uncertainties that lead to significant doubt about
the LLP's ability to continue as a going concern, but the going
concern basis remains appropriate; or

(c)   the use of the going concern basis is not appropriate.

Where there is significant doubt about the LLP's ability to continue as a
going concern, the disclosure made by the members will be considered by
the auditors. Such disclosure should be given reasonable prominence
within the accounts and will not normally be considered as adequate by the
auditors unless it contains the following:

(a)   a statement of the specific nature of the material uncertainties that
give rise to significant doubt;

(b)   a statement of the assumptions made by the members, which should
be clearly distinguishable from the relevant facts;

(c)   where appropriate and practicable, a statement regarding the members' plans for resolving the matters giving rise to the uncertainty;

(d)   details of any relevant actions taken by the members; and

(e)   an explanation of why the going concern basis has been adopted.

The auditors will then need to consider whether they agree with the
statement in the accounts, and how fundamental the uncertainty is, before
deciding upon whether there is any implication for the wording in their
audit report.

Related parties

14.31 LLPs are required to comply with FRS 8 'Related party disclosures'. The objective of FRS 8 is to ensure that financial statements contain the disclosures necessary to draw attention to the possibility that the reported financial position and results may have been affected by the existence of related parties and by material transactions with them. The FRS requires disclosure of a material transaction undertaken by the LLP with a related party, irrespective of whether a price is charged.

Where the LLP is controlled by another party, disclosure is required of that controlling party, irrespective of whether a transaction has taken place with it.

Transition from partnership to LLP

14.32 The transition from partnership to LLP should be accounted for using the merger basis, so long as it meets the criteria to be treated as a group reconstruction set out in FRS 6 'Acquisitions and mergers'. FRS 6 is worded in the context of corporate entities and states that, in order to qualify as a group reconstruction, the ultimate shareholders must remain the same, and the rights of each such shareholder, relative to the others, should be unchanged immediately before and after the transaction.

Putting this definition into the context of a partnership, in order for the transfer to an LLP to qualify as a group reconstruction and hence for merger accounting, the interests of all members in the LLP should be in the same proportions as their share in the partnership immediately prior to transfer. Both the amount of capital introduced and profit sharing arrangements will need to be taken into account when determining if the criteria have been met.

The application of this requirement means that transition to an LLP should not be combined with the retirement or appointment of partners or members, nor should the relative benefits of partners/members be altered at this stage. Such changes may also have consequences in respect of the exemption from stamp duty on incorporation. However, HMRC have stated that they will accept that there can be a change of partners taking place the instant before or after incorporation. HMRC can ask to see all associated documents affecting the change in membership prior to and/or after incorporation.

Where the requirements of FRS 6 are not met, the transfer should be accounted for as an acquisition, and the assets and liabilities transferred would need to be restated to their fair values and the consideration for the acquisition determined by reference to the value of the business of the partnership transferred. Goodwill will arise as a consequence of the difference between the two values, and this will have to be recognised on the balance sheet and amortised through the profit and loss account of the LLP. For professional practices, the value of the business taken as a whole compared to the value of its underlying assets and liabilities could well be significantly different. The amount of goodwill, and the impact of subsequent amortisation on the profit and loss account, could be substantial.

On transferring assets and liabilities to the LLP, the amounts at which they are initially recorded in the accounts should be calculated by reference to the accounting policies to be adopted by the LLP. Depending on the policies adopted, these could vary significantly from those shown in the accounts of the predecessor partnership. This will be particularly relevant where the partnership had prepared accounts for its own purposes other than on the true and fair basis, making adjustments to that basis only for the purposes of its tax return. Areas where differences are most likely to arise are as follows:

(a) Provisions for retirement benefits to former partners to the extent that the liability to meet the cost is transferred to the LLP.

(b) Valuation of work in progress and accrued income.

(c) De-recognition of provisions which do not meet the definition within FRS 12 (for example, provisions for possible future PI claims).

The members of the newly formed LLP will need to consider how they wish to deal with the increase (or decrease) in net assets that may arise upon conversion and whether any change is treated as a firm asset (or liability) or one that is allocated to the members.

The SORP requires that single-entity LLPs formed from the transfer or incorporation of an existing entity should present comparative pro-forma information for the previous period. The corresponding amounts should be stated using the same accounting policies as those adopted by the LLP. For the reasons discussed above, the amounts shown by the comparative figures may differ from those in the equivalent partnership accounts, resulting in a consequent difference between partners' interests and members' interests. This difference should not be reflected in the accounts of the LLP, which should be prepared on the basis that the LLP has always existed and always prepared accounts in accordance with its selected accounting policies.

Chapter 15   Financial Management

Introduction

15.1   This chapter examines the budgeting and financial monitoring process appropriate for a professional practice, the funding of partnerships and LLPs, and deals with banking issues, including financial products and treasury management.

Budgets

15.2   CHAPTER 10 looked at the need for a business to produce an overall strategic plan, recognising the need to consider the resources necessary in order to achieve the objectives. The plan should ideally cover a three- to five-year period and include broad reference to the financial needs of the business.

The strategic plan should be supplemented by a three- to five-year financial forecast based on a reasonably small number of broad assumptions. Its purpose is to demonstrate the financial implications of the firm achieving its objectives over the given period.

Objectives and definitions

15.3   The firm should produce an annual budget which is much more detailed than a long-term financial forecast. The objective of the budget is twofold. First, it is the means by which the objectives in the long-term plan can be converted into a detailed financial action plan. Secondly, it is a way of monitoring the firm's financial performance on a regular basis.

Generally, a forecast estimates the future state of the market and the economy and is used for long- or medium-range planning. However, a budget is a far more detailed document that includes a regular, usually monthly, analysis of fees, salaries, overhead costs, cash flows, capital expenditure and working capital requirements.

Budgets provide a clear picture of the firm's likely financial performance. They enable a view to be taken of income and overhead levels, likely profitability, capital expenditure and cash flow requirements. Preparing a budget provides a planning discipline that is useful in short-term decision-making and in controlling the allocation of resources. It also quantifies the likely effect of action plans. In addition, particularly for those whose performance might be assessed by reference to budget, it provides stimulation and motivation for the achievement of a good performance in the year. It is also a useful communication tool within the firm and is a key means of maintaining a focus on achieving the firm's aspirations throughout the financial year.

Perhaps more than any other financial tool used by a professional practice, the budget is able to affect the attitudes and behaviour of senior members of staff. As a motivational tool, research has shown that budgets tend to improve performance. In order to extract the maximum benefit, it is essential that each of the elements within the firm takes ownership of their particular part of the budget.

Budgets must be set at a level that is realistically achievable but nevertheless demanding, rather than be a statement of the ideal which all involved know to be unachievable. Demanding but achievable budgets tend to motivate, whilst less demanding or unrealistic targets have an adverse effect on performance. Care should be taken when setting and comparing budgets for different departments which may have differing levels of profitability but all contribute to the firm, in some cases in a way that cannot be shown in the budgets, such as giving the firm a high profile. Care must also be taken when a budget is not met. A critical approach may demotivate, and other factors, such as performance against the previous year, or factors outside the control of the firm, should also be taken into account when reviewing results. Ultimately, it is important that the budget is considered to be binding and attracts personal commitment from senior people in the firm.

Budget preparation

15.4   There are a number of critical steps to ensure that the budget process provides the greatest possible benefit to the firm. A formal budget committee will often need to be established to coordinate the budget process, although this role may be taken by the firm's finance function. Members of this committee will vary according to the size of the firm, the nature of its business and its management structure. However, in general, it is likely to include representatives of the executive management, department heads and accounting staff.

Key steps will include the following:

(a)   The committee, with guidance from the partnership board or management committee, should establish initial guidelines which can be used by departmental heads to prepare individual departmental budgets. The main parameters will include overall salary increases, charging structures and particular target growth rates for certain teams.

(b)   A timetable should be issued for the preparation of relevant information, reviewing first draft budgets and discussing with each department head the basis upon which their budget has been prepared.

(c)   The finance director or finance partner should coordinate the timetable and produce the first draft firm-wide budget.

(d)   The committee or management board should consider the first version of the firm-wide budget, to ensure inconsistencies and anomalies are removed and the budget is consistent with the firm's long-range plans. Discussions with department heads are likely to take place as the overall aspirations of the firm are matched to each fee-earning department's ability to deliver.

Content

15.5   The main elements of a budget include a detailed profit and loss account for the period and a cash flow statement. In a professional practice, the key areas of focus will include: the profit and loss account, the amount of value locked up in work in progress and debtors, the capital expenditure budget, and the financing facilities available to the firm.

The cash flow budget should be compared with the bank and other facilities available to the firm. The variation between these two numbers should be taken into account when finalising the budget for the year and determining the firm's funding arrangements.

Budgeting income

15.6   Within a professional practice, the income element of the budget is a key issue. This figure can be uncertain, due to external factors such as decisions taken by competitors, the general state of the economy, the effectiveness of advertising and marketing activities, and the stability of clients. Estimating professional practice income will often involve forecasting the value of time input and projecting the anticipated level of recovery of this time. However, in transaction-based practices, such as agency work for chartered surveyors and corporate finance work for lawyers, it is difficult to estimate with any degree of certainty the projected fee income over the forthcoming year. History and past experience may show that fee income will continue to come from a number of sources and, with a proper understanding of the marketplace within which the firm operates, this should be a good base from which to develop the budget.

When preparing a budget, firms should first consider the key drivers of their income generation. For some, this may be based on success fees or commission. However, for most firms the number of billable hours that individuals can work during the year will be the key driver of income. An alternative approach to forecasting the fees that can be generated from available resources is to ask partners to forecast the work that they expect to be forthcoming from existing and new clients, and then assess the appropriate level of resource that will be required to manage that work.

One of the key factors in a profitable firm is the extent to which professional staff are utilised in chargeable time working on behalf of clients. Clearly, the higher the utilisation of the individual, the more profitable and productive they will be, assuming this time is recoverable from the client.

Utilisation rates will depend on the seniority of the person involved; partners will spend more time on business development and management issues than junior staff. Professional practices should generally aim to achieve the highest level of utilisation possible without the firm becoming an unpleasant place to work. Therefore, when preparing an income budget, it is appropriate to consider potential chargeable hours by individuals multiplied by the charge-out rate.

Charge-out rates are normally expressed as a rate per hour or day. Firms will set rates to reflect their own cost structure and what the market will accept. One method is cost plus pricing. In simple terms, this means calculating the direct cost of servicing a client and then adding a fixed percentage to cover overheads and a further percentage to provide a profit. Provided that the percentage uplift to cover overheads and profit reflects fairly on the working practices of the firm, the relevant fee will represent the firm's expected profits on each transaction. However, firms which only utilise this approach risk being out of touch with the marketplace. They may miss the opportunity for extra profits by undercharging for the real value of their work or, alternatively, find that, where there is a shortage of work, they miss the opportunity of making a contribution to fixed overheads because they do not accept work for which they cannot achieve full recovery of their normal charge-out rates.

The marketplace for professional practices is changing dramatically, and firms' pricing policies must move to meet market needs. Increasingly, clients are requesting fixed fee arrangements for work, which provides certainty for the client, but with the professional practice bearing the risk that time costs will exceed the budget. However, it is still essential that firms set charge-out rates for each of their professional employees, and monitor and record the time charged by them to particular contracts or transactions. By setting charge-out rates that reflect a fair proportion of overheads and profit, and taking into account each person's salary costs, the firm will determine the cost of undertaking work for clients. In current market conditions, when bidding for proposals or undertaking work for clients, charge-out rates will provide an indication of the cost of the work and the effect of the pricing policy on the profits of the firm.

Budgeting costs

15.7 The main cost elements will be staff costs, followed by premises. It should be reasonably straightforward to budget for these costs over the next 12 months as, in the short term, they are essentially fixed. Where this is not the case, the financial effect of decisions that have been taken in respect of levels of human resources, premises and other overheads should be factored into the budget.

Management accounts

15.8 Once partners and staff are aware that budgets have been set and that their performance will be gauged against them, they will generally work to increase the probability of making budget and avoid alternatives which reduce it. The successful use of budgets as a control mechanism to improve the financial performance of the business depends on whether each department takes ownership of the costs under its control. However, mitigating factors should also be considered, such as costs outside the control of the department, and other priorities and responsibilities which may direct partners' attention away from client activity. In addition, the quality of the work being undertaken should not be ignored. Finally, it is often the case that the costs of support departments within the firm, such as marketing and personnel, attract particular attention and the effectiveness of their activities should be constantly evaluated.

The budget should be reviewed on at least a monthly basis, to compare actual results against expectations. An efficient way of doing this is to prepare management accounts which compare the budget and actual results for the period and for the year to date and include, where appropriate, the results of the prior year. A commentary highlighting the key areas where results do not meet expectations should be attached.

The monthly review of results should not only encompass the income and costs but also, particularly in professional practices, certain balance sheet items. The commentary should address capital expenditure and the level of lock-up included in work in progress and debtors. The main determinant of liquidity within a firm is the extent to which time has been incurred on client affairs but has yet to be billed and collected, and the management of the firm's investment in this working capital is crucial to the control of cash and borrowing requirements.

At the conclusion of this chapter are some example schedules for a set of management accounts. These show the way in which a profit and loss account may be presented, together with the additional balance sheet information which is needed.

Management of work in progress

15.9   The management of work in progress in a professional practice has as much to do with managing the client relationship as it has to do with a well-run accounts department. Before accepting and starting work for a client, the fee earner should, if possible, provide the client with a quote for the work and agree a billing and payment schedule in writing. If at any stage it appears possible that actual costs will exceed the budget, the client should be advised and a revised billing and payment schedule agreed. It is vital that professional staff manage effectively clients' expectations, not only on delivery and quality of professional work, but also in terms of fee arrangements.

Disbursements incurred by a firm on a client matter should be invoiced on a regular basis, to ensure the firm does not fund excessive amounts of expenditure on behalf of a client.

Partners and fee earners should be encouraged to make appropriate provisions against irrecoverable work in progress as soon as they are in a position to predict that a particular assignment's costs will not be recovered. Further analysis of the reasons for any cost over-runs compared to original estimates may provide opportunities for additional costs to be billed to the client or indicate areas where efficiency improvements could be made on future assignments.

Management of debtors

15.10   Fees and disbursements should be billed to clients on a regular basis in order to ensure cash is collected in a timely manner. It is appropriate to have a standard procedure for chasing up unpaid bills, through the issue of monthly statements, reminders and solicitors letters and, depending upon the size of the firm, a dedicated credit controller, to take responsibility for chasing outstanding invoices. Again, the monitoring of debtor days, perhaps by individual fee earners, will enable the firm to maintain better control on its working capital.

Cash flow forecast

15.11   In order to manage the cash requirements, it is usual to review the cash position on a regular basis, perhaps weekly but certainly no less than monthly, against the forecast. The forecast cash flow statement will be based upon information extracted from the income and expenditure budget, with assumptions on debt collection, payments to suppliers, the capital expenditure budget, partners' drawings and tax payments.

The more sophisticated the cash flow document is, the more effective it will be as a management tool. Whilst it can be difficult to forecast the cash flows arising out of income, taking into account seasonal variations and detailed assumptions, monitoring the results against these expectations on a regular basis enables the firm's financing requirements to be managed effectively. It also provides credibility when exhorting fellow partners to increase their billing and debt-collection levels.

Variances which will occur between budget and actual must be considered carefully, and action taken when appropriate. Some differences may merely be caused by timing, whilst others will arise from a difference in volume, perhaps caused by excess business or lack of it, both at income and cost level. As the projection of income will influence the level of associated costs, if the income forecast is grossly inaccurate, the operating and cash budgets will fail to produce a realistic plan for the period. Therefore, it is essential to undertake regular reviews of the budget, which may involve rolling forward the actual cash balance every month. This has the advantage that cash forecasts will never get hopelessly out of line, as can happen if they are prepared only once a year.

The accuracy of such information will offer the firm extra time to plan sourcing additional funds to cover any shortfalls in financial headroom or to take advantage of investment opportunities, knowing that funding of working capital will not be compromised.

Funding and banking matters

Partners' financing

15.12   Historically, the primary source of finance available to a professional practice came from the partners themselves, albeit in various different forms.

Partners' capital

15.13   There is no statutory or other requirement to use capital accounts to finance a firm. If, however, the firm chooses to use such a method, the partnership or LLP agreement will often contain a clause setting out details of the capital contributions to be made by the partners. If not, the partners are expected to contribute equally. The partners' capital represents the long-term capital base of the business; it also represents the cost of an individual's entry into the partnership or LLP which is returned upon retirement, subject to increases or decreases during the lifetime of the partner.

The capital to be put up by each partner may be based upon historic precedents within the firm. However, a number of firms also determine capital based on the level of profitability so that it reflects more closely the partner's share of the goodwill and value of the firm. Under this arrangement, capital may be calculated as a multiple of a number of years' profits. This approach takes into account that a new partner is buying into an existing business with a value attached.

Therefore, if, on his retirement, the business has expanded and become more profitable, he will be due his share of that enhanced value by way of the revised calculation of his capital. In this situation, whilst the balance sheet of the firm shows the considerably higher partners' capital base, it will also show a value under goodwill to reflect the non-cash element.

Where capital is held in profit-sharing ratios, it is often unnecessary to provide for interest to be paid. However, as capital and remuneration arrangements become more complex, it may be appropriate to allocate a prior share of profits as interest.

A new partner may find it prohibitively expensive to provide his share of capital immediately on joining, and the firm may consider that an incoming partner should be allowed to subscribe his share over a period of years by, for instance, not withdrawing part of his profit allocation. Alternatively, he may use his own personal wealth, savings, mortgage or other assets, or he may take out a personal bank loan (see **15.35** below).

Depending on the availability of tangible assets as security, the bank may prefer to assist a firm via personal loans to individual partners in addition to lending on the partnership or LLP account. If lending takes the form of unsecured loans to partners, the facility made available may only cover part of the overall requirement.

Partners' undrawn profits

15.14 In addition to the fixed capital provided by partners to fund the business, it is also common for partners to support the business through profits earned and left undrawn on current accounts. Every firm needs a policy on the level of partners' drawings. It is usual to provide that each partner may draw a sum on account of profits each month which represents a conservative estimate of his likely profit share for the year, subject to deduction of other expenses incurred on his behalf, eg health insurance, and after deduction of pension contributions and taxation.

There are many different practices as to when partners receive their profits over and above their monthly cash drawings. It is usual for firms to wait until the annual accounts have been produced, when final profit shares have been agreed and taxation provided in accordance with the firm's policy. Partners may then be entitled to draw the balance due to them in their current account. However, some firms will be able to make payments of the partners' profits on account, perhaps after the subsequent quarterly management accounts have been prepared, and again in stages during the preparation of the final annual accounts. The timing and extent of profit distributions will reflect historical practice, the level of partners' capital, third party finance and the cash flow forecasts.

As the current accounts also provide a form of financing the firm, most professional practices would expect partners' current accounts to remain in credit. Where overdrawn current accounts occur, these should be dealt with carefully as they may give rise to tax difficulties. There may be particular circumstances which have led to a partner's account being overdrawn and firms can, of course, agree specific procedures to deal with such a situation. Overdrawn balances may often arise on the more junior partners' accounts, where capital contributions are being transferred from the current account.

Retentions

15.15 A firm may also wish to restrict profit distributions by way of retentions, for example, where cash resources need to be built up for the purposes of funding capital payments to departing partners.

Partners' taxation reserves

15.16 The accounting policy for providing for tax varies from firm to firm, and will reflect historical practices and the culture of the organisation. Whatever the policy, it is essential to ensure that all partners understand the implications for their own personal position. Firms which have a prudent policy for providing for tax reduce the amount of cash available to partners on account of taxation payments which will be made perhaps one or even two years after the relevant profits have been earned. To the extent that such amounts are set up in advance of the payments to HM Revenue & Customs, it would normally be considered reasonable to refer to these balances as part of the partners' financing of the firm, ie within partners' funds, rather than as creditors. Ultimately, a prudent tax provisioning policy can provide additional, sizeable funding to a firm.

Financing by creditors

15.17 Creditors can provide a source of funding through the negotiation of terms of credit and the use of the related credit periods. The major creditors of professional practices are usually staff and the tax authorities which, apart from partners' taxation, do not provide much scope for credit beyond the usual monthly cycle, although there may be opportunities to utilise payments to suppliers of other services.

Choosing a banker

15.18　In addition to partners' financing, a firm may decide to utilise debt as a source of finance. As partnerships and LLPs are very different in structure, law and operation to limited companies, the firm would benefit from dealing with a banker who understands the peculiarities and nuances of professional practices.

It is important that the banker understands how a firm operates and, in particular, understands:

- the *Partnership Act 1890*;

- the *Limited Partnerships Act 1907*;

- the *Limited Liability Partnerships Act 2000*;

- the *Legal Services Act 2007*;

- the implications of limiting liability;

- how a firm finances its fixed assets and working capital;

- accounting and taxation principles and ongoing developments thereof;

- how the economic cycle affects each profession; and

- the client account requirements of the various professional regulators, such as the Solicitors Accounts Rules (see CHAPTER 17, REGULATION AND CLIENT MONEY).

Most corporate branches of the clearing banks now offer professional practice banking specialists. Firms holding significant client funds, however, should find themselves a more attractive proposition to most banks, and the cost of funding may as a result become more competitive.

Factors for success

15.19　The relationship between the firm and its banker, and the support that the firm receives, can be crucial to its success. The partners should be aware of the importance of this relationship and ensure that communication of key results and decisions is maintained.

In particular, the firm should look to demonstrate the following:

Management

(a)　an understanding of the performance on both a client-by-client basis and a departmental basis;

(b)　remuneration and training packages that ensure low staff turnover and the retention of key personnel, particularly major fee earners;

Financial Management

(c)   an appropriate, responsible and managed approach to professional indemnity issues with adequate cover;

(d)   efficient cost control systems to monitor overheads relative to fees;

(e)   regular production of management accounts for partners and the bank on a timely basis, including accurate and sufficiently detailed data;

(f)   good credit and accounting control, particularly in terms of:

    (i)   cash and cash flow management;

    (ii)   prudent and regular provisioning bases;

    (iii)   efficient billing and cash collection procedures; and

    (iv)   a sustained approach to lock-up reduction.

Structure

(a)   a workable partnership or LLP agreement;

(b)   taxation and drawings policies which are equitable between partners and prudent in terms of future liabilities and working capital requirements;

(c)   realistic policies for repayment of capital and current accounts as partners retire;

(d)   appropriate finance for known increases in capital expenditure;

(e)   efficient use and cost-effective nature of property commitments; and

(f)   procedures to avoid partners over-extending their personal financial position.

Market

(a)   market awareness;

(b)   good reputation within the marketplace;

(c)   expertise within the firm's chosen field(s); and

(d)   the ability to retain and build on client relationships.

While a firm may strive to achieve these goals, its ability to deal with a changing working environment will impact on the banker's assessment of creditworthiness. How the firm deals with the following issues will therefore be of interest to bankers:

- peer group competition and the impact on fee incomes;

- increasing client turnover;

- the cyclical nature of the marketplace and the type of work undertaken, such as consulting work; and

- potential downsizing to improve lacklustre performance.

The manner in which each firm deals with these issues will be influenced by its size and its extent of sophistication. However, the basic principles still remain.

Financing through external equity funding

15.20   External equity finance has historically been an option available to a number of professional practice sectors and has been embraced through the listing of firms on the stock exchanges and investment by private equity funds. However, following the issue of appropriate regulations after the enactment of the *Legal Services Act 2007*, the option of external equity funding is available to law firms. This is explored in more detail in CHAPTER 4, CHOOSING AN APPROPRIATE BUSINESS STRUCTURE.

Products and services available from financial institutions

Introduction

15.21   The following section highlights specific issues the firm should be aware of when considering various types of finance from a financial institution.

Working capital/short-term finance

15.22   Bank overdrafts are the most widely used form of external finance used by professional practices, with nearly all using or having access to such facilities. Whilst they are technically repayable on demand and negotiated with the bank on what is normally an annual basis, they are often used to provide the whole of a firm's external funding requirements. Firms which operate using external finance on a permanent basis may find that overdraft funding provides an essential element of their financing facilities. However, short- and medium-term loan facilities may also be needed to meet non-working capital requirements, and it should be borne in mind that overdrafts should never be regarded as a substitute for adequate medium-term finance. The principal costs of an overdraft will be the variable interest rate, generally calculated on a day-to-day basis with reference to the bank's base rate, together with an additional facility fee, usually a fixed percentage of the maximum facility. The overall interest rate charged by the bank will vary, depending on a number of criteria, including the historic and perceived profitability of the firm, its gearing levels, its relationship with the bank, its prospects, the quality of financial information it produces and, finally, the level of security provided to the bank.

There has been an increasing tendency, particularly among larger firms, to seek committed lines of credit as part of their funding arrangements, rather than relying solely on an overdraft, which provides greater certainty over the future funding of the firm.

Term finance

15.23   In general, loans are often used to finance specific projects, such as the cost of fitting out premises or enhancements to the firm's IT systems. A loan can be tailored to meet customers' capital expenditure needs, and loan facilities should be allied to the life expectancy of the asset or work being undertaken. In practice, medium-term finance loans are usually put in place for a period of up to seven years, and repayments are made on a regular basis to include both interest and capital. The interest cost can be either fixed at the beginning of the period of the loan or can be linked to the bank's own base rate in much the same way as an overdraft. Term documentation is more complex than for overdrafts and other demand facilities, as specific terms and conditions are included defining how both sides will act during the term of the loan, and setting out what will happen if the loan falls into default. The benefit of committed term facilities for the firm is that the bank can only withdraw the facility or demand repayment if the terms of the agreement are breached, so the firm knows that the finance is in place until expiry.

Hire purchase and leasing

15.24   Hire purchase and leasing facilities are available, with the former having the benefit of attractive capital allowances to reduce the tax liability. Hire purchase and leasing arrangements can be set up quickly and generally offer fairly flexible repayment terms. The security for the advance is provided by the asset being purchased. Leasing, while more commonly used as medium-term finance, can also provide shorter-term funds.

The cost of such finance is often more competitive than overdrafts, but is only available for the funding of specific capital items rather than general working capital needs. As a result, firms have used hire purchase and leasing finance principally for motor vehicles, IT equipment and major office refurbishment.

Contract hire and vehicle management services

15.25   Contract hire financial arrangements include a fixed monthly charge to reflect the capital costs of the vehicle, maintenance and depreciation. The contract would normally include a pre-determined mileage limit for each vehicle for the contract period.

On termination of the hire period, the contractor checks the condition of the vehicle and may look for a contribution in respect of damage beyond normal wear and tear, but otherwise would not look for further payments. Where the firm breaks the hire contract part way through the period, a payment would be due based on a number of months' hire charge.

The major benefits are that the firm knows the costs at the start of the contract period and so will not suffer from excess depreciation or maintenance expenditure, and the maintenance arrangements themselves are taken entirely out of the firm's hands, with commensurate savings and reduction in administration.

Firms which run fleets of ten or more vehicles can also be considered for specialist vehicle funding and management services, such as accident management and vehicle rescue and recovery at competitive, short-term rental rates.

Guarantees

15.26   In general, where firms have overseas offices, it may be necessary for banks to provide cross-border bonding or guarantees. In particular, requests may be received to provide guarantees in favour of overseas banks, to cover advances and general banking facilities provided by those banks. Guarantees may also be required to cover lease obligations on commercial premises. Where firms are involved in competitive tendering for overseas contracts, there may be a need for UK and overseas contract bonding facilities to be confirmed as part of the tendering process.

Invoice discounting and debt factoring

15.27   Funds can be advanced against invoices (often up to 80% of invoice value) immediately upon agreement of the facility and, in the case of factoring, the factor (usually a bank group company) takes on the responsibility of the sales ledger management, credit control and debt collection. Facilities can be varied to cover all invoices for all buyers, all invoices for agreed buyers, or selected invoices for agreed buyers. Both UK and overseas invoices can be covered by such facilities. Such financing arrangements would be most beneficial for firms that are expanding rapidly and require facilities to finance the increasing levels of their work in progress and debtors arising from this expansion. Factoring is becoming increasingly competitive, and fees should be comparable to an overdraft, together with a charge for cash advances. However, factoring has disadvantages, such as the loss of immediate contact with the client, who may (unfairly) see factoring as a sign of financial weakness. There are also some potential regulatory restrictions on using this type of finance, depending on the business of the firm. Credit insurance is also available, either to cover this type of finance or as a stand-alone product. For a fixed premium dependent on turnover, debtors can be insured up to agreed limits per buyer, and debt recovery is handled by the insurer.

An alternative to conventional factoring is now offered by some banks to provide client funding with recourse to the firm. This has the benefit of improving cash collections and passes the interest burden to the client. It is very flexible and can be used for specific clients or even for individual matters for clients. There is no cost to the firm as the bank lends direct to the client, but it is not a panacea for bad payers, as the bank does retain recourse to the firm. It has been shown to be effective as, frequently, clients will be more concerned about having a direct debit to a bank returned unpaid than about not paying their professional advisers promptly.

Payment and cash management services

15.28　A full range of inward and outward payment facilities is available for sterling, euro and foreign currencies, both within the UK and abroad. Electronic payment methods are increasingly being used with direct links between the firm and its bank, providing the facility to make payments directly into the banking system, to retrieve information on bank accounts, to reconcile accounts, and to download information directly into certain accounting software packages. For larger firms, there is a range of options for cash pooling and netting.

Lease incentives

15.29　While not strictly a form of financing, depending on the size and length of a new premises lease, landlords may provide financial incentives to take on the premises, which can reduce the cash flow impact of the move. Incentives can include rent-free periods and contributions to fit-out costs, but care needs to be taken when negotiating such terms to understand the accounting and post-tax implications.

Treasury management

15.30　Summarised below are a number of the options available to professional practices considering an appropriate place to deposit funds.

Cash flow budgets should reveal, among other things, the value of funds available for short-term investment. A professional practice should take opportunities to manage money effectively over short periods of time. This may mean investing overnight, or for longer periods where appropriate, into the money markets to obtain the best rate for the funds. Funds should be placed with creditworthy institutions. The overall aim should be to secure the maximum interest possible, consistent with a satisfactory level of risk and the required degree of liquidity, in the most appropriate currency.

When considering the appropriate investment method, the certainty and accuracy of the cash budget will determine the amount and the length of time for which funds are available for investment. In addition, where there is any possibility that cash may be required prematurely to make unexpected payments, consideration must be given to the costs in the event of an early termination of the investment arrangement. Differences between investment opportunities arise principally over rates of interest, periods to maturity and the risk element. In broad terms, the shorter the life of the investment, the lower the interest earned; and the riskier the investment, the higher the interest earned.

Banks can arrange for cleared funds in excess of a predetermined amount to be transferred automatically on a daily basis from the firm's current account to an interest-earning account. In addition, where the firm holds money on behalf of clients in general client accounts, they should discuss with the bank ways in which these funds can be used to offset, for interest purposes only, the cost of any borrowings the firm may have.

The professional practice, like any business, should be actively managing its cash balances on a regular basis to ensure that it is obtaining the best use of its funds out of the money market and banking system, and minimising the interest costs incurred on borrowings.

Managing surplus funds

Bank deposits

15.31 A range of commercial bank deposit products are available:

- variable rate deposit accounts, including instant access, for relatively small balances;

- money market term deposits at a fixed interest rate for a fixed period of between one day and five years. Withdrawals are not normally possible until the end of the term. The interest rate will depend on the length of the term and the size of the investment; and

- certificates of deposit issued by clearing banks. These carry a fixed rate of interest and are for a fixed term, normally between three months and five years, but can be sold by the investor during the term through the London discount market.

Special arrangements are available for a firm's clients' money whereby interest can be earned on cheque accounts. On groups of clients' accounts, higher interest rates can be obtained than would be available on each individual account.

Building society deposits

15.32 Competition for investors' deposits amongst building societies and between building societies and banks is keen, and as a result there are many different schemes.

Some societies (and banks) now offer current accounts linked to an interest-earning bank account, with automatic transfers between the accounts as required. This is a useful way for firms to ensure that excess funds in a bank account can immediately be transferred to the interest-earning account.

Money market accounts

15.33 Several financial institutions, among them unit trust groups, merchant banks, finance houses and several commercial clearing banks, offer schemes which provide access to money market rates of interest for deposits which are not fixed. Withdrawals are allowed. The rates of interest available fluctuate with the London money market rates, and the terms and conditions, which can vary substantially from scheme to scheme, need to be carefully reviewed.

Treasury bills

15.34 Treasury bills are issued by the Bank of England and are government guaranteed. They are issued at a discount and redeemed at par after one, three or six months. The bills can be bought or sold on the discount market at any time until redemption.

Personal financing to partners

15.35 Banks often provide facilities to partners personally in addition to, or instead of, providing facilities to the firm directly, and there are a number of related issues which arise. If structured correctly, the funds lent to partners and used in the business will qualify for tax relief in respect of the interest charges arising on personal borrowing.

It is important that the firm makes the bank aware of the total facilities available to the firm and to the partners as a whole, when banks are considering the partner's own personal position. It is vital for a banker to establish the proportion of partnership capital which has been funded by personal loans to the partners, before a decision on financing can be made.

While joint and several liability in traditional professional partnerships is attractive to a bank, partners may have committed personally or have ring-fenced their private assets without a banker's knowledge. It is therefore the overall position which will be considered when assessing where to position facilities.

The partner may find that the bank would prefer to arrange any new partnership debt with the partners personally if there is personal tangible security available, rather than lend directly to the firm, particularly if the firm is an LLP.

If the firm is considering refinancing which involves new facilities with the bank, then it may also be a good opportunity to consider 'recycling' partners' capital, as this may enable the individual partners to structure their borrowings more tax efficiently. Care must, however, be taken to ensure that any such recycling is undertaken correctly, as this is an area that HM Revenue & Customs often review and will seek to deny tax relief for interest if it is undertaken incorrectly.

Security

15.36 When lending unsecured to the partners personally to fund partnership capital, the bank may prefer to lend only part of the overall requirement, and therefore it may be necessary for the partner to provide part of the requirement from his own personal assets. Life cover may also be required by the bank to ensure that the partner's personal debts to the bank are cleared by the life assurance on death to avoid recourse to the firm or to the estate.

A banker may require a formal assignment of partnership capital to ensure that he has priority over other creditors in the event of death or bankruptcy. The partner can choose between several different types of facility when arranging finance and should be aware of the different characteristics of each. In particular:

- term borrowing (over 364 days) tends to be more expensive than short-term borrowing;

- uncollateralised borrowing is more expensive than secured debt;

- financial strength of the partner will impact upon the rate of interest charged by the bank;

253

- the lower the perceived risk to the bank, the lower the cost will be;

- facility arrangement fees are usually a feature of lending products and are most often calculated as a percentage of the maximum facility amount.

For larger firms, banks will often agree a loan scheme for all the partners of that firm. This has several benefits:

- all partners pay the same rate of interest;

- terms are identical;

- normally there will be no individual credit assessment of the partner; and

- normally there is enough headroom in the overall limit to accommodate new partners.

Partnership structures and legal matters in relation to banks

15.37 *Section 5* of the *Partnership Act 1890* and *s 6* of the *LLP Act* set out the general principles of agency which apply in the context of partnerships and LLPs respectively. These are discussed at **2.24** and **3.10**, and mean that the bank could simply assume that, provided a partner acts within his actual authority or acts in the ordinary course of the business (implied authority), the partner's actions will, in the case of partnership, bind the other partners jointly or, in the case of an LLP, bind the LLP.

Even where there is no actual authority, in practice it is generally assumed that the partner or member has implied authority to open bank accounts in the firm's name, write cheques and borrow money for the purposes of the business.

In practice, reliance on implied powers is not generally satisfactory to a bank. A bank can ensure that the partnership or the LLP is bound by insisting that the signing partners or members have express authority pursuant to a mandate signed by all the partners or members, or at least a certified copy of a resolution in the form required to confer such authority.

Where persons hold themselves out, or allow themselves to be held out, as partners, they may incur liability as if they were partners (see **2.25**). Common examples of these are 'salaried partners' who do not share in the partnership profits. However, commonly, the equity partners agree to indemnify such partners against liabilities arising against the partnership.

Extent and duration of an individual partner's or member's liability

15.38 As discussed at **2.23**, any partner in a partnership is generally liable without limit for the partnership debts. His/her liability may be restricted if he/she:

- is a minor;

- has limited liability under the *Limited Partnerships Act 1907* (but, in this case, he/she will not be allowed to take part in the management of the partnership); or

- has obtained the agreement of the other party to the contract that his liability is limited in some way. This will apply only to debts owed to that party and not to all debts generally. Also, such arrangements must not contravene the *Unfair Contract Terms Act 1977*, nor the *Solicitors Act 1974*, which prevents solicitors limiting their liability for *contentious* work.

When a partnership borrows money, everyone who is a partner at the date when the debt is incurred will normally be subject to the obligation to repay. Retiring partners will remain bound unless expressly released, but new partners will have no direct obligation to the lender unless they novate the obligation (see **2.28**).

Former partners may continue to be liable to those who dealt with the firm while they remained a partner for the partnership's debts incurred before their death (or dissolution in the case of a partner which is a company), insolvency or until actual notice is given on their retirement or replacement (see **2.29**).

The bank may control the duration and extent of any partner's liability through lending documentation signed by all the partners. For new partners, the bank could arrange for them to sign documentation agreeing to be bound to previously incurred partnership debt, and likewise arrange for retiring partners to be released from their liability.

Care is required with revolving debt facilities, such as overdrafts, as legally any credits to the accounts repay 'old' debt, and debits to the account create 'new' debt. Under this arrangement, new partners assume liability over a period, as the 'new' debt is incurred after they become a partner.

In contrast, a member of an LLP is not liable for the LLP debts, except if he/she:

- has assumed responsibility to meet them;

- has a duty in tort to the LLP's counterparty; or

- is a single member of an LLP which has carried on business for at least six months with only one member.

In theory, therefore, the members of the LLP should have little impact on the relationship with the bank. However, in practice this is often not the case, and banks frequently ask members to guarantee loans or overdraft facilities granted to the LLP personally.

Partnership property

15.39   Partners may agree amongst themselves which assets are to be treated as partnership property, and may change the ownership of that property from partnership property to that of a specified partner or partners, subject to laws governing this area such as the *Law of Property Act 1925*.

Many professional practices occupy leasehold premises. The *Law of Property Act 1925* states that a leasehold (or, indeed, a freehold) property cannot be vested in more than four people, hence usually four partners are identified to act as nominees or, alternatively, the lease is held in the name of a nominee company. Generally, modern leases provide for the other partners to guarantee the obligations of the nominee partners (see **2.29**).

As an LLP is a separate legal body, LLP property is owned by the LLP, and leases will generally be entered into between the landlord and the LLP itself.

Bank collateral

15.40   The firm should be aware of the following issues relating to any collateral that a bank may require:

(a)   Fixed security or charges given by a partnership to the bank should be executed or signed by all the partners on behalf of the firm, or pursuant to the authority of all the partners. Floating security is more difficult because a charge which affects chattels or book debts is subject to the *Bills of Sale Act* (which is the subject of a current consultation) and may contravene a solicitor's obligations of confidentiality. Enforcement of a floating charge by appointment of a receiver may contravene a solicitor's obligations of independence.

(b)   Security given by partners is generally taken in the same way as that given by tenants in common.

(c)   Land vested in some of the partners as trustees for themselves and the other partners can be charged using special trustees' charge forms.

(d)   Guarantees may be taken from parties other than the partners or members to secure partnership debt.

(e)   In some cases, the bank may obtain a formal assignment of a partner's rights to payment of partnership capital to secure the liabilities of that individual partner, and to prevent monies being released to third parties in the event of death or bankruptcy of that partner. However, such an assignment would breach professional rules in the case of a solicitor, and therefore banks frequently rely on a promise by the partnership to repay the bank.

The bank may also require the firm to produce regular management accounts for its review as well as the annual accounts. The nature of the accounting policies and the sophistication of the regular reporting will influence the bank's reliance upon the accounts and hence the level of collateral that may be required.

Bankers and other stakeholders have now become familiar with the LLP structure, but firms still considering conversion to LLP should review the impact of this legal entity on their creditors, most notably their bank and landlord who may require guarantees before accepting the covenant of the LLP in place of the partners. Any security given by an LLP is subject to registration requirements under the *Companies Act 2006*, which include delivering particulars of the charge to the registrar, together with a copy of the charging instrument. The current system for the registration of charges by companies and LLPs is the subject of a consultation (see www.bis.gov.uk/consultations/registration-of-charges).

ABC Partnership
A Department
Chargeable Time Summary

	May	Jun	Jul	Aug	Sep	Oct	Nov	Dec	Jan	Feb	Mar	Apr	Total to date	Total Year
2010/11														
Compliance	280,000	403,000	407,000	–	–	–	–	–	–	–	–	–	1,000,000	
Ad Hoc	135,000	106,000	155,000	–	–	–	–	–	–	–	–	–	396,000	
Total Budget	415,000	480,000	562,000	308,000	385,000	345,000	333,000	243,000	388,000	388,000	383,000	333,000	1,486,000	4,402,000
Compliance %	67%	79%	72%										73%	
Ad Hoc %	33%	21%	28%										27%	
2009/10 Actual														
Compliance	240,000	300,000	310,000	193,000	268,000	197,000	207,000	151,000	195,000	229,000	230,000	211,000	310,000	2,730,000
Ad Hoc	90,000	80,000	84,000	82,000	88,000	121,000	74,000	107,000	95,000	90,000	140,000	109,000	84,000	1,182,000
	330,000	380,000	401,000	275,000	364,000	318,000	281,000	258,000	280,000	313,000	370,000	320,000	404,000	3,312,000
Compliance %	73%	79%	77%										77%	
Ad Hoc %	27%	21%	23%										23%	

Chargeable Time – Variances

Bar chart. Y-axis: 20,000 · 40,000 · 60,000 · 80,000 · 100,000 · 120,000 · 140,000 · 160,000 · 180,000. X-axis: May Jun Jul Aug Sep Oct Nov Dec Jan Feb Mar Apr.
Legend: □ Last Year ■ On Budget

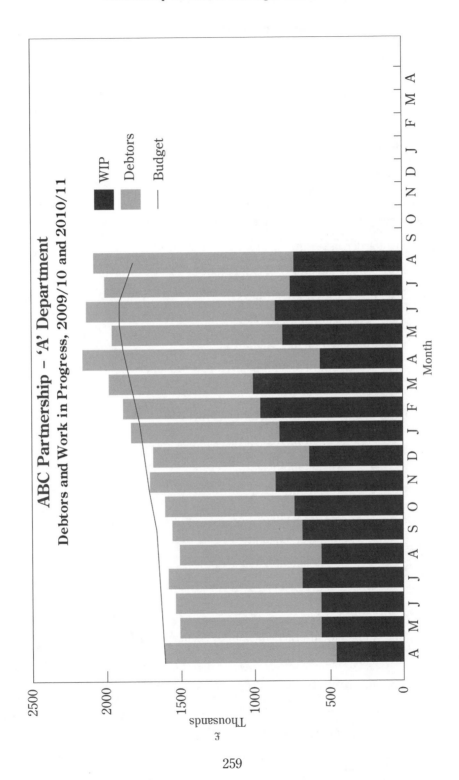

ABC Partnership – 'A' Department
Debtors and Work in Progress, 2009/10 and 2010/11

WIP
Debtors
Budget

£ Thousands

Month

Chapter 16 Insurance

Introduction

16.1 The insurance requirements of professional practices are varied, and a wide range of insurance covers are available. These are designed to protect the practice itself, individual partners and employees. Each firm must focus on the specific requirements of its business.

This chapter discusses the main insurance covers available.

(a) Professional indemnity (PI) insurance:

    (i) purchasing PI insurance;

    (ii) description of a PI policy;

    (iii) important elements of a PI policy;

    (iv) selection of the sum insured and self-insured excess; and

    (v) claims procedure.

(b) Other insurances for professional practices:

    (i) general insurance for professionals:

- office buildings;
- office contents;
- loss of income;
- employer's liability;
- public liability; and
- money;

    (ii) motor;

    (iii) employment practices liability insurance (EPLI);

    (iv) management liability;

    (v) income protection (IP);

    (vi) private medical insurance;

    (vii) protection for dependants:

- partners; and

- employees; and

(viii) critical illness.

This list is not exhaustive. Firms may have specific insurance cover that is not mentioned. We make no excuse for concentrating on professional indemnity cover, which is essential to most professional practices.

Professional indemnity (PI) insurance

16.2 Professional indemnity insurance has been described as an insurance which indemnifies the professional against pecuniary loss resulting from a breach of civil liability such as a negligent act, error or omission which causes their client or a third party to suffer loss. The standard of care required of the professional is that of a person who is reasonably competent or skilled in that particular profession. Excellence is not required, but merely the ability to exercise knowledge and skill by using a reasonable standard of care. It has been suggested that the professional should give the standard of professional service to their clients that they, when in the client's position, would be content to receive. Under English law, such a standard should avoid, or at least minimise, the risk of negligence. However, a professional could still be liable under the law of other countries, as required standards may differ.

The need for PI insurance

16.3 Professional indemnity insurance is available to those individuals who provide a professional service, eg solicitors, doctors, accountants, architects and consulting engineers, to name but a few, and is intended to protect them against claims from aggrieved clients or third parties, primarily, but not now solely, based on allegations of negligence in the performance of their particular duties.

The last few years or so have seen an alarming increase in claims against professional people. In many cases, the insurance market has provided the means of absorbing these claims and continues to do so. Therefore, the decision to have a PI policy should form a crucial part of a firm's commercial thinking, bearing in mind the increasing frequency of litigation.

Litigation is no longer the last resort for disgruntled clients who perceive they have received a substandard service or faulty advice, especially where these services have been provided for a fee.

The rules of certain professional institutes, including the Solicitors Regulation Authority, RICS and the ICAEW, make PI insurance a requirement for some professions. While it is not a requirement for all professionals, it is strongly advised for all firms which provide fee-based advice.

Even where the professional's innocence is upheld by a court, the costs of defending litigation can be very high, and frequently could cost hundreds of thousands of pounds. A PI policy provides the firm with access to advice on how best to defend such claims and protect its reputation.

Purchasing PI insurance

16.4   Having decided to purchase a PI insurance policy, the first aspect to consider is the completion of the proposal form which must be submitted to the underwriters. The proposal forms are designed to give the underwriters an understanding of the firm so they can assess the degree of exposure which might be presented. Questions are asked about the particular business activities, the size and scale of operations and the firm's claims history.

The information given is extremely important because it is used by underwriters to rate the risk, and therefore determine the premium, as well as the terms and conditions of the policy. Therefore, proposal forms must be completed with great care.

Non-disclosure

16.5   Insurance contracts are treated by the courts as a contract of the utmost good faith. This means that it is incumbent upon the firm to provide all relevant material information which a 'prudent insurer' would consider relevant to the underwriter on the risk which he is asked to accept. Therefore, any material non-disclosure or misrepresentation will entitle the underwriter to avoid meeting the particular claim he may be asked to consider, and he may be entitled to avoid the policy in its entirety. Non-disclosure or misrepresentation does not have to be deliberate to enable the insurer to avoid the policy. A positive duty to disclose material facts is imposed, not just to answer the questions asked.

All those within the firm who could be aware of material facts must have the opportunity to disclose any matters which need to be disclosed to underwriters. Therefore, it is vital to circulate to all appropriate partners, managers and employees before finally completing the proposal form. At renewal, there is effectively a double duty to notify all claims or incidents which may give rise to claims during the policy period, as well as to disclose these incidents to the new insurer.

The duty of disclosure to the underwriters does not end with the completion of the proposal form but continues right up to the date when the policy commences, which could be a number of weeks later. Therefore, full disclosure and prompt reporting of all circumstances which constitute a claim, or which might give rise to a claim, are absolutely essential.

Differentiating risk

16.6 The purpose of the proposal form is to provide the underwriters with sufficient information in order to differentiate the firm's risk from that of other firms in the same profession and to secure the most attractive terms and premium. Therefore, as much additional information as is appropriate must be provided. Some points of differentiation for underwriters are as follows:

(a)   provide underwriters with a copy of the firm's operation and procedures manual;

(b)   provide underwriters with details of the firm's approach to risk management;

(c)   provide underwriters with a copy of your corporate brochure;

(d)   try to meet with the underwriters to establish a face-to-face relationship; and

(e)   provide underwriters with copies of contract conditions used.

Access to underwriters

16.7 Considerably fewer underwriters write PI insurance than write some other general classes of insurance. Insurers also tend to specialise in particular professions. A specialist market exists and incorporates many of the traditional large UK insurers supplemented by major Lloyd's participation and the involvement of the UK offices of large international insurance groups. Internationally, many countries have their own domestic PI market, but only London and, to a lesser extent, US and Bermudian markets operate globally and insure worldwide risks.

Description of a PI policy

16.8 Professional indemnity policies operate on a 'claims made' basis, ie any claim will fall to be dealt with under the policy in force when such claim is 'first made' by a third party and notified to the underwriters during the policy period. Claims made after the period may not be covered, even if the work giving rise to the claim was performed in the period.

The assured should notify the underwriters as soon as any claim is made against them, and in some policies this is a condition precedent to the insurance coverage.

The aim of PI policies is to provide the assured with an indemnity in respect of the assured's legal liability to third parties for any third party claim which satisfies the following necessary requirements:

(a) The third party claim must be for compensatory damages, and such indemnity will include the claimant's costs, as well as the assured's costs and expenses of defending the proceedings. The question of costs is particularly important, as claims against professionals generate substantial legal fees and expenses.

(b) The claim must be made against the assured during the policy period.

(c) The policy will provide an indemnity in respect of financial loss arising from any claim in respect of any legal liability arising out of the professional's activities and duties.

(d) The claim arises out of the provision of the services described in the proposal form. This is a particularly important point and the firm should ensure that the business description provided is wide enough to encompass all of its activities. This is something that should be reviewed annually when the policy is renewed. For example, if a firm of solicitors takes the decision to offer personal financial planning services, this should be notified to the insurer.

(e) The claim relates to a negligent act, error or omission which is alleged to have occurred after the retroactive date specified in the schedule of the policy.

The retroactive date limits the time from when the policy becomes effective, so the further the date goes back, the better. If possible, a policy providing full retroactive cover, without limitation, is preferable.

Important elements of a PI policy

16.9 These elements comprise the following:

(a) Traditionally, policies are renewed annually. In certain cases, the period can be extended but this is dependent on prevailing market conditions.

(b) The policy will generally only respond to claims brought anywhere in the world other than the USA and/or Canada. Cover can be extended where necessary.

(c) The sum insured being provided can either be on an 'aggregate' or 'any one claim' basis. Having an aggregate sum insured costs less, but it also limits the sum insured available to pay claims in any one year to the limit chosen. For example, if a sum insured of £1 million in the aggregate was chosen, this would be the maximum amount the underwriters would pay in any one year towards one claim or all claims notified to them during the policy period. Selecting the sum insured on an 'any one claim' basis is the more expensive option, but allows the sum insured to apply to each claim that is notified during the policy period.

(d) The policy will also cover all costs and expenses incurred by underwriters in the investigation, defence or settlement of any claim made against the firm. These costs and expenses can either be included within the sum insured or be in addition to that sum. The difference can be significant.

The more restrictive option is to have the costs and expenses included within the sum insured. This means that the sum insured the firm chooses can not only be eroded by damages awarded against them, but also by costs and expenses incurred in defending the claim. The best cover option is to have the costs and expenses in addition to the sum insured.

(e) It is generally a requirement for the assured to carry a self-insured excess or a deductible. By carrying a self-insured excess, an assured has a vested interest in his own claims experience because, each time a claim is made, he has to contribute towards it. It also cuts out nuisance claims being notified under the policy which, if frequent and involving underwriters in incurring costs to defend them, could influence the premium that they may charge when the policy renews.

(f) While some underwriters can be approached directly, the majority of policies are purchased via brokers, who have access to all of the insurance underwriters both in the UK and overseas.

Why employ a broker?

16.10 Together with their broker, a professional practice might consider the following questions:

(a) What cover do we need?

(b) Which underwriter can offer the cover?

(c) Which underwriter can offer the broadest cover?

(d) Which underwriter is most competitive?

(e) Which underwriters have a reputation for not willingly paying claims?

(f) How does one keep up with changes in the insurance market and the law?

(g) Have we examined all our options?

Selection of the sum insured and self-insured excess

16.11   Some professional bodies give guidance to their members on this subject or specify minimum levels of insurance, often a multiple of the largest individual fee or annual fees. However, this is a very rough guide. Often this is a commercial decision, weighing up price against exposure but, when doing so, the firm must bear in mind that the sum insured must be adequate for a settlement that may well be made years after the initial notification was made under the policy.

The decision should also be influenced by other exposure factors, such as the nature of the firm's work, where it is being done (eg the USA), the nature of the firm's clients, protection (if any) given by contractual terms, and current legal precedents.

When considering the appropriate level of self-insured excess, again it is important to weigh up the premium savings against the extra exposure that will have to be faced, usually on a per claim basis. The self-insured excess required by the underwriters depends upon various factors. These sums can range from a couple of hundred pounds to millions of pounds, depending on the size and claims experience of the firm. If the self-insured excess requirement is potentially onerous, an alternative may be to establish a captive insurance company.

A captive insurance company

16.12   The objective of a captive insurance company is to create a formalised financing vehicle to support the firm's risk retention. The advantages and capabilities of such a vehicle over less formalised alternatives are as follows:

(a)   It provides a central focus for implementing a firm's risk management strategy, and complements the risk prevention efforts of management by providing a means of measuring the results of actions taken.

(b)   It allows the firm to participate in a variety of ways in its own insurance programme and, to varying degrees, as an insurer that issues a policy for 100% of the risk, as a co-insurer alongside the conventional market.

(c)   The firm can secure easier access to the reinsurance market, which may be cheaper and more flexible.

(d)   By acting alongside and/or in substitution for conventional underwriters, it may be possible to exert a competitive influence when premium rates are competitive, and a stabilising and smoothing influence when premium rates are increasing.

(e)   It could, over a period of time, reduce the level of premium paid to the commercial insurance market, thereby reducing the costs to the firm. If a firm decides that the captive insurance company option is viable for them, the specialist services of risk management advisers will be needed.

Claims procedure

16.13   It is now quite common for substantial claims to be made against professionals for a variety of complaints. Having a PI policy allows a firm to pass the claim to the underwriter, who will work in conjunction with the firm, advise and, where appropriate, contest the third party claim. Cover is usually inclusive of legal costs which have been authorised by the insurer. It is the firm's responsibility to notify its underwriters as soon as a claim is made, or as soon as it considers that there are circumstances which could give rise to a claim ultimately being made. Brokers can help with any notification given to underwriters, in its subsequent dialogue with them about the claim, and with any settlement.

Once the claim is made or the circumstances which might give rise to a claim are notified to the underwriters, the underwriters have the right to appoint their own solicitors and/or specialist representatives to act on their behalf. In these circumstances, the firm must actively cooperate with the underwriters' appointed representatives to enable the claim to be efficiently and effectively defended. It is important that the firm does not make any admission of liability or offer of settlement without the concurrence of its underwriters. This would be contrary to the terms of the insurance policy, and may in certain circumstances result in the rejection of the claim by the underwriters.

Other insurances for professional practices

General insurance for professionals

16.14   Firms can usually obtain most of the cover they need from a combined 'package' policy, available from many insurers. One document will provide most of the cover needed, eg office buildings, office contents, loss of income, employer's liability, public liability and money.

To ensure that the cover is purchased on the correct basis, points to consider include the following:

(a)   *Utmost good faith.* As is the case for PI insurance, general insurance contracts are determined by the doctrine of utmost good faith. The parties must disclose all material facts or the policy may be declared invalid. Particular care is needed to ensure that full and accurate details of the risk are provided, including previous claims. Where there is a question as to whether or not an aspect is material, it is best to disclose it.

(b) *Underinsurance.* Office combined policies will usually provide for the replacement of property on a 'new for old' basis. Allowance should be made for telephone equipment and other property such as photocopying machines and computers leased or rented unless the rental agreement states otherwise. Therefore, the sum insured must reflect the new replacement cost of all the contents. If not, the firm may be penalised should it need to make a claim.

(c) *Definition of business.* The definition that appears on the policy must embrace all the firm's activities. If a loss occurs that is outside the definition, the insurers may repudiate liability – a frequent omission is that of 'property owner', which is essential when buildings are owned.

(d) *Claims reporting.* It is important to notify claims promptly, as required by the policy conditions, so insurers are given a fair opportunity of mitigating their losses. In particular, claims involving injury to employees or third parties should always be notified to insurers without delay.

(e) *Terrorism.* For many firms, this will require negotiation of separate cover to ensure full protection.

Sufficient time should be devoted to fully reviewing the firm's cover at least once a year, to ensure that the cover is updated to reflect changes in the business.

Office buildings

16.15   Most policies will provide cover on an 'all risks' basis, rather than the contingency (eg fire, storm, etc) being specified. The cover operates in respect of all loss or damage, other than losses which are excluded. Therefore, the 'all risks' format is recommended and normally the difference in premium is small.

Buildings are usually defined to include outbuildings, walls, gates, fences and the owner's fixtures and fittings. Therefore, it is essential that the sum insured is calculated accordingly, with due allowance for professional fees and compliance with any local authority rebuilding requirements.

EXCLUSIONS

- Excess – the amount of the excess can vary, and different levels can be selected.

- Damage caused by thieves (usually covered by the contents section).

- Storm damage to fences and gates.

- Breakage of glass (usually covered by the contents section, or this can be included separately).

- Maintenance costs (the loss must be fortuitous).

- Subsidence (can be added).

EXTENSIONS

- Subsidence.

- Automatic provision for inflation of declared sum insured.

POINTS TO WATCH

- Some structures, particularly listed buildings, require special consideration to ensure the policy contains a local authority clause that allows for extra costs in rebuilding in accordance with revised planning requirements. Appropriate provision should be made within the sum insured.

Office contents

16.16 As with office buildings, the choice of cover is between 'all risks' and 'fire and perils'. The former is generally preferred. The office contents can normally be extended to include cover for reinstatement of documents, including client files and title deeds, plans and the like in the firm's trust.

EXCLUSIONS

- Excess – the amount of excess can vary, and different levels can be selected.

- Many policies will exclude theft losses which do not involve physical evidence, eg an actual break-in or break-out; therefore, a 'walk-in' theft is not covered.

- Losses from unattended cars.

- Electrical or mechanical breakdown, erasure of information, etc. A separate specialist policy can insure these risks.

- Theft of gold, silver, jewellery, etc whilst unattended or outside a safe when the premises are closed.

EXTENSIONS

- Some policies will provide for equipment such as laptop computers used away from the office on either a temporary or permanent basis, but this should be checked. The firm may also need to include items that are used at an employee's private dwelling.

- Damage to the building caused by thieves.

- Cost of replacing locks following theft or loss of keys.

- Damage to glass.

- Some policies give wider cover for computers, eg for reinstatement of data following erasure by any cause and increased cost of working cover following loss, damage or breakdown of the computer equipment. (A separate specialist policy may be the best option where high values are involved.)

POINTS TO WATCH

- Most policies provide cover for the contents whilst at the firm's specified premises, with an extension for a lesser amount whilst at other locations in the UK. A few provide the extension for cover in Western Europe. Cover for contents temporarily in use anywhere in the world can normally be purchased if required for portable computers, etc.

- Some policies require that computer equipment is specified within a separate sum insured.

- Some insurers impose a minimum standard of security expected at the premises within the text of the policy. Frequently, this is not well highlighted and could enable the insurer to repudiate a claim if the requirements are not being followed.

Loss of income

16.17 This provides an indemnity in respect of loss of income and the additional expenditure incurred in maintaining the business following a material damage loss. The cover operates for an agreed period following the loss, commonly between 12 and 36 months.

EXCLUSIONS

- Losses which do not follow a claim under the material damage section.

- Losses which result from incidents at customers' or suppliers' premises (cover might be available if requested).

- The accidental failure of public utilities due to a fortuitous event at the suppliers' premises.

- Accountants' costs in preparing a claim.

- Non-damage denial of access.

POINTS TO WATCH

- Some policies provide automatic cover with a pre-set limit of indemnity, although it is important to ensure that this limit is adequate for the firm's situation. Consideration needs to be given to the required level of indemnity. For example, if there is only a 12-month indemnity period, would the business be fully up and running in this time? If not, a longer indemnity period should be sought. Of course, if a 36-month indemnity period is given, the sum insured must be at least three times the annual figure.

Employer's liability

16.18 This provides an indemnity in respect of the professional practice's legal liability to employees in respect of death or bodily injury arising in the course of their work. The usual limit of indemnity is £10 million for each occurrence.

EXCLUSIONS

- Injury which occurs from activities outside the geographical limits of the policy. Usually, insurers provide 'anywhere in the world cover' for business trips, so long as no manual work is involved.

- Injury to employees as passengers of motor vehicles (this will be covered under the motor policy). However, your legal liability to an employee who is driving a motor vehicle in the course of your business is covered under the employer's liability policy.

EXTENSIONS

- Most policies give a wide definition of 'employee', which includes work experience and voluntary workers and can also include business partners.

- The legal costs for representation in respect of a prosecution under health and safety legislation.

- Whilst the standard cover of £10 million seems substantial, the limit may prove insufficient if an incident occurs involving several employ- ees, particularly if there is a delay in the case being decided by the court. Of course, it is the limit of indemnity in force at the time of the loss that is operative. 'Top-up' cover is available.

Public liability

16.19   The purpose of this section is to provide an indemnity to the firm in respect of its legal liability to third parties for bodily injury and loss/damage to their property. The limit of cover normally depends on exposure. The usual minimum limit is £10 million.

EXCLUSIONS

- The excess, normally £250 in respect of third party property.

- Liability for loss/damage to goods in your custody and control. (Usually, the exclusion does not apply to the personal effects of employees or visitors to the premises.)

- An incident that does not involve third party injury or damage.

- Liability in respect of any incident where the *Road Traffic Act* applies.

- The professional indemnity risk.

- Libel and slander.

- Breach of copyright.

EXTENSIONS

- Legal liability for injury or damage following the sale or supply of a product.

- Liability in respect of damage to rented premises (naturally, the cover provided is that which is outside the requirements of any lease), ie if a lease makes you responsible to insure the building, this extension will be insufficient.

- A cross-liability clause is needed where several companies are cov- ered under the same policy. (This allows each company to claim indemnity against actions brought by others who are joint insureds under the policy – as if they had separate policies.)

- Many policies specifically exclude liability arising from manual work away from the premises.

Money

16.20 This section will provide cover for 'money' as per the policy definition. The usual definition is: 'Current coin, bank notes, currency notes, cheques, giro cheques, travellers cheques, bankers drafts, giro drafts, bills of exchange, money orders, postal orders, current postage stamps, unused units on franking machines, revenue stamps, National Insurance stamps, National Savings certificates, premium bonds, luncheon vouchers, trading stamps, consumer redemption vouchers, gift tokens, credit card sales vouchers, VAT purchase invoices, airline tickets, machine tokens and telephone cards'.

EXCLUSIONS

- Losses which exceed the limits of cover. Typically, the following limits will apply as standard:
  - non-negotiables: £500,000;
  - money in transit: £1,500;
  - money on premises whilst open: £1,500;
  - money in safe: £1,000;
  - other money on premises when closed: £250;
  - money at a private residence: £500; and
  - theft involving employees, unless not noticed within the 'discovery period' of the policy – this is usually seven days in most policies.
- An overnight theft loss from a safe when the keys are left on the premises.

EXTENSIONS

- Personal accident assault benefit, which provides a lump sum benefit for serious injury and a weekly disablement benefit following an assault on an employee whilst carrying the firm's money. It should be noted that, frequently, the standard benefit is for minimal sums but these can be increased at nominal cost.

POINTS TO WATCH

- People travelling abroad on the firm's business will need additional cover, as cover normally operates only in the UK (a business travel policy is usually best).

Motor

16.21 Motor insurance cover is available at four levels: comprehensive; third party, fire and theft; third party only; and fire and theft only (for vehicles which are 'laid up' and not in use).

Liability to third parties is included under all covers (except fire and theft only) in respect of all sums for which the firm may be legally liable. The limit of indemnity for third party property damage is normally £5 million in respect of commercial vehicles, and many insurers apply a £20 million limit in respect of private cars and motor cycles. The limit of indemnity for third party injury is unlimited.

Exclusions

- Excess, can be own damage only or all claims, and may apply to windscreens.

- Loss of use, depreciation, wear and tear, mechanical or electrical breakdown.

- Loss of value following repair.

- Loss or damage arising from theft or any attempted theft whilst the ignition keys have been left in or on your vehicle.

Extensions

- Rugs, clothing and personal effects. However, insurers will not usually provide indemnity for the following:

    - mobile telephones, computers, gaming consoles, any portable or removable audiovisual equipment, navigation devices and traffic alert systems; and

    - any equipment, goods or samples carried in connection with any trade or business.

- Fitted audio and visual equipment.

- Territorial limits can be extended for foreign travel. EU countries are usually included within a European certificate in respect of private car types, whereas commercial vehicles are usually limited to cover in the UK, with prior notification required to extend.

- Unauthorised movement of third party vehicles.

- Contingent liability which provides an indemnity to the professional practice in respect of a third party claim following an accident when an employee was using their own vehicle on the firm's business without proper motor insurance cover.

- Loss or theft of keys.

- Courtesy car provision free of charge, or hire car provision at discounted rates.

- Breakdown assistance.

- Legal services and advice.

Points to watch

- Motor fleet insurance is generally only available where at least five vehicles are operated.

- Driving restrictions could apply to specific vehicles.

- A higher excess and other additional terms may apply to young or inexperienced drivers.

Cover will include use in connection with the policyholder's business. Any other business use is not included, although the insurers may provide specific extensions upon request.

Employment practices liability insurance (EPLI)

16.22 An emerging risk facing professional practices is the risk of being sued for employment law breaches by their own partners and employees or by third parties.

Employer's liability covers awards for bodily injury and failure to provide a safe working environment, but does not cover suits for breaches of employment law. Professional practices are now more vulnerable to such suits, as redundancies of professionals become more commonplace. EPLI will provide cover for situations such as unfair dismissal, failure to promote and employment contractual disputes.

Management liability

16.23   With professional practices increasingly being professionally managed and more partnerships adopting limited liability partnership status, there is increasing exposure to professional practices, and the individuals responsible for managing such entities, from liability incurred for wrongful acts and breaches of partnership agreements.

Management liability insurance (also referred to as 'Directors & Officers (D&O) insurance') protects the professional practice and the individual from claims by partners or employees such as mismanagement or breach of contract, claims by regulators for violation of professional regulations, and claims by competitors for predatory hiring and use of confidential information. This should include cover for 'insured versus insured' claims, by which partners sue the professional practice or the management of the practice. In addition, partner redundancies which are more commonplace may not strictly fall under employment claims, but evolve into a claim for breach of the partnership agreement.

Income protection (IP)

16.24   IP is protection against loss of earnings in the event of sickness, injury or disability. It can be effected by individuals, partners or by companies, partnerships or LLPs on behalf of their employees.

The maximum amount of cover available to partners is usually 50% of their normal net income from the firm, and this may be subject to averaging, eg over the previous three years. Net income means taxable earnings, after deduction for business expenses, derived by the partner from the firm. Should the IP benefit become payable, like individual policies, it is paid directly to the partner and is free of any income tax liability. Benefits under group policies for employees will be subject to tax.

For high earners, benefits may be restricted to a maximum cover ceiling. Benefits from all such policies are normally taken into account in calculating maximum benefits. The limits are set so as not to discourage an individual's financial incentive to return to work.

At the outset of the policy, it is necessary to select a 'waiting period'. This is the period during which an individual is unable to work before benefit payments commence. The longer the waiting period, the lower the premium. Waiting periods are commonly 8 weeks, 13 weeks, 26 weeks or 52 weeks.

Another factor affecting premiums is occupation. Insurers categorise occupations from lowest risk, eg professional/managerial/clerical duties, through to highest risk, eg unskilled manual work. Age at commencement and sex also affect the premium, as does an individual's state of health.

In the event of a claim, benefits are normally paid monthly. Benefits cease when the individual is able to return to work, dies or on reaching the selected termination date, whichever is the earlier. The age to which a policy can be written often aligns with normal retirement age.

It is possible to select a policy which automatically increases claims in payment by a fixed percentage such as 3% (5% in past years) or in line with the Retail Prices Index (RPI).

Some policies will pay claims if the individual is unable to follow his/her own occupation prior to the sickness, injury or disability, whilst, for other policies, claims will only be paid if the individual is unable to follow any defined occupation for which they are qualified (usually any suited). The definition of disability will need to be selected at the outset of the policy.

If an individual who is unable to return to full-time work does work on a part-time basis or takes a less well-paid job, a proportion of the benefit will normally be paid.

There is no tax relief on personal contributions. Following the *Finance Act 1995*, benefits paid from April 1996 will not be taxed.

A group IP (GIP) policy is an arrangement set up by an employer for its employees to replace salary in the event of sickness, injury or disablement resulting in the individual being unfit for work.

Through a mix of economies of scale, non-selection and commercial reality, premium rates for GIP cover are generally cheaper per individual than the cost of individual policies. Many professional practices establish such schemes for their employees. The same pricing principles apply to GIP schemes as for individual policies, in that the average age and sex of the employees will be considered, as will the occupations of the employees and the length of the 'waiting period' and the definition of occupation.

In addition to insuring a percentage of each employee's salary, it is possible to insure the employer pension contributions, either based on salary prior to disability or on notional pay in line with what the employee would have earned had he/she been fit to work. If the pension scheme is contributory, the employee pension contributions will normally be deducted from the salary continuance benefit. It is also possible to insure the employer's National Insurance contributions, but the employee's National Insurance contributions would be recovered from the salary continuance benefit.

The maximum level of cover can be subject to limit, and this will vary depending on who the insurer is.

GIP will normally be designed so that the 'waiting period' (the period during which an individual is unable to work before payments commence) coincides with company short-term sick pay obligations, during which the firm continues to pay an employee who is unfit for work.

There are three main types of GIP schemes for employees:

(a)   *Gross Pay.* This scheme provides a fixed percentage of pre-disability pay, eg 75% of salary less defined offset for state benefits, whether payable or not.

(b)   *Fully Integrated Pay.* This type of scheme provides a fixed percentage of pre-disability pay less any state incapacity benefit actually received.

(c)   *Net Pay.* Benefits are specified as a percentage of net pre-incapacity earnings, eg 90% of net pre-incapacity earnings after taking into account any state incapacity benefits actually received.

It is possible to select cover which does not increase in payment or only increases either by a fixed percentage or in line with the Retail Prices Index (RPI).

For schemes with a small number of employees, the premium is exact costed each year based on the cover and age of each employee, the waiting period and the benefit payment period. The termination date will normally be in line with state pension age, but it is possible to effect limited payment which will limit a benefit-paying period to two or five years.

For larger groups of employees, normally 20 or more, the premium is costed on what is known as a unit rate basis. This means that the premium is calculated based upon the total salary roll and is normally guaranteed for a two-year period, provided that there is not a material change in membership.

Free cover limit

16.25   Group schemes provide a free cover limit, which is the level of cover that the insurer is prepared to offer without requiring evidence of health (providing all entry conditions are satisfied). Cover in excess of the free cover limit is underwritten, which means that the individual is required to provide details of his state of health and may also be required to undergo a medical examination and other tests.

Taxation

16.26   Premiums paid by the employer are allowable as a business expense and are not taxed as a benefit-in-kind on the employee. Generally, any benefit payments are taxed under PAYE when passed to the employee.

Reducing partners' IP costs

16.27   A number of insurers of group schemes will allow a separate category of benefit to be created for partners, which sits on top of the employee GIP arrangement. In this way, partners can benefit from group premium rates and free cover levels. However, the cost of the cover is usually still the partner's personal responsibility and, in all other respects, the benefits are treated as though they are arising from an individual policy.

Private medical insurance

16.28   Private medical insurance provides for the cost of treatment of acute medical conditions on a short-term basis. It does not cover primary care or chronic conditions and may not cover pre-existing conditions. It is designed to complement the NHS rather than replace it.

Most schemes cover: hospital accommodation charges and surgeons' and anaesthetists' fees, operating theatre costs and consultants' fees on a full refund basis. Outpatient costs may be subject to limitations, although most of the diagnostic tests (including CAT scans, MRI and PET scans) are covered in full.

Most schemes do not cover: chronic (long-term or recurring) conditions, pregnancy or childbirth, cosmetic surgery, preventive or prophylactic treatment, out-patient drugs and/or dressings.

The core benefit designs are similar, with common variations including: excesses, psychiatric cover limits and controls, NHS cash benefits, home nursing allowance, GP referred physiotherapy and complementary therapies, overseas cover (emergencies only), and out-patient treatment limits.

The larger schemes will be rated on claims experience, have 'bespoke' benefits and can include treatments that would normally be excluded.

It is common for immediate members of the family (spouse and children) to be included in the arrangement, including non-married partners (aligning with current legislation).

The cost of medical insurance for partners would normally be deducted from profit share, with the individual partner responsible for their share of the premium cost, which might reflect age (smaller schemes) or the unit rate of a larger group arrangement.

Many professional practices put in place group arrangements for their employees. The cost of the arrangement is allowed as a business expense, and any employee earning in excess of £8,500 per annum would be liable to pay income tax on the cost of providing the insurance, as it is treated as a P11D benefit. The cost to the employer is allowable as a business expense.

Partners can normally effect cover for themselves through the employer arrangements, but their tax position would be exactly the same as for an individual policy. The major benefit to the partner is that this typically results in a substantial reduction in the premium payable.

There is also often preferential underwriting on entry. Many group schemes offer medical history disregarded entry to cover, whereas individual cover is typically subject to full medical questionnaire where specific treatment exclusions are applied or subject to a 'moratorium' where pre-existing conditions are excluded.

Professional practices provide PMI for many reasons, including: provision of a valued perk, to aid employee recruitment or assist in retention, as a risk management tool to get employees back to work, as a response to employee pressure in reward negotiation, and in recognition of loyalty.

The benefits are many too: cost effective purchase, promotion of healthy workforce, reduced sickness absence, and favourable tax treatment if funding care (P11D liability on shared premium, not specific claims treatment cost).

There are drawbacks, however: healthcare costs typically escalate above general inflation, costs are volatile under annual contracts, future costs are difficult to assess, and benefit commitment tends to be long term, with no easy way out once offered, due to emotive nature of healthcare cover.

The healthcare costs are increasing due to a number of reasons: increasing usage, changing culture in the NHS, increased technology, expensive equipment and drugs, more complex procedures being undertaken in private sector, and increased patient expectations.

Advice is often sought to: add value, offer independent cost review, carry out market tenders and assessments, undertake scheme audits, leverage more buying power, and provide expert intervention in specialist claims areas.

Protection for dependants

Partners

16.29 Any life assurance taken out by a partner to cover dependants is normally effected via individual life assurance policies (see also CHAPTER 26, BECOMING A PARTNER), with the partner being responsible for maintaining premium payments. Before considering the most appropriate policy, it is important to consider objectives. For example, if the requirement is to ensure that dependants are left with sufficient income to maintain their standard of living, it is important to assess the level of the income requirement and then capitalise this on the basis of annuity factors at the time.

The next question is to consider the term of the cover. If it is to provide for dependants whilst children are in full-time education, the policy term could be linked to when the youngest child might leave university. As a rule of thumb, most families' insurance requirements are at their height between the ages of 30 and 50, reduce between 50 and 60, and increase after 60 when issues such as inheritance tax planning raise their head.

The simplest form of life cover, which provides a lump sum on death, is term assurance. This is one of the cheapest forms of cover, as benefits are paid on the death of the life assured within a specified period and, at the end of the period, the cover simply expires with no investment value. There is no tax relief on premiums paid to the policy unless it is taken out under personal pension plan provisions (see CHAPTER 27, RETIREMENT PLANNING). However, the proceeds will be free of all tax if the policy is properly established in trust.

Placing a policy in trust for beneficiaries ensures that benefits will not form a part of the deceased's estate. Failure to place benefits under trust could result in inheritance tax being paid if the deceased's estate exceeds the inheritance tax threshold. The trust must be discretionary, which is favourable for term assurance policies as they have no investment value, or a flexible interest in possession trust, a *Married Women's Property Act* trust or other absolute trust. Writing the policy in trust ensures that the proceeds are paid in accordance with the policyholder's wishes.

There are several types of term assurance: the most common is level term assurance, where the level of cover is set at the commencement of the policy and it remains unchanged until the term of the policy, which is selected at the outset, expires.

To protect the cover from inflation, there is the option of taking out an increasing term assurance. As the name implies, the original sum assured may be increased at a fixed rate or in line with the RPI each year during the term of the policy.

An option to renew the policy at the end of the term may be attached to term assurances. Another option available is to convert the policy to either endowment or whole of life policies. These options have to be selected at the commencement of the policy. At the end of the term, the option to renew or convert will be available without any further medical underwriting, but the premium will be based on premium rates and the age of the life assured at that time. These options can be useful where cover may be required for longer than the original selected term, but premium rates are more expensive than for level term assurance.

Family income benefit may be taken out to provide an income instead of a lump sum on death. Again, at commencement the benefit and term must be selected. The benefit on death will be paid in the form of annual or monthly income from the date of death to the end of the term of the policy. It is, in effect, the same as lump sum assurance cover, but paid out in the form of a regular tax-free income.

It is also possible to provide for partners' death-in-service under a group arrangement (either registered, non-registered or 'excepted' group life). This offers the normal benefits of a unit costed group arrangement, such as levels of free cover (which can be extremely valuable) and simplified administration, plus an averaged cost for the professional practice grouping which may undercut the individual policy pricing. However, the specific approach adopted will depend on a number of factors such as how many partners, the levels of cover provided, and other benefits the partner may have that count towards the lifetime allowance. This necessitates specialised advice to devise an effective strategy for the arrangement.

Employees

16.30 A professional practice is allowed to provide death-in-service benefits for its employees. Benefits can be in the form of a lump sum, spouse's pension and/or dependant's pension. In summary, lump sum benefits up to the lifetime allowance (£1.8 million as at April 2010) can potentially be paid tax-free. For death-in-service pension benefits, the benefit limit is removed, although payments continue to be subject to PAYE.

The cost of providing the benefit is tax deductible as a business expense in the firm's accounts. Death-in-service schemes are established under trust, and the firm can appoint the trustees of the scheme. Employees should be encouraged to complete a 'nomination' form detailing to whom they would like the benefits to be paid in the event of death. The trustees would take these wishes into account when distributing the lump sum benefit in the event of a claim.

The principal advantage of a group arrangement, apart from the tax deductibility of premiums, centres on the relatively cheap cost of cover (in comparison to individual policies) and the fact that these schemes provide a free cover level, so that benefits below this level do not require underwriting regardless of the health of the individual (providing all entry and eligibility criteria are satisfied).

Most professional practices will wish to provide cover for employees as it is the cheapest form of employee benefit, does not require a great deal of administration and helps ensure that their employees' dependants are adequately covered in the event of the employee's death in service.

Critical illness

16.31   Critical illness cover has been available in the UK for individuals and employers for many years now.

Generally, it is not considered to be as vital as other forms of benefits such as pension, life assurance and income protection cover. Many people confuse the benefits being provided by income protection (IP) and critical illness cover. Income protection cover, as described above, is designed to pay a regular income, which can continue up until retirement, for someone who is unable to carry on with their occupation. The illness concerned may not necessarily be life threatening.

Critical illness cover is designed to pay a lump sum, free of tax, in the event of one of a defined list of critical illnesses being diagnosed. Generally, the medical conditions concerned are severe and potentially life threatening. The attraction of a tax-free lump sum in the event of a critical illness is the fact that it could be used for purposes such as repayment of a mortgage or other debt, or to help fund private medical care. In addition, many policies will provide cover in the event of total permanent disability (TPD).

Over time, model wordings for non-core conditions have been agreed with insurers, and these cover areas such as loss of limbs or deafness where specific levels of additional cover can be provided. In addition, model wordings have been agreed in relation to exclusions explaining in what circumstances they will apply.

For group schemes, the premium paid by the employer is tax deductible, but it is taxed as a benefit in kind on the employee. Many group schemes nowadays are established as voluntary arrangements, whereby the employee pays for the cover, normally as part of a flexible benefits package so that the premium is deducted from the payroll, and the employee then benefits from lower group rates.

In partnership situations, professional partners choosing critical illness protection will in most cases effect individual critical illness policies and set the level of cover to meet liabilities which might present a problem in the event of a critical illness diagnosis, such as repayment of a loan or payment of school fees. The premiums paid to individual policies are not tax deductible, but the benefit in the event of a claim is again tax-free.

Critical illness cover certainly can complement an individual protection package, which should also comprise life cover, private medical insurance, and permanent health cover; and, for this reason, it is commonly found amongst flexible benefit choices.

Chapter 17 Regulation and Client Money

17.1 Professional practices are regulated by professional or regulatory bodies which provide the framework through which professional services are delivered to clients. Membership of one of these professional bodies gives certain comfort to clients regarding the level of service that they should expect to receive.

Of particular importance to clients, and a key management issue for the professional practice, is the administration and safekeeping of client money by the firm. To this end, the majority of professional bodies have put in place specific rules regarding client money caretaking.

Fundamental principles

17.2 Certain basic principles are common to all the various client money rules:

(a) Client money must be separated and distinguished from the firm's money by the use of different bank and building society accounts.

(b) Proper books of account must be maintained.

(c) Client account balances belong to the individual clients. It is their money and can only be used as directed by them. Use of one client's money to settle the liability of another client is not permitted.

(d) For some professional bodies, when client money is held or received, an accountants' or auditors' report must be submitted, stating whether client money rules have been complied with.

The main objective of the various rules is therefore to ensure fair treatment of clients' money and to maintain adequate bookkeeping and recording systems in order to avoid any confusion of clients' money with the firm's own money.

Specific requirements – solicitors

Introduction

17.3 Solicitors are frequently responsible for large sums of their clients' money and must abide by rules aimed at preventing the solicitor mixing his own money with that of the client. The Solicitors Regulation Authority (SRA) monitors its members to ensure that the handling of money is being carried out in accordance with the rules. This is primarily achieved by an annual report by an independent reporting accountant.

Even though authority may be delegated to one partner, responsibility for maintaining a proper bookkeeping system is shared by all (including salaried partners or members). Any misappropriation or error by one partner is, therefore, the responsibility of all the partners. All partners are responsible for ensuring that any breaches of the rules are immediately remedied.

Current rules

17.4 The Solicitors' Accounts Rules 1998 (with consolidated amendments to 31 March 2009) ('SAR') regulate the accounts of solicitors and their employees, registered European lawyers and their employees, registered foreign lawyers, and recognised bodies and their managers and employees, in respect of practice in England and Wales.

The SAR include the following definitions:

(a)   *Client* – 'the person for whom a solicitor acts'.

(b)   *Client account* – 'a current or deposit account at a bank or deposit account with a building society in the name of the solicitor or his or her firm in the title of which the word "client" appears'.

(c)   *Client money* – 'money held or received for a client or as trustee, and all other money which is not office money'.

Clients' money

17.5 Whilst clients' money is defined in **17.4** above, specific instructions from a client take precedence over the rules. These instructions may be in writing or acknowledged in writing.

In general, a solicitor cannot treat himself or herself as a client or conduct personal or office transactions through a client account. There are, however, some exceptions, as follows:

(a)   If a firm is acting in a conveyancing transaction on behalf of both a principal and his or her spouse (not being a partner in the firm), the firm is acting for both jointly and the matter must be conducted through a client account.

(b)   If a conveyancing matter involves a building society or other lender for whom the firm is also acting, that part of the transaction involving the lender's money must be dealt with through a client account.

(c) Where the firm conducts a conveyancing transaction on behalf of an assistant solicitor, consultant or non-solicitor, he should be treated as a client and any money should be kept in a client account, even if it is the assistant solicitor who is handling the matter. Money held by a solicitor, consultant or non-solicitor in respect of PAYE and VAT is not the client's money and should not be processed through a client account.

Stakeholder money is client money unless it is placed in an account operated jointly by two firms. The latter is not client money because it is not under the control of either firm. This applies equally to any money held jointly with a third party. It is best practice for jointly held money to be recorded separately in the accounting records.

Payments into a client account

17.6 The rules specify circumstances in which money must or may be paid into a client account. No other receipts are permitted to be paid in.

(a) Client money received must be paid into a client account. This must be done without delay, which in normal circumstances means the day of receipt or the next working day.

(b) Money that may be paid into a client account at the discretion of the solicitor is:

   (i) trust money;

   (ii) the firm's own money for the purpose of opening or maintaining an account;

   (iii) money to replace any sum withdrawn in contravention of the rules;

   (iv) mixed receipts which contain a proportion of client money; and

   (v) settlement of bill of costs, provided this money is withdrawn within 14 days.

Withdrawals from a client account

17.7 The rules detail when money may be paid from a client account. Other withdrawals are not permitted without the express permission of the Law Society Council, although recent changes to the rules now permit some withdrawals where the rightful owner cannot be traced, on the SRA's authorisation and, in certain cases, without SRA authorisation. The rules allow clients' money to be paid from a client account as follows:

(a) to or on behalf of the client;

(b) for the reimbursement of the solicitor, provided the client's authority has been obtained;

(c) for the solicitor's fees, but only after a bill or written intimation of a bill has been delivered by him to the client; or

(d) into another client account.

Other payments allowed include:

(i) payments of trust money;

(ii) repayment of the firm's own money when no longer required; and

(iii) repayment of money paid in contravention of the rules.

Books of account

17.8 Solicitors are required to keep accounting records showing their dealings with all clients' money. The rules require that these records are properly written up at all times. The records should include, for each client:

(a) a client cash account or a column of a cash book; and

(b) a client's ledger or column of a ledger.

The records must be such that the account balance on each client's ledger can be extracted. Dealings with non-client money should be maintained separately but in the same manner.

In addition, solicitors are also required to keep a record of all bills of costs which distinguish profit costs and disbursements and all written intimations delivered by the solicitor to his or her clients.

At least once in every five weeks, the solicitor is required to:

(i) compare the total balances shown by the clients' ledger accounts (including trust money) with cash account balances;

(ii) prepare reconciliation statements explaining any differences; and

(iii) reconcile the cash account balances to the balances shown on bank statements and in building society pass books.

The reconciliation statements must be preserved. Other documents required to be preserved are as follows:

(A) accounting records for six years;

(B) bank statements for six years;

(C) all paid cheques for two years (these can be held by the bank); and

(D) copies of bank withdrawal authorities for two years.

Interest

17.9   The rules detail the circumstances in which a client should receive interest on clients' money:

(a)   When the solicitor places the money on deposit in a separate designated account, he must account to the client for the interest earned on it. In certain circumstances set out in the rules, he must also account for a sum equivalent to the interest which would have accrued if the money received had been kept on deposit, or its gross equivalent if the interest would have been net of tax.

(b)   Where sums are not held in a separate designated account, interest is based on the amount and the time held, as set out in the rules.

Except as provided by these rules, a solicitor is entitled to retain personally interest on clients' money placed in a general client account. However, where there are variable balances, or the money is held intermittently with no individual sum within the table in the rules, interest should be accounted for when it is fair and reasonable. The fair and reasonable basis also applies to money transferred to or from a designated account while it is undesignated. Detailed rules concerning the relevant rate of interest are also set out in the rules.

The accountant's report

17.10   Within six months of the end of the financial year, every solicitor who handles clients' money or money subject to a controlled trust, is required to submit to the SRA an accountant's report certifying that he or she has complied with parts A and B, rule 24(1) of part C, and part D of the SAR. The accounting period to which the report relates must normally cover not less than 12 months and should correspond to the period for which the accounts of the firm are ordinarily made up. However, some flexibility may be allowed in the first period with the agreement of the SRA, on merger or conversion to an LLP. An accounting period may be changed to a period longer than 12 months, up to a maximum of 18 months, provided that the SRA receives written notice of the change before expiry of the deadline for delivery of the accountant's report which would have been expected on the basis of the firm's old accounting period.

Part F of the SAR sets out the nature and scope of the work to be carried out by the reporting accountant, including: who is qualified to give an accountant's report; the work that the accountant must perform on the client and office accounts for both client money and controlled trust money; when an accountant's report is required; and the format of the accountant's report. The rules do not require a *Companies Act*-style audit of the solicitor's accounts, nor do they require that accounts be prepared. The rules specify a test examination of the solicitor's accounts. Evidence of failure to comply with the SAR by such tests would lead to further testing to ascertain the extent of and reasons for the failure.

The accountant is required to extract or check the extractions of balances on the client ledger on at least two dates selected by him or her during the accounting period. At these dates, the accountant must compare the total liabilities to clients with the cash account balances of client accounts. He or she must also reconcile those cash account balances to those confirmed direct to him or her by the bank or building society.

A solicitor may decline to produce to the accountant any document which the accountant may consider it necessary to inspect, on the grounds of confidentiality between the solicitor and client. In these circumstances, the accountant must qualify the report to that effect, setting out the circumstances.

In many practices, clerical and bookkeeping errors will arise. In the majority of cases, these may be classified by the reporting accountant as trivial breaches. The reporting accountant is not required to report on trivial breaches due to clerical errors or mistakes in bookkeeping, provided they have been rectified on discovery and the accountant is satisfied that no client has suffered any loss as a result.

To report under the SAR, a reporting accountant must be a member of the ICAEW, ICAS, ICAI, the Association of Chartered Certified Accountants or the Association of Authorised Public Accountants. The reporting accountant must not have been disciplined by his or her professional body and must not be a partner or employee of the solicitor.

The accountant must also be either a registered auditor under *s 35* of the *Companies Act 1989*, an employee of the registered auditor, a partner or employee of a firm which is a registered auditor, or a director or employee of a company which is a registered auditor. (The latest SAR rules have yet to be updated to refer to the *Companies Act 2006*.)

The accountant is required to use an appropriate work programme and to complete and sign a checklist produced by the SRA. This is kept by the solicitor for three years and has to be produced to the SRA on request.

The checklist is effectively a summary of the work required under the SAR. There are two conclusions for each test:

(a) whether the test is satisfactory; and

(b) if not, whether the breaches should be notified in the accountant's report.

The checklist also requires cross-references to the accountant's own working papers.

The reporting accountant is required to report on material departures from the SRA guidelines for procedures and systems for accounting for clients' money. The reporting accountant is not required to undertake a detailed check on compliance with these guidelines. Instead, the accountant only needs to report those matters which come to their attention during the course of the work required under the SAR.

The SAR require the rights and duties of the reporting accountant to be set out in a letter of engagement with standard terms, giving the accountant a right to report directly to the SRA where there appears to be cause for concern, and a duty to report on termination of the appointment.

The terms of engagement also include:

(a)   the requirement for the accountant to produce the 'checklist' to the solicitor; and

(b)   the requirement to provide any further relevant information to the SRA on request in response to a whistle-blowing report. The letter of engagement has to be signed by the solicitor (or a partner or member of the firm) and by the accountant. Both parties must keep it for three years from the termination of the engagement and produce it to the SRA on request.

The accountant has the right to report the following matters direct to the SRA:

(a)   evidence of theft or fraud affecting clients' money or money subject to a controlled trust; and

(b)   any other information likely to be of material significance in determining whether any solicitor is a fit and proper person to hold clients' money or money subject to a controlled trust.

The accountant also has a duty to report directly to the SRA if his appointment is terminated following:

(a)   the issue of a qualified accountant's report;

(b)   the indication of an intention to issue such a report; or

(c)   the raising of concerns prior to the preparation of an accountant's report.

The reporting accountant is also given a measure of protection from breaching client confidentiality. The solicitor has to confirm in the letter of engagement that he waives his right of confidentiality in respect of any report made, document produced or information disclosed to the SRA, provided that such reports, etc are made in good faith. This applies even if the accountant is later shown to be mistaken in his belief that there was cause for concern.

Specific requirements – chartered surveyors

Introduction

17.11   Chartered surveyors, as part of their work, often receive and hold money belonging to their clients.

Current rules

17.12   RICS's Rules of Conduct for Firms version 3 (with effect from 1 January 2010) states under Part II, Conduct of Business, rule 8 that a firm shall preserve the security of clients' money entrusted to its care in the course of practice business.

Rule 8

Aim

17.13   To ensure that clients' money can be clearly linked to the clients to whom it belongs and is protected on their behalf in the following circumstances:

- insolvency;
- misappropriation by any party; or
- death of a sole practitioner.

Managing clients' money effectively should deliver an appropriate level of confidence to RICS, firms' clients, potential clients and stakeholders.

What is clients' money?

17.14   Clients' money is any money received and held by a firm that does not solely belong to it. Examples may include:

- tenants' deposits;
- rents;
- service charges;
- interest (if in an interest-bearing client account);
- arbitration fees;
- fee money taken in advance;
- clients' money held but due to be paid to contractors;
- money held by members appointed as a Receiver; or

- sale proceeds.

Key elements of best practice

CLIENT ACCOUNTS

17.15   RICS indicates that best practice regarding the custody of client money is to:

- keep clients' money in a designated account(s);

- include the name of the firm and the word 'client' – to distinguish the account from the office account;

- obtain bank confirmation of account conditions, including making sure the bank does not combine or offset funds in the client account with any other account the firm holds;

- advise client and agree terms of account handling in writing;

- ensure there are sufficient funds in the account to pay amounts owing to clients as they fall due under the firm's terms and conditions of engagement; and

- obtain clients' written approval to make payments from their accounts.

CONTROLS IN THE FIRM

17.16

- Bank funds at the earliest reasonable opportunity.

- Nominate authorised staff to handle money.

- If the firm makes use of cash receipts to settle transactions by cash, make sure the records show all cash transactions.

SYSTEMS

17.17

- Manage transactions using an accounting system appropriate to the business.

- The system should enable the firm to keep adequate records of clients' money holdings.

- A suitable software package will enable the firm to manage money effectively.

The rule recommends that client accounts, together with bank and cash balances, are reconciled at regular intervals in order to demonstrate control over the accuracy and completeness of accounting records.

It is suggested that, for most firms, monthly reconciliation is an appropriate frequency to ensure suitable control.

COMPLIANCE

17.18   RICS does not expect members to submit a periodic report, certified by a registered auditor, to indicate compliance with rule 8. However, registered firms are visited at least once every 12 to 24 months by the RICS Regulatory Services department, at which time compliance with rule 8 is monitored.

Specific requirements – estate agents

Introduction

17.19   The *Estate Agents Act 1979* (*EAA*) and the accompanying *Estate Agents* (*Accounts*) *Regulations 1981* (*EAAR*) impose a statutory duty to pay into a separate client account without delay any pre-contract and contract deposits.

A pre-contract is a payment which a prospective buyer pays to an estate agent:

(a)   in whole, or in part, as an indication of his intention to acquire an interest in land;

(b)   in whole, or in part, towards meeting any financial liability which would arise once unconditional contracts are exchanged; or

(c)   in relation to a connected contract.

A contract deposit is defined as being any sum paid by a prospective buyer which, in whole or in part, is or is intended to form part of the consideration of an interest in land, and is paid on or after the time unconditional contracts are exchanged.

Any contract or pre-contract deposits must be paid without delay into a separate client account with an institution authorised by the *EAAR*. The account must include the name of the person or firm engaged in 'estate agency work' and have the word 'client' in the title. The client account must never hold money which the estate agent has received for any other purposes. This money will however be subject to the client money rules of the NAEA, RICS and ISVA. The *EAAR* strictly regulate when payments may be put into or drawn out of a 'statutory' client account.

Payments into a client account

17.20   The following money may be paid into a client account:

(a)   all contract and pre-contract deposits;

(b)   the minimum necessary to open, or maintain, the account; and

(c)   any sum needed to rectify an error immediately upon discovery.

Withdrawals from a client account

17.21   Money may only be withdrawn from a client account in the following cases:

(a)   where it is properly required for payment to, or on behalf of, the person entitled to ask for it;

(b)   for payment of any remuneration or reimbursement of expenses in relation to estate agency work, provided the estate agent is entitled to the payment and it is made with the agreement of the client;

(c)   in the exercise of any lien to which the agent is entitled;

(d)   for transfer to another client account;

(e)   to remove the minimum sum which was non-client money used to open or maintain the account; or

(f)   to rectify a mistake when non-statutory client money has been paid into a client account in error.

Books of account

17.22   The regulations do not specify what books should be kept, but they do specify what information the estate agent should record. At any time, these must show that the estate agent has paid the money into a statutory client account and show and explain readily all subsequent dealings with that money. In particular, these records must show:

(a)   the full title of the client account;

(b)   the authorised institution where it is held;

(c)   the amount received;

(d)   the name and address of the payer;

(e)   whether the sum received is a contract or pre-contract deposit;

(f)   in either case, whether it includes any sum in respect of a 'connected contract';

(g) if the sum includes any money which is not statutory clients' money, and if so, for what purpose and in what form that part is received;

(h) the interest in the land to which the sum relates;

(i) the identity of the person wishing to dispose of the relevant interest in the land;

(j) the capacity in which the sum is received;

(k) if the payee is himself an agent, the identity of the person for whom the sum is being received; and

(l) the date of receipt.

Interest

17.23 Under the *EAAR*, anyone who holds clients' money in the course of estate agency work which exceeds £500 must account to the person for interest which has been or would have been earned, unless the amount involved is less than £10.

The accountant's report

17.24 'Statutory client accounts' must be audited within six months of the end of an accounting period, which must not exceed 12 months. The auditor must report to the estate agent whether, in his opinion, the requirements of the *EAA* and of the *EAAR* have been observed or substantially observed. The auditor can report substantial compliance if, in his opinion, they have been so observed, or complied with except for trivial breaches – for example, due to clerical errors or mistakes in bookkeeping – all of which were rectified on discovery, and none of which resulted in any loss to the person entitled to the money.

The Act does not specify any particular form of auditors' report, but a model form has been produced by the accountancy bodies. As the *EAA* is worded, the auditor has considerable responsibility. If the estate agent's accounting system is non-existent, then it may be necessary to examine every file to check compliance.

It should be noted, however, that since the 1970s, when the majority of estate agents made it standard practice to take deposits, this is an area where practice has changed significantly. There has been a greater resistance to taking pre-contract deposits as a result of intervention of solicitors, and many firms have decided against taking them.

Specific requirements – residential lettings agents

17.25   The Association of Residential Lettings Agents (ARLA) code of practice includes guidance on client money:

'●   *For the avoidance of doubt, money held or rent collected for and on behalf of client landlords (including ex-clients) is considered as client money and this will include deposits or money held for and on behalf of an applicant, tenant or ex-tenant,*

●   *The Association's Client Money Protection Bonding Scheme (CMPBS) applies to all ARLA Member Firms and protects client money held by an ARLA Member Firm in the course of its normal business of Residential Lettings and Management of a landlord's residential property against wrongful and dishonest misappropriation of such funds by the Member Firm,*

I.   A Member Firm must promptly transfer client money to and must then hold client money in a specifically designated "Client Account" (separate from the firm's own Office, Business or Operating account). A Member Firm must be able promptly, by means of a reconciliation, to identify all individual amounts of client money held in a pooled Client Bank Account.

II.   A Member Firm should not deduct any fees, costs or charges from client money without having the contractual or lawful authority to do so from the person or body who has a beneficial interest in that money.

III.   A Member Firm must pay or repay money to clients (including ex-clients), applicants, tenants (including ex-tenants) as soon as is administratively practicable and/or in line with agreed contractual arrangements.

IV.   A Member Firm should take care when making payments to ensure that any cheque banked, against which the payment is dependent, has been cleared and will not be dishonoured. It is normal to allow five working days but this is, however, a matter for the commercial judgement of each Member Firm.

V.   Except in an emergency, a Member Firm must not authorise expenditure on a property where not satisfied that funds either are, or will very shortly be, in place to pay the invoice when it becomes due.

VI.   A Member Firm must only use money or funds held to the credit of an individual client to pay that particular client or invoices incurred on behalf of that client.

VII.   A Member Firm must provide a client with an appropriate, regular Statement/Invoice detailing Income and Expenditure. Other than for trivial or minor amounts, adequately detailed invoices or receipts should support payments made on behalf of a client and copies provided to the client upon request.'

Specific requirements – accountants

Introduction

17.26 The 'Clients' Money Regulations' introduced in April 1992 are applicable to all United Kingdom, Isle of Man and Channel Island offices of firms of chartered accountants, as defined below, and are set out in the relevant Institute's 'Members Handbook'. However, the regulations do not apply to monies defined as 'investment business clients' monies' under the Investment Business Regulations. The main elements of the Clients' Money Regulations as set out by the Institute of Chartered Accountants in England and Wales are summarised below.

Key definitions

17.27 These definitions are as follows:

(a) *Clients' money* – 'money which a firm holds or receives for or from a client and which is not immediately due and payable on demand to the firm for his own account and money held by a firm as stakeholder. Fees paid in advance for professional work agreed to be performed and clearly identifiable as such shall not be regarded as "Clients' Money" for the purposes of the "Chartered Accountants' Clients' Money Regulations" '.

(b) *Clients' bank account* – 'an account in the name of the firm separate from other accounts of the firm which may be either a general account or an account designated by the name of a specific client and includes the word "client" in its title'.

(c) *Firm* – 'a sole practitioner who is a Member, or a partnership or a body corporate comprised in whole or in part of Members, the main business of whom or of which is that of a public accountant'.

Payments into a client account

17.28 The regulations specify details of what must be and what shall not be paid into a client account as follows:

(a) Clients' money received must be paid forthwith into a client account.

(b)   If money for any one client in excess of £10,000 is held or expected to be held, the money should be held in a designated client account.

Withdrawals from a client account

17.29   The regulations set out the only permitted circumstances for withdrawing client money. These include:

(a)   monies paid into the client account in error;

(b)   non-client money paid in as part of a remittance consisting of client and non-client funds;

(c)   surplus funds remaining on the account after all amounts due to the client have been repaid to them;

(d)   money properly required to be paid to or on behalf of the client;

(e)   money required to pay the firm's fees, providing the firm has given the client a statement showing details of the work carried out, provided these have been agreed by the client, 30 days have lapsed since the statement has been delivered to the client, and the fees have been accurately calculated in accordance with a formula agreed in writing by the client; and

(f)   money properly transferred into another client account.

Records and reconciliations

17.30   Accountants are required to keep proper books of account showing their dealings with all client money. Cheques endorsed over to clients must be recorded, except for firms handling monies in an insolvency capacity provided other appropriate controls are implemented. Each client bank account is required to be reconciled against the clients' ledger at least every six months, and records should be kept of such reconciliations.

Interest

17.31   The firm is required to pay interest over to the client, unless agreement not to do so has been effected in writing with the client. The client bank account must be an interest-bearing account if 'material interest' would be likely to accrue. The regulations provide explanatory notes that set out, as a guide, minimum balances and lengths held for determining 'material interest'. The regulations are therefore reasonably concise and no reporting requirements exist. The regulations concerning client monies in relation to investment business are separately dealt with under the Financial Services (Investment Business Clients' Money) (Chartered Accountants) Regulations 1988 and the Institute's Investment Business Regulations.

Specific requirements – other regulated business

17.32 Depending upon the nature of the firm's business, it may be required to comply with the rules of other regulators, most notably those of the Financial Services Authority. It is important that not only are underlying rules followed, but also the firm has a clear and correct understanding of which authority it is regulated by.

Chapter 18　Taxable Income and Allowable Expenses

Types of income

18.1　The bulk of the income of a professional practice is likely to consist of fees for services to clients and customers. However, many other kinds of receipt may in practice find their way into a firm, for example, interest on cash deposits, dividends from investments and rental income. Partners or members may also generate income from individual activities which they are obliged under the firm's constitution to put into the common pool. The income tax system in the United Kingdom deals with various types of income under separate statutory headings. It is important to understand under which heading a particular item of income falls, because the rules which determine how much of it is taxable, and the periods on which the assessment is based, vary from one statutory heading, or type of income, to another.

The main statutory headings for income

18.2　The main types of income likely to be relevant to a professional practice are as follows:

(a)　'Trading Income', which covers income from the carrying on of a trade, profession or vocation.

(b)　'Property Income', which covers rental income and most other kinds of receipts from land and buildings.

(c)　'Savings and Investment Income', which covers interest and dividends.

(d)　'Employment Income', which covers income from offices and employments, including benefits in kind and share-based remuneration.

(e)　'Foreign Income', ie income with a foreign source.

(f)　'Miscellaneous Income', which is a residual category but also contains various anti-avoidance provisions.

The most common types of income

18.3　The most common types of income are normally:

(a)　Under the 'Trading Income' heading:

Profits from the carrying on of a trade or profession, which are taxable in full, where the activity is carried on at least partly in the UK.

Professional practices, inevitably, will have most of their income taxed under this heading. This will cover the profits of the practice from providing services to clients and customers. It may, however, also include various other items, such as, in some circumstances, money received as compensation for lost profits, or the proceeds of sale of a block of fees to another firm. There are rules governing what can be deducted in calculating the professional profit, and these are described in **18.4** below.

In general, the distinction between trades on the one hand, and professions or vocations on the other, is of little practical importance nowadays, and the tax treatment of both categories of activity is the same. However, the rules introduced in the *Finance Act 1998*, which brought to an end the so-called 'cash basis', require the distinction to be made, since only firms carrying on professions or vocations were allowed to defer the additional tax arising when a change was made from the cash basis..

(b)   Under the 'Property Income' heading:

A firm may have investment property producing rental income which will be taxed under this heading, although by HMRC concession, rents from surplus office space may sometimes be included as professional profit under the 'Trading Income' heading.

(c)   Under the 'Savings and Investment Income' heading:

(i)   Interest from UK sources, such as UK bank deposit accounts, UK gilts or loan stock issued by UK companies.

(ii)   Dividends from UK companies.

(iii) Many professional practices invest surplus funds on deposit, and the interest earned will be investment income for tax purposes. However, solicitors receiving interest on clients' money are subject to special rules.

(d)   Under the 'Employment Income' heading:

Partners may also receive income from professional engagements which are undertaken by them as individuals. For example, a solicitor may write a legal textbook, or a doctor may undertake medical examinations for a life assurance company.

Many firms' constitution agreements provide that income of this type must be brought into the 'common pool' and it may then be reflected, if significant, in the size of the individual's profit share. It thus becomes part of the firm's professional profit. If retained personally, however, it will need to be entered on the individual's tax return.

Some such 'personal' activities may, in law, be offices or employments under the 'Employment Income' heading; eg a solicitor or doctor who acts as a coroner, or an accountant who acts as a director of a company. Income tax normally has to be deducted under a PAYE code number from the fees received, although small directors' fees can often be paid gross of tax and NICs if the directorship is a normal incident of the profession and the firm, and the fees are pooled under the firm's constitution. (See CHAPTER 23 for the NIC treatment of such fees.) The impact of the 'IR35' rules, which came in from 6 April 2000, may have to be considered in relation to some income of this kind, a matter which is discussed in CHAPTER 19.

(e)   Under the 'Foreign Income' heading:

The most obvious type of income here will be income from foreign investments, but this heading also covers the profits of a trade or profession carried on wholly outside the UK.

Computing trading or professional profits

18.4   It has always been necessary to make adjustments, for income tax purposes, to the results shown by the accounts of a professional practice in order to comply with tax law. These adjustments can be very substantial, because many items included, quite properly, by accepted accountancy practice may not necessarily be taxable receipts or allowable deductions under tax law. The main types of adjustment are mentioned at **18.5** and **18.13** below, but this is only a very general description of this subject. What all partners must remember, however, when they see their firm's signed accounts, is that the profit share shown as allocated to them will almost always be less than the amount on which they will eventually be taxed for the year. If the accounts show significant depreciation charges or general provisions (neither of which is allowable for tax purposes), the difference could be substantial. Of particular relevance here are the effects of Financial Reporting Standards (FRS) 5 'Revenue Recognition', and 12 'Provisions, Contingent Liabilities and Contingent Assets', and Urgent Issues Task Force (UITF) Paper 40. These are considered in more detail at **18.7–18.11** below.

An additional requirement which has applied since 1999 is that the profits for tax purposes must be computed in accordance with generally accepted accounting practice, subject to any adjustment required or authorised by law in computing profits for tax purposes. In HMRC's view, this is no more than a statutory recognition of what the law, as interpreted by the courts, has always required, but its practical effect is to import into partnership taxation computations many of the accounting principles which are required for companies, although partnerships are still not required to draw up accounts under the rules of the *Companies Acts*. One very important consequence concerns the treatment of work-in-progress and debtors. This is discussed in more detail at **18.6** below.

Taxable and non-taxable receipts

18.5   There is a basic distinction between transactions of a revenue and a capital nature. Generally, the former are part of the taxable professional profits, whereas the latter are not, although they may well have other taxation consequences.

Therefore, fees for professional work will normally be taxable as professional profits, but if a motor vehicle owned by the firm is sold at a profit this will arise on a capital asset of the business and, although it is excluded from the professional profits, the transaction will usually affect the firm's capital allowances computation. A profit on the sale of a property would equally be excluded from the professional profits, but would enter into the partner's capital gains tax computation.

Some kinds of compensation payment may be 'revenue' in nature; for example, where compensation is received for loss of profits when builders damage the firm's offices and staff cannot work normally, the proceeds merely fill a hole in the firm's profits and are taxed just like the profits they replace. However, where almost all of a firm's profit arises from a single source, such as an agency contract, which is then cancelled, compensation for this is likely to be capital in nature and not part of the professional profits (although, again, it may be liable to capital gains tax).

Many types of grant or subsidy are taxable professional receipts, especially if they are intended to assist with 'revenue' type expenses (such as salaries); but, if they are to assist with the cost of a capital asset, they are not part of the professional profit but instead deducted in calculating the capital allowances on that asset.

Recognising taxable income

18.6   In practice, the correct time when income should be recognised for tax purposes is often a more difficult problem than whether a particular receipt is taxable. This is because of the treatment of accrued rights to income and work-in-progress.

Taxable Income and Allowable Expenses

The basic rules

The position until June 2005

18.7   Until 2005 the basic rule, derived from case law, was that a professional receipt should be recognised for income tax purposes when the recipient had done everything which he was obliged to do to earn it. Normally, a professional person acting for a client will issue a bill for his services at an agreed time, or at agreed intervals, as work is done. Everything necessary to earn that fee has therefore been done when the bill is issued. Therefore, the correct treatment until 2005 was to bring into the accounts all bills issued in the year (the 'earnings' basis or 'bills issued' basis) – which automatically meant that the taxable result included outstanding debtors, possibly subject to any specific write-offs or reserves for bad or doubtful debts. Some firms, until 1999, adopted a modified version of this practice, usually known as the cash basis. Although it no longer applies for tax purposes, its abolition has some ongoing implications for firms which previously adopted it.

The significance of work-in-progress

18.8   Conventional accountancy practice requires the matching of costs with revenues in a period. Therefore, although a firm has not yet billed a client for a particular job (let alone been paid), costs have been incurred on salaries and other overheads in doing that work. So, even if it is not yet appropriate to include any part of the expected fee income for this work in revenues (as to which, now see **18.10** below), an adjustment must be made to remove these costs from the accounts at the end of the year, known as work-in-progress (WIP). The opposite adjustment is made in the following year to bring the cost into the right place to match the expected income. However, since the time of equity partners does not represent a true cost to the firm for tax purposes, chargeable time recorded by them does not need to be included in the WIP adjustment.

Example 1 – Calculating profit for tax purposes

ABC & Co bill clients for £100 of work in Year 1, but also have £20 of chargeable time recorded, by fee earners other than partners, for further clients at the year end which will be billed in Year 2. They normally apply a mark-up of 66% to costs to arrive at their charge-out rates, so this £20 represents £12 of costs. The method of calculating the Year 1 profit for tax purposes will therefore be as follows:

Year 1	£
Bills issued	100
Costs incurred (say)	(30)
	70
Add Closing WIP as above	12
Taxable profit before other expenses	82

In Year 2, the work is completed and billed at £20, in addition to other work billed at £90. The taxable profit before other expenses will be as follows:

Year 2	£	£
Bills issued		110
Less costs		(30)
Opening WIP	(12)	
Closing WIP	15	
		3
Taxable profit before expenses		83

After June 2005

18.9 However, for accounting periods ending on or after 22 June 2005, the 'basic rule' has been significantly modified by the application of UITF 40, discussed in **18.10** below.

Revenue recognition and the valuation of debtors and work-in-progress in the light of UITF 40

18.10 The *Finance Act 1998* changes made the valuation of debtors and WIP very important for partnerships, both as regards the amount of the catching up charge and, going forward, the taxable profits in future years. It became vital for firms, especially those previously on the cash basis, to have good systems for recording both of these items, and for reviewing them regularly; this remains the case, because inadequate valuations will mean that taxable profits are understated and will open the partners to HMRC investigation and possible penalties, but over-valuation will cause needless acceleration of tax bills.

However, for accounting periods ending on or after 22 June 2005, the accounting practices in UITF 40 must also be considered. Because they reflect the principles of FRS 5 on revenue recognition, they became part of 'generally accepted accounting practice', and therefore have to be adopted for tax purposes in the absence of any statutory rule to the contrary (see **18.4** above).

Broadly, UITF 40 says that revenue should be recognised once the right to consideration has arisen as a consequence of the performance of contractual obligations.

Contrasting this principle with the former 'basic rule' mentioned in **18.7** above, under which income was recognised when the professional person had done everything necessary to become entitled to it, it can be seen that the key difference is this: under the former principle, it could be argued that, where the essence of a professional assignment was the delivery of a service such as a report or a set of accounts, or the accomplishment of a transaction such as the formation of a company or a trust, there was no entitlement to be paid until the service or transaction was completed, because until then the work done had no value to the client; however, under the new principles in UITF 40, where a service is provided over a period of time, or a transaction occurs in stages, the professional may be required to recognise the revenue which has accrued to date even though the 'product' is still incomplete, provided that the work done to date has given rise to a right to revenue which can be quantified with reasonable certainty.

The practical impact of UITF 40 will be on the WIP figures in accounts at the year end (and, therefore, on the taxable profit for that year). The fair value of the work done to date on uncompleted projects will need to be included in the 'top line' rather than being recorded at no more than cost in WIP. Another fundamental difference flowing from this is that, whereas partners' time can be excluded from WIP, because partners' costs are not included in expenses, that is *not* true where a 'fair value' figure is included in revenue on the 'top line' – that figure must include work done by partners.

However, that does not mean that uncompleted work necessarily has to appear at its full selling price. UITF 40 accepts that:

(i) where a fee is contingent on matters outside the professional's control (for example, on completion of a deal), it should not be recognised until the contingency is resolved;

(ii) if a differential fee arrangement has been agreed (for example, a lower level of fee if a transaction does not proceed), revenue recognition is based on the lower amount until completion; and

(iii) account must be taken of the client's ability and willingness to pay. This allows sensible provisions to be made for WIP which may not be fully recoverable.

Firms will need to take care with the UITF 40 adjustment, especially if most of their professional engagements span more than one accounting period. The effective advancement of taxable income may well encourage firms to review their billing arrangements in order to minimise unbilled time and debtors.

Taxation effect of UITF 40

18.11   As indicated above, the impact of UITF 40 means that taxable income is recognised earlier than would have been the case under the previous accounting rules. For firms in existence when UITF 40 was adopted, there was a one-off effect in the first year in which the new basis was adopted. The *Finance Act 2006* introduced a spreading relief similar to the relief that applied when firms switched from the cash basis. This relief allowed the additional tax resulting from the adoption of UITF 40 to be spread over three years or, for those firms most severely affected, over up to six years.

Each year, one-third of the UITF 40 adjustment was taxable, subject to an upper limit of one-sixth of that year's taxable trading profit. This continued for up to five years or until the adjustment had been fully taxed. After five years, any untaxed balance would be fully taxable in the sixth year. For a firm that changed its accounting practice in the year to 30 April 2006, giving rise to an adjustment of £30,000, the maximum amounts taxable in 2006/07, 2007/08 and 2008/09 would have been £10,000 (ie one-third) in each year. However, depending on the firm's taxable profit profile, the total adjustment income could conceivably have been spread into the years 2009/10, 2010/11 and 2011/12.

Non-professional income

18.12   The calculation of taxable professional profits will also need to eliminate any 'non-professional' income shown in the accounts, such as rent or interest. These amounts will be divided between the partners in the appropriate proportions and taxed on them separately under the appropriate statutory heading, eg 'Property Income' or 'Savings and Investment Income' (see **18.2** and **18.3** above).

The property income calculation may need to include an adjustment for reverse premiums or similar cash inducements paid by landlords to persuade a firm to occupy a property which might otherwise be difficult to let. These are taxed as if they were rental income received, but the tax bill will be spread over the period over which the receipt in question is treated as income in the accounts. The normal accounting treatment would be to treat it as arising evenly over the period of the lease or, if sooner, to the date of the next rent review, and the taxation treatment will follow this. (See **18.14**(c) below for the treatment of rent-free periods.)

Deductible expenses

18.13 As with taxable income (see **18.4** above), there is considerable case law on the expenses which can be deducted in calculating the taxable professional profit. However, here there are also statutory rules, although their interpretation often causes problems.

This is especially true of the rule which says that expenses not incurred 'wholly and exclusively ... for the purposes of the trade, profession or vocation' cannot be deducted.

This area is not discussed in detail here, but a summary is provided of the most common expenses likely to be incurred and their likely tax treatment.

Normally allowable

18.14 These include as follows:

(a) *Personnel and administration*

(i) Staff salaries (although there can be problems with salaries to partners' spouses who do not perform very substantial duties). This will include the costs relating to salaried partners who have been taxed under PAYE.

(ii) Staff benefit costs.

(iii) Staff training costs.

(iv) Pension contributions for staff (but not partners). Note that a deduction is only allowable if it is paid over by the year end.

(v) One-off payments for services, eg temporary staff and consultants.

(vi) Magazines, newspapers, etc related to the business and possibly books (but see **18.19** below).

(vii) Stationery, printing, photocopying, etc.

(viii) Legal fees relating to staff matters, eg disputes about unfair dismissal, but not disputes with partners.

(ix) Employment agency and headhunters' fees relating to staff.

(x) Staff entertaining, provided that clients, contacts and other outsiders are not present.

(b) *Marketing*

 (i) Costs of producing brochures, advertisements, etc for the firm and its services.

 (ii) Fees of PR consultants, etc.

 (iii) Some kinds of sponsorship (excluding entertaining) where there is a clear advertising aspect.

(c) *Property occupied for the business*

 (i) Rent (but not a premium on a lease). The timing of the rent deduction may be affected by any rent-free periods which are agreed with the landlord; the normal accounting treatment of these will be to spread the rent actually payable over the lease, after allowing for such inducements, evenly over the term, and tax relief will be given in the same way.

 (ii) Repairs and redecoration (which often raises problems of definition, on which there is much case law).

 (iii) Rates.

 (iv) Water charges.

 (v) Lighting and heating.

 (vi) Cleaning costs.

 (vii) Property insurance.

 (viii) Reserves for leasehold dilapidations, provided that the firm will have a legal obligation at the end of the lease term, and the reserve can be calculated with sufficient accuracy. This is an area where expert advice is essential, but it should be possible to provide for the whole expected liability at the start of the lease, subject to an annual review. See also **18.17** below.

 (ix) Reserves for expected losses on rented accommodation previously used for the business, which cannot be sublet, or only at a loss. See also **18.17** below.

(d) *Finance*

 (i) Interest on the firm's borrowings, whether for working capital or the purchase of capital assets used in the business.

 (ii) Specific bad or doubtful debts written off or provided against, so long as there is evidence to support this.

 (iii) Professional indemnity premiums.

Normally disallowed

18.15 These include the following:

(a) *Personnel and administration*

> (i) Expenses which have dual business/private purposes (though sometimes apportionment may be allowed, eg home telephones which are sometimes used for business calls).

> (ii) Expenses for the maintenance of the partners personally, eg their personal drawings.

> (iii) Partners' personal pension contributions.

(b) *Marketing*

> (i) Entertaining of clients, potential clients, suppliers and contacts (this is very widely defined and the argument that, say, a party for potential clients is 'advertising' is not accepted by HMRC. The position might be different for a seminar intended to impart information).

(c) *Property*

> (i) Improvements and new building costs.

> (ii) Lease premiums and associated legal costs.

> (iii) Leasehold redemption reserves (but see **18.14**(C)(VIII) above regarding dilapidation reserves).

(d) *Finance*

> (i) Depreciation of fixed assets.

> (ii) Interest on partners' personal borrowings (although this may be allowed against the borrowing partner's personal income).

> (iii) General bad debt reserves, ie not against specific bad or doubtful debts.

> (iv) Other non-specific reserves, eg retentions against possible unspecified negligence claims (although a specific and properly quantified provision for such claims should be allowed).

> (v) Taxes on profit, eg income tax, but employment costs such as employer's NICs are allowable.

> (vi) Interest and penalties in respect of overdue tax.

It should be stressed that this is only a very broad list, and there are many individual exceptions and special cases.

Only revenue expenses

18.16 It is, of course, fundamental that only revenue expenses are allowed. Therefore, for example, although fees paid to professional tutors for staff training courses will be allowable in calculating the professional profit, the purchase of a television set and video recorder on which training videos can be watched represents the acquisition of new capital assets and is not so deductible (although capital allowances should be available, see **18.18** below). This capital/revenue distinction is also relevant in deciding, for example, whether a piece of building work represents a repair (allowable) or an improvement (not allowable). In this case, there are no capital allowances on capital expenditure, so the distinction is of considerable practical importance.

It is the presence of 'nothings' – items of expense for which neither a revenue deduction nor capital allowances is available, such as property improvements and many legal costs relating to property matters – which makes the gap between the accounts profit and the taxable profit so crucial for partners. The choice of knowledgeable and effective advisers who can negotiate the many grey areas with HMRC is most important.

Timing of deductions

18.17 As with receipts (see **18.6** above), there are rules about when an expense can be recognised for tax purposes as a deduction in calculating taxable professional profits. Broadly, an allowable expense can be deducted when it would be charged in the accounts according to generally accepted accountancy principles, unless there is a statutory provision to the contrary. In one decided case (*Gallagher v Jones* [1993] STC 199), the Court of Appeal held that it was correct to spread the rental payments for an asset over the term of the lease, even though the actual payments were largely front-loaded.

Reserves and provisions for expected future expenses may be disputed by HMRC unless they can be justified under generally accepted accounting practice. Financial Reporting Standard (FRS) 12 deals with these items and requires that a provision can only be made where a business has a present obligation, legal or constructive, as a result of a past obligating event, and it is probable that a payment will be required to settle that obligation. The amount of that payment must also be capable of being reliably estimated. For tax purposes, HMRC will accept a properly estimated FRS 12 provision, provided it does not conflict with any rule in the *Taxes Acts*. It should, therefore, be possible to obtain tax relief for a properly calculated provision for leasehold dilapidations, or expected losses from being unable to sublet surplus space. In the past, HMRC tended to dispute these and allow relief only on a 'paid' basis when expenditure was incurred.

Taxable Income and Allowable Expenses

Example 2 – A profit computation adjusted for income tax purposes

The following example – necessarily oversimplified – shows how a firm's profit and loss account is adjusted to take account of some of the more common adjustments mentioned above.

Messrs Sue, Grabbit and Runne's profit and loss account shows, in summary, the following results for the year:

	£	£
Work done (adjusted for WIP)		400,000
Less		
Salaries and other staff costs	100,000	
Partners' motoring expenses	10,000 (*a*)	
Entertaining of clients and contacts	5,000 (*b*)	
Office rent	25,000	
Office repairs	1,000 (*c*)	
Specific bad debt provided	3,000 (*d*)	
General bad debt reserve	2,000 (*e*)	
Interest on overdraft	10,000 (*f*)	
Interest on partners' loans	5,000 (*g*)	
Depreciation of fixed assets	12,000 (*h*)	
Other allowable expenses	27,000	
		200,000
Profit divisible among partners		200,000

Notes

(*a*)   The detailed mileage records indicate that 50% of these expenses are 'private', so profit for tax purposes is increased by £5,000.

(*b*)   The entertaining expenses are disallowed by statute (see **18.15** above), increasing taxable profits by £5,000.

(*c*)   All are 'revenue' items except for £600 which is in fact the cost of a new desk for a partner and is disallowed for the purpose of the taxable profit, but will qualify for capital allowances.

(*d*)   If this all relates to specific debtors, properly evaluated, it should be allowed.

(*e*)   The general bad debt reserve of £2,000 is disallowed in full.

(*f*)   Interest on the firm's overdraft will normally be allowed (so long as partners' current accounts are not overdrawn).

(*g*)   Partners' personal borrowing costs of £5,000 are not allowable in computing the firm's profit, but may be allowed against their personal tax bills.

(*h*)   Depreciation of fixed assets is disallowed here, but may be reflected in the capital allowances (see **18.18** below).

The 'tax-adjusted' profit is, therefore, £229,600.

From this amount, any capital allowances (see **18.18** below) are then deducted.

Capital allowances

Introduction

18.18   As has been seen in **18.17** above, there are several types of capital expenditure for which no deduction is due when calculating professional taxable profits, but where some relief is available by capital allowances. These, in their different ways, all give some relief for the capital cost of an asset over a period of time, and so the practical difference between a deduction in arriving at the professional taxable profits and a capital allowance is measured in terms of cash flow.

The tax system gives capital allowances on plant and machinery, ships, scientific research, patent rights and other more rarely encountered assets. However, professional practices will be concerned normally only with allowances for plant and machinery, so what follows will concentrate on these.

Meaning of 'plant and machinery'

18.19   This expression has misleading overtones of large industrial processes. In fact, it was defined by the courts many years ago as 'whatever apparatus is used by a businessman for carrying on his business – not his stock in trade, which he buys or makes for sale; but all goods and chattels, fixed or moveable, live or dead, which he keeps for permanent employment in his business' (*Yarmouth v France* (1887) 19 QBD 647). In that case, the item held to be plant (which will be used here as a shorthand expression) was a horse. Its modern counterpart, the motor vehicle, is another obvious case of plant. In the present context, the expression also clearly includes the array of machinery such as computers, fax machines, photocopiers and telephone apparatus found in a modern office. Perhaps less obviously, the courts have held that a library of law books would be plant for a lawyer (although, in practice, the whole cost may be written off as a deduction in computing professional profits – see **18.17** above). There is now special legislation for intangible assets such as software. Arguments about what is plant usually centre on items which are arguably parts of buildings or closely associated with buildings.

The courts have drawn a distinction between the physical setting in which a business is carried on, which cannot be plant, and functioning apparatus with which it is carried on, which may be plant. Thus, for example, an immobilised barge, used as a restaurant, was held not to be plant, but a dry dock in a shipbuilding business was. These case law principles have been supplemented by detailed statutory rules, introduced after HMRC had become concerned about the increasingly liberal trend of recent court decisions. These are currently enshrined in the *Capital Allowances Act 2001.*

Very broadly, the Act declares that no expenditure on the provision of a building can be plant, and the same applies to assets incorporated or normally in buildings. Specific items are listed which are not to be plant, and there are lists of items which may be.

This development has not helped to clarify an already vague area of tax law. Firms which are contemplating a major building project or the purchase of office buildings must take good advice on how they can maximise the element of cost which qualifies as plant – remembering that the element which does not qualify will attract no income tax relief at all (see **18.16** above). In general, plant allowances will not be available for the cost of walls, floors, ceilings, doors or stairs; for mains services delivering water, electricity and gas; waste disposal, drainage and sewerage systems and fire safety systems such as escapes and fire doors (unless expenditure on them can be regarded as incidental to the installation of plant). However, many specific items are allowed, including space and water heating systems, air-conditioning systems, most kitchen equipment and sanitary fittings, lifts (but not their shafts), burglar alarms, safes, advertising displays, and partitions which are intended to be moved around to reconfigure working spaces. Most of these items reflect court decisions in the taxpayer's favour.

Since 6 April 2008, a new category of plant or machinery has been introduced – integral features. Integral features are typically, but not always, fixtures, and currently include plant in five categories:

- electrical systems (including lighting systems);

- cold water systems;

- space or water heating systems, powered systems of ventilation, air cooling or purification and any floor or ceiling comprised in such systems;

- lifts, escalators and moving walkways; and

- external solar shading.

Integral features qualify for capital allowances at a special rate (see **18.26** below). Where repair expenditure (when considered on a rolling 12-month basis) on integral features amounts to more than 50% of the cost of replacement at the beginning of the 12-month rolling period, it is regarded as capital expenditure and not revenue (repair) expenditure. In practice, it should be straightforward to assess whether repair expenditure on integral features breaches the capital expenditure limit; although, if the asset register of the business is large and complex, it may be necessary to have a complex recording and control system in place.

How plant allowances are calculated – first-year allowances, writing down allowances and the 'pool'

18.20   Assuming the expenditure in question is 'plant', the law then requires that it must belong to the partnership which acquired it as a consequence of capital expenditure having been incurred on it (other types of financing are considered below).

'Small or medium- sized' firms

18.21   Firms which qualify as 'small or medium-sized' businesses could claim a first-year allowance on certain items of plant acquired before 6 April 2008. Very broadly, a firm met these size criteria if, in the accounting period in question or the previous one, it met two of the following three conditions:

- turnover not exceeding £22.8 million for periods from March 2004 to March 2008;

- gross assets not exceeding £11.4 million for periods from March 2004 to March 2008; and

- not more than 250 employees, taking the average monthly figures in the period in question.

Firms which met the above criteria obtained a first-year allowance (FYA) of 40% of expenditure after 1 July 1998. The first-year allowances were not available on motor cars, expenditure in the period in which a business ceases, and certain other assets with a predictable life exceeding 25 years.

Where an asset qualified for the 40% allowance in its first year, the balance of expenditure (60%) attracted writing-down allowances (WDAs) on the reducing balance in later years, along with expenditure which did not attract the first-year allowance, as described below.

'Small' firms

18.22 Firms which qualified as 'small' could claim certain special rates of capital allowances on assets acquired up to 5 April 2008. 'Small' broadly meant a business which met at least two of the following criteria in the period in which the expenditure was incurred or in the previous accounting period:

- turnover not more than £5.6 million for periods from March 2004 to March 2008;

- the balance sheet total not more than £2.8 million for periods from March 2004 to March 2008; and

- the average number of employees, calculated on a monthly basis, did not exceed 50.

'Small' firms were able to claim an enhanced rate of FYAs at 50% on certain types of plant and machinery, although this has been available only during specific periods. The 50% rate was available for acquisitions after 5 April 2004 and before 6 April 2005, but was then withdrawn, only to be reintroduced for acquisitions after 5 April 2006 and before 5 April 2008

Temporary first-year allowance

18.23 A temporary 40% first-year allowance was introduced for businesses of all size, for expenditure on plant or machinery in the period 6 April 2009 to 5 April 2010.

Annual investment allowance

18.24 For expenditure incurred on or after 6 April 2009, partnerships of individuals could claim an annual investment allowance (AIA) of 100% of the expenditure on most plant or machinery (other than cars). The limit of expenditure for the AIA was £50,000 for expenditure between 6 April 2009 and 5 April 2010 and £100,000 after this date, with the limit time apportioned for periods crossing the date of change. The Chancellor announced in the June 2010 Budget that this limit will reduce to £25,000 with effect from 6 April 2012. If a partnership contains a corporate or trust partner, then it cannot claim AIA. There are also avoidance provisions to prevent a multiplication of claims from related businesses where the trade has been split. Only one AIA is available to more than one business where the same person carries on the businesses and controls them, and the businesses are related. Unincorporated businesses are related if, at the end of the accounting period, they operate from the same business premises or undertake the same EU NACE classification of activity.

Special allowances

18.25 There is also an Enhanced Capital Allowances scheme which lists classes of energy-saving or environmentally friendly technologies that can qualify for 100% first-year allowances, regardless of the size of the business. The types of energy-saving plant which can qualify have to be designated as such by Treasury Order, and a list of qualifying items is maintained. Full details of the qualifying technologies and products are available on the Internet at www.eca.gov.uk. Items of plant can be added to or removed from the list, so it is critical to ensure that the item is on the list when the expenditure is incurred. Advice can be obtained from the Environment and Energy Helpline (tel 0800 585794).

Cars with low CO_2 emissions also qualify for 100% first-year allowances. For expenditure incurred on or after 6 April 2008, the limit of emissions for cars in this category is a level not exceeding 110 g/km.

The 'pool' concept

18.26 Most expenditure on plant which qualifies for WDAs, along with the balance of expenditure which qualified for first-year allowances, goes into a 'pool', and the allowance is calculated on the total value of the pool after deducting items sold, destroyed or no longer used in the business. The sale price of items sold, or the open market value or insurance proceeds in other cases, has to be deducted. However, this cannot exceed original cost, since the purpose of the WDA is to allow tax relief for no more than the cost, and any 'profit' made may be subject to CGT. A point to note on the interaction with CGT is that, if capital allowances have been claimed on fixtures in a building which is subsequently sold, the cost of the fixtures still qualifies as a deduction in the CGT computation, notwithstanding that capital allowances have been claimed, as long as the CGT computation shows a gain. In this regard, it will be pertinent to ensure any election to treat the disposal value of fixtures at a set value is taken into account in order to secure a capital allowance deduction without clawback as well as a deduction for CGT purposes.

With the introduction of integral features in April 2008, and the change in rates of allowance, a new 'special rate pool' was established for expenditure incurred on or after 6 April 2008 (for unincorporated businesses) which qualified for plant or machinery allowances in the following categories:

- thermal insulation;

- integral features;

- long-life assets (unless used in a ring fence trade) for all expenditure incurred on or after 6 April 2009; and

- cars with a CO_2 emission level exceeding 160 g/km for expenditure incurred on or after 6 April 2009.

The rate of annual writing-down allowance for the special rate pool is 10%, but the Chancellor announced in the June 2010 Budget that this rate will reduce to 8% with effect from 6 April 2012.

For the main plant or machinery pool (for qualifying expenditure not in any other category of pool), the rate of annual writing-down allowance changed (for unincorporated businesses) on 6 April 2008 from 25% to 20%. The Chancellor announced in the June 2010 Budget that this rate will reduce to 18% with effect from 6 April 2012.

With effect from 6 April 2009, expenditure on cars with CO_2 emissions levels not exceeding 160 g/km is allocated to the main plant or machinery pool. A consequence of the pooling treatment for cars from April 2009 is that there is no longer a balancing allowance on disposal of these cars. There is avoidance legislation to prevent schemes aimed at crystallising a balancing allowance on such pooled cars.

'Non-pooled' assets and private use

18.27 Certain assets are not 'pooled' in this way because the WDAs given on them are calculated differently. The principal instances are pre-6 April 2009 expenditure incurred on motor cars (but not vans) which cost more than £12,000, where the WDA is limited to £3,000 (or 25% of the reducing balance if less), and other assets which are used partly for private purposes, where the WDA is restricted to the business proportion. Where there is such a restriction, the whole (unrestricted) WDA is deducted from the brought-forward value to give the value to carry forward to the next year, so the effect is that allowances are lost permanently to the extent that there is private use. Short-life assets (see **18.29** below) are also excluded from the main 'pool'.

Cars in single asset pools ('expensive cars') at 6 April 2009 continue to attract the main rate of annual writing-down allowance (a rate of 20% restricted to a maximum of £3,000 per year) and normal capital allowance disposal treatment. However, any balance left in these single car pools at 6 April 2014 will be transferred to the general pool.

Balancing adjustments

18.28 Where there is a sale or other event which requires a value to be deducted from the 'pool' (see **18.26** above), this may exceed the total 'pool' value. In that event, the excess is treated as taxable income and known as a 'balancing charge'. It simply claws back the tax relief which was given on the original expenditure to the extent that it has been recovered by selling the asset. A similar calculation applies where a 'non-pooled' asset is sold. Balancing charges on such assets, especially cars, are more common than balancing charges on the 'pool'. If the business has ceased, the market value of the 'pool' has to be deducted from its brought-forward value. This may give rise to a balancing charge or, if the market value is less than the brought-forward value, a balancing allowance, which simply gives additional relief for the paper loss thrown up on cessation in respect of those depreciated assets.

A balancing allowance can also arise on 'non-pooled' assets which are sold, but it cannot arise in respect of the 'pool' except on cessation. This has led to the creation of a useful facility to extract certain 'short-life' assets from the 'pool' – see **18.29** below.

Short-life assets

18.29 The standard method of giving WDAs at 20% (25% for periods prior to 6 April 2008) on the reducing balance each year may give a reasonable result for assets such as office furniture and fixtures, which often have a fairly long life. However, the reducing balance method may not reflect the economic reality for 'short life' assets, such as much modern computer equipment. Therefore, it is possible to elect for specified classes of assets of this type to be 'de-pooled'. This will ensure that a balancing allowance can be given immediately on sale (see **18.28** above), instead of having to wait until the business ceases. This treatment has to be claimed within two years of the tax year of acquisition. It is not suitable for assets expected to last for five years or more, since after five years any remaining cost is transferred back to the general 'pool', nor can this treatment be applied to motor vehicles. Expenditure on integral features cannot be allocated to a short life asset pool.

Other forms of ownership

18.30 Plant may not necessarily, of course, be purchased outright: it may be taken on hire-purchase or various types of lease arrangement.

Rules for claiming capital allowances on leased plant or machinery were significantly changed with effect from 1 April 2006. The changes transferred the ability to claim allowances from the lessor to the lessee where the lease met the conditions of a long funding lease (most operating leases of five years or more, certain finance leases between five and seven years in length, and all funding leases of seven years or more). Fortunately, there is an exemption from the long funding leasing rules (subject to certain requirements) for certain plant or machinery typically leased in a building.

Determining whether a plant and machinery lease is a long funding lease is a two-stage process. First, one must decide if the lease is a 'funding lease'. Secondly, if the lease is not a 'short lease', it is a long funding lease.

A funding lease is:

- a finance lease or loan in the accounts of the lessor under GAAP; or

- a lease where the present value of the minimum lease payments are equal to or greater than 80% of the fair value of leased plant; or

- a lease whose term is more than 65% of the remaining useful economic life of the leased asset.

Useful economic life begins with the term of the lease, and ends when the asset is no longer likely to be used by any person for any purpose as a fixed asset. Thus, the time period is not limited to the period of the current lease, nor to use of the asset in a particular trade. It is good practice to retain records demonstrating how it was decided whether or not the lease is a funding lease, as conclusions may change with the benefit of hindsight at a later point.

Having determined that the lease is a funding lease, it will be treated as a 'long funding lease' if it is not a 'short lease'. If treated as a long funding lease, the lessee will be entitled to the capital allowances, not the lessor.

A short lease is one which has:

- a lease term of less than five years; or

- a lease term of between five and seven years that satisfies all of the following three points:

    - is treated under GAAP as a finance lease, and

    - the residual value of the finance lease is less than or equal to 5% of the market value of the plant at the commencement of the lease term (as estimated at lease inception), and

    - total rentals in the first year are no lower than 90% of the rentals in the second year, with rentals in any year after the second year being no greater than 110% of those in the second year. This test excludes any rentals due on the first day of the lease.

An operating lease lasting more than five years which is a funding lease can never be a short lease and will always be subject to the long funding lease rules. There are circumstances, however, where a finance lease of plant or machinery lasting up to seven years could escape the long funding lease rules.

Sometimes, a firm which leases a building is required under the lease to fit out the building with fixtures of various kinds. Broadly, these are treated as belonging to the tenant, even though in law they belong to the landlord, as long as they are used in the tenant firm's business, and allowances can be claimed accordingly.

Where capital allowances can be claimed on leased assets that are not subject to the long funding lease rules, the allowances are claimed on the capital element of the lease expenditure. A more detailed discussion of the capital allowances of leased plant or machinery is outside the scope of this reference book.

Making claims and method of giving relief

18.31   Capital allowances are given as an expense item (or, in the case of balancing charges, as business receipts) in arriving at the taxable professional profit: if this computation shows a loss, they are simply components in arriving at that loss, like any other deductible expense.

Claims to capital allowances have to be specifically made in tax returns, which must be submitted by 31 January after the end of the tax year.

Example 3 – Typical computation of capital allowances

A partnership which is unable to use the annual investment allowance, as it has a corporate partner, has the following transactions in plant during the year ended 30 April 2010:

		£
July 2009	Purchase of car with emissions levels over 160 g/km for partner	26,000
Nov 2009	Purchase of general pool plant	20,000
Dec 2009	Disposal of general pool plant	30,000
Jan 2010	Disposal of office computer	3,000
Feb 2010	Purchase of office computer	8,000

Both the computers are treated as 'short life' assets (see **18.29** above). The car acquired for the partner is used privately for 30% of the time. The written-down value of the general pool brought forward as at 1 May 2009 is £180,000 and of the 'old' computer (1) is £5,000.

Taxable Income and Allowable Expenses

	General Pool	Computer (1)	Computer (2)	Private use single asset car pool subject to Special rate	Allow-ances Given
	£	£	£	£	£
Written down value b/fwd	180,000	5,000	–	–	
Additions				26,000	
Sale proceeds (restricted to original cost, if lower)	(30,000)	(3,000)			
Balancing Allowance		(2,000)			2,000
Remaining expenditure	150,000	–		26,000	
WDA to be restricted	–		–	(2600)	2,600
30% private use					(780)
Annual writing down allowance (20%)	(30,000)				30,000
Additions qualifying for temporary FYA	20,000		8,000		
Temporary FYA	(8,000)		(3,200)	–	11,200
Written down value c/fwd	132,000	–	4,800	23,400	
Total allowances to be given as an expense in arriving at 2010/11 taxable profits					45,020

Chapter 19 Income Tax

Introduction

19.1 Partnerships have their taxable profits calculated on the current year basis. It is an immutable rule of the current year basis that an individual will pay tax on all the taxable profits attributed to them from the date of commencement (or 6 April 1996, if later) to the date of cessation.

Although the computation of taxable profits is prepared at the partnership level, the partnership itself has no tax liability, and the taxable profits are allocated to the individual partners and taxed on them effectively as though they were sole traders.

The members of an LLP, like the partners of an unlimited partnership, will normally be subject to income tax on the firm's profits rather than corporation tax. Accordingly, the income tax treatment of equity partners in a partnership will usually be unaffected by the change to LLP status, but the tax status of salaried partners may change from being an employee taxed under PAYE to being regarded as self-employed.

Section 4(4) of the *LLP Act* states that:

> 'A member of a limited liability partnership shall not be regarded for any purpose as employed by the limited liability partnership unless, if he and the other members were partners in a partnership, he would be regarded for that purpose as employed by the partnership.'

Therefore, the LLP legislation clearly envisages circumstances where a member could be employed for tax purposes and therefore liable to employment taxes.

However, it appears that HMRC take the view that all members of an LLP are self-employed for tax purposes. The HMRC Business Income Manual at BIM72115 says: 'If an LLP carries on a trade then each registered partner is taxable on the income they derive from the LLP as self-employed trading profits notwithstanding the fact that the registered member may have been a salaried partner (an employee) in a predecessor general partnership'.

The members of a partnership are required to nominate one of their number to complete and file the partnership tax return. This partner is referred to as the nominated or representative partner.

If the nominated partner becomes unavailable, the members of the partnership may choose a successor and must notify the change to HMRC. In the absence of such notification, HMRC can make a nomination. In the event that HMRC propose to open an enquiry, the appropriate notice has to be issued to the nominated partner.

HMRC previously took the view that the other partners had no rights of appeal against the partnership profits allocated to them, but that view did not find favour with the First Tier Tribunal in the cases of *Graham Morgan and Heather Self v The Commissioners for HMRC* (TC00046) and *Raymond John Phillips v HMRC* (TC00276). It is understood that HMRC are reviewing their procedures in the light of those reported cases. In particular, it appears that HMRC now accept that, if an individual partner does not agree the amount of taxable profits allocated to them by the nominated partner, that individual cannot make what they regard as a complete and correct return unless they also show on their personal tax return what they consider to be the correct assessable profits.

The current year basis of income taxation for partnerships and limited liability partnerships

Overview of the present system

19.2 The main features of the current year basis are:

(a) current year ('CY') basis of assessment (see **19.3** below);

(b) special commencement and cessation rules (see **19.5** and **19.9** below);

(c) the concept of 'overlap' reliefs for profits taxed more than once (see **19.6** below);

(d) individual accountability for partners' tax and the concept of treating each partner as carrying on a notional separate business (see **19.23** below); and

(e) self-assessment compliance rules (see **19.35** below).

The 'CY' basis

19.3 The 'CY' basis ensures that partners are taxed on the profits of the accounting period ending in the current year (ie accounting year ended 30 April 2009 will be taxed in the tax year 2009/10).

Payment of tax and choice of accounting dates

19.4 Tax is due under the present regime via an instalment system which requires a final payment by 31 January following the end of the tax year (see **19.34** below). Therefore, there can be a considerable time-lag between the end of the accounting period and the date of payment of tax (see **19.30** below). The choice of an accounting date early in the tax year can have important cash flow advantages. With a 30 April date, the final tax payment for 2009/10 is due on 31 January 2011, ie 21 months after the year end.

Commencement rules

19.5 The current year basis deals with the opening years in the following way:

(a) *First tax year of business*

Based on the actual profit of that year, apportioned to 5 April.

(b) *Second tax year of business*

(i) If there is an accounting date in that year which falls less than 12 months after the starting date, the taxable profit is based on the first 12 months.

(ii) If there is an accounting date in the second year which is more than 12 months after the starting date, the taxable profit is based on the accounting period ending in the year. In other words, such a business reaches the 'CY' basis in the second tax year.

(iii) If there is no accounting date in the year (for example, where a business starts on 1 March 2008 and draws up a long account to, say, 31 December 2009) the 'fiscal year' basis is used.

(c) *Third tax year of business*

By the third tax year, the business should reach the 'CY' basis if it has not already done so in the second.

Example 1 – Start business on 1 May 2008 with 30 September accounting date

Bob, Carole, Ted and Alice started their firm on 1 May 2008 and draw up their accounts to 30 September each year, from 30 September 2008.

Their accounts show tax adjusted profits as follows:

1 May 2008 to 30 September 2008	£60,000
Year ended 30 September 2009	£108,000
Year ended 30 September 2010	£120,000

Their tax bills will be based on the following:

2008/09 (based on 1 May 2008 to 5 April 2009):	
Profit of initial period	£60,000
plus (say) ⁶⁄12 x £108,000	£54,000
	£114,000
2009/10 (based on year to 30 September 2009):	£108,000
2010/11 (based on year to 30 September 2010):	£120,000

Note that, in practice, apportionment of 'overlap' profits (see **19.6** below) is calculated in precise numbers of days rather than round months.

Also note that the accounting date in the second tax year, 30 September 2010, falls more than 12 months after the starting date, and thus the firm reaches the 'CY' basis by its second tax year.

The profits of this second accounting period are, clearly, taxed 1.5 times – partly in 2009/10 and wholly in 2010/11. The treatment of this 'overlap' profit is discussed below (see **19.6** and Example 3 at **19.10** below).

Example 2 – Start business on 1 March 2010 with 30 September accounting date

Atherton, Helsby and Cable started their firm on 1 March 2010 and also draw up accounts to 30 September, with the following profits:

1 March 2010 to 30 September 2010	£91,000
Year ended 30 September 2011	£144,000
Year ended 30 September 2012	£156,000

Their tax bills will be based on the following:

2009/10 (based on 1 March 2010 to 5 April 2010):	
(say) ¹⁄7 x £91,000	£13,000
2010/11 (based on 1 March 2010 to 28 February 2011 – see below):	
Profits of initial period	£91,000
plus (say) ⁵⁄12 x £144,000	£60,000
	£151,000
2011/12 (based on year to 30 September 2011):	£144,000
2012/13 (based on year to 30 September 2012):	£156,000

Here, the accounting date in the second tax year, 30 September 2010, is less than 12 months after the starting date, and thus the first 12 months' profit is taken. The 'CY' basis is not reached until the third tax year.

As in the previous example, some profits 'overlap' – here, the periods from 1 March to 5 April 2010 (falling in 2009/10 and 2010/11) and from 1 October 2010 to 28 February 2011 (falling in 2010/11 and 2011/12). This is discussed below (see **19.6** and Example 3 at **19.10** below).

This multiple taxation of the same profits means that the legitimate minimisation of taxable profits in the opening periods remains very important. There are many ways in which this can be done, including the use as employees or consultants of those who may later become partners. This will reduce initial profits by their salaries or fees.

Overlap profits

19.6   Both Examples 1 and 2 above showed that the same profits can be taxed more than once. The 'CY' basis identifies the over-taxed profit – called an 'overlap' profit – and gives relief for those actual amounts later, either on cessation or if the accounting date is moved to later in the tax year. However, the rules do not give any relief for inflation, so the real value of this relief may be substantially eroded if it is not given until many years later. However, the 'CY' basis ensures that partners pay tax on the full amount of their share of the taxable profit arising during their partnership career.

HMRC have confirmed that the incorporation of the whole of the business of an unlimited partnership to an LLP will not trigger any recovery of overlap relief for members or partners.

Subsequent changes to a later accounting date

19.7   If no subsequent changes to a later accounting date in the tax year occur, the overlap relief will be given in full on cessation. If the accounting date is changed to a date nearer to the end of the tax year, a pro-rata fraction of the relief is given. A change to a 5 April date will result in the whole of the relief being given, but a change from, say, 30 September to 31 December, roughly 'half way' to 5 April, would release roughly half the accrued relief.

'Reward' for those with late accounting dates

19.8   The intention of this system is, quite clearly, to 'reward' firms who choose late accounting dates, with the consequent acceleration of the receipts to the Exchequer. When selecting accounting dates, partners therefore need to bear in mind that the cash flow benefits of an early date may involve inability to recover 'overlap' relief until cessation. The minimisation of initial profits, and hence the amount of any overlap, is thus particularly important (see **19.5** above).

Cessations

19.9   In the tax year in which a partnership business ceases altogether, the tax bills for each partner are based on the profits from the end of the last preceding basis period to the cessation date. The last preceding basis period may have ended in the previous tax year and the basis period could exceed 12 months, but the taxed profits will be reduced by any 'overlap' relief from the opening years.

The incorporation of an existing partnership business into an LLP will not be treated as a cessation for income tax purposes. The exception to this rule is where only part of the business is transferred and, in such cases, specific advice should be sought.

No revision of earlier years' assessments

19.10   There is no revision of any earlier years' assessments as there was under the pre-'CY' basis. In addition, there is no deemed cessation of the business when there is a change of partners (see **19.26** below), although any retiring partner will then be subject to the cessation rules.

Example 3 – The overlap relief rules in relation to cessations

The following example illustrates how the overlap relief (see **19.6** above) feeds through into the treatment of cessations.

Bob, Carole, Ted and Alice (see Example 1), who started their business on 1 May 2008, decide to bring it to an end on 31 December 2011. Their profits from 1 October 2010 are as follows:

Year to 30 September 2011	£96,000
Period from 1 October to 31 December 2011	£24,000

The tax year of cessation is 2011/12, so the basis period for that year runs from 1 October 2010, immediately after the end of the basis period for 2010/11, to 31 December 2011, ie 15 months.

The profits taxed will be based on:

12 months to 30 September 2011	£96,000
3 months to 31 December 2011	£24,000
Total 15 months	£120,000

However, this is when the overlap relief from commencement is given. The period from 1 October 2008 to 5 April 2009, say six months, was taxed both in 2008/09 and 2009/10. So, relief for this profit is now given as follows:

15 months' profit to 31 December 2011, as above	£120,000
Less 6 months' profit from 'overlap' period, as above (say, 6/12 × £108,000)	£54,000
Total 9 months	£66,000

The tax bills for Bob, Carole, Ted and Alice for 2011/12 will thus be based on aggregate taxable profits of £66,000. Superficially, it may seem that nine months of profit, corresponding to the (roughly) nine months from 6 April to 31 December, have been taxed, but the relief does not take the form of taxing only 9/15 of the actual profits earned from 1 October 2010. It is based on the actual overlap profits from 2008/09. In the real world, Bob, Carole, Ted and Alice might continue as partners for nearly 40 years instead of less than four, and the real value of the 'overlap' profit of £54,000 in, say, 2050 might have little impact on taxable profit at that time. This is another argument for a late accounting date (see **19.8** above). It will also, of course, be important to record and carry forward any 'overlap' reliefs, so that they are not overlooked, and the tax return for partners includes a box to record this figure.

When overlap relief exceeds the profits

19.11   The overlap relief is deducted from profits of the final tax year, as illustrated above; if it exceeded those profits, a 'loss' would be created, which could then be relieved against other income or in the various ways described at **19.17** below.

Changes of accounting date

19.12   Businesses are free to choose their own accounting date, despite the obvious inducement in the 'overlap rules' to choose a late date in the tax year, and in general this will be respected for tax purposes, but HMRC have the power to disregard a change if certain conditions do not apply.

Conditions for change of accounting date

19.13   Except in the first three years of trading, in order to be a valid change of accounting date the following conditions apply:

(a) the first period ending on the new date must be 18 months or less; and

(b) notice of the change is given to the Inspector by 31 January following the 'year of change'; and

(c) unless there has been no change under these rules in the previous five tax years (in which case, no further steps are necessary), HMRC are satisfied that there are bona fide commercial reasons (unconnected with tax) for the change.

If the above conditions are not satisfied, the results of the new accounting period must be apportioned across the old periods, so compliance with the above is highly advisable.

The 'year of change' is the first tax year in which accounts are drawn up to the new date, or, if there is a long gap so that there is a tax year with no accounting date, it means that 'blank' year. Therefore, if the change is from 31 December 2009 to 30 April 2010, 2010/11 is the 'year of change'. If the change is from 31 March 2009 to 30 April 2010, the 'year of change' is 2009/10.

The effect of changing the date

19.14 Assuming that these conditions are all met, the effect of changing the date will be that the tax bill for the 'year of change' will be based on the profits as follows:

(a) if the period exceeds 12 months, from the end of the basis period for the immediately preceding tax year to the new accounting date in the year of change; and

(b) in other cases, of the 12 months ended on the year of change.

To a later or earlier date

19.15 This is simpler than it sounds. If the change is to a later date in the tax year, the gap between the old and new dates will exceed 12 months. If it is to an earlier date, it will be less than 12 months. A change to a later date involves a basis period of more than 12 months, and therefore 'overlap' relief can be deducted to reduce it to 12 months. A change to an earlier date leads to the extension of the 'gap' period to a full 12 months, and therefore a further 'overlap' for relief later.

Example 4 – Change of accounting date to later date

Atherton, Helsby and Cable (see Example 2) decide to change their accounting date from 30 September to 31 December. Their year to 30 September 2012 showed profits of £156,000 and their next accounts, for the 15 months to 31 December 2013, show profits of £240,000.

The 'year of change' is 2013/14, the first tax year in which the new date is used. So the bill for that year is based on 15 months from 1 October 2012 to 31 December 2013, less three months of 'overlap' relief from commencement. That 'overlap' profit was approximately:

1 March to 5 April 2010 (say ⅐ x £91,000)	£13,000
1 October 2010 to 28 February 2011	
(say ⁵⁄₁₂ x £144,000)	£60,000
Total	£73,000
So the 2013/14 tax bill will be based on:	
15 months profit to 31 December 2013 as above	£240,000
less overlap relief £73,000 x ³⁄₆	£36,500
	£203,500

The remainder of the 'overlap' relief (£36,500) is simply carried forward and can be given on another change to a later date (eg it would be fully available if that change was to 5 April or, in practice, to 31 March), or on cessation.

Example 5 – Change of accounting date to an earlier date

Suppose instead that Atherton, Helsby and Cable decided to change their accounting date to 30 June. Their next accounts after 30 September 2012 cover the nine months to 30 June 2013 and profits disclosed are £144,000. 2013/14 is still the 'year of change' but the 'gap' is less than 12 months from the old date. So, 2013/14 is based on the 12 months to 30 June 2013, ie:

³⁄₁₂ x £156,000	£39,000
plus 9 months as above	£144,000
	£183,000

There is now a new 'overlap', for the period from 1 July to 30 September 2012, producing an additional £39,000 as above. This is simply carried forward in addition to the 'overlap' relief accrued on commencement.

HMRC's view

19.16 These inducements to choose late accounting dates may well prompt a review of policy by firms which had high initial profits and thus high 'overlaps' on commencement. Fortunately, HMRC are unlikely to regard a change to a later date as objectionable and for non-bona fide reasons. However, it should be relatively simple to make one change, since it is not necessary to show bona fide reasons unless there has been a change within the previous few years under the 'CY' basis. Therefore, new businesses should be able to make a subsequent change to release large 'overlap' reliefs. Where profits fluctuate by high margins, good advisers would normally consider the impact of a change and make recommendations.

Losses

19.17 Business losses are generally relieved against other income for the tax year of loss or the previous year. Various permutations of claims are allowed.

Example 6 – Options when making a loss

Dead, Beat & Co make a loss of £50,000 in their year to 30 September 2010. This is the basis period for 2010/11, so the taxable profits for that year for the firm will be nil. Dead and Beat share losses equally. Dead has other (personal) income of £10,000 for 2010/11 and £15,000 for 2009/10 (this includes his share of the small profit the firm made in the year to 30 September 2009). He has the following options:

(a)   He can offset £10,000 of his allocated loss (£25,000) against his 2010/11 income, reducing it to nil and reclaiming any tax already paid, and carry the balance (£15,000) forward to set against his share of future profits.

(b)   As (a) for 2010/11, but he can also carry back the balance of £15,000 to offset his other income of 2009/10. This will also be reduced to nil and tax paid can be reclaimed. This uses up the whole of his losses, with nothing to carry forward.

(c)   He can set £15,000 of his losses against his 2009/10 income, claim relief as in (b) above, but then carry the remaining £10,000 forward. He might do this to avoid wasting other reliefs due in 2010/11, such as enterprise investment scheme investments or personal allowances.

It is not unusual for partners to share profits on the basis that some are entitled to a salary, with the balance then being shared in profit/loss sharing ratios. In the case of a hypothetical ABC partnership, partner A is allocated a salary of £150,000, B is allocated a salary of £100,000, and A, B and C then share the balance equally. Assuming that the net taxable profits of the ABC firm are only £40,000, the initial allocation would show A with taxable profits of £150,000 less £70,000 = £80,000, B with taxable profits of £100,000 less £70,000 = £30,000, and C with a loss of £70,000.

However, it is important to note that individual partners can only claim their allocated share of a net loss made by the partnership itself. In this case, C's loss would be reduced to nil for tax purposes, and the partnership's assessable profits of £40,000 would be split between A and B on a 60:40 basis (being the ratio of their salaries). Clearly, C is disadvantaged by this result, whereas A and B would pay less tax than expected on their actual earnings, and the partners might wish to consider making an equitable adjustment between themselves.

Relief for losses should be available to members of LLPs which carry on a profession, in the same way as it is available to members of an unlimited partnership. More complex rules apply if the LLP carries on a trade rather than a profession; these are beyond the scope of this book, and professional advice should be taken on such rules.

Anti-avoidance provisions for LLPs

19.18 The *Finance Act 2001* contained some measures designed to prevent tax loss through the use of LLPs. These anti-avoidance rules are aimed at investment and property investment LLPs.

Capital allowances

19.19 Capital allowances are given as a business expense, and balancing charges are treated as a business receipt. Thus, the firm's taxable profit figure will be net of allowances and include charges. If allowances are high enough, they could, like any other expense, turn a profit into a loss.

Accounting period of more or less than 12 months

19.20 This does, however, mean that, in accounting periods longer or shorter than 12 months, the allowances and charges have to be adjusted proportionately. In a six-month accounting period where there is a pool of assets with an opening tax written down value of £10,000, the writing down allowance (WDA), normally 20% (ie £2,000), will become an expense of £1,000. In a 15-month period, it would become ($15/12 \times$ £2,000 =) £2,500. No accounting period can exceed 18 months for this purpose.

Expenditure allowed before it is incurred

19.21 The apportionment of accounting period profits into tax years can mean that expenditure in the first year of a firm's business can be allowed in a tax year before it was incurred.

Example 7 – Relief in first tax year for item bought in second year

The firm of John Smith & Co began on 1 January 2010, and drew up its first accounts to 31 December 2010, spending £40,000 on plant and machinery on 1 December 2010. The accounts showed a profit of £120,000. After treating the capital allowances as an expense, the taxable profit becomes £80,000. Under the commencement rules (see **19.5** above), the first tax year, 2009/10, is based on the profits from 1 January to 5 April 2010, ie £20,000. This includes an element of relief for the plant and machinery, even though it was not bought until 2010/11. This could allow a useful element of flexible planning in the first year, as the plant and machinery could be purchased when the partners' other income and circumstances for 2009/10 were already known.

How the income tax system treats partnerships and limited liability partnerships

19.22 The change to the 'CY' basis made a fundamental change in the tax treatment of partnerships and their partners. The old system taxed the profits of the firm as a unit, and then allocated the taxable profits between those who were partners in the tax year concerned, regardless of the identity of the partners in the basis period. There was joint and several liability in law for the resultant tax.

Key implications of the present system

19.23 Under the present system, however:

(a)   Each partner is deemed to carry on a notional separate business, which begins when he joins the firm and ends when he leaves. The commencement, cessation and overlap rules will apply on an individual basis to these events.

(b)   The profit is allocated among the partners according to their shares in the accounting period on which the tax year is based.

(c)   Each partner is personally liable for tax on his share, but only for that tax.

Simpler allocation

19.24 In an ongoing firm with no partnership changes, this system produces a simpler form of allocation.

Example 8 – One partner reduces workload and profits

Peter, Paul and Mary have been in partnership for many years and, until 30 April 2010, they share profits equally. On 1 May 2010, Peter decides to reduce his workload, and profits are henceforth shared 10% to Peter and 45% each to Paul and Mary.

Profits are:

£180,000 to 30 April 2010
£200,000 to 30 April 2011

The 2010/11 profits, based on the year to 30 April 2010, will be taxed as follows:

Peter 33.33%	£60,000
Paul 33.33%	£60,000
Mary 33.33%	£60,000
	£180,000

The 2011/12 profits, based on the following year, will be taxed as follows:

Peter 10%	£20,000
Paul 45%	£90,000
Mary 45%	£90,000
	£200,000

If Peter fails to pay the tax on his £20,000, Paul and Mary have absolutely no responsibility.

Adjustments

19.25   There may be adjustments for fixed shares, such as salaries and partnership notional interest. These are made on the basis of the entitlement of the partners in the accounting period.

Leavers and joiners

19.26   This feature can become complex when partners join or leave a firm. The following example takes a firm from the commencement of the business through several partnership changes, to show how each partner is regarded as carrying on a notional separate business.

Example 9 – Commencement of a partnership

Edwards, Bairstow and Harrison began practising as a professional partnership on 1 October 2007. Edwards contributed more capital than the others, so profits were initially split 50% to him and 25% each to Bairstow and Harrison. Profits to 30 September each year are as follows.

2008	£270,000
2009	£300,000
2010	£320,000
2011	£360,000
2012	£375,000

(a)   *Opening years*

The allocation of profits for tax purposes in the opening years follows the principles in **19.5** above:

Tax Year	*Taxable Profits Allocated*	E £	B £	H £
2007/08	$^6/_{12}$ x £270,000 = £135,000	67,500	33,750	33,750
2008/09	Year to 30 September 2008 (£270,000)	135,000	67,500	67,500
Each partner also has a personal 'overlap' profit in respect of the period from 1 October 2007 to 5 April 2008 (see **19.6** above)		(67,500)	(33,750)	(33,750)

Each partner is treated as having begun his own notional profession on 1 October 2007.

(b)   *A new partner joins*

On 1 October 2009, the firm took in a new partner, Miss Rowlatt. Profits are now shared equally. Miss Rowlatt is regarded as beginning her own notional profession when she joins. However, she joins in 2009/10 so this is her first tax year, and the commencement rules apply to her share, even though the others are taxed on the 'CY' basis. Miss Rowlatt's tax bill for 2009/10 is therefore based on the period from 1 October 2009 to 5 April 2010, during which she has a 25% share. So she will be taxed on 25% of $^6/_{12}$ x £320,000, ie £40,000. This, of course, is based on the profits of the year to 30 September 2010. The three original partners, however, are in the third tax year of their notional professions when Miss Rowlatt joins. For them, the basis period for 2009/10 is the year to 30 September 2009, with profits of £300,000. Their 2009/10 tax bills will be based on their profit shares in that year, ie:

Edwards	(50%)	£150,000
Bairstow	(25%)	£75,000
Harrison	(25%)	£75,000

Moving on to 2010/11, this is Miss Rowlatt's second tax year as a partner, and her tax bill will be based on the year to 30 September 2010 (see **19.5** above). This gives her 25% of £320,000, ie £80,000. In addition, she also acquires a personal 'overlap' profit of £40,000, since the profits of her notional profession in the period from 1 October 2009 to 5 April 2010 have been taxed twice. The other partners will also have their tax bills based on the same year and will thus be taxed on £80,000 each.

To summarise the position for 2009/10 and 2010/11:

Tax Year	Taxable Profits	*Allocated*			
		E	B	H	R
		£	£	£	£
2009/10	Year to 30 September 2009				
	(£300,000)	150,000	75,000	75,000	–
	Period from 1 October 2009 to 5 April 2010				
	(25% x ⁶⁄12 x £320,000)	–	–	–	40,000
2007/08	Year to 30 September 2010				
	(£320,000)	80,000	80,000	80,000	80,000
Personal 'overlap' to carry forward		(67,500)	(33,750)	(33,750)	(40,000)

(c) *A partner retires*

On 30 September 2011, Edwards retires and the three remaining partners share profits equally thereafter.

Therefore, 2011/12 is Edwards' final tax year and his notional profession ceases. The cessation rules have to be applied to him only. His 2011/12 tax bill will therefore be based on the period from 1 October 2010 to 30 September 2011, ie 25% of £360,000 = £90,000. Now, however, he can deduct his 'overlap' profit from the first year of his notional profession, £67,500, to give a net taxable profit of £22,500. The other partners are simply taxed on their shares of the profit of the same year:

Tax Year	Taxable Profit	Allocated			
		E	B	H	R
		£	£	£	£
2011/12	Year to 30 September 2011 (£360,000)	90,000	90,000	90,000	90,000
	Less 'overlap' relief given on retirement	(67,500)			
		22,500	90,000	90,000	90,000
Personal 'overlap' relief carried forward		–	(33,750)	(33,750)	(40,000)

(d) Cessation of the whole business

In the year to 30 September 2012 (profits £375,000), there are no changes in the firm, but there is a dispute shortly after this and the partners decide to go their separate ways on 30 April 2013. Profits from 1 October 2012 to that date are £90,000 (having been adversely affected by the internal bickering in the period).

The effect of this is that all the partners' notional professions are deemed to end on 30 April 2013, and 2013/14 is the final tax year for each. The cessation rules are applied and, for each partner, the basis period for 2013/14 runs from 1 October 2012 to 30 April 2013. Each partner can deduct his or her accrued 'overlap' profits:

Tax Year	Taxable Profit	Allocated		
		B	H	R
		£	£	£
2012/13	Year ended 30 September 2012			
	(£375,000)	125,000	125,000	125,000
2013/14	1 October 2012 to 30 April 2013			
	(£90,000)	30,000	30,000	30,000
	Less personal 'overlap'	(33,750)	(33,750)	(40,000)
	Losses	(3,750)	(3,750)	(10,000)

It will be seen that the allowances for their 'overlaps' give each partner a loss in 2013/14 which can be used against any other income for the year or the previous year. If the losses were much larger, they could claim 'terminal' loss relief against the previous three years' profits, ie 2012/13, 2011/12 and 2010/11.

Cessation in a successful partnership

19.27   In a more successful scenario, however, such a cessation could involve substantial tax bills. Suppose that this partnership had made profits of £480,000 in the period from 1 October 2012 to 30 April 2013. Each partner would have been taxed on £160,000 less 'overlap' relief. Each would have been a partner for only a month in 2013/14, yet would have been taxed on seven months' profit before 'overlap' relief, and that relief, based on historical profits of an earlier period without indexation for inflation, would have been of much less value. However, this only reflects the taxable profits earned that have not been taxed in a previous tax year, and is therefore the 'unwinding' of the cash flow advantage of the choice of accounting reference date.

Retirement planning

19.28   This point needs to be borne in mind, since in the real world a partner might expect many more years of income from a firm and, in a successful career, would hope to retire with a much larger profit share, from a much larger pool of profits, than he started with. Provision will be needed for the substantial tax bills which will arise on retirement in such a case, and the choice of retirement date will need careful planning.

Cessation of the business of an LLP

19.29   An unfortunate aspect of the way in which the *LLP Act* was drafted can cause problems if an LLP ceases to carry on any trade, profession or other kind of business activity, but then there is a period during which it is wound up and dissolved. During this period, strictly, tax transparency is lost, and the LLP is taxed as a company, at corporate tax rates. More seriously, the rights of members would appear to be treated from that point as if they were shares, which could lead to double taxation when the LLP is finally dissolved and its assets distributed to members. It is understood, however, that HMRC will not apply the strict letter of the law regarding loss of transparency and the treatment of members' interests as shares where winding up takes place over a relatively short period, provided that it is done solely for commercial reasons and not for tax avoidance purposes. Also, any deferred CGT which members have claimed under the rollover relief rules would, strictly, appear to become taxable immediately on the cessation of any trade or business, even though no sale proceeds would be available. Great care and professional advice should, therefore, be taken when contemplating the cessation of an LLP's activities.

Taxable and actual earnings compared

19.30   Where profits increase year by year, the 'CY' basis produces a time-lag between when profits are earned and when they are taxed, which still provides an incentive to select an accounting date early in the tax year.

Example 10 – Time-lag between when profits are earned and taxed

The Sharp and Smart Partnership (consisting of Mr Sharp and Mr Smart) has a 30 April accounting date. The partners' final tax bills will be payable on 31 January following the end of the tax year. The partners' 2010/11 tax bills will be based on the results to 30 April 2010, and the final payment date will be 31 January 2012 (see **19.32** below). However, 'interim' payments will be due on 31 January and 31 July 2011, based on the bills for 2009/10 (see **19.32** below). The choice of an early accounting date has therefore given the firm the use of the funds for 21 months, insofar as profits are rising so that they exceed what is needed for the interim payments. By contrast, a 31 March accounting date would have reduced this time-lag to just ten months.

The comparison

19.31   It is useful to compare actual and taxable income.

Example 11 – Actual and taxable income

Profits of the Sharp and Smart Partnership are as follows:

Year ended 30 April	£
2010	350,000
2011	375,000
2012	400,000
2013	430,000

Assuming that the partners, Sharp and Smart, share profits equally, Mr Sharp's position is as follows:

Tax Year	Income enjoyed	Income on which tax paid for year	Tax deferred income – as % of A
	(A)	(B)	
	£	£	£
2010/11	187,500(1)	175,000(2)	6.6 (3)
2011/12	200,000	187,500	6.25
2012/13	215,000	200,000	6.97

Notes

(1)   Half of profit of the year to 30 April 2011.

(2)   Half the profit of the year to 30 April 2010, taxed in 2010/11.

(3)   £12,500 (£187,500 less £175,000), ie 6.6% of £187,500, is enjoyed in 2010/11 but not taxed until 2011/12.

Tax payments – compliance and administration

19.32   Tax payments are due for a tax year by a final payment date of 31 January after the end of the year. However, two interim payments must also be made, on 31 January in the year and 31 July after its end. Each of these is based on half the partner's final tax bill for the previous year. Credit is given for these payments against the final bill on the following 31 January.

For the fiscal year 2009/10, tax will fall due for payment as follows:

1st payment on account	31 January 2010
2nd payment on account	31 July 2010
Balancing payment	31 January 2011*

*   The 1st payment on account in respect of the 2010/11 year will also be due for payment on this date.

The interim payments on account also reflect any non-partnership income, such as bank interest, for the year, but not any capital gains. Tax on these is wholly collected in the final payment. If, because a partner's income has declined, the final bill is less than the interim payments, he will receive a refund (with tax-free interest). It is possible to reduce the interim payments if current income is thought to be reducing, but interest (and possibly penalties) can arise if this estimate proves incorrect.

Example 12 – Timing of payments

Mr Sharp, of the Sharp and Smart Partnership, has the following tax bills, on his income for 2010/11:

	£
On his share of the firm's profits (say)	70,000
On personal income from property	5,000
	75,000

Income Tax

On his 2011/12 income and gains, he has the following tax to pay:

	£
On share of profits	75,000
On income from property	5,000
On capital gains (say)	10,000
	90,000

He will have to make the following payments for 2011/12:

	£
On 31 January 2012:	
Interim payment equal to half the previous year's tax (and see below)	37,500
On 31 July 2012:	
Second interim payment as above	37,500
	75,000
On 31 January 2013:	
Final payment for 2011/12 on income and gains	90,000
Less interim payments as above	75,000
To pay	15,000

On 31 January 2012, Sharp will also have had to pay the final amount due for 2010/11 – the difference between £75,000 and the interim payments made in that year. On 31 January 2013, he will have to make the first interim payment for 2012/13.

Tax deducted at source

19.33   Credit is also given in the final bill for tax deducted at source, eg on UK bank interest or tax deducted under PAYE on director's fees, and for tax credits on dividends.

Late final payment

19.34   A late final payment, in addition to non-tax deductible interest, may incur a surcharge of 5% if paid after 28 February, which is doubled if payment is more than six months late (ie after 31 July).

Tax returns

19.35   The personal tax return is a 'self-assessment' return including income from all sources and capital gains. The return is due by 31 January after the end of the tax year if it is filed online – the same date as the final tax payment date (see **19.32** above). If the return is filed in hard copy format, the filing date is 31 October after the end of the tax year.

There is a penalty if the personal tax return is filed more than a day late, ranging from a flat £100, plus another £100 if it is six months late, to an amount of up to 100% of the tax due on the filing date if it is more than 12 months late. The flat £100 penalties in respect of a late personal tax return are capped at the amount of tax outstanding on the filing date.

Partnership returns

19.36　A partnership must also submit a return. It includes a declaration of the name, address and tax reference of anyone who has been a partner in any part of the period to which the return relates, a statement of the tax-adjusted profit of the firm, the shares allocated to all partners, and other information, such as details of capital gains on business assets. It also includes basic information about turnover and profits, derived from the accounts; the accounts themselves are not required unless turnover exceeds £15 million. The person making the return also has to make a declaration that it is correct and complete to the best of his knowledge. Where the partner responsible for dealing with any matters relating to the partnership return ceases to be available to do so, the remaining partners may nominate a replacement as 'successor'.

Penalties for delay and errors

19.37　As for an individual, the partnership return is due by 31 January after the end of the tax year if it is filed online – requiring third party software. If the return is filed in hard copy format, the filing date is 31 October after the end of the tax year. The same penalty rules apply as for an individual but, if the return is late, the penalty is multiplied by the number of partners, with no capping based on the tax outstanding.

Example 13 – Penalties for late submission of returns

Muddle, Shambles and Co is an old established firm with 25 partners. Its accountant, Ivor Crisis, prepares the firm's accounts and all the partners' individual tax returns. He is swamped with work in January 2010 and has not managed to collect all the information for the 2008/09 returns due on 31 January. Some partners are more dilatory than others and he decides to wait until he has each partner's figures – the last of which do not arrive until September 2010. He then submits the partnership return and accounts plus 25 individual returns.

The delay means that the firm and the partners could incur the following fixed penalties:

	£
Firm's return more than six months late (two penalties of £100 x 25 partners)	5,000
25 individual returns also more than six months late (maximum £200 x 25)	5,000
	10,000

Although the partnership return is delivered by the nominated partner, penalties for incorrect returns are personal to the individual partners. Penalties may arise on the individual partners if the nominated partner delivers an incorrect partnership return, makes an incorrect statement or submits incorrect accounts. The size of the penalty will depend on whether the inaccuracy is innocent, careless, deliberate, or deliberate and concealed, and will be based on the difference between the amount of tax payable by him or her for the relevant period and the amount which would have been payable if the return had been correct. Therefore, firms must have an efficient system of compliance and competent professional help.

The system also includes a tariff of penalties for inadequate business records (£3,000 per failure per partner),which must be retained for five years beyond the 31 January filing date each year; and, since there are similar requirements for VAT (see **CHAPTER 23**), failure could be expensive.

Personal Service Companies ('IR35')

What IR35 means

19.38 Some complex rules were included in *Finance Act 2000* to counter perceived tax avoidance by 'Personal Service Companies', typically one-person organisations where the only shareholder also performs all the work which produces the profits. These could be used to control the amount and timing of the proprietor's remuneration for tax purposes, particularly by paying out profits in the form of dividends which do not incur National Insurance Contributions (NICs). The then named Inland Revenue regarded many such proprietors as merely disguised employees of those for whom their company performed services, especially where the company had only one or a very few 'clients'. From 6 April 2000, this perceived abuse has been countered by rules which have become known as 'IR35', after the number of the Budget Day Press Release in 1999 where they were first announced. Despite the references to companies, these rules can sometimes apply to partnerships.

The essence of IR35 is that it 'looks through' the formal contractual relationship between the service company and its client, to the actual relationship between the person who performs the services ('the worker' –

who may often be the proprietor of the service company) and the client. It then asks whether, in the absence of the service company, the worker would be, in law, an employee of the client. This question has to be answered using existing case law on the distinction between a contract of service (employment) and a contract for services (self-employment).

If the answer is that the worker would be an employee when the relationship is 'looked through', the service company is deemed to have made a payment of taxable employment-style remuneration to the worker on the last day of the tax year in which the work is done. This requires the preparation of a 'deemed payment' calculation. This consists of the fees or other payments received from the client, less expenses which would be allowable if there really was an employment – such as travelling in the course of carrying out the work, pension contributions, any capital allowances which an employee could claim, NICs and a flat rate deduction of 5% (to cover all other expenses). The totals for all engagements which fall within IR35 have to be amalgamated, and PAYE and employers' NICs calculated as if the amount was being paid out on 5 April as salary. Any PAYE and NICs which have actually been deducted in the year are credited. The net amount then has to be paid to HMRC by 19 April after the year end. The liability for this payment falls on the service company, not on its clients.

How IR35 can affect professional partnerships and LLPs

19.39   HMRC were concerned that, if the IR35 rules applied only to service companies, they could easily be evaded by the use of service partnerships or LLPs. Thus, there are provisions which can catch partnerships and LLPs, and they are so widely drawn that they can apply even where there is no intention to avoid or delay any tax payments.

Does IR35 apply to the work?

19.40   The first question to ask is whether the relationship between a partnership or LLP and any of its clients is such that the person or persons who do the work would be employees of the client, in the absence of the partnership/LLP (see above). Examples might include:

(i)   A firm of accountants is asked to lend a client the full-time services of a partner for 12 months to replace a Finance Director who has died suddenly.

(ii)   A firm of solicitors is asked to make a partner with a reputation for expertise in a particular specialism available to lecture several times a week and conduct tutorials at the local university in that subject, to cover for an academic who is taking sabbatical leave.

(iii) Another firm of accountants is asked to undertake high-level financial modelling training for a group of senior executives in a client company, to replace the company's internal trainers who have been made redundant.

The fees received for work which is within the 'employment' category may fall within IR35, but this will depend on the status of the 'worker' and the nature of the firm, as explained below.

Does IR35 apply to the 'worker' and the firm?

19.41   IR35 can apply to the income from work within the 'employment' category if any of the following conditions apply:

(a)   The 'worker' is entitled to 60% or more of the profits of the partnership. For this purpose, rights of relatives have to be counted as well – this includes a spouse, parent or remoter forebear, child or remoter issue, brother or sister. 'Spouse' also includes an unmarried partner with whom the 'worker' lives as man or wife.

(b)   Most of the profits of the firm are derived from engagements with a single client, or associates of that client, within the IR35 rules. 'Most' in this context is undefined, and HMRC have preferred to leave it open for negotiation.

(c)   The profit sharing arrangements are such that the income of any partner is based on the income generated by him in providing services through engagements within the IR35 rules.

Condition '(a)' above will clearly apply to many family-based professional partnerships, as well as firms where one individual has a very large profit percentage.

Condition '(b)' is aimed at specifically created devices to circumvent the rules, but could of course also apply if a separate firm was created, perhaps for regulatory reasons, to take on work which happened to fall within IR35. Where the client is a company, its associates include any person connected with the company as defined in *s 839* of *ICTA 1988*.

Condition '(c)' is the least easy to understand. It appears to apply even if the income of a partner is 'based' to a small extent on IR35 income. However, it is thought that it is aimed at the direct passing through of IR35 income to the 'worker'. Unless either condition (a) or (b) is in point, it should not apply if the income of IR35 engagements is pooled in the normal way before profits are allocated.

Practical implications if IR35 applies

19.42 If IR35 does apply, separate records will be needed of the income and expenses involved and of who does the work. These will need to be kept for the tax year rather than the accounting year, as IR35 works on a cash basis rather than an accruals basis. This information will be needed to calculate the PAYE and NIC bill at 5 April each year. However, if the profits have been paid out as they come in with a PAYE and NIC deduction, no further payment will usually be needed.

The firm is entitled to deduct the deemed salary payment and the employer's NICs in calculating its taxable profits for the accounting period in which the relevant 5 April falls. This means that a firm with a 31 March accounting date will always obtain relief for the payment one year late, and a change to 5 April might be considered if the amounts are material. If the deduction of this payment produces a loss, the partners cannot set this against their other income (in the manner described at **19.17** above) – it can only be carried forward.

Partnership service companies and IR35

19.43 The above assumes that it is the partnership which provides services potentially within IR35. Many firms own companies which employ staff and provide common services, as well as perhaps holding properties from which the firm operates. These could, in theory, themselves be within IR35 if the work done through the company would represent an employment in the absence of the intervening company. However, the staff who actually provide the services in such companies will normally be paid through the PAYE and NIC system in the normal way for all the work they perform through the company, and no problems should therefore arise.

Where this is not the case, the IR35 rules can only apply to fees for work done through the company by individuals who hold, broadly, more than 5% of the ordinary share capital of the company, either alone or with associates. The latter expression includes not only relatives but also business partners. Thus, because one partner's ownership of service company shares will be attributed to all the other partners, it is likely that any fees for work done through a partnership-owned company by partners themselves will be within IR35 if the client relationship would be that of employer and employee in the absence of the company.

If this seems likely to be the case, it may be possible to avoid the rules by appropriate restructuring of the contracts. Failing this, the effects can be mitigated by making the maximum possible corporate pension contributions for those who undertake the work, since these are deductible in arriving at the amount which is subject to PAYE and NICs. Many of the running costs of the company – such as travelling and accommodation costs – can also be offset, and an additional 5% of the relevant fees can also be offset to cover other costs. IR35 is thus only likely to be a problem for partnership-owned companies where they receive substantial fees for work done by partners, or by staff with more than 5% of the shares who are not fully taxed under PAYE.

HMRC concessions

19.44   IR35 does not affect the tax authority practice of allowing small fees from directorships and other sources to be paid gross, provided that they are pooled with profits before allocation.

IR35 conclusions

19.45   Many firms will never encounter these complex provisions; but, when they do apply, their effects can be substantial. There are detailed rules affecting the calculation of the deemed payment required when IR35 'bites' and, for partnerships in particular, the treatment of expenses requires careful consideration. Instead of receiving fees which can be allocated, along with the rest of the general profit pool, among all partners, IR35 fees have to be taxed, in effect, as if they were paid as salary to a particular individual, and there will be interest and possibly penalty costs if the rules are not observed. Last, but not least, an additional NIC cost on the relevant fees will be incurred which would not arise under normal rules. Family-based firms, and smaller firms which could be caught by the 60% rule mentioned above, will therefore find it worthwhile to review current client engagements to see if any could fall within IR35 and, if so, whether the contracts can be restructured. Larger firms may need to review profit sharing arrangements to ensure that, even if they do have engagements within the rules, the income from them is genuinely pooled before profit shares are determined.

It was announced in July 2010 that the Office of Tax Simplification had been asked to explore alternative approaches to IR35, and further developments are expected in Budget 2011.

Settlements legislation

19.46   Partnerships and LLPs also need to remain aware of the anti-avoidance provisions of the settlements legislation (see *s 619* onwards of the *Income Tax (Trading and Other Income) Act 2005*, which was formerly *s 660A* onwards of *ICTA 1988*). Those who are caught by the settlements legislation will be taxed on income which they believed they had given away or diverted away from themselves.

In April 2003, the then Inland Revenue issued Tax Bulletin 64, setting out a number of examples of cases that it considered were caught by the legislation. It subsequently issued 'A Guide to the Settlements Legislation for Small Business Advisers', which included the following example of a partnership caught by the provisions:

'*Example 20 – Partnerships*

Mr F and Mr G are in partnership as second hand car dealers. They do not have any premises but buy and sell cars through auctions and the classified adverts of local papers. The partnership's only assets are some office equipment worth less than £1,000 and they usually have a couple of cars in stock at any one time.

They are successful and the profits of £80,000 a year are split equally between them. They decide to admit their wives to the partnership and amend the partnership agreement in order to split profits equally four ways. Mrs F and Mrs G do no work in the partnership and the partnership has no employees.

This is a bounteous arrangement transferring income from one spouse to the other. The settlements legislation will apply and Mr F and Mr G continue to be taxable on half the profits each.'

HMRC subsequently took the landmark case of *Jones v Garnett* (commonly known as the *Arctic Systems* case) through the courts, but they lost in the House of Lords. Shortly after the judgment, the Minister made the following statement:

'Some individuals use non-commercial arrangements (arrangements that they would not reasonably enter into with an arm's length third party) to divert income (which would, in the absence of those arrangements have flowed to them) to others. That minimises their tax liability, and results in an unfair outcome, increasing the tax burden on other taxpayers and putting businesses that compete with these individuals at a competitive disadvantage.

It is the Government's view that individuals involved in these arrangements should pay tax on what is, in substance, their own income and that the legislation should clearly provide for this.'

In 2007, the Government issued draft legislation designed 'to undo the tax advantage gained by income shifting arrangements'. In his Pre-Budget Report on 24 November 2008, the Chancellor of the Exchequer announced that the new proposals would be deferred as a result of the 'current economic challenges' and not introduced in the *Finance Bill 2009*, as previously planned. The 2009 Budget indicated that the matter was still under review, but no mention at all was made in the 2010 Budget.

Whilst the proposed new rules appear to have been shelved, the legislation in *s 619* onwards of the *Income Tax (Trading and Other Income) Act 2005* continues in force, and any partnership which believes it may be affected by the settlements legislation should take specific advice.

Chapter 20   Taxation of Corporate Aspects

Corporate partners

20.1   In general, there are no provisions in either the *Partnership Act 1890* or *Limited Liability Partnerships Act 2000* to restrict a company from being included as a partner or member in a partnership or LLP structure respectively.

The presence of a corporate partner in a structure can be useful for a number of reasons, discussed below, and a significant benefit has always been that the liability of a corporate partner to the partnership debts is restricted to its own resources.

Corporate partner's tax position

20.2   From a UK taxation perspective, a company incorporated (or tax resident) in the UK is liable to corporation tax on its global income. Where a company is a partner in a trading partnership, it will be assessed on its tax-adjusted share of profits arising, or obtain its share of a loss, in accordance with the rules set out in *Part 17* of the *Corporation Tax Act 2009* for accounting periods ending on or after 1 April 2009, and in *ss 114* and *115* of the *Income and Corporation Taxes Act 1988* for accounting periods ending prior to this date.

Note that, in general, a company becoming, or ceasing to be, a partner in a partnership will be deemed to commence or discontinue a trade, although this does not in itself bring to an end an accounting period for the company.

A partnership with a corporate partner has to adjust the partnership's total profits under corporation tax rules. This is likely to require a partnership to undertake two calculations of taxable profit to allocate to its partners: one under the income tax rules for individuals, and one under the corporation tax rules for companies. Typical differences that would arise between the calculations would be the treatment of interest under the loan relationship rules for a company and the treatment of amortisation on intangible assets.

The company is taxable on its share of the adjusted result of the partnership apportioned to each of its accounting periods. This is generally a separate and distinct calculation to the adjustment of the total profit for income tax purposes which follows the fiscal basis periods for individuals. In particular, prior to the rewrite in the *Corporation Tax Act 2009*, it was

351

specifically stated that references to capital allowances and charges on income were disregarded when preparing the computation. Separate computations were then prepared for these items for the corporate partner. Under the rewrite, the capital allowance rule was removed, and capital allowances are now treated as a deduction in the computation (although the net effect is similar). The rule regarding charges on income has been removed completely, as charges can no longer be a deduction in calculating the profits of a trade.

Corporate partners resident overseas are taxed on their share of the profits of a trade carried on in the UK through a permanent establishment.

Allocation of profits and losses

20.3   Specific anti-avoidance provisions have been introduced for corporation tax purposes, for periods ending on or after 1 April 2009, to prevent a partnership calculating a net loss to allocate to its partners, then allocating a profit to the corporate partner, ie thereby increasing a loss to other partners. Similarly, if a taxable profit is calculated and is available to be allocated to its partners, then it is not possible to allocate a loss to the corporate partner. The provisions are in *ss 1263* and *1264* of the *Corporation Tax Act 2009*, which detail how the allocation of a loss in a profit-making period (or vice versa) to a corporate member is treated. HMRC have commented that this change legislates the practice that they have historically adopted, and brings consistency as between income tax and corporation tax treatment.

Interest

20.4   A corporate partner brings into account, for corporation tax purposes, interest under the loan relationship provisions. Broadly, interest received or payable by the partnership, which is attributable to the corporate partner as its share of profits, is calculated on an accruals basis (as compared to a paid basis for individual partners).

Sideways loss relief and restriction

20.5   In general, where a corporate partner has a share of a trading loss from an interest in a partnership, it should be able to offset these losses against other income in the period ('sideways loss relief'). That said, anti-avoidance legislation was introduced to provide a restriction on the amount of sideways loss relief available. This is contained in *s 56* of the *Corporation Tax Act 2010*, and limits the loss available for sideways loss relief to the company's capital contribution to the partnership at the appropriate time of the claim.

Tax planning opportunities

20.6 Below are some of the potential tax planning opportunities that can benefit a structure with the inclusion of a company as a partner or member of a partnership or LLP respectively – the list is not exhaustive. For the purpose of this chapter, reference to a 'partner' is used throughout, but the discussion applies equally to members of an LLP (unless otherwise specifically stated).

- Depending on the cash requirements for the business and individual partners' needs, including a corporate partner can create cash flow benefits from the deferral of payment of tax. In particular, if cash can be left within the structure, for example, for working capital or future reinvestment, then profits that are attributable to corporate partners would generally suffer lower amounts of tax up front (although tax would be suffered again on extraction of profits). In particular, the inclusion of service companies in partnership structures is popular, which can provide cash flow benefits.

- Including a corporate partner can also provide opportunities to potentially plan for dividend payments to its shareholders/individual partners in the partnership, as compared to them receiving a full profit share year on year, or salaries/bonus payments. Including a company in the structure may also provide more opportunities for providing incentivisation to key employees and may act as a tool for staff retention.

- With the introduction of the higher 50% income tax rate that applies to individuals with income of more than £150,000 from 6 April 2010 onwards, tax planning around how individuals are remunerated and the timing of cash taken out of a business structure will play a bigger part. Including a corporate entity in the structure is likely to provide such opportunities.

- There can be a number of commercial and regulatory reasons as to why a structure may want to include a corporate partner, for example, for geographical spread of a business or different areas within a business. It can also provide structure to the natural expansion of a business.

- Corporate partners can be particularly useful as general partners in a limited partnership structure.

It should be noted that there are anti-avoidance provisions that may apply to broadly reclassify profits received by a partner in another form as income, in cases where there are arrangements in place to avoid or reduce a tax liability. An example would be the sales of occupation income provisions in *Chapter 4* of *Part 13* of the *Income Tax Act 2007*. These potentially catch transfers of income arising from professions or vocations which create rights to a capital sum.

Service company overview

20.7   For a number of reasons, including the perceived organisational problems of large partnerships, there has been a trend over some years for 'service companies' to be utilised. Service companies have traditionally been used for one or more of the following:

(a)   to employ some or all of the staff of a partnership;

(b)   to own the partnership's plant, machinery, motor cars, etc;

(c)   to own the property, take leases and generally deal with occupancy expenses;

(d)   to generally provide back office functions to the partnership;

(e)   to undertake certain segmental tasks (where there is a preference for these to be separated from the main partnership structure, or for geographical reasons); and

(f)   to provide a source of funding for short-term working capital for the partnership.

From a UK tax perspective, the inclusion of a service company in a partnership structure could provide benefits.

One of the benefits is to provide a deferral of tax where surplus cash is not required to be extracted from a business, which can potentially aid the accumulation of working capital in the company. By way of example, this could be structured as follows:

- the service company could be used to provide back office functions on behalf of the partnership. The partnership will therefore pay the service company for the provision of these services, and the cost to the partnership should reduce its profits available for allocation to members. If the service company is a partner, these costs would be treated as a priority profit share.

- the company could also provide short-term working capital loans to the partnership, for which the partnership would pay interest and fees at market rates (although see below regarding potential issues on funding from a company).

- charges for services should be made on an arm's length basis, and be sufficiently documented.

In this structure, the corporate partner will receive income from the partnership which would be liable to corporation tax at 21%/28% (see **20.13** below for details regarding rates) and save the individual partners National Insurance costs and income taxed at potentially higher rates. This would enable profits taxed at lower rates to roll up in the company, which would be available for meeting trading expenses and/or investing in assets, or lending back to the partnership.

This type of tax planning has certain uses in the UK, but there are a number of areas that need to be considered in detail and, as such, advice should be sought. In particular, the application of the transfer pricing rules would need to be considered (see **20.10** below for more details).

Company as member of partnership

20.8   Separate from including a service company in a LLP structure, individual partners could potentially incorporate and use their own corporate entity to become a member of the partnership, so as to undertake similar tax deferral planning as noted above. If a UK individual partner used a UK corporate, then profits could potentially be rolled up in their UK company, which would be subject to UK corporation tax.

Going forward, the UK individual could then take a distribution from the company if required, or cease operation and liquidate in due course. These companies are being used in the UK to aid individual deferral tax planning, given the new 50% top income tax rate, ie partners could potentially defer receipt of dividends to such periods when their income was lower.

However, care would be required to ensure that the relationship between the individual and the partnership could not be considered an employment, or else the intermediary legislation (IR35) could apply. Furthermore, the anti-avoidance legislation mentioned at **20.6** above would need to be considered.

Director status

20.9   The service company can also be used to provide director status for a level of senior staff just below partner, or professionally unqualified employees, so they can assume a role similar to that of a partner. The company clearly has to be funded to pay the payroll costs so, in general, a service company charges on a monthly basis the total costs of the payroll together with a profit margin.

The use of a service company can also give rise to income tax and reporting issues regarding employment-related securities. Shares, share options and other share-based transactions between a company and its directors and/or employees are potentially within the employment-related securities rules. If within the rules then providing, say, shares to a director at an undervalue will give rise to income tax and employees' National Insurance Contributions charges for the individual (potentially with employers' National Insurance Contributions for the company) on the amount of undervalue and would be reportable to HMRC. The tax and reporting implications are dependent on the specific circumstances and, therefore, each situation should be considered on its own merits.

Transfer pricing

20.10   Transfer pricing legislation for the UK, as set out in *Part 4* of the *Taxation (International and Other Provisions) Act 2010*, requires all transactions between related persons to be calculated on an arm's length basis for tax purposes (ie at prices which would be charged to unconnected persons), and sufficient documentation needs to be in place to support the prices used. This includes information to identify the transactions to which the transfer pricing rules apply, in addition to evidence to demonstrate that these transactions meet the arm's length test.

The transfer pricing legislation applies to corporate groups as well as to corporate entities within a partnership structure. Two persons are 'related' for these purposes if one controls the other or if they are under common control.

There are exemptions from the transfer pricing rules for small and medium-sized groups and companies.

A small company/group business is one with:

●   fewer than 50 employees; and

●   either turnover or assets of less than €10 million.

A medium-sized business is one with:

●   fewer than 250 employees; and

●   either turnover of less than €50 million or assets of less than €43 million.

Small and medium-sized groups are exempt from the transfer pricing legislation, unless they elect to be excluded from exemption, or the related party is an overseas party resident in a non-qualifying territory (ie one whose double tax treaty with the UK does not have a non-discrimination clause, or one designated by the Treasury as a non-qualifying territory). Medium-sized groups may also be required by HMRC to apply the transfer pricing rules through the issue of a transfer pricing notice, although this is unlikely unless there is a significant amount of tax at stake.

Partnerships are not normally treated as taxable persons separate from those who are partners in them. However, the transfer pricing rules are unusual in this respect and treat a partnership as a 'person'. Therefore, if, for example, goods or services are supplied between a partnership and a company, where the service company is a controlling partner in the partnership (which could be via common control), then the transfer pricing rules will apply to any transactions between them (subject to the exemptions noted above). In addition, the partnership structure could also incorporate a service company under the partnership's control, and the transfer pricing rules may similarly apply to transactions between them.

Furthermore, with regard to partnerships, the basic test of control is the right to a share of more than one half of the partnership's assets, or of more than one half of its income. The major participant rules also apply to partnerships, such that, in a partnership where two persons each have at least a 40% interest in the partnership, they will be treated as being in control for this purpose.

It is, therefore, essential to ensure that charges made between the professional practice, the partnership and the corporation are on a consistent and reasonable basis.

However, the application of the transfer pricing rules could create an opportunity for profits to be taxed in the corporate vehicle at corporation tax rates, and relievable in the partnership at income tax rates, potentially without the need for the partnership to make good the 'profit' element.

Example of charges between practice and company

20.11   In the case of *Stephenson v Payne, Stone, Fraser & Co*, a firm of accountants incorporated a service company which provided the firm with premises and its services as secretaries, registrars and executors. In the first year, the service charge paid was 1.47 times the actual cost incurred for the provision of the services. In the second year, the actual charge was less than the cost of the provision of the services, on the basis that the excess profit of the first year would be recouped. The High Court ruled that, for tax purposes, only the cost of the services plus a nominal profit could be charged across and could be properly attributed to the first year of operation.

Care should, therefore, be taken over the level of profitability in a service or an associated trading company, and that this is consistently applied.

Lending and financing issues

20.12   The use of a service company and the retention of lower taxed profits by the company can potentially lead to funding opportunities for typical partnership structures (where the service company is also a partner/member in the partnership/LLP).

The transfer pricing legislation can also apply to the lending of funds between related persons and require that arm's length interest rates are used and the terms are essentially on third party commercial terms.

In general, if the corporate partner is a close company and shareholders are partners, the surplus funds should not be lent to the partnership, since a 25% tax on the loan under *s 455* of the *Corporation Tax Act 2010* could arise, as it is likely to be considered a loan made by the company to one of its shareholders (being the partners/members of the partnership/LLP). Broadly, a company is considered close if it is under the control of five or fewer participators (shareholders) or any number of directors.

However, HMRC accept that there is some doubt as to whether this legislation can apply to a partnership, and indicate that, provided the partnership and loan are genuine and commercial, they will not take this point (CTM61515). Furthermore, *s 455* of the *Corporation Tax Act 2010* can apply to indirect loans made from a close company to one of its participators, potentially using a partnership.

If the loan is repaid within nine months after the end of the company's accounting period, no such tax is due; in addition, any such tax already paid becomes repayable.

There is an exemption under *s 456* of the *Corporation Tax Act 2010* for trading debts. This applies if the loan or debt arises from the supply by the service company of goods or services in the ordinary course of its trade or business, unless the credit given exceeds six months or is longer than that given to the company's third party customers. As most service companies would not have third party customers, invoices for supply of staff should be settled regularly. Surplus funds could then either be rolled up, or used to provide dividends to the company's shareholders (who are often partners in the partnership), or be utilised to invest in partnership property.

Corporation tax

20.13   As an overview, the profit retained inside the service company (or another general corporate entity in the structure) will be subject to corporation tax at the following rates:

	Year to 31 March 2010 and 2011
Standard rate of corporation tax	28%
Small profit rate for companies	21%
Lower limit on small profit rate	£300,000
Upper limit on small profit rate	£1,500,000
Marginal rate of corporation tax	29.75%

The standard rate of corporation tax applicable to taxable profits above £1,500,000 for the financial year commencing 1 April 2011 is to be reduced to 27% (other than for ring-fenced profits). The Government is also proposing to reduce the standard rate of corporation tax by 1% each year, until the standard rate for the year commencing 1 April 2014 is 24%.

Depending upon the size of the profits of the partnership and the service company concerned, the lower rate on a profit of £300,000 can be a method for reducing the overall effective rate of tax on the partnership structure. In addition, provided that cash can be left in the structure, for example, as working capital, then even if the service company is paying corporation tax at the current top rate of 28%, it could still provide a cash flow advantage through the deferral of tax.

The limits for application of the different rate of corporation tax are divided by the number of active companies that are associated to the service company. 'Associated' is defined as being under common control; control is as construed in *s 450* of the *Corporation Tax Act 2010*. From 1 April 2008, and for determining the number of associated companies for the purpose of the small profit rate only, a partner will only be treated as an associate of the company and/or another partner in a partnership if tax planning arrangements are in place. Arrangements are widely defined to include any agreement, understanding, scheme, transaction or series of transactions that involve the participator/shareholder of the company and the partner(s) to secure a tax advantage. At the time of writing, the Government has indicated that this 'tax advantage condition' will be replaced, from 1 April 2011, by a condition requiring substantial commercial interdependence, whether or not association is through the attribution of rights of partners.

In general, if a company's taxable profits for an annual accounting period are more than £1.5 million (divided by the number of associated companies), then the corporation tax for that accounting period is due for payment to HMRC in instalments (in accordance with *SI 1998/3175*). However, a company does not have to pay in instalments if one of the following exemptions apply:

- If a company's taxable profits are in excess of the limit of £1.5 million (divided by the number of associated companies) but were below this limit in the previous 12 months, then it does not have to pay in instalments, provided that the company's taxable profits for the accounting period do not exceed an annual rate of £10 million (also divided by the number of associated companies).

- There was any part of the previous 12 months when the company was not liable for, or 'within the charge to', corporation tax.

- The company's total corporation tax liability for the accounting period is less than £10,000.

If corporation tax needs to be paid in instalments, then the first payment is due on the 14th day of month seven of the relevant accounting period. Subsequent instalments are due on a quarterly basis thereafter. If instalments are not required, corporation tax is due for payment nine months and one day after the end of the accounting period.

In the context of a service company and the timing of corporation tax payments, care should be taken, where possible, to ensure that its profitability and that of associated companies does not exceed the £1.5 million limit, and hence accelerate the payment of tax.

Profits for corporation tax purposes are filed on a form CT600 under corporation tax self-assessment, which, together with the accounts and a supporting tax computation, are sent to HMRC on an annual basis.

In general, a corporation tax return is due for submission to HMRC within 12 months of the end of the relevant accounting period. Problems with timing can arise where a partnership includes both corporate and individual partners. In some cases, corporate partners may need the information of their partnership income before the partnership tax return is required to be filed. In some cases, estimated numbers have to be included in the returns.

For an accounting period ending after 31 March 2010, a company's corporation tax return must be filed online with accompanying computation and financial statements. With effect from 1 April 2011, HMRC will reject the submission if these documents are not in iXBRL format (inline eXtensible Business Reporting Language).

The iXBRL requirement only applies where tax returns and accounts are filed on or after 1 April 2011. Therefore, it should be possible for some businesses to defer the impact of the requirement by filing their tax return, computation and accounts before that date. For example, a company with a year end of 30 June 2010 will have to file its corporation tax return online, but if it does so for this period before 31 March 2011, it will defer the iXBRL requirement for a further year.

Example 1 – A tax reduction example

An example of the tax reduction arising from the use of a service company follows:

N & Co, a consultancy partnership, have made a level profit of £2,000,000 per annum for some years. The firm incorporates a service company to employ all staff, and the company makes a profit each year of:

(a)   £250,000;

(b)   £500,000; and

(c)   £750,000.

The profit margins are consistently applied and accepted by HMRC. Ignoring income tax reliefs, National Insurance contributions, and assuming an average rate of income tax of 40% for all partners, the income tax position would be as follows:

	No service company	*(a) Profit*	*(b) Profit*	*(c) Profit*
	£	£	£	£
Profit of service company	–	250,000	500,000	750,000
Profit in N & Co	2,000,000	1,750,000	1,500,000	1,250,000
Income tax at, say, 40%	800,000	700,000	600,000	500,000
Corporation tax at 21% to limit of £300,000	–	52,500	63,000	63,000
29.75% on profit over £300,000	–	–	59,500	133,875
Total corporation tax liability	–	52,500	122,500	196,875
Total tax liability	800,000	752,500	722,500	696,875
Reduction achieved	–	47,500	77,500	103,125
Percentage reduction	–	5.94%	9.69%	12.89%

For reasons of simplicity, this example ignores the impact of current year bases of assessment of the partnership's profits and the economic aspect of differing payment dates for income tax and corporation tax. The example also assumes that any profit arising in the company is retained within the company.

Consideration would need to be given to the extraction of profits, either by way of salaries, bonuses, pensions, dividends or rolled up, and a future liquidation of the company.

Payment of dividends

20.14   Assuming that the shareholders of the service company are the partners in the partnership, then the individual shareholders (ie the partners) will be subject to income tax on the payment of a dividend by the service company.

In a case where the partnership itself owns the service company, any dividend from the service company is excluded from the partnership's taxable profits and apportioned among the partners (in accordance with the partnership agreement).

In either case, if the individual partner's income is within the basic rate band (ie paying tax at 20%), then no further tax is due on the dividend. If the individual partner is a higher rate tax payer, paying tax at 40%, then the effective rate of tax on a dividend is 25%. If the individual partner is paying tax at the 50% rate, then the effective rate of tax on a dividend is 36.11%. The dividend will be subject to tax, for a 40% and 50% taxpayer respectively, as shown below:

Example 2

	40% taxpayer	50% taxpayer
	£	£
Dividend apportioned from service company distribution	90	90
Add tax credit at ⅑ of dividend	10	10
Income chargeable to tax	100	100
Income tax @ 32.5%	32.5	
Income tax @ 42.5%		42.5
Less tax credit	10	10
Liability to tax	22.5	32.5
Effective rate of tax on dividend cash receipt	25%	36.11%

Utilising surplus funds

20.15   As an alternative to paying dividends, a service company may be able to utilise surplus funds in providing benefits for partners and/or could use them to fund client entertainment costs or other disallowable expenditure. This is disallowable for both corporation tax and income tax purposes. The advantage here is that it may be possible that the disallowable expenditure incurred by the service company will be liable to the lower rates of corporation tax compared to the top rate of income tax. It is important to take good professional advice when considering such courses of action.

Provision of cars

20.16   Service companies have often been used to provide cars, not just for the employees of the company, but also for the partners of the partnership, which owns the service company. The objective here is to put the possession of the car or the benefit of the car onto the basis for employment income, ie as for all employees, rather than to have the complexity of being dealt with under the self-employment rules. Whether this is a positive income tax benefit to the individual partners is difficult to predict and will depend on a number of factors, including the usage and expense of the car concerned for the individual. Each case has to be dealt with on its own merits.

Plant and machinery

20.17 Where a service company owns plant and machinery and makes it available to the partnership, it should receive capital allowances in respect of that plant and machinery. In the case of items of expenditure which do not generate capital allowances, eg some leasehold improvements, it may be advantageous if these are incurred in a service company, as the lease charge would be tax deductible in the partnership at a marginal rate of 40%/50% and taxable at 21%/28% in the company, and can also be used to deplete the surplus of funds in the company. Again, each case has to be judged on its own merits. In the case of fixtures, it is important to ensure that the claimant of capital allowances (for example, the company) has an interest in the land or buildings to which the fixtures are attached.

Pensions

20.18 On the provision of pensions for employees, there is no real distinction between providing a scheme linked to a service company and one linked to the professional partnership. Advice should be sought for specific requirements. (See also **CHAPTER 27, RETIREMENT PLANNING**.)

Corporate structures

20.19 It is also now relatively commonplace for professional practices to consider entirely corporate structures.

Broadly, each company in the structure would be subject to corporation tax in the same way as noted above for a service company.

Benefits of corporate structures can arise where there are, for example, a number of segments (either business lines or geographically) in the overall business which, for commercial, or perhaps regulatory, reasons need to be to ring fenced. In addition, where a group is highly profitable, then the difference in the maximum current corporation tax rate of 28% is much lower than the maximum current income tax rate of 50%.

Even where losses are realised, corporate structures also generally able to share tax losses through group relief as set out in *Part 5* of the *Corporation Tax Act 2010*, provided that the relevant companies are in a 75% group. Broadly, a 75% group company is one that is owned 75% directly by another company, or by an effective 75% holding through a series of companies.

Benefits can also arise when a group company disposes of a capital asset, where they are able to elect for another group company to be deemed to incur the chargeable gain. This is of use where there are companies in the group with a lower current year tax rate or that have capital losses brought forward or arising in the year. A capital asset is also able to be transferred at nil gain/nil loss between relevant group companies.

Each company in the group will be associated with each other and, therefore, by including a large number of corporate entities, a group will reduce the limit at which quarterly instalment payments would be required and the level to which the small profit rate applies, which can impact on the cash flow position for the group.

Individuals could be directors or employees of the corporate structure and would be remunerated accordingly. It would also be possible to introduce employee incentives in the form of approved and unapproved share schemes, which can provide tax advantages for the individuals and, if set up correctly, act as a retention and incentivisation tool for the group.

If individuals are also shareholders in the group, then dividend payments and tax planning may also be possible.

A corporate structure is generally more rigid in how it is operated, ie it provides less flexibility, which is one of the main benefits of operating through a partnership structure.

Operating through a corporate structure should also provide for increased liability protection from a partnership's debts and obligations (where they are operating through a regular partnership).

Expansion

20.20 When a professional partnership expands, opportunities may arise in associated areas of activity that differ geographically or economically from the core professional activity. As an example, accountancy practices, solicitors and actuaries have tended to consider utilising separate companies for the provision of financial services. Having a separate company can also help with regulatory issues, as the company's activities could be ring-fenced and better controlled than having the provision of financial services spread throughout the partnership.

Funding for the acquisition of shares

20.21 Funding for the acquisition of shares in a trading company, or lending to such a company, can be problematic. If this is done using partnership funds, it could be deemed unnecessary for the partnership's business, particularly if a minority interest in the trading company is involved. The result could lead to a restriction on eligibility for deduction for tax purposes of interest on the partnership overdraft or on partners' borrowings for the provision of partnership capital. Therefore, it might be advantageous to have such an investment made by the partners directly, having withdrawn funds from the partnership.

Joint ventures

How they differ from partnerships

20.22 A joint venture should be distinguished from a partnership because, although both are governed by contract and are between two or more parties, the parties agree typically to split expenses and/or income in a defined basis for a joint venture rather than a share of profits (the result).

The result in financial terms may be the same – if a joint venture between three parties has each entitled to 33.33% of the income and 33.33% of expenditure of the joint venture, then this is effectively identical to a partnership with a profit-sharing/loss-sharing ratio of one-third each. Unlike a partnership/LLP, the joint venture is not generally a separate body (unless it is set up with a corporate structure). If the participator in the joint venture is a professional partnership or a corporation, it takes into its own accounts its share of the joint venture's income and expenditure. Commercially, joint venturers are not jointly and severally liable beyond their share of the income and expenditure of the joint venture.

The construction industry

20.23 Joint ventures are common in the construction industry, and may be preferable to partnerships, since the start of a new joint venture is not necessarily thought to be that of a new trade. The result is that separate and new accounts for the new venture do not have to be prepared, and the opening/closing years of assessment under the current year basis of assessment do not have to be invoked. A joint venture is usually looked at as being an extension of an existing trade. This has the additional advantage that there are generally no restrictions on tax losses arising from a joint venture; it forms part of the general activities of the professional partnership.

Bank interest

20.24 Joint ventures usually have bank accounts that are joint accounts for the joint venture parties. Care should be taken that the interest on cash deposits arising to the joint venture is included in the correct tax return periods of the joint venturers. This is a common cause of difficulties with such joint ventures.

VAT considerations

20.25 There are a number of factors that should be considered in relation to VAT and the choice of corporate, partnership, or joint venture structure. For a general description of VAT, see **CHAPTER 23**.

Care should be taken to consider the differing VAT treatment of supplies and intra-group/partnership/joint venture supplies, as well as the VAT registration considerations (some of which are mentioned below). An important aspect of this is whether a VAT group should be utilised (if possible) to try and avoid any unnecessary irrecoverable VAT costs (if there are any) being incurred. This is especially the case for service companies providing services to business entities that are unable to fully recover VAT incurred on costs.

The VAT registration of partnerships is treated differently from corporate structures. A partnership is treated as a single entity for VAT registration purposes, and the members of the partnership are treated as being jointly and severally liable for any debts and liabilities of the partnership.

Corporate entities, including LLPs, are VAT-registered as entities in their own right and have no joint and several liability issues.

Only the general partner of a limited partnership can normally register for VAT (as a limited partner is not treated as being able to control and be involved in the day-to-day running of the limited partnership).

Joint ventures are often the most complicated in relation to VAT registration unless a joint venture company is set up. Joint ventures will normally be treated as partnerships for VAT purposes by HMRC, but this is not always the case.

Chapter 21 Capital Gains Tax

This chapter outlines the main capital gains tax (CGT) issues which arise for partnerships (including LLPs) and partners (or members). This is a complicated subject, where there is not much statute law but a good deal of generally accepted HMRC practice. Most of the practical problems arise when partners leave a firm or change their profit-sharing arrangements.

Partnership assets and the nature of a partner's interest

Basic points

21.1   CGT is a tax on gains on the disposal of assets and, according to the legislation, 'all forms of property' are assets for CGT purposes unless specifically excluded. Clearly, a firm's activities involve some assets which most people would describe as partnership assets, eg office premises and, perhaps, its goodwill. However, the partners also have rights under the partnership agreement (if one exists) which could be treated as assets. The combination of law and practice effectively:

(a)   disregards the firm as such, and deems all dealings in partnership assets as dealings by the partners;

(b)   treats each partner as owning a share of the firm's assets and therefore realising a share of any gains or losses when they are sold; and

(c)   makes the partners personally liable to CGT on their individual shares of any gains made on these assets.

How is a partner's share of gains calculated?

21.2   A partner's share of any such gains will be his capital profit share as set out in the partnership agreement. If there is no agreement, capital profits will be shared equally. Capital profit shares do not have to be identical to income profit shares. It is quite common to find that, where, for example, a partner puts a property into a firm, the agreement provides for capital profits or losses on its sale to be for the account of that partner alone.

Indexation, taper relief and the introduction of the flat rate of CGT

21.3   Until 5 April 1998, indexation relief operated to remove the inflationary element of taxable gains. The acquisition expenditure (or 'base cost') of an asset was written up for tax purposes according to the increase in the Retail Prices Index between the date of acquisition and the date of disposal.

However, as a result of the *Finance Act 1998*, indexation was 'switched off' at 5 April 1998 for individuals and partnerships. The relief which had accrued up to that date was still available on disposals between 6 April 1998 and 5 April 2008. Indexation relief was replaced by a new 'taper relief' covering disposals in the period between 6 April 1998 to 5 April 2008. This operated by reducing the otherwise taxable gain – after any indexation up to 5 April 1998 for assets acquired before that date – by a percentage which increased the longer the asset was held.

Since 5 April 2008, a flat rate of CGT has applied to any gain, without regard to any taper relief or indexation allowance that might have accrued prior to that date.

From 6 April 2008 to 22 June 2010, the flat rate was 18%. The flat rate was increased to 28% for higher rate taxpayers in the Emergency Budget on 22 June 2010 for disposals on or after 23 June 2010.

The 18% flat rate continues for all basic rate taxpayers. The 28% rate applies where total taxable income and gains are in excess of the upper limit of the income tax basic rate band (£37,400 for 2010/11). The level of the basic rate band is determined by the legislation. This provides that, for 2010/11, the standard basic rate limit is set at £37,400 and that it is increased in some circumstances. The circumstances given are where there are grossed-up Gift Aid payments and grossed-up personal pension contributions.

For the purposes of calculating the rate for post-22 June disposals, one ignores pre-23 June disposals.

On the introduction of the flat CGT rate, entrepreneurs' relief was also introduced, which provided that, subject to a claim, gains on qualifying assets would have an effective CGT rate of 10% on a lifetime gains limit of £1 million. With effect from 6 April 2010, the lifetime limit for entrepreneurs' relief was increased to £2 million. It was increased from £2 million to £5 million with effect from 23 June 2010. In determining whether there is any basic rate band such that gains can be taxed at 18%, gains attracting entrepreneurs' relief are set against the basic rate band in priority to other gains.

Disposals of partnership assets to the 'outside world'

21.4   There are normally few tax problems where a partnership asset is disposed of to a third party. The capital gain is calculated under the usual rules and then divided among the partners as indicated at **21.2** above.

Example 1 – A disposal to a third party

Furniss, Dawson, Craven and White have been in partnership since 1984. They have always shared capital profits as to 40%, 30%, 15% and 15% respectively. In July 2010, they sell for £1,500,000 an office building acquired in July 1988 for £600,000 ('base cost'). The overall gain on the building is calculated under normal CGT principles, but divided in appropriate shares, ie:

	F 40% £	D 30% £	C 15% £	W 15% £	Totals £
Sale proceeds	600,000	450,000	225,000	225,000	1,500,000
Base cost	(240,000)	(180,000)	(90,000)	(90,000)	(600,000)
Chargeable gains	360,000	270,000	135,000	135,000	900,000

Each partner should include his share as above in his tax return, and tax will be payable by each accordingly.

Reporting by the firm

21.5   Gains or losses on disposals of partnership assets must be reported by the firm on the partnership return (see **18.35**), quite separately from each partner's responsibility to report his personal gains or losses, including shares of such disposals.

Transactions between partners

Change in capital and income profit sharing ratios

21.6   When income profit sharing ratios change, typically (but not only) when there is a change of partners, there may well also be a change of capital profit shares (see **21.2** above). This will affect the CGT base cost of each partner in respect of his share of any assets liable to CGT. Strictly, it amounts to a disposal by any partner whose share is reduced, and an acquisition by any whose share is increased.

HMRC practice

21.7   However, HMRC practice is not to make a CGT assessment on a partner who reduces his share in these circumstances, and to treat the transaction as giving rise neither to a gain nor a loss, subject to certain exceptions (see **21.10** and **21.11** below).

Instead, there is simply an adjustment to the base costs of all partners involved to reflect the altered entitlements to eventual capital profits.

Example 2 – When a new partner is admitted

Instead of selling their building in July 2010, the partners in Furniss, Dawson, Craven and White (see the example at **21.4** above) decide to admit a fifth partner, Templeman. Income and capital profits will hence-forth be shared respectively 36%, 27%, 13.5%, 13.5% and 10%. Assuming none of the exceptions in **21.11** and **21.12** below apply, no CGT assessments will be made, and the following adjustments should be recorded to the partners' CGT base costs:

	F	D	C	W	T	Totals
	£	£	£	£	£	£
Base cost b/f	240,000	180,000	90,000	90,000	–	600,000
'Disposal' to Templeman in July 2010	(24,000)	(18,000)	(9,000)	(9,000)	60,000	–
Revised base cost c/f	216,000	162,000	81,000	81,000	60,000	600,000

This calculation shows, as one would expect, that Furniss has 'disposed' of a 4% share (£24,000 being 4% of £600,000), since his profit share has declined from 40% to 36%. The other three original partners have respec-tively 'disposed' of 3%, 1.5% and 1.5%. Templeman has 'acquired' a 10% share of the original £600,000.

The effect of the indexation allowance

21.8   Prior to 6 April 2008, indexation allowance was taken into account when adjusting partners' base costs on a no gain, no loss transaction. However, with effect from 6 April 2008, indexation allowance is no longer relevant, and gains on disposals after that date are calculated using actual base costs only.

Assets acquired before 1 April 1982

21.9   Further considerations can come into play where the asset in question was acquired before 1 April 1982. Statutory rebasing of CGT to this date will mean that, for individual partners, calculations are based on the value of the asset at 31 March 1982 rather than historic cost (see Revenue & Customs Brief 9/2009). As inter-partner transfers on a change of sharing ratios are treated as 'no gain/no loss' events (subject to the exceptions noted in **21.10** and **21.11** below), the base cost transferred between partners in such a case will be part of the value at 31 March 1982, even where the transferee partner joined the firm long after that date.

Exceptions to the general rule

21.10   There are several exceptions to the general rule that inter-partner transactions in partnership assets take place on a 'no gain/no loss' basis. In these cases, the transaction will normally be deemed to take place at the open market value of the asset concerned, and tax may be payable by the disposing partner. These exceptions are:

(a)   where the parties are 'connected' with each other independently of the partnership, eg father and son; and

(b)   where a payment is made between the parties outside the accounts. Detailed professional advice is needed in these situations.

Revaluations of assets

21.11   A further, and often more important, exception to the general rule is where partnership assets, for example property or goodwill, are revalued in the firm's accounts. This event does not have any CGT implications at the time, because nothing has been disposed of. However, when there is a later change in sharing ratios (whether between existing partners or on a partner joining or leaving), partners whose shares are reduced will be regarded as having realised a gain (if the revaluation was upwards) or a loss (if it was downwards). The logic behind this lies in the accounting entries made when a revaluation occurs. Where an asset is revalued upwards, anyone who was a partner at the time will be credited with the surplus according to his sharing ratio. If his share of capital profits is later reduced, without such treatment his potential CGT bill on a sale of the asset (or on leaving the firm – see **21.12** below) would also be reduced, yet his capital account would still show the revaluation surplus which could be enjoyed tax-free.

Example 4 – Revaluation of an asset

Sam and Janet have been in partnership for many years, sharing income and capital profits equally. They paid £20,000 for the goodwill of another practice which they took over in 1984. Until 1992, they showed this asset at cost in their accounts but then decided that, since this side of the business had been very successful, they would revalue it to £100,000. £40,000 was credited to each partner's capital account. In December 2009, they admit a third partner, Arabella, and she takes a 20% share of profits, with Sam and Janet reducing their shares to 40% each.

Sam and Janet are regarded, in 2009/10, as having each disposed of a 10% share of the goodwill to Arabella, and as each making a capital gain as follows:

Deemed proceeds: 10% × £100,000 =	£10,000
Less 10% of original cost (£20,000) =	(2,000)
Capital gain	£8,000

This gain will be taxable in 2009/10 unless one of the relevant reliefs (see **21.19** below) applies.

Arabella is deemed to have a base cost of £20,000 (20% of £100,000).

It will be appreciated that this leaves the relevant partner with tax to pay, but no cash in his hand. Upwards revaluations should therefore be treated with great care, since they may have unpleasant consequences in future. In this example, Sam and Janet might have to withdraw funds from the firm, with consequent loss of working capital, to pay the tax. (See **21.15** below for the position when Sam retires.)

CGT implications of partnership retirements and goodwill

Typical arrangements

21.12   Firms make a wide variety of different provisions for a partner's retirement. The most common arrangements, however, are probably either:

(a)   the payment out of sums standing to the partner's credit (ie his capital and current account credit balances, if any) but no payment for goodwill, together with an annuity; or

(b)   a payment for goodwill, together with any credit balances as above, but no annuity – such a firm will have required partners to make their own pension arrangements out of their drawings.

No payment for goodwill

21.13   The first type of arrangement occurs either where no goodwill is thought to exist or where it is not recognised in the accounts as having any value, usually because it is declared in the partnership agreement as accruing to the firm as a whole. Where a partner leaves such a firm but the business continues, he will not have made any disposal of an asset recognised for CGT purposes. (The return of his capital and current account balances is simply, in effect, the withdrawal of his own money which has no CGT consequences – nor does it have any income tax consequences, because these funds include past profits on which he has already paid income tax.) However, advice will be needed where a partner extracts assets (eg a property) in kind on retirement. See **21.17** below on the treatment of annuities.

The partner pays for goodwill

21.14   It might, of course, be the case that a partner in a firm of this type originally paid for a share of goodwill, either when he joined the firm or perhaps when a new business was acquired (see the example in **21.11** above), but this value has later been written down to zero because of a change of policy. In this event, a retiring partner might be able to claim a loss for CGT purposes, against any personal gains he makes in that or a later tax year, although HMRC are likely to challenge this claim.

Payment for goodwill

21.15   In the second type of arrangement (described at **21.12** above), the retiring partner will realise a taxable gain on his share of goodwill, calculated by taking the amount paid to him less his accumulated base cost on the principle already described for changes in profit shares (see **21.7–21.8** above). This is, after all, simply another such change, the retiring partner's share reducing to zero.

Example 5 – Partner paid for share of goodwill on retirement

The partnership of Sam, Janet and Arabella which featured in the example in **21.11** above continues until July 2010 when Sam retires. He is paid £100,000 for his share of goodwill by Janet and Arabella, who henceforth divide profits equally. The CGT position is as follows:

	Sam £	Janet £	Arabella £
Share of goodwill before Arabella's admission (as **21.11** above)	10,000	10,000	–
Base cost used on disposal to Arabella	(2,000)	(2,000)	20,000
	8,000	8,000	20,000
Payment to Sam (July 2010)	(100,000)	50,000	50,000
Sam's gain	92,000		
Remaining partners' base costs		58,000	70,000

Sam may well, however, be entitled to one of the reliefs mentioned at **21.19** below.

Other 'no gain/no loss' situations

21.16 It may be asked at this point what happens, on a partner's retirement, to his share of other assets of the firm, such as property. If that property remains in the firm, as it normally will, and no payment is made to the retiring partner, for CGT purposes, nothing happens. The transaction is simply regarded as a reduction in profit share to zero on the part of the retiring partner, giving rise to neither a gain nor a loss.

Example 6 – Partner retires without property being sold

Returning to the firm of Furniss, Dawson, Craven, White and Templeman, suppose that Furniss retires in July 2011. No payment is made to him in respect of his share of the property, and the remaining four partners share profits thereafter as 36% to Dawson, 22.5% each to Craven and White and 19% to Templeman.

The position will be as follows:

	F	D	C	W	T	Total
	(£000's)	(£000's)	(£000's)	(£000's)	(£000's)	(£000's)
Base cost	216	162	81	81	60	600
'Disposal' by Furniss	(216)	54	54	54	54	–
Gain/loss to Furniss	NIL					
Base costs to c/f		216	135	135	114	600

The remaining partners have each increased their base cost by 9% of £600,000. Furniss has simply disposed of his share for its CGT base cost, in line with the treatment described earlier.

Annuities and CGT

21.17 Firms which do not make payments for goodwill to retiring partners tend instead to pay annuities in recognition of the retiring partner's contribution over the years. HMRC will regard such payments wholly as income in the recipient's hands, so long as they do not exceed a specified proportion of his recent shares of income profits. If more than these amounts are paid, HMRC may treat the capitalised value of the annuity as consideration for a disposal of the partner's share of the firm's assets, and CGT may be due accordingly.

Statement of Practice D12 revisited

21.18 In mid-October 2002, the Inland Revenue updated their Statement of Practice D12 relating to the capital gains tax treatment of partnerships, first issued in January 1975, to cater for limited liability partnerships (LLPs). The treatment set out in SP D12 is extended to LLPs as long as they remain fiscally transparent. Fiscal transparency is only lost if the LLP ceases to carry on any trade or business with a view to profit and, even then, it can remain transparent whilst in the course of an orderly and bona fide winding up.

The 2002 version of SP D12 meant that, where goodwill was recognised on a firm's balance sheet, it was treated as though that goodwill was a holding of shares. However, pooling was restored for fungible assets (including partnership goodwill) for disposals after 6 April 2008.

On 25 January 2008, HMRC issued Revenue & Customs Brief 3/2008 to clarify their interpretation of SP D12 in the context of assets contributed to a partnership. In contrast to previous decisions of some HMRC officers, their view was clarified to state that, when a partner contributes an asset to a partnership by means of a capital contribution, the correct application of the capital gains legislation is that the partner in question has made a part disposal of the asset equal to the fractional share that passes to the other partners.

The market value rule would apply, if the transfer is between connected persons or the transaction is other than by way of a bargain made at arm's length, Otherwise, the consideration to be taken into account in computing the chargeable gain or loss on the part disposal will be a proportion of the total consideration given by the partnership for the asset. That proportion will be equal to the fractional share of the asset passing to the other partners. HMRC take the view that a sum credited to the partner's capital account represents consideration for the disposal of the asset to the partnership.

CGT reliefs for partners

21.19   Partners may be able to claim several valuable reliefs from CGT, some of which are deferrals of tax rather than exemptions. Basic points in relation to individual partners appear below, but the conditions are complex and expert advice should always be taken.

Rollover and holdover relief on replacement of business assets

21.20   Partners can 'roll over' the capital gains they make on their shares of the gain into the purchase of new qualifying assets.

Where a firm sells:

(a) freehold land (or an interest in land such as a lease with more than 60 years to run), and/or buildings, which were occupied by the firm for its business; or

(b) goodwill of the business (and several other kinds of asset which are unlikely to be found in a professional partnership, such as fixed plant and machinery, aircraft or satellites),

the partners can 'roll over' the capital gains they make on their shares of the gain on the purchase of new assets in the same categories. The new assets must be acquired during the period beginning one year before, and ending three years after, the disposal of the old ones. Like-for-like replacement is not required (eg gains on a lease could be 'rolled' into an acquisition of goodwill, or vice versa). The effect is to reduce the base cost of the partners' shares of the new asset by their gains on the old assets. The relief is, therefore, a deferral of tax rather than an exemption.

There are special rules which apply where:

(i) the old asset has not been used wholly for the business;

(ii) not all the sale proceeds are reinvested; or

(iii) the new asset is a lease with less than 60 years to run.

These can restrict or eliminate any deferral. The relief can also apply to an asset owned personally by a partner but used by the firm, eg office premises. Where rollover relief was claimed on a new asset acquired between 6 April 1998 and 5 April 2008, however, the base cost of the new asset for CGT purposes was reduced by the full untapered gain (after indexation up to 5 April 1998).

Gifts of business assets

21.21 Another type of deferral relief is available where an asset of a partnership business is given away. Here, the disposal is deemed to take place at market value but any gain can be deducted from the base cost of the donee. Normally, of course, professional partners will not be able to make such gifts under the partnership agreement. However, if a partnership decides to incorporate, this relief can be a useful way of passing assets to the successor company without immediate CGT bills arising. For more details, see CHAPTER 24.

This relief does not apply where the asset given away is shares or securities, and the donee is a company. This restriction, introduced in 1999, was aimed at certain specialised methods of tax avoidance, but could also apply where a partnership holds shares, for example in a service company, and wishes to incorporate by means of a gift of assets to the new company. With careful planning, it should be possible to resolve this problem.

EIS deferral relief

21.22   This relief enables any capital gain, including one arising when a partner retires (see **21.12** above) or one of the exceptions to the 'no gain/no loss' rule for inter-partner transfers applies (see **21.10–21.11** above), to be deferred by the purchase of shares in an unquoted trading company. The time limits are the same as for the general rollover relief mentioned at **21.20** above.

This relief is only available for the acquisition of newly subscribed shares in companies which qualify under the Enterprise Investment Scheme, though it is not dependent on the availability of income tax relief on those shares. Certain trades, notably those with a substantial property element such as property development and farming, do not qualify. The gain on the 'old' asset, such as a partnership interest, is not exempted from tax, but merely deferred until the new shares are sold, or certain other events occur, such as long-term emigration from the UK. Numerous other detailed rules apply, and advice should always be taken.

Retirement relief

21.23   This formerly very valuable exemption was abolished for disposals after 5 April 2003. For details of how it operated and the way in which it was withdrawn, reference should be made to the fourth edition of this book.

Entrepreneurs' relief

21.24   As mentioned at **21.3** above, entrepreneurs' relief was introduced for 'qualifying business disposals' on or after 6 April 2008. In relation to partnership interests held by individuals, qualifying business disposals include a 'material disposal of business assets' and a 'disposal associated with a material disposal'.

A 'material disposal of business assets' means the disposal of the whole or part of a business owned by the individual throughout a one-year period ending with the date of disposal. It also covers the disposal of an interest in one or more assets in use for the purpose of the business, where the disposal occurs when the business ceases to be carried on, again with a one-year period of ownership condition ending with the cessation of business. The disposal must be made within the three-year period beginning with the date of cessation. A 'disposal associated with a material disposal' is made if the disposal is made as part of withdrawal from participation in the business of the partnership.

Entrepreneurs' relief needs to be claimed by the first anniversary of 31 January following the tax year in which the disposal takes place. For the tax years 2008/09 and 2009/10, there was a lifetime limit of £1 million of gains on which entrepreneurs' relief could be claimed. The relief was given by deducting losses arising on the disposal from the gains arising on the disposal, and then reducing the net gain by 4/9ths in order to arrive at an effective rate of 10% (18% × 5/9).

For disposals made between 6 April 2010 and 22 June 2010, the lifetime limit was increased to £2 million.

For disposals on or after 23 June 2010, there is a fixed rate of 10% on qualifying gains, regardless of whether the individual is a basic or higher rate taxpayer.

Entrepreneurs' relief is very different to the taper relief that it replaced and has more similarities to the old retirement relief. Care needs to be taken regarding assets owned by the individual for use in the business and, in particular, it should be noted that no entrepreneurs' relief will be available for a property which is let to the partnership at a market rent.

Taper relief

21.25   As indicated above, taper relief was available between 6 April 1998 and 5 April 2008 to reduce the gain subject to capital gains tax. There were two scales of tapering, one for business assets, and one for other assets. The distinction between the two classes could be complex. For the purposes of this chapter, it will be assumed in the main that the asset being disposed of qualified for the more generous business scale. That would have been the case for a disposal of a partner's interest in a partnership, and of an asset which had been used, throughout its ownership (or throughout its ownership since 5 April 1998, if acquired earlier) wholly for the purpose of the firm's business. From 6 April 2000 until 5 April 2008, it may also have been the case with shares in trading companies owned by partnerships.

For business assets held for just two whole years, an effective rate of CGT of only 10% was available. The taper scales which applied to disposals of business assets after 5 April 2002 and before 6 April 2008 are set out below. The amount of the relief depended on the length of the 'qualifying holding period' (QHP); this was the number of complete years after 5 April 1998 for which the asset had been owned by the person disposing of it at the date of disposal. The table also shows the effective tax rate after taper relief, based on a 40% rate for a higher rate taxpayer:

Number of whole years in qualifying period	Percentage of gain taxed	Effective tax rate
Less than 1	100	40
1	50	20
2 or more	25	10

For non-business assets, the scale was less generous:

Number of whole years in qualifying period	Percentage of gain taxed	Effective tax rate
Less than 3	100	40
3	95	38
4	90	36
5	85	34
6	80	32
7	75	30
8	70	28
9	65	26
10 or more	60	24

If a non-business asset was held at 16 March 1998 by the person disposing of it, an extra year's relief was given.

For disposals before 6 April 2000, the 'business' scale was also a ten-year one, with the effective minimum tax rate of 10% achieved only after ten years' ownership. No 'credit' was given for periods of ownership before 6 April 1998, since indexation operated for that period.

The *Finance Act 2000* altered the definition of a business asset for taper relief purposes. Notably, in relation to partnerships, it provided that shares or securities in an unlisted trading company would become business assets in relation to periods after 5 April 2000, regardless of the percentage owned or whether the shareholder worked full time, or even at all, in the company's trade. Thus, shares in a partnership service company which carried on a trade, such as the provision of staff and services to the firm, qualified for the much more generous scale of business taper relief. However, the definition of a trading company for this purpose was complex. Also, for periods of ownership before 6 April 2000, the shares might have only qualified for the less generous non-business scale, unless the partner in question owned more than 25% of the voting shares, or, if less, was a full-time employee of the company (not of the partnership). These conditions were rarely satisfied except in small firms, so the change was welcome.

379

An apportionment would be needed on the sale of service company shares held at 5 April 2000, which switched from non-business to business asset status as a result of these changes, between business and non-business periods.

A further expansion of the definition of a business asset took effect from 6 April 2004. Subject to certain restrictions, this allowed somebody who let property to a trading or professional partnership, for use in its business, to claim business asset taper relief for periods after that date, even if they were not themselves a member of the partnership.

Further advice should be taken where apportionment of a gain is required between a business and non-business asset. HMRC have contended that, where a disposed asset was partly non-qualifying and partly qualifying during its ownership, the gain must be apportioned between the non-qualifying and qualifying fractions of ownership. A Tribunal case (*Jefferies & Anor v HMRC* [2009] UKFTT 291 (TC), 29 October 2009) determined that, if the asset disposed of was a business asset at the date of disposal, business asset taper relief could apply to the full amount of business gain.

Chapter 22   Stamp Duty Land Tax

Introduction

22.1   When Stamp Duty Land Tax ('SDLT') first applied to land transactions in the United Kingdom with effect from 1 December 2003, transfers of land in and out of partnership, and transfers of interests in a partnership, were excluded from SLDT (*Finance Act 2003, Sch 15, Part 3*).

A consultative paper with draft clauses to amend *Part 3* of *Sch 15*, to bring certain partnership transactions within the charge to SDLT, was published in October 2003. Despite representations, the content was largely incorporated in the draft legislation in the 2004 *Finance Bill*. However, substantial changes had to be introduced at report stage, and the legislation (*Finance Act 2004, Sch 41*) was enacted with effect from 23 July 2004, the date of Royal Assent.

The *Finance Act 2004* legislation was extremely difficult to understand and threw up numerous inconsistencies and anomalies. Changes have been made in almost every *Finance Act* since. These have, on the whole, been helpful, although there are some areas that remain unclear.

In March 2005, HMRC published a draft Manual. As at October 2010, this draft Manual is the only interpretation of the legislation by HMRC in the public domain. However, it is dangerously out of date and should not be referred to. In 2009, a further draft was issued for consultation. It is anticipated that a revised draft will be published, with a final version sometime later. This lengthy timescale does suggest that HMRC have as much trouble with the legislation as do practitioners.

Rates

22.2   The amount of any SDLT payable on a partnership transaction will vary with the consideration, in the same way that a simple purchase of property does. The tax charge will depend on whether the property is residential, non-residential or mixed. The 'slab system' applies so that, if the consideration exceeds a certain threshold, that percentage applies to the whole consideration. The rates are not 'sliced' as they are for income tax.

The tax chargeable on the grant of a lease, where rent only is being received, is calculated by discounting the rent receivable under the lease by a discount rate of (currently) 3.5% back to the date of the grant of the lease. The capital value thus obtained is charged to SDLT at a rate of 1% to the extent that the discounted value exceeds the residential or non-residential threshold. This is an exception to the 'slab system'.

Scope

22.3 A partnership for SDLT purposes is defined (in *Finance Act 2003, Sch 15, para 1*) as:

(a) a *Partnership Act 1890* partnership;

(b) a partnership registered under the *Limited Partnerships Act 1907*;

(c) a limited liability partnership (under the *Limited Liability Partnerships Act 2000* or the equivalent Northern Ireland legislation); or

(d) a similar overseas body.

Ordinary partnership transactions

22.4 There are ordinary transactions where, for example, a professional practice operating as a partnership or LLP may buy or sell UK land or enter into a lease. If an interest is acquired, all the obligations and authorisations which fall on or attach to a purchaser (if, for example, land is acquired) fall on the responsible partners, who are those partners at the effective date of the transaction and any person who becomes a partner after the effective date of the transaction. A partner who joins after the effective date could be responsible for penalties, but not the SDLT itself or interest on late payment of SDLT.

Special provisions

22.5 The special provisions apply to certain transactions surrounding the transfer of:

- a chargeable interest to a partnership by a partner or connected party;

- an interest in a property investment partnership; or

- a chargeable interest from a partnership to any of its partners or persons connected with them.

Basic concepts for the special provisions

22.6 It is important to remember that SDLT is not applied in the same way to partnerships as capital gains tax (although market value for SDLT purposes is determined as for capital gains tax: *Finance Act 2003, s 118*).

The first point to note is that a person's partnership share is assessed by reference to income share not capital share. Worse still, this assessment is by relative income shares not residual income shares. So, in the case of a three-man partnership where the results are divided in the following manner, the income shares are not ⅓ each, but as set out in the final column below:

Profit

	Salary	*Share*	*Total*	*%*
Oliver	10,000	50,000	60,000	26
Dick	60,000	50,000	110,000	48
Annie	10,000	50,000	60,000	26
	80,000	150,000	230,000	100%

The second point to note is that, for the purposes of *Finance Act 2003, Sch 15, Part 3*, partnership property includes property held by the members of the partnership for the purposes of the partnership business. HMRC originally said that this (for relevant partnership property) included land held by any of the partners outside the partnership and used for the partnership business (SDLTM35100, www.hmrc.gov.uk/so/pftmanual.htm#20). However, HMRC's latest draft partnership guidance on their interpretation of *para 34(1)* indicates that a chargeable interest beneficially owned by some, but not all, of the partners in a partnership will not be classed as partnership property, even if the chargeable interest is used for the purposes of the partnership business. When all the partners own the property, it might or might not be partnership property, depending upon the basis of ownership. Even if all the partners own the property, HMRC now say that it is unlikely to be partnership property if it is subject to an express declaration of joint tenancy (www.hmrc.gov.uk/so/technewsletter5.htm).

Transfer of interests into a partnership

22.7 These provisions (contained in *Finance Act 2003, Sch 15, para 10*) apply where:

(a) a partner transfers a chargeable interest to a partnership;

(b) a person transfers a chargeable interest to a partnership in return for an interest in the partnership; or

(c) a person connected with a partner, or a person who becomes a partner as a result of or in connection with the transfer, transfers a chargeable interest to the partnership.

A 'chargeable interest' is broadly an interest in land in the UK. It can be a transfer to an existing partnership or the formation of a new partnership.

There can be a further charge to SDLT if there is a transfer into a partnership and, subsequently, there is a transfer of an interest in the partnership or a withdrawal of money, etc from the partnership.

The SDLT charge is based on the chargeable consideration (see *Finance Act 2003, Sch 15, para 10(2)*), calculated as follows:

The chargeable consideration for the transaction is MV × (100 − SLP)%.

MV is the market value of the interest transferred.

Where part of the chargeable consideration includes rent, separate computations will be needed for the MV of the premium and the MV calculated as the net present value of the rent, if this exceeds the current rent threshold.

SLP is known as the 'sum of the lower proportions'.

The calculation of SLP for a partnership consisting of individuals involves a series of steps (*Finance Act 2003, Sch 15, para 12*).

Essentially, what is required is to calculate the proportion that goes into the partnership from individuals who either are, or become, partners, or to partners who are connected with those individuals.

Determining SLP

22.8 Step 1 is to identify 'relevant owners'. These are persons who, immediately before the transfer, are entitled to a proportion of the chargeable interest and, immediately after the transfer, are a partner or are connected with a partner.

Step 2 is to identify the 'corresponding partner' or partners for each relevant owner.

A person is a corresponding partner if, immediately after the transfer, he is a partner and he is the relevant owner or connected with the relevant owner. For SDLT purposes, the normal income tax definition applies, except that partners are not treated as connected unless they are connected in some other way, such as husband, wife, son, daughter, etc.

Example 1

If Toby transfers property into the partnership consisting of Toby and others (unconnected persons), Toby is the corresponding partner to Toby the relevant owner.

If James transfers the property into a partnership consisting of James and his wife, both James and his wife are corresponding partners in relation to James.

Step 3 is to find, for each relevant owner, the proportion of the chargeable interest prior to the transfer.

That interest is then apportioned between the relevant owner's corresponding partners. In Example 1 above, James's 100% interest is apportioned between James and his wife.

Finally, Step 4 is to find the 'lower proportion' for each person who is a corresponding partner to the relevant owner.

The lower proportion is:

(a) The proportion of the chargeable interest attributable to the partner. This is the proportion apportioned to him at Step 3 above. This might be from one or more relevant owners.

(b) If lower, the partner's partnership share immediately after the transaction.

A partner's partnership share is defined by his share in *income* profits (see **22.3** above).

The draft HMRC SDLT Manual (see SDLTM33800) indicates that HMRC will allow apportionment in a way that produces the highest SLP.

Example 2

Frodo, Sam and Pip are all unconnected and in partnership together, sharing profits, both income and capital, equally. The total capital is £3 million.

Merry, who is also unconnected, joins the partnership, introducing land worth £1 million. The capital and income shares become 25% each.

75% of the property is transferred to Frodo, Sam and Pip and a charge arises on £750,000. SLP in this case is 25%.

$(100 - 25)\% \times £1,000,000 = £750,000$

1   Relevant owner is Merry.

2   Corresponding partner is Merry. (No connected persons.)

3   The portion of chargeable interest held prior to the transfer is 100%. This is apportioned wholly to Merry.

4   Find the lower proportion. This is the proportion that applies to him in Step 3 or, if lower, the partner's income share immediately after the transaction = 25%.

5   Add together lower proportions = 25%.

Example 3

Thomas, Edward, Gordon and Percy are in partnership, sharing profits and losses (income and capital) equally.

Thomas, Edward and Gordon are brothers, but Percy is unconnected.

Thomas transfers land into the partnership worth £800,000.

To calculate SLP, the following process applies:

1   The relevant owner is Thomas.

2   The corresponding partners are Thomas, Edward and Gordon.

3   Apportion 100% interest owned by Thomas to Thomas, Gordon and Edward ⅓ each.

4   Find lower proportion:

- the lower of 1/3; or

- income share of 25% each.

5   SLP = 25 + 25 + 25 = 75%

Transfer of partnership interest pursuant to earlier arrangements

22.9   Where a chargeable interest has been transferred to a partnership, and subsequently there is a transfer of a partnership interest by the person who made the initial transfer or someone connected with him, and arrangements were in place when the original transaction took place, then there will be an additional charge. This charge will be calculated as a proportion of the market value originally transferred, based on the reduction of the partnership share of the relevant person. The two transactions will be treated as linked transactions (*Finance Act 2003, Sch 15, para 17*).

Withdrawal of money from a partnership

22.10   Care needs to be taken where there is a transfer of a chargeable interest to a partnership, as described above, and, within a period of three years after that land transfer, money or money's worth is withdrawn from the partnership. This provision applies where the transfer of the chargeable interest to the partnership is after 19 May 2005.

These provisions broadly apply where the person who makes the transfer, or a person connected with him, withdraws money or money's worth which does not represent income profits.

These can include simply withdrawing capital from his capital account, reducing his interest, ceasing to be a partner or the repayment of any loan by the partnership.

Under these circumstances, the amount chargeable is equivalent to the amount withdrawn, but shall not exceed the market value of the interest transferred, reduced by the amount previously chargeable to tax.

This appears to charge consideration received within three years from the event, even though the withdrawal may be totally unconnected with the original transfer and despite the fact that the charge on the original transfer is now based solely on market value rather than consideration (*Finance Act 2003, Sch 15, para 17A*).

Concluding remarks on putting property into partnership

22.11 If all the parties are connected and no transfers of partnership interests have taken place within three years of the transfer, and no money or money's worth except income profits are withdrawn from the partnership within three years of the transfer in, there should be no charge to SDLT.

SLP = 100%. So, applying the formula:

$(100 - 100)\% \times MV = 0.$

Property investment partnerships

22.12 The *Finance Act 2006* made significant changes to the legislation, such that the complicated rules on the transfer of interests in a partnership now usually only apply to 'property investment partnerships'. The definition is, however, a misnomer, as it is defined as a partnership whose sole or main activity is investing or dealing in land, whether or not that activity involves construction operations. Suffice to say that professional partnerships are very unlikely to be property investment partnerships, so this chapter restricts the analysis of the SDLT problems associated with the transfers of partnership interests to the limited times when *para 17* applies.

Transfers of chargeable interest from a partnership

General

22.13 This applies where a chargeable interest passes out of the partnership to a partner or ex-partner, or a person connected with a partner or ex-partner.

On dissolving a partnership, partnership property will continue to be treated as partnership property until it is distributed. There is the justifiable view that SDLT should not be payable on dissolution, since this puts partnerships at a disadvantage to companies; and, where the property is distributed on a winding up in proportion to partnership income shares, there is no change of interest in the proportion of property beneficially held by an individual partner. However, HMRC may seek to use the transfer out of partnership rules to calculate the SDLT on a dissolution.

A similar formula applies to the formula used for transferring interests into a partnership, ie:

$$MV \times (100 - SLP)\%$$

The SLP is calculated in a similar way to the transfer into a partnership, the steps being set out in a reverse way to those set out in **22.8** above.

Where the chargeable consideration includes rent, then a proportion of the market value of the premium plus a proportion of net present value of the rent will be chargeable.

Calculating a partnership share

22.14   However, the calculation of the partnership share attributable to a partner, which is then used to calculate the SLP, is subject to further provisions.

Effectively, if the transfer into partnership was before 20 October 2003, or the instrument was stamped with ad valorem stamp duty or if any SDLT was paid, then the share is calculated using the steps set out below. Otherwise, it is zero. (Note that there does not seem to be any requirement that SDLT has to be payable: the legislation states that 'any tax ... has been duly paid'.)

The series of steps referred to above are:

1   Determine the partnership share attributable to the partner on the relevant date. This date is:

   (i)   if the chargeable interest was transferred before 20 October 2003 and the partner was a partner on 19 October 2003, that date; or

   (ii) if the chargeable interest was transferred on or after 20 October 2003 and the partner was a partner on the day the interest was transferred, the day it was transferred.

   In any other case, it is the date he became a partner.

2   Add increases in partnership shares from the relevant date up to the time the property is transferred out of partnership.

Increases only count if they are stamped with ad valorem stamp duty or, if they take place after Royal Assent (23 July 2004), any SDLT has been paid if due. If the transfer of partnership interest took place on or after 19 July 2006, then it is unlikely that any SDLT would be payable.

3   Deduct decreases in partnership shares between the relevant date and the time the property leaves the partnership. This cannot reduce the partnership share to below zero.

If the partner ceased to be a partner before 19 October 2003, or before the transfer of the interest to the partnership, the partnership share attributable is zero (*Finance Act 2003, Sch 15, paras 21* and *22*).

Example 4

Sauron, Saruman and Gandalf are in partnership. Neither Saruman nor Gandalf is connected with Sauron. The income shares are respectively 35%, 30% and 35%. The partnership was set up in 1990, when land worth £250,000 was transferred by Sauron into the partnership. The original income shares were Sauron 95% and each of Saruman and Gandalf 2½%. The partnership income shares have been amended since then up until 2000. The present shares have been in force since 2002. However, the capital shares remain Sauron 95% and Saruman and Gandalf 2½% each. The land is now worth £2 million, and Sauron, on retirement in 2005, pays the partnership £100,000 for the withdrawal of the land.

What is the chargeable consideration?

This is computed as a proportion of the market value, the proportion being (100 – SLP)%. In this case, the relevant owner is Sauron. The corresponding partner is Sauron alone (neither of the others being connected with him). The proportion of the chargeable interest to which Sauron is entitled immediately after the transaction is 100%. The partnership share attributable to Sauron is then found. Sauron's actual partnership income share on 19 October 2003 was 35%. There are no adjustments either to increase or to decrease this share under Steps 2 and 3 (see above), there being no changes in Sauron's partnership share between 20 October 2003 and the day of his retirement. The lower proportion under Step 4 above is therefore 35% (the lower of the chargeable interest and the partnership share). The sum of the lower proportions (SLP) is also 35%. Therefore, applying the above formula, the chargeable consideration is found as follows:

(65% x £2,000,000) = £1,300,000. This is despite the fact that, from a CGT point of view, Sauron 'owns' 95% of the property.

It should be borne in mind that a charge under this head can arise even if the transfer is to a former partner who retired many years ago.

In simple terms, if the property was in the partnership and the individual was a partner on 19 October 2003 and there have been no profit sharing ratio charges since then, the market value charge will be reasonably straightforward.

Concluding remarks on transfers out of the partnership

22.15 The mismatch between income and capital shares can produce unexpected charges, as can be seen from Example 4.

Similar to transfers into partnership, if all the partners are connected, SLP = 100% and there should be no SDLT charge. This is provided that appropriate stamp duty or SDLT has been paid, if due, on any changes since 20 October 2003.

Other areas

Exchanges

22.16 This provides that the exchange rules that apply generally for SDLT (contained in *Finance Act 2003, Sch 4, para 5*) apply equally to a partnership (*Finance Act 2003, Sch 15, para 16(1)*).

However, *Sch 15, para 16(3)* specifically disapplies the general partitions rules. This means that, if Andrew and Brian are in a partnership which owns two offices 50:50, and the partnership is dissolved such that Andrew ends up owning one office and Brian ends up owning the other, SDLT will be chargeable. This is in contrast to the position if Andrew and Brian owned the offices outside the partnership as tenants in common and let them to the partnership, in which case a partition would not give rise to a SDLT charge.

Transfers from a partnership to a partnership

22.17 Where there is a transfer from a partnership to another partnership where charges could arise on both the transfer from and the transfer to, only one charge, the higher one, applies (*Finance Act 2003, Sch 15, para 23*).

The only charging provisions

22.18 The legislation makes it clear that the acquisition of an interest in a partnership is not a chargeable transaction, except under the specific circumstances described above covering transfers of land into partnership and transfers of partnership interests.

Notification

22.19 Partnership transactions involving transfers into or out of the partnership only need to be notified if they exceed the limits set out in *Finance Act 2003, s 77A*. The current limit for freehold transfers is £40,000. Transfers of partnership interests only need to be notified if the consideration exceeds the zero rate threshold.

Continued application of stamp duty

22.20 The intention behind the legislation was to continue a stamp duty liability on a transfer of a partnership interest. With effect from 20 July 2005, where a partnership owns stocks and shares, the charge will be based on the share (income share) changing hands.

The linking provisions

22.21 If there is a transfer to or from a partnership and the partners are only connected as partners, it appears that the linking provisions in *s 108* cannot apply (*Finance Act 2003, Sch 15, para 39*). It appears that the linking provisions will only apply if the individuals are connected (such as husband and wife). Clearly, if, in a partnership situation, the value acquired by them jointly exceeds the threshold, then an SDLT charge will apply.

However, if a partnership acquires land, then it appears that this is no different to an acquisition by a joint purchaser and will be a single transaction.

Death

22.22 The situation on death is going to vary considerably, but a common situation might be as follows. Consider an example of a partnership consisting of Alpha, Bravo and Charlie all sharing profits equally, where the partnership owns land. Alpha dies, and the partnership agreement provides that his share vests in his personal representatives, but Bravo and Charlie have an option agreement along the lines suggested in *Lindley & Banks on Partnership* (18th edition), para 10–151. Does SDLT apply to the exercise of the option? The provisions governing the transfer of a partnership interest should not apply, since the personal representatives are not a partner and therefore these provisions cannot apply. HMRC have confirmed that SDLT does not apply to the exercise of the option. This issue was relevant if the land came out of the partnership on death.

Incorporation as a limited liability partnership ('LLP')

22.23 The incorporation of an LLP is exempt (under *Finance Act 2003, s 65*), provided the following conditions are satisfied:

(i) The date of the transfer of the land to the LLP is not more than one year after the date of incorporation.

(ii) The transferor is a partner in the partnership comprised of all the persons who are to be members of the LLP (or the interest is held in an identical way by the transferor as nominee or bare trustee).

(iii) The proportions of interest transferred to which the partners are entitled are the same after incorporation as they were before, or none of the differences in proportions have arisen as part of a scheme or arrangement whose main or one of whose main purposes is to avoid liability to any duty or tax.

Anti-avoidance

22.24 In addition to specific anti-avoidance rules, *Finance Act 2003, s 75A* applies so as to ignore transactions that have been inserted purely to reduce the SDLT charge. *Finance Act 2010, s 55* introduced a new rule, such that transactions that fall under the anti-avoidance rules could not benefit from the special rules for partnership transactions where the effective date of a notional transaction is on or after 24 March 2010. This could potentially catch many partnership transactions, although the explanatory notes to the *Finance Bill* indicated the change was to ensure that SDLT planning schemes which seek to exploit the partnership rules will be subject to the anti-avoidance rule in *s 75A*.

Chapter 23   Other Taxes

This chapter briefly reviews taxes, other than income tax and capital gains tax, with which professional practices may be concerned. These are:

- inheritance tax (**23.1** below);

- Value Added Tax (**23.7** below); and

- PAYE and National Insurance Contributions (**23.11** below).

Inheritance tax (IHT)

IHT generally

23.1   IHT is payable, very broadly, on the value by which someone's 'estate' (ie the assets he possesses) is decreased by gifts made either in his lifetime or on death. Transfers during a person's lifetime to another individual, or to a disabled person's interest, or to a bereaved minor's trust on the coming to an end of an immediate post-death interest, are normally potentially exempt, which means that no tax is payable if the donor survives for seven years after the gift is made. However, lifetime transfers in relation to professional partnership assets will not normally be gifts, in this sense, because there will be no element of gratuitousness. Transfers between partners will normally be made in consideration of the respective services provided or capital contributions made, and absolute gifts will typically be prohibited by the partnership agreement. Therefore, attention here will be concentrated on transfers made when a partner dies.

Value of deceased partner's interest in the firm

23.2   When a person dies, he is deemed to make a transfer, for IHT purposes, of all the assets he owned immediately before death. Therefore, if a partner dies, the value of his partnership interest, together with that of any asset which he owns but is used by the firm, will be liable to IHT, together with all his personal assets, less any debts owed. The net value of the estate is taxed, currently, at 40%, although this tax bill will often be reduced by the 'nil rate band' applicable to the first £325,000 (from 6 April 2010) of value. The exact liability will depend on any gifts made in the

393

previous seven years and a number of statutory exemptions, the most important of which, for present purposes, is Business Property Relief (see **23.4** below).

Valuing a partner's interest

23.3   There can be complications in valuing a partner's interest in the firm for IHT purposes. The key feature is the procedure specified in the partnership agreement on a partner's death. It is rare nowadays for an agreement to specify that a firm is dissolved when a partner dies (although this is the legal position if there is no provision about death, see *s 33(1)* of the *Partnership Act 1890*) but, if so, the deceased's share in all the partnership assets has to be valued together with any other amounts due, such as credit balances on capital and current accounts.

Usually, the agreement will provide that the firm will continue, but that an account is to be drawn up as at the date of death. This may require all the assets to be revalued, and for the deceased's estate to be paid out of that value. Alternatively, it may provide for a payment to be made in respect of the deceased's share of the firm's assets or, perhaps most typically nowadays, it may state that goodwill accrues to the firm. In the latter case, the deceased's estate will only be entitled to the credit balances on his accounts (which may include items such as surplus tax and pension provisions). Provisions which compel the surviving partners to buy out the deceased's share cause problems with Business Property Relief – see **23.5** below. Normally, HM Revenue & Customs will accept that the value of the deceased's partnership interest for IHT purposes is the amount which his estate receives for his share of the firm's assets and his capital and current account balances. There can, however, be complications where partners are 'connected' independently of the firm, eg in a family partnership. In any event, it is sensible to provide that any annuity payable on a partner's death is payable to the surviving spouse rather than the estate, because the value of the annuity rights will then normally be exempt from IHT.

Business property relief

23.4   Assuming that the relevant valuations have been established, the next step is to consider how much Business Property Relief (BPR) is due. BPR is given by a 100% reduction in the otherwise taxable value of the partner's 'interest in the business', and a 50% reduction for any land, buildings, machinery or plant owned personally by him, but used wholly or mainly for the firm's business immediately before his death. BPR is not due at all if the deceased had become a partner less than two years before his death. The 'interest in the business' is the value ascertained (see **23.3**

above), and any personally owned assets attracting the 50% relief are valued at their open market value. 100% relief may also extend to minority shares in an unquoted company.

Assets, whether partnership assets or personally owned, which are neither used wholly or mainly for the business nor required for future use, are also excluded from BPR, which means it may be undesirable for a firm to hold long-term investment assets such as quoted shares or let property in its balance sheet. Problems can also arise if an IHT event, notably a partner's death, happens to occur when substantial amounts of cash are held in the business. Such holdings should be supported by a clearly documented business plan for their reinvestment in the medium term (for example, in a projected acquisition of new offices on the expiry of a current lease).

Problems with the agreement

23.5   Problems can arise over BPR if the partnership agreement, or any side-agreement, provides that the continuing partners are required to buy out the deceased's share, either at market value or according to a formula. The HMRC view is that this constitutes a binding contract for sale. Assets subject to such a contract are statutorily excluded from BPR, presumably because they are regarded as virtual cash-in-hand. Clauses which provide for the automatic accrual of the deceased's share to the surviving partners in return for a payment to the estate avoid this problem. An alternative, which achieves the same commercial effect, may be to provide for 'cross-options' under which the surviving partners may buy, and the estate may sell, within defined periods, though legal advice will be essential.

IHT planning

23.6   Currently, BPR is extremely generous. In effect, the value of a deceased partner's share in the business is exempt from IHT altogether. However, this relief can be put at risk in various ways, the most obvious being a change in the underlying assets of the partnership to non-qualifying assets. On the death of a retired partner, BPR will not be available, since he will no longer have an interest in the business when he dies.

Value Added Tax

23.7   The general principles of VAT apply to professional practices in much the same way as to any other business. However, there are some issues specific to partnerships, limited partnerships and limited liability partnerships.

General background

23.8 For VAT purposes, partnerships are separate entities. Therefore, where a sole proprietor takes on a partner or where a partner retires leaving a sole trader, a business is deemed to be transferred for VAT purposes and a new registration is required. Changes in the composition of an existing partnership do not represent transfers of business. However, a retiring partner could cause two partnerships to become one for VAT purposes, eg where one firm consists of A, B and C, and the other of A and B, and C then retires. Each partner is jointly and severally liable for any VAT liability and, therefore, a retiring partner remains liable until HM Revenue & Customs ('HMRC') are notified of the departure, even if this occurred at an earlier date.

It is possible to treat changes from sole trader to partnership status, and vice versa, as a 'transfer of a going concern' and therefore outside the scope of VAT. However, application must be made to HMRC for this treatment. Where a transfer of a going concern takes place, the purchaser should beware of the dangers of taking over a VAT registration number, as this will make the purchaser liable for any VAT owed by the transferor.

Generally, professional practices are involved in the supply of services rather than goods, and therefore it is important that the 'tax point' rules for the supply of services are understood, to ensure the correct accounting for VAT. It is also important to remember that, where a member of a partnership is also an officer of another organisation, eg a company director, fees paid will usually be treated as if paid for supplies by the partnership and therefore subject to VAT.

Partnership registrations

23.9 In some cases, a number of individuals operating together without a formal partnership deed are treated by HMRC as deemed partnerships carrying on the business of a single taxable person. This is subject to a direction being made under *Value Added Tax Act 1994, Sch 1, para 2.* Directions are given in cases where business splitting or disaggregation has taken place, often in an attempt to keep below the VAT threshold. This is particularly common with husband and wife business activities, and in such cases it is important to look at the intentions of the individuals. For example:

(a)   Are profits shared gross or net of expenses?

(b)   Is there a written partnership agreement?

(c)   What do the annual accounts reflect?

(d)   How do business names appear on stationery?

(e)   In whose names are sales invoiced?

(f)   Who would be sued if an action was taken against the business?

(g)   Are separate bank accounts maintained?

(h)   Is there a common trading name?

(i)   How is the business taxed by HMRC?

If such a direction is made, it cannot operate retrospectively.

For limited partnerships, HMRC generally accept that it is the general partner that is deemed to undertake all activities for VAT purposes, therefore it is the general partner that should be registered for VAT. If a limited partner does become involved in the day-to-day running of the partnership, they will be treated as a general partner. Where there is more than one general partner, all the general partners will need to be registered as a partnership.

Limited liability partnerships are treated as corporate bodies for registration purposes, as the members of the LLP will be protected from debts or liabilities arising from negligence, wrongful act or misconduct of another member, employee or agent of the LLP. VAT grouping is possible for LLPs.

When a partnership becomes a limited liability partnership (see **CHAPTER 24**), the change in structure would normally be treated as the transfer of the business as a going concern, as noted above.

Joint ventures may be treated by HMRC as partnerships and registered as such. This will mean that all bodies will be jointly and severally liable for debts. There are cases where such a venture does not involve anything approaching a partnership, eg no sharing of profits and losses. In such circumstances, HMRC may treat one party as receiving and supplying goods, and making payments to and from other members as being consideration for services given and received. Care is needed, as, if the relationship is not clear, it may lead to situations where VAT is not charged where it should be, or is recovered where it should not be. Co-owners of buildings and land are treated as a single taxable person and registered by HMRC as if they were a partnership. All interested parties will be treated as jointly and severally liable.

Other VAT points to consider

23.10   The rules on the recovery of input tax for partnerships are the same as those which apply to all businesses. However, it is worth noting that, where exempt or partially exempt partnerships operate with service companies which recharge certain expenses, the non-recoverable VAT on the recharge will represent an expense to the partnership. This may be avoided in certain circumstances for limited liability partnerships by form- ing a VAT group with the limited liability partnership and the service company, so that any charges made are within the VAT group and thus outside the scope of VAT.

Partnerships should also note the need to account for output tax when assets are taken for personal use by a partner.

Following the European Court case of *KapHag Renditefonds* (C-442/01), partnerships should consider the VAT implications when partners join or leave a partnership, and the associated changes in partnership interests. Where an incoming partner is VAT registered and contributes assets, the admission to the partnership is not treated as a taxable supply by the partnership, but there may be VAT consequences for the disposal of the assets by the incoming partner. Where assets are passed to an outgoing partner by a partnership, this may give rise to a VAT charge, and also the possible right to recovery by the partner. For further details, please see HMRC Business Brief 21/04 and 30/04.

Another issue to consider is, where partners hold various offices, including acting as clerk and/or treasurer of various local charities and societies, HMRC may take the view that the partners have accepted the offices in the course or furtherance of their profession. This would result in the partner- ship being required to account for output tax on any payments which the partners receive in relation to those offices. However, if it can be shown that the duties involved were a reflection of the personal standing of the partner involved and were of an administrative nature, it may be possible to argue that the partnership should not be liable to account for output tax (see *Oglethorpe Sturton & Gillibrand* (VAT tribunal decision 17491)).

When a partnership comes to an end, the outgoing partners will remain liable for the VAT owed by a partnership until the date that HMRC are notified of the partnership's dissolution. Until that date, the partnership will be treated as continuing (see *Customs and Excise Comrs v Jamieson* [2001] SWTI 938, ChD).

With effect from 1 January 2010, and the introduction of the VAT Package, any professional services business engaged in advisory work for EU (non-UK) business clients will need to ensure that invoices raised show the client's VAT number, and advise that the business client is obliged to account for VAT on the value of the services supplied. Also, EC Sales Lists will need to be completed each calendar quarter, providing details of the clients and the value of services supplied. There are exceptions to this general rule, eg services related to land.

PAYE and National Insurance Contributions

PAYE and Class 1, 1A and 1B National Insurance Contributions

23.11   Firms with employed staff have the same obligations as any other employer to operate the PAYE system and administer the collection and/or payment of Class 1, 1A and 1B National Insurance Contributions (NICs). It should be noted that salaried partners are employees in law, and their pay will count as employment income subject to tax under PAYE and Class 1 NICs.

PAYE and Class 1 NICs apply to employee wages and salaries, to round sum expense allowances that have not been approved for payment by HMRC (under a form P11D reporting dispensation), to vouchers that can be exchanged directly for cash, and to the provision of 'readily convertible assets' (generally, items for which trading arrangements are in existence). Class 1 NICs, but not tax under PAYE, also apply to:

(a)   the provision of vouchers that can be exchanged only for goods or services (that are not tax exempt);

(b)   the reimbursement of expenses that are not tax exempt;

(c)   the direct payment to a third party, where the employee has made the contract for supply, of expenses that are not tax exempt; and

(d)   the writing-off of an employer provided loan.

Class 1 NICs are divided into primary (employee's, which are deducted from pay) and secondary (employer's) contributions. Class 1A NICs are payable by the employer only, on all taxable expenses and benefits in kind (that are not liable to Class 1 NICs) provided to employees. Class 1B NICs, again payable by the employer only, arise as part of a method of settling employees' income tax on certain taxable benefits and expenses covered under a PAYE Settlement Agreement (or 'PSA').

Tax under PAYE and Class 1 NICs may also be due on fees earned by partners if they arise from a client engagement that is caught by the IR35 rules. The circumstances in which this might arise are explained in detail at **19.38–19.41**.

Class 2 and 3 NICs

23.12   As self-employed people, partners are subject to Class 2 NICs (until the week in which they reach pensionable age), unless profit shares are small (below £5,075 in 2010/11) or they make a loss. Class 2 NICs are paid at a flat rate per week (in 2010/11, £2.40), either quarterly or monthly, by direct debit. These contributions secure entitlement only to state sickness and invalidity benefits, the state retirement pension and widow's benefit (they do not cover unemployment-related benefits, maternity or paternity benefits). In some circumstances, eg where a partner has spent some years abroad and did not pay Class 2 NICs, it might be worth paying Class 3 NICs (£12.05 per week in 2010/11). These contributions are voluntary and can be used to make up for 'lost' years of entitlement in respect of the basic state pension. Payment can be made at any time up to six years following the end of the tax year in question.

Class 4 NICs

23.13　Class 4 NICs are payable by the self-employed (until the end of the tax year during which they reach pensionable age), in addition to Class 2 NICs, but they secure no additional benefits. As self-employed people, partners are subject to Class 4 NICs, which are calculated on a tax year basis, as a percentage of their profits chargeable for income tax purposes. These are the partner's taxable profits for a tax year after adjustment for capital allowances, losses and interest on partnership capital loans. In 2010/11, the rates that apply are 8% on profits in the band from £5,715 to £43,875 and 1% on all additional profits. No Class 4 NICs are paid on the profits chargeable to income tax up to the lower profits limit (in 2010/11, £5,715). The contributions are paid along with income tax on the same payment dates.

HMRC are of the opinion that salaried members should be treated as self-employed members of the LLP for tax purposes, and therefore subject to tax on their share of the tax adjusted profit, together with a liability to Class 2 and 4 NICs. This view is referred to in *ICTA 1988, s 118ZA(1)(a)*, which provides that all the activities of the partnership are treated as carried on by its members.

LLP Act, s 13 provides that 'where income tax is (or would be) charged on a member of a limited liability partnership in respect of profits or gains arising from the carrying on of a trade or profession by the limited liability partnership, Class 4 contributions shall be payable by him if they would be payable were the trade or profession carried on in partnership by the members'.

For these purposes, a member of a limited liability partnership is stated within *s 4(1)* and *(2)* of the *LLP Act* as being '... the persons who subscribed their names to the incorporation document' and 'any other person ... in accordance with an agreement with the existing members'.

LLP Act, s 4(4) goes on to state that 'a member of an LLP shall not be regarded for any purpose as employed by the limited liability partnership unless, if he and the other members were partners in a partnership, he would be regarded for that purpose as employed by the partnership'. This would indicate a continuation of employment status.

This would therefore mean that, if previously salaried partners do not subscribe their name to the incorporation document and are not registered as members at Companies House, they would not be held out to be members of the LLP and, as such, would not fall within the provisions of *ICTA 1988, s 118ZA(1)(a)* and would not be chargeable to tax and NICs as a self-employed individual. They would, instead, fall within *s 4(4)* of the *LLP Act* and continue to be treated as employed.

It has been proposed that NIC rates (employee, employer and Class 4) should increase by 1% from 2011/12, although there may be relief from this increase available for businesses, depending on specific circumstances.

Employment income

23.14 Partners may also have employment income (see **18.3**), eg from directorships, which makes them liable to Class 1 employee's NICs in addition to the Class 2 and Class 4 NICs on their profit share. For individuals in this situation, a maximum amount of Class 1, Class 2 and Class 4 NICs for a tax year is prescribed, to ensure that liability at the main rates (on the band of income between the lower and upper earnings limits) is not duplicated. A complex formula is involved in computing the maximum amount (see *Tolley's Practical NIC Service*, section 7, for details), but if earnings from the employment exceed the upper earnings limit for the tax year, liability to Class 4 NICs is limited to 1% of all profits above the lower earnings limit. Where it is clear that this will apply, the partner can apply for 'deferment' of Class 4 NICs and, when granted, will pay Class 4 NICs only at 1% on profits above the limit. Class 1 NICs cease, for the individual, in respect of employment income paid after they reach pensionable age.

Fees from 'incidental' directorships

23.15 Some partners may acquire directorships as an incident of their professional work, eg with a client company, and become entitled to receive directors' fees (employment income). Where this is a 'normal incident' of the profession, and of the practice itself, and the amounts are an insubstantial part of the turnover of the firm, and the partner is required to account for the fees to the firm to be pooled and divided according to the partnership agreement, the fees can be received by the partnership without tax under PAYE or employee's Class 1 NICs being deducted (see also **18.3**). This treatment is concessionary as far as tax is concerned, and the paying company may need the partnership's assistance (with regard to the pooling issue) when applying to HMRC for permission to disregard the normal PAYE rules.

Chapter 24 Tax Aspects of Incorporation and Disincorporation

Tax considerations on incorporation as a company

Introduction

24.1   The major problems on incorporation as a company arise because of the impact of UK taxation of income and gains arising up to and on the act of incorporation, and the different treatment of the business after incorporation. By contrast, incorporation of a partnership as an LLP, as discussed in **CHAPTER 4**, is more straightforward.

Cessation

24.2   Incorporation as a company for income tax purposes by a professional partnership will be a cessation (see **19.9**). The possibility arises for partners to utilise overlap relief against the final period's profits from the partnership. Care should be taken that there are sufficient profits to utilise such relief (see **19.9** and **19.11**). If a partnership's taxation position is some years in arrears, then estimation of the tax effect of incorporation may involve an extensive exercise to get the partnership's and partners' tax affairs up to date. This can give rise to a situation where the tax position is imprecise and contains probability factors due to the presence of, for example, disputes regarding the treatment of expenditure or the analysis of items which are not clear.

Treatment of work in progress and stock sales or transfers

24.3   *Sections 173 to 185* of the *Income Tax (Trading and Other Income) Act 2005* provide for the treatment of work in progress and stock sales or transfers on incorporation: ie whatever figure is taken as the transfer value (unless it is unreasonable and excessive) is taken as the closing figure for income tax purposes in the partnership and the opening figure for the professional company for corporation tax purposes. This subject is dealt with in a Technical Circular TR 5/95 issued by the ICAEW in February 1995.

Alternative treatment for work in progress

24.4   Occasionally, on incorporating a professional partnership, the partners may not wish to dispose of the work in progress to the new entity. This may be because one near completed contract, for example, is particularly identified with one or two old or retiring partners, for example, a building project in the context of a firm of architects. Instead, the work in progress may be run off or collected subsequent to incorporation, in which case the benefit of the sale accrues to the 'old' partners as a group. This transaction does not escape the tax net – such post-cessation receipts are dealt with as income under the regime for post-cessation receipts in *ss 241 to 257* of the *Income Tax (Trading and Other Income) Act 2005*.

Treatment of assets liable to capital allowances

24.5   The professional partnership which incorporates would normally have assets which would be liable to capital allowances. These may be transferred over from the partnership to the company without unfortunate tax consequences. Such assets probably have four different figures attached to them as follows:

(a)   The value shown in the books of the partnerships, ie usually cost less depreciation.

(b)   Their tax written-down value; this would normally be cost less annual allowances and be encapsulated in various 'pools' constituting the residue of expenditure.

(c)   Their market value; this would be determined by a sale to a third party (and would not be replacement cost or value).

(d)   Cost.

Assets which have been subject to capital allowances under the code for plant and machinery (ie computer equipment, cars and so on) can be transferred to the professional company at tax written-down value, if an election is made under *s 267* of the *Capital Allowances Act 2001*. The result of this election is that there is no additional income or loss in this respect for the partnership as it incorporates, and the professional corporation takes over these assets for tax purposes at their tax written-down value. A similar election can be applied for industrial buildings and enterprise zone investments. Failing an election, the legislation would impute into the transaction the asset's market value. Given the nature of a professional partnership's assets, this may be troublesome, eg what is the market value of motor vehicles or computers? As a result, in almost all cases an election is made.

Goodwill and property

24.6 Other assets (which are not liable to capital allowances) and the goodwill of the firm have the capability of a market value significantly in excess of their cost. Furthermore, goodwill may not be recorded in the partnership's accounts. The cost of land and buildings owned by a partnership may be shown in the books, and could even be depreciated, but the market value may be significantly above cost. If, on incorporation, the land, buildings and goodwill are transferred into the company which is going to carry on the professional business, a disposal has been made for capital gains tax purposes by the partnership. Capital gains tax will, therefore, be due on the increase in the value of the asset from its cost or 31 March 1982 value to its market value at the date of incorporation. In such a case, market value would have to be substituted, because the partnership and the company which carried on the business will be connected persons, and the transaction is therefore deemed not to be at arm's length.

Applicable reliefs

24.7 Fortunately, there are several reliefs which apply, or can be made to apply, on incorporation of a professional practice. These usually avoid or defer the problem of a capital gain and the resulting payment of tax. These are as follows:

(a) *Transfer for shares relief – s 162* of the *Taxation of Chargeable Gains Act 1992*. Under this section, a relief is given if a person (or persons) which is not a company transfers, to a company, a business as a going concern, together with the whole of the assets of the business, for the issue of shares in that company. The relief is that the gain on the disposal into the company is calculated but is deducted from the cost, for capital gains tax purposes, of the shares issued. Effectively, the individual receives the shares at the same value for capital gains tax purposes as the cost of the old assets that were transferred into the company. The relief can still be obtained if the cash element in the old partnership is not transferred into the company and, under the Inland Revenue's Extra-Statutory Concession D32, HMRC are prepared not to treat liabilities taken over by a company as consideration. Further, relief is not precluded if some or all liabilities of the business are not taken over by the company.

It should be noted that, for entrepreneur's relief purposes, a new period commences with the acquisition of the shares through incorporation.

Before 5 April 2002, *s 162* relief had to apply to all partners on an incorporation. The *Finance Act 2002* provides an election for an individual partner to elect for the provisions of *s 162* not to apply. This may be beneficial, where incorporation is followed by a sale of some or all of the shares received, in order to maximise the relief from tax arising from the entitlement to entrepreneurs' relief. It may also be appropriate where the rates of tax applicable to CGT are to be higher in the period following sale (so that base cost of the shares is increased).

For the purposes of chargeable gains, the assets taken over by the company are acquired at their market value at the date of transfer, and not their historic cost to the partnership or partners. This can provide a useful tax-free uplift.

(b) *Relief for gifts of business assets – s 165* of the *Taxation of Chargeable Gains Act 1992*. This relief is claimable if a business asset is given to a trading company within the United Kingdom. The gain is held over and the trading company acquires the assets at the tax cost to the individual who disposed of the assets to the company for capital gains tax purposes.

(c) *Enterprise investment scheme – EIS relief.* Individuals investing in an EIS qualifying company may defer gains to the extent of the investment. Hence, the gain on incorporation might be deferred into the subscription for shares in the company formed. However, EIS companies do not include accountancy, legal or financial services companies so that, in the context of a professional practice incorporating, only a few qualify.

(d) The acquisition of goodwill by the company will bring the corporate goodwill within the intangible asset regime. If the goodwill was created or acquired by the predecessor partnership on or after 1 April 2002, then it can potentially qualify as goodwill under the intangible asset regime for companies. This will enable the company to take a tax deduction either based on accounting impairments and reversals of impairments, or (subject to an election) an annual 4% writing down allowance (*Corporation Tax Act 2009, Part 8*). Under the provisions for transactions with related parties, the transfer of goodwill to the company would be treated as made at market value for the intangible asset regime. Where such a deemed market value applies, then a corporation tax deduction for what would be the accounting deduction, or the 4% elected writing down allowance, can be taken, notwithstanding the fact that the accounts of the company show no goodwill recognised for accounting purposes. However, if a claim for gift relief is made (see (b) above)), then the tax value for the company will be the market value less the reduction for gift relief (*Corporation Tax Act 2009, s 849*). If the partnership carried on the business prior to 1 April 2002, then any goodwill of that business is treated as created before the commencement of the intangible asset regime and, therefore, non-qualifying for corporate purposes (in which case, it remains an asset chargeable to capital gains tax in the company).

For more details on capital gains tax treatment, see CHAPTER 21.

Annuities

24.8 It is difficult to predict what relief will best suit the incorporation of each and every professional firm or partner. The problem is exacerbated if the partnership pays annuities, normally to former partners. The liability in the partnership deed to pay a future annuity to retiring partners can create significant tax problems. Although the annuity liability may not be recorded in the balance sheet of the partnership, the current value of the future liability can be estimated and, in HMRC's view, this amount is consideration on incorporation. The assumption by the company of this liability is deemed to be consideration, as far as the old partners are concerned, on incorporation. It does not, therefore, satisfy the conditions for relief under *s 162* of the *Taxation of Chargeable Gains Act 1992*. Accordingly, the result would be a chargeable gain which should be liable to capital gains tax in those circumstances.

Comparison of tax costs of partnership versus company

Running tax cost

24.9 In deciding whether or not to incorporate, the tax cost on incorporation is a material factor. Another material factor is the running tax cost of the business as a company as opposed to a partnership. A partner's profit share can be taxed at income tax rates up of to 50% plus National Insurance Contributions for the 2010/11 tax year. A marginal rate of 60% applies to taxable income between £100,000 and £112,950 as personal allowances are withdrawn. The big difference that applies in a corporate setting is the fact that employers' NICs have to be paid on salaries distributed by a company to its employees. The employers' rate of NICs for 2010/11 is 12.8%, which is a significant tax cost on incorporation. Turning to the impact of income tax versus corporation tax, the rates of corporation tax are as follows:

		Year to 31 March 2011
Standard rate of corporation tax	–	28%
Small profits rate	–	21%
Lower limit on small profits rate	–	£300,000
Upper limit on small profits rate	–	£1,500,000
Marginal rate of corporation tax	–	29.75%

Examples of the impact of the small company rate are as follows:

Year end		31 March 2011	31 March 2011
Chargeable profits	–	£500,000	£700,000
£300,000 @ small profits rate	–	£63,000	£63,000
Balance @ marginal rate	–	£59,500	£119,000
Total corporation tax	–	£122,500	£182,000
Effective rate of corporation tax	–	24.5%	26.0%

The lower and upper limits, shown in the table above, apply if there is only one company involved. If there is an associated company (which means both the original company and the associated company are under common control), then the lower and upper profit limits are halved for each company. If the company has three other associated companies, then the lower and upper limit for each company is divided by one quarter. In determining control for the purpose of identifying an associated company, the rights of 'partners' are attributed to a person only where there are relevant tax planning arrangements that secure a relevant tax advantage. At the time of writing, the Government has indicated this 'tax advantage condition' will be replaced with effect from 1 April 2011 with a condition requiring substantial commercial interdependence, whether or not association is through the attribution of rights of partners.

It can be seen that, if a professional practice incorporates and the profit (after distribution of salaries to the partners) is under £300,000, a lower rate of tax at 21% on retained earnings is a useful advantage over the top rate of income tax. However, if there is no need to retain profits within the business, the funds distributed will be subject to a further layer of taxation upon extraction.

Dividends

24.10 A company has the option to pay dividends to its shareholders as an alternative to paying remuneration. A dividend, unlike remuneration, is not tax deductible from the company's profits. For the individual recipient, there is a notional tax credit of ⅑th of the actual dividend paid. The dividend plus tax credit will then be liable to tax at 32.5% for a taxpayer subject to the 40% income tax rate, and 42.5% for a taxpayer subject to the 50% rate of income tax. For taxpayers subject to a rate of income tax of 40%, the calculation shows that, as a percentage of the cash dividend, the tax payable is at a maximum of 25%, as follows:

	40% taxpayer	*50% taxpayer*
Cash Dividends paid	£1,000	£1,000
Income tax credit: ⅑	£111	£111
Taxable Dividend plus tax credit	£1,111	£1,111
Income Tax at 32.5%/42.5%	£361	£472
Tax payable after tax credit	£250	£361
Tax payable as a percentage of cash dividend	25.0%	36.1%

The total percentage tax suffered on company profits distributed by way of dividends to an individual who is subject to the 50% income tax rate is 49.5% for a small profits rate company for 2010/11, and 54% for a company taxed at the standard rate of 28%.

The overall position

24.11 It is difficult to generalise on the overall tax costs of operating a professional practice as a partnership as opposed to an incorporated entity; there is no simple rule, and the financial dynamics of each business have to be considered. However, the cost of National Insurance Contributions on salaries at 12.8% means that incorporation, and then distributing all income as salaries/emoluments, increases the tax cost accordingly. If the incorporated business retains earnings, the tax charge can be reduced, but professional practices may have commercial drivers which result in little desire to retain significant profits within the business.

NIC rates (employee, employer and Class 4) will increase by 1% for 2011/12, but the employers' NICs threshold will be increased to compensate those subject to rates of income tax below 40%. The standard rate of corporation tax will reduce to 27% for the year commencing 1 April 2011 and will reduce by 1% per annum until it reaches the rate of 24% with effect from 1 April 2014. The small profits rate will reduce to 20% for the year commencing 1 April 2011.

Incorporating a company to act as a partner within an existing business, either as one company owned by all partners, or an individual company for each partner (thus creating a partnership with both individual and corporate partners), would need careful consideration, particularly in view of the sales of occupational income legislation (*Income Tax Act 2007, ss 773–789*).

Interest relief

Purpose of borrowings

24.12 Inside a partnership, interest paid on its borrowings would be deductible if the borrowings were wholly and exclusively for the purpose of the professional activity carried on. If the borrowings are not exclusively utilised for business purposes, a certain amount of disallowance might occur in the partnership. For a company, tax relief for interest on borrowings depends on whether the interest is paid in respect of a loan relationship and/or a money debt (there is no relief for interest on loans for an unallowable purpose, which would include a purpose which is not amongst the business or other commercial purposes of the company).

Funds borrowed by an individual

24.13 There is a difference between the criteria for interest relief on funds borrowed by an individual to lend to a partnership or a company or, alternatively, to invest in the capital of a partnership or shares in a company. The relief given in *s 398* of the *Income Tax Act 2007* is for interest on a loan to buy into, or lend money to, a partnership and is conditional on individuals concerned being partners and not withdrawing any capital from the partnership. The relief for interest on loans utilised to buy shares in a company, or lend money to a company, is more restrictive. The company concerned has to be a close company (*Corporation Tax Act 2010, ss 439, 441* and *442*), or an employee-controlled company (*Income Tax Act 2007, s 396*). Few incorporated professional firms meet these definitions. Furthermore, the individual either has to possess a 'material interest' (simply put, 5% of the capital) or he or she has to have worked for the greater part of his time in the actual management or conduct of the company or an associated company (see *Income Tax Act 2007, ss 393, 397*). This latter requirement can prove restrictive, as HMRC have tried to interpret the requirement as relating to the management of the company as a 'whole', and a specialist technical director may not qualify.

Close company status

24.14 'Close company status' means that the incorporated professional firm has to be under the control of its directors who are participators, or of five or fewer participators taken together. For a partnership that is planning to incorporate, this is easy to achieve if there are ten or fewer former partners, but for larger partnerships this may be more difficult.

Partial incorporation as a company

Disadvantages

24.15 Incorporating half or part of a professional practice could well be tax disadvantageous for two reasons. First, the capital gains exemption under *s 162* of the *Taxation of Chargeable Gains Act 1992* would not be available, as it refers to the whole assets of the partnership. Secondly, the division of a profession or business into two parts, of which one is incorporated, would almost certainly lead to the cessation of both parts of the business or profession for tax purposes (Statement of Practice 9/86).

Existing service companies

24.16   If a professional firm has a service company, this company may be used as the vehicle for incorporation using the provisions of *s 165* of the *Taxation of Chargeable Gains Act 1992*. The position of service companies and of associated trading companies is considered in more detail in CHAPTER 20.

Transfer of a business from a company to an LLP

24.17   There will be many factors to consider in determining whether it is more appropriate to operate through a company or an LLP. This section considers some of the tax implications. When a business is transferred from an unquoted trading company to an LLP (where the company is the sole partner in the LLP, apart from a very nominal interest held by another member), then, under Statement of Practice D12 (SP D12), there is no disposal for CGT, as the company is disposing of assets to itself.

New members could then be introduced to the LLP, with a consequent change in partnership sharing ratios. SP D12 sets out the conditions where no CGT charge would arise at that point, and in summary these are where:

- no consideration payment is made outside the accounts,

- there is no revaluation of assets within the LLP accounts (resulting in no adjustment of capital accounts), and

- new members are introduced pursuant to genuine commercial arrangements.

The new members would, in this instance, acquire a fractional interest in LLP assets at the CGT base cost of the asset.

An LLP structure is transparent for tax purposes, and the LLP's assets would be deemed to be owned directly by the members. This means that the capital gain arising on the sale of an asset would be charged proportionately on the members. There is, thus, a possibility of disposing of assets at a lower tax cost than if the disposal was to take place through the company alone, with proceeds extracted from the company via distribution or return of capital.

Paragraph 7 of SP D12 also states that, where LLP assets were transferred between members under bone fide commercial arrangements, with no payment made either through or outside the accounts, the members would not be treated as connected for capital gains tax purposes. However, HMRC clarified their interpretation of this practice on 21 January 2008 (Revenue & Customs Brief 03/08). A previous practice had been to treat any asset introduced by the new member as introduced at his CGT cost, with no gain or loss at that point. The Brief clarified that, where a new partner introduces an asset to the partnership, that partner disposes of their interest in the asset given up to the other partners (using the A/(A + B) formula, with market value and capital gain base cost). That Brief indicated that, where confirmation of the old treatment had been given, HMRC would be bound by previous guidance given on an old transaction. Where no specific advice had previously been given, however, it suggested that the new interpretation would have applied.

The interpretation of SP D12 has not changed where it is the vendor member who transfers assets to the incoming new member.

In the context of disincorporation where, initially, the company is the only member of the LLP (apart from a nominal interest), it is important to bear in mind the comments in SP D12 that arrangements for the introduction of new partners must be subject to genuine commercial arrangements to avoid any CGT charges.

One of the side effects of this transaction is that the business owners may have lower NIC costs on extraction of remuneration through an LLP structure than through a company. Distributions to members in an LLP would not attract employer's NICs, whereas bonus payments to employee directors in a company would. There may, however, be other factors that affect the total tax cost for the business and the owners, including:

- expenses deductible on a different basis;

- disposal of assets pregnant with gain in a company could attract corporation tax in the company (possibly reduced by indexation); there may be a further level of tax on the shareholder on extraction of profits or return of capital from the company;

- tax on profits reinvested in the business may be higher in an LLP structure than a company structure;

- there may be SDLT implications arising from the transfer of real estate interests from the company to the LLP and the introduction of new members, subject to any specific SDLT reliefs;

- goodwill subject to the intangible asset regime (that was created or acquired on or after 1 April 2002, and which is not subject to capital gains tax in the hands of the company and therefore not covered by SP D12) would be transferred to an LLP at market value, and would become an asset subject to CGT in the hands of individual members of an LLP to the extent that interests in that goodwill is transferred to individual members;

- certain corporation tax provisions, such as research and development allowances and land remediation relief, would not be available to individual members of an LLP.

For capital allowance purposes, it may be possible to use the provisions of *ss 266* and *267* of the *Capital Allowances Act 2001* to transfer assets qualifying for capital allowances at tax written down value from the company to the LLP. It would be necessary to ensure that the successor (LLP) and predecessor (company) were connected.

Chapter 25   Changes in the Professional Practice

Planning for succession

25.1   In any professional practice, planning for succession should be an issue for management and certainly in the forefront of the minds of the senior management of the firm. Without young blood willing and able to take on the more senior positions of responsibility in the firm, there can be no continuing business. Without a continuing business, it is unlikely that retiring partners will receive full or satisfactory return of capital contributions, annuities or payment for goodwill (depending on the nature of arrangements for retiring partners). Whilst there may still be satisfactory exit routes available with mergers or sale of the practice, such methods rarely produce full value in the case of a forced sale. Retired partners will also often have a vested interest in the firm continuing successfully, so that it can maintain continuing professional indemnity cover.

A first step in planning for succession is an examination of the birth dates of all partners, together with planned retirement dates. This will show any bunching of retirements at particular times.

Plans for introducing new partners to the firm should bear in mind the likely retirement dates. Skeleton plans for transfers of responsibilities should be in place, not only to prepare for retirements or wind-downs in the run-up to retirement, but also to cope with emergencies such as death, disablement or other early departures of partners.

Finally, younger partners must eventually have the financial resources to take over the responsibilities for providing capital and enabling retiring partners to be bought out. This is a factor to be considered in profit-sharing arrangements.

Admitting new partners

25.2   Each firm will have a procedure, formal or informal, for agreeing which individuals should be admitted as new partners to a firm. There may be separate procedures for admission as full partners and admission as salaried partners. This is likely to be a matter on which the whole partnership votes or otherwise has its say, although in large firms it is sometimes a matter reserved for management. The candidates will generally be senior employees but, increasingly, candidates are existing partners in other professional firms who, for whatever reason, wish to leave their existing practices and generally have been introduced to the firm by intermediaries.

A new partner needs to absorb a significant amount of information prior to and at the time of admission. This will include details of the financial position of the firm, profit-sharing arrangements, capital provisions by the new partner, his tax position and additional responsibilities. He or she would also be well advised to enquire generally into the nature of these arrangements, seeking information from existing partners in the firm and, possibly, seeking permission to obtain information from the firm's accountants.

Expulsion of partners

25.3 Power to expel a partner is a reserve power that most firms generally hope will never be needed. It is, however, a very powerful tool for management.

There will be no power to expel a partner without an express power in the firm's constitution. It is sometimes said that professional practices find it very difficult to progress without the existence of this power. It is normally only exercisable with the consent of a significant proportion of the firm's voting rights, generally at least 75%. Larger firms have recently either moved this to a decision of the board or reduced the size of the majority required to remove a partner.

Providing the management has the full backing of most of the firm, the very existence of this power will help give it the necessary clout to exercise delicate negotiations with any partner, both on the question of departure and, more generally, on profit-sharing arrangements or other major issues.

In practice, it is rare for partners to be expelled, and withdrawals or resignation (albeit negotiated at the instigation of the management) are more normal.

Retirements

25.4 A wise professional practice will write a retiring age into its partnership deed. Such ages are normally chosen at between 60 and 65. Firms should be wary of age discrimination legislation in considering these issues (see also CHAPTER 5). Modern professional partnerships have tended to do away with provisions for partners' annuities or consultancies on retirement. Instead, they generally encourage or even require partners to make provision for their retirement during their time as a partner. Many partnerships have restrictive covenants in their partnership agreements to discourage partners leaving to join other firms and minimise the damage when they do leave. Restrictive covenants are considered further in CHAPTER 5. The use of notice periods during which the retiring partner is excluded from the office, clients and employees, often called 'gardening leave clauses', has also proliferated, as firms seek to prevent partners simply walking out to join their competitors. The combination of a notice period and restrictive covenants is a disincentive to poachers, as it can reduce the value of the incoming partner. Providing that the restrictive covenant and notice period are reasonable, they will generally be enforceable.

Demergers

25.5 A demerger is used to describe the situation when several partners in a firm, generally representing a branch or department, split away from the main firm to carry on their profession as a separate, smaller business. Such a circumstance may arise as a result of dissatisfaction over profit shares, how the firm is run, a desire for autonomy, or fundamental differences as to the firm's strategy or priorities.

Mergers and team moves

25.6 Mergers and team moves are common in professional practices. Whilst, within the corporate world, many mergers would be classified as acquisitions, the professional practices environment means that such transactions will nearly always be presented to clients (particularly of the smaller firm) as a merger. However, with the implementation of the *Legal Services Act 2007*, the manner in which law firms combine with other law firms or other professions is likely to be extended.

A merger is the coming together of two, or occasionally more, professional practices. In many cases, mergers are more akin to takeovers. True mergers occur where the two firms are of similar sizes. Contested takeovers of the kind that occur with quoted companies are unheard of, because the merger is unlikely to be a success unless the majority of partners in both firms wish it to take place. However, in some mergers, it is a precondition of the deal that some partners are not included. Some firm's constitutional agreements now have provisions designed to prevent the movement of whole teams to rival firms, as this is perceived to be more damaging than the loss of a single partner.

A firm may decide to take a merger partner, or acquire a smaller practice, as a result of its strategic plan (see CHAPTER 10). Alternatively, it may be approached and consider the merger to be a business opportunity. Whatever the reasons leading up to the merger proposal, a great deal of careful investigation, planning and implementation will be needed to ensure it is a success.

Why merge or acquire a team?

25.7   There are many reasons why a professional practice may wish to seek a merger or team acquisition, which may include a wish to:

(a)   expand or diversify client base;

(b)   increase income or profit growth;

(c)   increase depth of skills;

(d)   increase range of services; or

(e)   expand/diversify geographically.

Care should be taken to consider other factors that may be seen by the merger partner as a weakness. Some mergers fail as they are undertaken in order to resolve problems that should be addressed internally before considering a merger opportunity. Typical issues that can have a negative impact on the merger process are:

(i) failure to keep up with growth of clients;

(ii) ageing senior partner or partners failing to grasp the succession problem;

(iii) poor financial performance;

(iv) unutilised office space, tied into a long leasehold;

(v) culture clash between the firms;

(vi) client conflicts of interest;

(vii) inadequate due diligence, leading to unpleasant surprises about the other firm or its clients;

(viii) professional indemnity claims issues and the adequacy of insurance; and

(ix) establishing a commonality between the two sets of partners; will the merger be harmonious, or will some partners continue to create difficulties for the new firm?

If problems such as the above exist, it is better that they are considered and dealt with before the merger process is entered into.

Merger issues

Third party advice

25.8   Lack of external advice is often cited as a reason for difficulties arising, either during or after a merger. Firms should not be afraid of seeking advice from other members of their own profession more experienced in mergers, subject to obtaining appropriate confidentiality agreements. External advice may be required on a number of separate and distinct areas, and the use of an external independent adviser can, at times, assist in the negotiation process. External advice can also provide an objective assessment of the strategy driving the proposed merger, the likely compatibility of the two firms, and the likely market impact of the merger. The external adviser could be responsible for chairing meetings between the two parties and ensuring a proper exchange of information. It is important that information exchanged should be in a similar format, ensuring accurate comparisons can be made. For example, there is no statutory format for a partnership's accounts, and therefore each party may have accounting policies that would produce considerably different results from the same details. The external adviser should also be required to consider areas of dispute, with a view to providing a compromise solution acceptable to both parties.

As an alternative, or in addition, to having an external adviser appointed jointly by both parties, a firm may decide to appoint their own adviser to undertake appropriate due diligence on the merger target and advise them on the implications of the proposed combination.

Human resources

25.9 Interestingly, the most common underlying reasons for post-merger failure revolve around people issues. Some of the areas that should be considered on or prior to the merger are as follows:

(a) Remuneration and benefits. Should the best practices, and probably the most expensive, be adopted by the new firm?

(b) Appraisal and grading systems.

(c) Contracts of employment.

(d) Manpower planning. Will some staff be surplus to requirements, and how will this be dealt with?

(e) Management structure and style.

(f) New firm culture. Will this be dominated by one party and, if so, what will be the effect on the staff of the other party?

(g) Managing internal communications and post-transaction expectations.

Legal issues

25.10 As with all important transactions, it is important to ensure that what has been agreed is properly documented. Whilst minor issues may be documented by way of agreed minutes, more major issues should be agreed by way of either amendments to or a new constitution for the firm. Equally, there are various other legal issues that will need to be fully considered, such as the *Transfer of Undertakings* (*Protection of Employment*) *Regulations* and the professional indemnity insurance needs for the new firm and any necessary insurance for the original firms.

External and internal communications

25.11　The strategic reasons behind any merger will always include an aspect concerned with development of the external perception of the firm. It is, therefore, advisable to ensure that the merger is perceived in the marketplace as a significant move forward for the new firm.

Equally, communications with clients and staff should be considered carefully and worded to ensure a positive and constructive message is received.

Managing the communication process, particularly in the confidential negotiation phase, is crucial, and firms will need to have a plan in place to deal with the risk of news of the merger breaking, either internally or externally.

Information technology

25.12　Most businesses are reliant upon information technology systems to run their finances, billing system, document and case management, word processing and other key functions. It will, therefore, be necessary to consider the position of the new firm and, in particular, the following issues:

(a)　Are both parties using compatible equipment?

(b)　Should one of the existing systems be adopted? If so, when and how should this be implemented?

(c)　Is it appropriate to review the new firm's information technology structure, with a view to adopting a more advanced and integrated system?

Property

25.13　Physically relocating people following a merger can be key to ensuring successful integration, but this has obvious implications for space and property. Failure to deal with property matters up front in negotiations can often result in the failure of the merger discussions. It is important that these are discussed at the start, with consideration being given to areas where difficulties may arise. It may be worth seeking external advice to understand the size of any problem and what options may be available to resolve these issues. Possible options may include:

(a)   renegotiation of the lease term;

(b)   renegotiation of the rent payable; and

(c)   sub-letting of vacated space.

Pensions

25.14   If either firm has any staff final salary pension schemes (whether open or closed) or unfounded partner pension liabilities, these will need to be considered very carefully. These liabilities may be very substantial and will need to be properly identified and valued using realistic valuation and life expectancy assumptions.

Implementation

25.15   Assuming negotiations reach a successful conclusion and an agreement is signed, it is important to recognise that the process does not come to an end there. Indeed, the view is often expressed that completion of the merger only represents a small proportion of the effort required to make the merger successful. Arguably, the more crucial work needs to be carried out continually over the few years following the merger to maximise the benefit. Both parties should continue to work together to establish proper integration and the new culture for the success of the new firm.

Chapter 26 Becoming a Partner

General and financial considerations

Introduction

26.1 Becoming a partner, or member, of a partnership or limited liability partnership is a career ambition for the majority of professionally qualified individuals who work within such businesses. Partnership signals to their contemporaries that they have made the grade. It indicates to their clients that they have the authority and experience to make major decisions on the client's behalf. It confirms that the individual's colleagues consider him or her sufficiently able and experienced to join them within the partnership. Partnership is a privilege that is not easily achieved and which cannot be taken lightly.

There are various categories of partner. This chapter is particularly concerned with those who are invited to become equity or full partners, and is written from a prospective partner's perspective. However, a firm should address similar considerations when deciding who to admit to the partnership and what information it will need to make available.

Routes to equity partnership

26.2 There are generally two main routes to equity partnership:

(a) Perhaps the most common is to progress from salaried partner to equity partner within the same firm. While salaried partners are able to make the same commitments on the firm's behalf as equity partners, they are either employees in the partnership or partners whose profits consist principally of a fixed or prior share and, therefore, generally make no contribution, or at least no substantial contribution, to the firm's capital. Nor do they have any significant share in the partnership's profits. After a period as a salaried partner, an individual may be invited to become an equity partner.

(b) The second route is to be invited to join a partnership as an equity partner without going through the 'probation period' as a salaried partner. This may occur, for example, when a senior individual leaves one partnership and is invited to join another at a similar level. It may also occur when an individual joins a partnership from a senior non-partnership position, such as industry or local government.

What does equity partnership involve?

26.3 Becoming an equity partner requires a full understanding of the running of the partnership, its commitments and strategy. Although a new partner is often in a poor negotiating position and is not generally able to dictate terms, partnership is a serious commitment and a degree of due diligence is required. A responsible firm should respect the individual for asking reasonable questions. The following issues should be considered:

(a) *The existing partners.* Who are they? Do you respect them? Are you happy to join them in a relationship which will, for a partnership but not an LLP, involve you having joint and several liability for commitments they have entered into and/or will enter into? Most importantly, do you trust them? Becoming an equity partner involves a firm commitment from you, as well as from the present partners.

(b) *The financial strength of the business.* Are you given access to financial information? How profitable is the partnership? Has it got a reasonable capital base? Has it got any unreasonable borrowings or long-term commitments? Are any bank overdrafts, loan facilities or other sources of finance in place for the foreseeable future? What are the terms on which partnership premises are occupied, and when will they change? What is the position on retired partners' annuities? Are you confident that the partnership's finances are and will continue to be well managed?

(c) *Professional indemnity insurance.* Is the present level of cover adequate? You should be able to review details of the cover, claims record and any outstanding claims. Is there a material level of uninsured potential liability? What risk protection procedures exist?

(d) *Capital requirements for individual equity partners.* How and when will you be required to contribute capital to the business? Many partnerships have arrangements in place that enable equity partners to borrow money and obtain tax relief on the interest, or pay their capital in instalments out of profits.

(e) *Profit sharing arrangements.* What arrangements are in place at present? Is there a lockstep system? How might this change in the future? Is it fair? Will it reward you adequately for your contribution? What is the policy on drawings on account of such profits? Will this meet your immediate requirements for income?

(f) *Monthly income.* What effect will the change in status have on your monthly income? How are monthly drawings calculated? What events may reduce monthly drawings? When and what additional drawings will be allowed?

(g) *Provision for taxation.* How is taxation provided for within the partnership? Who will be responsible for payment of tax liabilities on partnership income? If a full reserve is made for taxation on all profits earned, over what timescale will you be required to build up this reserve?

(h) *Benefits and expenses.* How will pension contributions, private health insurance, permanent health insurance, critical illness insurance and life insurance be dealt with? Will you have a car paid for by the firm? A prospective partner is likely to require advice on his accrued rights under existing pension schemes as well as the position for the future.

(i) *The partnership agreement and other documentation.* Will you be able to review this fully before agreeing to become a partner? You should consider taking legal advice before signing the agreement.

(j) *Other partners' personal balance sheets.* Before joining the partnership, will you have access to any information on the financial position of existing partners? A new partner may wish to know whether the existing partners have been entering into asset protection arrangements that would reduce the partnership's ability to support future claims. This is a most delicate area and many firms do not provide the information to prospective partners. This should be less of a concern in the context of an LLP, as an individual's liability should be limited.

(k) *Partnership decisions.* How are decisions made that affect the way the partnership is run? Is there a management committee or board? If so, who sits on it and for how long? Is there provision for rotation of positions on the committee? Who has the final say in setting the direction of the partnership? How would a new equity partner make his or her views clear? How confident are you in the effectiveness of the partnership management?

(l) *Strategy documents.* Does the partnership have a strategy document? Are you able to review this before signing the partnership agreement? It is important that a new partner understands what his colleagues are planning to do with the business and the way it will develop in the future.

(m) *Business winning and retaining.* What fee target will you be set? What will happen if the target is not met? If your initial role is to inherit and retain clients won by an existing partner who is approaching retirement, will you be penalised for not winning new business? If you are expected to develop clients in a new sector in which the firm has no existing reputation, has this been taken into account? How will you be supported in this activity?

(n) *Management.* What percentage of your time is likely to be spent on management? Are these and other non-chargeable activities recognised as valuable? Will you also be asked to take on specific non-chargeable responsibilities? If so, how are these activities recognised in the reward system?

(o) *Retirement.* What are the terms on which you will be able to retire from the partnership in due course? What indemnities will be available for liabilities arising both before and after your retirement? Will there be continuing burdens such as restrictive covenants?

(p) *Personal finances.* Should you consider rearranging your personal and family finances in the context of the proposed partnership?

(q) *Advice.* Will you be able to have access to the firm's accountants or legal advisers to discuss any of the above? This is a route which professional firms are increasingly prepared to consider, to ensure that a prospective partner fully understands the firm's finances and his rights and obligations. You may like to consider obtaining independent advice rather than dealing with the firm's professional advisers.

Limited liability partnerships

26.4 If being invited to become a member in an LLP then all the above considerations remain in point. However, in this instance the level of exposure will be capped, subject to any 'duty of care' liability, to your investment in the firm. You should consider how the LLP has been set up and its engagement terms with clients, suppliers and landlords to understand any potential liability that may go beyond the LLP. Equally, you should be aware of any personal guarantees which partners have given in connection with the business. In view of the more restricted liability exposure, it may be preferable to join an LLP rather than an unlimited liability partnership.

Conclusion

26.5 Becoming an equity partner or member is a serious business decision. You should satisfy yourself about as many of the above questions as possible before accepting partnership or membership. This is a decision for which only you can take final responsibility. It is also a decision in which you must allow trust and instinct to play a major part. In some firms, it may be wiser to remain a salaried partner or even a well-paid employee than to take on the responsibility of equity partnership if you are not comfortable with the replies to some of the above questions.

Chapter 27   Retirement Planning

Introduction

27.1   6 April 2006 ('A-Day' as it has been designated) saw the most radical shake-up of pensions in the UK since 1970. Until A-Day, partners and the self-employed (both with earnings not taxable under Schedule E) and those in non-pensionable employment could only participate in personal pensions, which replaced 's 226' retirement annuities on 1 July 1988. Retirement annuity policies that were then in force could still receive further contributions, which were generally limited to a lower maximum percentage of net relevant earnings, but with no restriction on the level of earnings that could be taken into account. Most partners with such policies in force were, therefore, well-advised to maintain them.

Personal pensions were introduced under *Finance (No 2) Act 1987* with more generous maximum contribution percentages (eg 40% for someone aged 61 on 6 April 1987), but earnings were limited or 'capped' initially at £60,000 for these purposes. The 'earnings cap', as it became known, had been increased to £105,600 by April 2005, but was removed altogether from A-Day, with an entirely new tax regime replacing some eight existing regimes, covering both occupational pensions and personal pension arrangements.

The introduction of a single simplified tax regime swept away all of the previous contribution limits and benefit limits (applicable to occupational pension schemes) at a stroke. The niceties of 'carry-back' and 'carry-forward' provisions for tax relief associated with personal pensions and retirement annuities disappeared. We have, therefore, excluded reference to previous regimes in this chapter, other than to the extent they impact upon transitional protection, of which more later.

Post A-Day, the tax treatment of pension contributions is the same for all pension arrangements, although minor differences still exist over how this is claimed. Under registered pension schemes, basic rate relief (currently 20%) is deducted at source, and excess relief available to higher rate taxpayers is separately reclaimed, which may result in an adjustment of personal tax code.

Since A-Day, we have seen a number of changes to the pension regime that mean that, in many cases, pensions legislation could hardly be described as simple.

Pension regime

Scheme membership rules

27.2 To be eligible to receive tax relief on a pension contribution to a registered scheme before age 75, an individual must be 'a relevant UK individual' for the tax year in question. To meet this eligibility condition, there are the following requirements:

(a) the individual has relevant UK earnings chargeable to income tax in that tax year; 'relevant UK earnings' for this purpose are defined as employment income or income from a trade, profession or vocation or patent income; and

(b) the individual has to be resident in the UK at some time during that tax year;

or

the individual was resident in the UK at some time in the five tax years immediately before that year when the contribution was made; in these circumstances, contributions are restricted to a maximum of £3,600 per tax year or the level of taxable relevant earnings in the year of payment if higher, and the effective rate of relief is restricted to basic rate tax by deduction and, in addition, the individual must have been a UK resident at the time they joined the scheme;

or

the individual or their spouse has earnings in the tax year from an overseas Crown employment that is subject to UK tax.

Whilst individuals who do not meet such requirements can pay unlimited personal pension contributions to a registered scheme, they will not get any UK tax relief.

The annual allowance

27.3 The term 'contribution limits' was redefined under the 2006 Regulations as 'the annual allowance'. This effectively limits the amount of tax relief on contributions that can be paid from all sources into registered pension arrangements during a particular tax year.

The allowance was set at a much higher level than the previous allowances for personal pension and retirement annuity arrangements unless, in the case of the retirement annuity regime, the individual had very substantial earnings indeed.

The annual allowance limits were fixed through to the tax year 2010/11.

Contributions paid into a registered pension scheme in the year when the individual vests his benefits under that scheme are not subject to the annual allowance test.

In the April 2009 Budget, the Government announced its intention to restrict higher rate tax relief from 6 April 2011 for those individuals deemed to be 'higher earners' – individuals with income from all sources of £150,000. Higher rate relief will be tapered away for those with income over £150,000 until only basic rate relief applies to total income above £180,000.

At the same time, the Chancellor announced anti-forestalling provisions to ensure individuals did not bring forward their pension contributions in advance of April 2011 so that they would continue to benefit from higher rate tax relief on pension contributions.

Special annual allowance

27.4   A special annual allowance applies to individuals who:

- receive income from all sources in excess of £150,000 in the tax years 2007/08, 2008/09, 2009/10 and 2010/11; and

- increase their 'regular' contributions from 22 April 2009, or make contributions greater than £20,000 gross per annum from 22 April 2009.

The special annual allowance is £20,000, or may be up to £30,000, dependent on the individual's history of infrequent contributions.

Exceptions

27.5   High earners who were already making regular contributions in excess of £20,000 on 22 April 2009, that is quarterly or more frequently and either personally or via an employer, could continue to make these contributions at the same level and benefit from higher rate tax relief. Higher earners who were making regular contributions below £20,000 are free to increase these to this level without any tax penalties.

For those who were making one-off (infrequent) contributions in excess of £20,000 per annum, such as the self-employed where contributions were based on the level of annual profits, the special annual allowance is increased to up to £30,000.

The level at which contributions can be made and continue to benefit from higher rate tax relief is calculated by determining the average infrequent contributions from tax years 2006/07 to 2008/09. This average is then used as the amount that can be contributed in 2009/10 and 2010/11 while continuing to benefit from higher rate relief.

If an individual has both frequent and infrequent contributions, once the average level of contributions has been determined the frequent contributions are deducted to ascertain if there is any scope for further contributions.

If an individual is already making frequent contributions in excess of £20,000, these will be protected from any tax charges, but no other contributions can be made while benefiting from higher rate tax relief.

Change to 'high earner' definition on 9 December 2009

27.6 A further change was made to the 'high earner' definition in December 2009 that effectively reduced the definition of high earner to anyone with income in excess of £130,000 after allowing for pension contributions of up to £20,000. In one tax year, there was a situation where there could be three different regimes applying in respect of contributions paid between 6 April 2009 and 22 April 2009, contributions paid between 22 April and 9 December 2009, and for contributions paid between 9 December 2009 and 5 April 2010. Pension simplification has been consigned to the dustbin!

Tax penalties

27.7 If an individual who qualifies as a high earner exceeds the special annual allowance, a special annual allowance tax charge will apply. For 2009/10, this was 20%, rising to 30% in 2010/11. The effect of this charge is to reduce the relief the contribution receives to basic rate only.

The individual is personally liable for the charge that is collected via their self-assessment tax return. The effect of this is that any employer or other third party contribution that results in a special annual allowance tax charge has to be met by the individual.

The statutory lifetime allowance

27.8 The introduction of the lifetime allowance was designed to set an upper limit on the maximum pension fund that an individual can accrue during their working life. In design, it has been established to replace the earnings cap that previously applied to restrict the amount of contributions that could be paid by setting a maximum income level on which such contributions could be based. As we have seen at **27.3** above, there are generous annual contribution allowances, but with the caveat that, once the lifetime allowance is exceeded, there are potentially penal tax charges to pay. Again, the relevant allowance figures are set by the Treasury, and it has now been frozen at £1.8 million up until tax year 2015/16, but see **27.46** below in relation to recent measures to reduce the lifetime allowance.

Valuing pension rights against the statutory lifetime allowance

27.9   Most partners in professional firms will not have rights from occupational pension schemes. If they do, then these are quite complex to value in relation to the statutory lifetime allowance.

Defined benefits schemes

27.10   The pension payable from a defined benefit scheme is now known as a scheme pension and, for statutory lifetime allowance purposes, it is valued using a 20:1 factor. For example, if an individual has an entitlement to a preserved pension of £10,000 per annum, the capitalised value of this pension is taken as £200,000. This calculation will be applied purely on the first benefit crystallisation event post A-Day to establish the percentage of the lifetime allowance that has been utilised or for the purposes of electing for protection (see **27.37** below). If there is a pension already in payment that came into payment before 6 April 2006, then the factor applied is 25:1, as it is assumed that some elements of the benefits have been taken as tax-free cash.

Money purchase occupational schemes

27.11   This is relatively simple as, assuming that no benefits have been drawn, it is the value of the pension fund itself that counts towards the statutory lifetime allowance. If there is a pension in payment from, say, the purchase of an annuity with the proceeds of the money purchase scheme, then again a 25:1 factor to the annual pension annuity figure would be applied.

Unsecured income

27.12   Where an individual already has in payment an unsecured income scheme (formerly known as income drawdown) and this was in place before A-Day, then the factor of 25 times is applied to the maximum pension that an individual could take from the plan, regardless of the actual level of the income they are drawing. For unsecured schemes established after A-Day, the value of the pension fund at the time utilises part of the statutory lifetime allowance. For example, if an individual moved £500,000 into unsecured income in the tax year 2006/07, they have effectively utilised one third of the statutory lifetime allowance (which was £1.5 million in 2006/07). When they come to vest their other pension arrangements in, say, the tax year 2010/11, as the statutory lifetime allowance has increased to £1.8 million because a third of the allowance was used at the outset, the individual has £1.2 million of the allowance remaining in relation to the arrangements they are vesting at the time. See generally **27.25** below.

The lifetime allowance charge

27.13   Taking benefits from pension policies is now known as a benefit crystallisation event. The valuation of pension rights, as mentioned earlier, applies when a benefit crystallisation event occurs.

Having calculated the value of the individual's pension fund at the time of the benefit crystallisation, if it is in excess of the statutory lifetime allowance the lifetime allowance charge is applied to the excess, ie the chargeable amount.

The purpose of the charge is to recover tax relief that the individual enjoyed when making the pension contributions.

The chargeable amount is taxed at a rate of:

(a)   55% if it is drawn as a lump sum; or

(b)   25% if it is utilised to provide annual income.

The effective rate is 55%, whichever way benefits are taken, as the example below illustrates, based upon a chargeable amount of £100,000.

If taken as cash, £100,000 at 55% = £55,000.

If taken as pension income, £100,000 at 25% = £25,000.

Thus, assuming the individual is a higher rate taxpayer, the income fund produced by the fund will be taxed at 40%.

£75,000 at 40% = £30,000

Total tax = £55,000

This tax liability cannot be reduced in any way, as it is not income for the purposes of income tax and so cannot be offset by allowances, reliefs or losses.

Whilst the liability for the tax is joint and several between the scheme administrator of the registered scheme and the member, in practice it is best paid by reducing benefits; otherwise, additional tax liabilities could arise.

The annual allowance charge

27.14 If the annual allowance charge is exceeded in any tax year, the individual would be subject to an annual allowance charge on the excess at a rate of 40%. Therefore, it would be unwise for individuals to make contributions in excess of the annual allowance. As contributions cannot be related back to earlier tax years, most individuals will have to make an assessment of the likely income on which they will be subject to tax, rather than working on the basis of known figures, as in the past.

There will, therefore, be the need to ensure that any contributions they pay do not exceed the annual allowance or, if their earnings are below this figure, 100% of their annual earnings. Where the funds come from to pay the contributions is not too relevant, unless they are being paid from a tax-free cash sum taken out of an existing pension arrangement, in which case complex tax-free cash recycling rules apply to prevent this.

In the worst-case scenario, an individual could be subject to both a lifetime allowance charge and an annual allowance charge, that would effectively give rise to a tax rate of up to 90%, which must be avoided.

Careful planning is therefore necessary and, whilst this is reasonably straightforward as far as contributions are concerned, it may prove more difficult to plan for the lifetime allowance charge, as it is likely to be dependent upon factors such as the movement in investment values, which are, of course, unpredictable.

Taking benefits

27.15 For those with existing personal pensions in retirement annuity policies, the 2006 regime confirms that they will be entitled to take 25% of the accumulated funds as tax-free cash when they come to draw benefits. Similarly, in most cases those paying into registered pension schemes post A-Day will be able to draw 25% of the accumulated fund as cash.

Pension age

27.16 The *Finance Act 2004* introduced a new normal minimum pension age. This was set at 50 for those retiring between 6 April 2006 to 5 April 2010, and 55 thereafter, so 55 is now the minimum age at which benefits can be drawn.

The maximum retirement age for partners in professional firms is effectively 75, as tax-free cash must be paid out before the individual's 75th birthday. If it is paid on or after that date, it would be treated as an unauthorised payment and be subject to tax penalties.

We will review later in this chapter the retirement options, including the new alternatively secured pension which would be available at age 75.

Tax treatment

Contributions

27.17 With few exceptions, all pension schemes will have to operate a system of relief at source for personally paid contributions.

In essence, this means that the individual will be allowed to deduct tax at the basic rate on their contribution – as they did under the old regime for personal pension payments. For example, if an individual is contributing a gross sum of £10,000, they would deduct tax at the current basic rate of 20% that applies for the 2010/11 tax year from this payment, ie £2,000, and they would then pay a net sum of £8,000 to the scheme administrator. The scheme administrator would then recover the basic rate tax relief from HMRC.

The individual would then claim the difference between the basic rate and higher rate tax relief if he/she is paying tax at the marginal rates of 40% or 50% via their self-assessment tax return.

One exception that does apply to professional partnerships is that contributions to retirement annuities can continue to be paid gross, and in some cases will have to be, as the legacy computer systems operated by some pension providers will not permit them to collect contributions net of basic rate tax.

It should be remembered that any relevant UK individual can contribute up to £3,600 gross, regardless of the level of their earnings, and many individuals have taken advantage of this to finance pension arrangements for non-working spouses and children/grandchildren.

Investment funds

27.18 There has been little change to the taxation of registered pension scheme investment funds, as there is no liability to income tax in respect of income derived from investments or deposits, but do remember that the dividend tax credit on UK dividends can no longer be reclaimed since the relevant rules were changed in the 1997 Budget. There is no capital gains tax on gains but, clearly, there is no allowance for losses either. Trading income is taxable.

In the preamble to the 2006 changes in the pension regulations, it was proposed that all classes of investment would be permitted, which is covered at **27.33** below. However, at the last moment, the Chancellor stated that those who invested directly or indirectly in certain 'prohibited assets' within their pension fund would be subject to swingeing taxes which, to all intents and purposes, makes them a no-go area for investment within pension funds.

Benefits

27.19 All income payments are effectively treated as pensions and they are subject to income tax as earned income, regardless of what form of pension arrangement they are paid from.

Unauthorised payments

27.20 The A-Day regulations defined various authorised payments and there are tax sanctions if payments from a registered scheme fall outside this list, most of which was defined in the *Finance Act 2004*, namely:

(a) Pensions or pensions payable on death.

(b) Lump sums and lump sum death benefits.

(c) Pension transfers.

(d) Certain expenses involved in scheme administration.

(e) Payments resulting from divorce proceedings.

(f) Payments prescribed in HMRC regulations.

Where an unauthorised payment is made an income tax charge is levied at 40% on the recipient.

If the total of unauthorised payments made from a scheme in a year exceeds 25% of the fund value there is a further unauthorised payments surcharge of 15% of the unauthorised payment value, so that the total charge is 55%.

Unauthorised payments are also subject to scheme sanction charges payable by the scheme administrator. These would be offset by up to 25% of the unauthorised payment, but it does mean that the tax charge on all unauthorised payments is at least 55%.

Finally, where a scheme is deregistered by HMRC, as it may be if more than 25% of its fund is invested in a prohibited asset, a 40% tax charge will be levied on the total fund value immediately prior to de-registration.

Death benefits before taking benefits

27.21 Most registered schemes (other than defined benefit arrangements) will provide for a full return of the fund in the event of death before drawing benefits. Some older retirement annuity policies do not provide for a full return of the fund in this event, so it is worthwhile checking the position where it is unclear.

If no alternative arrangements are made, on death before drawing benefits the full value of the fund is payable to the individual's estate. Alternatively, the individual can nominate their proposed beneficiaries to the scheme trustee, who retains discretion over the disposal of the proceeds or, where the scheme rules permit it, creates an individual trust. The death benefit can then be paid into the trust and paid out to beneficiaries by the trustees appointed by the scheme member, thus avoiding inheritance tax liabilities.

The retirement options

27.22 Under the new regime, there are four methods of retirement income provision as follows:

(a) *Scheme pensions* – in practice, in most cases these are unlikely to apply for pension arrangements taken out by partners of professional practices as they are really only relevant for pensions being paid out under defined benefit occupational schemes, but see **27.29** below in connection with Family SIPPs.

(b) *Lifetime annuities* – these can only be provided by an insurance company.

(c) *Unsecured pensions* – which include pension fund withdrawals, ie income drawdown.

(d) *Alternatively secured pensions* – this is a special form of pension fund withdrawal that is only available from age 75.

Under the new regime, there is no requirement to take pension benefits before age 75 other than the requirement to take the tax-free cash sum before age 75 as mentioned earlier.

We look below at the various options.

Lifetime annuities

27.23 Other than the scheme pension, the lifetime annuity must be paid by an insurance company, and the individual can select the company effectively by utilising what is known as an 'open market option'. The annuity must meet certain conditions, as follows.

The minimum payment frequency period must be annually. It can be guaranteed for a period of up to 10 years from the date when the annuity first comes into payment.

If it is not a fixed annuity figure, it can vary in line with the various indices, namely:

(i)   the Retail Prices Index;

(ii) the market value of any freely marketable assets;

(iii) the index which reflects the value of freely marketable assets;

(iv) an insurance company's with-profits fund performance; or

(v)   any combination of (i) to (iv).

In establishing an annuity that relies upon one of the investment-linked methods above, when determining the initial annuity level an individual can make an assumption about future investment returns of between 0% and 5%. This assumption is similar to the return on gilts that an actuary has to assume for a conventional gilt-backed annuity. Clearly, if the assumptions used are over-optimistic, this will reduce future income; if they are exceeded, there is the prospect of income rising.

When purchasing a lifetime annuity, an individual could purchase an annuity which should be reviewable at least every five years, linked again to the performance of any of (i) to (iv) above. This annuity would be subject to a maximum income parameter of 110% of a single life level annuity and a minimum of half of this figure. The lifetime annuity could be transferred whilst in payment to another insurance company's registered pension scheme.

The annuity could include annuity or 'value protection' which, in essence, is designed to protect the capital value of the annuity. In addition, annuity rates could be improved if the individual has any health problems or, for example, is a smoker, as this could reduce their life expectancy. There are known as 'impaired annuities'.

Investment-linked annuities

27.24   Annuities in (ii) above are commonly known as investment-linked annuities. With falling conventional annuity rates, a number of annuitants are now looking at investment-based annuities. These rely on future returns to maintain or increase the underlying pension level, and so are not appropriate for those wishing to take no risk whatsoever. Pure investment-linked annuities will fall and rise in line with markets and so are potentially volatile. With-profit annuities sometimes have a guarantee that they will not drop below the starting level if 0% growth is selected at the outset.

The level of the initial annuity depends on the investment growth rate assumption that is selected when setting up the annuity. The annuity will remain level if the selected growth rate is achieved, but will fall if it is not, and rise if this growth is exceeded.

For with-profit annuities, an important factor is the financial strength of the underlying with-profits fund.

Unsecured pensions

27.25   There are two types of unsecured pension – income withdrawal and short-term annuities.

Income withdrawal

27.26   The idea here is that the individual transfers his pension funds into income withdrawal at the time he wants to draw benefits. He is allowed to take a tax-free cash sum either upfront or piecemeal through what is known as 'phased retirement'.

Each year, the individual can take income from the fund that is based on a maximum level calculated by reference to annuity tables produced by the Government Actuary's Department (GAD). The tables rely upon long-dated gilt yields at the time the individual enters into income drawdown, and the maximum level of income that can be drawn is calculated as 120% of the maximum income (broadly equivalent to a single life pension with no minimum guaranteed payment period) calculated by reference to the GAD tables.

The individual does not have to draw any income whatsoever, but if they wish to draw out a tax-free cash sum, which can be up to 25% of the fund value, they must do so when they convert the funds into income withdrawal.

For those with liabilities to meet on retirement, but who have ongoing income, there is the flexibility therefore to draw the tax-free cash sum to pay off such liabilities, whilst not being forced to draw pension income that would be taxable.

The parameters calculated by the GAD annuity tables must be reviewed every five years and will be based upon the fund value at the time of the subsequent review, as well as the age of the individual and gilt yields at that time. An individual can draw an income from the remaining fund in order to meet their income needs until age 75 when the unsecured pension must stop. However, at that stage there will be the option of an alternatively secured pension (ASP), which is described later.

If funds are being moved into income drawdown piecemeal, then the maximum income is constantly reassessed, normally at the time the transfer is made. In addition, an income withdrawal fund can be transferred to another registered scheme at any time.

Income withdrawal counters one of the principal historical objections to pension fund investment – namely, that individuals are not keen to buy annuities, particularly when annuity rates have fallen as much as they have in the last ten to 15 years. Under income withdrawal, there is no need to commit to the purchase of an annuity and the individual can continue to benefit from investment returns that would have a positive impact upon the likely income levels at each five-yearly review.

Short-term annuities

27.27 The concept here is that, after the individual has drawn their tax-free cash, the remainder of their fund remains invested and they can continue to have a say in how the funds are invested. However, some of the funds are then used to buy a temporary annuity and the individual can again select the company with which the annuity is purchased. The annuity itself must meet certain conditions:

(a) Minimum payment frequency of annually.

(b) The income payable must not be more than that permitted under income drawdown.

(c) It cannot be payable for more than five years.

(d) It cannot incorporate any annuity protection provisions.

(e) It can be transferred to another insurance company.

(f) It can have similar conditions to a lifetime annuity in terms of changes to the level of the annuity each year.

(g) It cannot continue beyond age 75.

Income reviews under short-term annuities will follow the same five-year pattern as for income withdrawal unless an event, such as pension sharing as part of a divorce procedure, should occur.

Alternatively secured pension

27.28 The genesis of alternatively secured pensions (ASPs) comes from lobbying by religious groups who explained to the Treasury that they could not purchase formal annuities. This is because their religious beliefs did not allow them to profit from someone else's death, which is implicit in the way that annuity funds are operated, as those who die early effectively subsidise annuity payouts to those who live longest.

ASPs are only available from age 75 and effectively mean that individuals no longer have to buy an annuity during their lifetimes in order to produce their pension income in retirement, as this can be done via income withdrawal before age 75 and by an ASP after age 75.

The maximum income is calculated as 90% of the appropriate GAD rate and the minimum is 55%. It is based upon an individual aged 75 and, whilst reviews must be carried out annually to reset the new maximum income limit, the annuity rate under the GAD tables must still be based on an age of 75 rather than actual age.

Family SIPPs and scheme pensions

27.29 A scheme pension is not available under all pension contracts but it is a feature of Family Self Invested Personal Pensions (SIPPs), which some partners may find attractive if they wish to run their family's pension fund on a collective basis. Where it is an option, it is available at any time from age 55. This option allows the individual to exchange their pension fund for an income that will be payable for life from the pension scheme without purchasing an annuity. The scheme pension fund remains invested in a tax-favoured environment, whilst providing a regular income each year. In very limited circumstances, it may enable them to pass any residuary fund on death to other members of the scheme as a lump sum, subject to tax charges.

It is possible to switch from an unsecured pension or an ASP to a scheme pension. It is not possible to switch from a scheme pension to an unsecured pension or an ASP.

At the outset, an actuary calculates the income that can be drawn. This calculation takes into account the value of the fund, assumed investment growth of the fund and life expectancy. A scheme pension can be set up for a fixed period of up to ten years, irrespective of whether you die during the period. The level of income is normally reviewed every three years by an actuary and could reduce.

Prior to age 75, an unsecured pension generally offers more flexibility to vary income than a scheme pension and has a more advantageous death benefit structure. In addition, depending on health, the maximum level of income that can be taken each year is usually more than the maximum permitted under scheme pension. These two factors mean it is unlikely that a scheme pension would be used prior to age 75. However, there will be certain instances, for example if a pension fund is of significant value, where it may be possible to avoid or reduce the lifetime allowance charge by vesting into a scheme pension as opposed to an unsecured pension.

From age 75, the maximum permitted income that can be taken under a scheme pension is likely to be greater than that allowed under an ASP. This, combined with the ability to guarantee the income payments for up to ten years, means that there is more scope for the members to extract money and, therefore, potentially greater value, from the pension fund than is available under an ASP.

Death benefits post taking benefits

27.30   The treatment of death benefits varies according to the retirement income options selected when the individual comes to take his benefits. This is explained below.

Death benefits under secured and unsecured income

27.31   The benefits available depend upon the type of annuity selected at the outset. There are two options here that could apply in terms of generating potential death benefits, namely a guaranteed minimum payment period or the inclusion in the pension of some form of annuity protection, and there are separate rules for unsecured pensions.

(a)   *Guaranteed periods* – Regardless of the individual's age at outset, a guaranteed minimum payment period of ten years can be selected. In the event of the individual's death during this period, the payments for the remaining period of the guarantee would be paid to the beneficiaries as income taxable under PAYE in their hands. There is no option to commute these income payments for a lump sum.

(b)   *Pension/annuity protection (value protected)* – Historically, in the annuity market this form of protection has been known as 'capital protection'. Under capital protection, on death the lump sum payable is equivalent to the original cost of the annuity less the total of gross income payments up to the date of death, and the resultant lump sum figure is subject to a 35% flat rate tax charge on payment to beneficiaries.

(c)   *Unsecured pension – the death position* – The value of the residual fund on death is subject to a lump sum flat rate tax charge as for the lump sum payment under annuity protection at 35%. It is possible that this would also be subject to a 40% inheritance tax charge if the lump sum is simply paid into the individual's estate and then passed on to beneficiaries. To avoid this IHT charge, it would be prudent to establish a trust at the outset in favour of the relevant beneficiaries or using standard nominations under the master trusts under which these schemes are established; although, as they give discretion to the scheme trustee, they cannot be wholly relied upon. However, there is the option to pass the income drawdown arrangement on to the spouse, who would then be able to continue drawing an income from that fund until age 75 if they do not wish to receive it as a lump sum at the outset. Any pension income they withdraw would be subject to income tax in their hands, and the surviving spouse would then have the option of moving the fund into an ASP at age 75.

The death position for ASPs

27.32 The death benefit position is complex. If the individual dies leaving financial dependants, the remaining fund must first of all be used to provide pension benefits for them.

On the financial dependant's death after the age of 75, or if there is no financial dependant, the only authorised payment that can be made is for the fund to go to charity. No tax charges are levied.

Transfer of the residual fund to another scheme member's pension, or payment of the funds to any individual, will be treated as an unauthorised payment. Many pension providers will not agree to make unauthorised payments. If they do, tax charges will be levied. A large part of this tax charge will be a personal tax liability payable by the individual who receives the fund. In addition, inheritance tax will be due in most cases. The combined effect of the taxes means that tax of approximately 82% of the fund will be paid.

If the financial dependant dies before reaching age 75, any residuary fund, after IHT, can be passed out as a lump sum, subject to a further tax charge of 35%, ie an overall tax rate of 61%. In these circumstances, there is no option to transfer the residuary fund to other members of the scheme or to a charity.

The death benefit position for scheme pensions

27.33 On death of the member in a scheme pension after age 75, on the basis that a fixed period (maximum ten years) has been selected at the outset, income can continue to be paid to any nominated individual(s) for the remainder of the fixed period selected if death occurs within this period. After the end of the fixed period, the scheme pension fund can be applied to provide an income for a spouse, civil partner and/or financial dependant.

Where the fixed period has expired and there are no surviving financial dependants, any transfer of the residual fund to another scheme member's pension, or payment of the funds to any individual, will be treated as an unauthorised payment and tax charges will be levied. A large part of this tax will be a personal tax liability payable by the individual who receives the fund. In addition, inheritance tax will be due in most cases. The combined effect of the taxes means that tax of either 73% or 82% of the fund will be paid under current tax rates, depending on whether or not a spouse or civil partner survives the individual concerned.

If the member's intention is to take as much as possible out of the fund to minimise the penal tax charges on death, in many cases from age 75, a scheme pension may be more appropriate than an ASP. There is also the possibility for payments during the fixed period to be made to nominated individuals who may not necessarily be financially dependent, eg grandchildren, without any inheritance tax implications.

Permitted investments

The permitted investment range

27.34   Originally, the new simplified regime was designed to remove the complex regime surrounding pension fund investment and make such investments easier to police in the future. This relaxation was widely praised, and asset classes such as residential property would have been permitted for the first time. However, as mentioned at **27.18** above, in the pre-Budget statement in December 2005, this expansion of the permitted investment range was widely curtailed.

It is true to say that all schemes are broadly subject to the same investment requirements; but, for those schemes which may fall outside the new provisions in relation to existing fund investments, there are transitional rules which cover this situation. However, there are controls being placed on permissible investments that will cover a number of areas, ie:

(a)   value shifting investments;

(b)   investment in prohibited assets;

(c)   loans made by a scheme to a member or his employer;

(d)   borrowings by the scheme itself;

(e)   investments where there is a sponsoring employer involved; and

(f)   investments that could in any way be seen to be benefiting the member personally.

Value shifting is essentially the idea that you can move an asset that is held within the scheme to a member so that they benefit from it in some way, shape or form. Where transactions are carried out on an arm's-length basis on totally commercial terms, then this is not value shifting.

Investment in unquoted shares within a SIPP is now permitted unless more than 50% is owned by the member, and the company, in turn, owns prohibited assets worth more than £8,000 and up to 100% of a SIPP could be invested in this way. Previously, only quoted shares could be held. The difficulty here would be how to establish the true market value of the asset at the time of the acquisition by the SIPP.

Commercial property has always been a permitted asset but, whilst investment directly in residential property is not permitted under the new rules, investment in a fund that invests in residential property is permitted, subject to:

(a) there being at least 11 investors in the fund;

(b) no one investor owning more than 10% of the fund;

(c) the total fund value being at least £1 million; and

(d) no one property asset within the fund representing more than 40% of the fund value.

On this basis, at least three residential properties would have to form part of the fund.

The range of prohibited assets, other than direct investment in individual residential properties as above, includes most forms of tangible moveable property. In translation, tangible moveable property means personal chattels. Previously, assets such as fine wine were going to be added to the list of acceptable investments.

Loans

Loans to a scheme

27.35 Borrowing within a pension fund is restricted to 50% of the net scheme assets before the loan, eg the maximum loan to a fund with a net value of £300,000 would be £150,000.

Where there are existing loans that fall outside these parameters, as the previous rules were more generous, these can remain in force, but will need to fall within the new regime if they are restructured in any way.

Transitional rules

27.36 Following the introduction of the A-Day changes, provision was made in the regulations to enable individuals to protect accrued pension rights if they are adversely affected by some of the changes. For example, if their fund was in excess of £1.5 million in 2006/07, rising to £1.8 million by 2010/11, they could be subject to a 55% lifetime allowance charge on the excess. This is one area where we can safely say that there was little simplicity involved! The time limit for submitting protection elections expired on 5 April 2009 but, in essence, where professional partnerships are concerned there are two areas of protection that are relevant, namely primary protection and enhanced protection, and some partners will be subject to these provisions.

Primary protection

27.37 Primary protection was only available where the individual had accrued pension rights that were in excess of £1.5 million as at A-Day. For partners who had accrued pension rights in occupational pension schemes, the basis of valuation was determined as set out at **27.10** above.

All of the individual's rights were aggregated for valuation purposes and, if the total capital value exceeded £1.5 million, the individual could apply for primary protection. So what does primary protection mean?

Let us assume that the individual at A-Day had an aggregate pension fund valued at £3 million. This would be twice the standard lifetime allowance of £1.5 million applicable in the 2006/07 tax year. When he comes to draw his benefits, assuming he draws all of his benefits at the same time, if his aggregate fund value calculated as explained above is less than twice the statutory lifetime allowance in that tax year, there would be no lifetime allowance charge of 55% applied. For example, let us say that the individual retires in tax year 2010/11 when the statutory lifetime allowance is £1.8 million. His aggregate fund could be valued at up to £3.6 million without incurring a 55% lifetime allowance charge on the fund. However, if the fund were valued at, say, £4 million, there would be a 55% tax charge on £400,000.

Those individuals who could apply for primary protection in the main did so, as they could apply for enhanced protection at the same time, and enhanced protection would take precedence in any event. Thus, they gave themselves maximum flexibility so, if, for example, there were a dramatic downturn in markets, they would be able to rebuild their pension fund by paying additional contributions to do so whilst retaining a significant level of protection on the accrued fund as at A-Day.

Enhanced protection

27.38 Individuals could apply for enhanced protection regardless of whether or not their pension fund exceeded £1.5 million as at A-Day. An application for enhanced protection appealed to those who wished to avoid the prospect of a 55% lifetime allowance charge applying at any time, regardless of the existing value of their fund.

The reason for this is that an enhanced protection claim effectively ring-fenced the accrued fund as at A-Day from any future lifetime allowance charge, regardless of the future level of growth in the fund. So, if an individual had a fund of, say, £1 million as at A-Day and, due to impressive investment performance, this grew to £5 million in the year he comes to take benefits, and the standard lifetime allowance in that year is £1.8 million, there would be no lifetime allowance charge on the excess above the standard lifetime allowance.

However, there was a catch. Those applying for enhanced protection avoid any lifetime allowance charge only if three conditions are met:

(i)   There is no relevant benefit accrual under a registered scheme after 5 April 2006. Under any form of money purchase arrangement, including personal pension plans, this simply means that no more contributions could be paid on or after 6 April 2006. For defined benefit arrangements, it would apply to any increase in excess of the lower of 5% and the increase in the RPI each year. Effectively, under such arrangements the benefits accrued at 5 April 2006 would be frozen, other than increases as above.

(ii) Only permitted transfers could be made post 6 April 2006. Here you have to transfer all of the benefits under the scheme into an alternative arrangement, and the transfers must be of equivalent value, ie if you transfer a sum of £20,000, the receiving registered scheme should receive £20,000 and not some higher figure.

(iii) You must not establish any new schemes other than those under the permitted transfer regulations.

There are some definitions of non-permissible transfers that would include transfers from another individual's pension, which would immediately invalidate the enhanced protection.

Enhanced protection could, of course, be revoked at any time simply by making a contribution or joining a new registered scheme. But this is only likely to occur where the hoped-for increase in fund value has not been attained in practice so that there are no adverse tax consequences involved. It is necessary to inform HMRC of any revocation of enhanced protection within 90 days or there is the potential of a fine of up to £3,000. If the individual has applied for primary protection as well, the primary protection will continue to apply going forward.

The Emergency Budget of June 2010

Transitional measures for individuals approaching age 75

27.39   The Government announced in the Budget on 22 June 2010 that the current requirement at an individual's 75th birthday to draw an income by means of a secured pension (lifetime annuity or scheme pension) or enter an ASP will be abolished.

Pending implementation of the changes, legislation will be introduced to increase to 77 the age by which members of registered pension schemes have to buy an annuity or otherwise secure a pension income. The increase in the age by which an individual must secure an income comes into effect after 22 June 2010; however, the change only applies to individuals who have not yet reached age 75 before 22 June 2010.

Scheme members with money purchase arrangements, who have not yet bought an annuity and reach age 75 on or after 22 June 2010, are able to enter income drawdown or purchase an annuity after their 75th birthday. The strict minimum and maximum income limits which previously applied under ASP will no longer apply.

Before turning 75, an individual still has to withdraw the maximum pension commencement lump sum in respect of those funds not previously made available for income withdrawal, or else the entitlement to do so is lost.

Death benefits

27.40   In the interim period before the main changes take effect in 2011/12, there will be a tax charge of 35% on lump sum death benefits paid in income drawdown by the scheme if the individual dies on or after 22 June 2010 and is aged 75 or over. There will continue to be no tax charge or IHT charge where any part of the deceased's pension fund is used to provide a dependant's pension.

For those individuals who attained age 75 prior to 22 June 2010 and are currently in an ASP, on their subsequent death any funds not used to pay a dependant's pension or charitable donation remain subject to potential tax charges of up to 82% on the value of the pension fund.

Proposed changes to retirement benefits beyond age 75 from 2011/12 tax year

27.41   In the Government's consultation document issued in July 2010, the main proposed changes were outlined which would come into effect from 6 April 2011. The document confirms that there will no longer be any specific date (for example, an individual's 75th birthday) by which members of registered schemes have to annuitise or otherwise secure pension benefits.

Currently, there appears to be no requirement to crystallise benefits at all, although there will still be a lifetime allowance test at age 75. It has also been implied that an individual's pension commencement lump sum can be taken when benefits are crystallised, even if this is after age 75.

Income limits are to be reviewed and there will be an option to take flexible drawdown amounts after age 75, provided the member can ensure they have secured sufficient income from other sources to prevent them exhausting their savings and falling back on the State. This is currently referred to as the minimum income requirement (MIR) and is taken at the point at which flexible drawdown begins. It is anticipated that any pension income will need to take into account reasonable expectations of the future cost of living.

ASPs will be abolished from April 2011, and existing members will become subject to the proposed flexible drawdown rules, including those for death benefits.

Death benefits

27.42 It has been proposed that any lump sum death benefit will be subject to a tax recovery charge of 55%, unless it is a lump sum paid in respect of uncrystallised benefits where the member dies before age 75. In this instance, the funds can be paid at the discretion of the scheme administrator/trustees and should be paid free of IHT. This is irrespective of whether the lump sum death benefit is paid before or after age 75.

Dependant's pensions will not be subject to the 55% tax charge or any IHT charge where any part of the death benefit is used to provide a dependant's pension.

Changes to post-6 April 2011 regime

27.43 The proposed rule changes announced by the Labour Government to apply from 6 April 2011 were complicated and likely to lead to confusion. This was acknowledged by the Coalition Government which, in the 'Emergency' Budget on 22 June 2010, announced its intention to rewrite the rules, replacing them with simpler measures which would restrict the 'tax cost' by a similar amount.

After a consultation period, the Government has published its proposed changes for tax relief on pensions announced on 14 October 2010, with an estimated reduction in the cost of pensions tax relief of about £4 billion per annum.

Proposals

27.44   Instead of a new set of rules to adjust the effective rate of tax relief on a sliding scale for those with high incomes, with anti-avoidance provisions, the plan is to primarily work within the existing regime and restrict the amounts to which the tax benefits apply.

The key restrictions will be to the annual and lifetime allowances.

Annual allowance

27.45   There is no limit on the contributions that can be paid to a pension scheme, but there is a limit on the amount qualifying for tax relief. One of the limits on the amount paid or rights accrued for a tax year in a registered pension scheme (relevant where earnings or pension payments exceed that figure) is known as the 'annual allowance'.

The key changes being made with regard to this allowance are:

- from April 2011, the annual allowance for tax-privileged saving will be reduced from its current level of £255,000 to £50,000;

- tax relief will be available at the individual's marginal rate;

- deemed contributions to defined benefit schemes will be valued using a 'flat factor' of 16, instead of 10;

- there will be a three-year carry-forward rule that allows individuals to carry forward unused annual allowance, which means that, even if the pension saving is more than £50,000, the annual allowance charge might not apply; and

- there will be no blanket exemption from the annual allowance in the year that benefits are taken, but there will, however, be an exemption in the case of serious ill-health as well as death.

Lifetime allowance

27.46   In addition to the changes to restricting tax relief on pension contributions, the lifetime allowance is to be reduced from its current level of £1.8 million to £1.5 million. The Government is minded that the reduced lifetime allowance will operate from April 2012 and has invited views on the detail of its approach, including on the relative burdens for schemes and employers of implementation in 2011 compared with 2012, as well as the impact on individuals whose pension funds are already at a level either above or close to the reduced allowance.

Anti-forestalling

27.47   The 2009 Budget introduced 'anti-forestalling' restrictions on tax relief on pension contributions in advance of the proposed changes; these remain in force and affect the 2009/10 and 2010/11 tax years.

Comment

27.48   The proposed changes will be easier to monitor and understand than those originally in place. This simplification has, however, come at a cost, as more people are likely to be affected. An annual allowance of £50,000 is more generous than the indicative figures in the consultation document and is at a level that will not impact on most taxpayers.

The ability to carry forward unused relief is welcome and will help those with fluctuating incomes and members of defined benefit schemes with large increases in the value accruing, such as on promotion.

One note of caution on this point: the individual must have been a member of a registered pension scheme in the three prior years to carry forward unused relief. Also, although the proposed draft legislation says that no pension input is necessary in those prior years, HMRC in their accompanying guidance say the opposite. HMRC will therefore need to revisit their guidance, but there is a concern that the proposed legislation could be changed in this regard.

The withdrawal of the exemption from the annual allowance in the year that benefits are taken will adversely affect those who had been waiting until near retirement to make a significant tax-efficient pension contribution.

Planning points

27.49

- Maximise available pension relief under the current regime, taking account of the effects of the anti-forestalling rules.

- Where the anti-forestalling charge would apply to contributions under £50,000, consider deferring that element of the payment until after 6 April 2011.

- Depending on circumstances, there may be a benefit in making a large one-off contribution within the current regime, with tax relief at the basic rate, before the reduced annual allowance applies.

- Start making pension provision as soon as possible.

Summary

27.50 A-Day was a major watershed in pension planning, but it is clear that politicians still wish to tamper with pension legislation, and this has made pension planning for partners extremely difficult. The changes announced by the Labour Government in 2009, and now the changes announced by the Coalition Government in 2010, seek to reduce the impact of the cost to the Exchequer of the various reliefs applying to pension provision and, in particular, reduce available relief on pension contributions.

It is a confusing landscape against which to plan for retirement, particularly with further changes planned in 2011, based upon a consultative document issued in July 2010. So it is important, therefore, that partners in professional practices seek advice to establish how the changes impact upon their pension position. Many will find that investing in pensions alone may not produce a level of income that will sustain their lifestyle in retirement. Increasingly, they will need to adopt a 'cafeteria' approach to retirement planning by investing in other tax-advantageous investments, such as ISAs (Individual Savings Accounts), alongside making their maximum allowable pension contributions.

Chapter 28 Death of a Partner

Introduction

28.1 A partner's or member's death can cause serious problems for the partnership or LLP. Quite apart from the practical difficulty of providing a continuing high standard of service to the deceased partner's or member's clients, the firm will often have an urgent need to replace the deceased's investment in the firm, in the form of undistributed profit and capital. In the context of a partnership, there may even be an automatic dissolution of the firm, with the tax consequences that follow.

All firms, however large or small, should therefore consider the consequences of a partner or member dying in office, and take steps to facilitate the continued smooth running of the business.

28.2 For general partnerships, but not LLPs, unless the partnership agreement provides otherwise, the death of a partner in a general partnership will cause an automatic dissolution of the partnership (*Partnership Act 1890, s 33(1)*). This is so, even if the partnership agreement states that the partnership will exist for a fixed term and that term has not yet expired. Special rules apply to limited partners (*Limited Partnerships Act 1907, s 6(2)*), but it is very unlikely that any professional partnership will be a limited partnership, because of the restriction on limited partners taking part in management and because this would be likely to mean that it was a 'collective investment scheme' with potentially serious regulatory consequences (see **2.44**).

A dissolution can cause serious difficulties between the continuing partners. For example, unless the agreement provides otherwise, there is generally an obligation to sell the goodwill and other assets at the highest available price, to pay and provide for all and to divide any surplus. The death of a partner may provide a recalcitrant partner with an opportunity to exploit this situation. In addition, a dissolution can have significant tax consequences. It is, therefore, important to provide in the partnership agreement that the partnership will not be dissolved on the death of a partner. If, however, the death of a partner leaves only one surviving partner, there can of course be no continuing partnership, and the provisions in the partnership agreement dealing with dissolution will then apply.

28.3 The death of a member of an LLP is a cessation of that member's membership of the LLP (*Limited Liability Partnerships Act 2000 (LLP Act)*, *s 4(3))*, but a member's death does not cause the LLP's dissolution, as the LLP is a body corporate. However, for the reasons set out in this chapter, it remains important that the LLP agreement sets out how that member's share will be dealt with on the death. Unlike a general partnership, if the death of a member leaves a sole member of the LLP, the LLP can continue to exist. However, if the LLP continues for more than six months without having two or more members, the sole member may be jointly and severally liable for the LLP's debts during that period (*LLP Act, s 4A*).

Partnership or LLP share of the deceased partner or member

28.4 The deceased partner's or member's beneficial interest in the partnership or LLP vests in his personal representatives. However, if the partnership or LLP owns land, and the individual who dies is one of those in whom the legal title to the land has been vested (which is more likely to be the case in a partnership than an LLP), then, on his death, legal title to the land will automatically devolve upon the other individuals who share in the ownership of the legal title to the land on his death, the land remaining beneficially owned by the partnership or LLP.

Unless expressly provided for by the deceased's will, the personal representatives of the deceased will not have power to engage in a business in partnership or through an LLP and, in the case of a partnership, they will be personally liable for losses arising in respect of the deceased partner's partnership share after his death if they do so without express authority. The terms of the will may, however, include an express power for the personal representatives to carry on a business alone or in partnership with others or through a corporate entity like an LLP. The partnership and LLP agreement may require the estate of the deceased partner to leave the deceased's capital contribution in the business as a loan (bearing interest), to allow time for alternative arrangements to be made by the continuing partners or members. Personal representatives cannot, therefore, generally be obliged to continue as partners in the partnership or to accede to an LLP as members, although the estate may be liable in damages to the partnership or LLP if they fail to do so in contravention of an express term of the written agreement.

Subject to any contrary agreement, personal representatives have no right to participate in the management of the partnership or LLP or to become partners or members (*Partnership Act 1890, s 31* and *LLP Act, s 7(2)*). However, they can be admitted as partners or members with the consent of the other partners or members. They should not agree to be admitted unless they have power to carry on business in partnership because they will, from the time of their appointment as partners or members, have personal liability for any liabilities incurred by the partnership or LLP. The personal representatives may also incur liability where they fail to exercise any right to recover the deceased's assets from the business where they should have done so, or, in a partnership, where they allow the deceased partner to be held out as a continuing partner and his estate becomes subject to any partnership liabilities as a result. However, in professional partnerships, the personal representatives are unlikely to share the skills of the deceased, and personal representatives will therefore rarely be able, or wish, to accede to the partnership or LLP. Moreover, members of some professions may be prohibited from practising in partnership or through an LLP which includes partners or members who are not also qualified members of the profession. For example, in the legal profession at the time of writing, an individual who is not a lawyer of England and Wales or a registered or exempt foreign lawyer must be approved by the Solicitors Regulation Authority in order to be a manager or owner of a recognised body or a manager of a body corporate which is a manager of a recognised body (*SRA Recognised Bodies Regulations 2009, reg 3*). This position may change when the provisions of the *Legal Services Act 2007* relating to alternative business structures come into effect (see CHAPTERS 4 AND 7) but, even then, it would be important to check that the continuing firm is compliant with the regulations.

Return of capital and withdrawal of profits

28.5 It is important to ensure that the written agreement sets out clearly how the deceased's investment in the firm (normally representing a share of capital and past profits) is to be realised by the personal representatives.

In the case of a partnership, in the absence of contrary provision in the partnership agreement (such as an 'automatic accruer' or an option discussed below), when the continuing partners carry on the business without any final settlement as between the firm and the estate of the deceased partner, the personal representatives have the right to elect to receive either a share of the profits since death attributable to the deceased partner's share, or interest at 5% (*Partnership Act 1890, s 42*).

Provisions regarding return of capital need to balance the interests of the estate of the deceased partner or member and those of the ongoing partners and members. The amounts of capital and profits that can be withdrawn need to be clear, as well as the timing of any withdrawals, and particular care needs to be taken to reduce any cash flow problems that might arise as a result of the death.

How the share of a deceased partner or member is dealt with will depend upon the provisions in the written agreement covering withdrawal of capital (see **5.12**). This may take the form of an automatic conversion of the deceased partner's share into an entitlement to the repayment of the sums standing to the credit of his capital and current accounts, coupled with the automatic vesting of his interest in the business in the continuing partners (an 'automatic accruer' arrangement). Alternatively, provision may be made for the firm to have an option so that it can force the sale of the interest to the firm for cash (an 'option' arrangement). The decision as to which provision is included will depend on the nature of the business but, in any event, care must be taken to ensure that such a provision does not, inadvertently, lead to an unqualified person becoming a partner or member where this is prohibited by the relevant professional rules. It is also important to note that provisions amounting to a 'buy and sell' arrangement may have adverse inheritance tax implications (see **28.6** below). In either case, the agreement must specify how the financial entitlement of the deceased partner's share is to be determined.

Inheritance tax business property relief

28.6 In general, business property relief at 100% is likely to be available on the net value of an interest in a professional partnership or an LLP which forms part of the estate of the deceased partner, if and to the extent that he has owned it for at least two years prior to his death (*Inheritance Tax Act 1984, ss 103–114*). If his share has increased as a proportion of the firm's capital during the two years prior to his death, relief will not be available to the extent of that increase.

However, it is important to note that, where a provision in the partnership or LLP agreement amounts to a binding contract for sale (known as a 'buy and sell' agreement), business property relief will not apply (*Inheritance Tax Act 1984, s 113*).

HMRC's Inheritance Tax Manual provides at IHTM25292:

'For the agreement to come within *s 113* of the *Inheritance Tax Act 1984* it has to provide:

- For the interest or shares of the deceased partner or shareholder to pass to his or her personal representatives

- That the personal representatives are required to sell the interest or shares to the surviving partners or shareholders

- Who are in terms obliged to buy it or them.

These requirements are rarely satisfied.'

It is strongly arguable that an automatic accruer arrangement is not the same as a binding obligation to sell the deceased's share, and that *s 113* should not apply in such cases. Indeed, the authors have in the past received confirmation from the HMRC Capital Taxes that a particular automatic accruer arrangement will not prejudice full business property relief. While the answers given were (in accordance with HMRC's usual practice) expressed to be limited to the circumstances of the particular case, it is thought to be likely that HMRC would normally adopt the same approach. Sub-clauses 22(5)–(7) of the model agreements, set out in APPENDICES 4 AND 5, operate as an automatic accruer arrangement if the words in square brackets are deleted.

Alternatively, it may be possible to put the inheritance tax position beyond doubt by the inclusion in the written agreement of an option arrangement. This would operate so that, on the death of a partner or member, his personal representatives would continue to hold the deceased's interest, but the continuing partners or members would have an option to acquire his interest from the personal representatives. The personal representatives should also have the right to realise their interest in the firm, and this could be achieved either by giving the estate a cross-option entitlement or, in the case of a partnership, by providing for a dissolution, if the continuing partners do not exercise their option. There would then be no binding buy and sell arrangement as such and, as noted above, it is the HMRC Capital Taxes' stated view that an option arrangement does not deny the availability of full business property relief (IHTM25292). Sub-clauses 22(5)–(7) of the model agreements, set out in APPENDICES 4 AND 5, operate as an option arrangement if the words in square brackets are incorporated. However, note that such an arrangement may result in the personal representatives themselves having an equity stake in the business, and that in some professions this may be prohibited, with potentially very serious consequences, as described at **28.5** above. In such cases, it would be better to rely on an automatic accruer.

Land or buildings owned by the deceased for at least two years before his death, but used by the partnership or LLP until the death, qualify for business property relief at 50% (*Inheritance Tax Act 1984, s 105(1)(d)*). If the property passes tax free to the surviving spouse, the relief would be unavailable in the widow's hands (eg on her death).

If payable, inheritance tax on a partnership interest may, at the option of the personal representatives, be paid by interest-free instalments over ten years.

Loans

28.7 If individual partners or members borrow in order to introduce capital to the firm, and secure these loans on their other non-business assets, the loan should reduce the value of those assets for inheritance tax purposes and maximise the value of the business property relief applicable to their business assets. The loan should actually be secured on non-business property, because otherwise the IR Capital Taxes is likely to argue that the loan should be attributed rateably to the whole of the deceased partner's or member's estate, including the business property.

Life insurance

28.8 A common method of funding the entitlement of the estate of a deceased partner or member who dies before retirement has been through life insurance, which is either effected by the partnership or LLP in order to fund its obligations on death of a partner or member, or effected by each partner or member who assigns it to a trust for the benefit of the business.

In the latter case, the policies are often held on discretionary trusts for the benefit of all the partners or members, with the intention that, on the death of any partner or member, his fellow partners or members are able to finance the acquisition of the deceased partner's or member's share in the business. However, the deceased partner or member will generally wish to remain a beneficiary of the policy taken out in case he leaves the partnership or LLP. The settlor would, therefore, be a beneficiary, either as a member of the discretionary class to whom appointments can be made, or as a beneficiary who will benefit on leaving the business when benefits revert to him automatically under the trust.

HMRC previously took the view that, provided the arrangement was a commercial transaction, and it was demonstrably on arm's-length terms, with no gratuitous intent (and therefore no transfer of value), the exemption in *s 10* of the *Inheritance Tax Act 1984* applied, no 'gift with reservation of benefits' arose, and the policy was not subject to inheritance tax on the death of the partner concerned.

However, the introduction of the income tax charge on 'pre-owned assets' (*Finance Act 2004, s 15*) has had an adverse impact on such arrangements where the partner can benefit under the trust relating to the policy on his own life. Following the introduction of the legislation, HMRC originally made the following statement with regard to such business trusts in their guidance notes:

> 'A partner in a business effects a life insurance policy subject to a business trust. The partner is a potential beneficiary. Provided the arrangement is commercial it is not a gift with reservation for inheritance tax. However the trust is a settlement for inheritance tax purposes and a charge to tax will arise under paragraph 8 of this schedule.'

This was superseded by guidance released by HMRC on 4 April 2005:

- '● In some cases, policies are taken out on each partner's life solely for the purposes of providing funds to enable their fellow

partners to purchase his/her share from the partner's beneficiaries on their death. The partner is not a potential beneficiary of
his/her "own" policy. In such circumstances, a charge to tax
under paragraph 8 of this schedule will not arise.

- However, in many cases, the partner retains a benefit for
themselves, for example they can cash in the policy during their
lifetime for their own benefit. In such cases, even if the arrangement is on commercial terms so that it is not a gift with a
reservation of benefit for inheritance tax, the trust is a settlement for inheritance tax purposes and a charge to tax under
paragraph 8 will arise.'

The result is that, where a partner remains a beneficiary under a trust
holding a policy on his own life, he may be subject to a charge to income
tax under the new rules. While it is possible that, if the policy is a term
policy and the life assured is in good health, the taxable benefits will fall
within the *de minimis* provisions, the taxpayer will still have to go to the
trouble of obtaining annual valuations and, given HMRC's stated views,
professional advice should be obtained before entering into such arrangements.

It is hoped that HMRC will issue further regulations in the future to exempt
these trusts from the 'pre-owned assets' tax rules, in line with the exemption for commercial arrangements from inheritance tax 'gift with reservation' rules, on the basis that such arrangements have not been entered into
deliberately to avoid the 'gift with reservation' rules.

Liability of personal representatives

Debts incurred prior to a partner's death

28.9   In a partnership context, there may, of course, be internal partnership rules about the sharing of debts incurred prior to the death of a
partner, but to the outside world the estate will remain jointly liable with
the surviving partners in respect of liabilities of the partnership incurred
before the date of death. This liability extends beyond simple debts to any
torts, frauds or breaches of trust that are committed before the partner's
death.

It follows that, where the firm is known to face the risk of large uninsured
claims at the date of death, the personal representatives may need to retain
the whole of the deceased partner's estate in order to fund these potential
liabilities. If the personal representatives make a distribution to the heirs,
and the amount retained proves to be insufficient, the personal representatives will be personally liable for the shortfall up to the amount distributed.

Even in relatively straightforward situations, it may be prudent for the personal representatives to retain part of the estate to make provision for unknown partnership liabilities.

The same considerations are unlikely to arise in the context of an LLP, unless the deceased member has somehow assumed personal liability for debts of the LLP (see **3.10**), as the debts of the business are debts of the LLP, for which the individual members are not generally liable.

Debts incurred after a partner's death

28.10 *Section 36(3)* of the *Partnership Act 1890* expressly provides that the estate is not liable to third parties for partnership debts contracted after the date of death, except those properly and necessarily incurred in connection with the winding up of the partnership on the death of the partner. Furthermore, most partnership agreements provide that the deceased partner's estate owes no obligation to the other partners to contribute to liabilities incurred after death.

However, this is subject to any contrary agreement, and the deceased partner's personal representatives may find that they became subject to liabilities incurred after death if, by their conduct, they effectively agree to become parties in that capacity. If the personal representatives are not expressly authorised to commit themselves in this way by the deceased's will, they may also incur personal liabilities for breach of trust, and considerable caution is advisable.

The deceased partner's family

28.11 Busy partners or members are often far less effective in managing their own affairs than they are in looking after their clients. If a partner or member dies without making proper provision for his family, his partners or members may feel committed to ensuring that his family is looked after properly, and this can be expensive, both financially and in terms of management time.

Prevention is much better than cure, and many of the best-run firms encourage their partners or members to provide for their families through appropriate pension and life insurance arrangements. For a fuller discussion of this, see CHAPTER 16. It is also important, for family and firm alike, that the partner's or member's tax affairs can be wound up and his share of the firm's capital and profits distributed as soon as possible after his death. Many firms, therefore, also encourage partners or members to make well thought out wills, often appointing a continuing partner or member as one of the executors. It is important to be aware that conflicts can arise between the interests of the estate and the interests of the firm. Where an executor is a partner or member, therefore, the will should allow the executors to enter into contracts even where they have a personal interest, although the executors' overriding duty will be to act in the best interests of the beneficiaries, which may not necessarily be the best interests of the partnership or the LLP.

Appendix 1   Partnership Act 1890

1890 Chapter 39 – Royal Assent 14 August 1890

ARRANGEMENT OF SECTIONS

Section

Nature of Partnership

1. Definition of partnership

(1) Partnership is the relation which subsists between persons carrying on a business in common with a view of profit.

(2) But the relation between members of any company or association which is–

    (a) Registered under the Companies Act 2006; or

    (b) Formed or incorporated by or in pursuance of any other Act of Parliament or letters patent, or Royal Charter; [...]

    (c) :

is not a partnership within the meaning of this Act.

2. Rules for determining existence of a partnership

In determining whether a partnership does or does not exist, regard shall be had to the following rules:

(1) Joint tenancy, tenancy in common, joint property, common property, or part ownership does not of itself create a partnership as to anything so held or owned, whether the tenants or owners do or do not share any profits made by the use thereof.

(2) The sharing of gross returns does not of itself create a partnership, whether the persons sharing such returns have or have not a joint or common right or interest in any property from which or from the use of which the returns are derived.

(3) The receipt by a person of a share of the profits of a business is prima facie evidence that he is a partner in the business, but the receipt of such a share, or of a payment contingent on or

varying with the profits of a business, does not of itself make him a partner in the business; and in particular–

(a) The receipt by a person of a debt or other liquidated amount by instalments, or otherwise out of the accruing profits of a business does not of itself make him a partner in the business or liable as such.

(b) A contract for the remuneration of a servant or agent of a person engaged in a business by a share of the profits of the business does not of itself make the servant or agent a partner in the business or liable as such.

(c) A person being the widow, widower, surviving civil partner or child of a deceased partner, and receiving by way of annuity a portion of the profits made in the business in which the deceased person was a partner, is not by reason only of such receipt a partner in the business or liable as such.

(d) The advance of money by way of loan to a person engaged or about to engage in any business on a contract with that person that the lender shall receive a rate of interest varying with the profits, or shall receive a share of the profits arising from carrying on the business, does not of itself make the lender a partner with the person or persons carrying on the business or liable as such. Provided that the contract is in writing, and signed by or on behalf of all the parties thereto.

(e) A person receiving by way of annuity or otherwise a portion of the profits of a business in consideration of the sale by him of the goodwill of the business is not by reason only of such receipt a partner in the business or liable as such.

3. Postponement of rights of person lending or selling in consideration of share of profits in case of insolvency

In the event of any person to whom money has been advanced by way of loan upon such a contract as is mentioned in the last foregoing section, or of any buyer of a goodwill in consideration of a share of the profits of the business, being adjudged a bankrupt, entering into an arrangement to pay his creditors less than 100p in the pound, or dying in insolvent circumstances, the lender of the loan shall not be entitled to recover anything in respect of his loan, and the seller of the goodwill shall not be entitled to recover anything in respect of the share of profits contracted for, until the claims of the other creditors of the borrower or buyer for valuable consideration in money or money's worth have been satisfied.

4. Meaning of firm

(1) Persons who have entered into partnership with one another are for the purposes of this Act called collectively a firm, and the name under which their business is carried on is called the firm-name.

(2) In Scotland a firm is a legal person distinct from the partners of whom it is composed, but an individual partner may be charged on a decree or diligence directed against the firm, and on payment of the debts is entitled to relief pro rat from the firm and its other members.

Relations of Partners to persons dealing with them

5. Power of partner to bind the firm

Every partner is an agent of the firm and his other partners for the purpose of the business of the partnership; and the acts of every partner who does any act for carrying on in the usual way business of the kind carried on by the firm of which he is a member bind the firm and his partners, unless the partner so acting has in fact no authority to act for the firm in the particular matter, and the person with whom he is dealing either knows that he has no authority, or does not know or believe him to be a partner.

6. Partners bound by acts on behalf of the firm

An act or instrument relating to the business of the firm and done or executed in the firm-name, or in any other manner showing an intention to bind the firm, by any person thereto authorised, whether a partner or not, is binding on the firm and all the partners. Provided that this section shall not affect any general rule of law relating to the execution of deeds or negotiable instruments.

7. Partner using credit of firm for private purposes

Where one partner pledges the credit of the firm for a purpose apparently not connected with the firm's ordinary course of business, the firm is not bound, unless he is in fact specially authorised by the other partners; but this section does not affect any personal liability incurred by an individual partner.

8. Effect of notice that firm will not be bound by acts of partner

If it has been agreed between the partners that any restriction shall be placed on the power of any one or more of them to bind the firm, no act done in contravention of the agreement is binding on the firm with respect to persons having notice of the agreement.

9. Liability of partners

Every partner in a firm is liable jointly with the other partners, and in Scotland severally also, for all debts and obligations of the firm incurred while he is a partner; and after his death his estate is also severally liable in a due course of administration for such debts and obligations, so far as they remain unsatisfied, but subject in England or Ireland to the prior payment of his separate debts.

10. Liability of the firm for wrongs

Where, by any wrongful act or omission of any partner acting in the ordinary course of the business of the firm, or with the authority of his co-partners, loss or injury is caused to any person not being a partner in the firm, or any penalty is incurred, the firm is liable therefore to the same extent as the partner so acting or omitting to act.

11. Misapplication of money or property received for or in custody of the firm

In the following cases; namely–

(a) Where one partner acting within the scope of his apparent authority receives the money or property of a third person and misapplies it; and

(b) Where a firm in the course of its business receives money or property of a third person, and the money or property so received is misapplied by one or more of the partners while it is in the custody of the firm;

the firm is liable to make good the loss.

12. Liability for wrongs joint and several

Every partner is liable jointly with his co-partners and also severally for everything for which the firm while he is a partner therein becomes liable under either of the two last preceding sections.

13. Improper employment of trust-property for partnership purposes

If a partner, being a trustee, improperly employs trust-property in the business or on the account of the partnership, no other partner is liable for the trust property to the persons beneficially interested therein. Provided as follows:

(1)   This section shall not affect any liability incurred by any partner by reason of his having notice of a breach of trust; and

(2)   Nothing in this section shall prevent trust money from being followed and recovered from the firm if still in its possession or under its control.

14. Persons liable by 'holding out'

(1)   Every one who by words spoken or written or by conduct represents himself, or who knowingly suffers himself to be represented, as a partner in a particular firm, is liable as a partner to any one who has on the faith of any such representation given credit to the firm, whether the representation has or has not been made or communicated to the person so giving credit by or with the knowledge of the apparent partner making the representation or suffering it to be made.

(2)   Provided that where after a partner's death the partnership business is continued in the old firm-name, the continued use of that name or of the deceased partner's name as part thereof shall not of itself make his executors' or administrators' estate or effects liable for any partnership debts contracted after his death.

15. Admissions and representations of partners

An admission or representation made by any partner concerning the partnership affairs, and in the ordinary course of its business, is evidence against the firm.

16. Notice to acting partner to be notice to the firm

Notice to any partner who habitually acts in the partnership business of any matter relating to partnership affairs operates as notice to the firm, except in the case of a fraud on the firm committed by or with the consent of that partner.

17. Liabilities of incoming and outgoing partners

(1)   A person who is admitted as a partner into an existing firm does not thereby become liable to the creditors of the firm for anything done before he became a partner.

(2)   A partner who retires from a firm does not thereby cease to be liable for partnership debts or obligations incurred before his retirement.

(3)   A retiring partner may be discharged from any existing liabilities, by an agreement to that effect between himself and the members of the firm as newly constituted and the creditors, and

this agreement may be either express or inferred as a fact from the course of dealing between the creditors and the firm as newly constituted.

18. Revocation of continuing guaranty by change in firm

A continuing guaranty or cautionary obligation given either to a firm or to a third person in respect of the transactions of a firm is, in the absence of agreement to the contrary, revoked as to future transactions by any change in the constitution of the firm to which, or of the firm in respect of the transactions of which, the guaranty or obligation was given.

Relations of Partners to one another

19. Variation by consent of terms of partnership

The mutual rights and duties of partners, whether ascertained by agreement or defined by this Act, may be varied by the consent of all the partners, and such consent may be either express or inferred from a course of dealing.

20. Partnership property

(1) All property and rights and interests in property originally brought into the partnership stock or acquired, whether by purchase or otherwise, on account of the firm or for the purposes and in the course of the partnership business, are called in this Act partnership property, and must be held and applied by the partners exclusively for the purposes of the partnership and in accordance with the partnership agreement.

(2) Provided that the legal estate or interest in any land, or in Scotland the title to and interest in any heritable estate, which belongs to the partnership shall devolve according to the nature and tenure thereof, and the general rules of law thereto applicable, but in trust, so far as necessary, for the persons beneficially interested in the land under this section.

(3) Where co-owners of an estate or interest in any land, or in Scotland of any heritable estate, not being itself partnership property, are partners as to profits made by the use of that land or estate, and purchase other land or estate out of the profits to be used in like manner, the land or estate so purchased belongs to them, in the absence of an agreement to the contrary, not as partners but as co-owners for the same respective estates and interests as are held by them in the land or estate first mentioned at the date of the purchase.

21. Property bought with partnership money

Unless the contrary intention appears, property bought with money belonging to the firm is deemed to have been bought on account of the firm.

22. [...]

23. Procedure against partnership property for a partner's separate judgment debt

(1) After the commencement of this Act a writ of execution shall not issue against any partnership property except on a judgment against the firm.

(2) The High Court, or a judge thereof, [...] a county court, may, on the application by summons of any judgment creditor of a partner, make an order charging that partner's interest in the partnership property and profits with payment of the amount of the judgment debt and interest thereon, and may by the same or a subsequent order appoint a receiver of that partner's share of profits (whether already declared or accruing), and of any other money which may be coming to him in respect of the partnership, and direct all accounts and inquiries, and give all other orders and directions which might have been directed or given if the charge had been made in favour of the judgment creditor by the partner, or which the circumstances of the case may require.

(3) The other partner or partners shall be at liberty at any time to redeem the interest charged, or in case of a sale being directed, to purchase the same.

(4) [...]

(5) This section shall not apply to Scotland.

24. Rules as to interests and duties of partners subject to special agreement

The interests of partners in the partnership property and their rights and duties in relation to the partnership shall be determined, subject to any agreement express or implied between the partners, by the following rules:

(1) All the partners are entitled to share equally in the capital and profits of the business, and must contribute equally towards the losses whether of capital or otherwise sustained by the firm.

(2) The firm must indemnify every partner in respect of payments made and personal liabilities incurred by him–

(a) In the ordinary and proper conduct of the business of the firm; or

(b) In or about anything necessarily done for the preservation of the business or property of the firm.

(3) A partner making, for the purpose of the partnership, any actual payment or advance beyond the amount of capital which he has agreed to subscribe, is entitled to interest at the rate of five per cent per annum from the date of the payment or advance.

(4) A partner is not entitled, before the ascertainment of profits, to interest on the capital subscribed by him.

(5) Every partner may take part in the management of the partnership business.

(6) No partner shall be entitled to remuneration for acting in the partnership business.

(7) No person may be introduced as a partner without the consent of all existing partners.

(8) Any difference arising as to ordinary matters connected with the partnership business may be decided by a majority of the partners, but no change may be made in the nature of the partnership business without the consent of all existing partners.

(9) The partnership books are to be kept at the place of business of the partnership (or the principal place, if there is more than one), and every partner may, when he thinks fit, have access to and inspect and copy any of them.

25. Expulsion of partner

No majority of the partners can expel any partner unless a power to do so has been conferred by express agreement between the partners.

26. Retirement from partnership at will

(1) Where no fixed term has been agreed upon for the duration of the partnership, any partner may determine the partnership at any time on giving notice of his intention so to do to all the other partners.

(2) Where the partnership has originally been constituted by deed, a notice in writing, signed by the partner giving it, shall be sufficient for this purpose.

27. Where partnership for term is continued over, continuance on old terms presumed

(1)   Where a partnership entered into for a fixed term is continued after the term has expired, and without any express new agreement, the rights and duties of the partners remain the same as they were at the expiration of the term, so far as is consistent with the incidents of a partnership at will.

(2)   A continuance of the business by the partners or such of them as habitually acted therein during the term, without any settlement or liquidation of the partnership affairs, is presumed to be a continuance of the partnership.

28. Duty of partners to render accounts, etc.

Partners are bound to render true accounts and full information of all things affecting the partnership to any partner or his legal representatives.

29. Accountability of partners for private profits

(1)   Every partner must account to the firm for any benefit derived by him without the consent of the other partners from any transaction concerning the partnership, or from any use by him of the partnership property name or business connexion.

(2)   This section applies also to transactions undertaken after a partnership has been dissolved by the death of a partner, and before the affairs thereof have been completely wound up, either by any surviving partner or by the representatives of the deceased partner.

30. Duty of partner not to compete with firm

If a partner, without the consent of the other partners, carries on any business of the same nature as and competing with that of the firm, he must account for and pay over to the firm all profits made by him in that business.

31. Rights of assignee of share in partnership

(1)   An assignment by any partner of his share in the partnership, either absolute or by way of mortgage or redeemable charge, does not, as against the other partners, entitle the assignee, during the continuance of the partnership, to interfere in the management or administration of the partnership business or affairs, or to require any accounts of the partnership transactions, or to inspect the partnership books, but entitles the assignee only to receive the share of profits to which the

assigning partner would otherwise be entitled, and the assignee must accept the account of profits agreed to by the partners.

(2) In case of a dissolution of the partnership, whether as respects all the partners or as respects the assigning partner, the assignee is entitled to receive the share of the partnership assets to which the assigning partner is entitled as between himself and the other partners, and, for the purpose of ascertaining that share, to an account as from the date of the dissolution.

Dissolution of Partnership, and its consequences

32. Dissolution by expiration or notice

Subject to an agreement between the partners a partnership is dissolved–

(a) If entered into for a fixed term, by the expiration of that term.

(b) If entered into for a single adventure or undertaking, by the termination of that adventure or undertaking.

(c) If entered into for an undefined time, by any partner giving notice to the other or others of his intention to dissolve the partnership.

In the last-mentioned case the partnership is dissolved as from the date mentioned in the notice as the date of dissolution, or, if no date is so mentioned, as from the date of the communication of the notice.

33. Dissolution by bankruptcy, death or charge

(1) Subject to any agreement between the partners, every partnership is dissolved as regards all the partners by the death or bankruptcy of any partner.

(2) A partnership may, at the option of the other partners, be dissolved if any partner suffers his share of the partnership property to be charged under this Act for his separate debt.

34. Dissolution by illegality of partnership

A partnership is in every case dissolved by the happening of any event which makes it unlawful for the business of the firm to be carried on or for the members of the firm to carry it on in partnership.

35. Dissolution by the Court

On application by a partner the Court may decree a dissolution of the partnership in any of the following cases:

(a) [...]

(b)   When a partner, other than the partner suing, becomes in any other way permanently incapable of performing his part of the partnership contract:

(c)   When a partner, other than the partner suing, has been guilty of such conduct as, in the opinion of the Court, regard being had to the nature of the business, is calculated to prejudicially affect the carrying on of the business:

(d)   When a partner, other than the partner suing, wilfully or persistently commits a breach of the partnership agreement, or otherwise so conducts himself in matters relating to the partnership business that it is not reasonably practicable for the other partner or partners to carry on the business in partnership with him:

(e)   When the business of the partnership can only be carried on at a loss:

(f)   Whenever in any case circumstances have arisen which, in the opinion of the Court, render it just and equitable that the partnership be dissolved.

36. Rights of persons dealing with firm against apparent members of firm

(1)   Where a person deals with a firm after a change in its constitution he is entitled to treat all apparent members of the old firm as still being members of the firm until he has notice of the change.

(2)   An advertisement in the London Gazette as to a firm whose principal place of business is in England or Wales, in the Edinburgh Gazette as to a firm whose principal place of business is in Scotland, and in the Belfast Gazette as to a firm whose principal place of business is in Ireland, shall be notice as to persons who had no dealings with the firm before the date of the dissolution or change so advertised.

(3)   The estate of a partner who dies, or who becomes bankrupt, or of a partner who, not having been known to the person dealing with the firm to be a partner, retires from the firm, is not liable for partnership debts contracted after the date of the death, bankruptcy, or retirement respectively.

37. Rights of partners to notify dissolution

On the dissolution of a partnership or retirement of a partner any partner may publicly notify the same, and may require the other partner or partners to concur for that purpose in all necessary or proper acts, if any, which cannot be done without his or their concurrence.

38. Continuing authority of partners for purposes of winding up

After the dissolution of a partnership the authority of each partner to bind the firm, and the other rights and obligations of the partners, continue notwithstanding the dissolution so far as may be necessary to wind up the affairs of the partnership, and to complete transactions begun but unfinished at the time of the dissolution, but not otherwise. Provided that the firm is in no case bound by the acts of a partner who has become bankrupt; but this proviso does not affect the liability of any person who has after the bankruptcy represented himself or knowingly suffered himself to be represented as a partner of the bankrupt.

39. Rights of partners as to application of partnership property

On the dissolution of a partnership every partner is entitled, as against the other partners in the firm, and all persons claiming through them in respect of their interests as partners, to have the property of the partnership applied in payment of the debts and liabilities of the firm, and to have the surplus assets after such payment applied in payment of what may be due to the partners respectively after deducting what may be due from them as partners to the firm; and for that purpose any partner or his representatives may on the termination of the partnership apply to the Court to wind up the business and affairs of the firm.

40. Apportionment of premium where partnership prematurely dissolved

Where one partner has paid a premium to another on entering into a partnership for a fixed term, and the partnership is dissolved before the expiration of that term otherwise than by the death of a partner, the Court may order the repayment of the premium, or of such part thereof as it thinks just, having regard to the terms of the partnership contract and to the length of time during which the partnership has continued; unless–

(a) the dissolution is, in the judgment of the Court, wholly or chiefly due to the misconduct of the partner who paid the premium, or

(b) the partnership has been dissolved by an agreement containing no provision for a return of any part of the premium.

41. Rights where partnership dissolved for fraud or misrepresentation

Where a partnership contract is rescinded on the ground of the fraud or misrepresentation of one of the parties thereto, the party entitled to rescind is, without prejudice to any other right, entitled–

(a) to a lien on, or right of retention of, the surplus of the partnership assets, after satisfying the partnership liabilities, for any sum of money paid by him for the purchase of a share in the partnership and for any capital contributed by him, and is

(b) to stand in the place of the creditors of the firm for any payments made by him in respect of the partnership liabilities, and

(c) to be indemnified by the person guilty of the fraud or making the representation against all the debts and liabilities of the firm.

42. Right of outgoing partner in certain cases to share profits made after dissolution

(1) Where any member of a firm has died or otherwise ceased to be a partner, and the surviving or continuing partners carry on the business of the firm with its capital or assets without any final settlement of accounts as between the firm and the outgoing partner or his estate, then, in the absence of any agreement to the contrary, the outgoing partner or his estate is entitled at the option of himself or his representatives to such share of the profits made since the dissolution as the Court may find to be attributable to the use of his share of the partnership assets, or to interest at the rate of five per cent per annum on the amount of his share of the partnership assets.

(2) Provided that where by the partnership contract an option is given to surviving or continuing partners to purchase the interest of a deceased or outgoing partner, and that option is duly exercised, the estate of the deceased partner, or the outgoing partner or his estate, as the case may be, is not entitled to any further or other share of profits; but if any partner assuming to act in exercise of the option does not in all material respects comply with the terms thereof, he is liable to account under the foregoing provisions of this section.

43. Retiring or deceased partner's share to be a debt

Subject to any agreement between the partners, the amount due from surviving or continuing partners to an outgoing partner or the representatives of a deceased partner in respect of the outgoing or deceased partner's share is a debt accruing at the date of the dissolution or death.

44. Rule for distribution of assets on final settlement of accounts

In settling accounts between the partners after a dissolution of partnership, the following rules shall, subject to any agreement, be observed:

(a)   Losses, including losses and deficiencies of capital, shall be paid first out of profits, next out of capital, and lastly, if necessary, by the partners individually in the proportion in which they were entitled to share profits:

(b)   The assets of the firm including the sums, if any, contributed by the partners to make up losses or deficiencies of capital, shall be applied in the following manner and order:

1.   In paying the debts and liabilities of the firm to persons who are not partners therein.

2.   In paying to each partner rateably what is due from the firm to him for advances as distinguished from capital.

3.   In paying to each partner rateably what is due from the firm to him in respect of capital.

4.   The ultimate residue, if any, shall be divided among the partners in the proportion in which the profits are divisible.

Supplemental

45. Definitions of 'court' and 'business'

In this Act, unless the contrary intention appears–

The expression 'court' includes every court and judge having jurisdiction in the case:

The expression 'business' includes every trade, occupation, or profession.

46. Saving for rules of equity and common law

The rules of equity and of common law applicable to partnership shall continue in force except so far as they are inconsistent with the express provisions of this Act.

47. Provision as to bankruptcy in Scotland

(1)   In the application of this Act to Scotland the bankruptcy of a firm or of an individual shall mean sequestration under the Bankruptcy (Scotland) Acts, and also in the case of an individual the issue against him of a decree of cessio bonorum.

(2)   Nothing in this Act shall alter the rules of the law of Scotland relating to the bankruptcy of a firm or of the individual partners thereof.

48. Repeal

[...]

49. Commencement of Act

[...]

50. Short title

This Act may be cited as the Partnership Act, 1890.

Appendix 2   Limited Partnerships Act 1907

1907 Chapter 24 – Royal Assent 28 August 1907

ARRANGEMENT OF SECTIONS

1. **Short title**

    This Act may be cited for all purposes as the Limited Partnerships Act, 1907.

2. **[...]**

3. **Interpretation of terms**

    In the construction of this Act the following words and expressions shall have the meanings respectively assigned to them in this section, unless there be something in the subject or context repugnant to such construction:

    'Firm', 'firm name', and 'business' have the same meanings as in the Partnership Act, 1890.

    'General partner' shall mean any partner who is not a limited partner as defined by this Act.

4. **Definition and constitution of limited partnership**

    (1) [...] limited partnerships may be formed in the manner and subject to the conditions by this Act provided.

    (2) A limited partnership [...] must consist of one or more persons called general partners, who shall be liable for all debts and obligations of the firm, and one or more persons to be called limited partners, who shall at the time of entering into such partnership contribute thereto a sum or sums as capital or property valued at a stated amount, and who shall not be liable for the debts or obligations of the firm beyond the amount so contributed.

    (3) A limited partner shall not during the continuance of the partnership, either directly or indirectly, draw out or receive back any part of his contribution, and if he does so draw out or receive back any such part shall be liable for the debts and obligations of the firm up to the amount so drawn out or received back.

    (4) A body corporate may be a limited partner.

5. **Registration of limited partnership required**

    Every limited partnership must be registered as such in accordance with the provisions of this Act [...].

6. **Modifications of general law in case of limited partnerships**

    (1) A limited partner shall not take part in the management of the partnership business, and shall not have power to bind the firm.

477

Provided that a limited partner may by himself or his agent at any time inspect the books of the firm and examine into the state and prospects of the partnership business, and may advise with the partners thereon. If a limited partner takes part in the management of the partnership business he shall be liable for all debts and obligations of the firm incurred while he so takes part in the management as though he were a general partner.

(2) A limited partnership shall not be dissolved by the death or bankruptcy of a limited partner, and the lunacy of a limited partner shall not be a ground for dissolution of the partnership by the court unless the lunatic's share cannot be otherwise ascertained and realised.

(3) In the event of the dissolution of a limited partnership its affairs shall be wound up by the general partners unless the court otherwise orders.

(4) [...]

(5) Subject to any agreement expressed or implied between the partners–

(a) Any difference arising as to ordinary matters connected with the partnership business may be decided by a majority of the general partners;

(b) A limited partner may, with the consent of the general partners, assign his share in the partnership, and upon such an assignment the assignee shall become a limited partner with all the rights of the assignor;

(c) The other partners shall not be entitled to dissolve the partnership by reason of any limited partner suffering his share to be charged for his separate debt;

(d) A person may be introduced as a partner without the consent of the existing limited partners;

(e) A limited partner shall not be entitled to dissolve the partnership by notice.

7. Law as to private partnerships to apply where not excluded by this Act

Subject to the provisions of this Act, the Partnership Act, 1890, and the rules of equity and of common law applicable to partnerships, except so far as they are inconsistent with the express provisions of the last-mentioned Act, shall apply to limited partnerships.

8. Duty to register

The registrar shall register a limited partnership if an application is made to the registrar in accordance with section 8A.

8A. Application for registration

(1) An application for registration must–

    (a) specify the firm name, complying with section 8B, under which the limited partnership is to be registered,

    (b) contain the details listed in subsection (2),

    (c) be signed or otherwise authenticated by or on behalf of each partner, and

    (d) be made to the registrar for the part of the United Kingdom in which the principal place

of business of the limited partnership is to be situated.

(2) The required details are–

    (a) the general nature of the partnership business,

    (b) the name of each general partner,

    (c) the name of each limited partner,

    (d) the amount of the capital contribution of each limited partner (and whether the contribution is paid in cash or in another specified form),

    (e) the address of the proposed principal place of business of the limited partnership, and

    (f) the term (if any) for which the limited partnership is to be entered into (beginning with the date of registration).

8B. Name of limited partnership

(1) This section sets out conditions which must be satisfied by the firm name of a limited partnership as specified in the application for registration.

(2) The name must end with–

    (a) the words 'limited partnership' (upper or lower case, or any combination), or

    (b) the abbreviation 'LP' (upper or lower case, or any combination, with or without punctuation).

(3) But if the principal place of business of a limited partnership is to be in Wales, its firm name may end with–

(a) the words 'partneriaeth cyfyngedig' (upper or lower case, or any combination), or

(b) the abbreviation 'PC' (upper or lower case, or any combination, with or without punctuation).

8C. Certificate of registration

(1) On registering a limited partnership the registrar shall issue a certificate of registration.

(2) The certificate must be–

(a) signed by the registrar, or

(b) authenticated with the registrar's seal.

(3) The certificate must state–

(a) the firm name of the limited partnership given in the application for registration,

(b) the limited partnership's registration number,

(c) the date of registration, and

(d) that the limited partnership is registered as a limited partnership under this Act.

(4) The certificate is conclusive evidence that a limited partnership came into existence on the date of registration.

9. Registration of changes in partnerships

(1) If during the continuance of a limited partnership any change is made or occurs in–

(a) the firm name,

(b) the general nature of the business,

(c) the principal place of business,

(d) the partners or the name of any partner,

(e) the term or character of the partnership,

(f) the sum contributed by any limited partner,

(g) the liability of any partner by reason of his becoming a limited instead of a general partner or a general instead of a limited partner, a statement, signed by the firm, specifying the nature of the change shall within seven days be sent by post or delivered to the registrar [...].

(2) If default is made in compliance with the requirements of this section each of the general partners shall, on conviction under the Magistrates' Courts Act 1952, be liable to a fine not exceeding one pound for each day during which the default continues.

10. Advertisement in Gazette of statement of general partner becoming a limited partner and of assignment of share of limited partner

(1) Notice of any arrangement or transaction under which any person will cease to be a general partner in any firm, and will become a limited partner in that firm, or under which the share of a limited partner in a firm will be assigned to any person, shall be forthwith advertised in the Gazette, and until notice of the arrangement or transaction is so advertised, the arrangement or transaction shall, for the purposes of this Act, be deemed to be of no effect.

(2) For the purposes of this section, the expression the Gazette means–

In the case of a limited partnership registered in England, the London Gazette;

In the case of a limited partnership registered in Scotland, the Edinburgh Gazette;

In the case of a limited partnership registered in Northern Ireland, the Belfast Gazette.

11. [...]

12. [...]

13. Registrar to file statement and issue certificate of registration

On receiving any statement made in pursuance of this Act the registrar shall cause the same to be filed, and he shall send by post to the firm from whom such statement shall have been received a certificate of the registration thereof.

14. Register and index to be kept

The registrar shall keep, in proper books to be provided for the purpose, a register and an index of all the limited partnerships registered as aforesaid, and of all the statements registered in relation to such partnerships.

15. The registrar

(1) The registrar of companies is the registrar of limited partnerships.

(2) In this Act–

  (a) references to the registrar in relation to the registration of a limited partnership are to the registrar to whom the application for registration is to be made (see section 8A(1)(d));

  (b) references to registration in a particular part of the United Kingdom are to registration by the registrar for that part of the United Kingdom;

  (c) references to the registrar in relation to any other matter relating to a limited partnership are to the registrar for the part of the United Kingdom in which the partnership is registered.

16. Inspection of statements registered

(1) Any person may inspect the statements filed by the registrar [...]; and any person may require a certificate of the registration of any limited partnership, or a copy of or extract from any registered statement, to be certified by the registrar, and there shall be paid for such certificate of registration, certified copy, or extract such fees as the Board of Trade may appoint, not exceeding 10p for the certificate of registration, and not exceeding 2½p for each folio of seventy-two words, or in Scotland for each sheet of two hundred words.

(2) A certificate of registration, or a copy of or extract from any statement registered under this Act, if duly certified to be a true copy under the hand of the registrar [...] (whom it shall not be necessary to prove to be the registrar [...]) shall, in all legal proceedings, civil or criminal, and in all cases whatsoever be received in evidence.

17. Power of Board of Trade to make rules

The Board of Trade may make rules [...] concerning any of the following matters:–

(a) [...]

(b) The duties or additional duties to be performed by the registrar for the purposes of this Act;

(c)   The performance by assistant registrars and other officers of acts by this Act required to be done by the registrar;

(d)   The forms to be used for the purposes of this Act;

(e)   Generally the conduct and regulation of registration under this Act and any matters incidental thereto.

Appendix 3   Limited Liability Partnerships Act 2000

2000 Chapter 12 – Royal Assent 20 July 2000

ARRANGEMENT OF SECTIONS

Introductory

1. Limited liability partnerships

(1) There shall be a new form of legal entity to be known as a limited liability partnership.

(2) A limited liability partnership is a body corporate (with legal personality separate from that of its members) which is formed by being incorporated under this Act; and–

    (a) in the following provisions of this Act (except in the phrase 'oversea limited liability partnership'), and

    (b) in any other enactment (except where provision is made to the contrary or the context otherwise requires),

references to a limited liability partnership are to such a body corporate.

(3) A limited liability partnership has unlimited capacity.

(4) The members of a limited liability partnership have such liability to contribute to its assets in the event of its being wound up as is provided for by virtue of this Act.

(5) Accordingly, except as far as otherwise provided by this Act or any other enactment, the law relating to partnerships does not apply to a limited liability partnership.

(6) The Schedule (which makes provision about the names and registered offices of limited liability partnerships) has effect.

Incorporation

2. Incorporation document etc.

(1) For a limited liability partnership to be incorporated–

(a) two or more persons associated for carrying on a lawful business with a view to profit must have subscribed their names to an incorporated document,

(b) the incorporation document or a copy of it must have been delivered to the registrar, and

(c) there must have been so delivered a statement [...] made by either a solicitor engaged in the formation of the limited liability partnership or anyone who subscribed his name to the incorporation document, that the requirement imposed by paragraph (a) has been complied with.

(2) The incorporation document must–

(a) [...]

(b) state the name of the limited liability partnership,

(c) state whether the registered office of the limited liability partnership is to be situated in England and Wales, in Wales, in Scotland or in Northern Ireland,

(d) state the address of that registered office,

(e) give the required particulars of each of the persons who are to be members of the limited liability partnership on incorporation, and

(f) either specify which of those persons are to be designated members or state that every person who from time to time is a member of the limited liability partnership is a designated member.

(2ZA)The required particulars mentioned in subsection (2)(e) are the particulars required to be stated in the LLP's register of members and register of members' residential addresses.

(2A) [...]

(2B) [...]

(3) If a person makes a false statement under subsection (1)(c) which he–

(a) knows to be false, or

(b) does not believe to be true, he commits an offence.

(4) A person guilty of an offence under subsection (3) is liable–

(a) on summary conviction, to imprisonment for a period not exceeding six months or a fine not exceeding the statutory maximum, or to both, or

(b)   on conviction or indictment, to imprisonment for a period not exceeding two years or a fine, or to both.

3.   Incorporation by registration

(1)   The registrar, if satisfied that the requirements of section 2 are complied with, shall–

   (a)   register the documents delivered under that section, and

   (b)   give a certificate that the limited liability partnership is incorporated.

(1A)   The certificate must state–

   (a)   the name and registered number of the limited liability partnership,

   (b)   the date of its incorporation, and

   (c)   whether the limited liability partnership's registered office is situated in England and Wales (or in Wales), in Scotland or in Northern Ireland.

(2)   The registrar may accept the statement delivered under paragraph (c) of subsection (1) of section 2 as sufficient evidence that the requirement imposed by paragraph (a) of that subsection has been complied with.

(3)   The certificate shall either be signed by the registrar or be authenticated by his official seal.

(4)   The certificate is conclusive evidence that the requirements of section 2 are complied with and that the limited liability partnership is incorporated by the name specified in the incorporation document.

Membership

4.   Members

(1)   On the incorporation of a limited liability partnership its members are the persons who subscribed their names to the incorporation document (other than any who have died or been dissolved).

(2)   Any other person may become a member of a limited liability partnership by and in accordance with an agreement with the existing members.

(3)   A person may cease to be a member of a limited liability partnership (as well as by death or dissolution) in accordance with an agreement with the other members or, in the absence of

agreement with the other members as to cessation of member-ship, by giving reasonable notice to the other members.

(4)   A member of a limited liability partnership shall not be regarded for any purpose as employed by the limited liability partnership unless, if he and the other members were partners in a partner-ship, he would be regarded for that purpose as employed by the partnership.

4A.   Minimum membership for carrying on business

(1)   This section applies where a limited liability partnership carries on business without having at least two members, and does so for more than 6 months.

(2)   A person who, for the whole or any part of the period that it so carries on business after those 6 months–

(a)   is a member of the limited liability partnership, and

(b)   knows that it is carrying on business with only one member,

is liable (jointly and severally with the limited liability partner-ship) for the payment of the limited liability partnership's debts contracted during the period or, as the case may be, that part of it.

5.   Relationship of members etc.

(1)   Except as far as otherwise provided this Act or any other enactment, the mutual rights and duties of the members of a limited liability partnership, and the mutual rights and duties of a limited liability partnership and its members, shall be gov-erned–

(a)   by agreement between the members, or between the limited liability partnership, and its members, or

(b)   in the absence of agreement as to any matter, by any provision made in relation to that matter by regulations under section 15(c).

(2)   An agreement made before the incorporation of a limited liabil-ity partnership between the persons who subscribe their names to the incorporation document may impose obligations on the limited liability partnership (to take effect at any time after its incorporation).

6. Members as agents

(1)   Every member of a limited liability partnership is the agent of the limited liability partnership.

(2)   But a limited liability partnership is not bound by anything done by a member in dealing with a person if–

(a)   the member in fact has no authority to act for the limited liability partnership by doing that thing, and

(b)   the person knows that he has no authority or does not know or believe him to be a member of the limited liability partnership.

(3)   Where a person has ceased to be a member of a limited liability partnership, the former member is to be regarded (in relation to any person dealing with the limited liability partnership) as still being a member of the limited liability partnership unless–

(a)   the person has notice that the former member has ceased to be a member of the limited liability partnership, or

(b)   notice that the former member has ceased to be a member of the limited liability partnership has been delivered to the registrar.

(4)   Where a member of a limited liability partnership is liable to any person (other than another member of the limited liability partnership) as a result of a wrongful act or omission of his in the course of the business of the limited liability partnership or with its authority, the limited liability partnership is liable to the same extent as the member.

7. Ex-members

(1)   This section applies where a member of a limited liability partnership has either ceased to be a member or–

(a)   has died,

(b)   has become bankrupt or had his estate sequestrated or has been wound up,

(c)   has granted a trust deed for the benefit of his creditors, or

(d)   has assigned the whole or any part of his share in the limited liability partnership (absolutely or by way of charge or security).

(2)   In such an event the former member or–

(a)   his personal representative,

(b)   his trustee in bankruptcy or permanent or interim trustee (within the meaning of the Bankruptcy (Scotland) Act 1985) or liquidator,

(c)   his trustee under the trust deed for the benefit of his creditors, or

(d)   his assignee,

may not interfere in the management or administration of any business or affairs of the limited liability partnership.

(3)   But subsection (2) does not affect any right to receive an amount from the limited liability partnership in that event.

8.   Designated members

(1)   If the incorporation document specifies who are to be designated members–

(a)   they are designated members on incorporation, and

(b)   any member may become a designated member by and in accordance with an agreement with the other members,

and a member may cease to be a designated member in accordance with an agreement with the other members.

(2)   But if there would otherwise be no designated members, or only one, every member is a designated member.

(3)   If the incorporation document states that every person who from time to time is a member of the limited liability partnership is a designated member, every member is a designated member.

(4)   A limited liability partnership may at any time deliver to the registrar–

(a)   notice that specified members are to be designated members, or

(b)   notice that every person who from time to time is a member of the limited liability partnership is a designated member, and, once it is delivered, subsection (1) (apart from paragraph (a)) and subsection (2), or subsection (3), shall have effect as if that were stated in the incorporation document.

(5)   [...]

(6)   A person ceases to be a designated member if he ceases to be a member.

9. Registration of membership changes

(1) A limited liability partnership must ensure that–

(a) where a person becomes or ceases to be a member or designated member, notice is delivered to the registrar within fourteen days, and

(b) where there is any change in the particulars contained in its register of members or its register of members' residential addresses, notice is delivered to the registrar within 14 days.

(2) Where all the members from time to time of a limited liability partnership are designated members, subsection (1)(a) does not require notice that a person has become or ceased to be a designated member as well as a member.

(3) A notice delivered under subsection (1) that relates to a person becoming a member or designated member must contain–

(a) a statement that the member or designated member consents to acting in that capacity, and

(b) in the case of a person becoming a member, a statement of the particulars of the new member that are required to be included in the limited liability partnership's register of members and its register of residential addresses.

(3ZA)Where–

(a) a limited liability partnership gives notice of a change of a member's service address as stated in its register of members, and

(b) the notice is not accompanied by notice of any resulting change in the particulars contained in its register of members' residential addresses,

the notice must be accompanied by a statement that no such change is required.

(3A) [...]

(3B) [...]

(4) If a limited liability partnership fails to comply with this section, the partnership and every designated member commits an offence.

(5) But it is a defence for a designated member charged with an offence under subsection (4) to prove that he took all reasonable steps for securing that this section was complied with.

(6) A person guilty of an offence under subsection (4) is liable on summary conviction to a fine not exceeding level 5 on the standard scale.

Taxation

10. Income tax and chargeable gains

(1) [...]

(2) [...]

(3) In the Taxation of Chargeable Gains Act 1992, after section 59 insert–

'59A Limited liability partnerships.

(1) Where a limited liability partnership carries on a trade or business with a view to profit–

    (a) assets held by the limited liability partnership shall be treated for the purposes of tax in respect of chargeable gains as held by its members as partners, and

    (b) any dealings by the limited liability partnership shall be treated for those purposes as dealings by its members in partnership (and not by the limited liability partnership as such), and tax in respect of chargeable gains accruing to the members of the limited liability partnership on the disposal of any of its assets shall be assessed and charged on them separately.

(2) Where subsection (1) ceases to apply in relation to a limited liability partnership with the effect that tax is assessed and charged–

    (a) on the limited liability partnership (as a company) in respect of chargeable gains accruing on the disposal of any of its assets, and

    (b) on the members in respect of chargeable gains accruing on the disposal of any of their capital interests in the limited liability partnership, it shall be assessed and charged on the limited liability partnership as if subsection (1) had never applied in relation to it.

(3) Neither the commencement of the application of subsection (1) nor the cessation of its application in relation to a limited liability partnership is to be taken as giving rise to the disposal of any assets by it or any of its members.'

(4) After section 156 of that Act insert–

'156A Cessation of trade by limited liability partnership.

(1) Where, immediately before the time of cessation of trade, a member of a limited liability partnership holds an asset, or an interest in an asset, acquired by him for a consideration treated as reduced under section 152 or 153, he shall be treated as if a chargeable gain equal to the amount of the reduction accrued to him immediately before that time.

(2) Where, as a result of section 154(2), a chargeable gain on the disposal of an asset, or an interest in an asset, by a member of a limited liability partnership has not accrued before the time of cessation of trade, the member shall be treated as if the chargeable gain accrued immediately before that time.

(3) In this section "the time of cessation of trade", in relation to a limited liability partnership, means the time when section 59A(1) ceases to apply in relation to the limited liability partnership.'

11. Inheritance tax

In the Inheritance Tax Act 1984, after section 267 insert–

'267A Limited liability partnerships.

For the purposes of this Act and any other enactments relating to inheritance tax–

(a) property to which a limited liability partnership is entitled, or which it occupies or uses, shall be treated as property to which its members are entitled, or which they occupy or use, as partners,

(b) any business carried on by a limited liability partnership shall be treated as carried on in partnership by its members,

(c) incorporation, change in membership or dissolution of a limited liability partnership shall be treated as formation, alteration or dissolution of a partnership, and

(d) any transfer of value made by or to a limited liability partnership shall be treated as made by or to its members in partnership (and not by or to the limited liability partnership as such).'

12. Stamp duty

(1) Stamp duty shall not be chargeable on an instrument by which property is conveyed or transferred by a person to a limited liability partnership in connection with its incorporation within the period of one year beginning with the date of incorporation if the following two conditions are satisfied.

(2) The first condition is that at the relevant time the person–

(a) is a partner in a partnership comprised of all the persons who are or are to be members of the limited liability partnership (and no-one else), or

(b) holds the property conveyed or transferred as nominee or bare trustee for one or more of the partners in such a partnership.

(3) The second condition is that–

(a) the proportions of the property conveyed or transferred to which the persons mentioned in subsection (2)(a) are entitled immediately after the transfer are the same as those to which they were entitled at the relevant time, or

(b) none of the differences in those proportions has arisen as part of a scheme or arrangement of which the main purpose, or one of the main purposes, is avoidance of liability to any duty or tax.

(4) For the purposes of subsection (2) a person holds property as bare trustee for a partner if the partner has the exclusive right (subject only to satisfying any outstanding charge, lien or other right of the trustee to resort to the property for payment of duty, taxes, costs or other outgoings) to direct how the property shall be dealt with.

(5) In this section 'the relevant time' means–

(a) if the person who conveyed or transferred the property to the limited liability partnership acquired the property after its incorporation, immediately after he acquired the property, and

494

(b) in any other case, immediately before its incorporation.

(6) An instrument in respect of which stamp duty is not chargeable by virtue of subsection (1) shall not be taken to be duly stamped unless–

(a) it has, in accordance with section 12 of the Stamp Act 1891, been stamped with a particular stamp denoting that it is not chargeable with any duty or that it is duly stamped, or

(b) it is stamped with the duty to which it would be liable apart from that subsection.

13. Class 4 national insurance contributions

In section 15 of the Social Security Contributions and Benefits Act 1992 and section 15 of the Social Security Contributions and Benefits (Northern Ireland) Act 1992 (Class 4 contributions), after subsection (3) insert–

'(3A) Where income tax is (or would be) charged on a member of a limited liability partnership in respect of profits or gains arising from the carrying on of a trade or profession by the limited liability partnership, Class 4 contributions shall be payable by him if they would be payable were the trade or profession carried on in partnership by the members.'

Regulations

14. Insolvency and winding up

(1) Regulations shall make provision about the insolvency and winding up of limited liability partnerships by applying or incorporating, with such modifications as appear appropriate–

(a) in relation to a limited liability partnership registered in Great Britain, Parts 1 to 4, 6 and 7 of the Insolvency Act 1986;

(b) in relation to a limited liability partnership registered in Northern Ireland, Parts 2 to 5 and 7 of the Insolvency (Northern Ireland) Order 1989, and so much of Part 1 of that Order as applies for the purposes of those Parts.

(2) Regulations may make other provision about the insolvency and winding up of limited liability partnerships, and provision about the insolvency and winding up of oversea limited liability partnerships, by–

(a) applying or incorporating, with such modifications as appear appropriate, any law relating to the insolvency or

495

winding up of companies or other corporations which would not otherwise have effect in relation to them, or

(b) providing for any law relating to the insolvency or winding up of companies or other corporations which would otherwise have effect in relation to them not to apply to them or to apply to them with such modifications as appear appropriate.

(3) In this Act 'oversea limited liability partnership' means a body incorporated or otherwise established outside the United Kingdom and having such connection with the United Kingdom, and such other features, as regulations may prescribe.

15. Application of company law etc.

Regulations may make provision about limited liability partnerships and oversea limited liability partnerships (not being provision about insolvency or winding up) by–

(a) applying or incorporating, with such modifications as appear appropriate, any law relating to companies or other corporations which would not otherwise have effect in relation to them,

(b) providing for any law relating to companies or other corporations which would otherwise have effect in relation to them not to apply to them or to apply to them with such modifications as appear appropriate, or

(c) applying or incorporating, with such modifications as appear appropriate, any law relating to partnerships.

16. Consequential amendments

(1) Regulations may make in any enactment such amendments or repeals as appear appropriate in consequence of this Act or regulations made under it.

(2) The regulations may, in particular, make amendments and repeals affecting companies or other corporations or partnerships.

17. General

(1) In this Act 'regulations' means regulations made by the Secretary of State by statutory instrument.

(2) Regulations under this Act may in particular–

(a) make provision for dealing with non-compliance with any of the regulations (including the creation of criminal offences),

(b)   impose fees (which shall be paid into the Consolidated Fund), and

(c)   provide for the exercise of functions by persons prescribed by the regulations.

(3)   Regulations under this Act may–

(a)   contain any appropriate consequential, incidental, supplementary or transitional provisions or savings, and

(b)   make different provision for different purposes.

(4)   No regulations to which this subsection applies shall be made unless a draft of the statutory instrument containing the regulations (whether or not together with other provisions) has been laid before, and approved by a resolution of, each House of Parliament.

(5)   Subsection (4) applies to–

(a)   regulations under section 14(2) not consisting entirely of the application or incorporation (with or without modifications) of provisions contained in or made under the Insolvency Act 1986 or the Insolvency (Northern Ireland) Order 1989,

(b)   regulations under section 15 not consisting entirely of the application or incorporation (with or without modifications) of provisions contained in or made under the following provisions of the Companies Act 2006 (c. 46)–

Part 4 (a company's capacity and related matters);

Part 5 (a company's name);

Part 6 (a company's registered office);

Chapters 1 and 8 of Part 10 (register of directors);

Part 15 (accounts and reports);

Part 16 (audit);

Part 19 (debentures);

Part 21 (certification and transfer of securities);

Part 24 (a company's annual return);

Part 25 (company charges);

Part 26 (arrangements and reconstructions);

Part 29 (fraudulent trading);

Part 30 (protection of members against unfair prejudice);

Part 31 (dissolution and restoration to the register);

Part 35 (the registrar of companies);

Part 36 (offences under the Companies Acts);

Part 37 (supplementary provisions);

Part 38 (interpretation).

   (c)   regulations under section 14 or 15 making provision about oversea limited liability partnerships, and

   (d)   regulations under section 16.

(6)   A statutory instrument containing regulations under this Act shall (unless a draft of it has been approved by a resolution of each House of Parliament) be subject to annulment in pursuance of a resolution of either House of Parliament.

Supplementary

18. Interpretation

In this Act–

[...]

'business' includes every trade, profession and occupation,

'designated member' shall be construed in accordance with section 8,

'enactment' includes subordinate legislation (within the meaning of the Interpretation Act 1978),

'incorporation document' shall be construed in accordance with section 2,

'limited liability partnership' has the meaning given by section 1(2),

'member' shall be construed in accordance with section 4,

'modifications' includes additions and omissions,

'name', in relation to a member of a limited liability partnership, means–

   (a)   if an individual, his forename and surname (or, in the case of a peer or other person usually known by a title, his title instead of or in addition to either or both his forename and surname), and

   (b)   if a corporation or Scottish firm, its corporate or firm name, 'oversea limited liability partnership' has the meaning given by section 14(3),

'the registrar' means–

    (a)   if the registered office of the limited liability partnership is, or is to be, in England and Wales (or Wales), the registrar of companies for England and Wales,

    (b)   if the registered office of the limited liability partnership is, or is to be, in Scotland, the registrar of companies for Scotland, and

    (c)   if the registered office of the limited liability partnership is, or is to be, in Northern Ireland, the registrar of companies for Northern Ireland;

'regulations' has the meaning given by section 17(1).

19. Commencement, extent and short title

    (1)   The preceding provisions of this Act shall come into force on such day as the Secretary of State may by order made by statutory instrument appoint; and different days may be appointed for different purposes.

    (2)   The Secretary of State may by order made by statutory instrument make any transitional provisions and savings which appear appropriate in connection with the coming into force of any provision of this Act.

    (3)   For the purposes of the Scotland Act 1998 this Act shall be taken to be a pre-commencement enactment within the meaning of that Act.

    (4)   This Act extends to the whole of the United Kingdom.

    (5)   This Act may be cited as the Limited Liability Partnerships Act 2000.

SCHEDULE

Names and Registered Offices

PART I — NAMES

1.   [...]

Name to indicate status

2.   (1)   The name of a limited liability partnership must end with–

    (a)   the expression 'limited liability partnership', or

      (b)   the abbreviation 'llp' or 'LLP'.

  (2)   But if the incorporation document for a limited liability partnership states that the registered office is to be situated in Wales, its name must end with—

      (a)   one of the expressions 'limited liability partnership' and 'partneriaeth atebolrwydd cyfyngedig', or

      (b)   one of the abbreviations 'llp', 'LLP', 'pac' and 'PAC'.

3.   [...]

Change of name

4.   (1)   A limited liability partnership may change its name at any time.

    (2)   The name of a limited liability partnership may also be changed—

      (a)   on the determination of a new name by a company names adjudicator under section 73 of the Companies Act 2006 (c. 46) as applied to limited liability partnerships (powers of adjudicator on upholding objection to name);

      (b)   on the determination of a new name by the court under section 74 of the Companies Act 2006 as so applied (appeal against decision of company names adjudicator);

      (c)   under section 1033 as so applied (name on restoration to the register).

Notification of change of name

5.   (1)   Where a limited liability partnership changes its name it shall deliver notice of the change to the registrar.

    (2)   [...]

    (3)   Where the registrar receives notice of a change of name he shall (unless the new name is one by which a limited liability partnership may not be registered)–

      (a)   enter the new name on the register in place of the former name, and

      (b)   issue a certificate of the change of name.

(4) The change of name has effect from the date on which the certificate is issued.

Effect of change of name

6.   A change of name by a limited liability partnership does not–

    (a)   affect any of its rights or duties,

    (b)   render defective any legal proceedings by or against it,

and any legal proceedings that might have been commenced or continued against it by its former name may be commenced or continued against it by its new name.

Improper use of 'limited liability partnership' etc

7.   (1)   If any person carries on a business under a name or title which includes as the last words–

    (a)   the expression 'limited liability partnership' or 'partneriaeth atebolrwydd cyfyngedig', or

    (b)   any contraction or imitation of either of those expressions, that person, unless a limited liability partnership or oversea limited liability partnership, commits an offence.

    (2)   A person guilty of an offence under sub-paragraph (1) is liable on summary conviction to a fine not exceeding level 3 on the standard scale.

8.   [...]

PART II — REGISTERED OFFICES

9.   [...]

10.   [...]

Appendix 4 Model Partnership Agreement

[NOTE: This model agreement has been prepared by Maurice Turnor Gardner LLP and is for illustration only. Every firm's needs are unique and it is important to obtain legal and accounting advice when preparing a partnership deed.]

THIS DEED OF PARTNERSHIP is made on [ ], 20[ ] **BETWEEN** the persons whose names and addresses are set out in Schedule 1:

WHEREAS:

(A) The parties carry on business together in partnership as [ ] and wish to enter into this deed for the purpose of setting out the terms and conditions under which they will carry on business together with effect from and including the Effective Date (as defined below).

(B) It is the intention of the parties that this document be executed as a deed.

NOW THIS DEED WITNESSES AND IT IS AGREED as follows:

1. **Interpretation**

    (1) In this deed:

    Accession Agreement means a deed by which a New Partner accedes to the Partnership and to this deed substantially in the form of Schedule 5 and which states his initial Profit Share and capital contribution;

    Accounts means the accounts of the Partnership prepared and approved in accordance with clause 8;

    Accounts Date means [ ] in each year or such other date as may be decided by General Decision;

    Accounting Period means the period of one calendar year ending on the Accounts Date, or such other period as is decided from time to time by General Decision;

    Admission Date has the meaning given to it in sub-clause 17(1);

    Appointment has the meaning given to it in sub-clause 13(1);

Approved Appointment has the meaning given to it in sub-clause 13(1);

Approved Liability has the meaning given to it in sub-clause 13(2);

Capital Account means the account to be established for each Partner under sub-clause 5(2);

Current Account means the account to be established for each Partner under sub-clause 6(5);

Effective Date means [ ];

Former Partner means a person who ceases to be a Partner after the Effective Date for any reason (other than the dissolution of the Partnership) and includes the personal representatives of a Former Partner;

General Decision means a decision of the Partnership taken as a General Decision under sub-clause 14(8);

Goodwill means the goodwill of the Partnership;

Losses means, in relation to an Accounting Period, the revenue and capital losses of the Partnership as shown in the Accounts for that Accounting Period;

Management Committee means the members for the time being of the committee constituted under clause 16;

Managing Partner means the person who holds office as Managing Partner from time to time under clause 16;

New Partner means any person admitted as a Partner on or after the Effective Date under clause 17;

Non-Approved Appointment has the meaning given to it in sub-clause 13(1);

Partners means:

(a) those persons listed in Schedule 1; and

(b) every other person who is admitted as a partner in the Partnership after the Effective Date

in each case only until he becomes a Former Partner and Partner means any one of them;

Partnership means the partnership carried on by the Partners under this deed;

Partnership Accountants means [ ] or such other firm of chartered accountants as may be decided from time to time by General Decision;

Partnership Bank means [ ] Bank Plc or such other additional or substitute bank as may be appointed as banker to the Partnership by [General Decision/the Management Committee];

Partnership Business means the business and practice of [ ], any ancillary or related business activity, and any other business or practice which the Partnership may resolve to carry on by [General/Special Decision];

Partnership Interest Rate means the base lending rate of the Partnership Bank plus [ ] per cent per annum or such other rate as may be determined by [the Management Committee/ General Decision/Special Decision];

Partnership Name means the name of [ ] or such other name as may from time to time be adopted by [General/Special] Decision;

Partnership Premises means the offices of the Partnership specified in Schedule 2 and such other offices as the Partners from time to time by [Special/General] Decision decide will be used by the Partnership Business;

Profits means, in relation to an Accounting Period, the revenue and capital profits of the Partnership Business as shown in the Accounts for that Accounting Period;

Profit Share in relation to a Partner means the percentage set out against his name in Schedule 1 or such other percentage as shall be determined from time to time under the provisions of this deed;

Retirement Date means the date when a Partner ceases to be a Partner and becomes a Former Partner by reason of death, expulsion, retirement or otherwise;

[**Senior Partner** means the person who holds offices as such from time to time under clause 16;]

Special Decision means a decision of the Partnership taken as Special Decision under sub-clause 14(9); and

Unanimous Decision means a decision of the Partnership taken as a Unanimous Decision under sub-clause 14(10).

(2)   In interpreting this deed the following rules will be applied unless the context otherwise requires:

(a)   words importing the singular include the plural and vice versa and words importing gender import all genders;

(b)   references to any clause, sub-clause, schedule, paragraph or sub-paragraph are references to that clause in this deed, the sub-clause in the relevant clause in which it appears, a schedule to this deed or the paragraph or sub-paragraph in the relevant sub-clause, paragraph or schedule in which it appears and any schedules to this deed form part of this deed;

(c)   references to statutory provisions, subordinate legislation or professional regulations will be construed as references to those provisions, legislation or regulations as they have been or may be amended or re-enacted or as their application is modified by other provisions from time to time;

(d)   headings to clauses are for reference only and do not affect their interpretation;

(e)   references to this deed or any other instrument include any variation, novation or replacement of any of them; and

(f)   if a period of time is specified and is expressed to run from a given day or the day of an act or event, it is to be calculated exclusive of that day.

(3)   In this deed, unless the context otherwise requires, any reference to:

an **agreement** also includes a contract, deed, licence, undertaking, or other document and includes that agreement as modified, novated or substituted from time to time;

a **law** includes common or customary law and any constitution, decree, judgement, legislation, order, ordinance, regulation, treaty or other legislative measure of England and Wales;

a **person** includes an individual and that person's executors and administrators;

professional regulations includes any directions, standards, rules or regulations of any professional bodies which govern the conduct of any Partner of the Partnership;

rights includes authorities, discretions, remedies, powers and causes of action; and

tax includes any present or future tax, levy, duty, rate, charge, fee, deduction or withholding imposed, assessed or levied by any governmental agency in any part of the world (including national insurance contributions and any other social security or similar contributions wherever imposed) and any interest, penalties, fines, costs, charges and other liabilities arising from or payable in respect of that tax.

2.   Commencement, Effect, Name and Duration

(1)   With effect on and from the Effective Date, the Partners will carry on the Partnership Business in partnership under the Partnership Name in accordance with the provisions of this deed.

(2)   The Partners agree that they will at all times comply with the provisions of the Companies Act 2006 and of any regulation, instrument, rule or order from time to time and for the time being made under that Act.

(3)   The Partnership Name and any abbreviation or combination of it or any registered trade or service marks including or associated with those names, abbreviations and combinations (in this sub-clause the **Names**) and any logos or registered designs derived from or associated with the Names are assets of the Partnership and the use of the Names (or any interest in the Names) may only be licensed, sub-licensed, assigned, transferred or sold to third parties or otherwise disposed of as the Partnership may by [Special Decision] decide. No Partner may sell or dispose of the Names (or any interest in the Names) or use the Names except in connection with the Partnership Business.

(4)   The Partnership will continue upon the terms of this deed for so long as there are at least two Partners or until dissolved under clause 24.

(5)   Subject to clause 2(4), no change in the constitution of the Partnership (whether by reason of death, retirement, expulsion or bankruptcy of any Partner, or appointment of a New Partner or otherwise) shall cause the dissolution of the Partnership.

3.   Place of Business

The Partnership Business shall be carried on in the Partnership Premises.

4. Property and Liabilities

(1) All the assets of the Partnership, including (without limitation) the Goodwill, the Partnership Premises and all property for the time being used for the Partnership Business (other than property belonging personally to any Partner but kept by him upon the Partnership Premises), will be the property of the Partnership.

(2) Any asset of the Partnership not held in the names of all the Partners will be held upon trust for the Partnership by the person in whose name that asset is held, and that person will be indemnified by the Partnership in respect of all liabilities arising in respect of that asset.

5. Capital

(1) The capital of the Partnership will be the sum of [   ].

(2) A Capital Account will be established in the name of each Partner and all amounts contributed to the capital of the Partnership will be credited to his Capital Account and all amounts withdrawn by him from the capital of the Partnership will be debited to his Capital Account. Each Partner will on the Effective Date [contribute] [be deemed to have contributed] to the capital of the Partnership the amount set out opposite his name in Schedule 3 and his Capital Account will be credited accordingly.

(3) With effect on and from the Effective Date, the capital of the Partnership will be contributed by the Partners in proportion to their Profit Shares. Accordingly, on any change in the Partners' Profit Shares, any Partner whose Profit Share has increased will contribute in cash the corresponding amount as additional capital to the Partnership and any Partner whose Profit Share has decreased will be entitled to withdraw the corresponding amount from the capital of the Partnership and his Capital Account will be adjusted accordingly.

(4) The Partners may from time to time decide by [General/ Special] Decision to increase or reduce the capital of the Partnership. Any additional capital which may be required will be contributed by the Partners, and any surplus capital no longer required will be repaid to the Partners, in proportion to their Profit Shares as at the date of that decision and each Partner's Capital Account will be adjusted accordingly.

(5) Where a Partner is shown in the Accounts to have contributed an amount to the capital of the Partnership that is less than the

amount which ought to have been contributed by him, the amount of such deficit will become a debt due by that Partner to the Partnership [and interest thereon will be payable to the Partnership at the Partnership Interest Rate from the time when the deficit first arose].

(6) Subject to clause 22 (Former Partners and their Entitlements) where a Partner is shown in the Accounts to have contributed an amount to the capital of the Partnership that exceeds the amount which ought to have been contributed by him, the excess will be paid out to him as soon as is reasonably practicable [with interest at the Partnership Interest Rate from the time when the excess first arose].

(7) Subject to clause 22 (Former Partners and their Entitlements) and except as expressly provided in this deed or [with the agreement of the Management Committee/by Special Decision]:

(a) no Partner may draw out or receive back any part of his capital contribution to the Partnership during the continuance of the Partnership; and

(b) no Partner is entitled to any interest on the contribution made by him to the capital of the Partnership and no Partner is entitled to any interest on any amount lent by him to the Partnership.

6. Profit Shares and Losses

(1) The Profits and Losses of the Partnership for an Accounting Period are to be shared or borne by the Partners in proportion to their Profit Shares for that Accounting Period.

(2) On the Effective Date the Profit Shares allocated to each Partner are as specified in Schedule 1.

(3) The Profit Share allocated to any New Partner will be as specified in his Accession Agreement.

(4) The Partners may by [General/Special] Decision increase or reduce a Partner's Profit Share from time to time, such increase or reduction to take effect on and from a date specified in that decision.

(5) A Current Account shall be established for each Partner. Subject to sub-clause 5(2), all amounts owed to a Partner the Partnership will be credited to, and all amounts owed by a Partner to the Partnership shall be debited to, his Current Account.

(6) Each Partner will be reimbursed all reasonable and proper out of pocket expenses incurred by him in the performance of his duties under this deed or otherwise on behalf of the Partnership. Each Partner will provide to the Partnership appropriate records of his expenses within such period after the time when those expenses were incurred as the Management Committee may determine.

(7) Each Partner will be indemnified by the Partnership in respect of any liability incurred by him in the ordinary and proper course of the Partnership Business or in or about anything necessarily done for the preservation of the Partnership Business, but any liability occasioned by a Partner by reason of his fraud, dishonesty, wilful default or failure to act in accordance with his duty to act in the utmost good faith in all transactions relating to the other Partners must be made good by that Partner alone.

7. Drawings

(1) Subject to clause 9 (Provision for tax liabilities), the Partners may in any Accounting Period make monthly drawings of such amounts as may from time to time be determined by [General Decision/the Management Committee] on account of their Profit Shares in the relevant Accounting Period.

(2) Any Partner who is shown in the Accounts to have drawn any amount in excess of his share of Profits for that period, after provision for tax liabilities under clause 9, will (within one month of the time when the Accounts have been approved by the Partnership in respect of that Accounting Period under clause 8) refund that excess to the Partnership as soon as is reasonably practicable [together with interest on that amount at the Partnership Interest Rate for the period from the date when he is requested by the Management Committee to make the refund to the date of repayment].

(3) Unless otherwise determined by [Special Decision/the Management Committee], if a Partner is shown in the Accounts to have drawn an amount less than his Profit Share, after provision for tax liabilities under clause 9, that undrawn balance will be credited, within one month of the time when the Accounts have been approved by the Partnership in respect of the relevant Accounting Period under clause 8, to his current account with the Partnership [together with interest on that amount at the Partnership Interest Rate from such date as is determined by the Management Committee to the date of repayment]. When

the Accounts for each Accounting Period have been approved under clause 8, each Partner may draw the amount of the credit balance on his current account (if any) as shown in those Accounts at the times and in the instalments determined by [General Decision/the Management Committee].

(4) Except as expressly provided in this deed, no Partner will be entitled to any interest on any undrawn balance of his share of the Profits.

(5) Losses will be debited to the current accounts of the Partners rateably in accordance with their Profit Shares. If the debit of a Loss to a Partner's current account results in a negative balance on that current account, that Partner will contribute to the Partnership on request by the [Management Committee] an amount equal to that negative balance [together with interest on that amount at the Partnership Interest Rate from the date of that request to the date of payment].

8. Accounts

(1) The Management Committee will ensure that proper books of account and records will be kept by the Partnership of all matters, transactions and things of any kind that are usually entered in such accounts by those engaged in a business similar to the Partnership Business (including details of acquisitions and disposals of Partnership assets).

(2) The Partnership will at all times comply with the requirements of all professional regulations from time to time in force relating to the keeping of records and books of account.

(3) The Management Committee will ensure that the books and records kept under this clause, together with any supporting documentation relating to the Partnership Business (including all those records specified by law) will be kept for at least [six] years after the end of the relevant Accounting Period or for any longer period required by law or professional regulations. The books shall be kept at the Partnership Premises.

(4) Each Partner, his agents and the Partnership Accountants will have access to the books at all times, and may take copies or extracts as they think fit but will be required to treat all those copies and extracts as confidential to the Partners, their advisers and the Partnership Accountants.

(5) Subject to sub-clauses 22(1) and 22(2) at the end of each Accounting Period, Accounts will be produced for the Partnership, comprising a profit and loss account, balance sheet and

any other information which the Partnership is required by law or professional regulations to produce from time to time. The Accounts will be prepared upon such basis and within such period, in accordance with generally accepted accounting principles and practices, as may be recommended by the Partnership Accountants or otherwise determined by [General/Special] Decision.

(6) No account will be taken in the Accounts of the value of Goodwill.

(7) As soon as the Accounts have been prepared, and not later than six months after the relevant Account Date, those Accounts will be submitted:

    (a) to each Partner; and

    (b) to any Former Partner in respect of whom a retention has been made under clause 9.

(8) The Accounts will be considered by the Partners at a general meeting and will only be binding on all the Partners once approved by [General/Special] Decision. Once approved, the Partners hereby authorise any two members of the Management Committee to sign the Accounts on behalf of the Partnership.

(9) If the Accounts are not approved by [General/Special] Decision, any Partner may refer any point of dispute for resolution in accordance with clause 25.

(10) The books of account and records maintained for the purposes of complying with this clause will be subject to audit by the Partnership Accountants in respect of each Accounting Period.

9. Provision for Tax Liabilities

(1) Except as otherwise determined by the Management Committee the Partnership will retain such proportion of each Partner's share of the Profits in any Accounting Period as the Management Committee recommends is appropriate to meet that Partner's individual tax liability (if any) in respect of those Profits (whenever and wherever that tax may be payable and whether payable by the Partners or the Partnership). Where Profits are allocated under this deed to Partners but tax is payable in relation to those Profits in a different Accounting Period [the Management Committee/ the Partners by General/ Special Decision] may make such adjustments as between Partners as,

so far as reasonably practicable, shall procure that, in accordance with prevailing rules of accounting for deferred tax, the burden of tax in relation to those Profits is borne by those Partners who have had the benefit of those Profits.

(2)   Sums retained in respect of a Partner under sub-clause (1) will (even if he has since become a Former Partner) be paid on his behalf to the relevant tax authority when and to the extent necessary to meet the liability for which retention has been made. Once and to the extent paid to the relevant tax authority the debt to the Partners shall be discharged if and to the extent that such payment is made.

(3)   Sums retained in respect of each Partner or Former Partner under sub-clause (1) will be paid or released to him only when and to the extent considered by the Management Committee to be in excess of the necessary retention. In the event of a dispute between a Partner or Former Partner and the Management Committee as to the amount of the retention that is necessary, the decision of the Partnership Accountants (acting as experts and not as arbitrators) will be final and binding in the absence of manifest error.

(4)   The Management Committee will make its recommendations under sub-clauses (1) and (3):

(a)   on a basis which is consistent between the Partners and Former Partners;

(b)   assuming that all personal allowances and reliefs available to a Partner or Former Partner will be set against his income and gains from the Partnership before being set against other income and gains.

10. Bank Accounts

(1)   The Management Committee will ensure that all bank accounts required for the purposes of or in connection with the Partnership Business will be maintained with the Partnership Bank and will include the Partnership Name. This requirement does not apply to an account in the name of a client of the Partnership.

(2)   All Partnership receipts will promptly be paid into and deposited with the Partnership Bank to the credit of the Partnership.

(3)   All cheques drawn on the bank accounts of the Partnership will be drawn in the name of the Partnership.

(4)   All cheques, bills of exchange and other bank transfers or other instruments pledging the credit or affecting the property of the

Partnership will be signed on behalf of the Partnership by any [two] Partners unless otherwise decided by [General/Special] Decision.

(5) All monies and all securities received on behalf or for the account of a client or third party will (except as required for the matter in hand on behalf of that client or third party) promptly:

   (a) be paid or delivered to that client or third party; or

   (b) be paid into or deposited with the Partnership Bank in a client account or statutory client account (as the case may be) which is separate and distinct from any account relating to the property of the Partnership; or

   (c) otherwise be dealt with in a manner authorised by any law or professional regulations.

11. Insurance

(1) The Management Committee will ensure that the Partnership is insured against the following:

   (a) employers liability and any other liability against which it is required to be insured by any law or professional regulations;

   (b) liability for professional negligence of the Partners, Former Partners and employees former employees of and consultants to the Partnership;

   (c) liability of the Partnership to third parties for death, injury or illness, and for damage to third party property;

   (d) loss or damage to Partnership assets, including Partnership Premises;

   (e) liability of the Partnership as occupiers of the Partnership Premises; and

   (f) such other risks as the Management Committee may determine.

(2) The Management Committee may arrange any insurance with any insurer, on the terms and subject to the conditions, exclusions, limits and deductibles (or any other self insurance or captive insurance arrangements), as it thinks fit.

(3) In respect of all insurances effected for the benefit of the Partners, Former Partners and employees, former employees of and consultants to the Partnership the following will be treated as expenses of the Partnership:

(a) all premiums payable in respect of those insurances and all broker and adviser fees;

(b) all sums expended pursuant to any deductible or excess borne by the Partnership; and

(c) all sums expended for the account of the Partnership by reason only of the insufficiency of the limit of insurance or the failure (for any reason) of the insurers to meet any valid policy claim.

(4) The benefit of any professional negligence or other liability insurance and of any claim or recovery made under it, will be held in trust for the Partners, Former Partners and employees and former employees and consultants to the Partnership rateably with their respective shares of liability for the matter that was the subject of the insurance claim under this deed.

12. Duties

(1) Each Partner will at all times:

(a) act diligently in the conduct of the Partnership Business;

(b) act with the utmost good faith in all transactions relating to the other Partners and the Partnership;

(c) disclose to the Management Committee on request full details of all business transactions by him or at his direction for the account of the Partnership;

(d) provide the Management Committee with the information concerning the Partnership Business in his knowledge or possession that the Management Committee requests;

(e) comply with any law or professional regulations to which the Partnership or the Partner is or may become subject in that capacity and use reasonable endeavours to comply with any other law or contractual or other legal obligations of which he is aware;

(f) use the Partnership Name in all business transactions of the Partnership;

(g) except as otherwise determined by the Management Committee, account to the Partnership for any money or thing representing money including all gifts and legacies received from a third party in the course of the Partnership Business.

(2)   Unless a [General Decision/the Management Committee] determines otherwise in any particular instance:

(a)   subject to clauses 21 (Gardening Leave) and 27 (Holidays, Maternity and Paternity Leave) each Partner will devote his whole time and attention to the Partnership Business during normal business hours and at any other time when it is necessary to do so to enable him to perform his duties to the Partnership or any of its clients;

(b)   subject to clause 13 (Appointments and Approved Liabilities) a Partner will not become a sole trader or a partner in any business other than the Partnership Business or be a director of any company other than a company owned by the Partnership or be a member of a limited liability partnership except on behalf of the Partnership or be or become a member of Lloyd's or hold any shares in any company with unlimited liability;

(c)   a Partner will not do or omit to do any act or thing the doing or omission of which will bring or tend to bring the Partnership into disrepute;

(d)   a Partner will not, otherwise than as required by law, assign, declare any trust of, transfer or create a security interest over any legal or beneficial interest in his share in the Partnership or any part of the Profits of the Partnership;

(e)   a Partner will not lend any money or other property of the Partnership or, in the context of the Partnership Business, give credit to or act for or have any dealing with any person, company or firm with whom the Management Committee has previously requested him not to deal;

(f)   except within his authority as Partner, insofar as his advisers and any court, expert or arbitrator need to be informed in order to resolve any dispute under this deed or as required by law, a Partner or Former Partner will not use to the detriment or prejudice of the Partnership (or divulge to any person other than another Partner in any way which could reasonably be foreseen to risk any detriment to the Partnership or any of its clients) any confidential information concerning the business, investment or affairs of the Partnership or any of its clients. In this paragraph confidential information includes (without limitation) any information relating to this deed, the Accounts, the books of the Partnership, the financial position of the

Partnership, any decision of the Partnership (including a decision of the Management Committee) or any matter affecting the rights and obligations of the Partners or Former Partners or the management of the Partnership. However, a Former Partner may disclose the terms of the restrictions imposed on Former Partners under this clause and clause 23 (Covenants); and

(g) all intellectual property rights created, directly or indirectly by a Partner and relating directly or indirectly to the Partnership Business shall belong to the Partnership.

13. Appointments and Approved Liabilities

(1) (a) Partners must not accept or hold any charitable or non-charitable trusteeships, offices or appointments including (without limitation) appointment as a director of a company, a member of a limited liability partnership, an executor, an administrator or trustee of any will, estate or settlement (**Appointments**) except in accordance with this clause.

(b) Unless otherwise agreed by the Management Committee, every Appointment will be deemed to be held for the account of the Partnership. Those Appointments that the Management Committee agree will not be held for the account of the Partnership are referred to in this clause as Non-Approved Appointments.

(c) A register (the **Register**) of all Appointments will be maintained by the Management Committee specifying whether or not an Appointment is a Non-Approved Appointment or an Appointment held on behalf of the Partnership (an **Approved Appointment**) and the Register will be open to inspection by all Partners.

(2) (a) If any Partner incurs a liability (otherwise than by reason of his own fraud or dishonesty) in connection with or as a result of an Approved Appointment (an **Approved Liability**):

(i) that Approved Liability and any costs or expenses incurred by that Partner in or about contesting, compromising, admitting or compounding it will be a liability of the Partnership;

(ii) that Partner will be entitled to the same rights of indemnity and contribution from the other Partners

516

as if that Approved Liability had been incurred by him in the ordinary and proper course of the Partnership Business; and

(iii) that Partner must take such action at the expense of the Partnership as any insurer which is on risk in respect of the Approved Liability or the Management Committee may from time to time require to recoup all or any sums within the scope of this clause from any assets (other than his own) or from any person (other than himself) who may be liable in respect thereof and he must account to the Partnership for all sums so recouped.

(b) If any Partner incurs a liability in connection with an Appointment which is not an Approved Liability, the Partnership will have no responsibility for that liability and he will not be entitled to any rights of indemnity and contribution from the other Partners.

(3) All Approved Appointments other than those which are required to be held in the name of an individual must be held in the name of the Partnership and not in the name of any Partner.

(4) Unless otherwise agreed by the Management Committee, all fees, profits, remuneration, emoluments or other benefits received by a Partner (including, without limitation, all fees and payments received by a Partner arising from his acting as a company director or dividends or other payments received by virtue of a Partner holding shares in any company on trust for the Partnership) in respect of:

(a) any Appointment which is not a Non-Approved Appointment, will be received by him for the account of the Partnership and must be paid by him to the Partnership within seven days of receipt;

(b) any Non-Approved Appointment, will not be received by him for the account of the Partnership but will be held for his own personal account.

14. Meetings and Procedures for Decision-Making

(1) A meeting of the Partners may be convened at any time by the [Senior Partner,] [Managing Partner, the] [Management Committee] or on the written request of any Partner to the Management Committee.

(2)   (a)   Subject to paragraph (b), the Management Committee will in all cases determine the time, date and place of each meeting of the Partners and the nature of the business to be transacted.

      (b)   Any Partner may submit a matter for discussion at a meeting of the Partners to the [Senior Partner] [or] the [Managing Partner] before commencement of that meeting.

      (c)   Any meeting of the Partners shall be chaired by the [Senior Partner] or in his absence [by the person appointed for the purpose by [General/Special Resolution].

(3)   Subject to sub-clause (4), each Partner will have one vote at any meeting of the Partners.

(4)   (a)   The chairperson of the meeting will have a casting vote where a deadlock exists and may cast his second vote as he thinks fit.

      (b)   No Partner who has been required to retire from the Partnership by a Special Decision under clause 19, no Partner who has served a notice to retire as a Partner under clause 20 and no Partner who is absent from the Partnership under clause 21 (unless otherwise agreed by the Management Committee), will be eligible to vote for any purpose but no decision may adversely affect his interests without his written consent unless it applies fairly to all Partners.

      (c)   A Partner subject to a Special Decision under sub-clause 18(1) or sub-clause 21(2)(a) will not be entitled to vote on that matter.

(5)   (a)   Any Partner may be represented at any meeting by appointing another Partner as a proxy and that proxy will vote on the directions of the Partner in favour of or against any decision taken at the meeting. Written proof of appointment must be presented by that proxy to the chair of the meeting prior to commencement of the meeting.

      (b)   A vote cast by a proxy which complies with the terms of his appointment will count as the vote of the Partner making the appointment, and that Partner will be deemed for all the purposes of this deed to have been present at the meeting and to have voted on the matter.

(6) The quorum for any meeting of the Partners will be fifty per cent of all the Partners.

(7) A Unanimous Decision, a Special Decision and a General Decision will bind all Partners.

(8) (a) For a General Decision to be validly taken [seven] clear days notice in writing must be given to all Partners. A lesser period of notice may be agreed in writing by [ninety per cent] in number of all Partners.

    (b) General Decisions must be made at a meeting of the Partners on a show of hands by a simple majority of those Partners present and voting at the meeting (whether in person or by proxy).

(9) A Special Decision will be taken in the same way as a General Decision except that at least [seventy-five per cent] by number of all the Partners (whether present and voting or not) must be present at the meeting (whether in person or by proxy) and vote in favour of the resolution.

(10) A Unanimous Decision may be taken:

    (a) at any meeting of the Partners on a show of hands provided all Partners vote in favour of the decision (whether in person or by proxy); or

    (b) with the written approval of all the Partners in which case no meeting of the Partners is required for the making of that decision.

(11) The accidental omission to give notice of a meeting to, or the non-receipt of notice of a meeting by, any [two] or less Partners entitled to receive notice will not invalidate the proceedings of a meeting or a decision made by the Partnership.

15. Unanimous and Special Decisions

(1) In addition to any other matters referred to in this deed, the following matters will be determined by [Unanimous/Special] Decision:

    (a) the transfer or vesting of any part of the Partnership Business to or into a body corporate, limited liability partnership or any analogous entity or the merger of the Partnership Business with that of any other person;

    (b) any acquisition by the Partnership of any business or part of a business or company or part of a company for valuable consideration or any disposal by the Partnership of any business or part of a business or company or part of a company for valuable consideration; and

(c)   any acquisition or disposal of freehold or leasehold property.

16. Managing Partner, [Senior Partner] and Management Committee

(1)   The Management Committee will be comprised of the [Senior Partner, the] Managing Partner and [ ] other Partners. With effect on and from the Effective Date the Management Committee will be comprised of the Partners specified in Part I of Schedule 4.

(2)   Except where otherwise specifically provided in this deed any matter connected with the conduct and management of the Partnership Business will be decided by the Management Committee which will exercise its powers and discretions in the best interests of the Partnership as a whole.

(3)   Any decision of the Management Committee made in accordance with this deed binds the Partners and the Partnership.

(4)   The quorum necessary at meetings for the transaction of business by the Management Committee is [ ] members present in person or by telephone.

(5)   (a)   A member of the Management Committee will cease to be a member on the earlier of his ceasing to be a Partner and the [ ] anniversary of his most recent appointment but in the latter case he shall be eligible for re-appointment. The Partners may from time to time by [Special/General] Decision (i) remove any member of the Management Committee (ii) appoint another Partner to replace that member so removed or to replace any member of the Management Committee who has ceased to be a member of the Management Committee for any other reason or (iii) appoint an additional member of the Management Committee. Nominations for all such appointments must be given to the continuing members of the Management Committee at least 14 days prior to a general meeting of the Partners.

(b)   A member of the Management Committee may voluntarily stand down from the Management Committee on giving at least 2 months notice to the continuing members and the Partners must replace that member in accordance with paragraph (a) above.

(6)   Subject to sub-clause (6), the Management Committee will meet together for the despatch of business, adjourn and otherwise regulate its meetings as it thinks fit.

(7)   Matters arising at any meeting of the Management Committee will be determined by a simple majority of votes of the members of the Management Committee who are present and voting thereon on the basis of one vote per member. For the avoidance of doubt, the Managing Partner [and the Senior Partner] will not have a casting vote for the purposes of this sub-clause.

(8)   (a)   With effect from and including the Effective Date, the offices of Managing Partner [and Senior Partner] will be filled by the Partner specified in Part[s] [II and III] of Schedule 4 respectively. The provisions of sub-clause (4) will apply mutatis mutandis to the removal, retirement and appointment of the Managing Partner [and the Senior Partner].

        (b)   The Managing Partner [and the Senior Partner] may delegate to any Partner anything required to be done by him and the actions of the delegate will bind the Partners and the Partnership as if they were carried out by the Managing Partner [or the Senior Partner (as appropriate)] himself. In the absence of [the Senior Partner], or if he is unavailable, and notwithstanding any delegation of his powers under this sub-clause, any notice required to be given to him must be given to any one or more of the other members of the Management Committee.

17. Admission of New Partners

(1)   A New Partner may at any time be admitted by Special Decision which decision will specify his date of admittance to the Partnership (his **Admission Date**).

(2)   The admission of a New Partner is conditional upon the execution by him of an Accession Agreement approved by the Partners (excluding the New Partner) by Special Decision, on or before his Admission Date or, if later, within [ ] months of the date of the decision referred to in sub-clause (1). This Agreement will then be construed as though he had been a Partner with effect from the Admission Date.

(3)   The Accession Agreement will state the New Partner's initial capital contribution and his Profit Share. The Profit Shares of

the existing Partners shall be reduced in proportion to their Profit Shares by the percentage necessary to accommodate the New Partner's Profit Shares.

18. Expulsion

(1) A Partner will immediately cease to be a Partner upon being served with a notice in writing of a Special Decision expelling him following any of the events listed below:

(a) if he wilfully or persistently acts in a manner contrary to his material obligations under this deed or is guilty of any grave professional misconduct; or

(b) if he is convicted (unless quashed on appeal) of any criminal offence involving dishonesty; or

(c) if he commits any act of bankruptcy or is adjudicated bankrupt or enters into any composition, scheme or arrangement with his creditors or the equivalent in any relevant jurisdiction; or

(d) if he creates or purports to create a security interest over any legal or beneficial interest in his share in the Partnership including (without limitation) his account with the Partnership or any part of the Profits of the Partnership for his separate debt; or

(e) if he has become incapacitated by mental or physical illness, ill-health, accident or otherwise from performing his duties, obligations or responsibilities hereunder for a continuous period of [ ] months.

(2) A Partner will immediately cease to be a Partner if the Partnership would otherwise be dissolved by operation of law because he has lost or fails to hold a relevant qualification or to satisfy a relevant professional regulation.

19. Compulsory Retirement and Retirement due to Death

A Partner will retire from the Partnership and cease to be a Partner and become a Former Partner on the earlier of his death and the expiration of [six] months from the date of a Special Decision requiring him to retire as a Partner.

20. Voluntary Retirement

Any Partner may retire from the Partnership by giving not less than [six] months previous notice in writing to the Management Committee expiring on an Accounts Date (but any General Decision to amend the Accounts Date that follows such notice will not affect the date of expiry of the notice) except that the Management Committee may agree a shorter period of notice in any individual case whether or not expiring on an Accounts Date.

21. Gardening Leave and Suspension

(1) Where a Partner has been required to retire from the Partnership by a Special Decision under clause 19 or where a Partner has served notice to retire as a Partner under clause 20, the Management Committee may direct by notice to him in writing that during the whole or any part of the period of his notice to retire the retiring Partner:

    (a)   will not enter any of the Partnership Premises;

    (b)   will not contact or have any communication (or may only communicate in specified ways) with any client or employee of the Partnership for any business purpose;

    (c)   will do, or omit from doing, all such things in connection with the Partnership Business as the Management Committee may reasonably require including, for example, carrying out administrative duties or working on non-client matters; and

    (d)   will be subject to the provisions of clause 23 (Covenants) (without prejudice to the application of that clause to him when he ceases to be a Partner).

(2)   (a)   Where there are reasonable grounds for believing that any of the events referred to in clause 18 may apply to a Partner, the Partners may by [Special/General] Decision decide that such Partner will forthwith take no further part in the Partnership Business for a specified period or for a period expiring on further notice (in either case such period not to exceed six months) on such terms as that decision shall determine.

    (b)   Without prejudice to the generality of paragraph (a), the decision may direct that the provisions of sub-clause (1) will apply to the suspended Partner.

    (c)   A Partner who is subject to this sub-clause will, at the expiration of six months from the date of the decision referred to in paragraph (a), be deemed to have retired from the Partnership unless that decision has ceased or been revoked at, or before, the expiration of that period.

    (d)   The revocation of a decision made under this sub-clause will be by [Special/General] Decision.

(3) During any period when sub-clauses (1) or (2) apply, the Partner concerned will continue to be entitled to his share of the Profits and liable for his share of Losses and to drawings on account of those Profits after providing for any amount owed by the Partner to the Partnership but he shall not be entitled to continue to receive any financial or other information circulated or otherwise made available to Partners generally and shall rely on the certificate of the Partnership Accountants as to his financial entitlement and obligations.

22. Former Partners and their Entitlements

(1) As quickly as is reasonably practicable following a Former Partner's Retirement Date which falls other than on the Accounts Date, the Partnership Accountants will prepare Accounts in accordance with the provisions set down in clause 8 as at the Retirement Date for the period from the preceding Accounts Date to the Retirement Date.

(2) The interim accounts prepared under sub-clause (1) will be prepared on the same basis as the Accounts.

(3) Within two months of the Accounts being approved under clause 8 (or otherwise finally determined in accordance with the terms of this deed) (in the case of a Partner who ceases to be a partner on the Accounts Date) or the interim accounts being approved by [Special/General] Decision (in all other cases) and after providing for any amount owed by the Former Partner to the Partnership, the undrawn credit balance, if any, on the Former Partners Current Account will be paid to the Former Partner.

(4) The Partners will [if they make the election specified in sub-clause (5)] pay to the Former Partner a sum equal to the balance, if any, standing to the credit of the Former Partners Capital Account less the debit balance, if any, on his Current Account. Such payment will be made as follows:

   (a) one half plus interest thereon at the Partnership Interest Rate will be paid [twelve] months after the Former Partners Retirement Date;

   (b) one half plus interest thereon at the Partnership Interest Rate will be paid [eighteen] months after the Former Partners Retirement Date

provided always that in the event of the dissolution of the Partnership (otherwise than for the purposes of amalgamation or reconstruction) any outstanding balance due to a Former Partner will immediately become due and payable.

(5) The share of the Former Partner in the capital and assets of the Partnership will [if the Partners so elect by written notice to the Former Partner within six months of his Retirement Date and with effect from his Retirement Date] accrue to the Partners rateably in accordance with their Profit Shares.

[(6) If the Partners make no election under sub-clause (5) then the assets of the Partnership will be realised as soon as may be practicable and in any event within twelve months of the Retirement Date. Any surplus or loss on such realisation will be credited or debited to the capital accounts of the Partners and the Former Partner and the Former Partner will be entitled to be paid the balance standing to the credit of his capital account within eighteen months of his Retirement Date together with interest from the Retirement Date at the Partnership Interest Rate.]

(7) (a) Subject to paragraph (b) the Partners will indemnify each Former Partner against all liabilities of the Partnership including (without limitation) liabilities in respect of leases under which the Partnership Premises are held. If and to the extent that the Former Partner is entitled to any right of indemnity, reimbursement or contribution in respect of those liabilities from any person other than the Partnership or any Partner (whether under a policy of insurance or otherwise), he will disclose details of any such rights of reimbursement, indemnity or contribution, and any claim made under it, to the Partnership, which will be entitled to exercise those rights by way of subrogation.

(b) Notwithstanding paragraph (a) and unless otherwise agreed by [Special/General] Decision, each Former Partner will remain liable for that share of any liability arising by reason of his own professional negligence or breach of duty corresponding to the proportion which his Profit Share allocated to him at the time when the liability was incurred bears to the aggregate Profit Shares of all the Partners in the Partnership at that time.

(c) For the purposes of paragraph (a), any liability will be reduced to the extent that insurance cover would have been in effect in respect of it if a claim had been made in respect of it on the Former Partners Retirement Date.

(8) The Profit Share to which a Former Partner was entitled immediately prior to his Retirement Date shall accrue rateably to the Profit Shares of the other Partners.

(9) A Former Partner will at all times comply with the obligations imposed on him as a Former Partner by this deed, including (without limitation) the obligations imposed by clauses 12 (Duties) and 23 (Covenants).

(10) A Former Partner is entitled to the payments described in this clause in full satisfaction of his interest in the profits of the Partnership, and in the Goodwill, the Partnership Name, Partnership Premises, the Partnerships furniture and equipment and other assets of the Partnership, and has no further rights in respect of those profits or assets.

23. Covenants

(1) In this clause:

    (a) **in any capacity** means on that Partners or Former Partners own account, or jointly, in conjunction with, or on behalf of any other person, firm or company; and

    (b) **Partnership Client** means any individual, partnership, body corporate or unincorporated association who or which has been a client of the Partnership and for whom the relevant Partner had carried out work at any time in the period of [two] years before his Retirement Date except that each distinct business unit of a client will be treated for this purpose as a separate Partnership Client.

(2) A Partner or Former Partner will not, without the prior agreement of the Management Committee do any of the following:

    (a) for a period of [one] year from his Retirement Date act for, solicit or accept instructions from or provide legal services to, any Partnership Client in a way which is likely to compete with the business carried on by him as a Partner or by the Partnership immediately before his Retirement Date;

    (b) for a period of [one] year from the Retirement Date employ, solicit or endeavour to entice away, offer partnership or employment to or enter into partnership or any other commercial arrangement with any person who, at the Retirement Date was a Partner in, an employee of or consultant to the Partnership;

    (c) at any time after his Retirement Date and in any capacity:

(i) represent himself as a Partner in, employee of or consultant to the Partnership or that he is in any way connected with, or has the authority to bind the Partnership or any Partner; or

(ii) use the Partnership Name or any name which may in any way be confused with the Partnership Name.

(3) Each of sub-clauses (2)(a) to (c) inclusive constitutes a separate and independent restriction on each Former Partner so that, if one or more are held to be invalid or unenforceable for any reason whatsoever then the remaining covenants will be valid and enforceable to the extent that they are not held to be invalid or unenforceable.

(4) Upon any Partner becoming a Former Partner, all deeds, drafts, letters and other papers or records belonging to the Partnership or any Partnership Client or relating to any Partnership Client or prospective client of the Partnership will remain in the possession of, or be delivered by the Former Partner to the Partnership and, at the request of the Management Committee, the Former Partner will certify in writing to the committee whether or not he is in breach of this sub-clause.

(5) When a Partner becomes a Former Partner, due notice that he has ceased to be a Partner will be given in the London Gazette and (so far as is reasonably practicable) by a circular letter in such form and sent to such persons, companies and firms as the Management Committee will in their absolute discretion determine. If a Former Partner (who is still alive) shall refuse to sign the notice for insertion in the London Gazette the Managing Partner may sign the name of the Former Partner on his behalf and each Partner irrevocably grants to the Managing Partner from time to time his power of attorney for the sole purpose of signing his name on such a notice and by way of security of his obligations under this sub-clause. Each Partners power of attorney shall expire automatically 30 days after his Retirement Date.

24. Dissolution

(1) The Partnership may be dissolved at any time by a Special Decision or, if the Partnership then comprises only two Partners, by either Partner.

(2) Upon the dissolution of the Partnership for any reason all the assets of the Partnership (including the right to use the Partnership Name) will be realised and the proceeds remaining after the discharge of all liabilities to third parties (including any

amounts outstanding to or in respect of any Former Partner) will be applied firstly in payment of the amount standing to the credit of the Capital Accounts and Current Accounts of each of the Partners at the date of dissolution. Any balance will be distributed to the Partners in proportion to their respective Profit Shares at the date of dissolution.

(3) Sub-clause (2) will have no application if the Partnership is dissolved on or after the assignment of the whole or substantially the whole of the Partnership Business to a body corporate, a limited liability partnership or any analogous entity in consideration for the issue to the Partners, rateably in accordance with their Profit Shares, of shares, membership rights or analogous rights in that entity and the Partners will accept those shares, membership or other rights in full satisfaction of their interest in the Partnership and the Partnership Business.

25. Arbitration and Dispute Resolution

(1) Where any question, claim, dispute or difference (**dispute**) arises between any of the Partners or Former Partners concerning or in any way arising out of this deed or the performance of the terms of this deed, those Partners or Former Partners will make a genuine effort to resolve the dispute without resorting to litigation, using the procedures set out in this clause.

(2) Any dispute in connection with this deed will be resolved as follows:

    (a) in accordance with sub-clause (3) below if the dispute relates to an accounting matter; or

    (b) in accordance with sub-clauses (4), (5) and (6) below, in the case of all other disputes.

(3) Disputes relating to an accounting matter will be referred, at the written request of any party to the dispute, for determination by an independent accountant (the **Independent Accountant**) who is a member of the Institute of Chartered Accountants in England and Wales (the **Institute**) appointed by agreement between the parties to the dispute within seven days of delivery of the written request or (in default of agreement) appointed by the President for the time being of the Institute on the application of any party to the dispute. The Management Committee will determine whether a dispute concerns an accounting matter or not and its decision will be final in the absence of a manifest error. The determination of the Independent Accountant is final

and binding on all Partners and Former Partners. In determining the dispute, the Independent Accountant will act as an expert and not as an arbitrator. All costs incurred by the Independent Accountant will be borne by the parties to the dispute as determined by the Independent Accountant.

(4)   Without prejudice to any right to seek interim relief all other disputes will be referred, at the written request of any party to the dispute, to mediation by a mediator appointed by agreement between the parties to the dispute within seven days of the written request or (in default of agreement) appointed by the Chief Executive for the time being of the Centre for Dispute Resolution (**CEDR**). The mediation will be conducted in London in accordance with the CEDR Model Mediation Procedure (together with any amendments and updates to that procedure that are adopted by the Management Committee before the appointment of a mediator in relation to a particular dispute), which is deemed to be incorporated in this deed. If an agreement is reached on the resolution of the dispute during the mediation, that agreement will be reduced to writing and, once signed by the parties to the dispute, will be binding on all the Partners. Unless concluded with a written legally binding agreement, the mediation will be conducted in confidence and without prejudice to the rights of any Partner or Former Partner in any further proceedings, and the contents of the agreement will remain confidential to the parties to the dispute and their advisers save for the limited purpose of enforcement.

(5)   Without prejudice to any right to seek interim relief in the event that the dispute has not been settled within sixty days after the appointment of the mediator, or if no request is made to refer that dispute to mediation, the dispute will be referred (by any Partner or Former Partner involved in the dispute) to arbitration in London to be conducted in the English language by a sole arbitrator appointed in accordance with the rules of the London Court of International Arbitration (the **Rules**) which Rules are deemed to be incorporated by reference into this clause.

(6)   The Partners agree that any party to an arbitration under this deed may appeal against any award of an arbitrator on points of law.

26. Alterations

(1)   Any of the provisions of this deed may be altered at any time by [Special/Unanimous] Decision.

(2) Notwithstanding sub-clause (1), any of the provisions of this deed may be altered at any time by the Management Committee if the alteration is of a minor or technical nature which either is not materially prejudicial to the interests of any of the Partners or is to correct a manifest error. Any such alteration will be made on the terms and subject to the conditions that the Management Committee determines, will be notified to Partners as soon as possible and will be binding on the Partners when notified to them.

(3) No alteration of this deed will invalidate any prior act which would have been valid if that alteration had not been made.

27. Holidays, Maternity and Paternity Leave

(1) In each calendar year, in addition to public holidays, each Partner shall be entitled to take such annual holidays not exceeding [five] weeks in the aggregate [of which not more than [three] weeks may be taken consecutively] or as shall be determined by [General/Special] Decision from time to time and may (subject to such determination) carry forward into the next calendar year any unused part of his entitlement.

(2) A female Partner may, in the event of her pregnancy and upon giving not less than [three months] prior written notice of her intention to do so to the other Partners, take a period of maternity leave of not more than [four months] duration and commencing at such time as is agreed between the Partner and the Management Committee.

(3) A male Partner may upon giving not less than [three months] prior written notice of his intention to do so to the other Partners, take a period of paternity leave of such duration as shall be decided between the Partner and the Management Committee and commencing at such time as is agreed between the Partner and the Management Committee.

(4) A Partner may agree flexible working arrangements by [General/Special Decision].

28. General

(1) None of the rights or obligations under this deed may be assigned or transferred without a [Special/Unanimous] Decision.

(2) Where an obligation is expressed to be undertaken by two or more parties they shall, unless otherwise expressly stated, be jointly and severally responsible in respect of it.

(3)   This deed may be executed in any number of counterparts, all of which taken together shall constitute one and the same deed and any party may enter into this deed by executing a counterpart as a deed.

(4)   Except as expressly stated in this deed, this deed and its schedules and the documents referred to in it [contain the whole agreement between the parties][1]

(5)   Each of the parties acknowledges that in agreeing to enter into this deed he has not relied on any representation, warranty or other assurance except those set out in this deed.

(6)   This deed and any non contractual obligations arising out of or in connection with it shall be governed by and shall be construed in accordance with English law.

(7)   Any notice required or permitted to be given under this deed shall be in writing and if posted by prepaid recorded delivery post to the last known address of the person to be served shall be deemed to have been duly served forty-eight hours after despatch.

(8)   The parties agree that subject to clause 25 the courts of England have exclusive jurisdiction to settle any dispute arising out of or in connection with this deed (including any dispute relating to any non-contractual obligations arising out of or in connection with this deed) and the parties submit to the exclusive jurisdictions of the English Courts.

(9)   Except as expressly stated on this deed no third party shall have any rights in respect of this deed whether pursuant to the Contracts (Rights of Third Parties) Act 1999 or otherwise.

IN WITNESS of which each of the parties has executed this document as a deed the day and year first above written.

---

[1]   and supersede all previous agreements between the parties.

SCHEDULE 1

Partners

Name   Address

Profit Shares

SCHEDULE 2

Partnership Premises

Address

SCHEDULE 3

Name

Initial Capital Contributions

SCHEDULE 4

Part I

Initial Management Committee

[Senior Partner]

[Managing Partner]

Part II

Initial Managing Partner

[Part III]

[Initial Senior Partner]

SCHEDULE 5

Form of Accession Agreement

This DEED is made on [ ], 20[ ] between:

(1) [ ] of [ ] (the **New Partner**); and

(2) the persons whose names and addresses are set out in [Schedule 1] (the **Continuing Partners**) carrying on business together as [ ] Partnership (the **Partnership**).

WHEREAS:

(A) The New Partner wishes to be admitted as a Partner of the Partnership with effect from [ ] (the **Admission Date**).

(B) The Continuing Partners have agreed that the New Partner may be admitted in accordance with the Partnership Agreement dated [ ], in the form set out in the Schedule to this deed, as varied and supplemented from time to time (the **Partnership Agreement**).

(C) The New Partner now wishes to enter into an Accession Agreement pursuant to the Partnership Agreement.

NOW THIS DEED WITNESSES THAT:

1. In this Accession Agreement, the following terms shall unless the context requires otherwise have (whether with or without the definite article) the following meanings:

[insert any additional definitions]

Capitalised terms not defined herein shall have the meaning given to them in the Partnership Agreement.

2. The New Partner will for all purposes be and become a party to the Partnership Agreement with effect on the Admission Date as if he had executed it on or before the Admission Date, and will accordingly be entitled to all the rights and subject to all the obligations provided for under the Partnership Agreement.

3. The New Partner shall make a Capital Contribution of £[ ] for the purposes of [Clause 5] of the Partnership Agreement on the date hereof.

4. The Profit Share of the New Partner shall be [ ] and Schedule 1 of the Partnership Agreement shall be amended as attached to this Accession Agreement.

5. [insert any special conditions]

6. Any alteration, deletion or amendment of this deed must be made in writing and by deed executed by both the New Partner and the Partnership.

7. This deed and any and any non-contractual obligations arising out of or in connection with it shall be governed by and construed in accordance with English law.

Model Partnership Agreement

SIGNED as a deed by

in the presence of:

Witness signature:

Name:

Address:

SIGNED as a deed by

in the presence of:

Witness signature:

Name:

Address:

SIGNED as a deed by

in the presence of:

Witness signature:

Name:

Address:

Appendix 5 Model Limited Liability Partnership Deed

[NOTE: This model deed has been prepared by Maurice Turnor Gardner LLP and is for illustration only. Every LLP's needs are unique and it is important to obtain legal and accounting advice when preparing an LLP deed.]

THIS DEED is made on [ ], 20[ ] BETWEEN

- (i) the persons whose names and addresses are set out in Schedule 1 (the 'Original Members'); and

- (ii) [ ] LLP, a limited liability partnership incorporated in England and Wales under the Limited Liability Partnerships Act 2000 with registered number [ ] and whose registered office is at [ ] (the 'LLP').

WHEREAS:

- (A) The Original Members have incorporated the LLP and have agreed to carry on the business of [ ] through the LLP and wish to enter into this deed for the purpose of setting out the arrangements agreed between them and the LLP with effect from and including the Effective Date (as defined below).

- (B) It is the intention of the parties that this document be executed as a deed.

NOW THIS DEED WITNESSES AND IT IS AGREED as follows:

1. Interpretation

- (1) In this deed:

   'Accession Agreement' means a deed by which a New Member accedes as a member of the LLP and to this deed substantially in the form set out in Schedule 6 and which states his initial Profit Share and capital contribution;

   'Accounts' means the accounts of the LLP prepared and approved in accordance with clause 8;

   'Accounts Date' means [ ] in each year or such other date as may be decided by [General/Special] Decision;

535

'Accounting Period' means the period of one calendar year ending on the Accounts Date, or such other period as is decided from time to time by [General/Special] Decision;

'Admission Date' has the meaning given to it in sub-clause 17(1);

'Appointment' has the meaning given to it in sub-clause 13(1);

'Approved Appointment' has the meaning given to it in sub-clause 13(1);

'Approved Liability' has the meaning given to it in sub-clause 13(2);

'Auditors' Report' means the report to the Members prepared by the LLP Auditors in accordance with clause 8;

'Capital Account' means the account to be established for each Member under sub-clause 5(2);

'Chairman' means the person who holds office as such from time to time under clause 16;

'Chief Executive' means the member who holds office as Chief Executive from time to time under clause 16;

'Companies Act' means the Companies Act 2006 as it applies to limited liability partnerships, as replaced and amended from time to time and any regulations published pursuant thereto;

'Current Account' means the account to be established for each Member under sub-clause 6(5);

'Designated Members' means those Members who are designated members for the purposes of sections 8 and 9 of the LLP Act and who are appointed under clause 4 from time to time;

'Dispute' shall have the meaning given to it in sub-clause 25(1);

'Effective Date' means [ ];

'Former Member' means a person who ceases to be a Member after the Effective Date for any reason (other than the winding up of the LLP) and includes the personal representatives of a Former Member;

'General Decision' means a decision of the Members taken as a General Decision under sub-clause 14(8);

'Goodwill' means the goodwill of the LLP;

'Insolvency Act' means the Insolvency Act 1986 as it applies to limited liability partnerships as amended or replaced from time to time and any regulations published pursuant to that Act;

'LLP Act' means the Limited Liability Partnerships Act 2000 as replaced or amended from time to time and any regulations published pursuant to that Act;

'LLP Auditors' means [ ] or such other firm of qualifying accountants for the purposes of the Companies Act as may be decided from time to time by the Designated Members;

'LLP Bank' means [ ] Bank Plc or such other additional or substitute bank as may be appointed as banker to the LLP by [General Decision/the Management Committee];

'LLP Business' means the business and practice of [ ], any ancillary or related business activity and any other business or practice which the LLP may resolve to carry on by [General/ Special] Decision;

'LLP Interest Rate' means the base lending rate of the LLP Bank plus [ ] per cent per annum or such other rate as may be determined by [the Management Committee/General Decision/Special Decision];

'LLP Name' means the name of [ ] or such other name as may from time to time be adopted by [General/Special] Decision and notified to the Registrar of Companies under the LLP Act;

'LLP Premises' means the offices of the LLP specified in Schedule 2 and such other offices as the Members from time to time by [Special/General] Decision decide will be used by the LLP Business;

'LLP Registers' means the register of members and the register of members' residential addresses required to be maintained by Sections 162 and 165 of the Companies Act;

'Losses' means, in relation to an Accounting Period, the revenue and capital losses of the LLP as shown in the Accounts for that Accounting Period;

'Management Committee' means the Members for the time being of the committee constituted under clause 16;

'Members' means:

(a)   the Original Members; and

(b)   every other person who is admitted as a New Member,

in each case only until he becomes a Former Member and 'Member' means any of them;

'New Member' means any person admitted as a Member on or after the Effective Date under clause 17;

'Non-Approved Appointment' has the meaning given to it in sub-clause 13(1);

'Predecessors' shall have the meaning given to it in sub-clause 11(1);

'Profits' means, in relation to an Accounting Period, the revenue and capital profits of the LLP as shown in the Accounts for that Accounting Period;

'Profit Share' in relation to a Member means the Percentage set out against his name in Part 1 of Schedule 1 or such other percentage as shall be determined from time to time under the provisions of this deed;

'Retirement Date' means the date when a Member ceases to be a Member and becomes a Former Member by reason of death, expulsion, retirement or otherwise;

'Special Decision' means a decision of the LLP taken as a Special Decision under sub-clause 14(9); and

'Unanimous Decision' means a decision of the LLP taken as a Unanimous Decision under sub-clause 14(10).

(2) In interpreting this deed the following rules will be applied unless the context otherwise requires:

(a) words importing the singular include the plural and vice versa and words importing gender import all genders;

(b) references to any clause, sub-clause, schedule, paragraph or subparagraph are references to that clause in this deed, the sub-clause in the relevant clause in which it appears, a schedule to this deed or the paragraph or sub-paragraph in the relevant sub-clause, paragraph or schedule in which it appears and any schedules to this deed form part of this deed;

(c) references to statutory provisions, subordinate legislation or professional regulations will be construed as references to those provisions, legislation or regulations as they have been or may be amended or reenacted or as their application is modified by other provisions from time to time;

(d)   headings to clauses are for reference only and do not affect its interpretation;

(e)   references to this deed or any other instrument include any variation, novation or replacement of any of them; and

(f)   if a period of time is specified and is expressed to run from a given day or the day of an act or event, it is to be calculated exclusive of that day.

(3)   In this deed, unless the context otherwise requires, any reference to:

a 'deed' also includes a contract, deed, licence, undertaking, or other document and includes that deed as modified, novated or substituted from time to time;

a 'law' includes common or customary law and any constitution, decree, judgement, legislation, order, ordinance, regulation, treaty or other legislative measure of England and Wales;

a 'person' includes an individual and that person's executors and administrators;

'professional regulations' includes any directions, standards, rules or regulations of any professional bodies which govern the conduct of any Member or the LLP;

'rights' includes authorities, discretions, remedies, powers and causes of action; and

'tax' includes any present or future tax, levy, duty, rate, charge, fee, deduction or withholding imposed, assessed or levied by any governmental agency in any part of the world (including national insurance contributions and any other social security or similar contributions wherever imposed) and any interest, penalties, fines, costs, charges and other liabilities arising from or payable in respect of that tax.

2. Commencement, Effect and Name

(1)   With effect on and from the Effective Date, the LLP will carry on the LLP Business under the LLP Name in accordance with the provisions of this deed.

(2)   The LLP will at all times comply with the provisions of the Companies Act and of any regulation, instrument, rule or order from time to time and for the time being made under that Act.

(3)   The LLP Name and any abbreviation or combination of it or any registered trade or service marks including or associated with

those names, abbreviations and combinations (in this sub-clause the 'Names') and any logos or registered designs derived from or associated with the Names are assets of the LLP and the use of the Names (or any interest in the Names) may only be licensed, sub-licensed, assigned, transferred or sold to third parties or otherwise disposed of as the LLP may by [General/ Special Decision] decide.

3. Place of Business

The LLP Business shall be carried on in the LLP Premises.

4. Designated Members

(1) The Designated Members on the Effective Date shall be the Members named in Schedule 3.

(2) A Designated Member will cease to be a Designated Member if he ceases to be a Member or if he gives at least [two] months written notice of his resignation as a Designated Member to the LLP Management Committee. The Management Committee may by written notice remove a Designated Member and appoint another Member to replace any person who has ceased to be a Designated Member.

(3) The Management Committee shall ensure that at all times there are at least two Designated Members.

(4) The Management Committee and Designated Members shall ensure that notice of the appointment in sub-clause (1) and of any change in the Designated Members is delivered to the registrar of limited liability partnerships within fourteen days, as required by Section 9 of the LLP Act.

(5) The Designated Members shall have such duties as are specified in the LLP Act or otherwise at law and in this deed.

(6) The LLP shall indemnify each Designated Member and former Designated Member in respect of any personal liability arising as a result of his position as Designated Member, other than as a result of his fraud, dishonesty, wilful default or failure to act in accordance with his duty to act with the utmost good faith in all transactions relating to the LLP and its Members.

(7) Unless otherwise stated in this deed or decided by the Members by [General/Special] Decision, each of the Designated Members is authorised to, acting alone, execute or authorise the execution of any documents or deeds on behalf of the LLP which have been approved by the Members or by the person or persons duly authorised to do so under this deed and shall

ensure that all such documents (including promissory notes, cheques or similar bills) contain such details as required by Sections 82 and 83 of the Companies Act in legible form.

5. Capital

(1) The capital of the LLP will be the sum of [ ].

(2) A Capital Account will be established in the name of each Member, and all amounts contributed by a Member to the capital of the LLP will be credited to his Capital Account and all amounts withdrawn by him from the capital of the LLP will be debited to his Capital Account. Each Member will on the Effective Date [contribute] [be deemed to have contributed] to the capital of the LLP the amount set out opposite his name in Schedule 4 and his Capital Account will be credited accordingly.

(3) With effect on and from the Effective Date, the capital of the LLP will be contributed by the Members in proportion to their Profit Shares. Accordingly, on any change in Members' Profit Shares, any Member whose Profit Share has increased will contribute in cash the corresponding amount as additional capital to the LLP and any Member whose Profit Share has decreased will be entitled to withdraw the corresponding amount from the capital of the LLP and his Capital Account will be adjusted accordingly.

(4) Subject to sub-clause 5(5), the Members may from time to time decide by [General/Special] Decision to increase or reduce the capital of the LLP. Any additional capital which may be required will be contributed by the Members to the LLP and any surplus capital no longer required will be repaid to the Members by the LLP, in proportion to their Profit Shares as at the date of that decision, and each Member's Capital Account will be adjusted accordingly.

(5) The Members shall not be required to increase or contribute to the capital of the LLP at any time when the LLP is unable to pay its debts as defined in section 123 of the Insolvency Act.

(6) Subject to sub-clause (5), where a Member is shown in the Accounts to have contributed an amount to the capital of the LLP that is less than the amount which ought to have been contributed by him, the amount of such deficit will become a debt due by that Member to the LLP [and interest thereon will be payable to the LLP at the LLP Interest Rate from the time when the deficit first arose].

(7)   Subject to clause 22 (Former Members and their entitlements), where a Member is shown in the Accounts to have contributed an amount to the capital of the LLP that exceeds the amount which ought to have been contributed by him, the excess will become a debt due to him from the LLP and will be paid out to him as soon as is reasonably practicable [with interest at the LLP Interest Rate from the time when the excess first arose].

(8)   Subject to clause 22 (Former Members and their entitlements) and except as expressly provided in this deed or [with the deed of the Management Committee/as agreed by Special Decision]:

(a)   no Member may draw out or receive back any part of his capital contribution to the LLP;

(b)   no Member is entitled to any interest on the contribution made by him to the capital of the LLP; and

(c)   no Member is entitled to any interest on any amount lent by him to the LLP.

6.   Profit Shares and Losses

(1)   The Profits of the LLP for an Accounting Period are to be shared by the Members in proportion to their Profit Shares for that Accounting Period.

(2)   On the Effective Date the Profit Shares allocated to each Original Member are as specified in Schedule 4.

(3)   The Profit Share allocated to any New Member will be as specified in his Accession Agreement.

(4)   The Members may by [General/Special] Decision increase or reduce a Member's Profit Share from time to time, such increase or reduction to take effect on and from a date specified in that decision.

(5)   A Current Account shall be established for each Member. Subject to sub-clause 5(2), all amounts owed by the LLP to a Member will be credited to, and all amounts owed by a Member to the LLP shall be debited to, his Current Account.

(6)   Each Member will be reimbursed all reasonable and proper out of pocket expenses incurred by him in the performance of his duties under this deed or otherwise on behalf of the LLP. Each Member will provide to the LLP appropriate records of his expenses within such period after the time when those expenses were incurred as the Management Committee may determine.

(7)   Each Partner will be indemnified by the LLP in respect of any liabilities incurred by him in the ordinary and proper course of the LLP Business or in or about anything necessarily done in the preservation of the LLP Business, but any liability occasioned by the Member as described in sub-clause 12(3) must be made good by that Member alone.

(8)   Subject to sub-clause (7), losses of the LLP shall be borne by the LLP but the Members may, subject to sub-clause 5(5), decide by [General/Special] Decision to increase their contributions to the capital of the LLP to meet that deficiency and any such decision shall bind all of the Members.

7.   Drawings

(1)   Subject to clause 9 (Provision for tax liabilities), the Members may in any Accounting Period make monthly drawings of such amounts as may from time to time be determined by [General Decision/the Management Committee] on account of their Profit Shares in the relevant Accounting Period.

(2)   Any Member who is shown in the Accounts to have drawn any amount in excess of his share of Profits for that period, after provision for tax liabilities under clause 9, will (within one month of the time when the Accounts have been approved by the LLP in respect of that Accounting Period under clause 8) refund that excess to the LLP as soon as is reasonably practicable [together with interest on that amount at the LLP Interest Rate for the period from the date when he is requested by the Management Committee to make the refund to the date of repayment].

(3)   Unless otherwise determined by [Special Decision/the Management Committee], if a Member is shown in the Accounts to have drawn an amount less than his Profit Share, after provision for tax liabilities under clause 9, that undrawn balance will be credited, within one month of the time when the Accounts have been approved by the LLP in respect of the relevant Accounting Period under clause 8, to his current account with the LLP [together with interest on that amount at the LLP Interest Rate from such date as is determined by the Management Committee to the date of repayment]. When the Accounts for each Accounting Period have been approved under clause 8, each Member shall be paid the amount of the credit balance on his Current Account (if any) as shown in those Accounts at the times and in the instalments determined by [General Decision/ the Management Committee].

(4) Except as expressly provided in this deed, no Member will be entitled to any interest on any undrawn balance of his share of the Profits.

8. Statutory Accounts

(1) The Accounts of the LLP shall be made up to the Accounts Date in each year.

(2) A profit and loss account shall be taken in every year on the Accounts Date and a balance sheet as at the same date shall be prepared.

(3) The Designated Members shall, in compliance with Section 485 of the Companies Act, appoint the LLP Auditors as the auditors for each Accounting Period of the LLP and shall have the power to fix their remuneration.

(4) The Designated Members shall ensure that the Accounts are drawn up in the format and giving the information required in the LLP Act and the Companies Act, and the Accounts shall be audited by the LLP Auditors. Except as otherwise required by law, no value shall be attributed to the Goodwill in the Accounts.

(5) The Designated Members shall ensure that all the necessary and proper financial records of accounts shall be kept to enable the Accounts to be made up as above and retained for at least six years after the end of the relevant Accounting Period or such periods of time as required by law at the registered office (or such other place as the Members may determine) of the LLP on behalf of the Members in compliance with the LLP Act and such records shall be available for inspection by each Member and by the LLP Auditors for the time being at all times. Each Member shall be responsible for ensuring that full and proper entries of all transactions entered into by him on account of the LLP are made.

(6) As soon as the Accounts have been finalised, and no later than three months after the Accounting Date, the Accounts will be distributed to each Member and will be presented at the next duly convened Members' meeting for approval.

(7) Once the Accounts have been approved by [General/Special] Decision, the Designated Members shall then sign the Accounts on the balance sheet as required by the Companies Act whereupon they shall be binding on the Members, save in the event that an error be discovered, in which event such error shall be rectified in the manner required by the Companies Act.

(8) If the Accounts are not approved by [General/Special] Decision, any Member may refer any point of dispute for resolution in accordance with the sub-clause 25(3), provided that all reasonable efforts are made to enable the Designated Members to comply with sub-clause (11).

(9) The Accounts shall, once approved under sub-clause (7), be submitted to the LLP Auditors who shall make a report on them to the Members and will state, as set out in their letter of appointment, whether or not the Accounts give a true and fair view of the profit or loss of the LLP for the Accounting Period.

(10) The LLP shall ensure that a copy of the Accounts as approved and signed, together with a copy of the Auditor's Report on the Accounts, shall be sent to every Member and any other person who is entitled to receive them under Part 15, Chapter 7 of the Companies Act.

(11) The Designated Members shall in respect of each Accounting Period deliver to the registrar of limited liability partnerships a copy of the approved Accounts and Auditors' Report as required by the Companies Act.

(12) Where additional reporting or accounting information is required by the LLP Auditors to allow them to complete the Auditors' Report or comply with any statutory requirement to which the LLP is subject (including the provision of any information requested by the inspectors of the Department of Trade and Industry), that information will be provided by the relevant Member or Members at the expense of the LLP as soon as practicable.

9. Provision for Tax Liabilities

(1) Except as otherwise determined by the Management Committee, the LLP will retain such proportion of each Member's Profit Share in any Accounting Period as the Management Committee recommends is appropriate to meet that Member's individual tax liability (if any) in respect of those Profit Shares (whenever and wherever that tax may be payable and whether payable by the Members or the LLP). Where Profits are allocated under this deed to Members but tax is payable in relation to those Profits in a different Accounting Period, [the Management Committee/the Members by General/Special Decision] may make such adjustments as between Members as, so far as reasonably practicable, shall procure that, in accordance with

prevailing rules of accounting for deferred tax, the burden of tax in relation to those Profits is borne by those Members who have had the benefit of those Profits.

(2)   Sums retained in respect of a Member under sub-clause (1) will be debts owed by the LLP to the Member and will (even if he has since become a Former Member) be paid on his behalf to the relevant tax authority when and to the extent necessary to meet the liability for which retention has been made. Once and to the extent paid to the relevant tax authority the debt to the Members shall be discharged.

(3)   Sums retained in respect of each Member or Former Member under sub-clause (1) will be paid or released to him only when and to the extent considered by the Management Committee to be in excess of the necessary retention. In the event of a dispute between a Member or Former Member and the Management Committee as to the amount of the retention that is necessary, the decision of the LLP Auditors (acting as experts and not as arbitrators) will be final and binding in the absence of manifest error.

(4)   The Management Committee will make its recommendations under sub-clauses (1) and (3):

(a)   on a basis which is consistent between the Members and Former Members; and

(b)   assuming that all personal allowances and reliefs available to a Member or Former Member will be set against his income and gains from the LLP before being set against other income and gains.

10. Bank Accounts

(1)   The Management Committee will ensure that all bank accounts required for the purposes of or in connection with the LLP Business will be maintained with the LLP Bank and will include the LLP Name. This requirement does not apply to an account in the name of a client of the LLP.

(2)   All LLP receipts will promptly be paid into and deposited with the LLP Bank to the credit of the LLP.

(3)   All cheques drawn on the bank accounts of the LLP will be drawn in the name of the LLP.

(4)   All cheques, bills of exchange and other bank transfers or other instruments pledging the credit or affecting the property of the

LLP will be signed on behalf of the LLP by any [two] [Designated] Members unless otherwise decided by [General/ Special] Decision. The Signatories shall ensure that such documents and instruments shall contain such details as are required by Sections 82 and 83 of the Companies Act in legible form.

(5) All monies and all securities received on behalf or for the account of a client or third party will (except as required for the matter in hand on behalf of that client or third party) promptly:

(a) be paid or delivered to that client or third party; or

(b) be paid into or deposited with the LLP Bank in a client account or statutory client account (as the case may be) which is separate and distinct from any account relating to the property of the LLP; or

(c) otherwise be dealt with in a manner authorised by any law or professional regulations.

11. Insurance

(1) The Management Committee will ensure that the LLP and (in the case of paragraph (b)) its Members, Former Members and all employees and former employees of and consultants to the LLP and any person or persons in succession to which the LLP Business is carried on (in this clause 11, its 'Predecessors') are insured against the following:

(a) employer's liability and any other liability against which it is required to be insured by any law or professional regulations;

(b) liability for professional negligence of the LLP or any of its Members, Former Members and employees and former employees of and consultants to the LLP and of its Predecessors;

(c) liability of the LLP to third parties for death, injury or illness, and for damage to third party property;

(d) loss or damage to LLP assets, including LLP Premises;

(e) liability of the LLP as occupiers of the LLP Premises; and

(f) such other risks as the Management Committee may determine.

(2) The Management Committee may arrange any insurance with any insurer, on terms and subject to conditions, exclusions,

limits and deductibles (or any other self insurance or captive insurance arrangements), as it thinks fit.

(3) In respect of all insurances effected for the benefit of the LLP and its Members, Former Members and employees and former employees of and consultants to the LLP and its Predecessors, the following will be treated as expenses of the LLP:

(a) all premiums payable in respect of those insurances and all broker and adviser fees;

(b) all sums expended pursuant to any deductible or excess borne by the LLP; and

(c) all sums expended for the account of the LLP by reason only of the insufficiency of the limit of insurance or the failure (for any reason) of the insurers to meet any valid policy claim.

(4) The protection provided by any professional negligence or other liability insurance purchased for the benefit of the LLP and its Members and employees and former employees of and consultants to the LLP and its Predecessors will extend to Former Members and Predecessors to the extent of their individual liabilities as such. The benefit of any professional negligence or other liability insurance purchased for the benefit of the LLP and its Members, Former Members, employees of and former employees of and consultants to the LLP and of any claim or recovery made under it, will be held in trust for such persons rateably with their respective shares of liability for the matter that was the subject of the insurance claim under this deed.

12. Duties

(1) Each Member will at all times:

(a) act diligently in the conduct of the LLP Business;

(b) act with the utmost good faith in all transactions relating to the other Members and the LLP;

(c) disclose to the Management Committee on request full details of all business transactions by him or at his direction for the account of the LLP;

(d) provide the Management Committee with the information concerning the LLP Business in his knowledge or possession that the Management Committee requests;

(e) comply with any law or professional regulations to which the LLP or the Member is or may become subject in that capacity and use reasonable endeavours to comply with any other law or contractual or other legal obligations of which he is aware and use all reasonable endeavours to ensure that the LLP complies with any law, contract or other binding obligation to which it is subject and of which he is aware;

(f) use the LLP Name in all business transactions of the LLP;

(g) not exceed the authority conferred on him by this deed when acting on behalf of the LLP;

(h) except as otherwise determined by the Management Committee, account to the LLP for any money or thing representing money including all gifts and legacies received from a third party in the course of the LLP Business;

(j) not hold himself out as being in partnership with the LLP, or as being in partnership with or authorised to act as agent for any other Member or Former Member; and

(k) notify the Designated Members of any changes to his personal details (name or addresses) within 10 days of the change.

(2) The LLP shall:

(a) comply with the statutory duties imposed on it from time to time; and

(b) indemnify and keep indemnified the Members in respect of payments made and personal liabilities incurred by them while acting:

(i) in the ordinary and proper conduct of the LLP Business; or

(ii) in or about anything necessarily done for the preservation of the LLP Business.

(3) Sub-clause 12(2) shall not apply to payments made and personal liabilities incurred by a Member in connection with his:

(a) fraud;

(b) dishonesty;

(c) wilful default; or

(d) failure to act in accordance with his duty to act with the utmost good faith in all transactions relating to the other Members and the LLP.

(4)   Unless a [General Decision/the Management Committee] determines otherwise in any particular instance:

(a)   subject to clauses 21 (Gardening Leave) and 27 (Holidays and Maternity Leave) each Member will devote his whole time and attention to the LLP Business during normal business hours and at any other time when it is necessary to do so to enable him to perform his duties to the LLP or any of its clients;

(b)   subject to clause 13 (Appointments and Approved Liabilities) a Member will not become a sole trader or a member in any business other than the LLP Business or be a director of any company other than a company owned by the LLP or be or become a member of an LLP or hold any shares in any company with unlimited liability;

(c)   a Member will not do or omit to do any act or thing the doing or omission of which will bring or tend to bring the LLP into disrepute;

(d)   a Member will not, otherwise than as required by law, assign, declare any trust of, transfer or create a security interest over any legal or beneficial interest in his share in the LLP or any part of the Profits of the LLP or any amount owed to him by the LLP;

(e)   a Member will not lend any money or other property of the LLP or, in the context of the LLP Business, give credit to or act for or have any dealing with any person, company or firm with whom the Management Committee has previously requested him not to deal;

(f)   except within his authority as Member, insofar as his advisers and any court, expert or arbitrator need to be informed in order to resolve any dispute under this deed or as required by law, a Member or Former Member will not use to the detriment or prejudice of the LLP (or divulge to any person other than another Member in any way which could reasonably be foreseen to risk any detriment to the LLP or any of its clients) any confidential information concerning the business, investment or affairs of the LLP or any of its clients. In this paragraph 'confidential information' includes (without limitation) any information relating to this deed, the Accounts, the books of the LLP, the financial position of the LLP, any decision of the LLP (including a decision of the Management Committee) or any matter affecting the rights and obligations of the

Members or Former Members or the management of the LLP. However, a Former Member may disclose the terms of the restrictions imposed on Former Members under this clause and clause 23 (Covenants); and

(g) all intellectual property rights created, directly or indirectly, by a Member and relating directly or indirectly to the LLP Business shall belong to the LLP or as it shall direct.

13. Appointments and Approved Liabilities

(1) (a) Members must not accept or hold any charitable or non-charitable trusteeships, offices or appointments including (without limitation) appointment as a director of a company, an executor, an administrator or trustee of any will, estate or settlement ('Appointments') except in accordance with this clause.

(b) Unless otherwise agreed by the Management Committee, every Appointment will be deemed to be held for the account of the LLP. Those Appointments that the Management Committee agree will not be held for the account of the LLP are referred to in this clause as 'Non-Approved Appointments'.

(c) A register of all Appointments (the 'Register of Appointments') will be maintained by the Management Committee specifying whether or not an Appointment is a Non-Approved Appointment or an Appointment held on behalf of the LLP (an 'Approved Appointment') and the Register will be open to inspection by all Members.

(2) (a) If any Member incurs a liability (otherwise than by reason of his own fraud or dishonesty) in connection with or as a result of an Approved Appointment .(an 'Approved Liability'):

(i) that Approved Liability and any costs or expenses incurred by that Member in or about contesting, compromising, admitting or compounding it will be a liability of the LLP;

(ii) that Member will be entitled to the same rights of indemnity and contribution from the LLP as if that Approved Liability had been incurred by him in the ordinary and proper course of the LLP Business; and

(iii) that Member must take such action at the expense of

the LLP as any insurer which is on risk in respect of the Approved Liability or the Management Committee may from time to time require to recoup all or any sums within the scope of this clause from any assets (other than his own) or from any person (other than himself) who may be liable in respect thereof and he must account to the LLP for all sums so recouped.

(b) If any Member incurs a liability in connection with an Appointment which is not an Approved Liability, the LLP will have no responsibility for that liability and he will not be entitled to any rights of indemnity and contribution from the LLP.

(3) All Approved Appointments other than those which are required to be held in the name of an individual must be held in the name of the LLP and not in the name of any Member.

(4) Unless otherwise agreed by the Management Committee, all fees, profits, remuneration, emoluments or other benefits received by a Member (including, without limitation, all fees and payments received by a Member arising from his acting as a company director or dividends or other payments received by virtue of a Member holding shares in any company on trust for the LLP) in respect of:

(a) any Approved Appointment, will be received by him for the account of the LLP and must be paid by him to the LLP within seven days of receipt;

(b) any Non-Approved Appointment, will not be received by him for the account of the LLP but will be held for his own personal account.

14. Meetings and Procedures for Decision-Making and the Chairman

(1) A meeting of the Members may be convened at any time by the [Chairman], the [Chief Executive], the [Management Committee] or on the written request of any Member to the Management Committee.

(2) (a) Subject to paragraph (b), the Management Committee will in all cases determine the time, date and place of each meeting of the Members and the nature of the business to be transacted.

(b) Any Member may submit a matter for discussion at a

meeting of the Members to the [Chairman] [or] the [Chief Executive] before commencement of that meeting.

(c) Any meeting of the Members shall be chaired by the Chairman or, in his absence, by the person appointed for that purpose by [General/Special Decision].

(3) Subject to sub-clause (4), each Member will have one vote at any meeting of the Members.

(4) (a) The chairman of the meeting will have a casting vote where a deadlock exists and may cast his second vote as he thinks fit.

(b) No Member who has been required to retire from the LLP by a Special Decision under sub-clause 19(1), no Member who has served a notice to retire as a Member under clause 20 and no Member who is absent from the LLP under clause 21 (unless otherwise agreed by the Management Committee), will be eligible to vote for any purpose but no decision may adversely affect his interests without his written consent unless it applies fairly to all Members.

(c) A Member subject to a Special Decision under sub-clause 18(1), or sub-clause 21(2)(a) will not be entitled to vote on that matter.

(5) (a) Any Member may be represented at any meeting by appointing another Member as a proxy and that proxy will vote on the directions of the Member in favour of or against any decision taken at the meeting. Written proof of appointment must be presented by that proxy to the chair of the meeting prior to commencement of the meeting.

(b) A vote cast by a proxy which complies with the terms of his appointment will count as the vote of the Member making the appointment, and that Member will be deemed for all the purposes of this deed to have been present at the meeting and to have voted on the matter.

(6) The quorum for any meeting of the Members will be fifty per cent of all the Members.

(7) A Unanimous Decision, a Special Decision and a General Decision will bind all Members and the LLP.

(8) (a) For a General Decision to be validly taken [seven] clear days' notice in writing must be given to all Members. A lesser period of notice may be agreed in writing by [ninety per cent] in number of all Members.

(b)   General Decisions must be made at a meeting of the Members on a show of hands by a simple majority of those Members present and voting at the meeting (whether in person or by proxy).

(9)   A Special Decision will be taken in the same way as a General Decision except that at least [seventy-five per cent] by number of all the Members (whether present and voting or not) must be present at the meeting (whether in person or by proxy) and vote in favour of the resolution.

(10)   A Unanimous Decision may be taken:

(a)   at any meeting of the Members on a show of hands provided all Members vote in favour of the decision (whether in person or by proxy); or

(b)   with the written approval of all the Members in which case no meeting of the Members is required for the making of that decision.

(11)   The accidental omission to give notice of a meeting to, or the non-receipt of notice of a meeting by, any [two] or less Members entitled to receive notice will not invalidate the proceedings of a meeting or a decision made by the LLP.

15. Unanimous and Special Decisions

(1)   In addition to any other matters referred to in this deed, the following matters will be determined by [Unanimous/Special] Decision:

(a)   the transfer or vesting of any part of the LLP Business to or into a body corporate, limited liability partnership or any analogous entity or the merger of the LLP Business with that of any other person;

(b)   any acquisition by the LLP of any business or part of a business or company or part of a company for valuable consideration or any disposal by the LLP of any business or part of a business or company or part of a company for valuable consideration; and

(c)   any acquisition or disposal of freehold or leasehold property.

16. Chairman, Chief Executive and Management Committee

(1)   The Management Committee will be comprised of [the Chairman] the Chief Executive and [ ] other Members. With effect on

and from the Effective Date the Management Committee will be comprised of the Members referred to in Part I of Schedule 5.

(2) Except where otherwise specifically provided in this deed any matter connected with the conduct and management of the LLP Business will be decided by the Management Committee which will exercise its powers and discretions in the best interests of the LLP as a whole and in accordance with the obligations of the Members under the LLP Act, the Companies Act and the Insolvency Act.

(3) Any decision of the Management Committee made in accordance with this deed binds the Members and the LLP.

(4) The quorum necessary at meetings for the transaction of business by the Management Committee is [ ] members of the Management Committee present in person or by telephone.

(5) (a) A member of the Management Committee will cease to be a member on the earlier of his ceasing to be a Member and the [ ] anniversary of his most recent appointment but in the latter case he shall be eligible for reelection. The Members may from time to time by [Special/General] Decision (i) remove any member of the Management Committee, (ii) appoint another Member to replace that member so removed or to replace any member of the Management Committee who has ceased to be a member of the Management Committee for any other reason or (iii) appoint an additional member of the Management Committee. Nominations for all such appointments must be given to the continuing members of the Management Committee at least 14 days prior to a general meeting of the Members.

(b) A member of the Management Committee may voluntarily stand down from the Management Committee on giving at least two months' notice to the continuing members and the Members must replace that member in accordance with paragraph (a) above.

(6) Subject to sub-clause (6), the Management Committee will meet together for the despatch of business, adjourn and otherwise regulate its meetings as it thinks fit and may appoint one of their number as Chairman.

(7) Matters arising at any meeting of the Management Committee will be determined by a simple majority of votes of the members of the Management Committee who are present and voting thereon on the basis of one vote per member. For the avoidance

of doubt, the [Chairman and] Chief Executive will not have a casting vote for the purposes of this sub-clause.

(8)   (a)   With effect from and including the Effective Date, the office of Chief Executive and Chairman will be filled by the Member specified in Part II and Part III of Schedule 5 respectively. The provisions of sub-clause (4) will apply mutatis mutandis to the removal, retirement and appointment of the Chief Executive and the Chairman.

(b)   The Chief Executive and the Chairman may delegate to any Member anything required to be done by him and the actions of the delegate will bind the Members and the LLP as if they were carried out by the Chief Executive or the Chairman (as appropriate) himself. In the absence of the Chief Executive or the Chairman, or if he is unavailable, and notwithstanding any delegation of his powers under this sub-clause, any notice required to be given to him must be given to any one or more of the other members of the Management Committee.

17. Admission of New Members

(1)   A New Member may at any time be admitted by Special Decision which decision will specify his date of admittance to the LLP (his 'Admission Date').

(2)   The admission of a New Member is conditional upon the execution by him of an Accession Agreement approved by the Members (excluding the New Member) by Special Decision, on or before his Admission Date or, if later, within [ ] months of the date of the decision referred to in sub-clause (1). This deed will then be construed as though he had been a Member with effect from the Admission Date.

(3)   The Accession Agreement will state the New Member's initial capital contribution (if any) and his Profit Share. The Profit Shares of the existing Members shall be reduced in proportion to their Profit Shares by the percentage necessary to accommodate the New Member's Profit Share.

(4)   The Designated Members shall ensure that:

(a)   the notice of any admission of a New Member is registered with the registrar of limited liability partnerships within 14 days, as required by section 9 of the LLP Act;

(b)   the New Member's details are recorded in the Registers of Members.

18. Expulsion

(1) A Member will immediately cease to be a Member upon being served with a notice in writing of a Special Decision expelling him following any of the events listed below:

(a) if he wilfully or persistently acts in a manner contrary to his material obligations under this deed or is guilty of any grave professional misconduct; or

(b) if he is convicted (unless quashed on appeal) of any criminal offence involving dishonesty or if he acts in a manner which has caused, or is likely to cause, serious prejudice to the reputation of the LLP; or

(c) if he commits any act of bankruptcy or is adjudicated bankrupt or enters into any composition, scheme or arrangement with his creditors or the equivalent in any relevant jurisdiction; or

(d) if he creates or purports to create a security interest over any legal or beneficial interest in his share in the LLP including (without limitation) his account with the LLP or any part of the Profits of the LLP for his separate debt; or

(e) if he has become incapacitated by mental or physical illness, ill-health, accident or otherwise from performing his duties, obligations or responsibilities hereunder for a continuous period of [ ] months.

(2) A Member will immediately cease to be a Member if the LLP would otherwise be conducting its business unlawfully or because he has lost or fails to hold a relevant qualification or to satisfy a relevant professional regulation.

19. Compulsory Retirement and Retirement due to Death

A Member will retire from the LLP and cease to be a Member and become a Former Member on the earlier of his death and the expiration of [six] months from the date of a Special Decision requiring him to retire as a Member.

20. Voluntary Retirement

Any Member may retire from the LLP by giving not less than [six] months' previous notice in writing to the Management Committee expiring on an Accounts Date (but any General Decision to amend the Accounts Date that follows such notice will not affect the date of expiry of the notice) except that the Management Committee may agree a shorter period of notice in any individual case whether or not expiring on an Accounts Date.

21. Gardening Leave and Suspension

(1)   Where a Member has been required to retire from the LLP by a Special Decision under clause 19 and where a Member has served notice to retire as a Member under clause 20, the Management Committee may direct by notice to him in writing that during the whole or any part of the period of his notice to retire, the retiring Member:

(a)   will not enter any of the LLP Premises;

(b)   will not contact or have any communication (or may only communicate in specified ways) with any client or employee of the LLP for any business purpose;

(c)   will do, or omit from doing, all such things in connection with the LLP Business as the Management Committee may reasonably require including, for example, carrying out administrative duties or working on non-client matters; and

(d)   will be subject to the provisions of clause 23 (Covenants) (without prejudice to the application of that clause to him when he ceases to be a Member) and for this purpose, references to Former Member shall be references to the relevant Member and references to the Former Member's Retirement Date shall be to the date of service of notice to the Member.

(2)   (a)   Where there are reasonable grounds for believing that any of the events referred to in clause 18 may apply to a Member, the Members may by [Special/General] Decision decide that such Member will forthwith take no further part in the LLP Business for a specified period or for a period expiring on further notice (in either case such period not to exceed six months) on such terms as that decision shall determine.

(b)   Without prejudice to the generality of paragraph (a), the decision referred to in paragraph (a) may direct that the provisions of sub-clause (1) will apply to the suspended Member.

(c)   A Member who is subject to this sub-clause will, at the expiration of six months from the date of the decision

558

referred to in paragraph (a), be deemed to have retired from the LLP unless that decision has ceased or been revoked at, or before, the expiration of that period.

(d) The revocation of a decision made under this sub-clause will be by [Special/General] Decision.

(3) During any period when sub-clauses (1) or (2) apply, the Member concerned will continue to be entitled to his share of the Profits and to drawings on account of those Profits after providing for any amount owed by the Member to the LLP but he shall not be entitled to continue to receive any financial or other information circulated or otherwise made available to Members generally except to the extent necessary to enable him to carry out his statutory duties as a member, and otherwise he shall rely on the certificate of the LLP Auditors as to his financial entitlements and obligations.

22. Former Members and their Entitlements

(1) As quickly as is reasonably practicable following Retirement Date of a Member which falls otherwise than on the Accounts Date, the LLP Auditors will prepare interim accounts as at the Retirement Date for the period from the preceding Accounts Date to the Retirement Date.

(2) The interim accounts prepared in sub-clause (1) will be prepared on the same basis as the Accounts.

(3) Within two months of the approval of the Accounts (if the Member ceases to be a Member on the Accounts Date) or of the interim accounts being approved by [Special/General Decision] (in all other cases) and after providing for any amount owed by the Former Member to the LLP (if applicable), the undrawn credit balance, if any, on the Former Member's Current Account will be paid to the Former Member.

(4) The LLP will [if the LLP makes the election specified in sub-clause (5)] owe to the Former Member a sum equal to the balance, if any, standing to the credit of the Former Member's Capital Account less the debit balance, if any, on his Current Account. Payment of such amount owed will be made as follows:

(a) one half plus interest thereon at the LLP Interest Rate will be paid [twelve] months after the Former Member's Retirement Date; and

(b) one half plus interest thereon at the LLP Interest Rate will be paid [eighteen] months after the Former Member's

Retirement Date provided always that in the event of the winding up of the LLP (otherwise than for the purposes of amalgamation or reconstruction) any outstanding balance due to a Former Member will immediately become due and payable.

(5) The share of the Former Member in the capital and assets of the LLP will [if the LLP so elects by written notice to the Former Member within six months of his Retirement Date and with effect from his Retirement Date accrue] to the Members rateably in accordance with their Profit Shares.

[(6) If the LLP makes no election under sub-clause (5) then the assets of the LLP will be realised as soon as may be practicable and in any event within twelve months of the Retirement Date. Any surplus or loss on such realisation will be credited or debited to the capital accounts of the Members and the Former Member (but not so as to reduce the balance below zero) and the Former Member will be entitled to be paid the balance standing to the credit of his capital account within eighteen months of his Retirement Date together with interest from the Retirement Date at the LLP Interest Rate.]

(7) The LLP will indemnify each Former Member against all liabilities of the LLP. If and to the extent that the Former Member is entitled to any right of indemnity, reimbursement or contribution in respect of those liabilities from any person other than the LLP or any Member (whether under a policy of insurance or otherwise), he will disclose details of any such rights of reimbursement, indemnity or contribution, and any claim made under it, to the LLP, which will be entitled to exercise those rights by way of subrogation.

(8) The Profit Share to which a Former Member was entitled immediately prior to his Retirement Date shall accrue rateably to the Profit Shares of the other Members.

(9) A Former Member will at all times comply with the obligations imposed on him as a Former Member by this deed, including (without limitation) the obligations imposed by clauses 12 (Duties) and 23 (Covenants).

(10) A Former Member is entitled to the payments described in this clause in full satisfaction of his interest in the LLP, its profits, and in the Goodwill, the LLP Name, LLP Premises, the LLP's furniture and equipment and other assets of the LLP, and has no further rights in respect of those profits or assets.

23. Covenants

(1) In this clause:

    (a) 'in any capacity' means on that Member's or Former Member's own account, or jointly, in conjunction with, or on behalf of any other person, firm or company; and

    (b) 'LLP Client' means any individual, membership, body corporate or unincorporated association who or which has been a client of the LLP and for whom the relevant Member had carried out work at any time in the period of [two] years before his Retirement Date except that each distinct business unit of a client will be treated for this purpose as a separate LLP Client.

(2) A Former Member will not, without the prior permission of the Management Committee do any of the following:

    (a) for a period of [one] year from his Retirement Date act for, solicit or accept instructions from or provide legal services to, any LLP Client in a way which is likely to compete with the business carried on by the LLP immediately before his Retirement Date;

    (b) for a period of [one] year from the Retirement Date employ, solicit or endeavour to entice away, offer membership or employment to or enter into partnership or any other commercial arrangement with any person who, at the Retirement Date was a Member in, an employee of or consultant to the LLP;

    (c) at any time after his Retirement Date and in any capacity:

        (i) represent himself as a Member in, employee of or consultant to the LLP or that he is in any way connected with, or has the authority to bind the LLP or any Member; or

        (ii) use the LLP Name or any name which may in any way be confused with the LLP Name.

(3) Each of sub-clauses (2)(a) to (c) inclusive constitutes a separate and independent restriction on each Former Member so that if one or more are held to be invalid or unenforceable for any reason whatsoever then the remaining covenants will be valid and enforceable to the extent that they are not held to be invalid or unenforceable.

(4)   Upon any Member becoming a Former Member, all deeds, drafts, letters and other papers or records belonging to the LLP or any LLP Client or relating to any LLP Client or prospective client of the LLP will remain in the possession of, or be delivered by that Former Member to the LLP and, at the request of the Management Committee, the Former Member will certify in writing to the LLP whether or not he is in breach of this sub-clause.

(5)   When a Member becomes a Former Member, due notice that he has ceased to be a Member will be given by the Designated Member to the Companies Registrar as required by the LLP Act.

24. Winding Up, Arrangements And Reconstructions

(1)   The LLP may, by a [Special/General] Decision, determine:

(a)   to wind up the LLP;

(b)   to propose a voluntary arrangement with the LLP's creditors under the Insolvency Act and the terms of that voluntary arrangement;

(c)   to approve the terms of a voluntary arrangement proposed by a liquidator or administrator under the Insolvency Act;

(d)   to make an application to the court for an administration order or to appoint an administrator under the Insolvency Act;

(e)   to make an application to the court for the sanctioning of a proposed compromise or arrangement between the LLP and the Members or the LLP and its creditors under Part XIII of the Companies Act and the terms of that proposed compromise or arrangement;

(f)   to confer upon a liquidator general authority or authority for a particular arrangement to be made by the liquidator pursuant to Section 110 of the Insolvency Act, or authority to exercise any of the powers specified in Part I of Schedule 4 to the Insolvency Act. In each case the liquidator will call the requisite Members' meeting to propose such resolutions; and

(g)   subject to any arrangement with creditors, fill a vacancy in the office of liquidator in accordance with Section 92 of the Insolvency Act.

(2)   If a [Special/General] Decision is taken under sub-clause 24(1), the Management Committee is authorised to take the necessary steps on behalf of the LLP pertaining to a particular action, proposal or application, such steps including:

    (a)   appointing a liquidator to wind up the LLP's affairs and distribute its assets (but not filling a vacancy in the office of liquidator); and

    (b)   approving modifications suggested by creditors to any voluntary arrangement proposed by the LLP under sub-clause 24(1)(b).

(3)   In making any decision or carrying out any function the authority for which is derived from sub-clause 24(2), the Management Committee may, if in its absolute discretion it sees fit, refer any decision back to the Members in which case the Management Committee shall determine the level of Decision required.

(4)   If a winding up is proposed by the LLP, the Designated Members (or if there are more than two, the majority of them) may make a statutory declaration of solvency in accordance with Section 89 of the Insolvency Act to the effect that they have made full inquiries into the LLP's affairs and that having done so they are of the opinion that the LLP will be able to pay its debts in full. If such a declaration is made the winding up will be a 'members' winding up' or, if no such declaration is made, the winding up will be a 'creditors' winding up' for the purposes of the Insolvency Act.

(5)   Subject to sub-clause 24(1)(f), upon a 'members' winding up', any surplus assets after the liquidator has applied the property of the LLP in satisfaction of the LLP's liabilities (including those to any Former Member) shall be applied first in payment of the amount standing to the credit of the Capital Accounts and provisions for taxation under clause 9 of each of the Members at the date of winding up. Any balance will be distributed to the Members rateably in proportion to their Profit Shares at the date of winding up, having made appropriate reservation for taxation in accordance with clause 9.

(6)   The LLP Business (or any of it) may be transferred to one or more limited liability partnerships, partnerships, bodies corporate or any analogous entity in consideration for the issue to Members of shares, membership rights or analogous rights in that entity which are broadly equivalent to their interests in the LLP upon such terms as shall be agreed by the Members.

(7) [Each Member agrees to contribute in cash £100 to the assets of the LLP on a winding up and shall be a contributory for the purposes of Section 79 of the Insolvency Act.]

(8) The Members covenant to each other that they will not seek to exercise any rights that they may have in any capacity, individually or as a group, under Sections 112, 124 or 212 of the Insolvency Act, other than under sub-clause 24(1) above, unless so agreed by a [Special/General] Decision.

(9) Notwithstanding that the LLP has been wound up in accordance with this clause or become insolvent, this agreement will remain in full force and effect to the extent that the obligations and covenants in it remain to be performed.

25. Arbitration and Dispute Resolution

(1) Where any question, claim, dispute or difference ('Dispute') arises between any of the Members, the Former Members and the LLP concerning or in any way arising out of this deed or the performance of the terms of this deed, those Members, Former Members and the LLP involved in that Dispute will make a genuine effort to resolve the Dispute without resorting to litigation, using the procedures set out in this clause.

(2) Any Dispute in connection with this deed will be resolved as follows:

(a) in accordance with sub-clause (3) below if the Dispute relates to an accounting matter; or

(b) in accordance with sub-clauses (4), (5) and (6) below, in the case of all other Disputes.

(3) Disputes relating to an accounting matter will be referred, at the written request of any party to the Dispute, for determination by an independent accountant (the 'Independent Accountant') who is a member of the Institute of Chartered Accountants in England and Wales (the 'Institute') appointed by deed between the parties to the Dispute within seven days of delivery of the written request or (in default of deed) appointed by the President for the time being of the Institute on the application of any party to the Dispute. The Management Committee will determine whether a Dispute concerns an accounting matter or not and its decision will be final in the absence of a manifest error. The determination of the Independent Accountant is final and binding on all Members and Former Members. In determining the Dispute, the Independent Accountant will act as an expert and not as an arbitrator. All costs incurred by the Independent

Accountant will be borne by the parties to the Dispute as determined by the Independent Accountant.

(4) Without prejudice to any right to seek interim relief all other Disputes will be referred, at the written request of any party to the Dispute, to mediation by a mediator appointed by deed between the parties to the Dispute within seven days of the written request or (in default of deed) appointed by the Chief Executive for the time being of the Centre for Dispute Resolution ('CEDR'). The mediation will be conducted in London in accordance with the CEDR Model Mediation Procedure (together with any amendments and updates to that procedure that are adopted by the Management Committee before the appointment of a mediator in relation to a particular Dispute), which is deemed to be incorporated in this deed. If an agreement is reached on the resolution of the Dispute during the mediation, that deed will be reduced to writing and, once signed by the parties to the Dispute, will be binding on all the Members. Unless concluded with a written legally binding agreement, the mediation will be conducted in confidence and without prejudice to the rights of any Member or Former Member in any further proceedings and the contents of the agreement will remain confidential to the parties to the Dispute and their professional advisers save for the limited purpose of enforcement.

(5) Without prejudice to any right to seek interim relief in the event that the Dispute has not been settled within sixty days after the appointment of the mediator, or if no request is made to refer that Dispute to mediation, the Dispute will be referred (by any Member or Former Member involved in the Dispute) to arbitration in London to be conducted in the English language by a sole arbitrator appointed in accordance with the rules of the London Court of International Arbitration (the 'Rules') which Rules are deemed to be incorporated by reference into this clause.

(6) The Members and the LLP agree that any party to an arbitration under this deed may appeal against any award of an arbitrator on points of law.

26. Alterations

(1) Any of the provisions of this deed may be altered at any time by [Special/Unanimous] Decision.

(2) Notwithstanding sub-clause (1), any of the provisions of this deed may be altered at any time by the Management Committee if the alteration is of a minor or technical nature which either is

not materially prejudicial to the interests of any of the Members or is to correct a manifest error. Any such alteration will be made on the terms and subject to the conditions that the Management Committee determines, and will be notified to Members as soon as possible and will be binding on the Members when notified to them.

(3) No alteration of this deed will invalidate any prior act which would have been valid if that alteration had not been made.

27. Holidays and Maternity Leave

(1) In each Accounting Period, in addition to public and religious holidays, each Member shall be entitled to take such annual holidays not exceeding [five] weeks in the aggregate [of which not more than [three] weeks may be taken consecutively] or as shall be determined by [General/Special] Decision from time to time and may (subject to such determination) carry forward into the next calendar year up to five days of the unused part of his entitlement.

(2) A Member who is female may, in the event of her pregnancy and upon giving not less than [three months'] prior written notice of her intention to do so to the other Members, take a period of maternity leave of not more than [four months'] duration or of such duration as shall be decided between the Member and the Management Committee and commencing at such time as shall be agreed between the Member and the Management Committee.

(3) A Member who is male may upon giving not less than [three months'] prior written notice of his intention to do so to the other Members, take a period of paternity leave of such duration as shall be decided between the Member and the Management Committee and commencing at such time as shall be agreed between the Member and the Management Committee.

[(4) The LLP, by [General/Special] Decision, and a Member may agree flexible working arrangements. At the Effective Date, the agreed flexible working arrangements shall be those set out in Schedule 7.]

28. General

(1) None of the rights or obligations under this deed may be assigned or transferred without a [Unanimous/Special Decision].

(2) Where an obligation is expressed to be undertaken by two or more parties they shall, unless otherwise expressly stated, be jointly and severally responsible in respect of it.

(3) This deed may be executed in any number of counterparts, all of which taken together shall constitute one and the same deed and any party may enter into this deed by executing a counterpart as a deed.

(4) Except as expressly stated in the deed, this deed and its schedules and the documents referred to in it [contain the whole agreement between the parties] and supersede all previous agreements between the parties.

(5) Each of the parties acknowledges that in agreeing to enter into this deed he has not relied on any representation, warranty or other assurance except those set out in this deed.

(6) This deed and any non-contractual obligations arising out of or in connection with it shall be governed by and construed in accordance with English law.

(7) Any notice required or permitted to be given under this deed shall be in writing and if posted by prepaid recorded delivery post to the last known address of the person to be served shall be deemed to have been duly served forty-eight hours after despatch.

(8) The parties agree that, subject to clause 25, the courts of England have exclusive jurisdiction to settle any Dispute arising out of or in connection with this deed (including any Dispute relating to any non-contractual obligations arising out of or in connection with this deed) and the parties submit to the exclusive jurisdiction for the English Courts.

(9) No third party shall have any rights in respect of this deed, whether pursuant to the Contracts (Rights of Third Parties) Act 1999 or otherwise.

(10) For so long as the LLP is in existence, no Member shall have any right to apply to the court by petition for an order under Section 994 of the Companies Act in relation to the LLP's affairs.

(11) If any provision of this agreement or its application to the LLP, any Member, Former Member or circumstance is or becomes invalid or unenforceable to any extent in any part of the world, the remainder of this agreement and its application will not be affected and will remain enforceable to the greatest extent permitted by law in that jurisdiction.

(12) Each of the Members and the LLP shall do or procure to be done all acts and things and/or execute or procure the execution of all deeds and documents necessary or desirable to establish and govern the relationship between the Members and the LLP and to give effect to the matters contemplated by the agreement within it or his power or control (in whatever capacity).

IN WITNESS of which each of the parties has executed this document as a deed the day and year first above written.

SCHEDULE 1

Original Members

Name   Address

SCHEDULE 2

LLP Premises

Address

SCHEDULE 3

Initial Designated Members

SCHEDULE 4

Name   Initial Capital Contributions   Initial Profit Share

SCHEDULE 5

Part I

Initial Management Committee

Part II

Initial Chief Executive

Part III

Initial Chairman

SCHEDULE 6

Form of Accession Agreement

This DEED is made on [ ], 20[ ] between:

(1)   [ ] of [ ] (the "New Member"); and

(2)   [ ] LLP, a limited liability partnership established under the laws of [ ] with registered number [ ] and having its registered office at [ ] (the "LLP").

WHEREAS:

(A)   The New Member wishes to be admitted as a Member of the LLP with effect on [ ] (the "Admission Date").

(B)   The LLP has agreed that the New Member may be admitted in accordance with the LLP Agreement dated [ ], in the form set out in the Schedule to this deed, as varied and supplemented from time to time (the "LLP Agreement").

(C)   The New Member now wishes to enter into an Accession Agreement pursuant to the LLP Agreement.

NOW THIS DEED WITNESSES THAT:

1.   In this Accession Agreement, the following terms shall unless the context requires otherwise have (whether with or without the definite article) the following meanings:

[insert any additional definitions]

Capitalised terms not defined herein shall have the meaning given to them in the LLP Agreement.

2.   The New Member will for all purposes be and become a party to the LLP Agreement with effect on the Admission Date as if he had executed it on or before the Admission Date, and will accordingly be entitled to all the rights and subject to all the obligations provided for under the LLP Agreement.

3.   The New Member shall make a Capital Contribution of £[ ] for the purposes of [Clause 5] of the LLP Agreement on the date hereof.

4.   The Profit Share of the New Member shall be [ ] and Schedule 4 of the LLP Agreement shall be amended as attached to this Accession Agreement.

5.   [insert any special conditions]

6.   Any alteration, deletion or amendment of this deed must be made in writing and by deed executed by both the New Member and the LLP.

7.   This deed and any and any non-contractual obligations arising out of or in connection with it shall be governed by and construed in accordance with English law.

IN WITNESS WHEREOF, this DEED has been executed as a deed and delivered the day and year first before written:

EXECUTED as a deed by [ ]

in the presence of:

Witness' signature:

Name:

Address:

EXECUTED as a deed by [ ] LLP

acting by [ ]

and [ ]

SCHEDULE 7

Flexible working arrangements

SIGNED as a deed by [ ]

in the presence of:

Witness' signature:

Name:

Address:

SIGNED as a deed by [ ]

in the presence of:

Witness' signature:

Name:

Address:

SIGNED as a deed by [ ]

in the presence of:

Witness' signature:

Name:

Address:

SIGNED as a deed by [ ] LLP

acting by [ ]

and [ ]

Appendix 6 ABC Partnership — financial statements for the year ended 30 April 201X

572

ABC Partnership

The accounts of ABC Partnership for the year ended 30 April 201X as set out on pages [ ] to [ ] were approved by the Partners on [ ] .

Signed on behalf of the partners (in accordance with clause [ ] of the partnership deed).

Partner A ... ...

Partner B ... ...

:

:

:

:

:

:

:

Chartered Accountants' Report to the Partners on the Unaudited Financial Information of ABC Partnership

In accordance with the engagement letter dated [ ] we have prepared for your approval the financial information of the partnership for the year ended 30 April 201X which comprises of the Profit and Loss Account, the Balance Sheet and the related notes 1 to 17 from the partnership's accounting records and from information and explanations you have given us.

As a practising member firm of the Institute of Chartered Accountants in England and Wales (ICAEW), we are subject to its ethical and other professional requirements which are detailed at icaew.com/membershandbook.

This report is made solely to you, in accordance with the terms of our engagement letter dated [ ]. Our work has been undertaken solely to prepare for your approval the financial information of the partnership and state those matters that we have agreed to state to you in this report in accordance with the guidance of ICAEW as detailed at icaew.com/compilation. To the fullest extent permitted by law, we do not accept or assume responsibility to anyone other than the partners for our work or for this report.

You have approved the financial information for the year ended 30 April 200X and have acknowledged your responsibility for it, for the appropriateness of the financial reporting framework adopted and for providing all information and explanations necessary for its compilation.

We have not verified the accuracy or completeness of the accounting records or information and explanations you have given to us and we do not, therefore, express any opinion on the financial statements.

Smith & Williamson Limited

25 Moorgate

London EC2R 6AY

ABC Partnership—profit and loss account for the year ended 30 April 201X

	Notes	201X £	201Y £
INCOME			
Turnover	1	12,647,254	10,549,140
Closing work in progress		1,882,418	1,853,610
Opening work in progress		(1,853,610)	(1,777,515)
		12,676,062	10,625,235
Other income	2	145,781	131,247
		12,821,843	10,756,482
EXPENSES			
Staff expenses—fee earners	3	3,149,879	2,614,561
Staff expenses—non fee earners	4	1,030,337	876,652
Premises expenses	5	1,374,188	1,054,427
Professional indemnity insurance		509,746	421,274
General expenses	6	1,836,364	1,324,801
Financial expenses	7	398,137	367,574
Annuities to former partners		47,804	43,458
		8,346,455	6,702,747
PROFIT AVAILABLE TO PARTNERS	15	4,475,388	4,053,735

ABC Partnership—balance sheet as at 30 April 201X

	Notes	201X £	201Y £
FIXED ASSETS			
Intangible	8	200,000	250,000
Tangible	9	2,100,772	1,929,759
Investments	10	30,695	30,695
		2,331,467	2,210,454
CURRENT ASSETS			
Work in progress		1,882,418	1,853,610
Debtors	11	3,804,664	3,102,428
Cash at bank		423,926	199,823
		6,111,008	5,155,861
CREDITORS: Amounts due within one year	12	(2,977,710)	(2,781,640)
NET CURRENT ASSETS		3,133,298	2,374,221
TOTAL ASSETS LESS CURRENT LIABILITIES		5,464,765	4,584,675
CREDITORS: Amounts due in more than one year	13	(1,200,000)	(1,100,000)
NET ASSETS		4,264,765	3,484,675
Financed by:			
PARTNERS' ACCOUNTS			
Capital accounts	14	2,500,000	2,220,000
Current accounts	15	1,764,765	1,264,675
		4,264,765	3,484,675
Client monies in hand		4,460,685	3,605,925

ABC Partnership — notes to the financial statements for the year ended 30 April 201X

1 Accounting policies

The following accounting policies have been used in dealing with items which are considered material in relation to the partnership's accounts.

(a) *Basis of accounting*

The accounts are prepared using the historical cost basis of accounting except for certain fixed assets which are included at valuation.

(b) *Turnover*

Turnover represents the right to consideration in respect of legal services performed during the year, net of VAT.

(c) *Goodwill*

Goodwill represents the excess over fair value of the cost of DEF Partnership. The cost is being amortised in equal amounts over a 10 year period.

(d) *Tangible fixed assets*

Depreciation is provided on all tangible fixed assets, except freehold property, at annual rates calculated to write off their cost, less estimated residual value, on a straight line basis, over their expected useful lives as follows:

Leasehold land and buildings – Over the term of the lease

Fixtures, fittings and equipment – 20% p.a.

IT equipment – 25% p.a.

Motor vehicles – 25% p.a.

(e) *Work in progress*

Unbilled work has been included in these financial statements at the valuation made by the Partners, based on the lower of cost and net realisable value.

(f) *Taxation*

Full provision is made for income tax for the 201X/1W tax year, which is based on the profit for the year ended 30 April 201X.

(g) *Leases*

Rental costs under operating leases are charged to the profit and loss account in equal amounts over the periods of the leases.

(h) *Pension costs*

The partnership operates a defined contribution pension scheme. Amounts charged in respect of defined contribution schemes represent the contributions payable in the year.

(i) *Retirement benefits of former partners*

The partnership has a liability to pay annuities to certain former partners and their spouses. These annuities become due following retirement (but no earlier than the age of 60). On initial recognition the estimated current value of the future pension is a provision for included in creditors.

		201X	201Y
2	**Other income**	£	£
	Deposit interest	102,047	87,498
	Commissions	15,410	24,032
	Other income	21,867	16,405
	Directors fees	5,000	2,000
	Dividends on investments	1,457	1,312
		145,781	131,247
3	**Staff expenses—fee earners**	£	£
	Salaries	2,677,398	2,222,377
	National insurance	283,490	235,310
	BUPA staff	12,500	11,000
	Temporary staff	32,795	22,205
	Recruitment costs	9,481	5,082
	Practising certificates	58,900	56,500
	Consultancy fees	50,500	41,328
	Costs, draughtsmans' fees	3,250	2,859
	Training	21,565	17,900
		3,149,879	2,614,561
4	**Staff expenses—non fee earners**	£	£
	Staff salaries	896,393	762,687
	Temporary staff	41,214	35,067
	National insurance	92,730	78,898
		1,030,337	876,652

5	**Premises expenses**	£	£
	Rent payable	618,385	527,215
	Repairs	219,324	158,164
	Rates and water	274,838	210,885
	Lighting and heating	48,098	42,178
	Insurance	34,900	33,200
	Professional fees	137,418	51,152
	Cleaning	41,225	31,633
		1,374,188	1,054,427

6	**General expenses**	£	£
	Accountancy and taxation fees	120,203	99,758
	Professional fees	69,195	36,510
	Hire of motor vehicles and equipment	126,730	80,736
	Office sundry expenses	202,768	152,149
	Photocopying	45,048	33,277
	Postage and courier charges	88,702	66,565
	Unrecovered expenses	101,367	76,038
	Computer expenses	202,770	123,178
	Other equipment	25,346	19,015
	Publications and subscriptions	76,037	57,057
	Stationery	214,311	171,167
	Telephone	189,251	142,600
	Travelling expenses	126,025	115,021
	Practising certificate—partners	40,810	36,625
	Entertainment	207,801	115,105
		1,836,364	1,324,801

7	**Financial expenses**	£	£
	Bank charges and interest	10,900	12,500
	Bad debts written off	32,597	27,500
	Provision for bad and doubtful debts	(15,950)	7,200
	Deprecia- – furniture fixtures and tion equipment	129,781	95,868
	– computer	80,565	78,525
	– goodwill	50,000	50,000
	– motor vehicles	60,244	45,981
	– leasehold land and buildings	50,000	50,000
		398,137	367,574

8 Intangible fixed assets – goodwill

	£
Cost	
As at 1 May 201Y and 30 April 201X	500,000
Depreciation	
As at 1 May 201Y	250,000
Charge for the year	50,000
As at 30 April 201X	300,000
Net book value	
As at 30 April 201X	200,000
As at 30 April 201Y	250,000

9 Tangible fixed assets

	Leasehold land and buildings £	IT equipment £	Furniture fixtures and equipment £	Motor vehicles £	Total £
Cost					
As at 1 May 201Y	1,250,000	518,945	1,335,155	344,900	3,449,000
Additions	–	86,296	255,442	149,865	491,603
Disposals	–	(120,000)	(99,990)	(74,900)	(294,890)
As at 30 April 201X	1,250,000	485,241	1,490,607	419,865	3,645,713
DEPRECIATION					
As at 1 May 201Y	300,000	209,561	837,755	171,925	1,519,241
Charge for the year	50,000	80,565	129,781	60,244	320,590
Disposals	–	(120,000)	(99,990)	(74,900)	(294,890)
As at 30 April 201X	350,000	170,126	867,546	157,269	1,544,941
NET BOOK VALUE					
As at 30 April 201X	900,000	315,115	623,061	262,596	2,100,772
As at 30 April 201Y	950,000	309,384	497,400	172,975	1,929,759

10 Fixed asset investments	201X	201Y
	£	£
Investment at cost in ABC Services Limited	30,695	30,695
(net asset value £110,000; 201Y: £90,000)		

11 Debtors

	£	£
Trade debtors	3,043,732	2,342,870
Disbursements	342,420	381,291
Other debtors	152,186	147,097
Prepayments	266,326	231,170
	3,804,664	3,102,428

12 Creditors: Amounts falling due within one year

	£	£
Bank overdraft	109,554	155,632
Current portion of long term loans	407,914	334,184
Purchase ledger	119,110	111,265
Counsels' fees	372,215	347,705
Income tax (note 17)	1,118,847	963,435
Other taxation and social security	406,485	289,082
Other creditors and accruals	208,400	194,957
Fees received in advance	129,775	187,820
Retirement benefits due to former partners	105,410	197,560
	2,977,710	2,781,640

13 Creditors: Amounts falling due after more than one year

	£	£
Retirement benefits due to former partners	1,200,000	1,100,000

14 Partners' Capital Accounts

	Balance as at 1 May 201Y	Transfer from current account (*note 15*)	Repaid in year	Balance as at 30 April 201X
	£	£	£	£
Partner A	120,000	–	(120,000)	–
Partner B	120,000	–	–	120,000
:				
:				
:				
:				
:				
:				
:				
:				
Partner Y	–	60,000	–	60,000
Partner Z	–	60,000	–	60,000
	2,220,000	400,000	(120,000)	2,500,000

15 Partners' Current Accounts

	Balance as at 1 May 201Y	Profit for the year	Transfer to capital account (note 14)	Drawings (note 16)	Provision for taxation (note 17)	Balance as at 30 April 201X
	£	£	£	£	£	£
Partner A	106,973	267,568	—	(226,292)	(67,951)	80,298
Partner B	87,916	232,345	—	(187,542)	(58,466)	74,253
.. ..						
Partner Y	—	109,723	(60,000)	(57,705)	(24,760)	(32,742)
Partner Z	—	109,723	(60,000)	(58,373)	(28,970)	(37,620)
	1,264,675	4,475,388	(400,000)	(2,545,377)	(1,029,921)	1,764,765

16 Partners' Drawings

	Cash drawings	National insurance	Pension and life policies	Partners expenses	Motor car cost (private element)	Total
	£	£	£	£	£	£
Partner A	145,000	1,230	52,500	14,500	3,062	216,292
Partner B	140,000	1,230	25,500	6,500	4,312	177,542
.. ..						
Partner Y	48,000	1,230	6,525	1,950	—	57,705
Partner Z	48,000	1,230	6,193	2,950	—	58,373
	2,100,000	32,000	277,928	99,995	35,454	2,545,377

17 Partners' income tax

Income tax balances at 30 April 201X
Balance sheet liabilities

	201Z/1Y	201Y/1X	201X/1W	Total Reserves 30/04/ 201X	Total Reserves 30/04/ 201Y
	£	£	£	£	£
Partner A	41,228	50,090	65,170	156,488	138,036
Partner B	35,291	49,815	57,050	142,156	125,133
.. ..					
Partner Y	–	1,740	22,100	23,840	43,125
Partner Z	–	2,100	29,505	31,605	4,059
Tax paid	478,407	617,674	1,005,486	2,101,567	1,758,587
	(646,643)	(336,077)	–	(982,720)	(795,152)
Tax payable/ repayable	(168,236)	281,597	1,005,486	1,118,847	963,435

Income tax charge for the year ended 30 April 201X
Current tax provision and prior year adjustments

	201Z/1Y Case II	201Y/1X Case II	201X/1W Case II	Total
	£	£	£	£
Partner A	575	2,206	65,170	67,951
Partner B	195	1,221	57,050	58,466
Partner Y	–	1,740	22,100	23,840
Partner Z	–	2,100	29,505	31,605
Tax paid	(4,455)	28,890	1,005,486	1,029,921
				(note 15)

Appendix 7 Example presentations under the LLP SORP

EXAMPLE BALANCE SHEET PRESENTATION FOR AN LLP WITH NO EQUITY

	201X £'000	201Y £'000
Fixed assets		
Tangible fixed assets	9,500	8,200
Current assets		
Amounts recoverable on contracts	8,000	7,500
Trade debtors	17,500	16,000
Amounts due from members	1,500	1,200
Other debtors and prepayments	4,000	3,800
Cash at bank and in hand	6,000	4,500
Current assets	37,000	33,000
Creditors: amounts falling due within one year		
Bank overdraft and loans	3,000	2,800
Other creditors and accruals	6,500	6,000
Current liabilities	9,500	8,800
Net current assets	27,500	24,200
Total assets less current liabilities	37,000	32,400

Creditors: amounts falling due after more than one year

Bank loans	4,000	3,200

Provisions for liabilities

Post retirement payments to former members	4,500	4,800
Other provisions	2,000	1,900
	6,500	6,700

NET ASSETS ATTRIBUTABLE TO MEMBERS	26,500	22,500

REPRESENTED BY:	**201X** **£'000**	**201Y** **£'000**

Loans and other debts due to members within one year

Members' capital classified as a liability	8,000	6,000
Other amounts	18,500	16,500
	26,500	22,500

TOTAL MEMBERS' INTERESTS

Amounts due from members	(1,500)	(1,200)
Loans and other debts due to members	26,500	22,500
	25,000	21,300

EXAMPLE BALANCE SHEET PRESENTATION FOR AN LLP WITH SOME EQUITY

	201X £'000	201Y £'000
Fixed assets		
Tangible fixed assets	9,500	8,200
Current assets		
Amounts recoverable on contracts	8,000	7,500
Trade debtors	17,500	16,000
Amounts due from members	1,500	1,200
Other debtors and prepayments	4,000	3,800
Cash at bank and in hand	6,000	4,500
Current assets	37,000	33,000
Creditors: amounts falling due within one year		
Bank overdraft and loans	3,000	2,800
Other creditors and accruals	6,500	6,000
Current liabilities	9,500	8,800
Net current assets	27,500	24,200
Total assets less current liabilities	37,000	32,400

Creditors: amounts falling due after more than one year

Bank loans	4,000	3,200

Provisions for liabilities

Post retirement payments to former members	4,500	4,800
Other provisions	2,000	1,900
	6,500	6,700

NET ASSETS ATTRIBUTABLE TO MEMBERS	26,500	22,500

REPRESENTED BY:	**201X** **£'000**	**201Y** **£'000**
Loans and other debts due to members within one year		
Members' capital classified as a liability	5,000	4,000
Other amounts	9,000	8,000
	14,000	12,000
Members' other interests		
Members' capital classified as equity	3,000	2,000
Members' other interests – Other reserves classified as equity	9,500	8,500
	26,500	22,500

TOTAL MEMBERS' INTERESTS

Amounts due from members	(1,500)	(1,200)
Loans and other debts due to members	14,000	12,000
Members' other interests	12,500	10,500
	25,000	21,300

EXAMPLE PROFIT AND LOSS PRESENTATION FOR AN LLP WITH NO AUTOMATIC DIVISION OF ANY PROFIT

	201X £'000	201Y £'000
Turnover	55,500	49,500
Other operating income	2,500	2,000
	58,000	51,500
Other external charges	(8,500)	(7,500)
Staff costs	(21,500)	(18,500)
Depreciation	(2,000)	(2,000)
Other operating expenses	(11,000)	(9,000)
Operating profit	15,000	14,500
Profit on sale of fixed assets	1,000	–
Interest receivable and similar income	1,000	1,000
Interest payable and similar charges	(500)	(750)
Profit for the financial year before members' remuneration and profit shares available for discretionary division among members	16,500	14,750

EXAMPLE PROFIT AND LOSS PRESENTATION FOR AN LLP WITH AUTOMATIC DIVISION OF ALL PROFITS

	201X £'000	201Y £'000
Turnover	55,500	49,500
Other operating income	2,500	2,000
	58,000	51,500
Other external charges	(8,500)	(7,500)
Staff costs	(21,500)	(18,500)
Depreciation	(2,000)	(2,000)
Other operating expenses	(11,000)	(9,000)
Operating profit	15,000	14,500
Profit on sale of fixed assets	1,000	–
Interest receivable and similar income	1,000	1,000
Interest payable and similar charges	(500)	(750)
Profit for the financial year before members' remuneration and profit shares	16,500	14,750
Profit for the financial year before members' remuneration and profit shares	16,500	14,750
Members' remuneration charged as an expense	(16,500)	(14,750)
Result for the financial year available for discretionary division among members	-	-

EXAMPLE PROFIT AND LOSS PRESENTATION FOR LLP WITH AUTOMATIC DIVISION OF PROFITS EQUIVALENT TO SALARIED REMUNERATION

	201X £'000	201Y £'000
Turnover	55,500	49,500
Other operating income	2,500	2,000
	58,000	51,500
Other external charges	(8,500)	(7,500)
Staff costs	(21,500)	(18,500)
Depreciation	(2,000)	(2,000)
Other operating expenses	(11,000)	(9,000)
Operating profit	15,000	14,500
Profit on sale of fixed assets	1,000	–
Interest receivable and similar income	1,000	1,000
Interest payable and similar charges	(500)	(750)
Profit for the financial year before members' remuneration and profit shares	16,500	14,750
Profit for the financial year before members' remuneration and profit shares	16,500	14,750
Members' remuneration charged as an expense	(3,000)	(2,500)
Result for the financial year available for discretionary division among members	13,500	12,250

EXAMPLE RECONCILIATION OF MEMBERS' INTERESTS

	Members' Other Interests				Loans and other debts due to members less any amounts due from members in debtors	Total*
	Members' Capital (Classified as equity)	Revaluation Reserve	Other Reserves	Total		
Amounts due to members					X	
Amounts due from members					(X)	
Balance at beginning of period	X	X	X	X	X	X
Members' remuneration charged as an expense, including employment and retirement benefit costs					X	X
Profit (loss) for the financial year available for discretionary division among members			X	X		X
Members' interests after profit/(loss) for the year	X	X	X	X	X	X

594

Other divisions of profits/losses			(X)	(X)	X
Surplus arising on revaluation of fixed assets	X	X			X
Introduced by members	(X)			X	X
Repayments of capital				X	(X)
Repayments of debt (including members' capital classified as a liability)					(X)
Drawings					(X)
Other movements	X	X	X	X	X
Amounts due to members				X	
Amounts due from members					(X)
Balance at end of period	X	X	X	X	X

* A comparative total column is also required

Index

[all references are to paragraph number]